Curriculum Handbook

The Disciplines, Current Movements,
and Instructional Methodology

Louis Rubin

Allyn and Bacon, Inc.
Boston, London, Sydney

For Nick, Lisa, Beth, and Jenna
who have taught me so much

Copyright © 1977 by Allyn and Bacon, Inc.
470 Atlantic Avenue, Boston, Massachusetts 02210. All rights reserved.
Printed in the United States of America. No part of the material protected
by this copyright notice may be reproduced or utilized in any form or by
any means, electronic or mechanical, including photocopying, recording,
or by any information storage and retrieval system, without written permission from the copyright owner.

Library of Congress Cataloging in Publication Data

Rubin, Louis
  Curriculum handbook.

  Includes index.
  CONTENTS: v. 1. The disciplines, current movements, and instructional
methodology.—v. 2. Administration and theory.
  1. Curriculum planning—United States. I. Title.
LB1570.R79   375′.00973   77–1192
ISBN 0–205–05723–3

3/31/78 Becker + Tylr 27.95

Contents

Contents

Contents

Contents

Preface

We tend to assume, too often, that schooling is always uniform, a changeless ritual submitted to by one generation after another, year in and year out. The same things are taught, seemingly, tests are given, grades assigned, and teachers maneuver to achieve a semblance of decorum, much as they always have done. But it is not so. Surface appearances may be similar but beneath the outer veneer there are a vast number of subtle permutations, perpetuated by a wide array of forces. The curriculum, consequently, is a topic for endless study.

Embodied in that which we call curriculum are considerations going far beyond the mere determination of what knowledge is to be taught. Also involved are methods of instruction, the organizational scheme through which students are grouped, time allotments, linkages with other learning experiences in the lives of students, the construction of instructional materials, and so on. The curriculum, in short, is at the heart of the educational enterprise and is, therefore, correspondingly complex. It is this comprehensiveness, in fact, that makes the *Handbook* sufficiently thick as to require publication in two volumes. There are, in all, 111 separate essays on various aspects of the subject.

To facilitate convenience, the essays have been grouped into five sections, the first two of which are in the volume, *The Disciplines, Current Movements, and Instructional Methodology,* and the remainder in the volume, *Administration and Theory.* Section 1, the largest of the five, deals with the subject-matter disciplines, with major objectives and ongoing trends in the various content areas. In Section 2, the focus is on prevailing movements. One can detect, at any given time, particular tendencies and predispositions in the curricular structure. An earlier emphasis upon the open classroom, for example, is now being followed by a perceptible leaning toward stress upon ethical values, practical competencies, and multicultural awareness.

In Section 3, the last of the three sections in the first volume, the essays center upon teaching methods. The manner in which intellectual concepts are taught can be as critical as the ideas themselves. A considerable amount of research, consequently, is devoted to assessing the comparative advantages of alternative instructional techniques. The results of these assessments serve as the nucleus for the variety of recommendations that are made in the collected articles. In turn, Section 4, the first section in the second volume, considers the problems of curriculum administration. What, as a case in point, is the role of leadership in promoting educational reform? How do politics and curricular change interact? Visionary notions, in and of themselves, do not necessarily beget progress. Even a useful new approach that fails to capture the interest of practitioners is likely to lie fallow. And, used badly, it may produce more chaos than improvement. Because the curriculum, like any other dynamic process, must be managed with imagination, care, and skill, the essential balance between stability and change must be carefully engineered. These and other related problems are treated operationally in the analyses. Finally, in Section 5, a number of theoretical issues are considered. Viewpoints differ regarding the purpose of education, the desirability of compulsory attendance laws, the extent to which legalities constrain curricular options, and so on. An assortment of such controversies are debated in this concluding series of nineteen articles.

It seemed important, in a work of this scope and complexity, to provide the reader with both a synthesis of the dominant themes and a brief summary of their practical implications. As editor, therefore, I have undertaken the task of extracting the key concepts inherent in each essay, and adding a statement regarding their application and implementation. Each essay, accordingly, is followed by both a concept page and a commentary page. It should be clear, in this regard, that the contributing authors are in no way responsible for either the concepts derived from their postulations, or the opinions and suggestions advanced in the commentaries. If the authors' meanings have been misinterpreted, or their convictions misapplied, the fault is entirely that of the editor.

I hope that the two volumes will provide those interested in curriculum matters with a relatively complete overview of the existing scene. Particular readers may see fit to quarrel with the inclusion of a given essay, with the topical coverage, or with the editorial license. As in most human endeavors, however, choices and compromises were necessary. These were made as rationally as the editor's intelligence permitted.

Louis Rubin
Urbana, Illinois

Louis Rubin

Section 1 The Curriculum in Perspective: Schooling and Subject Matter

GENERAL ISSUES

What Shall We Tell the Children?

From the moment, long ago in history, when the first group of parents gathered together to plan the first school, the critical question has always been: what shall we teach the children? The question remains as vexing today as it was then. We somehow have never been able to reach a universally accepted conclusion as to precisely what knowledge, skills, and beliefs are most conducive to a successful adulthood. Thus, it is hardly surprising that in the seventies—as in the sixties, fifties, and forties—we once again are engaged in unsettling debates as to the proper subject matter of teaching.

The ancient issues are familiar enough: should the curriculum change as society undergoes one transition after another; is good education general in nature or must it rather accommodate the traditional disciplines; should schools serve the public good or the personal aspirations of their clients; and, to note the classic dispute that has again become an issue in our time, is compulsory education even desirable?

What Are Schools For?

The answers to these dilemmas depend upon what we take to be the purpose of education. Much curricular controversy, in fact, stems from our fickleness regarding educational aims. One can trace, throughout the history of the school, a chaotic sequence of evolutionary phases. Assumptions and presumptions have tended to shift as theories ebb and flow in response to societal crisis. Thus, the vocational school of a half-century ago has reappeared as career education. The dress, to be sure, is more modern and the organization more sophisticated, but, at bottom, the goals are similar. It has been much the same with other instructional policies as, periodically, we realign the balance of emphasis among the child's

1

personal development, his stockpile of information, and his sensitivity to societal problems.

One can trace from the historical record, if only crudely, at least three contradictory rationales for making decisions about the utility of particular subject matter:

1. Content selected for its practical usefulness.
2. Content selected for its traditional nature.
3. Content selected for its perceived relevance.

We teach arithmetic and reading, for example, because their knowledge is useful in pursuing ordinary aspirations. The study of, say, calculus, on the other hand, may have less pragmatic utility, but it explicates a branch of higher mathematics. Similarly, the facts surrounding a constitutional convention neither do much in the way of conveying historical insight nor offer practical advantage, but they constitute an aspect of our conventional wisdom—knowledge vaguely associated with "the educated person."

Questions of Relevance

In our present uncertainty, therefore, the criteria for relevance pose special difficulties. It is hard to determine what serves as truly functional knowledge in an unstable society. Are we better advised, for example, to teach the young about the workings of computers or, instead, to teach them about the dangers of uncontrolled technology? Are we to judge relevance according to the preferences of students, parents, or teachers? When what seems relevant to the student is contrary to that which seems relevant for the society, how is the conflict resolved? Finally, since issues invariably occur whenever people debate learning goals, who among us is best fit to determine educational significance?

Teachers, after all, are not passive pawns content to act out the wishes of administrators. They bias their instruction toward the educational values they most esteem. The relevancy issue, therefore, may be minimal when a particular teacher defers to students' personal interests; when, however, the teacher has strong convictions about the kind of instructional experiences that offer optimal benefits, arguments easily develop.

What we are left with, then, is a new renaissance of an old dilemma: what is to be taught? But in the present instance, the dilemma is likely to be a good deal more troublesome than in the past. Affected by the same wave of rising expectations that has engulfed their elders, students are no longer willing to accept boredom as uncomplainingly as they once did. Reluctant to delay gratification, increasingly sceptical about the virtues of traditional life-styles, they clamor for classroom lessons that bear upon the urgencies of the moment.

At first blush, it might seem that there would be little disadvantage to serving student self-interests, particularly since it is hard to demonstrate that—the basics aside—a specific bit of learning has direct consequences during adulthood. When the matter is probed somewhat more deeply, however, three difficulties emerge: First, since learners' educational interests can be either irrational, inconsequential, or otherwise misconceived, are they to be gratified as a matter of course or, rather, are we better advised to insist upon careful judgment? Education is both expensive and important, too vital to be left entirely to chance. If, in short, we operate schools, we presumably have a particular set of purposes in mind, and if these purposes are not accomplished, what is the point?

Second, until the possibilities of lifelong, continuing education become more viable, the long-range utility of student interests is a crucial consideration. That is, if students should happen to choose their curricula haphazardly, on the basis of momentary mood, precious opportunity may be dissipated. One might argue, of course, that as the learners' intellectual appetites shift, instruction can be adjusted accordingly; but, alas, formal education is not yet so resilient: schools are complex organizations; new instructional materials cannot be developed and legitimized with ease; and teachers are specialists who master their craftsmanship over long periods of time.

Third, there is the basic question of educational aim; are the schools intended to serve private or societal needs? That is, if the schools exist, even in part, to perpetuate the objectives of the social order, curricular choice cannot be left to the child alone. We must instead mandate those elements of general education that we consider essential to effective participation in the social system. In view of these impediments to a student-determined curriculum, then what can be said about the child's dissatisfaction with his compulsory education?

The Complaints of Learners

Thousands of youngsters like school, learn effectively, and derive considerable satisfaction from their classroom hours. Others, however, are not so blessed. Particularly in the inner cities, where social inequities etch deeply into the environment of the school, the young are often hostile, rebellious, and alienated. And even in the more affluent suburbs, where most students have benefited from a comparatively privileged background, many students are disenchanted with the mandated program of instruction.

As the young continue to mature and become more socially aware earlier, they seem to find too little connection between what goes on in the school and what goes on in the world outside. Apprehensive over the social plight, concerned about poverty, political corruption, the

irrationality of war, and the abuses of power, many students find
little of worth in what they take as the triflings of past history. They
want, instead, a program of instruction bearing more directly upon the
contemporary scene, and more aligned with subjects and topics that they
find personally significant(*1*).

The prevailing grading systems, too, are a source of malcontent.
Touched by the wave of existentialism that has characterized the last
decade of American life, many students express moral outrage over grades
based upon competitive achievement. Accultured over their years in
school to the art of "psyching-out" teacher expectations, the more able
students often object to grades that reflect not conceptual knowledge, but
rather test-taking ability. They sense, moreover, that the free exercise of
their imaginative and creative powers could be viewed as nonconforming
behavior, opening them to penalty of one sort or another. Unimpressed
by the requirements of the organizational system or by the conventions
of tradition, they are inclined to question not only the fundamental
value of grading, but its methodology as well.

Many are further alienated by the suspicion that their courses of
instruction are riddled with hypocrisy, contrivances, and cant. In an age
of relatively advanced communication technology, even slight exposure
to the media precludes complete student naivety. Learners are thus quick
to recognize the discongruity between the ideals of democracy outlined in
their tests and the machinations of their government officials.

We have tended—as do most other nations—to commit certain sins
of omission in designing the curriculum, largely out of the conviction
that some human events are understood in proper perspective only after a
degree of maturity has been reached. But today's young grow up faster,
learn more quickly, and seem, at least in recent times, to be increasingly
idealistic. Curricular distortions of reality, hence, are more readily
detected and less lightly condoned than once was the case. Perhaps the
most serious dissatisfaction of all, however, lies in the belief—widely
held by many students—that the secondary school is little more than a
warm place of containment where they must serve out their adolescence
until the social system allows them more useful roles.

A related dissatisfaction stems from recent shifts in our occupational
patterns. In earlier times, when apprenticeships were the normal route to
vocational preparation, viable alternatives to a sustained program of
schooling existed. With the advent of postindustrial society, however, an
era of unprecedented professionalism has emerged. As a consequence of
an extended period of formal preparation, career choices must be made
at an increasingly early age. Indeed, in many instances, if a career pattern
is not selected in sufficient time, the range of options becomes greatly
constrained. The young—caught between an understandable desire for the
good life and the co-options of the system—are embittered by what seems
like manipulative coercion. It comes as no surprise, therefore, that the

present crop of high school graduates, having witnessed the obstacles encountered by those in the sixties who chose to reject the customary rituals of vocational preparation, are once again submitting to the demands of the system. They remain, nonetheless, angered by programs of professional preparation that are sometimes extraneous, occasionally irrelevant, and invariably superfluous.

Erik H. Erikson has described adolescence as a time of "psycho-sexual moratorium" during which the young should be free to experiment with new role behaviors(2). Today's young seem to be acutely aware that the opportunity for such experimentation has been seriously curtailed. There is little chance, for example, during the high school years, to participate meaningfully in the affairs of the society. Time spent in school is sometimes seen as a form of social exile as much as a period of formalized learning. Worse, from the vantage point of many critics, little of the required learning has practical application. In the existing curriculum, for example, the student may not learn anything about income tax laws, or the repair of a clogged drain, or the way in which mouth-to-mouth resuscitation is administered to the victim of a heart attack. Most instructional theorists have viewed the school not as a place for the acquisition of practical skills, but rather as a place for becoming familiar with the cultural heritage, for intellectual growth, and for self-development. Many students, nonetheless, probably would prefer to know more about clogged drains and less about the Byzantine Empire.

Heavily committed to autonomy and independence of action, and dedicated to self-sufficiency, those in late adolescence—like some of their elders—would like to reduce the now-almost-mandatory reliance upon professional experts in managing their circumstances. Hence, they covet more knowledge about basic medicine, constitutional rights, legal protection, the cultivation of home gardens, automobile repairs, and so on.

For much the same reasons, they also resent their financial dependence upon their parents, which sometimes impedes their quest for personal sovereignty. The passion to be free of parental dominance is, of course, hardly new; the impatience of adolescents for adulthood, in fact, is probably as old as man's history itself. Yet, in a technocratic age, when ascension to majority is delayed longer than ever before, youth's anger with its forced impotence is not difficult to understand. Thus, whenever and wherever schooling fails to facilitate liberation from the shackles of subordinacy, students are inclined to react negatively.

The dissatisfactions of students also are related to their consuming preoccupation with self. Given to an intensely personal response to the vagaries of life, prompted by an existentialist approach to survival, the young object to a curriculum that prohibits individuality. They seek, therefore, learning that facilitates greater self-awareness, self-expression, and self-fulfillment: the self, in short, is everything. The arbitrary requirements for college admission, the compulsory participation in prescribed courses of study, and even the mandatory stipulations for graduation are regarded, not uncommonly, as impingements on personal liberty. Although such resentments are not surprising, and are perhaps even reasonable, the extent to which they should be cause for change remains a major issue in curriculum theory.

The answer, seemingly, again depends upon how one defines the function of schools. If public education—to repeat an earlier principle—is intended to serve the individual, accommodating student expectations is rational. If, on the other hand, the educational requirements for responsible citizenship, in the broadest dimension of the term, are the dominant goal, student desires cannot serve as the sole curricular determinant. But if both purposes are seen as essential, a judicious balance between individual and societal need must be found.

The Complaints of Parents

The complaints of parents, significantly, tend to contradict those of students. A recent Gallup poll of public opinion is instructive in this connection(3). Ranked in order of importance, the major parental concerns regarding schools are (1) lack of discipline, (2) integration–segregation issues, (3) insufficient dollar support, (4) drug usage, and (5) the limited supply of "good" teachers. Almost a third of the parents sampled nationally believe, in addition, that the growing incidence of crime in schools has reached crisis proportions. Although parents generally recognize that student lack of interest in schooling has risen sharply, only one in five would approve of eliminating compulsory education. The over-whelming percentage of those interviewed, moreover, want more emphasis upon vocational education, on-the-job training, and school credit for volunteer work performed in community agencies.

With respect to remedial students, those unable to reach the anticipated degree of academic achievement, 90 percent of the sampling favor repeating failed courses rather than automatic promotion. When asked what should be done about recalcitrant students who break school rules and refuse to follow teacher directions, about half suggest punishment of some sort, and roughly half think that more would be gained from rehabilitation measures such as counseling, parental conferences, reassignment to another teacher, and so on.

Opinion regarding experimental programs is equally varied. According to the poll,

> parents with children in the public schools are more inclined to say that the schools are too ready to try new ideas . . . those without children in the schools, and parents of children in parochial–private schools, are inclined to say the schools are not interested enough in new ways and methods.

Presumably, therefore, parents are opposed to innovations that they think will interfere with the acquisition of a traditional education. Nonparents and parents with children in private schools would both prefer more innovation—aimed primarily, one suspects, at reducing dollar cost. Three-fourths of those interviewed would like prayers utilized in classrooms, about half disfavor teacher tenure, and three out of four are opposed to integration through busing. Judgments as to the quality of current schools varied: among those likely to be most knowledgeable— parents with children in schools—approximately half are convinced that most schools do a credible job.

Echoing the findings of several other surveys, the data demonstrate a high correlation between success in school and amount of leisure reading, and a low correlation between success in school and time devoted to the viewing of television. Asked what constitutes a "good" school, the typical answer went something like the following:

> The good school has . . . teachers who are interested in their work and in their students; teachers who make their classes interesting; enough variety in the curriculum to interest students who are not college-bound; good discipline, respect for authority; good student–teacher relationships; and good student-to-student relationships.

In sum, it seems safe to conclude that, although the public's attitude is far from uniform, the central tendencies are certainly discernible. The prevailing conception of a good education is pretty much what it has always been: rather than replace the traditional subject matter with something new, most adults would prefer that teachers work harder to make the content more interesting and relevant. There is a continuing fear that, instead of perpetuating healthy values, schools may become the training grounds for crime and civil disobedience. And, importantly, parents and students alike still regard schooling as the dominant means of vocational preparation and entry into the work world.

So, when the concerns of students and parents are weighed against the reality of the times, the future of the traditional classroom—at least in its present form—is uncertain. Some grievances, to be sure, arise out of ideological differences and are thus likely to remain points of dispute. Others, however, have reasonable legitimacy, and definitive revisions seem in order. Untapped potential, for example, could reside in new applications of technology, in the use of the external community for educational experience, and in altered organizational structures that increase learning options. It may also be advisable to reexamine the appropriateness of our grading mechanisms, the pervasive anonymity of school life, the scant emphasis given to nonverbal learning modes, the pale facsimile that passes for authentic instructional individualization, and the limited attention given to the personal concerns of students.

Above all, however, the indictments of irrelevance must be subjected to further scrutiny. Three correctives, seemingly, may be possible: (1) more attractive subject matter can be substituted for content that students find unappealing; and (2) where the designated content is essential to a sound general education, more stimulating instructional techniques can be devised; and (3) greater efforts to make the intellectual ideas more germane to the lives of students can be made.

Toward this end it might be useful to review, if only in general, the specific problems associated with the subjects constituting the heart of the traditional curriculum. Although these are treated in greater depth in the *Handbook* section that follows, a brief overview may serve to illuminate the needed renovations.

THE TRADITIONAL DISCIPLINES

Viewed in the aggregate, the substantive content of the curriculum has not changed significantly over the past several decades. In the main, today's students come to grips with pretty much the same intellectual fare as did their parents and, in some subjects, their grandparents. Essentially the same curricular lore has persisted, generation after generation, mainly because our conception of general education has remained relatively constant. We still expect, for example, the "educated" person to write with reasonable grammatical precision, to know a bit about his cultural past, to cope adequately with conventional mathematical applications, and so on. Although we have never been able to demonstrate a direct connection between such knowledge and successful adulthood, it generally has been assumed that plumber, physician, housewife, and secretary alike would benefit from such general education, irrespective of one's particular lot in life.

Reason dictates that if these assumptions were valid in the past they may be equally so in the present. It would be hard to prove that the virtues of good general education have dissipated over time. Much criticism leveled against the prevailing curriculum stems not from the indictment that such knowledge is no longer worthwhile, but from the presumption that it no longer is sufficient. Occasional disclaimers in the maverick literature notwithstanding, most people believe that the plumber should know something about history, just as the physician should know something about music, whether or not such knowledge bears upon their vocational tasks. The more abiding danger, in fact, is that the heavy stress upon technology-oriented subject matter has perverted what once was called "a well-rounded education." To compound matters further, there is a growing inconsistency in the teaching methods associated with different subjects, so that students are sometimes confused by varying pedagogical procedures and standards. These similarities and dissimilarities are apparent in the synthesis that follows.

Science

The great wave of reform that characterized science education during the late fifties and sixties emphasized a shift from memorization to process learning. Curriculum theorists reasoned that it was more advantageous for students to develop scientific literacy through inquiry and discovery rather than through the routine memorization of facts. The theorists also reckoned that—since some scientific ideas are more important than others—a grasp of the major concepts was more beneficial than a mastery of secondary detail.

As Hozinsky(4) has demonstrated, the rationale for science education rests upon three basic assumptions. First, because science and its by-product, technology, have great impact upon our lives, there are *practical* reasons for being scientifically knowledgeable. Second, since scientific research exerts massive influence upon the society, improving the quality of life on the one hand and creating problems of environmental control on the other, there are compelling social reasons for giving students an understanding of the ways in which science affects their lives. Third, inasmuch as the history of science involves the creative use of inventive talents, there are aesthetic reasons for familiarizing students with the imagined aspects of scientific endeavor.

Although the more able students appear to leave high school with a respectable knowledge of basic biology, chemistry, physics, and so on, the health of science education is something less than perfect. There is an imbalance to the overall K–12 curriculum (the consequence of conflicting beliefs as to the critical concepts to be taught), junior high school programs vary considerably from locale to locale, and the typical high school courses in biology, chemistry, and physics are traditionally scant in student appeal. Roughly, 90 percent of high school students receive some exposure to earth science and biology, about half learn some chemistry, and only one out of five take a class in physics. In most states, the study of science is required during the elementary and junior high school years but is largely optional during high school.

During the spate of curriculum revisions that transpired between 1955 and 1965, a number of new instructional programs were devised, such as PSSC physics, CBA chemistry, BSCS biology, and the Intermediate Science Curriculum Study Program for junior high school students. Some of these curricula reflected learning theories associated with Jerome Bruner, particularly the postulation that significant ideas can be learned at virtually any age and thus the task of curriculum is to reinforce these ideas, in progressively greater sophistication, throughout the elementary and secondary school. Others, in contrast, reflected a somewhat contradictory set of principles, those for example of Jean Piaget and Robert Gagne, suggesting that children progress through cumulative stages of readiness for abstract thought, thus making it essential that a given intellectual concept be introduced at an appropriate developmental point.

More recently, a number of efforts to program science education through computer-assisted instruction (CAI) have been launched. The results, although encouraging, are not yet conclusive. All in all, science education is a good deal more effective than it was a generation ago, but a number of unsolved problems remain. As the essay by Collette in the following section shows, most curricula lack practicality, adequate equipment for laboratory experiments has become prohibitively expensive, the rapidity of scientific advancement tends to make textbooks obsolete soon after publication, and science teachers sometimes lack sufficient technical background. More generally, science education seems to suffer from the same basic infirmities as do other segments of the curriculum: the learning materials are not relevant to student interests, instruction fails to cut across the various science disciplines and to highlight their interconnections, little flexibility exists in pedagogical method, and the selection of teaching content is inordinately influenced by custom.

Social Studies

The social studies, too, have been criticized for both their excesses and lapses. Although the fault-finding varies with the critic, there seems to be widespread agreement that the typical program suffers from an exaggerated preoccupation with the past and from undue factual detail. Most critics, moreover, are likely to acknowledge that, if the end goal of the social studies is that of cultivating worthy citizenship, the present curricula deserve poor marks.

By and large, most students are sensitive to blatant propaganda, resent patent indoctrination, and are alienated by study materials that have been abridged of human idiosyncrasies. Most, moreover, demand the right to form their own values; as a consequence, courses in civics normally have negligible effect upon out-of-school conduct. Of greatest moment, however, the research data suggest that the majority of high school students leave school politically naive.

It is in the social studies that public expectation and instructional theory are most likely to conflict. A majority of theorists, for example, are convinced that values—in the last analysis—are self-fashioned and it therefore is essential to expose students to the pros and cons of moot issues and controversial ideas. But the public, fearful that an open consideration of "dangerous" issues could breed deleterious consequences, leans toward instruction that involves a heavily flavored indoctrination into traditional values. Whereas a majority of the body politic believes that children should be told what to believe and what to value, most curriculum designers are more persuaded that, in the words of Hunt and Metcalf, "any belief that has not been subjected to rational examination is by definition a prejudice no matter how correct or incorrect it may be"(5). The natural result of these unresolved conflicts is a social studies program that is frequently riddled with myth, mystique, and, upon occasion, out-and-out hypocrisy.

Teaching materials, say Hunt and Metcalf,

should be drawn from a selection of conflicting propositions in such controversial areas as race and minority-group relations, social class, economics, sex, courtship and marriage, religion and morality, and national and patriotic beliefs, plus a wide range of relevant data to be used in testing them. Many of these propositions will be derived from, or correspond to, the values, beliefs, and attitudes of high school students. One might say, therefore, that in any given learning situation teaching materials should be drawn from (1) broadly social and highly controversial issues of the culture; (2) knowledges, values, and attitudes of students; and (3) relevant data of the social sciences.

Before these highly desirable ends can be accomplished, however, it will be necessary to convince parents that students think for themselves, that they are capable of strong convictions on social matters, and that they fabricate, through trial and error, a personal system of beliefs and values —whether or not the underlying principles are treated in the curriculm. The temptation to avoid issues, to resist controversy, to preach lofty but meaningless ideals, and to rest in the counterfeit serenity of factual trivia, hence, all must be resisted before real instructional vitality can be achieved in the social studies.

At bottom, the curriculum still suffers—despite the impressive strides of recent years—from our classic inability to relate the lessons of history to the dilemmas of the time; from insufficient stress on the skills of analytic reasoning; from a preoccupation with content and an underemphasis of process; and from a failure to dramatize powerful social science concepts that establish connective tissue among different subject-matter areas. Like general science, the social studies are an eclectic distillation of many disciplines, including history, political science, geography, anthropology, psychology, and economics. Until we become more adept at clarifying their interrelationships and underscoring the human chemistry that stems from their interaction, our teaching will continue to miss the point. Although the precise distinctions between the social sciences and the social studies are perhaps fuzzy, and the marriage is at best fitful, it is generally presumed that each of the social sciences represents a compendium of scholarly knowledge; the social studies, in contrast, are an amalgamation of this knowledge that bears primarily upon social problems. Whether or not this distinction is valid, it can hardly be denied that we do not yet involve the minds of students in the social problems of the day to a sufficient degree, and to this extent, at least, social studies instruction suffers.

It is this same amalgamation of social science principles, moreover, that poses the major obstacle to sound curriculum design, for good social education must go far beyond the mere communication of significant principles. It must, as well, incorporate preparation for citizenship, inculcation in rational thought, familiarization with cultural heritage, orientation to the social scene, and the formulation of sound values. Each of these obligations, moreover, must be met through instruction that respects student concerns, permits reasonable spontaneity in learning, accommodates individual differences among learners, and makes use of defensible teaching methodology.

It is in this last connection that a pervasive issue again comes to the fore: when the instructional purpose is that of exposing the student to a particular fact or generalization, didactic teaching (verbal explanations through book or lecture) probably is most efficient. But when the goal is to perpetuate critical thinking, heuristic teaching (requiring the learner to inquire into phenomena and to discover meaning for himself or herself) probably has more to offer. Achieving a suitable balance between didactics and heuristics, in social studies in particular and throughout the curriculum in general, remains one of our most challenging enigmas. It comes as no shock, therefore, that the teaching methods of the social studies are often indecisive, sometimes moribund, and occasionally in violation of what we take to be legitimate pedagogy. But, in all fairness, they are also, at times, marvelously inventive, incredibly potent, and spectacular in their effects.

Language Arts

Curriculum specialists are periodically accused of tinkering with inconsequential details instead of striving for definitive improvement. There may be some truth in the criticism, but the disingenuous critic often forgets that educational practitioners are a large, diversified, and periodically intractable lot, sensitive to the pitfalls of faddism, and thus not readily predisposed either to abrupt reversals or the exhortations of change-agents.

Recent movements in the language arts curricula reflect this cautiousness. Although some departures from past convention are perceptible, there is, on the whole, a conspicuous absence of innovative momentum. The gamut of elective courses has broadened, somewhat, and increasing numbers of schools are experimenting with minicourses and instructional programs of differential length, but the corpus is largely as before.

One also finds, as in other subject areas, a mounting interest in nontypical grading procedures. Teachers appear to be relying less on repetitive drill and stressing, instead, the conceptual growth of their students. In many secondary schools, moreover, heterogeneous grouping has replaced the time-honored practice of clustering students according to ability levels.

Even more dramatic is the trend toward humanism. Not long ago, for example, Alfred Groman, a respected senior statesman in language arts education, referred to English as "the central humanistic study" and argued that, through the study of language and literature, students could be helped to increase their knowledge of self and of human behavior generally. As elsewhere in the instructional program, efforts are underway to reduce depersonalization and to provide students with a greater depth of affective experience. These developments, however, are far from widespread, and must be regarded as experimental efforts rather than as major reforms.

Much of the resistance to humanism stems from the same double bind afflicting science and social studies education: time devoted to humanistic concerns limits the opportunity to attack cognitive objectives. Teachers—aware of the periodic complaints that they fail to accomplish a solid grounding in the basics—are understandably reluctant to pursue what a sizable portion of the citizenry would regard as frills. Students, on the other hand, continue to seek classrooms that are less tedious, more stimulating, and focused more directly on the pressing concerns of contemporary life.

The basic substance of instruction, nonetheless, remains about what it has always been. Textbooks dominate, there is great variation in teaching technique, and, more than anywhere else in the curriculum, student achievement is affected by a wide array of internal and external forces. In the typical eighth grade, for example, student reading ability can span a range from fourth to twelfth grades, and parallel differences are likely to exist in spelling mastery, writing skill, and verbal capacity. Similarly, student achievement can be influenced to a considerable degree by the extent to which leisure reading and discussion are endemic in the student's home life.

The language arts normally include the four basic applications of language: writing, reading, speaking, and listening. They embody, in sum, the verbal arts of human communication. Most schools tend to emphasize the fundamental skills—handwriting, spelling, and punctuation —during the early school years, and substantive content—literature, rhetoric, and public speaking—during the latter years. Each language skill, although dealt with separately for the purposes of drill and exercise, eventually is fused into the usage patterns of conventional human communication.

The organization of instruction, from kindergarten through the twelfth grade, is intended to facilitate continuous language development. There is a presumption, furthermore, that learning experiences in other segments of the curriculum will also help to improve the student's language mastery. Yet, although a goodly amount of reading and writing goes on in science, social studies, and foreign language study, they seem to contribute only negligibly to the cumulative improvement of technical skills. Students, to be sure, can develop their writing skills on virtually any topic, and read about an infinite variety of subjects in seeking to enhance comprehension but, in most instances, non-English teachers view language as a means rather than an end, and skill development is left chiefly to language arts specialists.

Enjoying perhaps the highest priority of all subjects taught in school, if only because language and thought are inseparable and effective communication is central to social living, the teaching of English is nonetheless as vulnerable to pedagogical uncertainly as any other subject. Despite a considerable amount of research, the overall findings do not add up to an adequate explanation of the effects of cultural deprivation. Cause and effect, in short, are uncertain. Furthermore, beliefs regarding the ways in which grammar and reading are best taught differ; stylistic preferences in punctuation, sentence structure, and paragraphing vary from school to school, and from teacher to teacher; and the selection of representative literature is based in the main upon whim, tradition, or the availability of books.

The needed improvements, therefore, would appear to parallel those in other subjects. The subject matter must be imbued with greater excitement, alternative learning experiences must be devised for students who find it difficult to learn through standard procedures, our failure to teach substantial numbers of children to read and write must be overcome, the humanities must prevail to a larger extent than they now do, and the teaching methods themselves must be made more precise, consistent, and potent.

Mathematics

Commenting upon the teaching of mathematics today, Bell and Usiskin(6) have this to say:

> To summarize, the present situation for large numbers of students seems to be characterized by (1) dislike of the subject, (2) lack of opportunities to become acquainted with any more than trivial foundations of the subject, (3) limited competence with even the meager amount of mathematics learned, (4) ignorance about the nature of mathematicians' work, (5) fear or puzzlement when understanding of mathematics is expected, and (6) memories of failure whenever the subject of mathematics is broached. It is no wonder that most people consider mathematics to be relevant to others (perhaps) but irrelevant to themselves (certainly).

As in the case of science education, the reforms of the sixties were aimed largely at the development of better college preparatory curricula. Consequently, the requirements of the college entrance examination board governed, in large measure, the direction of the revisions. University entrance, not practical need, served as the determining factor. The powerful domination of the K–12 curriculum by higher education entry conditions—the pernicious by-product of an archaic conception of the public school as apprenticeship for the "real" education that follows—was thus demonstrated yet again. For the college-bound student, high school courses are chiefly geared toward preparation for what is to come. In turn, elementary and junior high school programs to a considerable degree are designed to set stage for high school instruction.

Still, viewed in retrospect, the mathematics curricula were unquestionably improved by the reforms. As the recommendations of professional mathematicians were implemented, conceptual understanding took on greater importance, and emphasis upon the memorization of formal laws diminished. New subject matter—set theory, nonmetric geometry, and variable number bases—was introduced. Teachers began to focus upon the structure of mathematics as much as on the mastery of operational skills.

Despite these impressive improvements, not much was done in the way of improving the mathematics curriculum for noncollege students; the new materials did not seem to enhance the subject's appeal in any real way, and little effort went into the upgrading of courses in applied mathematics.

Even today, large numbers of students find mathematics distasteful. Many have a negative mental set regarding their learning capacity and lack the ability to use anything beyond the basic arithmetical skills. And, in the worst of circumstances, a few leave school with less than a workable command of decimals, percentage, and fractions. We have not yet succeeded, seemingly, in convincing remedial students that basic mathematical skills are valuable. Nor have we learned to motivate reluctant learners with any real efficiency, to deploy teaching procedures that capture the learner's imagination, or to prevent slippage—the peculiar phenomena through which learners "forget" what they have once learned. Above all, the evidence seems to suggest that we are in serious need of alternative teaching methodologies which can be used with students who find it difficult to learn customary instruction.

Current developmental efforts, consequently, are directed toward the required correctives: designers are seeking to invest the curricula with more real-life connection; the newer teaching units, now under experimentation, accent less in the way of routine exercise and more in the way of active problem solving; learning theorists are at work on diagnostic procedures that can be used to pinpoint reasoning errors more precisely;

the possibilities of cross-disciplinary uses are being explored more fully; and training programs are beginning to equip teachers with specific tactics for teaching specific mathematical functions.

These curricular weaknesses notwithstanding, mathematics education has come a long way from the primitive modes of a decade or two back. Some students fall short of expected achievement, but some learn monumental amounts and reach unprecedented levels of excellence. As elsewhere in the curriculum, then, it is our failures rather than our successes with which we must be concerned.

If these revisions are sustained, future mathematics curricula will give substantially greater attention to problem-solving capability, mathematical reasoning, the extended use of out-of-school resources, and additional motivational techniques. More than anything else, however, the next decade will witness the utilization of multiple instructional programs, permitting teachers to individualize the study of mathematics to a far greater extent than they now do. The programs are also likely to make greater use of games—pleasurable activities through which children acquire and use mathematical skills—as well as alternative methods of reinforcing learning.

Although the ability to use numbers effectively will remain a high priority, greater emphasis will be given to the application of mathematical ideas, the use of mathematics in solving "nonmathematical" problems, and mathematical models for representing and comparing abstract ideas.

The Arts

Virtually everyone who progresses through the American public school is exposed, in greater or lesser degree, to some form of art education. It is exceedingly difficult, however, to judge the ultimate benefits of such instruction. Although we can determine whether a child can read, how fast he can run twenty-five yards, how accurately he can spell a word, and the extent to which he knows historical facts, evaluating the consequences of art education is far more complicated. We can, of course, rate performance: the quality of a painting can be appraised, the voice quality and intonation of a singer can be evaluated, and the artistic merits of a sculpture or photograph can be determined according to conventional critical standards. The assessment of aesthetic sensitivity or artistic appreciation, in contrast, is quite another matter. Aside from the fact that yardsticks for measuring the depth of emotional response are nonexistent, beauty (and therefore artistic taste) resides, as the saying goes, in the eyes of the beholder or listener.

Traditionally, art and music education involve both content and process. Students are expected to learn something about form, color, and harmony, as well as to recognize and appreciate art and music of high artistic value. Describing the objectives of art education, for example,

Hausman(7) lists three kinds of activities: "forming–making activities" wherein students create a variety of images; "visual studies" wherein students judge the visual clarities of a particular environment; and "historical and critical studies" wherein students become familiar with artistic traditions and values. In the usual instance, most students engage in such activities during their elementary school years, but only those with a pronounced special interest continue art and musical experiences in the secondary school. Throughout the entire arts curriculum, whether the learning derives from performance or appreciation, there is a basic assumption that aesthetic experiences contribute to the training of the senses, offer students an opportunity to express ideas in symbolic form, and heighten their visual, tactile, and aural capacities.

The probabilities are high that, in the time ahead, art, music, and other forms of aesthetic education will assume greater importance than they have in the past. Three factors support this premise. First, we have entered an age in which people manifest a pronounced interest in self; hence, school experiences that enhance self-awareness, self-expression, and self-actualization are likely to attract more and more student interest. Second, as we penetrate more deeply into postindustrial society, human preoccupation with the requirements for sustenance and survival is likely to diminish, and a corresponding rise in aesthetic interests could ensue. Third, increased leisure may also lead, in time, to greater interest in the arts. Currently, people still tend to use their spare hours for subsidiary employment and increased income. There is reason to assume, however, that the trend may reverse in the future, and that the aesthetic life will claim a larger share of people's interests.

The prospective shift toward greater emphasis on the arts therefore has direct implications for the curriculum. Observing that artistic expression is a powerful vehicle for human communication, Marantz(8) contends that:

> Where art has been totally integrated into classroom work its unique qualities have been lost; where it has been isolated from the total educational stream, it has tended to become an excuse for skill development or study of a narrow range of elite artifacts. Rarely is art accepted as a fundamental human potential to be evoked, cultivated, and used in immediate practical ways. Art education must respond to the aesthetic needs of the individual and the broader society.

He also believes that the arts and art education must begin to center upon the dominant issues in the social scene. Human stability will depend not merely upon pure water and clean air, but upon the prevention of "aesthetic pollution" as well. Thus, Marantz calls for a curriculum that teaches the young about style and design, that induces a lasting taste for aesthetic stimulation, and that encourages the full use of the sensory apparatus in developing aesthetic understanding.

What this means is that simple exposure to good painting, good music, good dance, and so on is not enough. Instruction will need to go beyond exposure, to the cultivation of artistic values, the development of artistic sense, and a basic familiarity with the artistic process itself. To achieve these ends it will be necessary both to enrich the aesthetic environment of the school and to provide students with opportunities to whet their artistic appetites by creating, and responding to, art products that they themselves find stimulating.

It must be acknowledged in this regard that once again we lack a repertory of teaching skills to match our ambitions. Much must be done, consequently, to redefine the objectives of art and aesthetic education and to devise artistic experiences that are more appropriate, more seductive, and more useful in providing students with a shelter against the shallow, the banal, and the mundane.

Foreign Language

Turning, finally, to current practices in the teaching of foreign languages, the existing state of affairs offers a useful illustration of the general weaknesses that permeate the curriculum as a whole. In varying degree, the problems are characteristic of virtually every teaching area. Using foreign language study as a prototype case, therefore, we can trace the egregious curricular soft spots that require strengthening.

Throughout the early history of the public school, foreign language instruction was regarded as peripheral to basic education and associated primarily with "finishing schools." A knowledge of French, Spanish, or German was not considered vital to active participation in social life. In the period following World War II, as the one-world concept gained currency, the proponents of foreign language teaching were able to argue more persuasively that bilingual individuals among the citizenry would contribute to better international relations. It was not until the late 1950s, however, with the advent of the National Defense Education Act, that the protagonists were able to marshal a strong political force. As a result of their endeavors, large numbers of dollars were invested during the 1960s in the development of new teaching materials, the purchase of equipment for language laboratories, and additional research on teaching. Yet, however valid such claims regarding the benefits of foreign language study, the fact remains that a majority of students study language courses because they are required for graduation or subsequent college entrance. A much smaller percentage take foreign language courses out of a desire for personal enrichment, recognizing nevertheless that the prospects of becoming truly bilingual are dim.

Moreover, the logic through which foreign language study—and most other areas of instruction—is organized, suffers from serious inadequacies. To begin with, there is substantial disagreement among professionals over appropriate learning objectives and teaching methods. In the case of foreign language, for example, some specialists contend that reading mastery offers more long-term advantage than speaking mastery. Others contest this point of view and argue, instead, that bilingual fluency ought to serve as the dominant aim. Similarly, opinion is divided within the profession over the relative merits of audiolingual and cognitive-decoding theories. In the audiolingual approach, major emphasis is placed upon aural communication, grammatical structure is dealt with only incidentally, and conversational dialogues are related to real-life situations as much as possible. The cognitive-decoding method, in contrast, is based on the systematic introduction of syntax, rules, and structure and vocabulary development. In the absence of a general consensus regarding the means and ends of foreign language study, one finds, throughout the nation's classrooms, considerable diversity in teaching methodology.

Another inadequacy stems from the proneness to exaggerate purpose, and to extend the learning goals beyond that which can reasonably be accomplished. In foreign language programs, for instance, many schools seek to teach not only the language but also the culture of a foreign society. Thus, children may be expected to learn Spanish *and* the social customs of Spain and Mexico. As a result, time for language mastery is diluted, and the learner becomes neither fluent in a foreign tongue nor particularly knowledgeable about another culture. Reason would hence seem to suggest that—throughout the curriculum—it might be better to attack fewer priorities with greater fervor.

A third failing derives from our apparent reluctance to establish a continuum wherein instruction from the first through the twelfth grades is sequentially ordered. To wit, some students start foreign language study in elementary school, some in junior high school, and some in senior high school. Moreover, for those who commence in elementary school, there is no systematic provision for sustained development throughout the upper grades. Predictably, therefore, in the absence of a cohesive program of instruction over a sustained period of time, few students become genuinely fluent in a second language. Presumably, if a child were to study, say, French progressively—from the first through the last year of schooling—a much higher degree of lingual competence could be achieved.

Our striking inability to determine who should study what constitutes yet another difficulty. Teachers have long acknowledged that students vary in their affinity for language study. Some have considerable natural aptitude, others relatively little. We do not yet know, however, whether this aptitude is inherent, whether it can be cultivated, or whether it is dissipated through nonuse. Indeed, research of recent vintage suggests that the curriculum favors learners sufficiently flexible in personality to adjust easily to the existing instructional system. Youngsters who have equal or perhaps even superior potential, but who best learn through instructional procedures that are not utilized, are thus heavily penalized. Hence, until provisions are made for the careful nurture of each child's capacity to learn, and for the systematic use of alternative teaching techniques, many children will continue to be victimized by curricular rigidity.

A further impediment has to do with the lack of junction between the lessons of the classroom and the external social environment. The typical foreign language student, for example, rarely has an opportunity to speak the language outside the classroom, unless unique circumstances prevail. Scandinavian children who are taught English, in contrast, are blessed with a sequential period of study, spanning seven to ten years, and also have comparatively abundant opportunity to use their second language outside the school's walls. It is to be hoped, consequently that in a time of increasing ethnic pride and cultural identity, and in a time when the lines between school-based and community-based learning are becoming increasingly blurred, formal education may lose some of its ivory-tower complexion.

The curriculum is also weakened by a lack of internal consistency. Once students have been taught a language for three or four years, they might study literature by reading original rather than translated material, just as they could keep abreast of international affairs by reading foreign newspapers—thereby killing, so to speak, two curricular birds with the same stone. Because of the characteristic isolation that exists among subject areas, however, such linkages are infrequent. The coalescence of disparate knowledge into a broad general education, long championed in theory, has seldom penetrated practice.

Research, too, contributes its sins. Although a vast amount of investigation has been recorded, the answers to many critical questions are still wanting. How much drill, for example, carried out under what kinds of conditions, and at what time intervals, is most desirable? What represents the proper balance between self-directed and teacher-directed learning activities? How can particular teaching methods best be tailored to the unique learning requirements of a given child? Through what devices can the motivation to learn be enhanced? What is the optimum utility of machine-assisted learning? Practitioners, in a great many instances, are on legitimate ground when they complain that research delivers obvious conclusions, but ignores important unknowns.

Finally, to touch upon two further limitations, the profession has been lax in familiarizing parents, and the public in general, with the rationale underlying many curricular innovations. Changes, resultingly, are often viewed with suspicion and disaffection. Second, too little effort has gone toward retraining teachers to make effective use of the innovations. A few years ago, for example, foreign language in the elementary school (FLES) was introduced. The reasoning was credible:

the cumulative study of a language over a sustained period of years would produce substantially more skill. The basis of the rationale, however, was not made apparent to parents; a vast number of teachers were required to teach a foreign language without adequate preparation; virtually nothing was done to assure a systematic sequence of instruction throughout the grades; and the programs were organized in such fashion that children found little cause for joy in striving for bilingual dexterity. As a result, the bulk of the programs launched are no longer in existence.

All in all, these various deficits—in foreign language and elsewhere—cause the curriculum to lose a good deal of its force. What, then, lies ahead?

The Short-Range Future

Over the past several years, the federal government has contributed to the support of a number of laboratories for educational development, as well as a number of centers for educational research. The curricular clout of their endeavors, now beginning to emerge in perceptible degree, is likely to influence instructional change, at least in the short-run future. The government's projection called for the centers to produce new research findings that could be fabricated into usable programs. As things worked out, however, many of the laboratories found it necessary to engage in basic research, and many of the centers exercised considerable control over the applications resulting from their data. Although the curricular products have not been available for sufficient time to test their ultimate utility, some have already demonstrated impressive potential. But, like curricula created by school districts and those fashioned by commercial textbook publishers, much will depend upon the commitment and expertness of the teachers in whose hands they eventually fall.

Among the more notable programs is a series of instructional units called *Humanizing Learning,* produced by Research for Better Schools in Philadelphia. The teaching materials facilitate the effective integration of affect and cognition, and are aimed primarily at the enhancement of children's interpersonal skills. Through the instructional tools provided, children are helped to achieve greater initiative, to sharpen their perceptions of self and others, and to be more self-directive in resolving personal life problems.

Similarly, the Wisconsin Research and Development Center for Cognitive Learning has developed an extensive curriculum known as Individually Guided Education (IGE). Intended as an authentic alternative to conventional age-graded classrooms, the learning materials emphasize concept learning and cognitive development. Heavy effort has been made to increase the student's motivation and to extend learning retention. In IGE schools, learners are grouped according to age, aptitude, and stage of personal development. New instructional materials,

21

incorporating these concepts, have been developed in mathematics, science, reading, and reading readiness.

The CEMREL laboratory has worked extensively on a K–6 curriculum in aesthetic education. Designed to provide learners with a basic "vocabulary" in six art areas—dance, music, film, literature, theater, and the visual arts—the instructional mechanisms include slide-tape presentations, games, workbooks and texts, masks, photographs, and light-color projections. It is of interest to note that the teaching units are directed toward the nonarts teacher, and are arranged to permit easy integration into existing instructional programs.

The Southwest Educational Development Laboratory, in Austin, Texas, has refined an instructional program for Spanish-speaking children. Intended for use in grades K–3, the materials emphasize oral language development, bilingual reading, mathematics, and bicultural social studies. All instruction materials are in both Spanish and English, making it possible for children from Spanish-speaking homes to be taught in their native tongue. In a related enterprise, the Northwest Regional Educational Laboratory has evolved an instructional sequence, Intercultural Reading and Language Development. The intent is to make better materials available for teaching reading and English skills to children from culturally different backgrounds.

In other innovative efforts, the Far West Laboratory for Educational Research and Development, in San Francisco, has invested considerable effort in the development of new systems for instructional management, and engineered, as well, an instructional "toy library" for preschoolers and a series of training kits for midlevel administrators. The Stanford Center for Research and Development in Teaching has done extensive research on teacher effectiveness; the Wisconsin center has focused upon new instructional strategies; and the Learning Research and Development Center, at the University of Pittsburgh, has devoted its endeavors to the design of organizational patterns that make the elementary school more responsive to individual differences in children. Working in tandem with the Philadelphia laboratory, Research for Better Schools, innovative programs in science, social studies, mathematics and reading, intended primarily to enhance the individualization of learning, have been developed and field tested. Other organizations, moreover, are engaged in experiments that may help to determine learning readiness, to counteract limited aptitude, and to create prototypes of alternative schools for the future.

The evidence is not yet in with respect to the impact these various programs will have upon contemporary practice, but it seems reasonable to assume that, overall, they will leave their mark upon the educational scene. The curriculum, as educational historians frequently lament, changes with stupefying slowness. As a result, to judge before sufficient gestation has occurred would be to judge prematurely. Nonetheless, the early signs suggest that many of these recent inventions—as well as those produced by school districts, publishers, and others—will influence the curriculum of the near future.

Curriculum in the Long-Range Future*

Teaching in the long range, however, will need to center more upon active and less upon inert knowledge. Subject matter that is more decorative than functional, or that owes its existence chiefly to tradition, will need to be abandoned in favor of knowledge that helps youth to better cope with the changing world. Because tomorrow's citizenry will be called upon to make sensitive choices among conflicting priorities, life-styles, and social patterns, the curriculum of subsequent decades will need to treat, in varying contexts, the processes through which people identify problems, gather and verify related evidence, judge the probable consequences of alternative choices, and reach decisions. And, if current trends are any index, citizenship education will assume renewed importance, first, because of the likelihood of prolonged internicine social strife, and, second, because social alienation has become a hallmark of our time.

The cultural barometers suggest that we are moving toward a period of extreme pluralism in human concerns. As people come, more and more, to embrace diverse values, the development in youth of a greater tolerance for cultural difference will take on increased importance. People are likely to find it necessary, for example, either to shape their beliefs in accordance with the expectations of the groups to which they belong, or to reject group identity in favor of personal integrity. Determinations of this sort are not easily made, because the risks of alienation and identity loss are high. To counteract these risks, it may be necessary to build a curriculum that gives greater attention to the skills of managing emotional stress and which provides cognitive insights regarding the self-control of psychological turbulence.

The shift toward polarized values may give rise to an additional mandate. Should ethnic and cultural group aspirations run opposing courses, should the balance and distribution of desirable goods and services provoke dispute and conflict, a sustained period of internal political wars are presumable. The processes for the nonviolent resolution of these disputes and conflicts, therefore, may become another indispensable element in future curricula. Schooling could, in short, seek to develop a reasonable adeptness in the techniques of compromise and negotiation, a larger capacity to tolerate divergent points of view, and a willingness to grant others the privilege of differences.

* Adapted from Louis Rubin, ed., *The Future of Schooling: Perspectives on Tomorrow's Education* (Boston: Allyn and Bacon, Inc., 1975).

Rilke once observed that "the future enters into us, in order to transform itself in us, long before it happens." Curricular evolution will not come in dramatic waves; it will, instead, flow steadily along a predictable path, diverted here and there by momentary interruptions, yet moving inexorably along its plotted course. The direction of the flow is already becoming manifest: the exclusive use of competitive grading systems will become increasingly suspect; expectations regarding classroom discipline will remain high, but the controlling devices will be less harsh and spartan; natural learning will come, increasingly, to be viewed as explorations into self as well as into organized knowledge; and the individuality of the child will grow in importance. The cumulative result of these transitions may be the gradual evolution of a variant curriculum and a greater emphasis upon autonomous, independent study.

If, as is certainly possible, schooling becomes a diminishing factor in socialization, teaching will need to couple more closely with outside learning experiences. For that matter, even if the significance of formal education remains high, a continuing demand for relevance will make it necessary to strengthen the ties between the traditional disciplines and the student's personal search for meaning. Home, school, church, job, and street corner may thus constitute an enlarged classroom wherein critical ideas and values are tested against one another in varying contexts. Unless a major reversal occurs, the ongoing rebellion against depersonalization and regimentation will enlarge, forcing educational institutions to reassess —crisis by crisis—the proper mix between a good general education, distilled from the accumulated wisdom of the race, and spontaneous learning emanating from the pursuit of personal interests.

The young now in school will find it necessary, during adulthood, to make hard decisions regarding the use of scant natural and economic resources, the division of political power, and the definition of their own identities and life-styles. They best can be prepared for these obligations by a school that itself is symbolic of the healthy society, affording authentic engagement with real events. As many of the essays that follow make clear, our conceptions of the educational process are still remarkably primitive.

There is much to suggest, in sum, that youth can learn significant lessons not only from work experience and community service, but also from a more direct participation in the social scene. Is there any reason, for example, why high school students could not work for political candidates of their choice, debate social issues, or participate in civic action programs? What would be the overall educational consequences, for example, if, as Leet and Schure suggest in Section 5, three years of social service were substituted for existing junior high and middle schools? How much real loss would occur in intellectual knowledge? Would the educational cost factor rise or fall? What would be gained in the way of active commitment, sophistication, and a personal sense of usefulness? How much more meaningful might the abstractions of book learning become?

A radical reorientation of this sort, of course, may not be possible. Nonetheless, the low ebb that portions of the curriculum have now reached are testimony to our tireless worship of custom and our reluctance to look outward rather than inward. If the revisionist critics are guilty of excess, as may be the case, they nevertheless demonstrate that it is time to summon our imaginations to new flights. The world that gave rise to the traditional curriculum is no more. What we most need, consequently, is to activate the human regenerative capacity.

The quality of human decisions largely depends upon a body of underlying values. On this basis alone, what we call values education— so much talked about in recent years—must, of necessity, play a prominent part in the succeeding generation of curricula. If our forecasting social scientists are correct, the time ahead will require individuals to make difficult choices on parenthood, marriage, and divorce; on leisure versus affluence; on conventional as opposed to unconventional living patterns, and so on. The ancient virtues of honesty, integrity, compassion, and dignity are as likely to be essential in the year 2000 as they are today. Other values, in contrast, may need to be refashioned to fit a new day. The school we shall need, therefore, must serve two requirements: it must be organized so as to transmit (at least for consideration) the cardinal values of the present, and, at the same time, it must afford practice in the construction of new ethos.

Our greatest difficulty in reorganizing the school will be to somehow escape the shackles of conformity. In its broadest dimension, education is any process or experience through which useful learning takes place. It follows, consequently, that we could conceive of an almost infinite number of activities which are educational in nature. Parents educate, as do games. Learning happens morning, noon, and night, in storefronts, movies, grocery stores, swimming pools, and playgrounds. Families learn together as well as separately. It is paucity of imagination, not of opportunity, that most stands in our way. There is something to be said, in this regard, for the criticism voiced by the more deviant reformers. They may well be right when they argue that we have worried too much about redressing the defects of existing institutions—and too little about the invention of new ones.

Left to caprice, the future curriculum could easily be more chaotic than the present. But because the future does not yet exist, all problems are open to creative solution; there are no irrevocable mandates, no fixed specifications; we are free to envision and create the best schools our ingenuity can spawn. Curricular confusion stems not from an inventive attitude, but from an absence of form and structure.

Institutions, as a general rule, are not renovated in bold strokes. Rather, they are changed piecemeal, as tolerance for successive alterations is achieved. Such is likely to be the case with the schools; as inroads are made here and there, the heart, muscle, and bones of a new system will begin to take shape. We would do well to remember, however, that, as history tells us, since improvement is mainly the by-product of desire, until the need for reform is widely acknowledged by the citizenry proper, the evolutionary pace is likely to be slow.

The most profound need, at the present moment, is to convince both school people and lay people of the need for experimental openness. The condition bearing upon the needed experiments is that the reorganized school must overcome present infirmities without sacrificing present achievements, and without violating the moral obligation of public agencies to serve the common good. Reformation merely for the sake of reform will not do. The reforms, in short, must fit the failings: boredom can be defeated by a more stimulating atmosphere, alienation can be countered by a curriculum better attuned to the concerns of students, childhood anxiety can be reduced by greater compassion, dehumanization can be reduced by a larger respect for human dignity, academic failure can be lessened by perseverance and alternative teaching procedures, and the learner's dwindling faith in education can be reversed by lessons that relate more directly to the real world.

In recent time, for example, a striking interest in affective education has developed, with a corresponding curricular injunction to deal more adequately with the emotional lives of children. Although we are beginning to recognize that much of affective education must be dealt with cognitively, our need for manageable teaching procedures borders upon the desperate. We lack, in brief, a finesse to match our ambition. It is shortsighted, then, to assume that suitable pedagogy for the future school will materialize as a matter of course. We must, instead, extrapolate from the present, think creatively about what is possible, and set to work testing the potential of these possibilities. Two overriding research questions are hence at stake: what kind of teaching will the available technology permit, and what kind of teaching will a reformed school need? Until these questions are answered, the design of a fitting curriculum for the time ahead will elude us.

What might help, in this connection, is a set of contrasting scenarios depicting potential new organizations. Given such scenarios, much perhaps could be gained in the way of opening our vision to new possibilities. Conceive, for example, of an educational system in which primary learning is facilitated by a variety of entertaining and instructive home games—games in which parents, using prepared guides, aid and abet the school's objective. Conceive, as well, of a secondary school in which students pursue independent learning activities through electronic tutors and video-cassette instruction, and of an adult school in which older students enroll in comprehensive, easily accessible courses linked to their vocational pursuits, and taught, in part, through texts published in daily newspapers.

Conceive, further, of a public school where each student has an opportunity to participate in community improvement programs, where a portion of the curriculum is based upon annual summaries of the human condition, where the lessons of history are applied to existing social problems, where conflicting societal goals are analyzed and compared, where the cognitive progress of students is monitored by computers that diagnose learning difficulties and prescribe remediating exercises, where academic credit is given for demonstrable knowledge gained through out-of-school experiences, and where the curriculum itself is sufficiently elastic for students to involve themselves in whatever kinds of academic endeavors that are germane to their interests.

Such a scenario is hardly inspired or even ingenious; it leaves, in fact, much to be desired. Nonetheless, even so feeble an illustration serves to illuminate the kinds of directional signs that could facilitate our task. Without such models it will be difficult to mount a cohesive thrust, and whatever future planning we undertake will be random and haphazard. If, on the other hand, we can test a number of rational designs that, in large dimension, portray prospective new kinds of schools, we may discover through trial and error what will and will not work. Should these scenarios ultimately prove unfeasible, we shall scarcely be worse off than if we had functioned mindlessly.

There is, finally, the problem of transitional spirit. The youth of today are inclined to fault us for the shoddy legacy we are leaving: for a spoiled environment, unspeakable war tools, and an overmaterialistic culture. They are, as a result, quietly despairing on the one hand and excessively preoccupied with self-service on the other. Both are understandable, but both also diminish the desire to work for something better. Both, therefore, are of curricular concern.

The mood, in varying degrees, is exaggerated existentialism— excessive faith in the belief that each of us can direct, privately, the total course of our existence. An identification with social goals, with freedom qualified by responsibility, and with obligation to society as well as self has become more rare, and an acceptance of powerlessness, defeat, and self-indulgence more common. There is the smell of counterfeit, and therefore unfulfilling, hedonism in the air and a simultaneous denial of the ancient essentials for the satisfying life. True self-realization does not occur without the gratification that comes from constructive work, from the use of one's talents in accomplishing a worthwhile task, from the willingness to accept challenge, and from personal contribution, howsoever small, to the making of a better world.

It is not crisis but the way human kind responds to crisis that determines survival. Thus, the current psychological malaise must be countered by a rekindling of spirit, by the cultivation of resilience and commitment, and by experiences that energize the will through demonstrations of man's ability to overcome.

The schools can help considerably in this regard. The present crop of first graders will reach their mid-twenties by the year 2000—time enough, almost certainly, to make a difference. The necessary attitudes of mind, however, cannot be achieved through the preaching of dogma. They must, instead, be the by-products of authentic encounters that teach directly the joys of hard-won success and the satisfactions of rigorous effort.

A curriculum in anticipation of the future, hence, must afford children a chance to pit their physical and intellectual muscles against manageable but demanding tasks—tasks that gradually extend their zeal and endurance and nurture a sense of power and control over circumstance. If the goals are personally rewarding, hard work neither bores, brutalizes, nor alienates. It is the curriculum's failure to free, and its lack of freedom to fail—not its softness—that we must overcome.

The essays that follow are intended as a representative overview of the general curriculum. The reader may quarrel either with the particular selection, or with the concepts and implications derived from the arguments. If nothing else, however, the articles furnish a reasonable perspective on the basic substance of contemporary instruction.

References

1. See the *School Review*, Vol. 79, No. 3, May 1971, for a series of articles by Edgar Bernstein, Murray Hozinsky, Eunice McGuire, Kenneth Marantz, Max Bell, and Zalman Usiskin.

2. Erik H. Erikson, *Identity: Youth and Crisis* (New York: W. W. Norton & Co., Inc., 1968), p. 157.

3. George H. Gallup, Sixth Annual Gallup Poll of Public Attitudes Toward Education, *Phi Delta Kappan*, Sept. 1974.

4. Hozinsky, op. cit.

5. Maurice T. Hunt and Lawrence E. Metcalf, *Teaching High School Social Studies* (New York: Harper & Row, Inc., 1968), p. 27.

6. Max S. Bell and Zalman Usiskin, Improving Mathematics for All Students, *School Review*, Vol. 79, No. 3, May 1971.

7. Jerome J. Hausman, Art; in *The Teachers Handbook*, Dwight D. Allen and Eli Seifman, eds. (Glenview, Ill.: Scott, Foresman and Co., 1971).

8. Kenneth Marantz, Aesthetic Alternatives: From the Private "I" to the Public "We," *School Review*, Vol. 79, No. 3, May 1971.

Harry A. Greene
Walter T. Petty

The Language Arts Teacher and the Curriculum

LANGUAGE

While the fundamental role that language plays in listening, reading, speaking, and writing may be recognized, what language actually is and what its fundamental role means may not be understood. In fact, this lack of understanding probably has caused many language arts programs to be less effective than possible.

What Is Language?

What is this basic component of the language arts? What is language? Most people would probably say it is "all the words and sentences we use as we talk with one another." Or they might say "as we communicate verbally with one another," thereby including writing as well as speaking. These are, of course, satisfactory definitions for everyday situations but they are not sufficiently accurate to satisfy the language arts researcher, the linguist, or the teacher of the language arts.

According to the first defining statement in *Webster's Third New International Dictionary,* language is "audible, articulate human speech as produced by the action of the tongue and adjacent vocal organs." A second statement describes language as "any means, vocal or other, of expressing or communicating feeling or thought." The first definition limits language to a human activity and to vocal sound. The second is more inclusive, implying that the waving of an arm or the furrowing of a brow is language, but at the same time limiting language to a conscious act, thus excluding the instinctive communicative acts one generally associates with animals.

An involuntary cry of pain or fear, the bark of a dog, or the wail of a hungry baby—all are sounds that may be heard and may attract the atten-

Reprinted from Harry A. Greene and Walter T. Petty, *Developing Language Skills in the Elementary Schools,* © 1971; by permission of Allyn and Bacon, Inc., Boston.

tion of a human being within hearing range, but they are not necessarily language. If the baby wails because he has learned that if he makes enough noise he will be given food, if the dog barks because he has learned that as a result his master will open the door and let him into the house, then these sounds may be considered means for communicating and a kind of language according to the dictionary definition.

The Linguist's Definition of Language

The linguist, the student of language, is precise in his definition of language. Linguists stress certain assumptions concerning language which in effect define language for their studies. The most important is that "the fundamental forms of language activity are the sequences of sounds made by human lips, tongues, and vocal cords . . ."(1). The linguist says that language is speech, pointing out that speech is as old as human society but that writing is only about seven thousand years old. While the statement of the relative ages is a fact, writing thus being a derivative of speech, teachers and curriculum authorities should not make a fetish of saying that language is speech(2). Certainly, language programs need to give greater attention to oral language that they traditionally have; however, the linguistic concerns of written expression must not be ignored. This is not to deny that speech is *the* language, but for school purposes, as opposed to the purposes the linguist has in his studies, it is convenient to refer to oral language and to written language.

From the basic assumption of the oral nature of language, the linguist moves to identifying certain characteristics. One source lists the five most important of these as follows(3):

1. Language is symbolic. It is a thing of itself, quite distinct from the matter to which it relates. Such a relation is purely arbitrary and may change with time. The nature of the symbol differs in form depending on whether one is speaking or writing.
2. Language is systematic. For this reason it can be learned. For the same reason it can be described and must be described in terms of a system. Languages are universally orderly, but there is not, as was once supposed, a universal type of order to which all languages aspire.
3. Language is human. It is the most characteristic human activity, completely different in kind from the "language" of animals.
4. Language is a social instrument. Our social relationships are achieved by it and through it, on the whole, and their perpetuation is heavily dependent upon it. Social differences and language differences almost invariably go hand in hand.
5. Language is noninstinctive. It needs to be learned. The child gains control of the structure of the language in association with parents, brothers and sisters, and playmates. Much of the vocabulary, particularly that reflecting social attitudes, is acquired through the schools.

Linguists usually add the terms *arbitrary* and *complete* to *symbolic,* pointing out that the attachment of words to objects or ideas represents an arbitrary act and that such attachment has been made to express every idea or feeling that the users of the language need. The arbitrary nature of language is illustrated by the symbol attached to the object we know as a dog. In French it is *le chien,* and in English it might as well be *neg* as *dog.* Since the attachment of symbols to things is arbitrary, the attachments must be learned—that is, someone who knows must tell the learner what the symbols are. The complete nature of language is shown in the fact that words and expressions are coined to take care of the language user's needs. For example, the Wichita language of the Oklahoma Indian tribe does not include *nuclear physics* or *celestial navigation,* because the speakers of Wichita have never needed these terms when using their native language(4). Similarily, the word *acrylic* never existed in the English language until the need for it arose.

Increasingly, linguists give less stress to noninstinctiveness as a characteristic of language. The point is generally made that young children are not taught a language but that they learn it by themselves(5). That is, there is no conscious effort and application; they seem to possess an inborn faculty for learning language in general, not any one particular language. The innateness of this faculty is questioned, but it is certainly true that exposure to a language or languages results in learning them quite rapidly.

Most persons realize that language is systematic, even though this knowledge is often unconscious. Because language entities may be arranged in recurrent patterns, a person presented with only part of a pattern can make predictions about the rest of it. He knows, for example, that the *ed* suffix is usually added to form the past tense of a verb. He knows that in the sentence "Bill_____s Jim an_____," the first blank must be filled with a verb and the second with a noun. He knows further that not all verbs can be used in the sentence (this one must be third person singular, must end with *s,* and must be able to take both direct and indirect objects) but that words such as *gives, throws, offers,* and *takes* would fit. And he knows that the noun must begin with a vowel (or silent *h*) and take an article—a noun such as *apple, illustration, orange,* or *example.*

Recognizing that language is systematic does not necessarily indicate that the system is actualized in specific instances or manifestations. That is, a language has several varieties as it is used. Thus, in speaking of the English language, we are referring to a kind of synthesis of common denominators in all of its varieties which makes these varieties generally and mutually intelligible(6).

Still another characteristic of language—related both to its symbolic and its systematic nature—is the fact that it changes. Evidence of the change in English is apparent if one compares that used in a page of the King James version of the Bible with one in the works of Shakespeare, the Declaration of Independence, or a modern novel. In addition, we all know that English has been changed by influxes of people and ideas. Lamb points out that the changes are "not haphazard or accidental," that they "are the hallmarks of a living, growing, healthy organism"(7).

Most linguists stress that language is a system of human communication originating in the sound stream produced by the organs of speech (8). Observers generally believe that animal cries and actions are instinctive and do not constitute language, though the close observer of nature might question this belief as he watches a mother hen call her chicks under her wings at the approach of danger, a colony of ants at work, or a mother quail lure a hunter away from her nest by appearing to be crippled. However, these are instinctive acts—responses to cues, like a dog's responses to a whistle, a pointing finger, or a traffic light. Even the myna bird who says, "When do we eat," while obviously vocalizing, is responding instinctively to a cue rather than consciously using language as a result of thought. Therefore, though some might argue that they have conversed with chimpanzees, dolphins, and so forth, most persons agree with the linguists that man alone possesses language.

Apparently there is no human action so complicated or requiring so much coordination as producing language. As several linguists have so aptly put it: "sounds are nothing but organized noises"(9). To coordinate the tongue, jaws, teeth, palate, and lips in adjusting the air that is forced through the larynx to produce sounds which are varied in quality, volume, and pitch requires an intelligence that only mankind appears to have. How did man learn to use this equipment to produce language? Was there a stage in development that might be called "pre-speech"? And how rapidly was the passage from such a stage to the first words? As one source questions, "Did it take centuries—millennia—from the time he could say, 'I'm hungry,' until he worked himself up to such profundities as, 'Woman, bring me my knotty pine club' "(10)?

No one knows the origin of language. Language is possible because everyone in a particular culture or setting agrees that certain sounds or combinations of sounds represent things about which they need to communicate with one another. The use of language is such an integral part of our everyday lives that we rarely think of it as something uniquely human. We rarely think of the immense consequences of man's invention of language—by the use of language babies become human beings; without language, becoming an adult would mean achieving only an aborted form of fulfillment(11).

The Uses of Language

Language is the fundamental means by which ideas, thoughts, feelings, and emotions are communicated. It is a vital part of every human activity. Universally humans talk, and almost invariably they utilize some form of recorded or written expression. The Congo tribes, the Ecuadorian Indians, the residents of Los Angeles, Brooklyn, London, Moscow, Cairo, Hong

Kong, or Tokyo all talk, all communicate by means of language. The language forms used depend entirely upon the culture-area in which the individuals are located. As soon as primitive men began to live together, first in families and then in tribes, there was a need for some means of making their intentions and desires clear to one another. Warnings of danger had to be given and sources of food reported; orders had to be given for group protection from enemies. Probably the earliest communication was by the use of natural signs—cries, gestures, and facial expressions, which at first were made spontaneously in response to natural situations to indicate needs, emotions, and feelings. From these early and surely accidental beginnings, meanings were refined for the signs and sounds. Vocal utterances, substituted gradually for manual signs, were found to be more effective, especially in combat and in the dark. Gradually man recognized the need for the creation of graphic symbols (writing) to represent the natural signs. Down through the ages language has been developed and refined until a rather intricate but reasonably effective means of communication has evolved. This development and evolution is still going on and will doubtless continue to do so as long as man's small segment of the universe survives.

The first purpose for language, then, is *communication*. Communication involves at least two persons, one to present the idea or thought by means of speaking or writing, and one to receive the idea or thought by means of reading or listening. The effectiveness with which the actual communication takes place depends entirely upon the knowledge of the language and its skillful use of both of the individuals involved. The individual who has a good command of language and its use for communication will be able to express his ideas and convey the desired meaning to someone else. Likewise, if the reader or listener has an adequate command of language, he will be able to comprehend the intended meaning speedily and correctly.

Using language as a means for releasing tensions or reacting to a specific personal incident is a second use of language. This expression is a very personal use which may range from the ludicrous to the sublime. Thus, it may range from muttering under one's breath or uttering an oath when the hammer hits the thumb instead of the nail to a poetic thought simply written for one's own enjoyment or saying "magnificent" at the brim of the Grand Canyon.

A related use of language that is possibly the most important of all uses is thinking. While thinking involves the mental manipulation of symbols which represent certain meanings, not all of the symbols are language symbols. Some are mental images, such as those of the artist as he thinks of line and color. Most of our thinking, though, makes use of language symbols, which means that an individual's thinking is controlled to a considerable degree by the qualities and categories of his language(*12*). This fact possibly accounts for the development of language and its growth as a primitive society became somewhat complicated. Primitive man probably had little difficulty thinking in terms of mental images as he went into the jungle to hunt for food. But the process of living with others of his kind brought the need for rules, generalizations, laws, customs—the development of social mores. Such abstractions as truth, honesty, love, honor, and courage are not easily expressed or comprehended by means of mental images. As mankind evolved, society became more and more complex and new concepts and experiences required the creation of new symbols to represent them. These language symbols have become the tools by which the individual forms an opinion or draws a conclusion; they are the means by which new meanings and new principles are constructed.

A fourth purpose of language is the *transmission of culture*. Many ideas, bright or dull; thoughts, brilliant or biased; deeds, heroic or cowardly; mistakes, stupid or profitable, are accessible today as a result of the literature society has left us. This trail has been left principally by language, although art and music, also forms of expression, have made their contributions. *Through recorded language the accumulation of human experience is shared and conveyed to posterity.* It would be difficult to imagine what it would be like to live without being able to profit from the experiences and contributions of our ancestors recorded in history and in literature. Without language we would be isolated, we would not be able to share the thoughts and ideas of others living during the same period as ourselves. We would know nothing of history, nothing of the marvelous literature of our own and other cultures. The preservation of the record of man's thoughts and deeds is vitally necessary to education and to the future development of man and society.

LINGUISTICS

Every teacher has heard the term *linguistics*. The interest in linguistics has penetrated most schools, and to some extent this interest has affected most language arts programs. Some observers regard the interest as present and growing, with various aspects of linguistics being reflected in programs (*13*). Others think of the interest today as being of a historical nature regarding the impact, or lack of impact, of the "linguistic revolution"(*14*). In our view, however, casting aside the "revolution" aspect and that of accepting a fad as an indication of interest, linguistics must be considered in planning and developing effective language arts programs.

What Is Linguistics?

Linguistics was defined earlier as "the scientific study of language." This is the definition most often found in educational literature, but it is one that needs explanation and extension for most persons. Postman and

Weingartner suggest that "any definition of linguistics depends upon who is doing the defining"(*15*). That is, to many teachers the term linguistics is equated with *grammar;* to others it is the relationship of sound symbols to graphic symbols. To many linguists a definition broadened to include studying the entire culture is most suitable. To the man on the street linguistics may mean the study of dialects or the determining of dictionary definitions.

The Nebraska curriculum guide defines linguistics as: "The study of human speech; the units, nature, structure, and modifications of language, languages, or a language, including especially such factors as phonetics, phonology, morphology, accent, syntax, semantics, general or philosophical grammar, and the relation between writing and speech"(*16*).

Lamb extends her "scientific study of language" with the statement: "Such study may concentrate on the sounds of language (phonology), the origin and changing meaning of words (etymology and sematics), or the arrangements of words in a meaningful context in different languages (syntax-structural or transformational grammar)"(*17*).

Guth says, "Linguistics is the study, according to rigorously defined methods or principles, *of language as a system*"(*18*).

A particularly useful definition of linguistics is that of Postman and Weingartner. They say that "Linguistics is a way of behaving . . . it is a way of behaving while one attempts to discover information and to acquire knowledge about language"(*19*). They proceed to discuss the behavior in terms of attitudes and procedures. Their emphasis is upon the inductive approach to learning, a spirit of discovery, a rejection of dogmatism, and the verifying and revising process identified with scientific study.

Linguistic Study

Linguistic study is done by linguists, though accepting the Postman and Weingartner definition means that anyone, including children in the elementary school, may do linguistic study if it is done in the spirit described. In a more restricted sense, however, linguistics is the study of language by language scientists—the linguists. A linguist may study any language—living or dead—and he may specialize in a particular field of study. He may study the history of a language; he may compare languages, examining such aspects as grammar, phonology, morphology, semantics, or dialects. Linguists subscribe to different theories related to their particular interests. For example, there are a number of widely differing theories (structural and transformational-generative are best known) upon which anlayses of language structure are based. The theoretical differences lead to differences in definitions, terminology, and procedures used in language study.

Linguistic study is being extended most recently into language behavior and learning (psycholinguistics), society and language (sociolinguistics), and the more totally inclusive "study of mutual relationships between language behavior and other modes of human behavior" (metalinguistics)(*20*).

Linguistic study in the schools ranges from the study of grammar, usually a new approach—in either a formal deductive manner or a functional inductive way—to the somewhat incidental introduction of the concept of language change by finding new words and identifying words brought into English from other languages. Later chapters in this book, as well as sections of this chapter, further specify what linguistics means to the school curriculum.

The Study of Language

The "scientific study of language" has most often been introduced into the school curriculum in the form of a study of language *structure*. That is, the greatest impact has been in the study of the system of language rather than in other areas of language study. This new approach to language structure, in fact, any approach to studying language structure, achieved a great deal of interest because of the traditional role of the teaching of grammar in schools for the purpose of helping pupils write "better" and speak "correctly." The issue of the teaching of grammar is discussed in the following chapter, as are matters relative to "correctness" of usage. Language learning, including the understanding young children have of the language system, will be discussed in Chapter 4. Other aspects of "the scientific study of language" are presented in most of the remaining chapters.

The study of language structure generally starts with *phonology*—the study of the sounds of the language. The basic sounds, called *phonemes,* described as the smallest units of sound by which different meanings may be distinguished, are the core of this study. Most linguists identify twenty-four consonants and nine vowels as the segmental phonemes(*21*). That is, through phonation and articulation, the stream of sound uttered by a human is divided into segments that are recognizable as units of meaning. In addition, there are suprasegmental phonemes which also describe the language. These are four degrees of *stress* given to segmental phonemes, three levels of *pitch,* and four *junctures* or interruptions and suspensions in the stream of sound (identified as breaks between words or the greater ones usually signaled in writing by punctuation marks).

The second area of study is usually *morphology*—the study of word forms. Morphology deals with the meaningful groupings of sounds, but with emphasis upon grammatical factors of grouping rather than upon meaning as we commonly think of it. *Morphemes* are described as the smallest meaningful units in language(*22*). Thus, the word *hat* is one morpheme, but is made up of three phonemes; *boy* is one morpheme and two phonemes; and *I* is one morpheme and one phoneme. Morphemes include word bases (or roots), prefixes, suffixes, and word-form changes or inflections. A *free morpheme* is one that may stand by itself in larger language structures, and a *bound morpheme* is one that must combine with another morpheme. The words above (boy, hat, I) are free morphemes; *pre-* and *-ness* are bound morphemes.

A third concern in studying language structures involves the forms of words. Words, of course, differ in meaning but they also differ in other characteristics. Language study based upon traditional or Latin-based grammar classified words according to their meaning (i.e., "A noun is the name of a person, place, or thing") or their function (i.e., "An adjective modifies a noun or pronoun"). Linguists who do not hold to traditional grammar classify words in a different way. They speak of *form classes*—which are the traditional parts of speech in English: nouns, verbs, adjectives, and adverbs, although they are sometimes identified by the words *form class* and a number (i.e., form class 1 = verbs) instead of by the traditional terms. Words are classified as to form class by testing them in "slots" (The _____ ran fast. A _____ truck approached.), by determining if they will "take" certain suffixes, and by relating the stress given them to other words given like stress in sentences of the same pattern. Related to word-form classes is a fourth area of study of the language system known as *syntax,* or word order. Syntax is defined as the study of the meaningful combinations of words—the study of the ways that words can be ordered or arranged significantly(23). This study involves classification of sentences and parts of sentences. *Structural linguists* use several classification systems to categorize sentences. These include relating each sentence to certain basic patterns or sentence skeletons or to the method of expansion of a skeleton by substitution or modification. Syntax can also be studied by a *transformational-generative* approach; this is used by another group of linguists known as transformationalists(24). Transformational study begins with the assumption that sentences are of two basic types: kernel sentences and transformed sentences(25). The transformationalist has rules concerning language which show that certain words or phrases can be grammatically moved. The approach is synthetic rather than analytic, as is the approach followed by structuralists. The transformationalist begins with the rules about the phrase structures, the possible transformations, and effects of transformations upon meaning and sound.

Other Linguistic Study

Studying language structure in terms of its phonology, morphology, and syntax is not the only concern of the linguist. As suggested above, the study of language structure (really its grammar) is most likely to receive attention in language arts programs, and for the reasons suggested; however, there are other areas of investigation which interest linguists and are of importance to the language arts.

Historically a major area of interest to linguists has been the geography of language—dialect differences by region and changes related to the movements of people. This area of study is known as *dialectology(26)*. To-day, major interest in dialects is shown by *sociolinguists;* these linguistic scientists are primarily concerned with social, racial, and ethnic differences as they relate to language usage. These linguists also investigate the atti-tudes people have toward variations in their language. They do not make judgments as to what is "right" or "wrong" but simply report the attitudes people in differing circumstances have about certain words and expres-sions. Their investigations of usage are closely akin to traditional dialect studies in that they seek pronunciation, syntax, and vocabulary commonal-ities related to economic, racial, and social groups, to urban and rural regions, and to modern-day migrations of people. In quite recent times many linguists studying dialects have become concerned with learning problems and the relation of a dialect to widespread or standard usage.

Another major area of study is *psycholinguistics,* which is the study of how language is learned and how language interacts with learning. Principal attention is given to the language development of infants and young children, but increasingly greater attention is being given to learning by school age children.

Another major interest of linguists is *semantics.* Postman and Wein-gartner say, "Perhaps the most important branch of linguistics . . . is semantics"(27). In general, semantics is concerned with meaning. Semanti-cists make inquiries into varieties of definitions, what really constitutes meaning, and the problems of communication in instances in which sup-posedly known words are used.

Linguistic study of the historical development of a language is an-other appealing area of study—one that has always been of interest in schools and which may have even greater appeal now that "stories about words" are appearing and scholarly works on such word studies are more available. Learning that commonplace words, such as *potato, chocolate, canoe, cannibal,* and *barbecue,* moved from the New World to England is of interest to teachers and children. Tracing the origins of many, many words—ranging from *gumbo, yam, chigger,* and *voodoo* to *flabbergast, cab,* and *grovel*—may arouse even greater interest.

There are elementary school teachers teaching the terminology (and more) given on the preceding pages. There are others teaching children to work as beginning linguists to discover facts about language, with varying degrees of reference to the terminology. Finally, there are textbooks and curriculum guides being developed by linguists for use in elementary school teaching; these, of course, make much use of terminology new to teachers and to students preparing for teaching(28).

References

1. Archibald A. Hill, *Introduction to Linguistic Structures* (New York: Harcourt, Brace & World, Inc., 1958), p. 1.

2. David Reed expands on this in "A Theory of Language, Speech, and Writing," *Elementary English* (December, 1965), p. 346.

3. Taken from Appendix B, *The Language Component in the Training of Teachers of English and Reading: Views and Problems*. Mimeographed material prepared by the Center for Applied Linguistics and the National Council of Teachers of English for a conference at Washington, D.C., April 28–30, 1966.

4. Jacob Ornstein and William W. Gage, *The ABC's of Languages and Linguistics* (Philadelphia: Chilton Books, 1964), p. 11.

5. William G. Moulton, "Language and Human Communication," *Linguistics in School Programs*, ed. Albert H. Marckwardt. The Sixty-ninth Yearbook of the National Society for the Study of Education, Part II (Chicago: The University of Chicago Press, 1970), p. 27.

6. Sumner Ives, "The Nature and Organization of Language," *Language Arts Concepts for Elementary School Teachers*, eds. Paul C. Burns et al., (Itasca, Illinois: F. E. Peacock Publishers, Inc., 1972), pp. 34–41.

7. Pose Lamb, *Linguistics in Proper Perspective* (Columbus, Ohio: Charles E. Merrill Publishing Co., 1967), p. 4.

8. No one—and teachers especially—should overlook nonverbal or "silent" language. We often communicate a great deal by what we do not say, by our actions, by our behavior. See Edward T. Hall, *The Silent Language* (in paperback by Fawcett: first published by Doubleday & Co., 1959).

9. Ornstein and Gage, *ABC's of Languages*, p. 68.

10. Ibid., p. 15.

11. Carl A. Lefevre, "Language and Self: Fulfillment or Trauma?" *Elementary English* (Feb. 1966), pp. 124–28.

12. W. Nelson Francis, "The Uses of Language," *Language Arts Concepts for Elementary School Teachers* (Itasca, Illinois: F. E. Peacock Publishers, Inc., 1972), pp. 42–46.

13. Paul C. Burns, "Linguistics: A Brief Guide for Principals," *Linguistics for Teachers*, ed. John F. Savage (Chicago: Science Research Associates, Inc., 1973), p. 33.

14. Albert J. Griffith, "Linguistics: A Revolution in Retrospect," *Linguistics for Teachers*, p. 16.

15. Neil Postman and Charles Weingartner, *Linguistics, A Revolution in Teaching* (New York: Dell Publishing Co., Inc., 1966), p. 3.

16. The Nebraska Curriculum Development Center, *A Curriculum for English: Language Explorations for the Elementary Grades* (Lincoln: University of Nebraska Press, 1966), p. 2.

17. Lamb, *Linguistics*, p. 4.

18. Hans P. Guth, *English Today and Tomorrow* (Englewood Cliffs, N.J.: Prentice-Hall, 1964), p. 25.

19. Postman and Weingartner, *Linguistics, A Revolution in Teaching*, p. 4.

20. Ibid., p. 197.

21. The Nebraska Curriculum Development Center, *A Curriculum for English*, p. 18.

22. Defined in Ornstein and Gage, *ABC's of Languages,* p. 81, as follows: "Roughly speaking, a morpheme is any of the pieces that has a function in a word."

23. The Nebraska Curriculum Development Center, *A Curriculum for English,* p. 94.

24. A more detailed explanation of transformational grammar, as well as other grammars, is given in Chapter 2.

25. Paul M. Roberts, *English Sentences,* Teacher's Manual (New York: Harcourt, Brace & World, Inc., 1962).

26. H. Rex Wilson, "The Geography of Language," *Linguistics in School Programs,* pp. 64–84.

27. Postman and Weingartner, *Linguistics, A Revolution in Teaching,* p. 122.

28. For example: Paul Roberts, *The Roberts English Series* (New York: Harcourt, Brace & World, Inc., 1966); *Linguistics in the Elementary Classroom* (Los Angeles County Superintendent of Schools Office, 1965) ; *Curriculum for English.*

Operational Concepts

1. The intellectual skills used frequently in life situations are learned easily.

2. The skills and understandings of language are best taught directly rather than as the by-products of other educational objectives.

3. The ability to use language expressively is most effectively learned through imitation and through repeated use in realistic situations.

4. Language is an indispensable vehicle for thinking.

Implications

What should be done with respect to altering the language arts curriculum depends, in considerable degree, upon the rationale one chooses to embrace. Those, for example, who believe that skill mastery should take precedence over a more general development will choose to continue instruction aimed at specific learning objectives. Those, on the other hand, who choose to believe that instruction in the use of language has either been overformalized or overemphasized will wish to place greater reliance upon the indirect learning that stems from rich experiences. In this regard, what is true for the language arts is equally true everywhere else: the curriculum can (1) attack predetermined goals, (2) avoid predetermined goals in favor of unstructured experience, or (3) seek a balance between the two.

My own preference, as the commentary at the beginning of the section indicates, is for the latter course. The elements of basic education are too important to be left to chance and thus must be approached systematically. This does not mean, however, that instruction must of necessity be dreary, boring, or brutal; nor does it mean that provisions for student autonomy, the pursuit of personal interest, or humanistic concerns are unessential.

It would be equally foolish to ignore new technological devices as they become available. Should computer-managed instruction prove to be an advantage in the teaching of, say, grammar, the advantage should be capitalized upon. One would hope, moreover, that such devices will make more time available for symbolic and self-instructive experiences.

In a more general vein, the language arts curriculum could be greatly improved by efforts to eliminate meaningless—as opposed to meaningful —drill, by greater emphasis upon the skills of listening and speaking and by efforts to make the subject matter more relevant to student interest. Moreover, although it is unlikely that competitive grading systems can be done away with, much might be done to make examinations less superficial, less punitive, and more diagnostic. The fundamental obligation to teach children to write effectively, read critically, and reason efficiently will almost certainly continue, but humanistic matters, too, have their place in the language arts curriculum.

42

Ruth C. Cook
Ronald C. Doll

Reading as a Receptive Art

No area of curriculum has received more attention than reading has, and despite the alarmists, this attention is getting results. Standard tests have been found to need more difficult items, and norms have needed revision upward because children reach the ceilings earlier. Tests given to servicemen during the last fifty years have shown a steady increase in reading ability. Scores on old tests have been compared with those earned on the same tests by children in recent years and the former have been found significantly lower although the modern school is recognized as less selective in pupil population than that of fifty or even twenty years ago.

Reading is a complex task. The skilled reader must be able to locate materials through use of indexes, tables of contents, center heads, topical sentences, and reference sources. To comprehend what he reads, he must have acquired a background of concepts and experiences, possess skill in recognition of words and their meanings, and be able to make inferences. In addition, he must be able to select and evaluate, organize facts or ideas, remember, and draw conclusions. He must also have ability to choose the most efficient method for the purpose, say, skimming or reading for detail, and then apply what he reads if his purpose so indicates. Tinker and McCullough have listed eighty-three discrete reading skills with as many as twenty-five devoted to study skills alone. Most of these skills are similar to those found in indexes of well-known teachers' manuals(1). Curriculum workers must realize that reading is a developmental skill and as such continues indefinitely. In the modern program, meaning is stressed from the beginning, and the children receive ideas and pleasure from what they read as they acquire skills.

READINESS AND EARLY INSTRUCTION

Most educators agree that readiness involves multiple factors, many of which are so interrelated that it is difficult to determine the factor oper-

Reprinted from Ruth C. Cook and Ronald C. Doll, *The Elementary School Curriculum,* © 1973; by permission of Allyn and Bacon, Inc., Boston.

ating at any one time. Language experiences, physical proficiency, motor development, interest, and social, emotional, and intellectual readiness are all important considerations. Much has been written recently, with opinion divided, on the advisability of a structured program of instruction in reading at kindergarten level. According to the Harvard Report, only 24 of 407 educators favored formal reading experiences for all kindergarten children (2). Several longitudinal studies, such as the Denver Study, on teaching kindergarten or preschool children to read are now under way, but they have not progressed sufficiently to make any claims. The Denver program has a planned program of beginning reading instruction in the kindergarten and preschool years with parents as participants. Results to date indicate that parent involvement is of value and that most kindergarten children can be taught to recognize letter forms and their names, and associate their sounds with the symbols. Research also indicates that children coming to first grade with some knowledge of letters and their names get off to an earlier start in first grade reading than those without such ability.

Children today, because they frequently travel extensively and normally experience the printed word in a variety of situations, become familiar with many words and letters at early ages. They see labels on packages, words in television advertisements, and on billboards. They speak glibly of television channels, radio stations, jet planes, and space travel. They watch and listen to adults read; they imitate, memorize, and sometimes surprise those about them by building up quite a stockpile of printed words both recognized and understood. Some even read from children's books. Either the number of children who enter school knowing how to read is increasing or our awareness of such individual learners is increasing. Durkin in a longitudinal study of ninety-eight early readers found that the children came from homes and kindergartens where parents and teachers read to them and where their questions were answered, although phonics and reading drills were not emphasized(3). The existence of individual differences in mental ability is known, but research has not established the optimum mental age at which teaching of reading should begin. Other factors such as ability to adjust the eyes to near vision, patience on the part of parents in answering questions, the understanding and warmth of the teacher, and type of reading experiences provided are all important.

Readiness is not a sudden thing, nor is the act of reading. Hearing many stories and discussing what they hear and see usually propel young children faster toward subsequent success in reading than a formal reading curriculum with phonics, drills, and workbooks before the readiness for such activities. Popular periodicals, Sunday supplements, and extravagant claims to the contrary, most very young children are not ready for formal instruction in reading. A child who has difficulty in distinguishing between a butterfly and an oriole, or between the sound of a dime and a heavy key as they strike a tile floor, is scarcely ready to see or hear the difference between a *b* and a *d,* or between a short *i* and a short *e.* This does not imply that children who are ready for reading and who ask questions about words and letters should be denied help, either at home or at school. Many children, with a little help at home, come to school knowing how to read and write their own names, and are able to recognize many letters of the alphabet, plus words common to their environments, such as *Walk, Don't Walk, Stop,* and *Go.* No child is known to have been frustrated by such help. The danger comes when early reading becomes a status symbol, and ego-centered parents, teachers, and administrators exert pressure on children to support a boast of either very bright offspring or a "forward-moving program." When pressure comes from a fear that children will not be able to cope with today's world unless they get a very early start in reading, it should be remembered that coping with problems requires imagination, ability to think critically, the understanding of self and relationships with others, and ability to interpret and draw inferences from what is read.

It would be difficult to find a modern kindergarten where the teacher is not nurturing individual reading interests or providing a rich environment for all pupils by experiences related at once to reading and their normal childhood activities. Experience reports are dictated to the teacher and "read" by the children; coat hangers, lockers, and pictures are labeled with the names of their owners; the days of the week are recognized on the calendar and the date is marked daily; and well before the end of the year most of the children are writing their own names, recognizing the individual letters, and frequently reading the names of their classmates or titles of favorite books or stories.

Most kindergarten teachers report that they do not hesitate to help interested children take initial steps in learning to read. Most, however, feel that the kindergarten program is so crowded with necessary developmental activities that formal instruction in reading must be approached with caution. They readily agree that they can teach kindergarten children to recognize many words and also letter sounds; however, they fear that such instruction might displace other activities basic to learning in general. As another consideration, ambitious adults might subject all children in a group to a program geared only to a few, possibly at the expense of social consciousness and the understanding that reading is getting meaning and can be fun. The teachers agree that kindergarten is a time for assessment and that a situation provided for determining readiness in one child may constitute reading instruction for another. Kindergarten teachers usually balk at the use of flash cards and phonics workbooks, not because children cannot learn from such procedures, but because they may build antagonistic attitudes toward learning, school, and society.

Educators who have made an extensive study of young children and who have had experience working with many children usually agree that very young children can, through vigorous effort on the part of both children and adults, learn to read, or repeat words; the educators usually question the procedure, however. They point out that pediatricians and psychologists frequently report adverse outcomes, such as ulcers or anti-social behavior on the part of pressured children.

INNOVATIONS AND ISSUES IN BEGINNING READING

Apart from the early introduction, several other innovations and resulting issues have been introduced into beginning reading instruction. Some will, no doubt, make lasting contributions either directly or indirectly. Others, it is safe to say, will fade from the scene.

Language Experience Approach

This approach is not new, modifications of it having been used for several decades. It would be difficult to find a classroom from kindergarten through fifth or sixth grades where children's experiences are not used for writing charts, reports, and stories to be read by the children. Recently, the use of language experiences of the children as the basic reading program, especially for the culturally deprived, has received renewed emphasis. As an introduction to reading, it has many advantages. It relates directly to the young reader because it is his own experience. He becomes oriented to the idea that reading proceeds from left to right and from top to bottom. He gradually understands that whatever he says can be written and subsequently read. As he is introduced to the symbolic nature of reading, he recognizes that others who have not had the same experience as he can learn of it vicariously, and that he can share, through reading, the experiences of others.

Most teachers, although they use the language experience approach, reject it as a completely dependable method for teaching reading; the concepts and numbers of words are frequently too numerous to insure sufficient repetition and they are not adaptable to phonic instruction. The material lacks literary quality and the attractiveness of most children's books and does not give practice in handling books. In adition, many teachers feel they lack skill and time to produce sufficient material of a balanced nature.

Not a great deal of research has been done on the language experience approach to teaching reading. In the majority of the studies, the teacher and not the material has been the influencing factor. When the teacher factor has remained constant, the basal-reader approach has produced results superior to the language experience approach.

Linguistic Innovations

Most scholars in linguistics have refrained from advising others in the field of teaching young children, because, as they freely admit, they have never studied children nor taught any to read. Recently, however, several persons have taken issue with the eclectic approach in the usual basal readers and have become quite vocal in expounding the belief that reading is merely a process of responding to sets of patterns in written words. They have urged, therefore, that children's first attempts to read should be with words of regular spelling. In one linguistic approach, the reading curriculum begins with capital and lower case letters that the child must name accurately before being introduced to words. Next are presented the short sounds of five vowels as they appear in two- and three-letter words. When these are mastered, consonant blends and pairs of vowels, plus irregular spellings, are introduced. There is heavy dependence on oral responses with meaning and story content basically ignored(4).

A similar program by Charles Fries, "Linguistics and Reading," concentrates on high-speed and accurate response to upper case letters presented singly and then in groups with no attention initially to words or meanings. Next are included the principal English spelling patterns, beginning with the simplest vowel-consonant and consonant-vowel-consonant patterns with sufficient drill to assure an automatic response.

The reading curriculum built around the ideas of a third linguist enthusiast, Henry Lee Smith, begins through the use of films with sight words in meaningful contexts somewhat similar to well-known basal preprimers, except that only one sound of a letter is included until it is sufficiently mastered to be recognized in words of similar spelling.

In addition to the sponsors of these methods, several others have prepared materials or suggested how they may be structured. The names of Carl LeFavre, Agnes Fries, Mae Carden, Donald E. Rasmussen, Rosemary Wilson, Lenina Goldbert, Christine Gibson, I. A. Richards, and Clara Stratemeyer are frequently associated with linguistic approaches to reading.

Many of these "new" programs, especially in their initial stages are reminiscent of the McGuffey Eclectic First Reader of 1879. In this, on page 4, is the alphabet in upper and lower case, and on page 8.

Is the cat on the mat?
The cat is on the mat.

In the following, selected at random from recent books and out of context, it is true, we find:

The cat is fat Nat.
Pat fat Nat on the mat(5).
The fat cat, the thin cat, and
the tan cat sat on Nip's mat(6).
A man ran.
A ram ran(7).

It must be remembered that to the linguist language is oral. To the curriculum worker trying to construct a reading program, it is written. Each, the linguist and the reading teacher, can learn from the other. Certainly, the reading program must provide experiences that will build and maintain the oral cadence and melody of the language. At the same time, it must build a lasting attitude toward reading that will emphasize getting meaning, allow for critical analysis of thought expressed, and satisfy various purposes, such as enjoyment.

Critics claim that the linguist entering the field of reading with such sentences as "The tan man can fan Nan" is defeating the purpose of maintaining the intonation patterns of the language with which the child is already equipped. He may establish the habit of acceptance of the printed word as a reproduction of meaningless speech. Assuming that early ability to "crack the code" is defensible "reading," we have no scientific evidence to support the theory that children exposed to an extreme linguistic approach are more efficient at decoding words than children are who have been exposed to a more gradual approach, in which meaning is stressed. Measuring results at the end of the first grade on word-recognition skill is not a satisfactory answer, in that skills not yet taught in the more gradual approach are measured.

Initial Teaching Alphabet

This alphabet began in England as the Augmented Roman Alphabet and has been an attempt to surmount barriers presented by the inconsistencies of English spelling. It consists of forty-four symbols, each representing just one sound. The short sounds of the vowels are left to the traditional alphabet; the long sounds are represented by a combination of the regular letter, plus a superimposed *e,* and all words are spelled phonetically in lower case only. The system, represented by the symbol *i/t/a* has been widely publicized and warmly proclaimed by its proponents. Mazurkeiwicz, in reporting on the Lehigh-Bethlehem study, concluded in his preliminary report that the i/t/a group was significantly superior to a matched group receiving instruction in the traditional alphabet(8). In a subsequent report, however, when method was controlled, he reported no significant difference in the groups in reading achievement as measured by the subtests on paragraph meaning, vocabulary, and word study skills of the Stanford Achievement Tests. The i/t/a group was superior in word reading, but significantly poorer in spelling after having transferred to the traditional alphabet(9).

There have been several other studies, published and unpublished. Most have been rather sketchily done with a distressing failure to rule out several contributing factors, such as the enthusiasm and efficiency of the teachers, differences in methods and in content, and attention to word analysis. Time elements per day or week have not been accurately reported, scores on pretests have been ignored, and most important, teachers using either of the systems have not been given equal instruction in the use of the materials.

Chasnoff, in one of the few, well-designed studies, carried out an experiment in each of seven schools. The teachers were carefully prepared in the use of the i/t/a and the same teachers taught both the experimental and the control groups. Children in the experimental group were housed in a classroom environment in which only the initial teaching alphabet was used, and the control group in a room in which only the traditional alphabet was used. Both classes were instructed in the same way, by the same teachers, with the same time scheduled, and the same material, except that one was in i/t/a. Children were matched according to sex, chronological age, mental test scores, scores on initial tests, reading opportunity at home, kindergarten records, placement in family, and data from children's drawing of six figures. The seven schools represented communities of various socioeconomic statuses.

The results of the final tests, which were transliterated for the experimental group, showed no difference at the end of the first grade in the groups in oral reading. The control group was significantly ahead in spelling, and the experimental group ahead in creative writing. This last finding may need modification in interpretation since the experimental group had received more opportunity to write freely, being told to pay no attention to spelling, and since it was i/t/a, children were not hampered by concern over capital letters or margins. At the end of the 140th day in second grade, there was no significant difference between groups using the i/t/a and those using the traditional alphabet. By the end of the 160th day, neither group was superior to the other on mean ratings of writing samples designed to test ability to express oneself in writing. Thus, according to Chasnoff's study, the initial teaching alphabet showed neither poorly nor to advantage in similar school populations. The study did show, as may be guessed, that the teacher was an important ingredient(10).

The initial teaching alphabet seems to be losing some of its following. It is considered an artificial and unnecessary crutch by many. In England, where it made its initial impression, it has apparently been losing ground. Lady Plowden, in her interim report to Her Majesty the Queen, indicated that i/t/a had attracted great public attention with the claim that only a small minority would find reading difficult if i/t/a were used. She also hinted that a substantial minority were finding reading difficult, and the claims merited careful scrutiny. A recent count in England reveals that the number of schools using i/t/a has been lowered to 5 percent(11).

Unifon

Another attempt to solve the phoneme-grapheme problem is Unifon, in which forty printed symbols are used, each of which has a one sound–one symbol correspondence. Malone, its author, claims it can be mastered in one hour by any English-speaking person, can be used on computers, and should be a permanent alphabet. For example, the *ch* digraph is represented by an inverted *c,* and long *e* by *I;* the word *read* would be *RID(12).* Research to date, does not indicate any advantages for its use in beginning reading. Also it is unrelated to any present reading environments.

Diacritical Marking System

Because the English alphabet is inadequate in itself to represent English sounds, and because irregular English orthography has long been resistant to reform, it has occurred to educators that a system of diacritical marking might aid beginning readers in deciphering symbolic language. McGuffey in his first readers used certain diacritical marks to introduce new phonic elements at the beginning of each lesson. Most teachers use the common diacritical marks, such as those to indicate short and long vowel sounds, the schwa, and accent, when demonstrating methods of analysis in word recognition. These are usually used on the chalkboard, or on worksheets.

Fry, working on the assumption that if a little is good, more might be better, felt that by adding diacritical marks to the regular alphabet the phoneme–grapheme relationships would be sufficiently regularized to aid young readers in doing much deciphering on their own. In the material prepared by Fry for children, all marks were those able to be reproduced on a standard typewriter, for example, time, write, lived, her, food and look. The schwa was represented by a single dot and other consistent variations by a bar under the letter. Exceptions were marked with an asterisk above the letter, for example, would or once. As the learner acquired power, the marks would be gradually abandoned. Fry made a study of DMS, or the diacritical marking system, in twenty-one first grade classrooms from three middle-class suburban school districts in New Jersey over a two-year period. Three systems were employed, the DMS, i/t/a, and basal readers. None of the three methods revealed superior or inferior results for slow or bright children, and sex was not a factor. The quality of the teacher was an important ingredient, especially at first grade level(*13*).

Programmed Reading

In programmed reading, the learning steps are laid out in a precise, structured pattern. There are many such programs, not all so labeled. Many workbook exercises from basal readers are types of programmed reading. The highly publicized programmed approaches to beginning reading such as the *Sullivan Associates Programmed Reading* all rely on a phonic-linguistic treatment, with most starting on isolated letters and regularly spelled one-syllable words. During the initial stages, which could be several weeks for some children, words are presented in isolation and story content is missing. In the Sullivan Associates material, the content is presented in short units called frames, with the words in each frame designed to elicit a constructed, or a discriminatory, response on the part of the child. Reinforcement is immediate by the manipulation of a strip of heavy paper to the left of the text that reveals the correct response when moved down. The authors of the material suggest its use as a basic text in kindergarten, first grade, and remedial classes(14). In addition to the prereading materials and the programmed primer, there are fourteen books of progressive difficulty. The pictures, described by the proponents of the program as "delightful" are somewhat grotesque and lack variety.

Programmed reading is linguistic in nature, differing in format rather than method from other linguistic programs. To the programmed reading proponents, reading is a decoding process with the process of decoding the chief motivating factor. Programmed materials can relieve the teacher of some aspects of drill and provide for individual needs, if the material fits the children's needs and they are allowed to progress at their own rates. However, "progressing at their own rates" does not necessarily mean that all children must pass through the same routines. Some children may not need any programmed material because they seem to grasp large blocks of learning quite readily. Their eagerness to read content with considerable meat makes programmed material seem anemic to them. Other children find the manipulation of such materials outside their abilities or interests and become frustrated in their use. Programmed material thrust at some children results in tears or other manifestations of emotional distress. In a large group of first graders, one boy of six repeatedly soiled his clothing when placed at a desk by himself with a sheet of programmed material before him, even though it seemed he was able to do the work. A second invariably developed a headache. Another, because he seemed to have difficulty manipulating the materials, was given a crayon, which he immediately melted on the nearby radiator. When moved from the vicinity of the radiator he ate the crayon. Assuming that the teacher's handling of the situation was effective, programmed material for such children would need to be postponed or abandoned. There is no one best way to teach every child to read.

In the case of the three children cited above, all learned to read by a multiple approach using a basal reader plus supplementary aids. A girl in the same group found some advanced programmed material from the same program used by the boys and completed it in one day. She was using the material as a challenging game and probably did not need it as a learning device.

Programmed material, whether in the commercially available form—booklets, machines, or television—or teacher-constructed worksheets and charts, will continue to be used. Certainly, all such materials must be studied with a view toward improvement, but the curriculum worker should realize that programs, goals, and children cannot be molded to fit specific materials. Rather, the materials must be designed for specific needs and objectively evaluated with other materials accorded similar attention as to time and enthusiasm.

Words in Color

Gattegno, believing that initial instruction in reading would profit by the addition of color to letters, has prepared large wall charts on which discrete speech sounds are represented by color in an attempt to represent nonphonetic English as phonetic without changing traditional spellings. Starting with the short *a* sound, all letters or combinations of letters representing it are shown in white. Thirty-nine different colors, including ten shades of green, are used and appear only on the wall charts that are used as keys. Color and pictures do not appear in the children's booklets and meaning is ignored(*15*).

It seems that although phonics instruction is given, children see and write combinations of letters that do not appear in phonetic elements; thus they might acquire the concept that the combinations of *aaa* or *aeiu* actually appear in words. Because the child does not ordinarily meet print in which most of the letters have a different color, the system relates poorly to any reading environment the child encounters. Because "reading" by this system is divorced from meaning, early practice in critical and creative thinking in relation to reading and opportunity for discussion of ideas gained in reading are impossible.

Studies, with adequate controls, on young readers in the United States using *Words in Color* are not available. The system lacks the balance of a good program, thus most curriculum workers at present are rejecting its inclusion in the communicative arts program.

Individualized Programs

Individualized instruction in America is not new. The pendulum has swung from the completely individual teaching by tutors, such as the housewives in the dames' schools, to a minute or two of attention given a child in a group of fifty or more, back to the one-to-one approach. Assuming that all teachers using any form of grouping and a basal reader exercised a lock-step procedure with all children, extremists insisted on the abandonment of all basal readers and grouping. Extreme positions have now been largely abandoned, and most teachers enjoying success in the field of reading presently use a multiple approach.

Knowing what skills are necessary to reading and how to teach them, the teacher plans work commensurate with the needs of an individual or those common to a group, whether that group consists of only two or more than a dozen. Grouping is undertaken for those who have selected the same story, in that discussion is fostered when there are common elements in reading experience. At other times a discussion is enriched by a diversity of experiential background in reading. Self-selection assumes the child is able to choose wisely but until he has had some guidance and experience, this is difficult for him to do. Therefore the teacher cannot abandon a planned program of skills development. Neither can she, in one hour, give ten minutes of individual help to each of twenty-five children.

In its extreme interpretation, individualized instruction is as inflexible as any system that has been under criticism by proponents of individualism. In its more modified form, teachers find individualized reading a motivating device. Relieved of pressure to read something beyond them or not within their immediate interests, many children develop sufficient confidence and concern to apply themselves to the learning task, whether that learning is secured within a group or by an individual approach. In the second quarter of the present century, completely individualized programs in reading were either abandoned or greatly modified, but beginning in the early 1950s, interest in individualized reading increased, with most of the emphasis on self-selection of material and individual conferences with the teacher. There is certainly no dearth of studies, but recent research is for the most part poorly controlled and poorly reported, or else it covers a period of too short duration for definite conclusions.

Grouping for Individual Needs

Homogeneous grouping according to intelligence has already been discussed. Scores on achievement tests administered to children so grouped have shown no significant difference over those not so grouped.

In some schools children move to classrooms other than their own for reading only, on a so-called modified Joplin plan. This system has its problems in that a teacher may work with a group of children for less than an hour out of the day, and yet the remainder of the day's work involves much reading under a teacher not well acquainted with individual needs in reading. Also, experienced teachers have long been aware that growth in reading can vary surprisingly and a child assigned to a specific group may very soon be misplaced within one or more levels of reading achievement. Yet reassignment is infrequent and may even be upsetting to the child.

Probably the most popular method, and most effective for children when well handled, is the organization of small, flexible groups within one heterogeneous class. For some skills a group may be very small, for others quite large. In some cases a child needing specific help may work on a task alone, or another may read and share material several grade levels beyond his classmates. Some groups may be interest groups, others organized around needs in critical reading or the social skill of oral reading.

53

Nongraded Plans

The nongraded plan has been another attempt to take care of individual differences. In some cases, this plan can be rigid in that children must move in prescribed steps from one level or book to another, making progress tantamount to as many as seven or eight promotions per year. Ideally, the child in the ungraded plan moves at his own best pace, feels no stigma attached to reading at a different level from that of his classmates, and does not experience frustrating failure. All of these attributes are equally possible in a graded system if the philosophy and skill of the teacher permits.

Basal Readers

In many school systems, the program presented by the selected basal reader accurately describes the curriculum in reading. If the selection has been wise, the basal reader does provide balanced, sequential learning experiences and guides the teacher in developing a sound program. It is economical in the use of the teacher's time, since materials for developing necessary skills are readily available and suggested plans are included. In addition, most basal reader programs today are rich in variety and provide for a wide range of interests and individual differences.

Good teachers select readers and workbook exercises on the basis of children's abilities, use those suggestions in the manuals that will help meet specific needs, and recognize that some children do not need to complete every exercise whereas others need more.

With few exceptions, basal readers are organized around a developmental approach. The readiness books commonly used in kindergarten or first grade try to develop auditory and visual discrimination, to enlarge vocabulary, and to orient the child to the idea that English is read from left to right and top to bottom. Usually, the more advanced readiness books introduce the child to the names of the characters he will meet in the first preprimer; the alphabet; a few commonly used words; and exercises to help the child detect rhyme and discriminate between the sounds and symbols of initial consonants and digraphs. The books in most series are multiethnic in character and contain stories of high interest set in both urban and rural environments. Decoding skills, comprehension skills including critical reading, study skills, and literary appreciation skills are sequentially presented and all included in the major series. Depth and scope are also characteristic of the offerings, which include poetry, humor, material stressing democratic values, depiction of human nature, adventure, biography, inspirational stories, and documentary accounts of current affairs.

Basal readers are popular. A recent survey, including 2,418 teachers from seven widely separated states, revealed more than 85 percent of the teachers were using basal readers. Adroitly employed, the basal reader is a strong asset in implementing the curriculum, but it should not be considered the entire curriculum in reading.

Word Recognition

Many curriculum innovations in reading and resulting issues have been concerned with instruction in word recognition. While inclusion of phonics and other word recognition techniques in the reading program has never been seriously questioned by the majority of curriculum workers, opinion is divided about the placement and stress accorded such instruction. A small minority present a heavy program of decoding symbols before words or books are introduced. Some begin with vowel sounds, others with consonants. A few present open syllables and have the child associate the consonant–vowel combination with the short sound of the vowel. The final consonant, in what would be a single-syllable word, is included either in an isolated manner such as

> *me t* and *be t*   or   *me*   *be*
> *met*   *bet*

Another small minority present all letters of the alphabet in isolation.

The large majority of curriculum workers prefer to begin with easy, highly meaningful material, giving instruction in phonic principles in conjunction with that material as children give evidence of readiness and need. Such workers believe that children beginning to read have a very limited ability to apply phonic principles and that when the reading curriculum includes drill on many phonic generalizations at the early levels, it not only takes the life and meaning out of the program but may confuse the child. Clymer, in testing the utility of commonly taught phonic generalizations, found many to be of doubtful value, anyway. Thus the curriculum worker's task of selecting content for an effective program in the development of word recognition, skills including phonics, structural analysis, syllabication, and accent is not an easy one(*16*).

Opinion is also divided over whether the analytic or synthetic approach in phonic instruction should prevail. To date, well-controlled research points to the evidence that a synthetic approach produces superior results at first grade level, with diminishing returns apparent later. Those who use the synthetic approach should earnestly question their definitions of reading and their knowledge of human nature. Should the ability to recite lists of words substitute for comprehension? In our society, shouldn't the child, from his initial steps in reading, be taught to demand meaning, draw conclusions, make inferences, and read creatively and critically? If interest and joy in reading are ignored, are they likely to be captured later? If an individual can decode word symbols with speed and accuracy, does it necessarily insure an abiding desire to read?

The writer followed two equated groups of twenty-five children in the same community, one of which had been exposed to a heavy program consisting of drills in a synthetic phonics program, and the other to easy, meaningful material, with an analytic approach to word recognition. At the end of the first year, the group using the synthetic approach was significantly ahead in word recognition skills on standardized tests. The second group was significantly ahead in reading for meaning. However, without the teacher participants of the plan being informed, the summer withdrawals from a nearby library were checked and it was found that of the fifty children, 100 percent of those in the second group read, and most of them prodigiously. Only one child in the group exposed to the heavy synthetic phonics program withdrew a book. Summer vacation activities are difficult to control or evaluate, but the above finding might stimulate further studies relative to interest and tastes in reading.

CRITICAL READING, THE ESSENCE OF A STRONG PROGRAM

The term *critical reading* may be interpreted in a variety of ways, but for purposes of most persons constructing a reading curriculum, the process begins early in the first grade and continues in developmental progression indefinitely, with each reader pursuing possible interpretations of printed matter as far as the material and his abilities permit. Thus, the child reading in a preprimer may be guided in interpreting the few lines and the accompanying picture to determine, for example, that the chief character is justifiably cross with his younger sister but gentle in his treatment of her. He can be led to see that the story was realistic or fanciful, that a commonly used persuasive device was used, or that the title was not in harmony with the content.

By third grade, most children reading sentences such as "She dropped her eyes in confusion," or "He flew out the door, picked up his friend, and shot questions at him with machine-gun rapidity," are able to infer that the author is speaking figuratively to create a mood. In a sufficiently rich and flexible curriculum, children at quite early ages will read advertisements with a discerning eye and quickly detect in a newspaper report of a "con game" the obvious fraud before it is stated in the article. Given a rich background of experience, they can learn to separate fact from fiction, detect propaganda techniques, and enjoy the fanciful and the realistic, differentiating between them. Critical reading requires the application of every reading skill, lively practice in meaningful situations, and an opportunity to react creatively.

References

1. Miles A. Tinker and Constance McCullough, *Teaching Elementary Reading* (New York: Appleton-Century-Crofts, 1962), pp. 23–24.

2. Mary C. Austin and Coleman Morrison, *The First R. The Harvard Report on Reading in the Elementary Schools* (New York: Macmillan Co., 1963), pp. 12–15.

3. Dolores Durkin. Unpublished address given at an American Education Research Association meeting in Chicago, February, 1966.

4. Leonard Bloomfield and Clarence L. Barnhart, *Let's Read: A Linguistic Approach* (Detroit: Wayne State University Press, 1961).

5. Charles Fries, Agnes Fries, and Rosemary G. Wilson, *Reader I*, "Merrill Linguistic Readers, a Basic Program" (Columbus, Ohio: Charles E. Merrill Books, 1966), p. 14.

6. *Sullivan Associates Reader Storybook I* (New York: Webster Division, McGraw-Hill, 1964), p. 14.

7. Glen McCracken and Charles C. Walcutt, *Basic Reading Pre-Primer* (Philadelphia: J. B. Lippincott Co., 1963), p. 9.

8. Albert J. Mazurkeiwicz, "Teaching Reading in America Using i/t/a," *Elementary English* 41 (November 1964):766–72.

9. Albert J. Mazurkeiwicz, "ITA and TO Reading Achievement When Methodology Is Controlled," *Reading Teacher* 19 (May 1966):606–11.

10. Robert Chasnoff, "Two Alphabets: A Follow Up," *Elementary School Journal,* February 1968, pp. 251–57.

11. Lady Bridget Plowden, *Children and Their Schools: A Report of the Central Advisory Council for Education* (England), Vol. I Report (London: Her Majesty's Stationery Office, 1967).

12. John Malone, "The Larger Aspects of Spelling Reform," *Elementary English* 39 (May 1962):435–45.

13. Edward B. Fry, "First Grade Reading Instruction Using Diacritical Marking System, Initial Teaching Alphabet and Basal Reading System," *Reading Teacher* 20, no. 8 (May 1967):687–93.

14. Cynthia Dee Buchanan, *Programmed Reading,* Sullivan Associates (New York: Webster Division, McGraw-Hill, 1966).

15. Caleb Gattegno, *Words in Color* (Chicago: Encyclopaedia Britannica Press, 1962).

16. Theodore Clymer, "The Utility of Phonics Generalizations in the Primary Grades," *Reading Teacher* 12 (January 1963):252–58.

Operational Concepts

1. Parental involvement is a significant factor in improving reading skills in the primary grades.

2. Premature emphasis on reading skills (during the preschool years) appears to offer little real advantage.

3. Prevailing theories on the teaching of reading conflict; it cannot be assumed, therefore, that any one method is superior to all others.

4. No known teaching method produces superior results with every child.

5. Used properly by skilled teachers, basal readers seem to yield consistently satisfactory results.

Implications

It seems reasonable to assume that the quality of reading instruction will improve only as we learn more about techniques for the individualization of learning. Not only do all the acceptable methods produce some successes and some failures, but children vary considerably in their kinesthetic, auditory, and visual development during the early stages of reading instruction. Moreover, since the desire to learn is even more crucial in reading than in other aspects of the curriculum, efforts to solve the problem of limited motivation must continue.

Our greatest liability, however, lies in the fact that we still fail to teach a very large percentage of our youth to read effectively. The bulk of these students stem from poverty-stricken families and from the ethnic minorities. Since no learning is more fundamental than basic literacy, everything possible must be done to correct the deficiency.

Again underscoring the importance of greater individualization, the research evidence makes it abundantly clear that some children learn to read more quickly than others, and, as a consequence, instructional time must be allotted accordingly. The evidence also indicates that efforts to prove one method of teaching reading superior to others are largely futile. What works for one child—or teacher—is ineffectual for another, and it would thus make more sense to focus our energies upon determining which particular method works best for each child and each teacher.

Despite a substantial increase in the use of remedial reading centers in schools, much more needs to be done. A great array of corrective materials is now available, and more are likely to be developed as research on reading continues. Nonetheless, despite the increase in resources, the school's success record is far from spectacular. Hence, the cultivation of children's desire and self-confidence remains *the* dominant goal. Once these two essentials are assured, the quality of the teacher appears to make the greatest difference. As a result, continuing efforts to extend the competence of reading teachers will probably yield the greatest payoff.

Margaret Early

Important Research in Reading and Writing

In this decade, the teaching of reading and writing has been influenced by two movements that seem at first to be at odds with each other. About ten years ago, teachers were told that to teach well they must know the structure of English, its phonology, morphology, and syntax. Very soon thereafter, they were told to pay more attention to how and why children learn to use and understand language and to remember that how children feel is more important than what they know. Good teachers learned both lessons and have shaped their teaching to take both into account. In the growing back-to-the-basics mood, they will view both "structure" and "feeling" as basic.

The purpose of this article is to review some of the studies, both empirical and theoretical, which seem to me to illuminate the changes affecting reading and writing in this decade.

In the movements noted in the first paragraph, both linguistics and psychology played influential roles. Indeed, the recent research of greatest potential significance to teachers of language arts has emerged from a union of these two disciplines. Psycholinguistics is just beginning to influence school practice. Teachers are reading texts like Frank Smith's *Understanding Reading* (1971) and Courtney Cazden's *Child Language and Education* (1972) and learning from them of the many studies which describe and systematize language development from infancy to adolescence(1). But having learned, for example, that learning to read is a further extension of learning to speak, teachers are still not sure how that nugget of information should modify their methods of teaching.

The implications of psycholinguistic studies often seem to run counter to what teachers have been taught, especially about reading instruction. Having learned that pupils fail in reading when pushed beyond their "mastery level," teachers are confused by advice suggesting that children should be allowed to get what they can out of books that may be "above their level." Nor are they happy to be told now that they may be doing

Reprinted from Margaret Early, "Important Research in Reading and Writing," *Phi Delta Kappan*, January 1976; by permission of the publisher.

more harm than good by piling on phonics instruction, especially when they were so recently (1967) told by Jeanne Chall in *Learning to Read: The Great Debate* that "code-emphasis" reading programs tend to produce better overall reading achievement, at least in the beginning, than do meaning-emphasis programs(2).

While the psycholinguistic studies of the past decade may have only potential significance, there is no doubt that Chall's work overturned beginning reading instruction. Not by itself, of course. *Learning to Read* is a review of methods of teaching reading from 1910 to 1965; it was inspired by the controversy set aflame by Rudolf Flesch's 1955 best seller, *Why Johnny Can't Read*. Chall's reading of the research led her to recommend a return to code emphasis in beginning reading methods, but she acknowledged that she was influenced also by the mood of the time in which she wrote, a time "when excellence in academic work is highly valued, when intellectual precociousness is viewed as promise of later accomplishment. . . ." The shift to code-emphasis methods had already begun by the time *Learning to Read* was published. It accelerated thereafter. But by the late sixties, even as basal series were becoming code oriented, the mood of the times was changing.

One signal of that change—especially as it affects the teaching of reading and writing—was the Anglo-American Seminar in the Teaching of English at Dartmouth in 1966. The shots fired at Dartmouth were not heard round the classrooms immediately, however.

While American and British educators were contrasting the values of knowing and feeling, debating open education versus more traditionally structured styles, elementary schools were buying instructional materials inspired by the previous decade's admiration for structure and academic excellence.

Reading, per se, played a minor role at Dartmouth. But in the nation as a whole, teaching how to read is always front and center. While Chall's book was in the making and the Dartmouth papers were emerging, the U.S. Office of Education was conducting and publicizing a spate of studies of first-grade reading, some of which continued into second and third grades(3). These studies reflected the decade's overriding concern with method, pitting one approach against another. Altogether, five different basal series, three phonics programs, two linguistic programs, and two i/t/a programs were tried out in classrooms across the country. The results were evaluated with the same tests. Among classes using the same methods, sharper differences showed up in end-of-the-year testing than appeared between classes using the different methods under comparison. This surprising result led many to infer that teachers, not methods, were responsible for the differences. Beyond this inference, the data offered some support for code-emphasis programs but not enough to be conclusive.

With or without support from research, phonics returned to reading instruction not only in new and revised basal series but also on TV's "Sesame Street" and "The Electric Company." No one suggested that ability to identify words would insure comprehension; so it should have come as no surprise in the early seventies that while primary-grade reading scores were rising, means were falling on middle-grade tests which measure comprehension. But if stressing phonics in beginning reading doesn't insure successful comprehension, neither can it be blamed for comprehension's falling off in the middle grades. Rather, evidence accumulated in this decade suggests that when comprehension scores decline on a national scale—and they seem to be doing just that—factors outside the school contribute as heavily as in-school practices.

Home and family background are dominant in determining achievement in reading, wrote Robert Thorndike in 1973, summarizing an extensive international evaluation of reading comprehension(4). In the United States, the 1974 National Assessment of Educational Progress reported that differences in reading performance were related consistently to level of parents' education, community, region, race, and sex(5). Neither these studies nor those summarized in 1972 by Christopher Jencks(6) should be construed as absolving schools of influence or responsibility. However, they suggest that more factors are at work than unsuccessful experiments with open education, as some critics have alleged. Failure to teach how to comprehend, using any method or in any kind of classroom setting, must be one of the reasons for low achievement, but there are many reasons why teachers fail to teach. Ignorance is only one of them. In this decade, we must consider also the direct effects on teaching of social and political issues such as busing and integration, unions and strikes.

Research has not been very helpful to teachers in this matter of comprehension. We still know next to nothing about the process, even though we are continually devising new measures of whatever it is. Frederick Davis's 1944 factor analysis of comprehension yielded nine subskills, which Louis Thurstone claimed could be subsumed into one or at most two: word meaning and "another factor." More than twenty years later, in 1968, Davis reaffirmed eight of his original nine subskills(7); but in 1972 John Carroll concluded from the amount of variance residing in the tests of these skills that "perhaps only four or five merit recognition as distinct skills"(8). These are remembering word meanings; following the structure of a passage; finding answers to questions answered explicitly or in paraphrase; recognizing a writer's purpose, attitude, tone, or mood; and drawing inferences from the content.

Accumulated research on comprehension tells teachers that behavioral objectives related to comprehension should be few and that measurement of these objectives should be interpreted warily.

Obviously, the next major goal of reading research must be unraveling the mysteries of comprehension. To date, psycholinguistic studies have ventured only as far as the sentence, depending too heavily perhaps on transformational analyses for insights that must also include examination of intention, memory, experience, and knowledge. Present studies try to simulate the process in slow motion. For example, some investigators have fed readers various "chunks" of sentence matter, chunking sometimes by syntax, sometimes by meaning, sometimes by neither(9). Others have experimented with the systematic deletion of words (CLOZE techniques) for clues to process.

While psycholinguistic studies try to determine what's happening when students comprehend, other researchers have been investigating the conditions under which students comprehend certain subjects (always measuring the intake by the output). Such studies have not proved very fruitful, because they have not defined carefully what was being measured, because they pitted one complex teaching method against another without being able to sort out the variables, or because they evaluated specific material rather than generalizable principles. Future studies will make greater use of observational techniques, interviews, introspection, and laboratory simulations employing computers and recording devices.

Kenneth Goodman and his students have recently contributed the concept of "miscue analysis" to the diagnosis of reading performance(10). Based on psycholinguistic principles, miscue analysis tries to determine the reasons for errors in oral reading. Which of these errors are a result of a mismatch between a nonstandard dialect (e.g., black English) and the dialect of the reading text? Which reveal that a rule for recoding from print to speech has not yet been learned? Goodman's research refines diagnostic techniques that teachers have long been urged to use. In essence, Goodman says to teachers: Meaning is more important than coding. If the reader accurately translates the printed message into his own dialect, he is reading successfully.

Restoring importance to "reading for meaning" does not dismiss the need for teaching decoding skills. Sensitive analysis of miscues helps the teacher to know which skills are functioning well and which need further support.

Successful individualizing of instruction depends on diagnosis but also on follow-through. What IGE (Individually Guided Education) seems to offer is systematic follow-through, as subskills pinpointed by diagnosis are keyed to instructional materials. Students stay with a subskill until it is reinforced to the point of mastery as evaluated by a criterion-referenced test. Do systems approaches work? Research usually shows that children learn what they have been taught. But pupil progress toward narrowly defined goals is only one answer to "Does it work?" This question also implies measuring what the system costs, not only for materials and personnel but in teacher morale and efficiency and in students' attitudes and overall intellectual curiosity. Systems approaches may be teaching and evaluating only peripheral aspects of what successful readers are really learning as they master the process of comprehension.

One questionable side effect of diagnostic-prescriptive instruction is that it can give numerical scores a spurious significance. Scores from a computer seem somehow more reliable than personal judgment. But nothing is less true. Diagnosing reading performance and choosing instructional materials are not a matter of matching reading scores to readability scores. From Winnetka in the twenties to IPI in the seventies, individualizing instruction has spawned readability formulas as an easy way to select books that children can comprehend. But all readability research, and there have been important additions to it in the decade under review(*11*), stresses the extreme limitations of the formulas and begs teachers not to substitute computationally derived ratings for experience and judgment.

My next topic is motivation. In introducing it here, I don't mean to suggest unfairly a polarity between diagnostic–prescriptive teaching and an approach that is centered less on skill than on children's interests. Although coming from different perspectives (to which I refuse to attach such convenient labels as Skinnerian and Piagetian), both approaches partake ultimately of many of the same practices: diagnosis, materials relevant to children's interests, goal setting, recording of progress. (In England recently, I visited infant schools stoutly defended as "traditional" and found practices there which were as "open" as many in other schools that were displayed as showcases of open education.) But, on the surface, IPI and SSR (to use another set of labels) appear to be movements and countermovements, and I cannot mention individually prescribed instruction and omit the impact of, say, *Hooked on Books*(*12*) or Lyman Hunt's sustained silent reading. Though not supported by massive research, the message from both of these quite different sources has come through clearly to teachers: Surround children with books, mostly paperbacks; set aside time for them to read; nudge them into books but let them find their own level; and talk to them about their reading.

Reading has taken the lion's share in this review, just as it usurps more than its share of language arts time in the classroom. Yet the really significant research in this decade is in language as it variously affects school learning. This research springs from Noam Chomsky's analyses of language in terms of transformational grammar, and much of it investigates speech from infancy to age 5. As this research moves into the language of older children, more of it has to do with children's writing as well as their speech and with the comprehension of language through listening and reading. As the studies accumulate, it becomes increasingly clear that children acquire language in sequence—moving, for instance, from understanding simpler to more complex constructions(*13*), from writing shorter to longer sentences(*14*), from using little to much subordination. The point is that such sequences are set, are not skipped, and cannot be force-fed.

Analyses of children's writing and speaking have often been limited to single situations: one kind of writing, for example, or an interview in a laboratory setting. Newer research asks whether children's language

64

changes according to its purposes and the situations in which it occurs and suggests, not surprisingly, that the forms change to suit the content(*15*). Much situational research has involved black dialects and has revealed their range and complexity(*16*).

How should these many studies affect the teaching of comprehending and composing in language? Perhaps the best summary answer, and the most influential one in this decade, is the theory developed by James Moffett in *Teaching the Universe of Discourse*(*17*). Drawing upon the language research and theories of the fifties and sixties, Moffett proposed a curricular structure that moves with the child along two dimensions of increasing abstraction. On the first dimension, the distance between speaker and audience widens (egocentric speech to public statement). On the second dimension, the child moves into participating in what is happening, then to reporting, on to generalizing, and finally to theorizing. Moffett's theories are by no means presented in the abstract, for they undergird not only a handbook on curriculum development but also instructional materials for stimulating the uses of language on the dimensions he has conceptualized.

Moffett says that, aside from art, music, and physical education, the only subject of the schools is language, since all other subjects are learned in and through language. "As content, they are what one discourses about; as process they are acts discoursing." This is another way of saying that reading, writing, speaking, and listening should be taught through content. Somehow, that sane idea strikes terror in the hearts of teachers, because the doing proves so much more complicated than the saying. Or at least it has so far. But here and there across the country, ready to be researched or at least minutely observed, are programs that variously implement Moffett's ideas and may indeed point the way to elementary curricula in which language learning is central.

If research says anything to teachers, it is, "Don't go overboard." In reading, keep an eye on decoding *and* meaning. Realize that long lists of behavioral objectives relating to comprehension fly in the face of what little research can tell us about this mysterious process. Look for psycholinguistic studies to reveal more about the process, and in the meantime teach four or five skills consistently and repeatedly in all subjects of the curriculum. Balance skills teaching with reading for personal motives and pleasures.

Remember that language is learned sequentially and that sequences cannot be reversed or stages skipped. But encouraging children to write and speak for many different purposes will cause them to use different forms and expand their language repertoire.

Good teaching of reading and writing can occur in several different settings, no one of which is best for all children. Thus, for growth in reading and writing, a sound educational system offers alternative programs and claims no one best method.

References

1. Frank Smith, *Understanding Reading* (New York: Holt, Rinehart and Winston, 1971); Courtney B. Cazden, *Child Language and Education* (New York: Holt, Rinehart and Winston, 1972).

2. Jeanne Chall, *Learning to Read: The Great Debate* (New York: McGraw-Hill, 1967).

3. Guy L. Bond and Robert Dykstra, *Coordinating Center for First-Grade Reading Instruction Programs,* Final Report, USOE Project No. X-001 (Minneapolis: University of Minnesota, 1967); also in *Reading Research Quarterly,* Spring, 1967, pp. 5–142.

4. Robert L. Thorndike, *Reading Comprehension Education in Fifteen Countries,* International Studies in Evaluation III (New York: John Wiley & Sons, 1973).

5. National Assessment of Educational Progress Report 02-R-30, *Recipes, Wrappers, Reasoning, and Rate: A Digest of the First Reading Assessment* (Washington, D.C.: U.S. Government Printing Office, April, 1974).

6. Christopher Jencks, *Inequality: A Reassessment of the Effect of Family and Schooling in America* (New York: Harper & Row, 1972).

7. Frederick B. Davis, "Research in Comprehension in Reading," *Reading Research Quarterly,* Summer, 1968, pp. 499–545.

8. John B. Carroll, "Defining Language Comprehension," in *Language Comprehension and the Acquisition of Knowledge* (Washington, D.C.: V. H. Winston and Sons, 1972), pp. 1–29.

9. Roy Oliver Martin Latham, "Cognitive Synthesis and the Comprehension of Written Language" (Ph. D. diss., University of Alberta, 1973).

10. Kenneth S. Goodman, ed., *Miscue Analysis: Applications to Reading Instruction* (Urbana, Ill.: ERIC Clearinghouse on Reading and Communication Skills, NCTE, 1973).

11. G. R. Klare, "Assessing Readability," *Reading Research Quarterly,* vol. 10, no. 1, 1974–75, pp. 62–102.

12. Daniel N. Fader and Elton B. McNeil, *Hooked on Books: Program and Proof* (New York: G. P. Putnam's Sons, 1969).

13. Carol S. Chomsky, *The Acquisition of Syntax in Children from 5 to 10* (Cambridge, Mass.: MIT Press, 1969).

14. Kellogg W. Hunt, *Grammatical Structures Written at Three Grade Levels,* NCTE Research Report No. 3 (Champaign, Ill.: National Council of Teachers of English, 1965); Roy C. O'Donnell, William J. Griffen, and Raymond C. Norris, *Syntax of Kindergarten and Elementary School Children: A Transformational Analysis,* NCTE Research Report No. 8 (Champaign, Ill.: National Council of Teachers of English, 1967).

15. Christine M. San Jose, "Grammatical Structures in Four Modes of Writing at Fourth-Grade Level" (Ph.D. diss., Graduate School of Syracuse University, August, 1972).

16. William Labov, *Language in the Inner City: Studies in the Black English Vernacular* (Philadelphia: University of Pennsylvania Press, 1972).

17. James Moffett, *Teaching the Universe of Discourse* (Boston: Houghton Mifflin, 1968).

Operational Concepts

1. Teachers, not methods, seem to produce differences in reading achievement.

2. Although failure to teach comprehension skills has contributed to falling scores on standardized reading tests, factors outside the school also have been heavily contributory.

3. Scores on primary-grade reading tests, emphasizing word recognition, appear to have risen; scores on middle-grade tests, emphasizing comprehension, in contrast, seem to have fallen; the resulting conclusion is that word-recognition skill does not guarantee parallel comprehension skill.

4. As comparatively greater emphasis is placed upon the teaching of reading, it is important to maintain a proper balance between the teaching of comprehension and the teaching of decoding skills.

5. The use of behavioral objectives in teaching reading comprehension can be problematic; the assessment of learner outcomes, on the basis of such objectives, should therefore be approached prudently.

Implications

Virtually any survey of test results can be controversial. Experts easily disagree as to validity and reliability of the test, the accuracy of the interpretations, and the causal factors relating to the results.

Be this as it may, the research reviewed by Early deserves serious attention. It seems clear, for example, that further developmental work is needed to improve the teaching of comprehension. It also is apparent that perhaps the greatest error in reading instruction is excessive and unwarranted stress upon one element at the expense of another. The teaching of skills must be balanced with attention to the pleasurable aspects of reading, considerable attention must be given to the clarification of what children infer from their reading, and the learner's mastery of fundamental decoding skills cannot be slighted.

Continued research on methods of teaching reading also seems desirable. In particular, more must be learned about the perceptual processes through which children derive meaning from content. And, as we perhaps have always suspected, the efficiency, effectiveness, and commitment of the teacher are of far greater importance than the method deployed.

Spelling

Harry A. Greene
Walter T. Petty

Developing Spelling Skills

SPELLING IN THE SCHOOL CURRICULUM

As children record and exchange their ideas and information by writing, they need to spell correctly the words they are using. Writing is done for the purpose of transferring thought from a writer to an audience. While it is possible to communicate in writing without all of the words used being correctly spelled, such communication lacks something in effectiveness. Too, spelling all words correctly in many instances is crucial. Correct spelling not only gives the individual confidence and independence in his writing and is often essential to his success in a vocational or social sense, but it also represents a reasonable if not necessary courtesy to extend to readers.

Goals of the Program

In most schools the instructional program in spelling centers in the use of a textbook or a workbook; in some of these the teacher supplements the instruction suggested in these materials. In a few schools the spelling program (largely the selection of words to learn) is taken from the daily work of the children. However, regardless of the materials or the basis for the selection of the words, too often the spelling instruction is limited and not really correlated with the general program in language. The basic goal in spelling is, of course, to teach children to spell correctly every word that they write. This goal is interpreted in two ways by spelling authorities. Some say that power in associating letters with sounds should be developed so that a general spelling ability is achieved(1). Others say that such associations may be misleading and that the words most commonly written should be taught, along with certain attitudes and habits that would lead to the learning of words not directly taught(2). Both points of view (which are discussed further later in the chapter) only set the general pattern for

Reprinted from Harry A. Greene and Walter T. Petty, *Developing Language Skills in the Elementary Schools,* © 1971; by permission of Allyn and Bacon, Inc., Boston.

the spelling program and must be expressed in specific objectives if effective instruction is to be achieved. The authors of this text believe that the following basic objectives should be a part of every spelling program:

1. To develop in each child an attitude that
   a. recognizes that correct spelling is important to effective communication
   b. creates a desire to spell correctly all the words he writes
   c. instills a desire to spell correctly an increasing number of words and to understand and use words more effectively
2. To develop in each child the ability to
   a. recognize all the letters of the alphabet in capital and lower case forms in both printed and handwritten materials
   b. write all the letters of the alphabet in a legible manner in both capital and lower case forms
   c. alphabetize words
   d. hear words accurately as they are spoken
   e. pronounce words clearly and accurately
   f. see printed or written words accurately
   g. group and connect the letters of a word properly
   h. use properly any punctuation elements important to spelling
   i. use a dictionary, including the use of diacritical markings and guide words
   j. use phonetic aids in arriving at the proper pronunciation of unfamiliar words
   k. use applicable knowledge of sound and symbol correspondence
   l. use the most effective spelling rules
   m. use effective procedures in learning to spell new words
3. To develop in each child the habit of
   a. proofreading his writing carefully
   b. using reliable sources to determine the correct spelling of unknown or doubtful words
   c. following a specific study procedure in learning the spelling of new words

A Basic Vocabulary

Research has established that approximately 3,000 words are so frequently written that they may be considered basic for every child to learn. In addition, there are words of particular relevance to writing and those are frequently misspelled. In the primary grades children need to learn to spell the words they are currently using in their writing—and usually in their reading. However, adding words to the basic list should be done carefully, as one curriculum guide points out(3):

> A word of caution needs to be given in regard to the list compiled from misspelled words. The teacher must [also] differentiate between words used so often in all writing that spelling mastery is both necessary and desirable and words that are peculiar to a given topic and are, therefore, needed only temporarily by pupils.

This advice as to lists is extended with reference to subject matter words(4):

> The latter words are not taught formally but they are listed on the chalkboard or on charts so that they can be made readily available to all members of the group.

Most commercial spelling programs provide a basic list of words in their books for the elementary grades, most of which reflect consideration of the research concerning the most frequently written words. Some books include additional words in attempts to teach generalizations about sound representations and structural patterns.

The principal point regarding a basic list of spelling words is that the teacher or local school staff should not be responsible for the compilation of the basic vocabulary forming the heart of the spelling program. Not only is this an expensive and technical task, but it might lead to grave omissions in words chosen. Moreover, the results of extensive research in this area are not readily available to the teacher, yet most commercial spelling materials have utilized this research.

The particular words taught in the spelling program are important but so is the stress upon correct spelling in all writing activities and upon the supplemental spelling skills of proofreading, using the dictionary, and learning to apply spelling generalizations. Also important are the adjustments teachers must make in the list of words to be taught, unless the spelling books they are using do so, in order to care for the needs and abilities of slow and gifted learners. When such adjustment is needed, it should be done on the basis of evidence of the relative importance of the words in the basic list for a specific grade level or for the school. Teachers should turn to basic reports for this help and not attempt to decide subjectively the importance or suitability of a particular word(5).

The Importance of Attitudes

Being a good speller is not simply a matter of ability to spell a basic core of words correctly, or even to spell many words. Certainly it is not a matter of making a perfect score on a spelling test. The good speller is the person who recognizes the importance of correct spelling, who endeavors to spell correctly each word that he writes, and who is equipped to learn how to spell new words independently. He knows that correct spelling will improve the quality of his written expression. He believes that the spelling words he is called upon to learn are important words that he will need to use frequently in his written work. In other words, the good speller has an attitude conducive to learning both through direct instruction and incidentally. Thus, while an important objective of the spelling program is to teach children to spell the words in a basic vocabulary list, that is not the sole major objective. The development of a favorable attitude toward spelling is also of great importance.

To develop in children a good attitude toward spelling, the teacher himself must regard spelling as important, as something that really matters. He should endeavor to spell correctly all words that he writes; when he has doubt as to the spelling of a word, he should use a dictionary to check himself. He should show children that the words they are learning to spell are words that they consistently use in writing and need to spell correctly. Simple investigations directed at their own and their parents' and friends' writing will show this.

Each child should learn to use a specific and efficient method of learning to spell a word, and should be required to study only those words which spelling tests and actual writing situations have shown that he is unable to spell. Asking pupils to study words they already know is a major deterrent to the development of favorable attitudes.

The teacher should require a high standard of neatness and accuracy in all written work. The standards should be developed cooperatively by teacher and pupils and should be consistently observed. Developing these standards will encourage in the class a spirit of mutual pride and cooperation in spelling achievement. To further this spirit, children should be allowed to help one another study and proofread for spelling errors and to give encouragement to those needing it.

The teacher should immediately attack any negative attitudes by encouraging and stimulating the children's efforts. Fault-finding should be eliminated in favor of determining the cause of spelling failure. Negative attitudes are also discouraged if the achievement of the class is emphasized and if individual pupils can see their own progress. Records of progress may be kept by the pupils themselves and any achievement appraised in the light of earlier efforts.

The Role of Habits

A good attitude toward spelling is basic to a successful program, but merely desiring to spell correctly will accomplish little unless certain habits such as those described below have been established.

1. *Being concerned about the spelling of words used in written expression.*
   For the child, this means teaching him to think "Is the word spelled correctly?" and "Am I sure?" This habit is established by the development and maintenance of standards in written work and by the teacher's repeatedly calling attention to the standards.

2. *Carefully proofreading all written work.* This means examining each word carefully to see if it is spelled correctly. The teacher must insist that a misspelled word is a mistake in spelling, whether the child knows better or not, and that the only way to avoid the making of such mistakes is to proofread for spelling errors.

3. *Checking the spelling of all words about which the child is in doubt.* The pupil should ask the teacher the spelling of such words, or when skill in use of the dictionary is developed, he should consult that authority.

4. *Using a specific procedure for learning the spelling of new words.* Such a procedure may vary from child to child (as is discussed later) but the particular steps a child follows should be thoroughly known by him.

Spelling and the Other Language Arts

Research has shown that spelling ability is related to abilities in reading, handwriting, speech, and written composition(6). Correlations between scores on reading and spelling tests have been reported at, for example, .48, .51, .61, and .63, so it is not surprising that children learn to spell many words by reading them(7). However, the act of meeting a new word in reading does not automatically mean that its spelling will be learned. Words must be met frequently through reading for this to occur, and even then one study showed that 63 of the 222 most frequently misspelled words are among the 1,000 words of highest frequency in reading(8). Thus, while there is a good deal of transfer of learning between spelling and reading, to teach spelling through reading activities interferes with the process of getting meaning by reading and is not an effective way to teach spelling. Furthermore, contrary to the opinions voiced by some persons, there is little evidence to suggest that spelling instruction promotes growth in reading(9). It is particularly important to remember, too, that spelling is an encoding act while reading is a decoding one. The child attempting to gain meaning from graphic symbols uses a set of clues which are entirely different from those available to the speller as he attempts to write a word.

Speed and legibility of handwriting are factors commonly mentioned as affecting spelling achievement. Certainly in spelling test situations in which time is a factor—and it often should be to prevent fostering poor listening habits—a faster writer obviously has an advantage over a slower one. It is equally obvious that an illegible word must be considered to be incorrectly spelled. Writing activities which give some emphasis to speed will aid spelling instruction by enabling pupils to write with greater facility. As suggested in the discussion of handwriting instruction, pupil self-evaluation will improve legibility. Most commercial spelling materials make provision for some handwriting instruction and practice, and most handwriting programs provide for writing practice using words which are most frequently written. While some questions have arisen concerning the relationship between the form of handwriting used and spelling achievement, there appear to be no differences in achievement which can be attributed to either manuscript or cursive form or to the time at which children were changed from using manuscript to cursive(*10*).

Speech problems also affect spelling achievement, with improvement in pronunciation and articulation and the development of the use of standard English resulting in growth in spelling ability(*11*). Again, while the relationships between the language skills exist and a program which seeks to foster their mutual development is desirable, neither the relationships nor the integrated program will take the place of direct instruction in each area. This does not mean that spelling, or any other language skill, should be taught in a meaningless and rigid environment. Systematic instruction does not preclude a teacher's capitalizing upon the important role the interrelatedness of the language arts can play in the total curriculum.

THE INSTRUCTIONAL PROGRAM

Although the teaching of spelling may be regarded as a relatively simple matter in comparison to instruction in such areas as social studies and science, the recurring expressions of concern, complaint, and even frustration indicate that the attainment of desirable instructional results is apparently not a simple matter. The difficulty seems to be that too little knowledge of the research on spelling instruction is possessed by teachers and too little is reflected in the commercial spelling materials that so greatly affect teaching practices. Certainly much research has been done, with a recently published comprehensive review of this research listing 244 studies in its bibliography(*12*). Not all of the spelling research has been good research, nor are all questions answered. However, a thorough critique of this research by Sherwin indicates that there are many instructional practices that should be followed(*13*). The extent to which teachers in one state are aware of practices based upon research findings and those not so supported has been reported by Fitzsimmons(*14*). He found that over 50 percent of the teachers either did not know or did not support the research findings in such instructional areas as time allotted for spelling, studying hard spots in words, taking spelling words from curricular areas, and teaching by phonics rules. Virtually all other practices established by research were not known to at least one-fourth of the teachers sampled.

The Problem of Spelling

Of course, no instructional procedures can ever alleviate frustrations traceable to the complexity and illogicality of the spelling of our language. However, excessive concern with the hybrid nature of the English language, with the fact that it is studded with words lifted bodily or adapted from other languages, or with the lag in changes in spelling as compared to changes in pronunciation will not solve the instructional problems(*15*). It is highly unlikely that it will ever be possible to change spelling to conform to pronunciation, and some authorities argue that this is not desirable even if it were possible(*16*). Nor does it seem profitable to attempt to alleviate frustration regarding an inconsistent sound-to-letter relationship by teaching many generalizations about how sounds are represented. This would appear to be primarily the substitution of one source of frustration for another, though this conclusion is disputed by some spelling authorities, as will be shown later.

Frustration is largely eliminated through the instilling of confidence in spelling. In spelling instruction confidence can be instilled in each child by (1) providing him with a definite and efficient method of learning; (2) providing words to be learned that are most needed in his writing activities; (3) making him aware of his skill in spelling and the progress he is making in learning new words; (4) making the spelling instruction period meaningful and interesting; and (5) developing in him an interest in his language and a desire to spell and use each word correctly.

Particular attention should be given to the development of a *spelling consciousness* or the ability to know whether a word is spelled correctly or that the spelling is doubtful and should be checked. This is not a new concept, but as pointed out by Valmont, it is one that has been neglected(*17*). What should be done to develop spelling consciousness is less well known. Valmont suggests that it is related "to intelligence, overall academic achievement, and abilities such as visual discrimination, a functional knowledge of phonics, and correctness in using homonyms"(*18*). Some of these factors, of course, are amenable to instruction.

An Instructional Plan

Although spelling programs in elementary schools may vary from the informal and incidental to those in which time is set aside for specific instruction, the majority fall into the latter category. This is proof of teachers observing the research evidence, but perhaps tradition is the major influence(*19*). It should be remembered, however, that systematic instruction does not mean that the learning cannot be correlated with other parts of the school program nor that differences among children need be ignored. In fact, good plans attend to these differences and relegate systematic study to proper portions of the school day.

Spelling is most often taught in periods set aside for that purpose, using spelling books which determine the basic words taught and suggest the learning procedures to be followed. For this instruction two general plans have been identified and one or the other is typically used. These are the *test-study* and the *study-test* plans. Sherwin says, ". . . the evidence is fairly consistently in favor of test-study. The poorer studies are the ones on the other, study-test, side"(*20*). In teaching spelling by the test-study plan, the teacher tests the pupils first to determine the words that each pupil does not know how to spell. Thus interest in spelling is not lost by those pupils who know how to spell all or many of the words in the spelling lesson, nor is instructional time wasted. The test-study plan of spelling instruction consists of these features:

1. A preliminary term or monthly test is given to determine the general level of spelling achievement of the class and of the individuals within the class.

2. A test on each weekly (or other instructional period) assignment is given before instruction is begun on that assignment. Sometimes the test is preceded by the teacher's pronouncing each word as the pupils look carefully at it. Following this the pupils pronounce the words themselves. The pretest procedure may also be modified prior to the first testing by the teacher's explaining the meanings of words which in his judgment pupils may not know. Usually the first step of the test-study plan should not be modified, however, since both meaning and pronunciation of properly chosen words will probably be known.

3. The words that each pupil misspells on this pretest are identified by the child and become his study list for the lesson.

4. In learning to spell each word, each child uses the steps that have been worked out by the class, or by the teacher and himself if modifications have been necessary to fit his particular needs.

5. A mid-lesson test is given to determine progress made since the pretest. A final weekly or lesson test shows the total progress made during the lesson and identifies words for later review.

6. Each child keeps his own record of spelling achievement on a chart or similar device.

7. Any words that the child misspells on the final test are recorded by him in a special review word list.

8. Each child studies the words in his review list in the same manner as he studied them in their original presentation.

9. At regular intervals testing of the review words for each child is done until all such words are mastered.

10. A final term or monthly test is given to measure the progress made since the administration of the first test.

The major difference in the study-test plan is that no pretest is given. The pupils begin the study of the words as the first step in the lesson. Thus all words in a lesson become the study list for each pupil whether he needs to study them or not. Also, usually only two tests are administered—a mid-lesson and a final one.

The Spelling Lesson

Many spelling textbooks or workbooks present the weekly list of words in context; that is, the words are introduced by their inclusion in a story or paragraph. This procedure, within limits, has value in making sure that pupils know the meanings of words to be learned. However, research has shown that the most efficient and economical method of presenting spelling words is by a list. This does not imply that meaning is of no concern; but it is wise to remember that if the words are carefully selected, they will be words whose meanings are known to children or which may be readily learned since they will be used in children's writing. Too much attention to a contextual presentation may simply be a waste of the pupils' time.

As to the amount of time to devote to spelling lessons, principles of learning and research in spelling indicate that no more than seventy-five minutes per week should be devoted to the spelling period(21). Time allotment is related, of course, to objectives of the total program sought to be accomplished by spelling periods, to the abilities of the pupils, and to the efficiency of the instruction. With a favorable attitude on the part of the pupils and a spirited attack upon the learning of the words in the lesson, as little as sixty minutes per week may be allotted to learning these words. Certainly efficient procedures and good attitudes and habits prevent dawdling and loss of interest.

A typical weekly spelling program, which has taken into account research evidence regarding instruction, has these features:

First Day. Administering the pretest on the words in the lesson. (See the form of test below). Checking the tests, each pupil checking his own, Making individual study lists of words misspelled. Discussing the words as necessary—their meanings and use, any unusual spellings, the application of any spelling rules, or etymological matters that are appropriate and of interest.

Second Day. Visual and auditory study of structural and phonemic elements in the words. Study of the words on the individual spelling lists.

Third Day. Administering of a test (usually including all words in the lesson as a means of insuring that guessing did not account for some correct spelling on the pretest). Checking the test, again each pupil checking his own. Studying the words misspelled.

Fourth Day. Continued practice in visual–aural analysis of the words. Learning new meanings for the words. Extending word knowledge through practice in using linguistic principles. Studying words misspelled on the third-day test.

Fifth Day. Administering the final test. Checking the tests, still each pupil checking his own. Writing words in a review list. Marking achievement on a progress chart.

In addition, most programs provide for handwriting diagnosis and practice, practice in using a dictionary, and various word building activities. Newer spelling textbooks provide listening and writing activities, the study of word origins, spelling games, and special exercises and activities for the less able and more able children(22).

Study Steps

Modern spelling programs incorporate the findings of research in presenting the steps in learning to spell a word. The steps involve visual, auditory, and kinesthetic imagery as well as an emphasis on recall. Most of the children will need to follow all the steps, although the best spellers will learn the words primarily by visual imagery, and thus quite rapidly. The poorer spellers will need extra help and encouragement in learning the steps; they may also need to have the steps individualized, such as adding extra ones to help them say the words properly or to gain better auditory or kinesthetic impressions. The poorer achievers in spelling should be particularly encouraged to use the systematic study steps, with special attention being given to those which require recall since recalling a spelling is the principal ability needed to spell words correctly in actual writing.

In spite of the fact that most spelling books list learning steps and suggest that pupils refer to these often, the best procedure is for the teacher and the class to develop their own steps and use them without reference to the book. Teachers can guide children into thinking about how a word should be studied and from this guidance and the resulting discussion the children can themselves state the necessary steps. The statement of the children can then be written on a chart and hung in a place in the room where it can be readily referred to. Through their experience in studying words, the children may want to modify or revise their statement from time to time. This should be encouraged if any of the steps generally suggested have been omitted in the children's statement or if local conditions or individual problems seem to warrant some change. Each child should be encouraged to determine for himself whether the steps listed by the class are those he should follow or if some modification would be an aid to him.

The following method of studying the spelling of a word is suggested as a model for guiding the class to develop its own statement of steps.

1. Look at the word carefully and pronounce it correctly. If you are not sure of the pronunciation, look it up in the dictionary or ask someone who is sure to know. Say the word slowly, naturally, and clearly, looking at the word while it is being said.

2. Cover the word or close your eyes, pronounce it, and think how it looks. Try to visualize just the way the word is written as you repeat each letter in sequence to yourself.

3. Look at the word again to be sure that you said it and spelled it correctly. If you did not, start over with the first step.

4. Cover the word and then write it, thinking carefully how the word

looks. Check the accuracy of your spelling. If you misspelled the word, begin again with the first step.

5. If you spelled the word correctly, write it again without looking either at the book or at your previous attempts. Again, check your accuracy.

The Lesson Test

In life situations words are seldom spelled orally or written in a list or columnar form. Aside from situations in school, the need for accurate spelling arises when an individual is writing connected discourse in which he chooses his words and writes them without giving undue thought to the correctness of their spelling. Because of this fact some educators favor teaching and testing of spelling words in contextual form. That is, the words to be learned or to be tested appear in connected discourse—sentences and paragraphs—as they are introduced in lessons and as they are given to children as a test. This practice is defended on the ground that it provides training in handwriting, punctuation, capitalization, and the form or appearance of a manuscript as well as making spelling more natural. Procedure of this sort, however, should be used sparingly. The experimental evidence favors a column or list presentation and testing of the words(23). The list approach is also less time consuming and the other skills which are reputed to be taught along with the spelling are taught more effectively when specific focus is given to each of them.

Ernest Horn summarized the evidence on the question of the form in which spelling words should be presented in the following statement:

> Written tests are to be preferred to oral tests. . . . Recall tests are superior to and more difficult than recognition tests. The evidence indicates that the most valid and economical test (in spelling) is the modified recall form, in which the person giving the test pronounces each word, uses it in an oral sentence and pronounces it again. The word is then written by the students(24).

However, the instructional program in spelling certainly should not ignore the pupil's need to spell words in context in all his normal writing activities in other school subjects. This suggests that a combination of list and context dictation activities may provide the most effective teaching.

Particular attention should be given in spelling instruction to the correction of the tests. In the first place, tests should be regarded as learning activities as well as a means for measuring spelling achievement. The most important aspect of the testing is the "correcting" or evaluating that takes place after the test has been given. This evaluating should be done by the pupils—each pupil evaluating and correcting his own paper. Ernest Horn stated that "when corrected by the pupils and the results properly utilized, the test is the most fruitful single learning activity per unit of time that has yet been devised"(25). The efficacy of this procedure continues to be supported by research(26).

To utilize the testing procedure most profitably as a learning activity, the teacher should show the children how testing identifies the words they need to learn to spell, how it is a learning procedure in that it calls their attention to the way they have misspelled a word and what they need to do to spell it correctly, how it forces them to recall either the actual spelling of the word or those associations which are useful in spelling it. As stated above, pupils should correct each of their own tests and record their own scores, with only an occasional rechecking by the teacher to see that the checking has been carefully done.

Practices to Avoid

Observations of the authors and others lead to the following suggestions concerning practices in spelling instruction that some teachers use but which should be avoided.

The teacher should probably not waste time calling attention to known hard spots in words. While known hard spots for many words have been determined, a more positive approach is needed. Attention should be focused upon looking carefully at the word as it is pronounced, noting the structure of the word, the sequence of the letters, and the letter representations given to sounds, rather than upon watching for a particular place of possible error.

The practice of writing words in the air is of doubtful value. This practice takes time and does not give the child a realistic image of the word. Supposedly this practice is to give a kinesthetic impression of the word, but the result is questionable, since the arm and hand movements are generally not the same as in writing a word. A kinesthetic impression is useful to a few very poor spellers but this practice does not provide it. A tactile-kinesthetic impression can be gained through finger-tip impression in sand or on the chalkboard.

Children should not be required to make repeated writings of words without intervening attempts at recall. The practice of having a child copy a word five times, or ten times, encourages poor habits and attitudes.

The teacher should avoid condemning children for asking how to spell a word. Of course, this does not mean fostering the habit of some children who always ask, particularly for the spelling of words that have been in their spelling lessons. However, asking how to spell a word is an expression of concern with spelling correctly and should lead to using the dictionary and other sources for checking spelling.

When a word is spelled by the teacher for a child, this spelling should be given in written form on a slip of paper or on the chalkboard—rather than orally. The effort of the teacher should always be to get the child to look at the word and thus gain a visual impression.

The teacher should not use the studying or writing of spelling words as a form of punishment. This practice will certainly not aid the spelling program, and it is even highly doubtful if it serves as a very meaningful punishment.

SPECIAL CONSIDERATIONS IN SPELLING INSTRUCTION

Perhaps the greatest area of controversy "centers on the question of whether competency in spelling can be obtained through a general use of spelling generalizations (rules) or not"(27). This is not a new issue since reports by Turner in 1912 and Archer in 1930 showed generally negative results from rule teaching, while Lester in 1917 and Watson in 1926 reported positive results(28). Opinion at the present time is probably reflected in Sherwin's statement that, "After examining the studies and weighing their methodological virtues and defects, it appears that rules offer limited help in the teaching of spelling"(29). It should be added, however, that some spelling researchers today emphasize the *learning* of sound-to-letter generalizations rather than the *teaching* of rules. This question is discussed further in the following section.

Linguistics and Spelling

Before the advent of the interest in linguistics the question of the regularity or irregularity of sound and written symbol correspondence was generally associated with "phonics" rather than with "linguistics." Hanna and Moore reported from a study of a 3,000-word vocabulary, for example, that "Nearly three-fourths of the vowel phonemes are spelled by their regular representations from about 57 percent to about 99 percent of the times they occur"(30). Horn reported from the study of a larger list of words that "The sound of long *a* (a) . . . was found 1,237 times, with 601 exceptions to the commonest spelling; the sound of *k* was found 2,613 times, with 932 exceptions; and the sound of *s* in *sick*, 3,846 times, with 1,278 exceptions"(31). From these studies and the conclusions of the investigators, differences in the interpretation of results and their implications for classroom instruction is clearly shown. On the one hand, it was suggested that the degree of "regularity" was great enough to warrant "grouping words about a phonemic family for a week's lesson and teaching the pupil inductively to *hear* the phoneme, then to *write* that phoneme with alphabetical letter or letters . . ."(32). Horn, on the other hand, stated that "One is hardly justified in calling spellings 'regular' or in teaching the commonest spelling as principles or generalizations when the exceptions are numbered not merely by the score but by hundreds"(33).

More recently, researchers at Stanford University conducted extensive studies involving the computerized analysis of a vocabulary of 17,000 words. From this analysis these investigators(*34*) report

that the great majority of individual phonemes of oral American-English are indeed consistently represented in writing by particular graphemic options when the main components of the phonological structure underlying the orthography are taken into consideration. Without regard to their occurrences in respective positions in syllables, consonant phonemes collectively were represented by an equal number of graphemic options over 80 percent of the time in the selected list of words.

As a second phase of this study, the investigators devised a set of rules for spelling the 17,000 words. This programming took into account "(1) the simple phoneme–grapheme relationships, (2) the effect of position of a phoneme in a syllable, and (3) the effect of syllabic stress upon choice of graphemic option." A fourth factor, identified as "internal constraints"— such as a particular phoneme following another in a word—was also used. Results from this computerized spelling showed that 49 percent of the words were spelled correctly, 37.2 percent with only one error, 11.4 percent with two errors, and 2.3 percent with three or more errors(*35*).

From these studies the investigators report that "even a limited knowledge of the phonological relationships between the sounds and the letters of the orthography can provide the power to spell literally thousands of words . . .(*36*).

Certainly these newer studies represent constructive and substantial evidence which may prove useful to instruction in spelling. However, as pointed out by Fries and others, spelling patterns (i.e., consistency of sounds and symbols relationships) to which *readers* must respond are something different from spelling patterns to be produced by writers(*37*). Too, it is important to remember that any analysis of how a phoneme is represented in writing usually does not recognize dialect differences in speech, that the same individual varies his pronunciation of many words depending upon their context (e.g., *and* in snow and ice, head and arm, man and beast, rod and gun), and that decisions as to the graphic representations of sounds call for a great deal of subjective judgment which may vary from investigator to investigator(*38*).

There has been little investigation of the success from actually teaching children to arrive at linguistic principles which may aid them in spelling, even though a good many commercial spelling materials profess to have selected words which teach generalizations. However, Maier developed a procedure for analyzing spelling programs with respect to linguistic variables, which showed when applied that many linguistic characteristics are overlooked in programs(*39*). There has been at least one study directed at determining the effectiveness of teaching sound–symbol correspondences (*40*). This researcher, Yee, reported that the "use of generalizations for spelling instruction appears to be less useful than test-study methods." Yet this study has been subject to criticism, including that by Personke, who found major fault with the "method used to teach the generalization"(41).

The analysis of the issue by Plessas perceptively points out once again the difference between the reading and spelling acts in using grapheme–phoneme relationships(42). Plessas suggests that proper and thoughtful attention to the amount of stress given to teaching generalizations "may prevent the phonemic cues in reading from becoming graphic miscues in spelling"(43).

A good example of what Plessas means is shown in Personke's study of using nonsense words to test generalizing ability in spelling(44). The generalizations tested included: (1) "Before *a, o,* and *u,* or a consonant, *g* has a hard sound. Before *e, i,* or *y, g* has the soft sound of *j.*" (2) "The *c* spells the soft sound of *s* before *e, i,* or *y.* Before any other letter, *c* spells the hard sound of *k.*" These are useful generalizations for deciding how to pronounce words beginning with *g* or *c,* but how do they help children spell jar, jewel, sight, kayak, etc.? Similar questions might be asked about the other "generalizations."

Even more sophisticated statements of generalizations are subject to question. For example, "final /k/ is usually spelled *ck* in a stressed syllable (smock), and *c* in an unstressed syllable (plastic)"(45). How many children would recognize *-tic* as unstressed? The same authors suggest using such words as *pick, rock, pack,* and *truck* in their "level 1" program to teach the generalization that /k/ "may be spelled *ck* in final position"(46). While this is a valid generalization, one wonders about the appropriateness of this instruction since the more commonly written *make* is left until "level 2"(47).

Furthermore, thoughtful examination should be given to statements by some linguists and others regarding "regularity" and "system" in orthography. For example, saying that "all the vowel letters can represent both full vowels and schwa without sacrificing regularity" does not tell what generalizations might be taught or when—or even if any need to be taught (48). Knowing the facts about our language system—at the verbalizing and conscious level—has historically never made any difference in how language is used by most persons.

On the other hand, children do make generalizations, in the same manner as all of us have learned to do as we transfer spelling knowledge of some words to new words that we encounter. In many spelling programs the children also learn to be cautious about the applicability of these generalizations, a fact that most adults learned in spelling programs in which there was no great emphasis upon spelling patterns. Of course, for years teachers and programs have taught children to note sound and symbol relationships by teaching word "families," the adding of suffixes, the building of compound words, the analysis of words into syllables, and the influence of context (as in choice among homonyms). Too, spelling authorities have long stressed the importance of careful pronunciation and the need for sight, sound, and taction in gaining images of words. The crucial aspect of teaching a program as suggested by linguistic findings, however, comes in determining which generalizations are actually helpful and how these may be learned in an efficient, economical manner that results in ability to spell correctly the words children write.

References

1. Paul R. Hanna, Richard E. Hodges, and Jean S. Hanna, *Spelling: Structure and Strategies* (Boston: Houghton Mifflin Company, 1971), p. 245.

2. Thomas D. Horn, "Spelling," *Encyclopedia of Educational Research,* 4th ed., ed. Robert L. Ebel (New York: Macmillan Publishing Co., Inc., 1969), pp. 1282–1299.

3. *Guidelines to Spelling Instruction,* Curriculum Bulletin 2–71–16 (Houston, Tex.: Northeast Houston Independent School District, n.d.), p. 3.

4. Idem.

5. Probably the easiest for a teacher to use, and likely the most available, is Harry A. Greene, *The New Iowa Spelling Scale* (University of Iowa, 1954). The most comprehensive report of word frequency available is the list of 86,741 words presented in rank order in John B. Carroll, Peter Davies, and Barry Richman, *Word Frequency Book* (Boston: Houghton Mifflin Company, 1971). This list was assembled from textbooks, however, rather than from the writing of either children or adults generally. The historical basic studies are Ernest Horn, *A Basic Writing Vocabulary* (University of Iowa, 1926) and Henry D. Rinsland, *A Basic Vocabulary of Elementary School Children* (New York: Macmillan Publishing Co., Inc., 1945).

6. T. Horn, op cit., p. 1289.

7. Idem.

8. James A. Fitzgerald, *A Basic Life Spelling Vocabulary* (Milwaukee, Wis.: Bruce Publishing Co., 1951).

9. Albert J. Harris, *How to Increase Reading Ability,* 5th ed. (New York: David McKay Company, Inc., 1970), p. 344.

10. Lois Ann Bader, "The Effects of Manuscript-Cursive Combinations of Instructional Treatments on Spelling Achievement" (Ph.D. diss.), University of Maryland, 1970; see also June M. McOmber, "A Study of the Relationship Between Handwriting Form and Spelling Performance of Intermediate Grade Pupils Using Manuscript and Cursive Handwriting" (Ph.D. diss.), Utah State University, 1970.

11. Jon Eisenson and Mardel Ogilvie, *Speech Correction in the Schools* (New York: Macmillan Publishing Co., Inc., 1963), p. 200.

12. T. Horn, op. cit., pp. 1294–1299.

13. J. Stephen Sherwin, *Four Problems in Teaching English: A Critique of Research* (Scranton, Pa.: International Textbook Company, 1969), pp. 29–108.

14. Robert J. Fitzsimmons, "A Study of the Attitudes of a Representation Population of Iowa Elementary Teachers Toward Spelling Theory and Practice" (Ph.D. diss.), University of Iowa, 1971.

15. Jean S. Hanna and Paul R. Hanna, "Spelling as a School Subject: A Brief History," *The National Elementary Principal,* May, 1959, p. 9.

16. William J. Stevens, "Obstacles to Spelling Reform," *English Journal,* February, 1965, pp. 85–90.

17. William J. Valmont, "The Effects of Searching for Spelling Errors on Spelling Consciousness and Achievement" (Ph.D. diss.), The University of Delaware, 1969.

18. William J. Valmont, "Spelling Consciousness: A Long Neglected Area," *Elementary English,* December, 1972, p. 1221.

19. T. Horn, op. cit., p. 1295.

20. Sherwin, op. cit., p. 107.

21. Walter T. Petty, "Handwriting and Spelling: Their Current Status in the Language Arts Curriculum," *Research on Handwriting and Spelling,* ed. Thomas D. Horn (National Conference on Research in English, 1966), p. 2.

22. For example, see Walter T. Petty and Gus P. Plessas, *You Can Spell,* Grades 1 through 8 (Boston: Allyn and Bacon, Inc., 1964, 1966).

23. Sherwin, op. cit., p. 107.

24. Ernest Horn, "Spelling," *Encyclopedia of Educational Research,* 3d ed., ed. Chester W. Harris (New York: Macmillan Publishing Co., Inc., 1960), p. 1340.

25. Ernest Horn, *What Research Says to the Teacher: Teaching Spelling* (Washington, D.C.: National Education Association, 1954), p. 17.

26. Robert W. Ash, "A Comparison of Various Procedures for Using the Corrected Test as an Instructional Device in Fifth Grade Spelling" (Ph.D. diss.), University of Minnesota, 1970.

27. Albert H. Yee, "The Generalization Controversy on Spelling Instruction," *Elementary English,* February, 1966, p. 154.

28. Ibid., p. 155.

29. Sherwin, op cit., p. 106.

30. Paul R. Hanna and J. T. Moore, "Spelling—from Spoken Word to Written Symbol," *Elementary School Journal,* February, 1953, pp. 329–337.

31. Ernest Horn, "Phonetics and Spelling," *Elementary School Journal,* May, 1957, pp. 424–432.

32. Jean S. Hanna and Paul R. Hanna, op. cit., p. 16.

33. E. Horn, "Phonetics and Spelling," p. 430.

34. Paul R. Hanna et al., "Linguistic Cues for Spelling Improvement," Report to U.S. Office of Education on Project Number 1991 for the period January 2, 1963 to December 31, 1964 (mimeograph), p. 4.

35. Richard E. Hodges and E. Hugh Rudorf, "Searching Linguistics for the Teaching of Spelling," *Research on Handwriting and Spelling,* ed. Thomas D. Horn (National Conference on Research in English, 1965), p. 34.

36. Ibid., p. 532.

37. Charles C. Fries, *Linguistics and Reading* (New York: Holt, Rinehart and Winston, Inc, 1963), p. 170.

38. Walter T. Petty, "Research Critiques—II," *Elementary English,* May, 1965, pp. 584–587.

39. Julius C. Maier, "Analyzing Linguistic Characteristics of Spelling Programs" (Ph.D. diss.), State University of New York at Buffalo, 1973.

40. Albert H. Yee, "Is the Phonetic Generalization Hypothesis in Spelling Valid?" *The Journal of Experimental Education,* Summer, 1969, vol. 37, p. 91.

41. Carl Personke, "Generalization and Spelling: Boon or Bust?" in Martha L. King, Robert Emans, and Patricia J. Cianciolo, *A Forum for Focus* (Urbana, Ill.: National Council of Teachers of English, 1973), pp. 148–157.

42. Gus P. Plessas, "Cues or Miscues in Spelling," *A Forum for Focus,* pp. 159–164.

43. Ibid.

44. Carl Personke, "The Use of Nonsense Words to Test Generalization Ability in Spelling," *Elementary English,* December, 1972, pp. 1233–1237.

45. Hanna, Hodges, and Hanna, *Spelling: Structure and Strategies,* p. 187.

46. Ibid., p. 142.

47. John B. Carroll et al., *Word Frequency Book,* gives these frequencies: pick 459, rock 925, pack 197, truck 410, and make 8333.

48. Fred Brengelman, "Roundtable Review," *Research in the Teaching of English,* Fall, 1971, vol. 5, no. 2, p. 220.

Operational Concepts

1. Many teachers seem to disregard the basic research implications on the teaching of spelling.

2. Studies show that spelling ability is related to speaking, reading, and writing ability.

3. The teaching of reading does not seem to improve spelling ability, and the teaching of spelling does not seem to improve reading ability.

4. Effective spelling depends as much upon attitude as technique.

5. Opinions on the value of teaching spelling rules differ; there is, however, at least some evidence to indicate that rule knowledge is beneficial.

Implications

It has become common, in the recent past, for professionals to contend that the teaching of spelling is overemphasized in the school curriculum. Because the time of student and teacher is limited, instructional theorists are forced to make hard choices of priority. The basic question of rationale, referred to earlier, is again applicable: if one assumes that the ability to spell correctly is a mark of the educated person, formal instruction in the rules of orthography and repeated opportunity for practice and drill are desirable. Conversely, if one believes that the ability to spell is of no particular virtue, such instruction can be regarded as insignificant.

Although it is true that many people learn to spell indirectly through repeated use of the language, my own conviction is that at least some emphasis upon spelling competence is desirable. Aside from the fact that spelling errors are habitually used as an indictment of educational systems, the effort required to master correct spelling is so slight that it would be illogical to settle for less.

Most adults, for example, work within a limited vocabulary of words, the spelling of which can be learned with relative ease. And since most spelling errors can be detected through simply checking, the largest part of the battle consists of developing a pride in accuracy.

Many successful teachers have come to conclude that time devoted to routine drills, dictionary assignments, and word copying yields less benefit than the acquisition of good spelling habits through writing activities. Some teachers, to be sure, still use word games to provoke interest and alleviate drudgery. Others, however, are convinced that the best strategy lies in (1) encouraging children to experiment with the use of new words, (2) insistence upon proper spelling, (3) ready access to dictionaries, and (4) the periodic analysis of repeated mistakes. Although opinion is divided, the incorporation of spelling instruction in general language development seems to be replacing the use of isolated spelling exercises.

English

Harry A. Greene
Walter T. Petty

A Functional Approach to Teaching English Usage

Current social acceptability—as broad in definition as that term is—is the principal criterion for what is acceptable or standard usage; only a small part of what is variously labeled as "standard," "correct," or "good" usage is justified by any historically grounded evidence or logical principle. Language usage is largely a personal matter, with each person using language to express his own thinking, but with the effective user of language recognizing that the language used in any communicative act is dependent upon the purpose of the communication, the meaning to be communicated, and the effect desired by the communication.

TEACHER ANALYSIS OF TEACHING REQUIRED

Items of usage that might need instructional attention in the elementary school were discussed [previously]. Also listed were usages that should not receive teaching emphasis in the elementary school. However, it is not actually possible to indicate the specific items of usage to be taught at particular grade levels and in a specific classroom. Textbooks, of course, do provide exercises and activities directed at specific usage items, but these should be used by a teacher only if the children in his class have problems with these usages—and then only if these are the grossest deviations they make. Every teacher should survey the oral and written usage of his class to determine the specific emphasis he needs to provide. The example of a survey record form (Figure 1) shows how a teacher recorded usage and indicates in a compact and concrete manner the direction the class and individual instructional efforts should take.

Another form for teacher recording of usages for instructional attention is shown in Figure 2; it focuses upon items previously selected and provides an easy means of noting particular improvements by pupils.

Surveys of instructional needs should be made by teachers several times during a school year, though some teachers prefer to keep a running record in a notebook, with a page for each child. The initial survey of a class may show many items of usage needing instructional attention, but a teacher should not attempt to change all of these. Thus, until the surveying procedure shows that change has occurred for the specific items selected, records need to be kept only for that limited number of usages, simplifying the record-keeping considerably.

THE ROLE OF HABIT

Teachers are generally aware that dialects are ingrained; that usage habits of children persist from year to year in spite of efforts to bring about changes. Moreover, the habits which are less acceptable tend to be most difficult to eradicate. Several reasons have been suggested for this: (1) the habits which the child has acquired in the five or six years of his life before school entrance have become firmly fixed; (2) these habits tend to be strengthened even after coming to school, since the child usually continues to live in the same environment as that into which he was born; (3) the

FIGURE 1

Usage survey for OCTOBER					
	verb forms	pronouns	redundancy	double negatives	illiteracies
JOHN	he done	her & me	this here	don't have no	youse hisn
HARVEY	they knowed brung	they's	this here		
LUCILLE	she don't				
PEGGY	has took				onct
MARY			John he		
DOUGLAS	has took	it's			
CYNTHIA					

child whose usage habits may be most in need of change is likely not to be interested in changing them, since to do so would set him off from his environment; (4) the school generally does not provide enough active language situations for real exercise of acceptable usage; and (5) many of the lessons on usage taught in the school are ineffectively motivated and taught.

In addition to these reasons, and perhaps of even greater importance, is the emphasis the school typically gives to changing usage through written drill, even though the particular usages may be more prevalent in the children's speaking than writing. The problem, of course, is to eliminate undesirable usage habits and to substitute more desirable ones. This is a difficult task, considering the fact that the school can do little about the influences of out-of-school environment. However, the school (every teacher) can do something about the reasons for the persistence of undesirable usage habits that are related to instruction.

A teacher can provide many active language situations for the genuine exercise of desirable habits. Every teacher should understand, as Blair has pointed out, that "the chief cause of deficiency in oral and written expression is probably *lack of experience and practice in using correct form*"(1). He further stated that

evidence from the field of psychology clearly indicates that pupils *learn to do what they do*. If a pupil learns a rule of grammar, he will be able to repeat that rule, but he will not necessarily be able to apply the rule in his speaking and writing. Transfer of training takes place only between elements and situations which are approximately identical. If pupils are to speak and

FIGURE 2

	HARRY	CHAS.	HARRIETT	Jo	BETTY	ROY	DORIS	TOM	GUS	HENRY	SALLY	ALMA	BOB
we was	✓			✓	✓			✓	✓				
have saw	✓	✓		✓		✓	✓			✓	✓		
me and	✓			✓		✓							
brung		✓						✓					
haven't no			✓										
he don't	✓												
hisself	✓												

write correctly they must be given practice in speaking and writing correctly (2).

Every teacher must recognize, too, that it is a basic instructional principle to apply remedy to the exact fault. Thus it is imperative that the usages that are departures from acceptable language must be identified for each child. The surveying and recording suggested in the preceding section should provide the basis that is needed.

BASIC INSTRUCTIONAL PROCEDURES

A teacher who recognizes the role habit plays in a child's usage, the importance of using language for genuine communicative purposes, and the need for a direct and systematic attack upon the usage items selected for instructional emphasis can achieve measurable success by following the steps suggested in the succeeding paragraphs(3).

The first step is to appraise the usage problems of the class and of each individual in it through the use of checklists and the cataloging of usages (as suggested above). This cataloging applies to both oral and written usages. With the completion of this survey, the deviations from standard usage found should be compared with [other] such lists to determine which require instructional attention.

The next step is to select the most frequent and grossest departures from acceptability for consistent attack. After being selected, they should be made known to the children (how they look and how they sound) in addition to the reasons for their selection. From the time of their selection, the teacher should strive to allow no deviation or lapses from the acceptable forms, even though this will call for diligent effort. When the new habits have become reasonably fixed, other items may be selected for attack.

As many opportunities as possible should be provided for the children to practice the usage items being taught in natural communication. These opportunities should call for both oral and written expression and should appeal to children.

It may be of considerable help if parents are made aware of usages under attack and are asked for their cooperation. This may be done at a group conference, at a PTA meeting, or by letter. Pupils may also write letters to their parents explaining what they are trying to accomplish with respect to learning usage. However, care must be exercised that usages selected for attack do not represent those commonly used in the community and not regarded as "errors."

As much responsibility for improvement as possible should be placed upon the children themselves. They may make individual lists of troublesome items and individual charts of usages that they have mastered.

An essential part of the process is building interest in words and expressions, and an enjoyment of the fitness of words in their uses.

A Functional Approach to Teaching English Usage

Perhaps the most vital point involved in developing acceptable usage habits is motivation. Pupils must be stimulated to want to use English effectively, or little benefit will result from teaching efforts. Teachers must utilize every possible device to relate the activities of the classroom to the basic goals of each pupil. A child must be made to feel that working on his English usage will benefit him personally. He must be convinced that his communication is more effective when he uses acceptable English, that most people actually do use it, and that these are the people with whom he will be associated. Efforts of the teacher to motivate pupils will of course be geared to each pupil's individuality. It is true, too, that efforts to change or expand usages in the lower grades will not depend so greatly on the pupil's actually feeling a need to do so, for he may be too immature to realize their importance. At this level, major dependence must be placed on simply making usage changes through continuous attention, perhaps oral drills, and providing many genuinely communicative situations for speaking and writing.

While written drills or practice exercises have been used for many years—and generally without much success—oral drills have only recently come into use. Examples of such drills are given in the following section. The section which follows that suggests how drills and practice activities and exercises may best be used.

References

1. Glenn Myers Blair, *Diagnostic and Remedial Teaching* (New York: Macmillan Publishing Co., Inc., 1956), p. 343.

2. Ibid., p. 355.

3. A number of linguists and others interested in language usage in schools hold that many "errors" and "deviations" need not be dealt with in an instructional sense as suggested here. Labov states that "In cold fact, the number of differences between most nonstandard dialects (especially those of middle-class speakers) and standard English are relatively few. In one way or another, most students have gradually learned to approximate the teacher's style, more or less. More important, their dialects have not obviously interfered with the learning of reading and writing to any serious degree." (William Labov, *The Study of Nonstandard English*. Champaign, Ill.: National Council of Teachers of English, 1970, p. 4.)

Operational Concepts

1. A small number of common errors in English usage, habitually repeated, create most of the difficulties in elementary school teaching.

2. Because of great variation in children's language backgrounds, multiple techniques for teaching correct English usage must be used in the elementary school.

3. When the acceptable language usage, taught in school, deviates from the usage children learn in their out-of-school environments, impetus to change is minimal, continuous inconsistency is inevitable, and there is little opportunity to practice school-learned skills.

4. Improvement in language usage remains marginal when children lack motivation and incentive to change.

5. If opportunity for repeated practice is not available, the development of better language usage is impeded.

6. Involvement in active communication—if proper usage is modeled—produces superior results to formal instruction in grammatical rules.

Implications

A major problem in teaching English usage is that much of the instruction seems to have limited utility. Although controversies regarding the substance and form of good teaching are endless, most experts are willing to concede that care must be taken to distinguish between what is significant and trivial in teaching grammar and usage.

Whether the teacher elects to work with transformational or generative grammar, whether the teaching emphasis is upon structure or function there is good reason to believe that instruction could be made more efficient. Those, for example, who contend that instruction in usage should be delayed until the seventh or eighth grade are convinced that the dominant objective is to ensure mastery of a comparatively small number of concepts. The trick, in short, is to teach fewer rules, more thoroughly, through whatever method seems most appropriate.

Two other implications are also worthy of note. First, the youth culture being what it is, students will undoubtedly continue to communicate in two separate languages: the formal language of conventionally correct practice and the informal language of their own subculture. The fact that adolescents sometimes prefer to converse in the picturesque colloquialisms which set them apart from their elders, however, does not mean that they should be freed of the responsibility for learning "proper" form.

Second, there is only a partial correlation between a knowledge of grammatical rules and the ability to express oneself articulately. Hence, correct language usage and writing clarity must be viewed as separate goals, although the former probably is best taught in conjunction with the latter. The available evidence seems to suggest, in fact, that the teaching of grammar, separated from practice in writing, brings very little real gain. Grammar is best treated not as an end in itself but as a means to a larger end—skill in the use of the written and spoken word.

Edward M. Anthony
William E. Norris

Method in Language Teaching

WHAT METHOD IS

Participants in discussions of the methodology of language teaching frequently lack the common ground upon which to build fruitful debate. At one extreme is a philosophical and psycholinguistic dialogue, largely on the axiomatic level—a level which may provide an approach to methodology, but which cannot in itself be labeled method. On the other hand, anecdotal presentations of pedagogical tricks, however well classified and no matter how diverting and perceptive, are not really methodological. Classroom techniques may reflect a particular method, or may implement a method—they may even provide data to evaluate a method, but they are not, in and of themselves, method.

Method is, then, neither the intricate set of assumptions, explicit or implicit, about language and language acquisition that characterizes a particular approach to language teaching, nor is it the list of drills, exercises, diagrams, and explanations that makes up the technique of the talented classroom teacher. Method lies somewhere between the labyrinthine algebra of the grammarian and the psychologist and the actions of an overworked teacher industriously following her lesson plans.

It is possible to initiate discussions of method in the philosophical labyrinth or in the classroom; to begin with approach or with technique. For example, let us begin with the classroom teacher. A skilled teacher may develop over the years certain techniques that "work"—that bring about a desired language learning event—that guide the behavior of the student in the direction the teacher wants. If these classroom strategies show structurally unifying characteristics and tend to form a coherent procedure, they may come to be regarded as components of a method. This route to method has been traveled time and again, as is evident from those many methods which are named after one of their successful practitioners or after

Reprinted from Edward M. Anthony and William E. Norris, "ERIC Focus Reports on the Teaching of Foreign Languages, No. 8," Modern Language Association of America, New York, 1969.

a characteristic technique. But though a particular method may historically derive from a set of techniques, a method may, by definition, be found only where pragmatically acceptable techniques are supported by theoretical assumptions.

As one of the authors of this article has written elsewhere: "Method is an overall plan for the orderly presentation of language material, no part of which contradicts, and all of which is based upon, the selected approach. An *approach* is axiomatic, a *method* is procedural"(*1*). In a perfect world an assembly of savants might decide for all time just what language really is, and how we acquire a first language, or learn a second. These precious truths would then be passed on to an ominscient language-pedagogy engineer who would transform them into an all-purpose, foolproof method for language teaching. The set of procedures, in the form of a syllabus, textbook, program, curriculum, or whatever, would be passed on to the teacher, who then could choose the weapons to accomplish the high purpose of language teaching. But, in our less than perfect world, instead of a smooth one-way route from approach through method to technique, we find a busy intersection where each of these three aspects of the total language learning process is continually modifying the others.

Language teaching methods come and go, ebb and flow. Some achieve wide popularity, then decline. Why the swing from oral learning to rule learning, back to oral learning, and yet again to rules? If a method is successful, why doesn't it remain in wide favor? The reasons do not lie in the failure of any particular set of techniques, for often the same techniques reappear in the next method to gain favor. The reasons are rather to be found in the shifts in linguistic, psychological and pedagogical concepts which in turn cause corresponding shifts in notions of what it means to acquire, teach, or learn a language. For example, language learning tended to mean quick and accurate translations or readings in the 1930s, but by the 1950s it meant facile ability in aural comprehension and oral production.

As our beliefs about the nature of language change, our faith in a method is affected, since we all value consistency. When language is seen as a closed system of contrasting patterns of phonology and syntax, a method which aims to teach aural–oral mastery of a finite set of sentence patterns enjoys theoretical support. But if we accept the view that language is a small set of basic relationships capable of infinite variation through expansion and transformation, we will feel constrained to adjust our methods to fit these new "facts" of linguistic theory.

Again, as the psycholinguists' view of language acquisition processes changes, so must classroom teaching techniques. If language is a set of habits, then mim–mem and stimulus–response practice to shape new habits dominates the lessons. Some recent psycholinguistic theory, however, holds that children are born with an innate set of linguistic universals which they use to acquire their first language. Stimulus–response explanations are alien to this theory and consequently, as applications of the theory are extended to second language teaching, the value of learning through habit formation and the most common practice procedures of the audiolingual approach are brought into question(2). Methods, then, are shaped by many different theories, and the popularity of a method may depend on the popularity of any of these theories.

Nevertheless, all language teaching worthy of the name must follow some sort of method. That method must include, as does all teaching, the selection of materials to be taught, the gradation of those materials, their presentation, and pedagogical implementation to induce learning(3). Method, we repeat, is by definition procedural, it is the sum and structure of the selection, gradation, and characteristic pedagogy which is carried out on the basis of certain axioms which form the underlying approach.

TWO EARLIER METHODS IN PROTOTYPE

Man can study his principal means of communication in three different ways. One of these is traditionally considered "training," while the other two are usually considered "education."

First, an individual may study a foreign language so that he can participate in the cultural affairs of the society which uses that language. Whether the society is living or long dead is irrelevant to this particular reason for study. The Peace Corps candidate who studies Hausa in order to teach Africans malaria prevention, and the scholar who studies Hittite in order to read history in cuneiform inscription are brothers under the skin. Each wishes to use the language he studies as a means to a basically non-linguistic end. Each neeeds to control the language sufficiently well to operate in some corner of the culture. He must be trained in some skill-building way designed to help him accomplish his specific goals. Indeed, we often speak of the "four skills" of aural understanding, oral production, reading ability, and writing ability. The Peace Corps candidate may have an interest only in the first two; the scholar, with access only to written records, has interest only in the third and, perhaps, the fourth.

Second, and usually considered "educational," is the study of artistic language. Certain gifted individuals respond to their environments with greater sensitivity than do we ordinary mortals, and some of these individuals (whom we often call poets), are able to communicate their sensitivity to the rest of us through language. Their language is considered worthy of educational academic study, both by those who speak the poets' native languages and by those who do not, in an effort to arrive at a wider understanding of the meaning of life.

Third, some students of language are interested in gaining insights into how language works—its peculiarities, its geographical, temporal, or social spread, and how it is acquired, either as a native or as a foreign language. This is generally considered educational study as well.

We will, within our present discussion, call these three ways of investigating language the study of *language,* the study of *literature,* and the study of *linguistics* respectively. It is useful to keep them separate in speaking of language teaching—especially in discussing earlier methods—because the proponents of these methods did not always separate them on the approach level, and did not always take advantage of the findings of one kind of language study to benefit another kind of language study. This is evident in the two central methods described in this section. While they are referred to as "earlier" methods, they are still, in some instances, followed today.

The first of these methods is often called the *grammar–translation* method. By *grammar* here is usually meant the series of rules or generalizations that is intended to describe the target language. A successful "grammar" performance by the student usually means his ability to recite the list of German prepositions which take the dative, or to give the forms of the Latin verb "to be" in the particular arbitrary order *sum, es, est . . . ,* or to name the conjugation to which the Spanish verb *cantar* belongs. In a more sophisticated use, it may mean that the student is successful if he can puzzle out a fill-in-the-blanks exercise, oral or written, on the model "el perro_____ un animal." That is, he must extract from his *soy, eres, es* conjugation the form that is labeled third person singular present and fit it into the blank. His performance is then judged by the speed and accuracy with which he can do these tasks.

The question that is always raised about the grammar portion of this method is "Is this the study of language or the study of linguistics?" If it is the former, it should, according to our earlier statement, enable the student to operate in some or most of the aspects of the society in which the language is used to conduct its cultural business. But it is doubtful if the Germans spend much of their time discussing the prepositions used with the dative case, or if Spanish speakers ask each other to fill in the blanks in sentences. To the extent that they do so, the study is valuable and relevant. Some teachers would see that this kind of study of grammar provides only the basis for studying the language rather than the language itself. To this extent, it is a sort of study of low-grade linguistics—that is, it gives some insights into how the language under study works, even though these insights are often phrased in terms more appropriate to the native language grammar than to the target language grammar.

But what of the other end of the grammar-translation method? How does *translation* fit in? When students of the grammar–translation method are not reciting rules or filling in blanks, they are frequently rendering foreign language passages into English or putting English passages into the foreign language. Again, one must ask, what is this the study of? Is it language? If it enables the student to operate in the society which uses the language, such translation must become an instantaneous skill, as indeed it may for some students after long years of agonizing practice. Is it the study of literature? Marginally perhaps, if one begins with a literary work to translate. Is translation the study of linguistics? Again, the answer must be that the linguistic insights gained are elementary and are on the truistic level for most linguists: perhaps that decent word-for-word translation is impossible; that different languages use different structures to express different things differently.

All this is not to say that it is impossible to learn a language through the grammar–translation method. The above-average student can gain a good deal from the method, can collect a vast amount of information that some day, somewhere, given the right circumstances, just might "nucleate"(4) into a useful command of the language. The odds, however, are not attractive. A good deal of the difficulty with the grammar–translation method seems to arise from the confusion of linguistic, literary, and language aims—possibly out of a misguided effort to include respectable "educational" material in a "training"-centered academic exercise.

The *direct method,* the second of two central methods, is much more focused and makes no pretension toward literary or linguistic aims, nor does it take into account literary or linguistic findings. Direct method teachers attempt to use only the target language on all levels, ask for no statements about grammar, proceed through conversation, reading, and writing in the target language, and give no attention to translation. It is, in its purest form, the direct antithesis of the grammar–translation method. The direct method is clearly aimed at giving students sufficient control of a language to operate in the society which employs that language. The direct method teaches without the emphasis on choice of materials that characterizes the method described in the following section. The valuable increase in relevance and efficiency that arises from the linguistic description and comparison of the target and native languages is lacking in the direct method. Nevertheless, it clearly shows an advance over the grammar–translation method when the goal is language control.

Although we have commented here upon two widely used and well-established methods as if they occurred only in pure form, a cursory examination of texts and syllabuses will show many that illustrate a mixed language-teaching methodology. It is perhaps unnecessary to mention that such mixed methods often reflect a curious inconsistency at the approach level.

THE DOMINANT METHOD TODAY: AUDIOLINGUAL

"What teaching method do you use?" Ask this question of almost any foreign language teacher in our schools today, and the reply will be "the audiolingual method," "oral approach," "aural–oral method," "linguistic method," or one of the other terms used to indicate certain procedures which share the same approach level assumption(5). An examination of current journal articles, a look at the introduction to new textbooks (and even revisions of old ones) will confirm this—the currently accepted method is audiolingual. Nearly all of us use it, or claim to use it.

What then is this method? Certainly the question should not be hard to answer considering the number of articles, books, lectures, conferences, and courses on the subject in recent years. But these discussions are often overly concerned with techniques. Perhaps it would be worthwhile to reconsider the basic assumptions of the audiolingual method before we take a look at the techniques most commonly employed to implement it.

This modern method has its theoretical base in an understanding of the nature of human language and the psychology of second language learning quite different from that underlying grammar–translation or even the direct method. Twentieth-century linguistic science has been the main source of the new ideas and knowledge from which language teachers have developed this method. Charles C. Fries set forth the implications of linguistics for language teaching most forcefully and effectively in his now classic 1945 monograph *Teaching and Learning English as a Foreign Language*. He there insists that the initial tasks in learning a new language are "first, the mastery of the sound system . . . second, the mastery of the features of arrangement that constitute the structure of the language." Thus Fries applies to language teaching two basic premises of structural linguistics concerning the nature of language: language is primarily oral, and language is a system of contrasting structural patterns. To this is added a third premise: language is a communicative activity of human societies, and therefore "accuracy," not mere "correctness," must be the standard for mastery from the beginning, "an accuracy based upon a realistic description of the actual language as used by native speakers in carrying on their affairs."(6).

These linguistic premises are reflected in the audiolingual method by the following requirements, at least for the first stages of language learning:

1. The student must learn to use orally with normal speed the foreign language response that is required by any of the situations he has studied.
2. The major structural patterns of the linguistic system, presented in meaningful contexts, are the language materials to be learned(7).

The psychological assumptions about the nature of human language acquisition and behavior which have influenced the method have been drawn from behaviorist theory. Its influence is clearly seen in Bloomfield's description of language behavior in stimulus–response terms, and his view that language consists of a great many complex activities united into a single far-reaching complex of habits(8). Psychologists themselves, although long interested in child language development, until recently took little direct interest in problems of second language learning; however, they assented to the linguist's and language teacher's assumption that "language is a system of extremely well-learned habitual responses"(9). A more direct application of psychological theory has come from the concepts of operant behavior and instrumental learning formulated by B. F. Skinner, who first pointed out that verbal behavior exemplifies operant behavior, thereby describing the mechanism for establishing new language habits. Moreover, in learning a second language it is assumed that the already established first language habits tend to interfere with the process of acquiring the set of second language habits wherever the native language and foreign language systems are in conflict.

These psychological conclusions are reflected in the method in the following ways:

1. Memorization and practice drills are used extensively to establish the new language skills as habits.
2. Materials take into account contrasts between the native language and the foreign language systems.

Over the past twenty-five years, these few assumptions by linguists and psychologists about language and language behavior have been the source from which modern teaching methods have developed, methods which have brought far-reaching changes in classroom procedures (emphasizing oral language habit formation) and teaching materials (employing sound linguistic description and contrastive analysis to select and order the language features to be taught).

The terms "mimicry–memorization" and "pattern practice," which are frequently used in describing the new methodology, each reflect the influence of both linguistic and psychological concepts. "Mimicry" recognizes the linguists' assertions that language is primarily oral and that native speaker models are ultimately the only completely acceptable models for imitation. "Pattern" represents the system of the language, each pattern a part of the system of systems of which the language is constructed. The language "item" to be learned is not an individual sound, word, or sentence, but that sound in contrast to other sounds of a phonological system; that word as the member of a lexical cluster; that sentence pattern in relation to other sentence patterns. The influence of behaviorist psychology is shown by the second term in each pair—"memorization" and "practice" are the chief mechanisms for establishing habit. "The command of language is a matter of practice . . . language learning is overlearning, anything less is of no use," says Bloomfield(10), echoing three hundred years later the words of Comenius, "Every language must be learned by practice rather than rules . . . ."

"Mim–mem" and "pattprac" are two important and complementary classroom tools of an audiolingual method. One or the other may dominate in a given lesson or even a whole set of lessons, but fundamentally they can be viewed as steps in a procedure by which the student is first presented with the new foreign language item and gains familiarity with and conscious control over it (through mim–mem), and then progressively gains language mastery as recognition and production of the item are made unconscious habit (through pattern practice). The precise steps in this procedure are recognition, imitation, and repetition, followed by variation and selection(*11*). To these steps we may add another which is commonly used with older students: explication. Usually coming between repetition and variation, explication typically consists of linguistic comments about the pattern or item, often elicited from the students as an inductive generalization from examples. The approach principle here seems to be that mature students, at least, are helped in language learning by some sort of systematic organization, overtly presented.

SUMMARY

Our purpose here has been to present a concept of method in terms of its relationship to the other components of language teaching. We have, hopefully, demonstrated that method, while it exists apart from basic theoretical assumptions on the one hand and day-to-day teacher–pupil interaction on the other, is nevertheless dependent upon them. We can make assumptions without feeling obliged to invent procedures to implement them; we can use classroom techniques without relating them to a particular method. But method must be based on axioms, and it must be implemented through techniques selected to lead the student to the desired language behavior, as defined by those axioms.

We believe that keeping these interrelationships in mind will clarify discussions of a particular method.

Notes and References

1. Edward M. Anthony, "Approach, Method and Technique," *English Language Teaching,* 17 (January 1963), 63–67.

2. Leon A. Jakobovits, "Implications of Recent Psycholinguistic Developments for the Teaching of a Second Language," *Language Learning,* 18 (June 1968), 89–109.
   David McNeill, "Developmental Psycholinguistics," in *The Genisis of Language: A Psycholinguistic Approach,* Frank Smith and George A. Miller, eds. (Cambridge, Mass., 1966), pp. 67–73.

3. William F. Mackey, *Language Teaching Analysis* (London, 1965), pp. 156–157.

4. Kenneth L. Pike, "Nucleation," *The Modern Language Journal,* 44 (November 1960), 291–295.

5. For us the use of a term like *audiolingual* alternatively with *approach, method,* or *technique* never implies that these combinations are synonymous. *Audiolingual approach* embraces an intricate series of postulates and

assumptions about language and learning, a number of possible methods, and innumerable techniques. *Audiolingual method* is used to describe a set of cumulative curricular procedures toward a stated language goal, again involving a large number of varying techniques. An *audiolingual technique* may be merely a classroom procedure during which the teacher and student talk and listen, and might easily be used in, for example, grammar–translation methodology:

> *Teacher:* Alvin, list the German prepositions which govern the dative.
> *Alvin: aus, ausser, bei, mit, nach, seit, von,* and *zu.*
> *Teacher:* Very good. You may to the head of the class go.

This use of the technique would, of course, be completely at odds with the aural–oral approach as usually understood.

6. Charles C. Fries, *Teaching and Learning English as a Foreign Language* (Ann Arbor, Mich., 1945), p. 3.
7. Fries, "On the Oral Approach," *ELEC Publications,* 4, 2 (Tokyo, 1960).
8. Leonard Bloomfield, *Language* (New York, 1933), pp. 22–37.
9. John B. Carroll, *The Study of Language* (Cambridge, Mass., 1953), pp. 99, 191.
10. Leonard Bloomfield, *Outline Guide for the Practical Study of Foreign Languages* (Baltimore, 1942), p. 12.
11. Freeman W. Twaddell, "Preface to the First-Year Seminar Script, 1958," *ELEC Publications,* 3, 2 (Tokyo, 1959).

The concepts and implications related to the teaching of foreign languages appear on pages 142 and 143.

Renée S. Disick

Performance Objectives in Foreign-Language Teaching

DEVELOPMENT OF PERFORMANCE OBJECTIVES

Until the late 1960s efforts to improve foreign-language instruction centered mainly on analysis of the teaching situation: What methods and texts produce optimum results? What are the characteristics of good teachers? What classroom conditions are most conductive to learning? Research along these lines, however, has failed to provide conclusive answers. The mere fact that teaching occurs does not guarantee that learning has also taken place.

Clearly, a new line of inquiry is needed. For this reason, interest has shifted from the process of foreign-language instruction to the measurable *outcomes* of that instruction. Attention centers less on the teacher and more on the learner. In the evaluation of instruction, the most pertinent question is no longer, "What has the teacher done?" Rather, it is "What will the learner be able to do as a result of the instruction he receives?" These concerns have been especially important in the development of programmed materials and computer-aided instruction.

Pressures from several areas have lent added impetus to this movement. The "New Student" demands more individual attention to his particular needs; he wants courses relevant to him—now! Parents refuse to tolerate educational programs which fail to equip their children with the skills promised them. School boards and taxpayers are increasingly reluctant to approve growing education costs without measurable proof that their money is well-spent. The national government, too, has drawn tighter the post-Sputnik purse strings and insists that federally supported researchers be held accountable for their work.

In addition, the trend toward considering higher education as the right of every child has created an urgent need to find ways of educating

Reprinted from Renée S. Disick, "ERIC Focus Reports of the Teaching of Foreign Languages, No. 25," Modern Language Association of America, New York, 1969.

all students. Screening out low-aptitude students can no longer remain the foreign-language teacher's privilege. Instead, finding ways of teaching both rapid and slow language learners must be his new challenge.

In view of these considerations, individualization of foreign-language instruction has become a necessity(*9, 17*). But before teaching pace, methods, and materials can be made flexible, instructional goals need to be clearly formulated. One step toward accomplishing this is by implementing performance objectives in the foreign-language curriculum.

SCOPE OF THIS REPORT

This report will explain what performance objectives are and how they may be classified. Ways in which performance objectives may be used to improve instruction will then be discussed and some arguments for and against them set forth. Sources which treat at greater length each of the topics mentioned will be indicated where relevant to the text as well as listed in a bibliography at the end of the report.

PERFORMANCE OBJECTIVES VERSUS GOALS

Performance objectives (also called "behavioral objectives" and "instructional objectives") differ from traditional goals, objectives, or purposes in two important ways. First, performance objectives are stated in terms of overt, measurable behavior. If learning is defined as a change in behavior, then it is difficult to determine if learning has occurred unless the new behavior is observed and measured. Second, performance objectives are stated in terms of desired *student* behavior, rather than teacher behavior. For example, the following purposes may *not* be considered performance objectives:

1. To teach the present tense of the verb *être*. This purpose is stated in terms of *teacher* behavior. It does not communicate to students what *they* are expected to do.
2. To pronounce accurately. Though this purpose is stated in terms of student behavior, it is vague; it does not include what will be pronounced, under what circumstances the pronunciation will occur, or how it will be evaluated.
3. To know the vocabulary in the lesson. This purpose fails to indicate how students are to demonstrate their knowledge and how well they must "know" the vocabulary words.

The purposes listed above are too ambiguous to be useful in promoting learning. The vague wording leaves room for different student interpretations of what the teacher wants. In such cases it becomes as important to "know the teacher" as it is to know the course material. Conceivably, two or more teachers would differ on what behaviors may be considered as fulfilling these ambiguous goals. They could also disagree on how to evaluate student performance. Vaguely stated purposes are detrimental to learning since they fail to communicate clearly the teacher's expectations.

STATING SUBJECT-MATTER GOALS AS PERFORMANCE OBJECTIVES

The limitations of the purposes above may be overcome by rewriting them as performance objectives(7, 20) composed of these four parts:

1. Purpose—the reason to engage in the learning activities.
2. Student behavior—what the student must do to show that he has accomplished the purpose.
3. Conditions—what the test and the test situation will be like.
4. Criterion—the minimal level of acceptable performance.

For illustration, the three goals listed above will be restated as performance objectives. Each part of the objectives will be identified in parentheses.

1. To demonstrate knowledge of the present tense of the verb *être* . . . (Purpose)
   . . . write the appropriate form of the verb . . . (Student behavior)
   . . . on a test of ten items such as: (Conditions)
   Je_____chez moi . . .
   . . . making not more than one error. (Criterion)
2. To demonstrate ability to pronounce accurately . . . (Purpose)
   . . . read aloud at least three sentences of recombined material . . . (Student behavior)
   . . . in class . . . (Conditions)
   . . . without any phonemic errors, or errors in rhythm and intonation. (Criterion)
3. To demonstrate knowledge of the following vocabulary words (list attached) . . . (Purpose)
   . . . circle the correct synonym . . . (Student behavior)
   . . . on a twenty-item test. Sample item: (Conditions)
   Il est arrivé *tout de suite*. (a) en retard, (Criterion)
   (b) immédiatement, (c) trop vite. No more than two errors are allowed.

Renée S. Disick

STATING HIGHER GOALS AS
EXPRESSIVE OBJECTIVES

Though many instructional goals can be set forth in the four-part format of a performance objective, there are others which are harder to state in this manner. For example, it may be difficult to specify exactly the student behavior, conditions, and criteria of subject-matter goals such as "to speak the foreign language fluently," or "to analyze a work of literature." With higher level, more complex behaviors like these, statements regarding percentage of accuracy are often irrelevant. In oral communication objectives, for example, it may be hard to predict exactly when the behavior will occur, or what its precise nature will be. In some cases, the mere fact that it occurs at all may be taken as proof that the requirements of the objective have been fulfilled.

For these reasons, it is helpful to state subject-matter goals set for advanced student behaviors as open-ended, expressive objectives. Here, the student behavior, conditions, and criteria are expressed in a general rather than specific manner. In some instances, the conditions and criteria might even be omitted altogether. This allows for greater freedom in student performances as well as for more subjective appraisals of them.

Expressive objectives are also useful when determining affective goals —the attitudes, feelings, and values which students should develop as a result of foreign-language study. Affective purposes commonly set for students often include these:

1. To develop awareness of the foreign culture.
2. To enjoy foreign-language class.
3. To appreciate the foreign language and culture.
4. To learn more on one's own about the foreign language and literature.

Some student behaviors which may be accepted as evidence that each affective purpose is being achieved might be, respectively:

1. The student keeps a scrapbook of news items related to the foreign country (or countries).
2. The student participates actively and willingly in all class activities.
3. The student corresponds regularly with a foreign pen pal.
4. The student voluntarily reads newspapers, magazines, and books in the foreign language.

Affective goals are a necessity in foreign-language courses. Unless teachers specify behaviors which demonstrate the achievement of affective goals, and unless they develop ways of determining this accomplishment, it is hard to know if the desired changes in student attitudes, feelings, and values are really occurring. Since affective goals such as those mentioned above are often presented as prime justifications for studying foreign languages, it is necessary that teachers state these goals in terms of student behavior and measure student achievement of them(*12, 20*).

TAXONOMIC CLASSIFICATION OF PERFORMANCE OBJECTIVES

Performance objectives vary considerably in the types of behavior they prescribe. Subject-matter goals range all the way from mechanical repetition to liberated self-expression. Affective goals progress from passive awareness to active leadership in foreign-language study. In view of the sequential nature of language learning, it is helpful to classify the objectives for each area in ascending order from the simplest to the most complex stages or levels of behavior. Such a classification system is called a taxonomy, a term originally used to designate biological classification of all life.

Taxonomic classification of foreign-language objectives is useful in the improvement of instruction. It can help a teacher determine the stage of behavior at which his teaching is aimed. Are his students engaged solely in the early stages of memorization and drill, or do they also have opportunities for more advanced free expression? Do his students perform only the minimum of assigned work or do they seek out opportunities for additional independent study? Once a teacher determines the stage at which his students are functioning, he can then set objectives which lead them toward higher behaviors. He can also find out if his goals relate solely to the subject matter or if his teaching also aims to develop positive attitudes, feelings, and values toward the foreign language and culture. Finally, taxonomic classification of test items permits a teacher to determine if his tests are appropriate measures of the skills his students have developed.

There is no one right way of classifying objectives and several systems have been proposed. One of these devised specifically for the subject-matter and affective goals of foreign-language teaching is presented in Valette and Disick(*20*).

SOME APPLICATIONS OF PERFORMANCE OBJECTIVES

Taxonomically classified performance objectives can improve instruction by facilitating communication between the people involved in the educational process: teachers, students, administrators, school boards, and local and national governments. Well-defined performance objectives enable a teacher to let his students know what is expected of them. Students are given a precise idea of *what* will be tested, *how* it will be tested, and *how well* they must do in order to pass. In this way, considerable anxiety is removed from the teaching situation. Furthermore, since students understand *why* they must do certain assignments, performance objectives work to increase student motivation(4).

Performance objectives also play a central role in the creation of criterion-referenced tests. Whereas norm-referenced tests rank all students according to a prefixed normative standard, criterion-referenced tests show whether or not students have achieved a specific knowledge or performance capability toward which the teaching has been directed(18, 19). Rather than "failing" the slow learner, criterion-referenced tests determine which students have succeeded in acquiring a certain skill and which need additional practice so that they too may eventually pass when retested.

Teaching for mastery is another possible application of performance objectives(14). Under this system a teacher does not begin the new material until 90 percent of the class has achieved at least an 80 to 90 percent mastery of each objective. In view of the wide range of learning time which different members of the class would need before reaching this standard, considerable individualization of instruction is necessary. Once a student achieves this performance standard, he may be freed to work independently. Conversely, the slower student is given more time to master the objective.

Continuous progress, a further development of this idea, allows each student to advance as far as he can as fast as he is able with his promotion based on demonstrated achievement, not on time spent sitting in a classroom. If individualization of instruction is to become a reality, however, then the traditional, lock-stepped nature of most schools needs to be altered radically and new techniques need to be developed for informal, or "open-classroom" instruction(2, 11, 16, 20). Furthermore, student involvement in the selection of individual course goals offers a promising way of making foreign-language study more relevant to the needs of today's learners.

A curriculum based on performance objectives can help alleviate many of the problems of articulation between different schools and different levels. Students would move on to the next level only if they had mastered the skills specified for their present level. By administering pretests at the beginning of the school year, teachers can ascertain which skills each new student already possesses and which ones he may need to review(1, 5, 13, 15).

Performance objectives can make possible the educational accountability increasingly being demanded of school programs. Since instructional goals are stated in terms of student behavior, it is relatively simple for administrators, school boards, taxpayers, or other interested parties to determine from student performance whether or not schools are teaching effectively and are accomplishing the purposes they have set for themselves.

Finally, performance objectives are useful in training foreign-language teachers. Several teacher-training institutions have developed lists of behaviors which candidates must demonstrate before gaining admission to student teaching. In addition, there has been a growing trend toward establishing performance objectives which student teachers must achieve before receiving state certification(8, 20).

LIMITATIONS AND ADVANTAGES OF PERFORMANCE OBJECTIVES

No new idea in education can possibly be worth its paper and ink unless it is vehemently opposed. Performance objectives are no exception to this rule. Some of the arguments for and against them are summarized in Table 1(*3, 10*).

TABLE 1

CON	PRO
1. Specification of student behaviors results in long lists of trivial and picayune goals.	1. Though this is possible, it need not be inevitable. Intelligent use of expressive objectives and taxonomical classification can promote the formulation of high-level goals. In fact, the precision demanded in performance and expressive objectives can often facilitate clarification of abstract and sometimes meaningless goals.
2. The emphasis on observable, measurable behavior neglects abstract, humane values which cannot be measured.	2. Unless higher orders of behaviors are specified, teaching will not progress from the memorization of facts toward more advanced, creative activities. Though some goals are indeed hard to measure with precision, subjective judgments are nevertheless being made constantly in the classroom. Surely, it would be helpful to students if the criteria for these judgments were communicated to them.
3. Performance objectives lead to rigid, standardized education in which machines take precedence over people.	3. Though it is true that performance objectives are needed for programmed instruction, this is not their only use. While performance objectives can lead to mastery of basic skills, expressive objectives can facilitate the development of original and highly creative activities.
4. It is unsound to teach toward a test.	4. Toward what else *can* you teach? If teacher-made tests are reliable measures of both simple and complex behavioral goals, then there is every reason to direct class activities toward them.
5. These new-fangled ideas won't work.	5. First of all, they *have* worked for many students and teachers. Second, are the current achievements in for-

6. A teacher need not justify his actions or be accountable to anyone for the learning which he produces. Performance objectives represent a threat to academic freedom and the sovereignty of the teacher in his classroom.

eign language instruction so impressive that one can afford to be complacent and not even *try* a new approach?

6. The purpose of education is to teach students, not to protect monarchies. Like members of other professions, teachers need to be held responsible for the quality of their work. Performance objectives offer the possibilities of pride in one's accomplishments and recognition of superior teaching efforts.

SUMMARY AND CONCLUSION

Educational goals stated in terms of formal performance objectives must specify the instructional purpose, student behavior, conditions under which the behavior is to occur, and minimal criteria of acceptable performance. In expressive objectives, these items may be stated generally rather than specifically, and the conditions and criteria may, in some cases, be omitted entirely. Classification of objectives and test items according to subject matter and affective taxonomies enables a teacher to determine the behavioral stage of his goals as well as the validity of his tests. This can lead to the development of higher orders of behavior as well as performance measures which reflect accurately what has been taught.

The use of performance objectives can lead to the improvement of instruction by providing a means of communicating clearly to all those interested in a teaching situation exactly what the outcomes of instruction are to be. Specific applications of performance objectives include criterion-referenced testing, teaching for mastery, a performance-based curriculum, and individualization of instruction.

While performance objectives offer considerable promise for increasing the effectiveness of foreign-language teaching, more research is needed in the areas of both theory and practice before definite conclusions can be drawn. Hopefully, some of these answers will be provided in the next few years.

References

1. Capper, Michael R., comp. *Instructional Objectives for a Junior College Course in French: First Semester.* Los Angeles: University of California, 1969. (Also in this series: *German: First Semester; Japanese: First Semester; Spanish: First Semester; Spanish: Second Semester.*)
2. Fitzgibbons, Nancyanne. "The Open Classroom: A Case-Study." *Leadership for Continuing Development.* Reports of the Working Committees of the 1971

Northeast Conference on the Teaching of Foreign Languages. New York: The Conference, 1971, pp. 97–107.

3. Hoetker, James. "The Limitations and Advantages of Behavioral Objectives in the Arts and Humanities: A Guest Editorial." *Foreign Language Annals,* 3 (1970), 560–65.

4. Jakobovits, Leon A. "Physiology and Psychology of Second Language Learning." *Britannica Review of Foreign Language Education, Vol. 1, 1968.* Ed. Emma M. Birkmaier. Chicago: Encyclopaedia Britannica, 1968 (1969), pp. 181–227.

5. Logan, Gerald E. "Curricula for Individualized Instruction." *Britannica Review of Foreign Language Education, Vol. 2, 1970* (1969). Ed. Dale L. Lange. Chicago: Encyclopaedia Britannica, 1970, pp. 133–55.

6. Mager, Robert F. *Developing Attitude Toward Learning.* Palo Alto, Calif.: Fearon. 1968.

7. ———. *Preparing Instructional Objectives.* Palo Alto, Calif.: Fearon, 1962.

8. Politzer, Robert F. *Performance Criteria for Foreign Language Teachers.* Stanford, Calif.: Stanford University, 1967.

9. ———. "Toward Individualization of Foreign Language Teaching." *Modern Language Journal,* 55 (1971), 207–12.

10. Popham, W. James. "Probing the Validity of Arguments Against Behavioral Goals." *Behavioral Objectives and Instruction.* Ed. Robert J. Kibler et al. Boston: Allyn and Bacon, 1970, pp. 115–24.

11. Reinert, Harry. "Practical Guide to Individualization." *Modern Language Journal,* 55 (1971), 156–63.

12. Seelye, H. Ned. "Performance Objectives for Teaching Cultural Concepts." *Foreign Language Annals,* 3 (1970), 566–78.

13. Smith, Alfred N. "Strategies of Instruction for Speaking and Writing." *Britannica Review of Foreign Language Education, Vol. 2, 1970* (1969). Ed. Dale L. Lange. Chicago: Encyclopaedia Britannica, 1970, pp. 113–31.

14. Smith, Melvin I. *Teaching Spanish by Being Responsible for Specific Objectives.* Modesto, Calif.: Stanislaus County Schools, 1968.

15. Steiner, Florence A. "Behavioral Objectives and Evaluation." *Britannica Review of Foreign Language Education, Vol. 2, 1970* (1969). Ed. Dale L. Lange. Chicago: Encyclopaedia Britannica, 1970, pp. 35–78.

16. ———. "Performance Objectives in the Teaching of Foreign Languages." *Foreign Language Annals,* 3 (1970), 579–91.

17. Strasheim, Lorraine A. "A Rationale for the Individualization and Personalization of Foreign Language Instruction." *Britannica Review of Foreign Language Education, Vol. 2, 1970* (1969). Ed. Dale L. Lange. Chicago: Encyclopaedia Britannica, 1970, pp. 15–34.

18. Valette, Rebecca M. *Directions in Foreign Language Testing.* New York: MLA/ERIC, 1969.

19. ———. "Testing." *Britannica Review of Foreign Language Education, Vol. 1, 1968.* Ed. Emma M. Birkmaier. Chicago: Encyclopaedia Britannica, 1968 (1969), pp. 343–74.

20. ———, and Renée S. Disick. *Individualizing Foreign Language Instruction Through Performance Objectives.* New York: Harcourt, 1971.

Operational Concepts

1. Methods of teaching change, not only because new techniques evolve, but also because our notions regarding the purpose of foreign language study shift.

2. The critical curricular questions have to do with the selection of learning objectives, teaching materials, instructional tactics, motivational devices, and evaluation procedures.

3. When the instructional objective is language control, the direct teaching of conversational skills is more advantageous than the teaching of grammatical rules and translation.

4. Memorization and practice drills are valuable in developing language mastery.

5. The selection of teaching methods cannot logically be separated from the selection of educational purpose.

6. Performance objectives tend to increase the efficiency of foreign language teaching.

Implications

Two articles on foreign language (one on methods and one on objectives) have been included so as to illustrate a number of general issues. Once again, as in so many other curricular dilemmas, opinion is divided, and, once again, the resolution of the dilemmas depends largely upon one's philosophical point of view.

When the objective is that of language mastery, time devoted to familiarizing students with a foreign culture is obviously nonproductive. When, in contrast, the objectives involve both cultural sophistication and language fluency, two kinds of instructional tactics are necessitated. The evaluation of student achievement, consequently, must be congruent with the intended instructional outcomes.

Whatever the objectives, however, a number of implications can be extracted from the research evidence. One, more must be done to correlate foreign language study with other curricular subjects. Two, to better accommodate individual difference, a larger range of teaching methodologies should be devised. Three, in view of the changing international scene, designers would do well to consider the wide-scale introduction of different languages, Chinese and Russian, for example, which are likely to increase in transnational significance.

Since skills that are not used regularly tend to grow fallow, efforts should be made to devise school experiences through which students can both sustain and extend acquired language facility. Finally, to again reinforce what will become a pervasive theme in the *Handbook,* the intellectual ideas upon which instruction is based must be more reflective of student's personal interests, foreign language classrooms must somehow be made more pleasurable and inviting, and the learner's personal objectives in studying another language must be clarified, student by student. Some are primarily interested in developing reading skill, some seek to become truly bilingual, and some wish merely to gain a repertory of basic phrases and greater sophistication regarding a foreign life-style. These clarifications, rather than endless debate over teaching objectives and teaching methods, are likely to spawn the greatest improvement.

Walter T. Petty   Marjorie F. Becking
Dorothy C. Petty

Second Language Teaching

Foreign languages have traditionally been taught in American schools by a grammar–translation method. This approach has fundamentally the same base as that of the traditional teaching of English grammar—defining parts of speech, memorizing conjugations, and learning rules. This approach has not worked satisfactorily in improving the writing and speaking of native speakers of English, and neither has it been very successful for teaching a foreign language, especially in terms of speaking that language.

Since about World War II the grammar–translation method for foreign language teaching has largely been supplanted by an approach that focuses upon imitation and memorization of basic elements of oral communication as they are used by native speakers. The essence of the procedure is the identification of the points of difference or interference between the two languages, followed by the developing of an aural–oral program for dealing with these points.

PRINCIPLES OF SECOND LANGUAGE TEACHING

This aural–oral method is also generally recognized as the procedure that is most effective in teaching English as a second language. This approach stresses the importance of hearing and speaking with purpose and understanding. It avoids many of the problems that arise when emphasis is given to grammar study and to writing and reading the new language. The following are recommended guides for teaching English as a second language:

1. The focus should be on oral activity. Specific English expressions should be listened to and spoken.

Reprinted from Walter T. Petty, Dorothy C. Petty, and Marjorie F. Becking, *Experience in Language Tools and Techniques for Language Arts Methods,* © 1973; by permission of Allyn and Bacon, Inc., Boston.

2. The language forms or patterns taught should be taken from the natural English speech of children, with attention given to the conversational speed, intonation patterns and stress, and idiomatic uses of the native child speaker of English.

3. The tape recorder provides a good means for gaining samples of speech, for listening to the forms being taught, and for allowing the child to listen to himself. Other audiovisual aids are particularly helpful in teaching meanings of words and expressions through pictures and actual objects.

4. The teacher sets a model for quality of speech, thus he must actually be this model or provide for the model by means of tapes and records.

5. The child should not be pushed into reading. Not only does he have the language handicap but he has had a different experiential background from that of native speakers of English. Attempting to teach a child to read before he has the language and experiential readiness for it is an inexcusable waste of both your time and the child's.

6. The basic procedure is one of drill upon language patterns selected on the basis of a contrastive analysis of English and the child's native language. The emphasis in the drill is upon the language patterns known to be the most difficult to learn.

7. Language drills should be related as closely as possible to actual classroom experiences. The emphasis in the drill is imitation of the model, including the pronunciation the model gives to words. Some separate drill upon making particular sounds will probably be needed.

8. Making the sounds of English is difficult, so a sympathetic, noncritical climate in the classroom is important. That is, overcorrecting a child's pronunciation, accent, or speech patterns should be avoided.

9. The child's native language should not be used during the teaching or drill sessions, since translation interferes with the automatic responses that are necessary.

TECHNIQUES FOR TEACHING ENGLISH

There are many techniques for presenting English to a nonspeaker that are based upon the aural–oral approach. A number of these are suggested below. Each one may lead to teaching situations made unique by the personalities, attitudes, and interactions of the individuals involved. That is, these are not "patterns" or "the way to do it" but are suggestions that may be useful in developing procedures for a specific classroom.

Teaching Vocabulary and Language Structure Directly

This is essentially a drill procedure in which an object, a specific action, or an idea is associated with the word or expression that names, describes, or explains it. A very useful plan for this is to have an "object box" (see Table 1) in which many objects are included(*1*). Objects may be selected from the box and identified by a simple sentence—for example, "This is a spoon." At first, the teacher should select the object, but later a child may select, or two children can use the box for a game (one should be a native speaker of English). The child should repeat the sentence, usually while he handles the object.

For direct teaching of action words and expressions, objects will not be helpful (except, of course, for words such as *cut,* in which case scissors, a knife, etc., would be needed). Many actions can be demonstrated by the teacher, an aide, or other children.

Ideas can be directly shown by placing something *in* a box, holding an object *above* a desk, taking a book *from* a shelf, etc. Of course, more complicated ideas are difficult to show directly because they involve several concepts. Some of these—for example, "helping one another"—can be shown in the classroom itself if time is taken to do so.

Other Teaching Techniques

Pictures may be used in somewhat the same way as objects to show actions and ideas. Pictures can be the basis for stories and games in which the idea or action is pointed to and appropriate sentences constructed for the child to repeat. Pictures can also be used as the basis for questions which require the beginning speaker of English to formulate responses. A picture file (added to regularly) is of course helpful to every teacher, whether he has non-English speakers in class or not. The file should be organized by major topics—communciations, sports, animals, ways people live, bodies of water, foods, etc.—with subdivisions for each and perhaps some cross-referencing so that pictures can be readily found and related to the vocabulary and structures that need to be taught.

TABLE 1

Suggested Items for an Object Box	
knife	mirror
fork	comb
spoon	hairbrush
plate	watch
glass	button
chalk	eyeglasses
notebook	purse
scissors	string
key	hammer
soap	nail
money	shoelaces

In a similar way, other materials may be used for children to talk about and as a basis for the construction of drill sentences. These include advertisements, news items, comic strips, games, and books.

Stories and poetry may also be used to present new vocabulary and structures. In using either literary form, the selection should be read and reread—possibly only one section at a time—until the children show understanding by their ability to answer specific questions. Using several readings will also help lead children into understanding new concepts by relating them to known ones, and will aid them in memorization of many structures. If this memorization does not occur from the repetition of the reading, memorization drills may be used for teaching the structures which have the most value.

Pattern Drills

Pattern drills are used to teach structures basic to communication in standard English through repetition until these structures are learned. The drills should be simple and easy so that children have the opportunity to use the language successfully and should focus upon stress and intonation given to commonly used English expressions. They should include sentence patterns in which a substitution is made for one of the words in the pattern (This is a *ball,* This is a _____; John *runs* fast, John _____ fast); questions which force a response of a particular pattern (Are you going to the store? *Yes, I am*); and sentences which call for a response in which the word order is changed (Joan has a torn dress, *Joan's dress is torn*), the sentence is expanded or reduced (There is a box on the table, *There is a big, red box on the center table*), or two sentences are combined into one (Bill has a bicycle. The bicycle was lost. *Bill's bicycle was lost*).

Perhaps the most important type of drill is that in which specific contrasts in pronunciation are emphasized. The drill material may be words, phrases, or sentences, but in each case the entire context is the same except for one sound. For example:

bat	my bell	We will shop here.
hat	my ball	We will stop here.

TEACHING STANDARD ENGLISH AS A SECOND DIALECT

The problem of teaching standard English to children who speak a nonstandard dialect is not unlike the problem of teaching English (also "standard") to speakers of foreign languages. That is, the nonstandard dialect and standard English differ at specific interference or contrast points, and these are the points that must receive particular instructional attention. On the other hand, there are differences between learning a second language and learning a second dialect. Probably the most important of these is that it is more difficult to motivate the learning of a second dialect. Also, a speaker of a nonstandard dialect has little or no trouble understanding most speakers of standard English—or at least grasping their fundamental meaning (though the opposite is less likely to be true). Further, the level of understanding suffers even more as standard English is met in print.

The points of interference or difference between standard English and nonstandard Negro dialect have been identified by some linguists(2). In addition, there are many features which are common to most nonstandard dialects. These features or points of interference may serve as the bases for teaching standard English by using foreign language teaching procedures.

The work of linguists is helpful, but teachers can determine in a non-technical way the features of two dialects that are different. Both phonological and grammatical differences should be noted if they appear consistently and are such that their use would sound out of place in conversation among educated Americans.

In essence, the strategy for teaching a second dialect "amounts to teaching the smallest possible number of vitally significant items—and *teaching each of them hard*"(3). Implementing this strategy successfully requires a long-term teaching effort that helps children recognize that the dialects are different, understand the reasons for language differences between people, and know the social situations in which it is appropriate to use the second dialect rather than the first. That is, while children can be taught to hear phonological differences and to recognize grammatical ones and can be drilled so that they repeat phrases and sentences in the second dialect, the new dialect will not be effectively used without attention to the attitudes of the children toward it.

Pitfalls to Avoid

The ability of a child who does not speak English or who speaks a nonstandard dialect should not be underestimated. Since many judgments in school are based upon intelligence tests, it is well to remember that such tests are related to a particular culture, with even the nonverbal tests retaining the cultural basis. A low score on an intelligence test, therefore, may reflect only a different cultural background rather than a degree of mental inability.

Further, time spent on pattern practice and the other teaching techniques may curtail or exclude other activities in which English may be learned and which are important to the child as he seeks to become an accepted member of the group. Therefore, an overemphasis upon activities that have characteristics of formality and/or predictability should be avoided.

A FINAL WORD

The objective of teaching English as a second language is for the child to learn to understand what he hears, and to speak so that he is understood by native speakers of English. In this way he will be better able to adjust to the school and its language as well as to the society in which he lives. In the same way, the child who speaks a nonstandard dialect can avoid the handicap which this may cause by learning standard English as a second dialect.

In either case, the younger a child is when the teaching begins, the better he is able to hear and imitate effectively. In addition, the young child generally has fewer conflicting feelings about learning the new language or dialect. Procedures for teaching each child will need to vary, but should the need arise, the procedures and techniques suggested in this chapter may prove helpful in selecting, devising, and planning a program for effective teaching of English as a second language or dialect.

References

1. This suggestion comes from Nina Phillips, *Conversational English for the Non-English-Speaking Child* (New York: Teachers College Press, 1968). This publication has many other good suggestions.

2. See Kenneth R. Johnson, "Standard English and Disadvantaged Black Children: Teaching Strategies," in William W. Joyce and James A. Banks (eds.). *Teaching the Language Arts to Culturally Different Children* (Reading, Mass.: Addison-Wesley Publishing Co., 1971), p. 123. Some linguists, however, do not generalize that there is a single nonstandard Negro dialect.

3. Virginia F. Allen, "Teaching Standard English as a Second Dialect," *Teachers College Record* (February 1967).

Operational Concepts

1. In the teaching of English as a second language, oral activity should predominate.

2. In the teaching of English to foreign-speaking students, the teacher serves as the primary model for imitating.

3. Teaching standard English to children who speak a nonstandard dialect poses problems similar to those encountered in teaching English to foreigners.

4. The efficient teaching of standard English—as a second dialect to those who speak a nonstandard dialect—requires repeated emphasis upon a small number of basic skills.

Implications

Teaching English as a second language remains a comparatively small, but nonetheless vital, aspect of the curriculum. Closely related to bilingual education, the teaching device of greatest value is that of providing students with abundant opportunity to hear and use correct English.

In common with other aspects of the language arts curriculum, there is an abiding need to develop more efficient techniques. Although English teachers undoubtedly will need to fight the battle of excessive class size for a long time to come, too little attention has been given to the development of imaginative teaching tactics that circumvent existing difficulties. As in the case of punctuation, rhetoric, and grammar, fewer skills need to be emphasized in greater depth. For the child who is learning English as a second language, punctuation and vocabulary extension can be treated in a variety of creative ways: radio and televison offer accessible listening experiences, native-speaking students can be pressed into services as peer tutors, benefit can be derived from practice with tape recorders, and so on.

Efforts should also be made to relate the learner's listening–speaking experiences to topics of high personal interest. Just as the learning of literature and composition can be enhanced by a more exciting and humane environment, and by content of greater relevance, it is *what* foreign-speaking children talk about, in their study of English as a second language, that may constitute the surest path to healthy motivation. Not in the study of English alone, but everywhere in the curriculum, the school must dispel—once and for all—the myth that one must suffer in order to learn.

Alvin M. Westcott
James A. Smith

Basic Principles of Mathematics Programs

A revolution in the teaching of mathematics in the elementary school has occurred in the past decade. In periodical literature throughout the country abundant references are made to the "new math." A decided change in the methodology and content of mathematics programs has been wrought in a relatively short period of time.

The impetus for this movement, like the interest in creativity, was in part prompted by the launching of Sputnik. The need for a sound understanding of mathematical processes in our highly technological society and the need for mathematics as a tool for science became apparent to everyone.

Increased interest in mathematics brought a flood of new programs for teaching mathematics, and a variety of modifications, additions, and devices were invented to augment existing programs. We are currently interested in the Madison Plan, the Cuisenaire Number-in-Color Plan, the Stanford Project, the Illinois Project, the School Mathematics Study Group Program, and the Greater Cleveland Mathematics Plan(1).

Many of these programs, and the ideas inherent in them, have met with fine success—if one is willing to accept the criteria for measurement that are applied to them. The effectiveness and justifications of some of the new programs have been challenged and remain to be proven. The introduction of "modern" math in many schools throughout the country has created a great deal of controversy among educators as to the effort such methods and resultant learnings have on the total growth of the elementary school child. One such controversy centers around the advisability of teaching geometry, algebra, and abstract math algorisms to kindergarten children, who have limited experiential backgrounds. It is extremely difficult to compare the effectiveness and utility of the older math programs with the new. More often than not, their primary objectives are different, which makes comparisons very complex. Unfortunately, some school systems have adopted new math programs based on very superficial comparative data.

Reprinted from Alvin M. Westcott and James A. Smith, *Creative Teaching of Mathematics in the Elementary School,* © 1967; by permission of Allyn and Bacon, Inc., Boston.

No one program of mathematics teaching will develop in every child all the mathematical concepts called for by his existing and future needs and abilities. But any plan, to be successful, must be based on general principles of child development and learning as well as on basic principles inherent in mathematics as an academic discipline.

From the writings of mathematicians and educators and from research in the area of mathematics teaching, the authors have selected the following principles as guides for the teaching of mathematics.

1. *Mathematics should be taught in a meaningful manner to children.* Children learn mathematics best when they understand the meanings behind what they learn. Meaningful math implies that, among other things, children understand the language of mathematics and care to know the intrinsic beauty and poetic qualities of mathematics. Equally important, children need to learn mathematics for use as an intellectual tool and social utility.

Mathematical understandings are an outgrowth of meaningful learning experiences. They are not "rules" to be memorized by children. Understandings usually grow slowly and as a result of many and varied positive reinforcement experiences.

2. *Mathematics should be taught through a structural developmental sequence.* Research indicates that one of the prime reasons for mathematical disability among children in the later grades is a lapse of instruction in the earlier grades. In a modern curriculum, it is recognized that the growth of many concepts in mathematics is a gradual process and takes place over a period of years. Understanding of upper-level concepts relies on mastery of earlier concepts.

3. *Meaningful mathematics makes provision for the application of quantitative procedures in social situations both in and out of school.* A practical balance must be achieved between the teaching of basic number facts and processes, and the social applications of mathematics. Motivation to learn mathematics becomes intense when the children identify mathematical problems that arise from a felt need in a social situation.

4. *Sound mathematics teaching incorporates learning experiences that relate to the nature of the learners, including their mental, emotional, and social development.* It is important that children experience success in their work in mathematics. Success sponsors positive attitudes toward mathematics. Attitudes relative to mathematics are as important as computational skill. When poor attitudes are formed, especially from too many failure experiences, children are prompted to build emotional blocks against mathematics.

5. *Modern mathematics programs include a wide variety of carefully selected learning experiences in which number functions directly(2).* Mathematics skills and computation must be taught in a sequential manner in school each day, probably in a given period. Opportunity should be found to apply the children's learnings to other aspects of the curriculum whenever possible.

6. *Mathematics programs usually emphasize the element of "discovery."* Guided experiences in learning promote progress toward desirable goals. In guided learning, the fact that all children do not learn in the same way or with the same speed is taken into account. Nevertheless, all can be led to discover meanings, facts, and understandings. In problem solving, the element of discovery tends to make the learnings more permanent and highly motivational. The mathematics classroom should be regarded by the teacher and children as an exciting discovery laboratory.

7. *Meaningful mathematics programs are built around "problem-solving situations" rather than problem solving as drill.* Creative problem solving should serve as the base upon which appropriate computational skills are brought to bear.

8. *In mathematics programs a systematic series of steps are established to make learning progressive and logical to the learner.* All children within a classroom do not receive the same mathematics instruction. In some instances instruction may be on an individual basis.

9. *Mathematics programs provide "practice" for the mastery of facts to be learned rather than "drill."* Practice implies that new skills are put to use at once in situations where they have significance to the learners. The necessary reinforcement for habituation is provided through the application of the new skill to many situations, rather than that application and memorization to one situation which is characteristic of drill.

10. *Sound mathematics programs employ the nomenclature of mathematics so that children learn to use it with understanding.* The processes and operations of mathematics are made more lucid by the language of mathematics when it is properly used. Children learn this nomenclature in meaningful context.

11. *Highly effective mathematics programs involve evaluation as a continuing process in which both teacher and pupil participate.* They include a broad range of educational outcomes and are not limited to tests of computational skill.

12. *In mathematics programs diagnostic procedures are continuously applied in the course of the learning activities so that difficulties will be promptly detected and remediation begun.* This procedure in some instances replaces the general tests given periodically to the total group of children in the classroom.

References

1. Clyde G. Corle, *Teaching Mathematics in the Elementary School* (New York: The Ronald Press, 1964), pp. 35–56.
2. Foster Grossnickle and Leo Brueckner, *Discovering Meanings in Arithmetic* (New York: John Winston Co., 1959), p. 4.

The concepts and implications related to the teaching of mathematics appear on pages 142 and 143.

Klaas Kramer

The Search for Improved Programs

Several developments have been responsible for the search for improved mathematics programs. Important factors that caused and are giving impetus to the movement are: the increased need for mathematics skills in society, the need for more mathematicians, the merger results of mathematics teaching(*1*), and the consistency of sizable differences, in favor of foreign students, in mathematics achievement tests administered to samples of pupils in the United States and abroad(*2*). Experimental programs were launched in the late 1950s and in the 1960s. The preparation and teaching of such programs and materials were often made possible or facilitated by financial grants of the federal government and of private agencies.

NEW MATHEMATICS PROGRAMS IN THE ELEMENTARY SCHOOL

Experimental mathematics programs for the elementary school that have been in the limelight for some time include the following:

1. *School Mathematics Study Group* (SMSG): The SMSG, directed by E. G. Begle, began its work in 1959, and produced a mathematics program for grades K–12. Mathematicians, educators, and psychologists were involved in the writing, countrywide teaching, and revising of the units.

The SMSG program is designed to guide pupils to a better understanding of the basic concepts and structure of mathematics. It covers topics in more breadth and depth than has been done in previous times, it includes new topics, it emphasizes principles of mathematics, and it stresses precise language. Materials for the teacher are available.

The program appears to have been the most influential experimental

Reprinted from Klaas Kramer, *Teaching Elementary School Mathematics,* 2nd ed., © 1970; by permission of Allyn and Bacon, Inc., Boston.

mathematics program. It was also planned to assist commercial publishers and authors in the preparation of new materials.

2. *Greater Cleveland Mathematics Program* (GCMP): The major purpose of the Educational Research Council, the parent organization of the GCMP, is to develop improved curricula for grades K–12.

Work on the GCMP was begun in 1959, at which time B. H. Gundlach was its director. In the mathematics program for grades K–6 efforts have been made to lead pupils to understand concepts before computational algorisms are stressed.

In the GCMP several new topics are presented. The discovery approach is used extensively. Proper sequence and mathematical correctness are stressed. The materials have been tested in the classroom. Comprehensive teachers' manuals are provided and many in-service programs have been conducted.

3. *Madison Project:* The Madison Project originated in 1957 at Syracuse University under the direction of R. B. Davis. The first experiments with the project were conducted in Madison Junior High School, Syracuse, New York. A second center was developed later at Webster College, Missouri, where prospective teachers can learn to work with the materials.

The program contains supplemental and enrichment materials for children in grades 2–9. Its purposes include: to build a sound background for future mathematics, to stimulate creativity in children, and to develop a greater interest in mathematics. Many of the materials deal with algebra and geometry. Concepts are introduced early; discovery of patterns is encouraged; the inductive approach is stressed; conversations and class discussions are preferred to lectures; and games are used to assist the learning of mathematics.

4. *University of Illinois Arithmetic Project:* Since 1959 D. Page and his staff have been working on this project to prepare supplementary mathematics materials that allow children to pursue mathematics beyond the usual limits of the elementary school.

The authors of the program hope that children by exploring and experimenting with the materials will develop insight and acquire an intuitive understanding of mathematical concepts. Thus, the discovery approach is emphasized.

5. *Stanford Projects:* The project *Sets and Numbers,* directed by P. Suppes, was started in 1959. Suppes holds that operations on sets can be better understood by young children than abstract operations on numbers.

The project *Geometry for the Primary Grades* is directed by N. S. Hawley. It is intended to stimulate the reasoning and the analytical and creative thinking of able learners. Children get a great deal of practice using pencil, straightedge, and compass, and learn the needed technical vocabulary.

6. *Minnesota Elementary Curriculum Project:* The Minnesota Elementary Curriculum Project originated in 1962 under the direction of P.

C. Rosenbloom. A main goal of the project is to introduce children early to a geometrical model of the real number system, and to assist them in visualizing relations between numbers and operations on numbers. The child is to apply the mathematics he has learned. One of the aims of the project is to coordinate mathematics with the natural and social sciences. A program for grades K–9 in mathematics and science is planned.

Experiments in mathematics learning are conducted in several countries. Information on several programs abroad is presented in a report published by the Unesco Institute for Education, Hamburg. This publication is identified at the end of the chapter.

The characteristics of the new programs as described by authorities include the following:

1. The programs have been produced by mathematicians or with their assistance.
2. Precise language and terminology are emphasized.
3. A main objective is to teach the child to think logically by developing skill in following and building patterns of organized thought.
4. New content has been added. Examples of topics included in all or many of the new programs are: prime numbers, composite numbers, factors, exponents, different numeration systems, properties of numbers, additional terms and symbols, algebraic equations, inequalities, mathematical sentences and frames, number patterns, the number line, logic, simple probability, sets, graphing, modular arithmetic, and geometry. It should be noted, however, that a number of these topics have already been included in good "traditional" programs for several years.
5. Efforts have been made to improve methods of teaching the subject matter.

The new mathematics programs have met with objections. Criticisms that have been directed at some or all of the new materials are:

1. New programs have a tendency to be unbalanced. Topics such as sets, notation systems, and geometry may have been overemphasized in some programs.
2. Authors who know about teaching elementary school children should have had a greater part in the preparation of the materials.
3. The typical classroom teacher is not able to teach a new program before he has thoroughly studied the new content and vocabulary. Examples of topics with which the typical teacher has to become acquainted are: different systems of numeration and notation, sets, mathematical sentences, modular arithmetic, and geometry.

Some claims made by advocates of exploratory programs do not do justice to several textbook series which antedated these programs:

1. It has been suggested that the new mathematics stresses concepts rather than rote memorization of the proper steps to perform, as in the old system. A careful study of good "traditional" programs will reveal that they also are emphasizing understanding of processes and are paying a great deal of attention to proper formation of concepts.

2. The implication has been made that the "discovery" method is a unique characteristic of experimental programs. However, the "discovery" method has long been used and is being enployed in many recent "traditional" mathematics curricula.

It should be acknowledged that experimental programs and conferences dealing with the improvement of the elementary school mathematics programs have been serving a very useful purpose. Professional people representing various disciplines have attacked the problem of how to improve the mathematics curriculum and have made a number of valuable contributions. New enthusiasm for mathematics in many schools, better attitudes among teachers, the addition of content, the presentation of several topics at lower grade levels, the refinement of terminology and vocabulary, the stimulation of the child's imagination, a desire among authors and publishers to produce superior materials, the creation of workshops for teachers of mathematics, and other undertakings have been a result of the promotion of experimental programs. These efforts should produce better teaching and learning through the use of improved, properly balanced programs. For attainment of this goal, promising new materials should be tried out in the classroom under carefully controlled conditions, before they are promoted for countrywide use or rejected as inferior.

THE CAMBRIDGE REPORT

An issue that has invited widespread discussion concerns the goals for elementary school mathematics. During the summer of 1963, twenty-nine mathematicians and scientists met at Cambridge, Massachusetts, to review school mathematics and to establish goals for mathematics education. The conference resulted in the bulletin *Goals for School Mathematics, The Report of the Cambridge Conference on School Mathematics,* commonly called "The Cambridge Report." It includes proposals for mathematics curricula for the elementary school and the high school. If a student should work through the proposed thirteen years of mathematics in grades K–12, he would be expected to have a level of training comparable to three years of top-level college training today; in fact, he would be expected to have the equivalent of two years of calculus, and one semester each of modern algebra and probability theory. In the report it is suggested that the curriculum be brought into being over the next few decades, and it is stated that the expressed views are intended to serve as a basis for further discussion and experimentation. As could be expected, the report has received praise and criticism(3).

NEEDED REVISIONS

A study of the research conducted in the field of mathematics reveals several shortcomings in the mathematics curriculum of the public school. The remediation of these diagnosed weaknesses should result in a distinct improvement in the program. In the following paragraphs some issues related to the teaching of mathematics in the elementary school are presented and research on the topics is reported.

1. Meaning Theory

The superiority of insight over rote memorization, of understanding the reasons why a process is performed over mechanical manipulation, and of encouraging children to form their own generalizations over dictating the rules has been demonstrated repeatedly. Thiele(4) conducted an experiment with two groups of beginning second-graders, totaling 512 pupils. The 100 basic addition facts were taught to one group by the "generalization (meaning) method" and to the other group by a drill method. The "generalization method" resulted in significantly better performance and in better transfer of training than the drill method.

Swenson(5) taught the 100 basic addition facts to three groups of second-graders, totaling 332 pupils. Three different methods were used: (1) the generalization (meaning) method; (2) the drill method; and (3) the drill-plus method. The drill-plus method was a drill method with certain concessions made to the ideas of concrete meaning and organization. The following findings stand out: (1) The generalization group was significantly superior to both of the other groups on the net total achievement. (2) The order of performance on tests that were to determine the amounts of transfer of training was, from highest to lowest, generalization, drill, and drill-plus.

Brownell, Moser, and others(6) investigated the effectiveness of four methods of teaching borrowing in subtraction: (1) the equal additions method, taught rationally; (2) the equal additions method, taught mechanically; (3) the decomposition method, taught rationally; and (4) the decomposition method, taught mechanically. Of the several findings, the following are important for the purpose of this chapter: (1) The meaningfully taught sections quite consistently excelled the mechanically taught sections. (2) There was some evidence that rational instruction produced greater uniformity in accuracy of computation than mechanical instruction did.

Though the importance of meaningful teaching has been shown in such studies as these and has been emphasized by an increasing number of educators, there still is a question as to which arithmetic teaching is done meaningfully in practice. There are indications that much mere lip service is being paid to the meaning theory and that in practical situations many teachers still use the drill method. In 1949 Glennon(7) concluded a study in which he sought to determine the degree to which persons above the level of grade 6 have possession of the meanings and understandings basic to the several computational skills commonly taught in grades 1 through 6, as follows(8):

> The data ... are limited evidence of the meager degree with which teachers are succeeding in bringing about growth in meanings and understandings. The evidence does not lend much support to the argument often heard that we are already teaching meanings.

More recent research has corroborated the findings of Glennon.

2. Readiness Program

At present practically all educators insist upon systematic instruction in mathematics in the first grade of the elementary school. When this systematic instruction is planned, it is of great importance to determine the mathematical background of the pupils, so that no time will be lost by presenting topics which children already have mastered. Much of the content in the typical first-grade textbook is too easy to challenge the average first-grade pupil. Research has demonstrated that entering first graders know more about arithmetic than is expected.

Brownell made an extensive study of arithmetic known by school beginners. He also summarized several investigations already made in this area. Some findings of these studies are presented below. Since the data were taken from several studies (as reported by Brownell), the percents and the ratios are approximations.

1. Nine out of every ten preschool children tested could count by rote to 10, and one out of every ten to 100.
2. Ninety percent of all the preschool children tested could count rationally to 10, and more than fifty percent to 20.
3. Eighty percent of the school entrants tested were able to identify a group of 5 and seventy percent could identify a group of 10.
4. Sixty percent of the preschool children tested could reproduce a group of 10.
5. Nine out of every ten school entrants tested knew the meaning of the words *longest* and *shortest*.

6. More than fifty percent of a group of preschool children tested could solve verbal problems in which the combinations $2 + 2$ and $3 - 2$ were individually presented.

7. The numerals from 1 to 9 could be identified by two out of every three preschool children tested.

8. Twenty percent of a group of school entrants tested could write the numerals 4, 7, 2, 5, 9, and 6.

9. Three out of every four children of a group of school entrants tested knew the terms *square* and *circle*.

10. Half of a group of school entrants tested could tell time to the hour.

11. Nine out of every ten of a group of beginning first-graders tested could identify a penny, a nickel, a dime, a quarter, and a half dollar.

More recently, Priore(9) conducted a study to determine how much arithmetic children know when they enter the first grade. The children tested (seventy) were only those enrolled in one school and, by request, these children had not been instructed in arithmetic in kindergarten. The following findings were revealing:

1. The average number to which children could count by rote was 30.

2. The average number to which they could count rationally was 30.

3. Over seventy-five percent of the children tested could reproduce numbers to 10 by selecting the correct number of blocks.

4. Sixty percent of the children could identify all the numbers up to 10. This was determined by showing the child a specific number of beads and asking him to tell how many there were.

5. Fifty percent knew the value of the fractions ½, ¼, and ⅓.

6. Forty-three percent of the children recognized the numerals through 10.

7. Forty-four percent of the children could estimate which of four boxes contained a pound of candy.

8. Over seventy-five percent of the children knew which is more—3 pennies or a nickel.

Miller(10) after reviewing the results of some studies on the background of entering first-graders, wrote:

> Thus a comparison of the arithmetical ability of entering first-grade children and the requirements of the general proposed curriculum in arithmetic shows that well over 50 percent of the students can already do the work which is required for the first grade. It appears that the majority of first graders simply review, for one year, material which they have already mastered.

Schutter and Spreckelmeyer(11) concluded, after comparing European and American textbooks for the primary grades:

By requiring additional time per week on arithmetic in the primary years, and by simultaneous development of concepts of numbers and operations with them, European texts permit the child to develop a broad background in a briefer span of time than do accepted American texts. The European children are more strongly challenged.

3. Grade Placement

In the 1930s the grade placement of arithmetic topics was changed partly as a result of the influence of the Committee of Seven(12). This committee sought to determine the mental-age level at which specific topics could be taught to completion. The findings of the committee seemed to indicate that many topics were introduced too early. Though critics offered valid objections to the findings and exposed some serious limitations of the study, the report had a tremendous influence. The teaching of several topics was postponed until higher grades. As a result, a heavy burden was placed on pupils, by requiring them to study more material at a faster rate in the upper grades.

More recently, a trend to move topics down in the grades has been evident. The new emphasis on science and mathematics, the experiences of teachers indicating that many children can do more in mathematics than is required of them, and comparisons of mathematics programs of the United States and foreign countries have been influential in establishing this new trend. Schutter and Spreckelmeyer(13) prepared a table presenting a summary of the grade levels at which selected basic topics are principally studied in seven European countries and in the United States. Where the grade levels for the topics are the same, the European students have had a longer acquaintance with concepts and skills that serve as foundations for the development of these topics. Buswell(14) found that many arithmetic topics had been studied by English children for a longer period of time than by the California children. The author(15), after a study of comparative curricula, concluded that Dutch schools were about a year ahead of Iowa schools in the grade placement of concepts and processes in arithmetic.

4. Time Allotment

The meaning method consumes a great deal of time because of added pupil activities and class discussions. The necessity of practice after a new process has been understood by the pupils is also realized. Some time ago Buckingham(16) stated: "Our position is not that drill should be avoided but rather that it should be made more intelligent in the fields to which it is now applied and that it should be applied still more widely." In the opinion of the author of this volume, the meaning method tends to consume more time than the drill method. In practice, however, the third R does not seem to have received its due share of time. Even before the

meaning method had become evident in children's textbooks, the time allotted to arithmetic had been gradually reduced. Sueltz(17) noted:

> During most of the nineteenth century, arithmetic occupied at least 25
> percent of the total school time. In 1928, this had been reduced to 11.6 per-
> cent as shown in a study of how schools use their time by Carlton H. Mann.

Miller(18) studied the time allotments for arithmetic in thirty-four
large school systems and forty-four small school systems in the United
States, and reported the following findings:

> (1) The amount of time spent in arithmetic ranged from a median score
> of 23 minutes per day to 45 minutes per day in the large city school systems,
> and 30 minutes per day to 47 minutes per day in the small school system.
> (2) There is a marked difference in the amount of time spent in the lower
> grades (1st, 2nd, and 3rd). The lower the grade, the less time devoted to
> arithmetic.

The same investigator(19) compared the time allotments in arithmetic of
thirty-two foreign countries and the United States. The data for the Amer-
can schools were taken from the study quoted above. He concluded that
other countries devote a greater amont of time to arithmetic during the first
six years of school than the United States does. Schutter and Spreckel-
meyer(20) stated that it is evident that European schools spend more time
on the study of arithmetic than American schools do. They felt that this
extra time has an effect both on the pace at which the subject is developed
and on the challenging achievement levels to which the basic topics are
carried. One of their recommendations was that more time be allotted to
arithmetic in the elementary school.

The author(21) found that in The Netherlands the average pupil
spends 1064 hours of class time on arithemtic in six years of elementary
school, whereas the Iowa pupil spends, during these six years, 537 hours
on arithmetic. Jarvis(22) conducted a study in which the achievement of
329 sixth-grade pupils who had spent 55 to 60 minutes daily in studying
arithmetic through grades 4, 5, and 6 was compared with the achievement
of 384 sixth graders who had studied 35 to 45 minutes daily over the same
period of time. The difference in intelligence between the groups was not
statistically significant. However, it was found that, without exception,
achievement of the pupils who had studied under the longer daily class
periods of 55 to 60 minutes exceeded that of the children of the group with
the shorter 35- to 45-minute periods. The difference was statistically significant. It was concluded that, for the average, the dull, and the bright pupils,
the longer periods in arithmetic resulted in substantially more significant
arithmetic achievement.

5. Training of Elementary School
Mathematics Teachers

The results of several studies indicate that the typical elementary school teacher does not possess an adequate background in mathematics. Time and again it has been demonstrated that teachers need to know more mathematics and understand mathematical processes better than they do. After reviewing several studies on the mathematical background of elementary school teachers, Sparks(23) noted:

> The most general conclusion that can be drawn from these studies is that teachers are considered by all of these authors to be:
> 1. Particularly deficient in understanding of underlying principles;
> 2. Deficient in computational skills, particularly with decimals and percents;
> 3. Deficient in problem-solving ability.

Sparks sees the need for a long-term investigation with sound theoretical bases and sound experimental design to determine what content material and types of presentation provide teachers with the knowledge found most valuable for elementary school teachers.

In a chapter dealing with background mathematics for elementary teachers, Ruddell, Dutton, and Reckzeh(24) present the results of a survey of research and literature on the problem, identify current practices in teacher training, and report the results of a questionnaire. The questionnaire was submitted to the elementary teacher training department of all members of the American Association of Colleges of Teacher Education. The purpose of the questionnaire was to establish a solid base of professional opinion for recommending a background course in mathematics for all elementary school teachers who are to be certified to teach in grades 1 through 8. Among the recommendations of the investigators were the following:

1. Each student admitted to the elementary teacher training program should be required to take a minimum of six semester hours of background mathematics.
2. Teachers of arithmetic in grades seven and eight should complete a minor in college mathematics.
3. All elementary school teachers should have a course in the teaching of arithmetic which should follow the background sequence in mathematics.

Important work with hopefully far-reaching consequences is being done by the Committee on the Undergraduate Program in Mathematics (CUPM), P.O. Box 1024, Berkley, California 94701, which is a committee of the Mathematical Association of America and which is supported in part by the National Science Foundation. This committee aims to develop a broad program of improvement in the undergraduate mathematics curriculum of the nation's colleges and universities(25). For college training of teachers of elementary school mathematics, the following courses are recommended by the committee:

1. One or two courses—depending upon the previous preparation of the student—in the structure of the real number system and its subsystems.
2. A course devoted to the basic concepts of algebra.
3. A course in informal geometry.

Another report on mathematical education of elementary teachers was presented by the Cambridge Conference on Teacher Training. The student is referred to the report and to an article of Morley in *The Arithmetic Teacher,* identified at the end of the chapter.

In 1968 *The Arithmetic Teacher* introduced a new department, "Forum on Teacher Preparation," edited by Francis J. Mueller. It is expected that this department will make valuable contributions. For example, the student is referred to Spitzer's article in the February 1969 issue of the magazine.

RECOMMENDATIONS

The results of the research studies reported in this chapter and the recent emphasis on mathematics seem to warrant the following recommendations for the improvement of the elementary school mathematics curriculum:

1. Teachers should introduce mathematical processes meaningfully, stimulate children to see relationships, encourage them to form generalizations, and guide them to an understanding of the structure of the real number system.
2. A sufficient amount of practice should be provided, in order to anchor needed skills.
3. The arithmetic readiness program should be reconsidered. Apparently, most first graders do not need many of the arithmetic readiness exercises the typical program presents.
4. Several arithmetic topics should be introduced or mastered sooner. This should result in more challenge to the lower grade pupils, in a less heavy load for the upper grade pupils, and in the carrying of topics to a greater depth.
5. More time should be alloted to elementary school mathematics, or al-

lotted time should be used more wisely. This will allow the teacher to use the meaning method to better advantage and to set aside a sufficient amount of time for practice exercises.

6. Mental computation should be taught systematically in all grades.
7. Proper methods for dealing with individual differences should be identified and used.
8. Prospective teachers should be required to take a sufficient number of semester hours of mathematics, followed by a course in the teaching of elementary school mathematics.
9. Teachers in the field should prepare themselves better by taking college courses or workshops in the content and the teaching of elementary school mathematics. Such preparation should include the study of modern mathematics topics.
10. The findings of exploratory programs in elementary school mathematics should be used to advantage. Modern topics presented in these programs should be included in the curriculum when their effectiveness has been proven.

SELECTED RESEARCH

KRAMER, K., "Arithmetic Achievement in Iowa and The Netherlands." *The Elementary School Journal,* February, 1959, pp. 258–63.

The purpose of this study was to compare achievement in arithmetic in the upper grades of schools in Iowa and in The Netherlands.

To collect data for comparing achievement, two tests—modifications of the arithmetic sections of the Iowa Tests of Basic Skills for grades 6, 7, and 8—were used. Test 1 (fifty-seven items) was a test of problem-solving ability. Test 2 (fifty-nine items) was designed to measure understanding of concepts and processes in arthmetic.

The tests were administered to a total of 1511 pupils in forty fifth- and sixth-grade classes in The Netherlands, and to a total of 1530 pupils in grades 5, 6, 7, and 8 of fifteen Iowa schools.

On both tests, pupils in grades 5 and 6 in Dutch schools performed considerably better than their Iowa counterparts. The differences were significant at better than the 1 percent level. In fact, average performance for the Dutch sixth grade was somewhat higher than the Iowa average for the eighth grade.

In the discussion of the study it is emphasized that in the interpretation of the findings, several matters should be considered, for example, time allotment for arithmetic (at the time of the study almost twice as much in The Netherlands as in Iowa), grade placement of arithmetic topics, and promotion policies.

HUNGERMAN, A. D., "Achievement and Attitude of Sixth-Grade Pupils in Conventional and Contemporary Mathmematics Programs." *The Arithmetic Teacher,* January, 1967, pp. 30–39.

The purpose of this study was to compare results of contemporary and conventional programs. Specifically, these matters were compared: (1) computational skills; (2) suitability of newer mathematical ideas, symbols, and vocabulary for various intelligence levels and socioeconomic backgrounds; (3) effect on attitude towards mathematics; and (4) relationship of conventional arithmetic achievement, contemporary arithmetic achievement, and attitudes.

References

1. L. J. Brueckner, "Testing the Validity of Criticism of the Schools," *Journal of Educational Research,* February, 1943, pp. 465–67; Admiral C. W. Nimitz, in "The Importance of Mathematics in the War Effort," *The Mathematics Teacher,* February, 1942, pp. 88–89; J. S. Orleans and J. L. Sperling, "The Arithmetic Knowledge of Graduate Students," *Journal of Educational Research,* November, 1954, pp. 177–86.

2. G. T. Buswell, "A Comparison of Achievement in Arithmetic in England and Central California," *The Arithmetic Teacher,* February, 1958, pp. 1–9; N. H. Tracy, "A Comparison of Test Results—North Carolina, California, and England," *The Arithmetic Teacher,* October, 1959, pp. 199–202; K. Kramer, "Arithmetic Achievement in Iowa and The Netherlands," *The Elementary School Journal,* February, 1959, pp. 258–63; T. Husén (ed.), *International Study of Achievement in Mathematics. A Comparison of Twelve Countries,* Vols. I and II (New York: John Wiley & Sons, Inc., 1967).

3. M. H. Stone (H. Tinnappel, ed.), "Reviews and Evaluations," *The Mathematics Teacher,* April, 1965, pp. 353–60; I. Adler, "The Cambridge Conference Report: Blueprint or Fantasy?" *The Arithmetic Teacher,* March, 1966.

4. C. L. Thiele, "The Contribution of Generalization to the Learning of the Addition Facts," Contributions to Education, No. 763 (New York; Bureau of Publications, Teachers College, Columbia University, 1938).

5. E. J. Swenson, "Organization and Generalization as Factors in Learning, Transfer, and Retroactive Inhibition," *Learning Theory in School Situations,* University of Minnesota Studies in Education, No. 2 (Minneapolis: University of Minnesota Press, 1949), pp. 9–39.

6. W. A. Brownell, H. E. Moser, and others, *Meaningful Versus Mechanical Learning: A Study in Grade III Subtraction,* Duke University Research Studies in Education, No. 8 (Durham, N.C.: Duke University Press, 1949).

7. V. J. Glennon, "Testing Meanings in Arithmetic," *Arithmetic 1949,* Supplementary Educational Monographs, No. 70 (Chicago: University of Chicago Press, 1949), pp. 64–74.

8. W. A. Brownell et al., *Arithmetic in Grades I and II: A Critical Summary of New and Previously Reported Research,* Duke University Research Studies in Education, No. 6 (Durham, N.C.: Duke University Press, 1941).

9. A. Priore ,"Achievement, Entering Grade I," *The Arithmetic Teacher,* March, 1957, pp. 55–60.

10. G. H. Miller, "Shall We Change Our Arithmetic Program?" *The Arithmetic Teacher,* April, 1962, pp. 193–97.

11. C. H. Schutter and R. L. Spreckelmeyer, *Teaching the Third R* (Washington, D.C.: Council for Basic Education, 1959), p. 23.

12. C. C. Washburne, "The Grade Placement of Arithmetic Topics: A 'Committee of Seven' Investigation." *Report of the Society's Committee on Arithmetic.* Twenty-ninth Yearbook, Part II, National Society for the Study of Education (Bloomington, Ill.: Public School Publishing Co., 1930), Chap. XIII.

13. Schutter and Spreckelmeyer, op cit., pp. 17–18.

14. Buswell, op. cit., p. 7.

15. Kramer, op. cit.. p. 260.

16. B. R. Buckingham, "What Becomes of Drill?" *Arithmetic in General Education.* Sixteenth Yearbook, National Council of Teachers of Mathematics (New York: Bureau of Publications, Teachers College, Columbia University, 1941), p. 200.

17. B. A. Sueltz, "Arithmetic in Historical Perspective," *The National Elementary Principal,* October, 1959, p. 14.

18. G. H. Miller, "How Much Time for Arithmetic?" *The Arithmetic Teacher,* November, 1958, pp. 256–59.

19. G. H. Miller, "Shall We Change Our Arithmetic Program?" *The Arithmetic Teacher,* April, 1962, pp. 193–97.

20. Schutter and Spreckelmeyer, op. cit., pp. 32–33.

21. Kramer, op. cit., pp. 261–62.

22. O. T. Jarvis, "Time Allotment Relationships to Pupil Achievement in Arithmetic," *The Arithmetic Teacher,* May, 1963, pp. 248–50.

23. J. N. Sparks, "Arithmetic Understandings Needed by Elementary-school Teachers," *The Arithmetic Teacher,* December, 1961, pp. 395–403.

24. A. K. Ruddell, W. Dutton, and J. Reckzeh, "Background Mathematics for Elementary Teachers," *Instruction in Arithmetic,* Twenty-fifth Yearbook of the National Council of Teachers of Mathematics (Washington, D.C.: The Council, 1960), Chap. XIII.

25. "Recommendations of the Mathematical Association of America for the Training of Mathematics Teachers," *American Mathematical Monthly,* December, 1960, pp. 982–91; CUPM Report Number 13, April, 1966; CUPM, *Course Guides for the Training of Teachers of Elementary School Mathematics,* 1968.

Operational Concepts

1. The conceptual understanding of mathematical principles is preferable to the rote memorization of rules.

2. The individualization of mathematics teaching, so that instruction fits the learner's particular stage of development, remains an important goal in curriculum improvement.

3. The research evidence suggests that some teachers are handicapped by an inadequate grasp of mathematical theory.

4. The tendency to "teach" some children that they lack "a mathematical mind" and the capacity to learn mathematics must be prevented.

Implications

Experts often contend that mathematics' greatest failing is reflected in the number of students who find the subject distasteful and are convinced that they have little mathematical ability. Over the years, we have had relatively little success in making the subject more interesting and less awesome. It is reasonable to argue, therefore, that such efforts should take continuing priority in future developmental endeavors.

Despite the wide assortment of truth and myth that surrounds modern math, the plain facts are that all children must master basic arithmetical skills, that these skills are best developed through repeated drill and practice, and that—once learned—the skills can be made relevant to an almost infinite number of student interests.

A rather different problem has to do with the arbitrariness of current instructional methods. It is commonplace that simple mathematical problems can be solved in a variety of ways. Yet, however good their intentions, teachers sometimes insist that there is only one "right" way, and a correct solution—reached in the "wrong" manner—is penalized. Considerable good might occur if teachers taught their students alternative ways of solving a problem, and allowed the individual learner to select a method of choice.

Yet another implication stems from the frequent assertion that since some teachers are lacking in mathematical sophistication, students do not acquire an adequate understanding of the function of mathematics. While a variety of in-service endeavors have, in recent years, helped to upgrade the competence of teachers, the consensus among observers is that much unfinished business remains.

Finally, the technological breakthroughs now on the horizon, involving, among other things, computer-assisted diagnosis and drills, are likely to set off a new revolution in mathematics teaching. For all the latent potential, however, a fundamental difficulty likely will remain: students have traditionally learned mathematical skills by memorizing a sequential series of operational steps; rarely, however, have they learned a fundamental understanding of the mathematical properties that cause these steps to work. Teachers and researchers alike, consequently, may need to give renewed attention to teaching programs—machine and otherwise—that substantially enlarge the learner's conceptual understanding of mathematical functions. Put another way, students not only need to master the use of mathematical tools, they must also learn how the tools work and when and where they are applicable.

Vincent J. Glennon

Mathematics: How Firm the Foundations?

Parents' interest in mathematics in the elementary school is second only to their concern for reading. How good is our math program? Are we teaching the new math? Are we getting back to the basics? Are we preparing for high school? For life situations?

Answers to these deceptively simple questions have not come easily in recent years. The math revolution of the past quarter century has been characterized by a kaleidoscope of change in many educationally significant variables which affect why Johnny can or cannot add. Shifting emphases in theories of curriculum are primary, but change is also occurring in theories of methodology, motivation, classroom organization, cognitive development, and learning generally. Acting singly and in combinations, these shifts change the programs of classrooms, schools, and school systems, and hence determine how much Johnny does in fact learn, retain, and transfer.

Beginning in 1958–1959, the new math moved into high gear. A concerted effort began to shift the theory of curriculum upon which the programs of the 1930s to the 1950s were based—a mixture of mathematically meaningful and socially relevant theories—to a theory which gave priority to the logical structure of mathematics. By the mid-sixties, many different modern math programs were in wide use. Each stressed to varying degrees a more formal development than earlier programs.

This increased emphasis on mathematics *as mathematics* concerned many who feared a concomitant lessening of emphasis on other aspects of the program. Their concern was in some instances well founded. For example, on the computation sections of standardized achievement tests, scores derived in a typical city or town were generally lower than scores on the concepts and problem-solving sections. Also, mean test scores on the mathematics part of the Scholastic Apitude Test taken by many high school students have fallen steadily from 502 (on a range of 200 to 800) in 1962–1963 to 472 in 1974–1975. Obviously, the causes of these two situations are not single and simple but subtle and complex.

Reprinted from Vincent J. Glennon, "Mathematics: How Firm the Foundations?" *Phi Delta Kappan,* January 1976, pp. 302–305; by permission of the publisher.

144

Morris Kline attributes the decline in computation scores to the new math programs of the 1960s(*1*). This is an oversimplification and reflects a failure to take account of the many variables (sets of theories) mentioned above which impinge upon the learning, retention, and transfer of learning in mathematics.

In almost every mathematics program, it became quickly apparent that the rigor, the formalism, the reading level, and the great number of separate lessons (as many as 400 in, say, a fifth-grade book) raised the difficulty level to the point where only the top third of the children seemed to cope successfully.

Among psychologists, Benjamin Bloom expressed the concern this way: "There seems to be little reason to make learning so difficult that only a small proportion of the students can persevere to mastery."(*2*). And David Ausubel stated that "much of children's alienation from school is a reflection of the cumulative effects of a curriculum that is too demanding" (*3*).

Among mathematicians, Carroll V. Newsom came to the same conclusion that many teachers had already made when he said, "I must confess an early satisfaction [with the new elementary mathematics curricula]. Now, however, we are learning that good mathematicians had too free a hand in the development of the programs"(*4*). And Henry VanEngen commented, "Most certainly there is reason to question the degree of formalism that is creeping into the elementary school [mathematics program]. Furthermore, the rapid pace of the more usual programs is questionable"(*5*).

The School Mathematics Study Group (SMSG), so very influential in the 1960s, reported in its evaluation of modern math textbook programs that

> not all modern textbooks produced the kind of results that were expected for them. Some in fact did rather poorly on *all* [cognitive] levels—from computation to analysis. These textbooks which did not do very well were for the most part considerably more formal and more rigorous than the SMSG books(*6*).

SOME RECENT EVIDENCE

While the above statements are in some instances judgmental, all are based on quantitative data and/or well-informed backgrounds. Of greatest interest in recent months have been the hard data revealed in the first report of the National Assessment of Educational Progress (NAEP) on mathematical achievement. The NAEP surveyed the attainments of 9-year-olds, 13-year-olds, 17-year-olds, and young adults (ages 26–33). Some of the findings are:

1. Only 40 percent of the 9-year-olds could do this addition correctly

$$\begin{array}{r} \$\ 3.09 \\ 10.00 \\ 9.14 \\ \underline{5.10} \end{array}$$

2. Only 33 percent of the 13-year-olds could find the answer to the problem: "If John drives at an average speed of 50 miles per hour, how many hours will it take to drive 275 miles?"

3. Only 10 percent of the 17-year-olds could correctly calculate a taxi fare.

4. Only 1 percent of the 17-year-olds could balance a checkbook.

As represented by these NAEP findings, the foundations of school mathematics would seem a bit shaky.

Virginia H. Knauer, director of the Office of Consumer Affairs, reacted to the findings of the report: "This report brings home the hard fact that consumers do not have the math skills necessary to solve the day-to-day problems we face in today's economy. Yet the importance of developing these skills is indisputable"(7).

THE "BACK-TO-THE-BASICS" TREND

During the 1960s one could hardly pick up an editorial, slick magazine, or Sunday supplement without finding articles on the new math written by persons of widely varying interests, ranging from those genuinely concerned with finding a better balanced program to faddists and opportunists. Today we rarely find such articles. Instead, we have a new spate of articles with the same range of scholarship represented by the writers in earlier years, but this time calling for a return to the basics.

For some, this trend means a shift away from the curriculum theory which supports the new math (i.e., heavy emphasis on logical structure) and toward a sociological theory which places major emphasis on socially useful mathematics. For others, a return to the basics means a shift away from the psychological, or needs-of-the-child, theory as evidenced in some informal or open classrooms and toward the socially useful or career education-oriented programs. In both trends the "back-to-the-basics" movement urges school personnel to find more time and better methods for mastering the common skills and abilities used in everyday computative and quantitative thinking situations.

To educators who know the history of mathematics education in this century, this new trend must recall Mark Twain's comment on New England weather: "If you don't like it, wait a few minutes." The back-to-the-basics trend had great visibility as a result of the World War II GI testing program, accompanied by the condemnation of the schools in the writings of some military personnel (most notably Admiral Hyman Rickover) and the work of the Council for Basic Education. The same concerns were evinced a decade or two earlier in the form of "100 percent mastery of adult socially useful arithmetic" under the leadership of Guy M. Wilson(8). In those years of progressive education and the Great Depression, a curriculum which stressed utilitarianism seemed consistent with the instrumentalism of John Dewey's philosophy of education in a democracy(9).

This constant change in emphasis in curriculum theories (from psychological to sociological to logical structure) makes it difficult to evaluate any overall curriculum progress. Joseph Featherstone recently commented on this situation:

> In one sense, it seems discouraging that our efforts to improve practice have not gone beyond the formulations of the Progressives. The general lack of cumulative development makes a good deal of our educational reform seem terribly faddish. In what I sometimes think of as the United States of Amnesia, we keep rehearsing the dilemmas of the past, and I suppose we will continue to start from scratch each generation until we develop a sixth sense of the past to add to our other five senses (10).

Perhaps the most recent application of this "back-to-the-basics" trend is the recent widely publicized *Project One* of the Education Development Center (EDC)(11). In the past decade, EDC has become known in mathematics for its development and distribution of teaching materials and films which adhere closely to a curriculum philosophy stressing the logical structure, the formalism of the subject. Now, under a USOE grant exceeding $4 million and with additional foundation funds, EDC is developing a series of sixty-five half-hour television shows aimed predominantly at minority children ages 8 through 11. The philosophy of curriculum upon which the program is based is very similar to Guy M. Wilson's utilitarianism of the 1920s to 1940s, mentioned above, although some of the specific topics differ from Wilson's. *Project One,* seeking to strengthen the knowledge of math foundations among its target population, has listed the following goals as the "basic literacy" of mathematics along with "problem-solving methods"(12).

1. Counting and ordering; the number system, decimal notation and powers of 10; very large and very small numbers, such as 6×10^6 and 6×10^{-6}. Arithmetic with small integers, such as 5×6. Approximate arithmetic, such as $31 \times 49 \cong 1,500$. (We do not include, for example, set theory, number systems other than base 10, arithmetic with elaborate fractions . . . , or long division.)
2. The concept of measurement; i.e., the description of real objects and situations. Units of measurement.
3. The ability to make reasonable, off-the-cuff estimates, e.g., of size, place, time, and quantity. (This is important to a casual, intuitive use of mathematics.)

4. The concept of size-scaling and mapping; the underlying concept of ratio.

5. Graphs in one dimension (number lines), and in two dimensions (crossed number lines).

The cumulative impact of career-oriented education for "basic literacy" and the "back-to-the-basics" trend on the future mathematics program of the elementary and middle schools remains to be seen.

THE INFLUENCE OF JEAN PIAGET

During the most intense years of the mathematics revolution, 1952–1965, the mathematicians who led the movement paid little heed to either the sociological or the psychological rationale for curriculum building. Apparently, logical structure *alone* was a sufficient basis for deciding what mathematics was of most worth. Eminent cognitive/developmental psychologists such as William A. Brownell(13) in this country and Jean Piaget in Switzerland were like voices crying in the wilderness, despite the fact that they had earlier produced major theories and research on cognitive development.

Here we are concerned, albeit too briefly, with the implications, if any, of Piaget's psychology (genetic epistemology) for the school mathematics program. While it is too early to make any strong statement on how it will affect the firmness of the foundations in the future, a substantial amount of research and opinion has appeared in the literature which *may* have implications for future directions.

Both Piagetian epistemology and progressive education grew out of the same basic assumption: that man, properly conceived, is spontaneously active and goal seeking rather than passive and receiving. This basic assumption has implications for both the learning environment of the child and the principles and methods of the teacher.

Willis Overton studied the interrelationship of these two systems of ideas and concluded that

curriculum development should consist of a progressive organization of subject matter involving the matching of particular content to the thought structures of the child at each stage of development. . . . Through his numerous works on specific content such as classification, space, geometry, and number, Piaget also provides valuable suggestions for the substantive implementation of such a child-oriented curriculum(14).

And for the teacher, Overton suggests that

Piaget's functional position contributes primarily to educational foundations and methods. . . . The detailed analysis of the nature of the activities involved in adaptation stresses the significance of discovery-oriented methods

148

in which the teacher actively participates by presenting appropriate materials and setting appropriate problems over methods of rote drill, training, or enriched environments.

However, Hermine Sinclair, an established member of the "Geneva Group," does not believe it to be a sound educational practice to "teach" Piagetian tasks or problems in the classroom.

> There seems to be a regrettable tendency to take Piaget's problem situations and convert them directly into teaching situations . . . . A child's reactions to a few Piagetian tasks will enable a well-trained psychologist to give a fair description of a child's intellectual level; but teaching the solutions of these same Piagetian tasks to a group of children does not mean that the children will thereby attain the general intellectual level of the child who can solve the tasks independently(15).

And Harry Beilin denies the importance of the very basic assumption of the need for activity-oriented experiences as necessary for the growth of logical thinking: "The idea that the child has to be active in contrived situations involving conflict to acquire logical reasoning is not substantiated by the available research. Neither active problem-creating conditions nor conflict-creating situations are necessary for logical thinking to be acquired"(16).

Just how essential is the Piagetian idea of, say, conservation of number to establishing a firm foundation in arithmetic? B. D. Mpiangu and J. R. Gentile in a recent research study(17), investigated Piaget's thesis that "conservation is a necessary condition for all rational activity . . . [and] arithmetical thought is no exception to the rule"(18).

The results of their well-designed study constitute evidence that the Piaget thesis above is false. Mpiangu and Gentile conclude that, rather than think of conservation as being crucial to good learning, "It would be more profitable to consider arithmetic and conservation of number as conceptualizations that develop simultaneously. Conservation of numbers . . . has little practical use in school."

In the light of presently available information, of which the above is a very small part, school personnel would be well advised to refrain from a headlong rush into a Piaget-based mathematics program if their purpose is to strengthen the existing foundations (see reference 19)

ON CONSOLIDATING THE FOUNDATIONS

Well-designed programs of preservice teacher education of the 1930s to early 1950s included specific training in how to teach a drill lesson, later called a practice lesson. In learning theory, practice is known as overlearning, and in our time it is usually referred to as consolidation of learning.

The major books on pedagogy of the 1930s to 1950s, most notably William H. Burton's *The Guidance of Learning Activities,* clearly identified the psychological principles of teaching essential to the consolidation of "mental skills." Perhaps because drill was misused and abused under Thorndikian connectionist psychology of the 1920s and 1930s, and hence rejected by the Progressives as contrary to sound child development, it lost its rightful place in the teacher's repertoire. It is a rare teacher trainee today who understands and practices well the psychological principles essential for the efficient consolidation of learning. And learning that is not consolidated cannot be well retained or transferred to new, related learning situations.

Yet the role of consolidation experiences is just as essential in the cognitive domain as it is in the psychomotor domain for the development of a Jack Nicklaus in golf or a Chris Evert in tennis. Until such time as the function of the brain chemistry in the storage and retrieval processes is better understood and controlled, in what David Krech refers to as the future science of education—psychoneurobiochemeducation(*20*)—it will still be necessary to firm up the foundations with appropriate consolidation activities. Conceptualization without consolidation is not enough. Maintaining a balance is most essential (see reference *21*).

The National Council of Teachers of Mathematics, recognizing this imperative need, recently authorized the preparation and publication of a yearbook on the theme, *Computation and Practice.* If implemented in classrooms, it should contribute to strengthening the foundations.

DOES INDIVIDUALIZING HELP?

The term "individualizing," like "charity," "justice," and "freedom," seems to refer to a concept that must be a good in itself, in need of no justification. In school programs, nothing could be further from the truth. Individualizing instruction, through whatever program, is far from being established as a good. On the contrary, it is in great need of justification, if that is ever possible.

Programs of individualized instruction, or programmed learning materials whether commercially produced or teacher made, may be contributing to the weaknesses of our educational foundations, broadly conceived. In the language arts, for instance, James Moffett notes that "programmed learning is isolated rather than individualized learning and hence utterly lacks the *interaction* so vital to learning language"(*22*).

In mathematics, Joseph Lipson, a developer of the IPI (Individually Prescribed Instruction) Mathematics Program, recently expressed his belief that "the program did *not* produce the dramatic gains that had been hoped for . . . because the program, and many like it, was built on false assumptions"(*23*).

And Eugene P. Smith, in his role as president of the National Council of Teachers of Mathematics in 1973, expressed his concern: "I do deplore the wholesale imposition of the technique (of individualized instruction) on teachers and students with the tacit assumption that the method is superior to any method they have used before. The evidence does not support the assumption"(24).

Most significantly, at the 1975 Annual Meeting of the National Council of Teachers of Mathematics, the Delegate Assembly *recommended* for consideration by the Executive Board the following resolution:

> That the NCTM should recognize the magnitude of the problems arising from the widespread and often precipitous adoption of programs described as "individualized instruction" in school mathematics by undertaking, without delay, a short-term study of such programs, with results to be published as soon as possible.

Obviously, this resolution shows a substantial concern for the quality of such programs.

DOES ABILITY GROUPING HELP?

In one of the best-designed research studies on the subject of grouping children for instructional purposes, Miriam Goldberg et al. demonstrated that ". . . ability grouping, by *itself,* has no important effect on the academic achievement of students . . . . It is . . . *what* we teach that matters, not . . . how we sort out the students. It is on the differentiation and appropriate selection of content and method of teaching that the emphasis must be placed"(25).

Logically, then, if we wish to firm up the foundations, no *single* mathematics program will fit children of all abilities. Moreover, no *single* mathematics program will fit all handicapped children—the mentally retarded, the emotionally disturbed, the sensory deprived, and those with specific learning disabilities.

A FINAL WORD

I believe that in the years immediately ahead we can stop reinventing the wheel and stop repeating the mistakes of our past. In tomorrow's school math program we will, I hope, find continued emphasis on sequential, systematic, and structured teaching using a variety of programs, working in settings of individualizing through small-group instruction in a socioemotional climate reflecting the new humanism.

References

1. Morris Kline, *Why Johnny Can't Add* (New York: St. Martin's Press, 1973).
2. Benjamin S. Bloom, "Learning for Mastery," *University of California Evaluation Comment,* vol. 1, 1968, pp. 1–12.
3. David P. Ausubel, *Urban Education,* vol. 1, 1964, pp. 16–38.
4. Carroll V. Newsom, "The Image of the Mathematician," *American Mathematical Monthly,* vol. 79, 1972, pp. 878–82.
5. Henry VanEngen, "The Next Decade," *The Arithmetic Teacher,* vol. 19, 1972, pp. 615, 616.
6. E. Begle and J. Wilson, eds., "Evaluation of Mathematics Programs," *Mathematics Education* (Chicago: University of Chicago Press, 1970).
7. *National Assessment of Educational Progress: Math Fundamentals* (Washington, D.C.: U.S. Government Printing Office, 1975).
8. Guy M. Wilson, *Teaching the New Arithmetic* (New York: McGraw-Hill, 1951).
9. John Dewey, *Democracy and Education* (New York: The Free Press, 1930).
10. Joseph Featherstone, "Notes on Educational Practice," *Harvard Graduate School of Education Association Bulletin,* Spring–Summer, 1975, pp. 2–5.
11. See, for instance, Mitchell Lazarus, "Rx for Mathophobia," *Saturday Review,* June, 1975, pp. 46–48.
12. "EDC's New Program in Mathematics: Purposes and Goals," *National Elementary Principal,* January–February, 1974.
13. J. Fred Weaver and Jeremy Kilpatrick, eds., *Selected Theoretical Papers of William A. Brownell* and *Selected Research Papers of William A. Brownell* (Pasadena, Calif.: A. C. Vroman, Inc., 1972).
14. Willis F. Overton, "Piaget's Theory of Intellectual Development and Progressive Education," *A New Look at Progressive Education* (Washington, D.C.: Association for Supervision and Curriculum Development, 1973).
15. Hermine Sinclair, "Piaget's Theory of Development: The Main Stages," *Piagetian Cognitive Development and Mathematical Education* (Reston, Va.: National Council of Teachers of Mathematics, 1971).
16. Harry Beilin, "The Training and Acquisition of Logical Operations," *Piagetian Cognitive Development and Mathematical Education* (Reston, Va.: National Council of Teachers of Mathematics, 1971).
17. B. D. Mpiangu and J. R. Gentile, "Is Conservation of Number a Necessary Condition for Mathematical Understanding?" *Journal for Research in Mathematics Education,* May, 1975, pp. 179–91.
18. Jean Piaget, *The Child's Conception of Number* (London: Routledge & Kegan Paul, 1964).
19. James E. Inskeep, Jr., "Building a Case for the Application of Piaget's Theory and Research in the Classroom," *The Arithmetic Teacher,* April, 1972, pp. 255–62; J. Fred Weaver, "Some Concerns About the Application of Piaget's Theory and Research to Mathematical Learning and Instruction," *The Arithmetic Teacher,* April, 1972, pp. 263–69.

152

20. David Krech, "Psychoneurobiochemeducation," *Phi Delta Kappan,* March, 1969, p. 370.

21. William A. Brownell, "Meaning and Skill: Maintaining the Balance," *The Arithmetic Teacher,* October, 1956, pp. 129–36.

22. James Moffett, *A Student-Centered Language Arts Curriculum—Grades K–13: A Handbook for Teachers* (Boston: Houghton Mifflin, 1973).

23. Joseph I. Lipson, "I.P.I. Math—An Example of What's Right and Wrong with Individualized Modular Programs," *Learning,* March, 1974, p. 60.

24. Eugene P. Smith, "A Look at Mathematics Education Today," *The Arithmetic Teacher,* vol. 20, 1973, pp. 503–8.

25. Miriam Goldberg, A. Harry Passow, and Joseph Justman, *The Effects of Ability Grouping* (New York: Teachers College Press, 1966).

Operational Concepts

1. Scholastic aptitude test scores in mathematics have fallen consistently from 1962 through 1975.

2. A recent National Assessment of Educational Progress Study suggests that many students lack the mathematical skills essential to the solving of day-to-day problems.

3. Piagetian-based mathematics, although useful in other ways, does not appear to contribute significantly to the mastery of basic mathematics skills.

4. The mathematical reforms of the 1960s were aimed at a conceptual understanding of logical structure. Proportionately less attention was given to the sociological and psychological dimensions of mathematics learning. In view of current achievement scores on standardized tests, a rebalancing in emphasis may be in order.

Implications

As interest in career-oriented education and basic social literacy mounts, a "back-to-basics" trend has occurred. The effect of this trend on future mathematics instruction is not entirely certain, but it is probable that somewhat less emphasis will be placed upon conceptual understanding, and comparatively greater emphasis will be placed upon functional mathematical skills. Perceptualization, we now seem to believe, is not enough: a repertory of applicable skills is equally essential to a good general education.

It has become apparent, moreover, that cognitive consolidation experiences (practice and drill) are as necessary in the effective learning of mathematics as in any other skill. Consequently, subsequent curricular revisions are likely to aim toward a better blend of theoretical understanding and practical utility.

As in any other readjustment intended to realign excesses, the danger is that through misplaced zeal one kind of imbalance will be replaced with another. The major need of the moment, therefore, is to fabricate instructional programs that provide the learner with an appropriate blend of technical skill and intellectual awareness.

Social Studies

Shirley H. Engle

Exploring the Meaning of the Social Studies

DEVELOPMENT OF THE CONCEPT "SOCIAL STUDIES"

The term "social studies" has now persisted in our language for over fifty years. It was first used in an official or public sense as the name of a committee, the Committee on Social Studies, which was part of the Commission on the Reorganization of Secondary Education appointed by the National Education Association in 1913. This committee, composed of twenty-one persons, mostly high school teachers and administrators, was chaired by a sociologist, Thomas Jesse Jones, and had as dominant members James Harvey Robinson, a noted historian, and Arthur William Dunn, a specialist on Civic Education in the United States Bureau of Education. The report of the committee, which was published in 1916 as a Bulletin of the Bureau of Education of the Department of the Interior, set the general direction of social studies education from that time to the present day(1).

The committee declared that the conscious and constant purpose of the social studies is the cultivation of good citizenship. The committee further declared the good citizen to be one who appreciates the nature and laws of social life, one who has an intelligent and genuine loyalty to high national ideals, one who has a sense of the responsibility of the individual as a member of social groups, one who is characterized by a loyalty and a sense of obligation to his city, state, nation and to the human race, and one who has the intelligence and the will to participate effectively in the promotion of the social well-being. The committee defined the social studies as all subject matter relating directly to the organization and development of human society and to man as a member of social groups.

The committee refrained from offering detailed content outlines, and

Reprinted from Shirley H. Engle, "Exploring the Meaning of the Social Studies," *Social Education*, March 1971, pp. 280–288, 344; reprinted with permission of the National Council for the Social Studies and Shirley H. Engle.

declared that the selection of topics and the organization of subject matter should be determined in each case by immediate needs.

Heavily influenced by the teaching of John Dewey, the committee opted for the principles of immediacy and utility in the instruction of the citizen over that of the teaching of formal disciplines. Decrying the notion that everything that is taught is learned, they quoted John Dewey as saying(2):

> We are continually uneasy about the things we adults know, and are afraid the child will never learn them unless they are drilled into him by instruction before he has any intellectual use for them. If we could really believe that attending to the needs of present youth would also provide the best possible guarantee of the learning needed in the future, transformation of educational ideals might soon be accomplished, and other desirable changes would largely take care of themselves.

In this vein, the committee report was clearly a manifesto of freedom from the control of college-entrance requirements and college and university scholars over the curriculum of the school. The social studies were to be directed to the education of all citizens, and not just to a cultivated elite. The social studies were to be especially tailored with the general education of all citizens in mind, and immediate need and utility were to be the guiding principles. The committee saw that there was more to the education of a citizen than merely the mastery of particular subject matter, and attached little importance to so many hours of this and so many hours of that in the education of citizens. It called upon the social scientists to stop contending over the extent to which each social science discipline was to be included in the curriculum and to unite among themselves to determine how all such subjects could be made to contribute most effectively to the purposes of secondary education.

In the end, however, the committee proposed a general outline of social studies for the secondary schools which has been widely followed to this very day. The cycling of geography, European history, American history, and civics in the junior high school years and the recycling of European (now world) history, American history, and problems of democracy in the senior high school, suggested by the committee, is all too familiar to most of us.

The high resolve of the committee to develop new programs in social studies that would focus directly on the development of good citizenship fell victim to the traditional belief that knowledge, as derived from the social science disciplines, was the road to good citizenship. Only the most daring departed from the safe haven of history. Thus, the committee, in effect, fastened on the social studies noble and distinctive purposes trapped in the rigidity of the subjects.

In 1899, the American Historical Association issued the first of a series of reports on the Study of History in Schools. Between 1916 and 1926, the American Political Science Association and the American Sociological Society, partly out of fear that their disciplines were being short-changed in the schools, set up committees and issued reports on the teaching of these subjects in the elementary and secondary schools. In 1921, a small group of professors concerned with teacher education founded the National Council for the Social Studies, which became the special "pleader," as it has remained to this day, for the social studies in the schools. Finally, in 1929, the American Historical Association established the first interdisciplinary Commission on the Social Studies. Between 1932 and 1941, this commission published a seventeen-volume report covering a wide range of problems relating to citizenship education and the social sciences but skirting the question of the content necessary to attain the objectives of citizenship education. From the scholarly standpoint, the commission membership was impeccably correct. It included the names of some of the most eminent historians, economists, political scientists, sociologists, geographers, school and university administrators, and educators of that day. Among them towered the figure of Charles A. Beard, who drafted much of the report. A significant result of the commission's report was the sanctioning, by an eminent group of scholars, of the term "social studies." A still more important result was the reiteration of the goal of social studies as being that of citizenship education, and the broad definition of this goal as including not only the transmission of the requirements of scholarship but also the comprehension of the social realities of the times and the climate of American ideals(3). Both the commission and the earlier committee understood that there was more to citizenship education than merely the mastery of subjects—history, economics, government, and the like—but it was not clearly understood then or even now what that something else was to be.

SOCIAL SCIENCE AND SOCIAL STUDIES

The commission and the earlier committee visualized the good citizen as having certain desirable attributes. He should look at things with a democratic slant; he should believe in decency and fair play, forbearance and respect for others; he should acquire the customs, traditions, and nationalistic ideals of his country; he should believe in the idea of progressive improvement of society; he should desire to promote the general welfare and be pledged to raise and safeguard standards of living for all; he should believe in universal education; and so forth(4). These attributes of the good citizen, paraphrased from "A Charter for the Social Sciences," Part I of the Report of the Commission on the Social Studies, clearly raise ethical, moral, and philosophical questions which fall well outside of the scope of the strict social science. If these are attributes of the good citizen, if social studies is supposed to develop such attributes, and if social sciences are indeed sciences, then social studies is a broader field than that covered by the social sciences. It is more accurate to think of the social studies as an applied field which attempts to fuse scientific knowledge with ethical, philosophical, religious, and social considerations which arise in the process of decision making as practiced by the citizen.

We, of the profession, have not immediately and clearly grasped this distinction between social science and social studies. We have devoted our major energies, including our efforts in the "new" social studies, to making the social sciences alone suffice for the broader needs of citizenship education. In this vein, we have tried to organize the teaching of the social sciences in all kinds of orders, sequences, and cycles; we have tried to organize teaching around concepts, generalizations, problems, and values; we have tried fusion, integration, and correlation of the social science disciplines; we have tried cases, projects, and contracts as organizing principles; we have prettied up our textbooks with maps, pictures, diagrams, graphs, charts, and a dozen other paraphernalia; we have thrown in audiovisual aids; we have "Brunerized" the subjects and made inquiry our god. These attempts to fit square pegs into round holes have never been entirely successful. It should be apparent that the social science disciplines, by themselves, do not constitute the whole of citizenship education. The effort to force citizenship education into a strict social science mold either does violence to social science, asking more of it than it has to offer, or it neglects the ethical component of citizenship altogether.

Because we continue to profess a goal inconsonant with the means we adopt, all efforts to define and give sanction to the term "social studies," following those of the committee and the commission, have ended in failure. The so-called "new" social studies of the 1960s, while laudably embracing the principle of inquiry over that of rote memory in teaching the social sciences, has largely skirted or ignored the question of the ethical component of citizenship education.

The social studies enterprise has never clearly decided whether it is primarily engaged in describing and explaining the society, which is the concern of the social sciences, or whether it is primarily engaged in transmitting and forming the values of citizens, which is the concern of ethics, philosophy, and religion. Since values are so clearly involved in citizenship formation, it is difficult to see how we can continue to turn our backs on the value component of citizenship education. Indeed, if it turns out that both scientific and ethical considerations are essentials for the development of good citizens, then it is high time that social studies turn its attention to the problem of how the realms of science and morality can be made to complement one another.

Nor should we compound our confusion in this matter by ambivalence as to what constitutes good citizenship. Is good citizenship a set of fixed attributes to be transmitted, that is, is the development of good citizenship a matter of prescription and the propagandizing of youth, or is it primarily

159

an intellectual task? Furthermore, if it is an intellectual task, is this task primarily one of mastering subject matter or the acquisition of certain intellectual skills, habits, and dispositions? These are tough questions, which the profession has never clearly answered and which it cannot, in good conscience, continue to avoid.

It may be useful to inquire at this point whether the social studies have been used in the past as a propaganda agent or, rather, as the means of developing critical intelligence. As the commission suggested(5), we have generously used the social studies to advocate a particular view of American life. Our purpose has been to unite and nationalize a people around certain preferred values. Under the guise of teaching history, government, economics, and the like, we have actually taught an incomplete, over-simplistic and in some respects mythological version of America. In describing American life, we have tended to emphasize national unity over conflict and dissension, a national character over cultural pluralism, general welfare over genuine and irresolvable conflict of interest, freedom and opportunity over the plight of minorities too weak to get a hearing at the bar of history, the inevitability of progress under the free enterprise system over deep-seated ills and problems which beset our society. We have given one simplified version, the correct or official version of affairs, ignoring that the scholars are deeply divided and continually at odds about interpretation of American affairs(6). Further, we have taught citizenship differently to different social groups, emphasizing obedience and conformity to the underprivileged while emphasizing use of power among the elite(7).

In contrast to social science, we have used social studies to advocate public policies that are deemed desirable at a particular time; likewise, the social studies have been used to oppose policies deemed undesirable. The social studies tended to support war aims during World War I. Current events courses were established to clarify these war aims, which were to make the world safe for democracy, and were thus deemed laudable and necessary. The social studies cooperated in the effort to gain support for the League of Nations. The social studies tended to support the numerous nationwide efforts during the depression to lift the country back onto the road of economic prosperity. Prior to World War II, the social studies responded to the growing threat of Communism and Fascism by stepping up the teaching of democratic principles; later we stepped up our friendly treatment of Russia when she became our ally. As American interests have grown in the Far East and the Middle East, we have increased our treatment of non-Western studies(8).

To point out these characteristics of social studies is not to criticize the enterprise for getting involved in the ethics of individual character and public policy. Intelligent and socially responsible involvement is the ultimate goal of citizenship education. Advocacy and commitment for good reason is to be cultivated rather than avoided. But this is a different role from that of social science, which is presumably value free, seeking to understand, describe, and explain the passing human scene without sitting in judgment on it. To quote Charles A. Beard in *A Charter for the Social Sciences*, "Insofar as social science is truly scientific, it is neutral; as taught in schools it is and must be ethical; it must take choices and emphasize values with reference to commanding standards"(9).

The error is in confusing the two kinds of activity. We confuse analysis and explanation on one hand with advocacy on the other. As a result, we frequently palm off factual description of states of affairs as if they constituted moral judgment. The going state of affairs in economics, or government, or social arrangement is described and accepted unknowingly as the necessary and therefore the good state of affairs. This is a perversion of the use of science to maintain the status quo. By avoiding the ethical questions which could be raised, and by refusing to speculate about future states to which human beings could conceivably aspire, the social studies tend to conserve rather than to participate in the reform of society. A social studies enterprise which ignores or glosses over this distinction does a disservice to both science and morality. The most important lesson we can teach our students is to make the distinction between fact and opinion, analysis and advocacy. Social studies would do well to recognize, embrace, and emphasize its ethical component, exposing this side of its character to the same critical analysis to which it presumedly exposes the more factual, scientific side.

More clarity and light would be thrown on the relationship between the social studies enterprise and the social science enterprise by asking how they are different than by merely saying that social studies is based on social sciences, or that the social studies are the social sciences simplified for pedagogical purposes(10). In contrast, it can be demonstrated that the two enterprises are very different but complementary enterprises with different goals, different content, and different methodologies.

The goal of social science is the discovery of knowledge describing and explaining human phenomena. Social scientists are engaged, primarily, in the search for new knowledge and the continual reexamination of human affairs from the new knowledge base. The aim of social science is to establish general laws of human society which may be used to explain and predict human behavior. Although the search is for orderliness, there is, presently, no agreement among social scientists as to what that order is. Prediction in social science is, at best, hazardous. As a result, the social sciences embrace many competing theories, each with some support in logic and empirical data but none, as yet, with a sure footing in facts. We have "new" historians and "progressive" historians and "consensus" historians and now "revisionist" historians. Keynesian economic theory replaces or modifies classical economic theory. Interactive geography supersedes geographic determinism. "Behaviorist" political scientists contend with "institutional" and "legalistic" political scientists, etc.

In searching for new knowledge, the social scientist follows any theoretical lead which holds out promise of insight into human affairs. There need not be any immediate, practical use for the knowledge sought. Because of its highly tenuous nature, social science tends to divide and proliferate, and new fields of inquiry are continually being developed, each with its own specialists who follow their line of inquiry to great depth. Specialization may even reach the point where an expert in one social science field cannot communicate readily concerning his specialization with an expert in another social science field.

Social science avoids closure, holds all findings tentatively until a new theoretical and factual assault can be launched against them. Social scientists pride themselves on objectivity, do not engage in advocacy, and view the human scene with an unbiased eye. They may describe values but they do not, as social scientists, engage in valuation.

In contrast to social science, the goal of social studies is the development of good citizens. The primary concern of social studies is the utilization of knowledge. The aim is to improve the process by which citizens use knowledge from the social sciences *and other sources* in making decisions concerning their individual behavior, and concerning questions of public policy.

While the social sciences deliberately delay closure, the social studies must help the citizen to bring public and private questions to some kind of closure. Decisions cannot wait until all the facts are in. Decisions must be made on the basis of the best possible evidence available or determinable at a particular time. The citizen must decide what information is relevant to the problem at hand. He must know how to find the information necessary to the decision. He must be familiar with the common categories under which social scientific and other information is classified. He needs to have mastered some of the less sophisticated tools used by social scientists and others in collecting and organizing information. Possession of facts already discovered by social scientists is, of course, useful to the citizen, but access to the systems by which such facts are stored and organized would be a higher priority. To know all is impossible for citizens, even as it is for scientists.

The social studies enterprise is further distinguished from the social science enterprise by its concern for valuation. Practical decisions always involve valuations. Socially responsible decision making requires the same care in grounding values as that taken in grounding facts. The values involved in a decision may be tested against facts, that is: Does the consequence claimed for the value actually follow from that value? Values may be compared for consistency with other values and with higher or more general values. In turn, more general values can be investigated for consistency with facts, etc. Social science information and modes of inquiry may be useful in the factual investigation of values, but social science does not tell us what to value, nor can it do so. The citizen's act of decision making requires a synthesis of fact and valuation. With respect to valuation, the citizen is not bound by social science, which prides itself on being value free, impartial, objective, descriptive merely of the passing human scene but never sitting in judgment on it. As an individual citizen, the social scientist may behave as any other citizen would behave, albeit more skillfully, synthesizing valuation with facts, but he does so as a citizen and not as a social scientist. As a social scientist, he is neutral, uncommitted to any value save that of complete objectivity.

Further, the problems which citizens face, and the decisions which they must make in real life, are usually global problems and global decisions. Global problems are always complex problems, cutting across subject matter lines, involving both beliefs about fact and beliefs about values. Global problems are never resolved merely by marshalling the facts or within the confines of a single discipline. The facts about pollution in this country are well-known and are becoming more so every day. The hang-up over pollution is basically one of the proper allocation of values. For example, certain of our valuations, such as the belief in individual freedom or the free enterprise system, are on a collision course with other valuations, such as the belief in one's right to live a long and healthful life or the belief in one's right to enjoy and have access to natural beauty. The social and also the biological sciences can help us to narrow and define the value problem but it is conceivable that the individual or the group might choose free enterprise and a shorter life span over regulated enjoyment of long life and natural beauty. It is also possible that some new value which merges the alternatives might be worked out.

The social scientist has never claimed citizenship education as his goal. To quote Pendleton Herring(11), himself a social scientist, on this matter:

> The problem of method in the social sciences . . . is best understood in relation to purpose. The more scientific the bent of the investigator, the less he is concerned with overall social problems or broad dilemmas that invite speculative thinking. His quest is for the concrete, the observable, the measurable, the definable.

Herring continues, "The social sciences are not the rival, but rather the auxiliary, of moral purpose and of normal judgment!" And again, "Social science research can limit the scope for guessing and for uninformed speculation." And finally:

> Social science knowledge can contribute, in some measure, toward the realization of the goals of government or religion or industry, but it cannot function as a rival or a substitute. Should Social Science be conceived in such terms, it would cease to be science, and should social scientists contrive to such ends, they would find themselves becoming politicians, theologians, or entrepreneurs.

Social scientists may claim, as Berelson does in the Introduction to the book, *The Social Studies and the Social Sciences(12)*, that social science is the best available knowledge upon which to base citizenship education. Berelson, however, does not make the claim that the social sciences are a sufficient or even necessary basis of good citizenship(13). There are many good citizens and many good politicians who have never formally studied the social sciences. Alternative routes to good citizenship do, therefore, exist. We should show more respect for the integrity of social science and cease asking of it more than it has to offer.

THE NATURE OF THE SOCIAL STUDIES

If the social studies are not merely the social sciences simplified for pedagogical purposes, what, then, is the nature of the social studies? Perhaps greater clarity can be thrown on this matter by considering the following questions. First, what are we to take as given (or what do we take for granted) in the social studies enterprise? Secondly, what does a citizen do? Thirdly, from what sources does the citizen get the beliefs which he uses in making practical decisions? Fourthly, how is formal education usefully related to the total learning process of the citizen? Lastly, what are the parameters of a necessary and sufficient social studies program?

What are we to take as given in the social studies enterprise? There *are* alternatives at this point. We either believe in a method of intelligence, or we do not. If we accept the scientific method and the democratic ideology, which is taken as basic in this analysis, then we must cease demonstrating ambivalence toward intellectualism, now rewarding, then punishing students for intelligent and socially responsible behavior. Unfortunately, social studies as frequently taught today bears a closer resemblance to propaganda and fiction than to fact(14). Schools, as they exist, frequently bear a closer resemblance to autocracies than to democracies(15). In a climate ambivalent to intellectualism, social sciences and scientific methodology are reduced to impotence, and the social studies enterprise becomes utterly chaotic. To say it another way, we are either committed to free inquiry or we are not.

On these axiomatic matters underlying what constitutes the good citizen and how he is nurtured, there should be no equivocation in the profession. These are difficult times which call for resolute and certain action. Student unrest should not be allowed to rattle us into abandoning our belief in intelligence, but should be seized upon as the harbinger of social concern. Crime in the streets, which no one takes lightly, should not blur our vision concerning justice. The drug society, which threatens to engulf us, should be seen not as a cause but as a symptom of serious ills that only deep-going social reform will heal.

What does the citizen do? If we take the democratic ideology as given,

164

the citizen is called upon to make myriad decisions, large and small, concerning social goals and the means of their attainment, as well as decisions with respect to his own personal behavior in these matters. He makes these decisions on the basis of his beliefs.

His beliefs are of two kinds. He may have beliefs of how things are, were, or came to be, or he may have beliefs of how they ought to be, or ought to have been. The first kind of belief is a matter of fact (or what citizens think are facts). The second kind of belief is a valuation, the citizen's conception of what is good, best, or what should be. The first of these may be thought of as being descriptive or explanatory of a state of affairs or of what is thought to be a state of affairs, or of how a state of affairs came to be; the second is prescriptive of what ought to be done about a state of affairs.

In reaching his decision, the citizen uses beliefs he feels are relevant to the problem. He is frequently confronted with relevant beliefs that are in conflict. He then, more or less knowingly, works out an accommodation between the conflicting beliefs, assigning to some a lower priority than to others. It is always possible that, were he better informed, a different priority among competing beliefs would be assigned.

From what sources does the citizen get the beliefs which he uses in making practical decisions? There is, of course, no way of knowing this precisely, but in today's world it is fairly obvious that the citizen gets the bulk of his beliefs from the world outside and beyond his formal education. Knowledge gained in the home and on the street has a tremendous advantage over formal education in that it is usually immediately relevant to something the learner needs to know and, therefore, is more easily assimilated into the mind. One lesson on the street is worth several lessons in a classroom atmosphere. Beliefs are formed as if by osmosis, that is, they are literally soaked up by the learner from elders, peers, and teachers. Not to be underestimated in this respect is the world of advertisement and entertainment, the theatre, television, radio, the music of youth, and the sources of instant news. Beliefs are transmitted by overt behavior, word of mouth, connotation, expressed and unspoken attitudes, and by outright advocacy of those looked upon as exemplars in the society. Business, the home, the church, and the school offer models, which are often accepted without question as prescriptions of how life should be lived. Serious literature, art, and music, as well as religion, vie with the forces of scientific study in the race to capture the minds of our students.

Not to be underestimated among the sources of the citizen's beliefs is his life in the school. The school is the one institution in which all young citizens spend the greatest portion of their waking hours. The general nature and tone of life in the school, the way power is exercised, the way rewards and punishments are allocated, the attitudes displayed toward intelligent behavior both inside and outside the classroom—all of these and a myriad of other matters experienced in school are more powerful in belief formation than are the more abstract and highly verbal experiences constituting the formal content of learning in the classroom.

To the extent that education fosters a kind of rote mediocrity in learning, neglecting to raise really important questions; to the extent that education consists of colorless textbook recitation of what Alfred North Whitehead years ago called inert ideas, ideas merely received into the mind without being utilized, or tested, or thrown into fresh combinations; to the extent that the cram, exam, grade system is fastened on the school; to the extent that school officials ignore or violate the civil and human rights of students; to the extent that student government, because of its phoniness, remains contemptible in the eyes of students; to the extent that teachers allow their own right to academic freedom to be restricted—to that extent a credibility gap will exist in the minds of students, which they will resolve by giving a higher value to "this is the way it actually is" over "this is the way they say it is."

A commitment to intelligence and social responsibility requires that the school be an open-ended and free institution where students are treated with respect rather than condescension. There is little hope for the development of intelligence and democratic responsibility in an institution built on a military model or even on that of a benevolent dictatorship.

How is formal education usefully related to the total learning process of the citizen? Looking at the sources of the beliefs of citizens, we are faced by the somewhat frightening probability that students learn more outside the classroom than they do inside. Despite our frequent lament about how poorly students master whatever is taught in history, government, geography, etc., it is obvious that these same students do learn much outside the classroom. They master a social system complete with its own history, sociology, economics, and system of values. On a particular day, the student carries in his mind, quite innocently, a complete picture of society which, however inaccurate and limited, nonetheless, in terms of his insights, can be used to explain any situation which he may meet.

Obviously, social systems are not beyond learning by most students. We seem to make our mistake by trying, possibly too energetically, to impose foreign and abstract models on students without making contact with the beliefs they already hold—beliefs they have learned without the strain that is characteristic of formal schooling. Students may come to social studies with many erroneous and poorly founded beliefs, but they do not come with empty heads.

While a citizen's beliefs may be impressionistic or, for that matter, merely the idle fictions of his imagination, it *is* possible for the citizen to have thought out his beliefs. He may have compared his conceptions of reality and desirability to those held by others. Or, he may have inquired systematically into his beliefs, grounding them in logical systems of thought and/or facts. From specific beliefs, the individual builds systems of beliefs, theories, and abstract models of behavior. Generalizing, theorizing, and modeling come quite naturally to him. He does it so smoothly, he may not be fully aware of the experimental bases of his models.

To the extent that the citizen has stopped to think about his beliefs, the various systems and subsystems or models, which each individual carries in his mind, may be consistent one with another. The individual, however, is fully capable of harboring in his mind many inconsistent beliefs about reality, and conflicting beliefs about what is good or what ought to be.

In the light of this analysis, the central strategem of formal education is confrontation. The structure of learning is mose usefully thought of as the system of beliefs, theories, or abstract models in the mind of the learner rather than outside his mind in a body of content. Teaching is manipulation of the environment of the learner so that the existing structure in his mind will be challenged by other structures including, importantly, those provided by the disciplines. We ignore, at our peril, the system of beliefs which the student brings to class about any subject being studied, for this is the most vital structure upon which significant new learning can be built. In this sense, the job of education is to bring the model-making process out into the open where the validity of beliefs can be tested against objectively established facts and values. This clearly is not a matter merely of imparting information to be used later, but rather of utilizing information in testing and modifying one's previously held beliefs. It is at this point that the disciplines become relevant and useful to the student. The grounding of beliefs of a descriptive and explanatory nature is the business of the social sciences, the special function of which is to discover the factual relationships in human affairs, past or present. The grounding of beliefs of a prescriptive nature is the business of philosophy and ethics, whose special function is to examine, factually and logically, the grounds for valuation in human affairs, insofar as this is possible.

Formal education is usefully seen as a continuous process through which individuals are helped to correct and extend their present beliefs, and to broaden their perspectives so as to include considerations not presently comprehended; formal education is not a matter merely of filling empty vessels. In this vein, the formal disciplines serve to afford alternative models, better grounded and more accurate ones at that, against which the beliefs of citizens may be compared and contrasted. The models afforded by the disciplines include not only claims to knowledge made by experts but also the conceptual tools and methods of inquiry used by each discipline to validate claims. The utility in the disciplines does not rest so much on their being compendiums of knowledge, but rather that they afford more objective ways of looking at beliefs.

May I turn to my last question? *What are the parameters of a necessary and sufficient social studies program?* Except as a noble purpose recognized and proclaimed by numerous committees and commissions on the social studies over the years, the social studies do not, in fact, exist today. The social studies enterprise is captive of the subjects and only a few of the

167

subjects at that. In some ways, the new social studies has taken a long step forward, but this enterprise falls far short of the goal in at least three respects. First, the new social studies is subject-centered. The number of alternative disciplines offered for inclusion in the curriculum has been increased and the treatment of each has been improved, but the separate disciplines do not constitute a social studies program. Little thought has been given to how all the social sciences are to be included in the curriculum, or how a selection is to be made among them, or how the separate disciplines are to be related, or how the lot is to be meshed together into a social studies program which contemplates the total and unified education of citizens. In the absence of such thinking, history, and not really history at that, but a kind of oversimplified mythical version of history written from a Western bias, still drives out most of the other social sciences. The behavioral social sciences, vying among themselves, get only a scant toehold in the social studies door.

Secondly, the new social studies, as did the old, continues to ignore or minimize the central position of values and valuation in the life of the citizen. Values are either taken for granted or values may be treated in a shallow and sentimental fashion, out of context with social problems and without any real recourse to the factual undergirding, which the social sciences might conceivably supply.

Thirdly, it is well-known that the mastery of social science content, even if done in an enlightened way, as is largely the case with the new social studies, cannot be equated directly with good citizenship. If the social science disciplines are to play a part in forming the beliefs of citizens they must be put to practical use by the students in defining their real life problems. The probability of such utilization taking place is nil if the social sciences are each taught as separate entities removed widely in time from any practical application to the social problems of youth and society.

THE KEY QUESTIONS

As we confront the problem of what a necessary and sufficient social studies program should be, it is helpful to begin by thinking of the social sciences, history, and the like as being instrumental to the large task of citizenship development rather than as subject matter to be learned for its own sake or for some remote and unforeseen future use. Such an approach immediately gets us out of three boxes in which we are presently deeply trapped. In the first place, the question of which social sciences to teach and which to leave out of the curriculum would no longer be an appropriate question. Obviously, each of the social sciences, in somewhat equal measure, has a contribution to make to the grounding of beliefs. None can be ignored. We thus have to rephrase our question to read: "How can each of the social sciences and all of them together be brought in a balanced way to contribute to the refinement of the beliefs of citizens?". This is not an easier question to resolve than the one it replaces, but it is at least the right question to ask if we are to move ahead in the social studies enterprise.

Treating the subjects as instrumental to citizenship development gets us out of a second box, that which equates the social studies with the social sciences merely. I have demonstrated earlier the paucity of this view. The appropriate question becomes: "How can the social sciences taken together and in concert *with other subjects* be made to contribute in a balanced way to refining the beliefs of citizens?". Thus literature, and the serious arts, religion, philosophy, and ethics come into the social studies door, and social science is relieved of carrying the unnatural load it was never intended to carry in the first place but which we have insisted on foisting off on it. This, too, is a big order. It is not an easy question but at least it is the right question to be asking.

Looking upon the subjects as instrumental to citizenship development rather than ends in themselves allows us to escape the third box in which we are entrapped, that of disallowing or ignoring the heterogeneous experiences of youth outside the classroom as a bona fide part of the curriculum. We are forced to look at citizenship education as a unitary enterprise. We are reminded that the growing citizen will continue to get most of his beliefs from outside of formal education. We are strongly impelled to admit these out-of-class experiences as being instrumental to our goal. The right question then becomes: "How can we systematically relate outside experiences with the organized work of the classroom?".

SOCIAL STUDIES IN THE FUTURE

I do not know what the social studies response to these three key questions will look like once it has been developed. I believe it would include, among others, these features:

The social studies will be brought to focus continually on social questions, problems, and issues, large and small, which youth articulates or can be helped to articulate. Social and individual problems will provide the linking thread of the curriculum. Consideration of such problems, appropriate to maturity levels, will be continuous throughout the grades. Treatment of problems will not be delayed until the upper grades on the grounds that children do not have the necessary background. Background will be sought as needed. Social science research tools will be used by students in studying social problems. Social problems will be treated in a free and open-ended manner, with full resort to both fact and values. Public closure on such questions will be avoided. Grading of students on their performance in handling such questions will be eliminated. Scholars drawn from several fields, including humanists as well as scientists, will afford models of how disciplined minds attack a global problem. These model discourses will be recorded and distributed to schools for purposes of instructing youth in the intellectual processes involved in global problem solving.

History, much broader in scope than that which is usually offered in schools today, will be used to probe the backgrounds of persistent social problems and to indicate broad trends and social drift in the context of which social problems can be understood. Or, history will focus on classes of events such as industrialization, urbanization, nationalization, democratization, and the like. Purely local and national history will be offered as electives.

At an early age, children will be helped to use simple social science research techniques, such as the sample survey, to investigate questions arising out of their current life and study. Somewhat later, formal instruction will be offered on the nature of social science, including the conceptual schemes used in the various social sciences and the inquiry techniques used to collect and verify social science information. Students will be encouraged to use more and more sophisticated conceptual tools and inquiry techniques from the social sciences in furthering their own problem-based inquiry. Social science will be treated separately insofar as this is necessary, but the effort will be made to identify conceptual tools, as, for instance, the "culture concept" and the concept of "social power and its allocation," which are useful in more than one discipline as well as in the resolution of practical problems. Likewise, inquiry techniques, such as the sample survey and the case study, that are useful in more than one discipline or in the general study of society, will be emphasized. Additionally, all of the major social science disciplines will be offered as electives.

To accompany firsthand experience in valuing, growing out of the consideration of individual and social problems, systematic study of public and personal values and value systems will be provided. Provision will be made for the comparative study of value systems. Study will include not only the historical development of values but analytical treatment of values as well. There will also be instruction from ethics and philosophy on the processes by which values are grounded in facts and in comparison to other values. The relation of science to valuing will be emphasized at the same time that children and youth are confronted with value issues in their lives, both inside and outside the classroom. Every effort will be made to help children apply formal instruction in values and valuing, as directly as possible, to the resolution of value conflicts present in their own lives. Systematic study of values will also include analysis of the genuine and spurious use of value exemplars in the society through such media as television, radio, the newspaper, the theater, and other elements of the world of entertainment.

Lastly, the school will be made to exemplify, in every respect, including that of its governance, a society of intelligent and responsible citizens working to improve the life which they are living. The school will be used as a laboratory where students can openly investigate the workings of a human community.

If the social studies develop along lines like these, we of the profession will at last be true to our long acclaimed goal, the development of good citizens.

References

1. Bureau of Education, "The Social Studies in Secondary Education," Bulletin No. 28. Washington, D.C., 1916.
2. Ibid., p. 11.
3. Charles A. Beard, *A Charter for the Social Sciences in the Schools*, Report of the Commission on the Social Studies, Part I (New York: Charles Scribner's Sons, 1932).
4. Ibid., pp. 46–81.
5. Ibid.
6. Robert D. Hess, "Political Socialization in the Schools," *Harvard Educational Review*, Summer, 1968, pp. 528–535.
7. Edgar Litt, "Civic Education, Community Norms, and Political Indoctrination," *American Sociological Review*, February, 1963, pp. 69–75.
8. Erling M. Hunt, "Changing Perspectives in the Social Studies," in *High School Social Studies Perspective* (Boston: Houghton Mifflin Co., 1962), pp. 18–20.
9. Charles A. Beard, op. cit., p. 94.
10. The shortcomings of this definition, attributed to Edgar B. Wesley and popularized through his textbook, *Teaching Social Studies in the High School*, published by D.C. Heath in 1937, are pointed out by James P. Shaver, "Social Studies: The Need for Redefinition," in *Social Education*, November, 1967, pp. 588–592 and 596.
11. Pendleton Herring, "Toward an Understanding of Man," in Roy A. Price, editor, *New Viewpoints in the Social Sciences,* Twenty-Eighth Yearbook. (Washington, D.C.: National Council for the Social Studies, 1958), pp. 1–19.
12. Bernard Berelson and others, *The Social Studies and the Social Sciences* (New York: Harcourt, Brace & World, Inc., 1962), pp. 3–19.
13. The inadequacy of the social sciences as a basis for social education is developed by Fred M. Newmann, "Questioning the Place of Social Science Disciplines in Education," *Social Education*, November, 1967, pp. 593–596.
14. Alan Westin, "Responding to Rebels with a Cause," in *The School and the Democratic Environment* (New York: Columbia University Press, 1970), pp. 65–82.
15. Gerald W. Marker and Howard D. Mehlinger, "School Politics, Rebellion, and Other Youthful Interests," in *The School and the Democratic Environment* (New York: Columbia University Press, 1970), pp. 65–82.

Operational Concepts

1. The primary function of social studies education is the cultivation of good citizenship.

2. Knowledge is an essential prerequisite to good citizenship.

3. In view of their purpose, the social studies cannot be value free; they must allow the learner to construct a behavioral code by which to live.

4. The instructional materials used in social studies education should include relevant material—intellectual ideas that bear upon fundamental values and beliefs—outside the scope of the social sciences proper.

5. Social studies instruction that equivocates, propagandizes, or defects—in any way—from free and honest intellectual inquiry may do more harm than good.

6. Confrontation, through which the learner clarifies his existing beliefs and compares them with alternative ones, is an indispensable element in good instruction.

Implications

Although the social studies have always, to greater or lesser degrees, been concerned with citizenship education, we are now in a time when the attack must be renewed with stepped-up vigor. Not only have the ethics and morals of responsible behavior been somewhat downplayed in recent curricula, but the hard social problems of the future will demand a lasting commitment to the common good and to human welfare. Teachers must seek to develop a belief in the virtues of moral behavior, an interest in the societal condition, and a sense of social responsibility— not through ritualistic catechisms and banal patriotic slogans—but through authentic involvement in the basic democratic processes.

To achieve these ends, considerable emphasis must be given to the strengthening of personal and public values. These values should stem not from moral abstractions or routine ideology, but from meaningful knowledge—in the form of concepts, principles, and generalizations— which students have internalized into their own cognitive maps. These ends could be greatly facilitated if schooling itself constituted a substantive experience in democratic life.

Many of the young seem to be at socially loose ends; they view the society's possibilities of survival with scepticism and thus question the meaningfulness of their lives. Feelings of despair and latent despondency among adolescents must be counteracted in all possible ways. If we cannot rekindle a faith in the society's future, much of our socialization endeavor will come to little good, and we will have failed the current generation of young.

At the same time, however, it is equally essential that those now in school not be caught socially unaware, and that they become familiar with the critical problems of the time. On this account, the trend toward increased pluralism, the rising degre of human interdependence, the dilemmas of environmental conservation, population control, dwindling world food supplies, and so on, must repeatedly be dealt with in the curriculum. Above all, however, social studies education must take, as one of its dominant goals, the cultivation of a desire and ability to meet oncoming social problems with confidence and competence.

Science

Alfred T. Collette

The Science Program

Curriculum experts believe that science courses should be developed which provide students with experiences that show how facts are obtained and new techniques are developed. These experts also believe that science programs developed in this manner can produce a more scientifically literate citizen who is better able to cope with the problems of everyday living and of the future.

Significant curriculum changes have occurred in science teaching. New, untraditional approaches in teaching elementary science, biology, chemistry, physics, earth science, physical science, and general science have now appeared, and more are being developed in all areas of science. The most noticeable trend in science education at the present time is the attempt to develop a kindergarten through grade twelve sequence that will coordinate and direct the efforts of science teachers to achieve the overall desired goals of the science program.

THE ELEMENTARY SCIENCE PROGRAM

Secondary school science teachers should become well acquainted with the science program of the elementary schools of the system in which they work. Pupils often enter the seventh grade with strong interests and a rich background of experience in science because of the elementary school program. Secondary school science teachers can utilize these interests and experiences in teaching their own courses.

Elementary teachers have a flexible schedule—no bells tell them when to start studying science and when to stop. If something of value arises in the early morning, they may take advantage of it, or they may shift the science lesson to late afternoon if this change is advantageous. They can extend a science lesson as long as they consider it profitable. They can weave science into areas of other subject matter.

Reprinted from Alfred T. Collette, *Science Teaching in the Secondary School*, © 1973; by permission of Allyn and Bacon, Inc., Boston.

The major objective of elementary school science is to use the materials of science to develop the individual child. Science, like all other areas, is included in the program to help pupils learn more about their own interests, abilities and limitations, to help them learn to work with others, and to give them help in solving their everyday problems.

Elementary science is not primarily designed to prepare pupils for secondary school science. It does not try to build up special vocabularies, techniques for handling specialized equipment, or ready verbalization of scientific principles. Instead, it provides the pupils with accomplishments of far greater value. It develops strong interest in science. It helps pupils approach problems intelligently and gives them confidence in their ability. The elementary science program can provide them with a rich and well-rounded background of experiences. These are the products upon which secondary school science teachers can capitalize.

Well-organized elementary science programs are not common throughout the country. Like other divisions of the science program, elementary school science teaching varies in its effectiveness from school to school and from teacher to teacher. The variation in the elementary school may be somewhat greater because of the variation in the backgrounds and interests of the teachers. Some elementary teachers like to teach science and have an adequate background to do a good job. However, most elementary teachers feel inadequate and teach little, if any, science.

At present, elementary school science is in a state of flux. It is not a required subject in all schools throughout the country. It does not have the status in the elementary school curriculum that many other areas have. Some state departments of education and local school systems have made it a requirement for all grade levels, but they are encountering many problems. The problems in implementing programs will be overcome someday so that organized and coordinated kindergarten through twelfth grade science sequences will be common throughout the country.

A well-organized, high quality elementary school science program can help secondary school science teachers. They will know the science backgrounds of their pupils and can capitalize on this background. They will be able to teach their courses of study using the foundation their pupils acquired through the elementary program. Secondary school teachers should regard elementary science as an important part of the elementary school curriculum. They should do all that they can to help implement an elementary science program in their own school systems.

New Developments in Elementary Science

Many active scientists are concerned about the errors in concept and in fact which have been and are still being taught by elementary school teachers. Scientists contend that elementary science textbooks and other science books are inaccurate and do not clearly show how the scientist finds out what he knows. In the majority of these books science is presented as a collection of disparate facts; no picture is given of the concepts and principles which clarify the subject. These scientists are seeking to help improve elementary science by contributing to the development of units which are scientifically accurate and demonstrate the nature of scientific inquiry.

Several elementary school science projects have been developed to date and are considered to be in final form. Others are still underway and are in various stages of development. The approaches have several common points.

1. Less emphasis is placed on subject matter per se than is found in traditional elementary science textbooks.
2. Discovery experiences receive major emphasis. Pupils use the methods of the scientist to uncover "new" facts.
3. Pupils have an opportunity to use their own materials to perform their experiments.
4. Students are given an opportunity to gather, to graph, and analyze data. They draw their own conclusions.
5. The material written is for the "average" elementary school student.

The common points of these curricula stated above were derived from research studies to determine how children learn science. Very little was known about how children learn before the new approaches to elementary school science were being developed. Psychologists who were interested in the problems of learning became associated with the curriculum projects and made many significant contributions to them. Various research studies by psychologists produced certain ideas which were used in the development of the new curriculums. These include:

1. Children should ask questions and find the answers to these questions.
2. They should make their own hypotheses, test them through observations and experimentation.
3. They should do this exploring on their own in order to learn how scientists approach problems.

Psychologists do not agree on how much time should be devoted to this "discovery" type learning in elementary science. Psychologists like Gagné, Piaget, Bruner, Ausubel(1), and others have all made important contributions to the psychological bases of a number of these elementary science programs. They have also been involved in the evaluation of some of them.

THE JUNIOR HIGH SCHOOL PROGRAM

The junior high school science program has been the most neglected area of science education. The most poorly prepared teachers and the most inadequate facilities are usually found in the junior high school science program. General science was the most popular science offering in the 1960s junior high school and probably the most poorly taught of all the science offerings. It is amazing that such a large percentage of the school population should be exposed to courses which are poorly developed, poorly taught, and outdated. Hurd describes the situation well when he states that

> Fifty years have elapsed since the first courses in general science were developed. We have described the goals and content at several intervals in this span of time. Over the fifty year period general science has not changed radically in either purpose or content though the forces determining contemporary society and the modern enterprise have(2).

Some changes are taking place in the junior high school but not at a very rapid pace. One reason for this is the instability of organizational patterns of the schools. There has been a great deal of controversy regarding the functions and goals of the junior high school even to the point where some educators say that it should not exist. Consequently school districts are now experimenting with organizational patterns which eliminate the junior high school completely. For example, some districts have organized into a K–5, 6–8, 9–12 pattern. Grades 6, 7, 8, in this pattern, constitute the so-called middle school and the junior high school is eliminated. Other districts have gone back to the K–8 and 9–12 pattern which also eliminates the junior high school. This state of flux is causing a great deal of difficulty in establishing a junior high school science program. An effective junior high school program can only materialize when the educational purposes of the junior high school, if there is to be one, are firmly established. Once this is done, then only the best qualified teachers should be recruited to teach science in this neglected area.

The greatest number of changes have occurred in grade 9. For example, earth science is replacing ninth grade general science in many schools, in an effort to provide students with a more meaningful science experience. Innovative approaches have been introduced in grade 9 which stress the processes of inquiry.

Courses for grades 7 and 8 are now appearing which emphasize the processes of science and attempt to prepare students for change and for the future as well as help them develop a positive attitude toward change. The curriculum writers of these new approaches have profited from the strengths and weaknesses of the new curriculum approaches which have already been introduced in the elementary and high school.

General Science

General science occupies a critical position in the secondary school curriculum. It is required of nearly all students. It is the first experience most students have with science as a special subject, and it may be the only science course that some students will take during their total high school experience.

General science determines the attitude that many students develop toward science. When the course is exciting, satisfying, and rewarding, boys and girls look forward to further science study. When the course is poorly taught, students will most likely look to other fields for satisfaction. General science deserves the best teaching and the best facilities that can be provided.

As its name implies, general science has a broad scope and can be applied to a broad range of interests. It was never intended, however, that general science be made up of a smattering of the specialized sciences. It has its own body of subject matter that is chosen to meet the needs of the students who take it. Nor should a general science course touch upon every aspect of science. To do so would result in superficiality and would cause feelings of frustration and dissatisfaction on the part of the students. General science is "general" only in that it is free of the traditional boundaries of the various areas of science.

General science was introduced into the curriculum as part of a general effort to humanize the secondary school curriculum. The courses offered at the beginning of the century were far from suitable for the great majority of students entering high school. After a brief taste of what was being offered them, boys and girls were leaving school in large numbers. Hunter states that during 1908 in New York City 43 percent of the enrolled students had left by the end of the ninth year, and 70 percent by the end of the tenth(3). The formal science courses of the time were in part responsible for the high dropout rate.

Educators felt the need at that time for a different type of science course, one designed for students who would elect no more science: a course designed to help them understand and use the things of science commonly encountered in daily life. These educators also recognized the need for a course in science for students who would continue their study of the subject, a course that would permit exploration of interests and abilities and the building of a background of experiences.

Early courses of study and textbooks show considerable diversity in content and approach. Some teachers emphasized the exploratory function of general science, presenting samplings of the various specialized sciences loosely tied together. This type of course was of little value to students who would not study science further.

Other teachers emphasized the preparatory function of general science, building the course from the introductory phases of physics, chemistry, biology, physical geology, and astronomy. They developed specialized vocabularies, skills in the use of formulas, and basic information. Such a general science course was of even less value to students who would not enter science fields.

A large number of teachers emphasized the practical applications of science. They taught their students how to stop faucets leaking, how to repair lamp cords, and how to choose a proper diet. Students probably benefited from this treatment, but formally trained science teachers considered the courses to be a "hodgepodge" of little value.

Gradually the idea grew that general science needed broader goals. A study made in 1930 showed that science teachers were thinking in terms of the development of interest, desirable attitudes, and certain general skills(4). Some were still thinking of the preparatory function of general science, but most were thinking in terms of giving an understanding and an interest in the environment. It is significant that few considered general science to have any responsibilities toward helping young people to cope with social problems, to help them with problems they would be faced with in the future and to show how man fits into his physical and biological environment. General science teachers were thinking as science specialists and not as educators.

In 1932 there appeared the *Yearbook of the National Society for the Study of Education*—a publication that was to have a strong effect on general science. This *Yearbook* proposed for the twelve years of public schooling a science program based on the major concepts of science. The *Yearbook* listed thirty-eight generalizations to be used as objectives for science instruction throughout the entire sequence of elementary, junior high, and senior high school science.

There have been objections to the proposals outlined in the *Thirty-first Yearbook* from the beginning. Hunter in 1932 said, "These generalizations completely leave out applications of science to the lives of children, no reference to health or citizenship objectives as such being found. Intellectual objectives hold complete domination over practical ones"(5).

Despite the objections of Dr. Hunter and others, general science continues to be dominated by intellectual objectives. Courses of study and textbooks emphasize generalizations rather than discovery. Demonstrations and experiments are used to "prove" that what the books and teachers say is true rather than to permit problem-solving situations.

General science has another handicap, which is a result of the times —a superfluity of material. As each major development of science has been brought to the attention of the public—television, jet planes, nuclear reactors—teachers and authors of texts have hastened to add them to the curriculum without considering the suitability of the added material. As a consequence, courses of study and textbooks have been filled with information that is "up-to-date," but which has little or no function in meeting the general objectives of education.

Courses in general science vary from school system to school system and from teacher to teacher. Some are well-planned and excellently taught. Others are taught by teachers who are not prepared in science. In fact, a report of the U.S. Office of Education(6) indicates that an overwhelming

179

proportion of general science teachers assigned to part-time teaching in science are *not* trained in science. This area of inadequacy, according to the report, presents a dismal picture of the staffing of general science courses(7).

Other information concerning general science is worthy of mentioning. Homogeneous grouping in general science is reported from about 60 percent of the schools, but the trend appears to be toward use of ability grouping(8). Some type of laboratory facility for general science was reported by 75 percent of the schools. Because of the large size of classes, many large schools in certain geographic areas are discouraging meaningful student laboratory activities(9). About half of the schools are using a coordinated series of textbooks for grades 7, 8, and 9. The large schools in general use recent texts and many of the smaller schools use textbooks which are fourteen years old or older(10).

The picture which general science presents is one of a course which is not realizing its potentialities. Symptoms of this failure include a low interest in senior high school sciences and the diversion of capable students into fields other than science. Some of the failures of general science are related to circumstances beyond the control of the individual teachers. Large classes, heavy class loads, and inadequate facilities are the inevitable results of a rapidly expanding school population.

RECENT DEVELOPMENTS IN JUNIOR HIGH SCHOOL SCIENCE

A survey by the U.S. Office of Education shows that general science was the most popular offering in the mid-1960s. This course took care of about 94 percent of the junior high school population at that time. Since then, general science has gradually been replaced by courses in earth science, life-science biology, and physical sciences. In addition, a number of schools and school systems throughout the country are introducing some of the new approaches especially developed for the junior high school science program. These courses develop inquiry skills and concepts in one or more science disciplines. The implementation of these courses is not extensive, however, and varies considerably throughout the country.

The most recent figures regarding the implementation of these new curricular approaches show that an estimated 26 percent of ninth grade students are taking earth science(11). Approximately 7,000 junior high school teachers are using Intermediate Physical Study materials (IPS)(12) and about 622 teachers are using the Intermediate Science Curriculum Study Program(13).

Even though the new programs have not been widely accepted, they are important for several reasons. They involve a philosophy which is different from that of traditional courses. They stress "discovery" and "inquiry" and de-emphasize facts per se. They require that students raise questions and use the various science processes to find answers to the questions. They provide for opportunities for students to make their own hypotheses, make their own observations, set up their own experiments, and draw conclusions based on their results. The content of the courses is rigorous and requires that a teacher must keep up-to-date in his subject and teaching methods. These modern curriculum programs are causing an impact which will be with us for many years to come. There is no question that science teachers will someday be forced to teach courses of this type in order to meet the demands of a rapidly changing scientific age.

The choice of electives in most high schools is usually limited to three: physics, chemistry, and biology. Some offer courses in advance general science, physical science, earth–space science and national curriculum projects in biology, chemistry, and physics.

[From] 1964 to 1965(14), in terms of enrollment, biology was by far the most popular science, chemistry attracted about 40 percent of the pupils who reached grades 11 and 12, while physics attracted about 20 percent. Earth science and advanced general science did not attract many pupils. Figure 1 shows the trends in the past five years in the State of New York based on the number of pupils taking statewide examinations in the various science areas. Again, biology is the most popular science—of the total number of state-wide examinations written, a little less than half were in biology. Chemistry is the next popular science offering in New York while physics and earth science are the least attractive.

Developments in Biology

The increasing percentages of students taking biology during the past sixty years attest to its appeal to young people. One can only speculate as to why biology has been more popular than physics and chemistry. Perhaps biology teachers have been less hampered by tradition and by the influence of college science. Perhaps pupils find the subject matter more meaningful than the content of chemistry or physics or earth science. Perhaps biology lends itself successfully to the teaching of classes having pupils with a wide range of abilities.

High school biology today bears little resemblance to its forebears of the nineteenth century. Previous to 1900, schools offered separate courses in botany and zoology, and later in human physiology. These courses emphasized classification and morphology. Laboratory work was primarily concerned with detailed studies of structural types. Teaching was strongly influenced by the doctrine of formal discipline which held that the mind could be trained through special exercises.

The closing years of the century saw two significant developments. Teachers began using experiments in physiology in place of studies of structure alone. The rising nature study movement, which emphasized the study of living things in their natural environment, stimulated field work and

FIGURE 1 Trends in the Past Five Years for Enrollments in Regents: Physics, Biology, Earth Science, Chemistry [Based on state-wide examinations (Regents) administered]

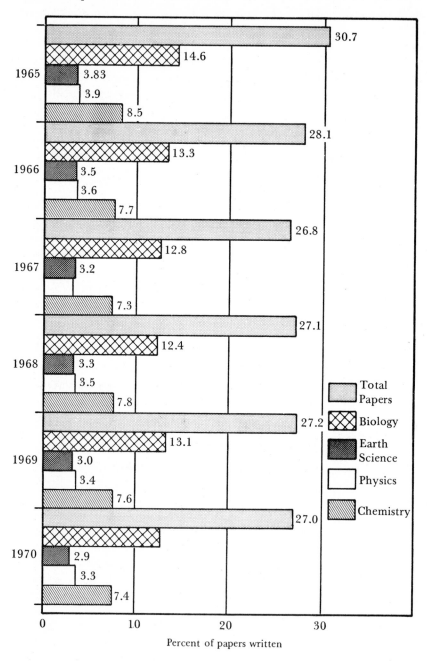

Percent of papers written

the study of interrelationships. These two factors greatly changed the pattern of biology courses.

In 1900 the move to unify the several phases of biology into a single course gained momentum. At first the resulting courses consisted of distinct sections devoted to zoology, botany, and human physiology, respectively. In these courses, type studies were often used, with perhaps an apple tree to illustrate a woody plant and a grasshopper to illustrate an insect. Field trips were taken to see these organisms in their natural environment. Laboratory exercises gave detailed studies of their structure and experiments with their physiology.

Such courses persisted into the 1920s. In many ways they were excellent courses, interesting and effective in meeting the goals of science education. Unfortunately, it was all too easy for type studies to become formalized into the pattern of college sciences. And the lack of integration between the separate sections of the course disturbed many educators.

The *Thirty-first Yearbook* of the National Society for the Study of Education had as great an impact on secondary school biology as it did upon general science. A number of the thirty-eight major generalizations of science listed in the *Thirty-first Yearbook* as objectives for a twelve-year science program were derived from the field of biology(15).

Courses built upon these generalizations differed completely from earlier biology courses. They were well integrated. Plant and animal cells were studied at the same time to make comparisons easier. All forms of reproduction were combined into one unit. Such biology courses were systematic, highly logical, and generally appealing to secondary school science teachers. Today most high school biology courses and most textbooks are organized on this plan although in recent years modifications are increasing.

As excellent as a course based on major generalizations may appear on superficial examination, serious defects show up in actual use. The use of major generalizations as goals effectively eliminated the discovery approach to science. No pupil can possibly discover enough in one year to arrive at even one major generalization. Experiments, demonstrations, and field work must be used chiefly as illustrations of the ways generalizations apply. Indeed, laboratory and field work can be minimized or even eliminated in such a course because books, films, and slides are able to present applications of generalizations much more quickly and effectively and without the problem of introducing confusing exceptions.

Much that was good in earlier biology courses was lost in using major generalizations as objectives. Type studies were abandoned, although type studies give the best concepts of an organism as a whole, since an organism is more than the sum of its parts or the sum of its processes. Lost too has been the emphasis upon the place of living things in their natural environment, a loss that cannot be replaced by a single unit on the principles of ecology.

On the whole, the recommendations of the *Thirty-first Yearbook* improved high school biology greatly by providing an effective organization. Major generalizations and concepts are excellent centers about which to build a course, but the discovery approach to biology requires more specific objectives.

Concern over the limitations of secondary school biology has produced some interesting trends in the biology offerings in the high schools. Courses have been developed which are organized around broad concepts and present biology as a changing body of knowledge. The pupils work out their own experimental procedures in the laboratory and answer questions and draw conclusions based on the data they collect. The most significant contributions to the teaching of biology were made by the Biological Sciences Curriculum Study (BSCS) Project, which produced three new approaches to teaching biology.

Physics

The relative unpopularity of physics is not because of the nature of the subject itself. No area has more application to everyday living. No subject deals with more exciting ideas. The fault lies in the goals of the teacher.

The college preparatory function of high school physics continues to dominate the thinking of physics teachers despite the efforts of many scientists and science educators to revitalize the subject.

> Physics as a college entrance requirement has been so firmly entrenched that teachers have had little opportunity to do more than follow a rather definite course of study based on factual information and laws which college professors deemed necessary as a basis for achievement in college. Physics teachers must discard the artificial standards established by colleges and universities and make physics a vital and exciting subject (*16*).

The following are some of the causes for the inadequacy of secondary school physics:

1. Emphasis upon principles and "laws" rather than upon the concrete things of the environment.
2. Insistence upon memorization of formulas and standardized ways of solving problems.
3. Excessive use of mathematical exercises in order to develop skills with formal science problems.
4. Employment of stereotyped laboratory exercises and materials of the type used in formal college classes.
5. Failure to provide for individual differences.
6. Inability to stimulate original thinking.

184

7. Refusal to accept responsibility for social and emotional growth of pupils.

Some new approaches to the teaching of physics have been produced in recent years which drastically deviate from traditional approaches. These new approaches utilize the inquiry and discovery techniques in the laboratory in order to permit students to learn how a scientist goes about his work.

A number of practicing physicists, and a group of secondary physics teachers recognizing the inadequacy of high school physics, established a study committee to reorganize its teaching. In the middle 1950s, the Physical Science Study Committee (PSSC) began writing materials for this new approach. Other approaches have since been produced to take care of students who are not able to handle PSSC materials. Harvard Project Physics (HPP), which is now on the market, is intended for the "average" high school student. This program is still in the process of development and testing.

Chemistry

Chemistry has fared better than physics in popularity during the past few decades. It has continued to attract about the same percentage of pupils from the general school population for about 60 years. Traditional courses are still popular although other approaches to chemistry are available. As in the case of physics, chemistry is failing to direct an adequate number of young people into scientific vocations. Students take the course and turn to other fields for their life vocation.

The criticisms that have been leveled at physics apply equally well to chemistry. The usual chemistry course is still concerned almost completely with abstractions. Students must memorize endless laws, principles, minor facts, symbols, formulas, and equations. From the very beginning they are drilled in chemical shorthand until they assume formulas and equations *are* chemistry.

Much laboratory work in traditional chemistry courses consists of sets of exercises. Some of these are designed to teach pupils the use of chemical apparatus and procedures. Others are designed to illustrate generalizations made in books and lectures. In general, the pupils do not carry out true experiments in which they are trying to find the answers to real problems.

It is interesting that with these serious faults chemistry has been able to maintain its enrollments. Anyone who knows junior high school pupils, however, may suspect the answer. To boys and girls of the early secondary school grades, chemistry suggests all kinds of exciting things—explosions, color changes, strange bubblings, startling transformations—strongly tinted with the romance that science fiction gives to chemistry. What a pity so many of them are disillusioned!

Traditional chemistry courses have needed the same reorganization that is suggested for high school physics. More attention should be given to materials with which the pupils are familiar. True experiments should replace many of the stereotyped laboratory exercises. The problem-solving approach should be used extensively throughout the course. Pupils should be encouraged to engage in extensive project work. Most important of all, the preparatory function should be minimized and pupils should be allowed to follow up special interests and develop along lines in which they show special ability. New courses have been developed using this approach, but teachers are hesitant to use them. Many teachers think that they lack the chemistry background needed to teach the new approaches as well as the training in the procedures and methods to handle the materials.

New approaches in chemistry which emphasize laboratory work and discovery are now part of the high school offerings. Like BSCS and PSSC programs, these chemistry approaches are organized around broad concepts.

COMMENTS REGARDING THE NATIONAL CURRICULA

A great amount of time, effort and money was spent during the 1960s to develop new approaches to the teaching of science. But very little effort was made to formally evaluate these courses of study along the way. Very little research data is available which tells us about the effectiveness of the new courses. Most of the information available is from personal observations and teacher feedback. In spite of the lack of reliable research data, enough time has now passed so that some of the major strengths, weaknesses, and limitations of the courses have been identified. These strengths and weaknesses are now redirecting our thinking in science education. Consequently many of the conflicts on issues which presently exist are the direct consequence of the curriculum movement of the 1960s. The debates and disputes are centered around issues pertaining to the purposes and goals of science education, the nature of learning and the learner, the training of teachers, the styles of teaching, the structure of a course of study, and topics of study to be covered in a science discipline.

Some of the strengths which are presently identified relate to the following points(*17*).

1. A course of study should be based on the concepts and principles of the discipline and organized around conceptual schemes. The knowledge presented should be up-to-date, accurate, and fit within the conceptual schemes.

2. Students should learn how scientific knowledge is obtained. This requires that they be involved in discovery and problem-solving activities in which they are on their own. In this way certain intellectual and cognitive skills are developed which cannot be accomplished through a series of set steps which are involved in problem-doing exercises.

3. Science should be presented as an ongoing, changing enterprise.

4. The authoritarian approach to the teaching of science does not give young people a feeling of what science really is. It does not expose them to its processes, its unifying principles. It does not permit them to ask questions nor does it present the uncertainty of science, or the ways which motivate scientists to work.

5. It is best to teach a few important concepts in depth than to cover many superficially. In this way, students understand something well and obtain a better feeling for a discipline or topic.

6. A science curriculum should not be static. It should be based upon the up-to-date knowledge of the discipline. Continuous revision is sound and is a good way for the teacher to stay informed on the state of science. It also permits the teacher to better understand the research in the field.

7. Students should be exposed to the important and outstanding principles of a science discipline. They should understand the unifying ideas, the abstract ideas, and its symbolisms. This kind of knowledge will be more useful than a collection of facts for generalizing, interpreting, and explaining.

The following are some of the weaknesses and inadequacies of the new science curricula(18).

1. The courses often omit treatment of whole areas of a modern discipline. For example, heat and alternating currents have been omitted from the PSSC approach.

2. Courses are geared for potential scientists. The needs of the average high school student have been disregarded. The courses are too difficult and abstract for him.

3. Courses cover a great many areas, are overwhelmingly encyclopedic, and are too long. Students become lost, bored, and alienated from science.

4. General education in the sciences has been disregarded. The subject matter lacks the social, humanistic, and historical points of view.

5. The new curriculum presents traditional topics—topics found in the old curricula. There are some exceptions in earth science courses which present topics in ecology, biophysics, and oceanography, but in general these areas and others are not represented, or poorly represented, in most of the curricula.

6. Goals of teaching are not clear in these approaches. Teachers have a difficult time in presenting the course of study.

7. The courses were designed to accommodate the existing organization of a school day—five days per week, five classes per week, one teacher per course, one laboratory per week. Consideration was not given to

other types of scheduling which allow for flexibility and better conditions for science teaching.

8. The new courses were developed independently of each other and are highly specialized. The topics from other science areas are used only to explain the meaning of an area within the discipline and not used to show unity between the sciences.

9. The broader meanings of science are not made clear to the student since the curricula are so highly specialized.

10. The projects have not clearly defined their goals, philosophy rationale, concepts, and skills. Consequently, in-service programs have been useless in preparing teachers to handle the materials since these programs stress subject matter background.

11. Instructional materials for the teacher are not clear. Goals of instruction are not identified or else very poorly presented. The textbook and instructional materials are difficult to use.

12. The training of teachers for these approaches has been difficult. Most of the effort has been placed on subject matter background of teachers and not the methods and styles of teaching. Subject matter background *alone* does not contribute significantly in implementing the new curricula.

13. The courses of study were prepared without regard to principles of psychology of learning. Very little regard was given to how boys and girls learn science.

14. Courses were prepared by scientists with little aid from teachers who know students, the school organization, and the conditions under which science could best be taught.

15. The new curricula cover the same topics as those found in traditional courses. No effort was made to cover areas which have interests for students.

In summary, these courses met the demands of the age and we have learned a great deal about science teaching because of them. Now we are in another generation and the demands of our society are different and the approaches to the teaching of science should be different. But we can capitalize on the experience of the sixties. In the past decade we have gathered more knowledge about schools, teachers, and students than ever before through these national curriculum projects. We have learned some new guidelines about curriculum development. We have learned that courses of study must be developed for all types of students—the average, the slow learner, and the disadvantaged. Through these first-generation courses we have learned a great deal about the use of conceptual schemes and principles in building a curriculum. We have learned that the "discovery method" has many different meanings and that there is much to learn about concept formation. We have also realized the importance of the teacher in curriculum development and implementation. Finally, we have learned that many types of experts are needed to write a course of study. Science teachers, practicing scientists, science educators, learning psychologists should all be involved in curriculum development. The expertise of all of these individuals is needed to produce a well-balanced curriculum.

References

1. Ausubel, D. P., *The Psychology of Meaningful Verbal Learning,* Grune & Stratton, New York, 1963.
2. Hurd, Paul DeHart, *New Curriculum Perspectives for Junior High School Science,* Wadsworth Publishing Co., Belmont, Calif., 1970.
3. Hunter, G. W., *Science Teaching at Junior and Senior High School Levels,* American Book, New York, 1934.
4. National Society for the Study of Education, *Thirty-first Yearbook,* Part I, "A Program for Science Teaching," Public School Publishing Co., Bloomington, Ill., 1932.
5. Hunter, op. cit.
6. U. S. Office of Education, *Science Teaching in the Public Junior High School,* Government Printing Office, Washington, D.C., 1967.
7. Ibid.
8. Ibid.
9. Ibid.
10. Ibid.
11. *ESCP Newsletter* No. 20, Boulder, Colo., Oct. 1969.
12. Lockhard, *Seventh Report.*
13. Ibid.
14. Other estimates have been made regarding enrollments. The U.S. Bureau of the Census projected that about 14.8 million students were enrolled in the high schools in 1970 and about 36.4 million pupils were enrolled in the elementary schools (Ronneberg, Conrad E., "Chaos in Science Teaching," *C and E N,* June 1, 1970, p. 51). According to a recent BSCS publication, *About BSCS Biology,* published by Biological Sciences Curriculum Study, Boulder, Colo., June 1969, estimates for science enrollments in 1969 were as follows—about 2.5 million tenth grade students take biology, about 850,000 students enroll in chemistry, and 400,000 students take physics.
15. National Society for the Study of Education, *Thirty-first Yearbook,* Part I, "A Program for Science Teaching," Public School Publishing Co., Bloomington, Ill., 1932.
16. Hunter, G. W., *Science Teaching at Junior and Senior High School Levels,* American Book Co., New York, 1934.
17. For further amplification see: Hurd, Paul DeHart, *New Directions in Teaching Secondary School Science,* Rand McNally, Chicago, 1969, pp. 93–114.
18. Ibid.

Suggested Readings

Biology

AUSUBEL, DAVID P., "An Evaluation of the BSCS Approach to High School Biology," *American Biology Teacher*, 28:176–186 (March 1966).

BLANKENSHIP, JACOB W., "Biology Teachers and Their Attitudes Concerning BSCS," *Journal of Research in Science Teaching*, 3:54–60 (No. 1, 1965).

CALANDRA, ALEXANDER, "Foundation Sponsored Programs" (in TST Forum), *The Science Teacher*, 36:73 (Feb. 1964).

COLBY, EDWARD, "The New Science Curriculums—A Loud Hurrah," *School Management*, 8:83+ (Nov. 1964).

CROSSLAND, RICHARD W., "The American Biological Sciences Curriculum Study," *American Biological Teacher*, 26:348–353 (May 1964).

EARLE, A. H., "Review of the BSCS Second Year Course," *American Biology Teacher*, 29:295–296 (April 1967).

EARLE, A. H., "A Decade of Advanced Placement Program in Biology," *American Biology Teacher*, 26:357–362 (May 1964).

GEORGE, KENNETH D., "The Effect of BSCS and Conventional Biology on Critical Thinking." *Journal of Research in Science Teaching*, 3:293–299 (No. 4, 1965).

Glass, H. Bentley, "Most Critical Aspect of Science Teaching," *The Science Teacher*, 34:19–23 (May 1967).

GROBMAN, HULDA, "Assignment of Students to Tracks in Biology," *American Biology Teacher*, 27:762–764 (Dec. 1965).

GROBMAN, HULDA, "Identifying the 'Slow Learner' in BSCS High School Biology," *Journal of Research in Science Teaching*, 3:3–11 (No. 1, 1965).

Chemistry

ANDERSON, ROBERT H., and STOWE, DONALD, "The Curriculum in Chemistry," *School Science and Mathematics: A Report of a Conference for School Administrators*, Western Michigan University, Kalamazoo, Michigan, 1965.

BASSOW, HERBERT, "The CHEM Study Course—An Objective Appraisal," *Science and Math Weekly*, 3:n.p. (Jan. 30, 1963).

BENNET, LLOYD M., and PYKE, BARBARA KINNARD, "A Discussion of the New Chemistry Programs (CHEMS and CBA) and the Traditional Programs in High School," *School Science and Mathematics*, 66:823–830 (Dec. 1966).

CAMPBELL, J. A., "Chemical Education Materials Study," *Journal of Chemical Education*, 38:2–5 (Jan. 1961).

"CBA Produces Research-Minded Students," *Chemical and Engineering News*, 40:38+ (March 12, 1962).

"CHEM Evaluation 1960–61," *Chemistry*, 35:15–17 (Oct. 1961).

"Chemical Bonds: A Central Theme for High School Chemistry," *Journal of Chemical Education*, 35:57 (Feb. 1958).

GROVES, CONSTANCE, "Nuffield Trials at Canterbury." *Education in Chemistry*, 4:125–126 (May 1967).

HALLIWELL, H. F., and VAN PRAAGH, G., "The Nuffield Project II: Chemistry 11–16," *The School Science Review*, 48:332–336 (June 1967).

"Honors for CBA and CHEM Study," *Chemistry*, 38:5 (Jan. 1965).

LIVERMORE, A. H., and FERRIS, F. C., "Chemical Bond Approach Course in the Classroom," *Science,* 138:1077–1080 (Dec. 7, 1962).

MABERLY, NORMAN C., "Chemistry Curriculum Patterns in High School," *Science Education,* 51:334–346 (Oct. 1967).

SALSTROM, DAVID, and EPPENSCHIED, JAMES, "An Experimental Use of the CHEM Study Program," *Ideas Educational,* n.v.:9–18 (1964).

SEABORG, G. T., "New Currents in Chemical Education," *Chemical and Engineering News,* 38:97 + (Oct. 17, 1960).

WESTMEYER, P., "Chemical Bond Approach to Introductory Chemistry," *School Science and Mathematics,* 61:317–322 (May 1961).

Physical Science

BEAIRD, ROBERT W., "The Introductory Physical Science Course in Junior High," *School Science and Mathematics,* 67:7:624–630 (Oct. 1967).

SMITH, M. K., and CROSS, JUDSON B., *Introductory Physical Science: A Progress Report,* Educational Services Inc., Watertown, Mass. (no date). The following articles on IPS are in this report:

    Haber-Schaim, Uri, "Objectives and Content of the IPS Course."

    Dillon, Thomas J., "The First Trial of the Course at Concord-Carlisle High School."

    Dodge, John H., "Introductory Physical Science and the Average Student."

    Shore, Edward A., "Introductory Physical Science in a Ninth to Twelfth-Grade School."

    Walter, James A., "Introductory Physical Science as a Terminal Course."

    Wilson, M. Kent, "Relationship of the IPS Course to the New Chemistry Curricula."

    Welch, Claude, "IPS and the New Biological Sciences Curriculum."

    Nelson, Nancy, "Feedback: Its Form and Function."

    Thompson, Raymond E., "IPS Achievement Tests."

Physics

ARONS, ARNOLD, "The New High School Physics Course," *Physics Today,* 13:20–25 (June 1960).

BAKER, J. R., "How Can Teachers Keep Up to Date," *Physics Education,* 1:241–246 (Nov. 1966).

BRAKKEN, E., "Intellectual Factors in PSSC and Conventional High School Physics," *Journal of Research in Science Teaching,* 3:19–25 (No. 1, 1965).

BRAUER, O. L., "Attempts to Improve High School Physics Education," *Science Education,* 47:372–376 (Oct. 1963).

BRAUER, O. L., "Conventional Physics Against PSSC Physics," *Science Education,* 49:170–171 (March 1965).

CALANDRA, ALEXANDER, "New Science Curriculums—A Sharp Dissent," *School Management,* 8:76–82 (Nov. 1964).

CALANDRA, ALEXANDER, "Some Observations of the Work of the PSSC," *Harvard Educational Review,* 29:19–27 (Winter 1959).

COLBY, EDWARD, "The New Science Curriculums—A Loud Hurrah," *School Management,* 8:834 (Nov. 1964).

CRUMB, GLENN H., "Understanding of Science in High School Physics," *Journal of Research in Science Teaching*, 3:246–250 (No. 3, 1965).

"Declining Physics Enrollment," *Science*, 155:984 (Feb. 24, 1967).

DETENBECK, R. W., and DiLAVORE, P., "Harvard Project Physics," *The Physics Teacher*, 5:233 (May 1967).

DROZIN, V. G., "Need for Multiplicity of Physics Courses," *The Physics Teacher*, 3:371 (Nov. 1965).

FERRIS, FREDERICK L., JR., "An Achievement Test Report," *The Science Teacher*, 26:576–579 (Dec. 1959).

FERRIS, FREDERICK L., JR., "The Physical Science Study—Will It Succeed?" *Harvard Educational Review*, 29:29–32 (Winter 1959).

FINGER, JOHN A., JR., DILLON, JOHN A., and CORBIN, FREDERIC, "Performance in Introductory College Physics and Previous Instructions in Physics," *Journal of Research in Science Teaching*, 3:61–65 (No. 1, 1965) .

FINLAY, GILBERT C., "Physical Science Study Committee," *School Review*, 70:63–81 (Spring 1962).

FINLAY, GILBERT C., "Physical Science Study Committee: A Status Report," *The Science Teacher*, 26:574–576 (Dec. 1959).

FINLAY, GILBERT C., "Physical Science Study Committee: Summary of Judgments Made by Teachers," *The Science Teacher*, 26:579–581 (Dec. 1959).

FINLAY, GILBERT C., "The Physical Science Study: What Are the Questions?" *The Science Teacher*, 24:327–329 (Nov. 1957).

FINLAY, GILBERT C., "Secondary School Physics: The Physical Science Study Committee," *American Journal of Physics*, 28:286–293 (March 1960).

HABER-SCHAIM, URI, "The Physical Science Study Committee: The Working Session on Physics Teaching at the Cavendish Laboratory, Cambridge," *Contemporary Physics*, 3:368–374 (June 1962).

HARRIS, JOHN, "The Laboratory and Project Physics," *The Physics Teacher*, 5:224–229 (May 1967).

HEATH, ROBERT W., "Comparison of Achievement in Two Physics Courses," *Journal of Experimental Education*, 32:347–354 (Summer 1964).

HOLTON, GERALD, "Harvard Project Physics," *Physics Today*, 20:31 + (March 1967).

HOLTON, GERALD, "Project Physics: A Report on Its Aims and Current Status," *The Physics Teacher*, 5:198–211 (May 1967).

HURD, PAUL DeHART, "The New Curriculum Movement in Science," *The Science Teacher*, 29:7–9 (Feb. 1962).

KIMBALL, MERRITT E., "Student Opinion Changes During a Year of Studying the Harvard Project Physics Course," *Journal of Research in Science Teaching*, 4:173–174 (1966).

NEWTON, DAVID E., "A New Look at Physics: Harvard Project Physics," *Michigan Science Teachers Bulletin*, 14:7–9 (Sept. 1966).

"Physical Science Study Committee: A Planning Conference Report," *Physics Today*, 10:28–29 (March 1957).

"Project Physics," *American Institute of Physics Educational Newsletter*, 7:n.pp. (Sept. 16, 1964).

"PSSC Versus Conventional Physics," *The Science Teacher*, 29:47 + (Feb. 1962).

"Review of the Nuffield Books," *Physics Education*, 2:292–294 (Sept. 1967).

ROGERS, ERIC M., "The Nuffield Project," *Physics Today*, 20:40 + (March 1967).

RUTHERFORD, F. JAMES, "Flexibility and Variety in Physics," *The Physics Teacher,* 5:215–221 (May 1967).

RUTHERFORD, F. JAMES, and WELCH, WAYNE W., "Evaluation Activities of Harvard Project Physics," *Science Education News,* American Association for the Advancement of Science Publication No. 67–7, pp. 5–6 (June 1967).

SCHWOB, TIMOTHY J., "Physics Teaching: An Alternative Method," *The Physics Teacher,* 10(2):98–99 (Feb. 1972).

TANNER, LAUREL N., "The Swing Away from Science," *The Education Forum,* XXXVI(2):229–238 (1972).

"A Third Course" (editorial), *The Physics Teacher,* 3:169 (April 1965).

WASIK, JOHN L., "A Comparison of Cognitive Performance of PSSC and Non-PSSC Physics Students," *Journal of Research in Science Teaching,* 8(1):85–90 (1971).

WATERMAN, ALAN T., "The Education and Training of Physicists" (editorial), *Physics Today,* 20:144 (Nov. 1967).

WATSON, FLETCHER G., "Comments on the Program of the Physical Science Study Committee," *Harvard Educational Review,* 29:12–15 (Winter 1959).

YOUNG, VICTOR J., "A Report on Pre-College Physics," *The Physics Teacher,* 4:20–22 (Jan. 1966).

ZACHARIAS, JERROLD R., "The Physical Science Study: Into the Laboratory," *The Science Teacher,* 24:324–326 (Nov. 1957).

Operational Concepts

1. Present science curricula appear to suffer from a lack of diversity in subject matter.

2. In the teaching of a particular science, it is important to relate the dominant concepts to the student's general education.

3. More variation in teaching methodology is essential to the continued improvement of science education.

4. Curriculum designers must strive for greater consensus regarding the optimum balance between inductive and deductive learning.

Implications

As in the case of mathematics, much of the problem with science education lies in its seeming lack of relevance and student appeal. At the secondary level in particular, an effort must be made to attract more students, especially among females. And, at all levels, teachers must look for more opportunities to relate scientific principles to such current problems as pollution, food production, and energy conservation. Moreover, as humans adjust to an altering planet, the traditional sequence of chemistry, biology, and physics must be broadened to incorporate significant concepts from the other sciences.

It also seems reasonable to conjecture, from the existing state of affairs, that a contemporary version of what once was known as the "general science" course would do much to fill an existing void. Many secondary school students would profit greatly from a comprehensive course in which the significant concepts from a variety of physical and biological sciences were brought together under a common conceptual structure. The shift toward inquiry-based learning, launched during the 1950s, appears to have produced relatively good results, as has the more recent emphasis upon the intellectual processes associated with science. These, therefore, seem to warrant further development.

Finally, as the body of scientific knowledge expands, science teachers might be well advised to concentrate upon ensuring the mastery of the powerful ideas related to a given science—the "cognitive organizers"—rather than to worry excessively about breadth of coverage. Science educators might also explore more fully the potentials inherent in peer tutoring, multiple learning units aimed at the same basic objective, and, importantly, teaching procedures through which the student's capacity for studying science can be enlarged.

Art

W. Dwaine Greer

Curriculum in the Visual Arts

During the latter part of the fifties, a national concern for educational quality came to public attention along with Sputnik. There was not only a consensus that something was wrong with education, but also a general consensus about how to remedy the situation. What was needed was an infusion of rigor from the academic disciplines. Experience was not enough; the content of education should provide a logical means of organizing the information of experience. Subject matter organized with the structure of a recognized discipline was the key to quality education. Curriculum reform was *the* way to improve education.

Within subject areas, perceived as the core of the general curriculum, this reform movement had a profound effect. Large conferences were called and projects undertaken that resulted in the large-scale development of curricula. Although there was less activity within the arts, a kind of spillover did take place.

Though not as large an effort as in other areas, *A Seminar in Art Education for Research and Curriculum Development(1)* was held at Pennsylvania State University in 1966 that has had some far-reaching effects in art education. The rethinking of what art education should be, resulting from beginnings made at that conference, has shaped where we are and has implications for future directions.

The general view of the focus and content of art programs that pervaded art education before the conference can be explained to some extent in terms of its history. The "image" that dominated the thinking about teaching art to children was that of the "child art" movement.

Based largely upon the earlier work of the Child Study Movement and the work of Viktor Lowenfield(2) and Sir Herbert Read(3), the movement had established by the 1960s the legitimacy of children's art products as art works. What emerged from the rethinking was a move away from the educational assumption that had accompanied the philosophical commitment and psychological investigation of children's art work—that childlike works should be the long-range result of art teaching. While it may well have been a misrepresentation of what Lowenfield and Read had said, the general position came to be that represented by writers like Natalie Cole(*4*) or Rhoda Kellog(*5*). Art works are a "natural expression" at their best before the stultifying effects of learning. Give the children motivation, draw out their expressive needs, provide some materials, and turn the children loose without interference to produce works everyone of which was to be accepted and praised. Creative expression would be the result, and such activities would be the foundation of the child's learning to understand the world as an artist does, having experienced the thrill of artistic creation.

Art programs designed to give substance to such a view have a particular character. The emphasis is placed on providing a variety of materials, the idea being that exposing children to a wide variety of materials will develop their sensitivity and creativity. The artistic content of such a program is almost exclusively children's imagery. If adult art works are shown, they are provided as motivational materials. Statements of goals for such programs are usually broad abstract generalizations about developing creativity and expression. There is little sense of art presented as a discipline with a content that children should learn.

Curricula, as the written form of plans for educational activities in such programs, do not have the character of materials in other subject areas. They are usually limited to curriculum guides that list kinds of activities and provide recipes for the various media used. The teacher was expected to choose activities and draw upon her own expertise to build them into an educational event.

There are few written examples of attempts to build a program around such a base. Each classroom should build its own curriculum. However, the Blanche Jefferson series(*6*), published in 1964, does provide teachers' manuals and books for children to use in an ordered series for grades 1 through 6. The materials are well done, and the statements made in the teacher's guide are an able presentation of the view of art education upon which they are based.

The premise from which the program starts is that "art is an outpouring of the child's ideas and feelings"(*7*). There is an emphasis on variety that is the hallmark of such programs, and care is taken to suggest that there is no special content and sequence is impossible. "The wide range of abilities within any group means that there can be no rigid standard for each grade level, no specific knowledge to be learned, and no level of quality to be attained in one grade or another"(*8*). Discussing the role of the teacher and the use of adult imagery, the view is that "Art does not depend on putting learned forms together in new ways"(*9*).

The author's description of the series as an ordered set of plans for activities is also consistent with the premises of the program. Organization of the program is focused on variety in art experience. In the section headed "Core Art Experiences," there is the notion that the program's "art problems" are the core of an adequate program. Yet there is also the notion that they are not to be followed as patterns but to serve as a springboard for the

197

teacher. In the "Sequence" section, there is a suggested arrangement of the activities, but a direction to study the materials ". . . changing the sequence of projects to suit the interests and needs of children"(*10*).

The rest of the guide is made up of hints for using the materials in the children's books to start the children making an artwork. A series of suggestions to teachers constantly reminds them to ". . . let the children follow their impulses, . . . avoid a structured art lesson," and statements like "You can make anything or do anything you want to with your crayons on this paper"(*11*) are given for teacher use.

Alternative positions that have risen in the decade since the Pennsylvania State Conference also have a history. However, it is important to note that there appears to be little change in the "image" of the child artist as the dominant one in school practice. A reading of any issue of *Instructor* or *School Arts* magazine will quickly confirm that "making" and "doing" projects that bear little resemblance to anything in the world of art are still the focus of most general art education activities.

What emerged as a basis for both research and curriculum work was a general position that chose premises different from those of the child art movement. There was recognition of the legitimate need to gain the knowledge of art obtained by performing as an artist. However, there was also the suggestion that childlike expressions of mature artists are not the same thing as expressions by children. The aim of art education would be the gradual acquisition of a developed adult understanding of works of art. Thus, children's products, while often interesting to perceive, would be seen as interim steps on the road to adulthood rather than as ends in themselves.

There was the further notion that for most people, as adults, the model of the artist is not entirely appropriate. The limiting of art activities to a making and doing framework defines art education too narrowly. The image of the artist, as the art education model was reconstituted, included images of the critic and the historian. The idea was that a fully developed adult understanding would also require critical and historical study. The content of these additional activities would come from appropriate disciplines: their bases would be the encounter with works of art and their focus more explicitly aesthetic experience.

The development of curricula that would set out the plans for new programs took a new form. This was not only due to new content, because the "accountability" charge was also being felt at this same time. The first publications following the redefinition of art education were guidelines that attempted to define and bound what should be included in a program to lead to developed adult understanding. These efforts were useful in causing people in the field to think through the redefinition that field leaders had gone through. They have been influential in stimulating support for the reconception and redefinition of art program contents. This is evident in documents such as California's "Art Education Framework"(*12*), Florida's "Catalog of Art Objectives"(*13*), Michigan's "Minimal Performance Objectives for Art Education"(14), and similar efforts in Ohio, Pennsylvania, Texas, and Utah. The approaches taken to build programs that would develop these broader understandings have been varied.

For some, adding new study materials to the already accepted "doing" kind of projects was the approach. These have taken the form of programs that can be used in addition to regular classroom activities. Two examples of this kind of program are *Learning to See* by Kurt Rowland(15) and *Teaching Through Art* by Robert J. Saunders(16).

In these materials there is the notion of content present: ". . . in producing the pattern the child will acquire a basic visual vocabulary"(17). And, there is an emerging emphasis on sequential development: "The exercises and lessons in each unit are prepared in the sequence in which they should be taught"(18). Both programs are only partial answers in that much of the organization and presentation must still depend upon their use by a teacher trained in art.

There have been other additions to school programs, notably the "Artist in the School"(19) work of the National Endowment for the Arts. The introduction of practicing artists into schools has achieved some notice where it has taken place. The excitement and interest generated have meant that this program is continuing and growing. Questions raised are those of long-term student commitment and the learning of content that leads to a full understanding. The visits of artists to schools still require an ongoing program.

Some attempts have been made to develop broader sequential program materials of the type found in the sciences(20). Although they were small in size, two efforts made in this mode have received attention. The "Kettering Project"(21) at Stanford was one attempt to build materials quite different from those normally found in the elementary classrooms. The curriculum was to have objectives, be sequential, and have instructional support of a kind not usually found in schools. There was a broader range of activities: ". . . we have attempted to organize learning activities into groups that are *dominantly* or *primarily* productive or critical or historical"(22). The purpose was to have the child develop a mastery of problems and tasks. Boxes of atypical instructional materials with over 500 individual pieces were tried out in classrooms.

The "Art Education for Disadvantaged Seventh-Graders"(23), developed at California State University, Los Angeles, shared many of the features of the Kettering project. Focus of the curriculum development was different, however. Major effort was given to having teachers develop their own curriculum that would be effective with children from minority-culture backgrounds. The conclusions from the study state that the outcomes were related to structure, sequence, and in-depth instruction, with a clear specification of goals the major factor for teachers' effectiveness.

Both programs were well-done experiments but did not extend much beyond their initial participants. Neither follow-through to publication nor wide-scale dissemination took place subsequent to development.

In response to the "accountability" charge, one series of texts was developed that has had wider distribution than most. *"Art—Meaning, Method, and Media: A Structured Art Program for Elementary Classrooms"(24)* was prepared, tried out, and published. There are objectives for activities, a range of activities, and sequence to the activities. One difficulty with this series of texts is that the development toward an adult statement is not evident. There appear to be careful directions provided for achieving standard "child-art" images, yet character of the content remains much like the earlier Jefferson series.

Perhaps the largest and most widely known effort to build new curricula and new program materials was that of CEMREL(25). The initial structuring work resulted in a set of "Guidelines"(26) for curriculum development for aesthetic education. Use of the guidelines generates task statements for curriculum development. However, the number of possibilities makes the ordering and sequencing of tasks a major problem that has not been solved. The materials developed from this framework are a series of parts to a system. It is intended that a teacher will be able to select from "instructional packages" the resources needed for an overall program. Difficulty arises because the materials do not provide the overall structure needed for this task; the teacher must still create the instructional program.

An effort, parallel to that at CEMREL, has been underway at SWRL(27). This effort was focused on building materials and procedures for sequenced, systematic art instruction. Materials were designed to be used by a nonspecialist teacher, and the range of student activities is referenced to the roles of artist, critic, and historian. Provision of images of works of art and instructional materials at reasonable cost was a premise of the work. The program has been in large-scale tryout, and plans call for wide distribution.

In summing up curriculum work in art, it appears that there are many promising beginnings available. However, if we look for curricula that form the basis for a complete program, there are still few materials available. A recent report by Educational Products Information Exchange would suggest that there are few materials found in schools that clearly identify conceptual content learning experiences for art students(28).

Undoubtedly, there are differing views of what should be the focus of art education programs. The reported development of the different programs indicates that there is still work to be done at a theoretical level. The ways in which programs differ and distinctions between underlying views or stances need to be clarified and written about. The development of complete programs that meet the demands of any particular stance is needed. And the way in which evaluation, verification of learning, and accountability can be accomplished remains an unanswered question.

Perhaps one of the most profound effects of the curriculum work that has taken place will be changes in the role of art supervisors. Efforts to revise local guides and produce local resources may no longer be the appropriate major focus of curriculum work. It may well be that the management, utilization, and adaptation of available materials by supervisors can achieve more than either revising guides or efforts to upgrade teacher expertise in special workshops. What will be required is knowledge of resources and the ability to analyze, utilize, and incorporate them into programs aimed at producing "developed adult understandings" of the world of art.

References

1. Matil, Edward L. *A Seminar in Art Education for Research and Curriculum Development*. University Park, Pa.: Pennsylvania State University, 1966.
2. Lowenfield, Viktor. *Creative and Mental Growth*. New York: Macmillan Publishing Co., Inc., 1947.
3. Read, Herbert. *Education Through Art*. New York: Pantheon Books, Inc., 1943.
4. Cole, Natalie R. *The Arts in the Classroom*. New York: The John Day Company, 1940.
5. Kellog, Rhoda. *What Children Scribble and Why*. San Francisco: N-P Publications, 1959.
6. Jefferson, Blanche. *My World of Art*. Boston: Allyn and Bacon, Inc., 1964.
7. Jefferson, Blanche. *My World of Art Book* (Teacher's Manual). Boston: Allyn and Bacon, Inc., 1964, p. 3.
8. Jefferson, Book 1 Teachers' Manual, p. 4.
9. Jefferson, Book 1 Teachers' Manual, p. 4.
10. Jefferson, Book 1 Teachers' Manual, p. 16.
11. Jefferson, Book 1 Teachers' Manual, p. 34.
12. Art Framework Subcommittee of the Fine Arts and Humanities Framework Committee. *Art Education Framework for California Public Schools*. Sacramento, Calif.: California State Department of Education, 1971.
13. Florida Department of Education. *The Florida Catalog of Art Objectives*. Tallahasee, Fla.: Department of Education, 1974.
14. Michigan Department of Education. *Minimal Performance Objectives for Art Education in Michigan*. Lansing, Mich.: Michigan Department of Education, 1974.
15. Rowland, Kurt. *Learning to See*. New York: Van Nostrand Reinhold Company, 1971.
16. Saunders, Robert J. *Teaching Through Art*. New York: American Book Company, 1971.
17. Rowland, Kurt. *Learning to See, Book 1 Teachers' Book*. New York: Van Nostrand Reinhold Company, 1971, p. 6.
18. Saunders, Robert J. *Teaching Through Art Series—A Manual*. New York: American Book Company, 1971, p. 3.

19. Madeja, Stanley S., et al. *The Artist in the School—A Report on the Artist-in-Residence Project.* St. Louis, Mo.: CEMREL, Inc., 1970.

20. Hurwitz, Al. *Programs of Promise: Art in the Schools.* New York: Harcourt Brace Jovanovich, Inc., 1972.

21. Eisner, Elliot W. *Teaching Art to the Young: A Curriculum Development Project in Art Education.* Stanford, Calif.: Stanford University, 1969.

22. Eisner, Elliott W. *Teaching Art,* p. 3.

23. Silverman, Ronald H. *Art Education for Disadvantaged Seventh-Graders.* Washington, D.C.: U.S. Office of Education, Department of Health, Education, and Welfare. ERIC No. ED 030 707.

24. Hubbard, Guy, and Rouse, Mary J. *Art—Meaning, Method, and Media: A Structured Art Program for Elementary Classrooms.* Westchester, Ill.: Benefic Press, 1969.

25. Central Midwestern Regional Educational Laboratory.

26. Barkan, Manuel, Chapman, Laura H., and Kern, Even J. *Guidelines Curriculum Development for Aesthetic Education.* St. Louis, Mo.: CEMREL, Inc., 1970.

27. Southwest Regional Laboratory for Educational Research and Development—SWRL Educational Research and Development.

28. Educational Products Information Exchange Institute. *EPIE Educational Product Report,* No. 46, "Evaluating 'Individualized' Materials." New York: Educational Products Information Exchange Institute, 1972.

Operational Concepts

1. The content of art education should provide a logical basis for organizing the child's artistic experience.

2. Prior to recent innovations in art education, instruction emphasized artistic creation, that is, painting, sculpting, and so on. As a consequence of recent changes, however, emphasis has shifted to the teaching of art as a formal body of knowledge containing substantive information, generalizations, and principles essential to the general education of children.

3. A basic objective of art education is the gradual development of a knowledge and appreciation of mature adult art.

4. As new curricula, directed toward these objectives, are produced, the roles of both art teachers and art supervisors are likely to change.

Implications

Again, in art education, as in so many other areas of the curriculum, we have testimony to the fact that curricular change tends to polarize from one extreme to another. In the 1940s and 1950s, when "learning by doing" ascended into high popularity, the teaching of art began to center upon instructional activities wherein children modeled, sculpted, painted, and engaged in similar artistic production. As a result, many students gained creative experience, some took great joy in inventive activity, but few learned the fundamental concepts underlying fine art.

What is now under way, resultingly, is a reversal intended to overcome this deficiency. Present curricula are beginning to treat art as a systematic discipline with its own vocabulary, structure, and aesthetic underpinnings.

Although there is less than definitive agreement as to whether art appreciation is best nurtured through the creation of art images or through the formal study of good art per se, the new mode supports the assumption that both are contributory. The major implication, correspondingly, is that teachers must do more than distribute the art materials; they must, themselves, have a fundamental grasp of art theory and be adept at transmitting this knowledge to their students.

Gilbert A. Clark

Expanding Conceptual Understanding in the Arts

To become educated—to engage in learning—is basically a process of developing and improving our discriminating use of concepts. Whether studying art or any other subject matter, we must master a complex of interrelated concepts. We understand and act in our world by the concepts we hold, but our concepts may be meager or rich, provincial or cosmopolitan, naive or sophisticated. Education is the expansion of conceptual understanding so that we move from a meager, provincial, or naive level to the fullest possible level of sophistication obtainable.

We conceptualize by seeing likenesses and differences, categorizing our perceptions, relating our experiences, and generalizing the relations. "Perceptual appearance is the spawning ground of all cognitive understanding"(1). It is important to recognize that conceptualization is a recurring cycle on a funded continuum from the tangible (the seen, felt, heard —sense experience) to the intangible (the highly symbolic or "desensed" experience). This concrete to abstract continuum is often violated in the classroom. The naive learner must be allowed to begin at the tangible, concrete level and progress, cyclically, to a sophisticated level of mastering the intangible abstract. Alfred North Whitehead's "Rhythm of Education"(2) characterizes a similar cycle as describing *the* process of learning.

Somewhere, between the tangible concrete and the intangible abstract, there is an area that Edgar Dale and John Belland(3) call the "semiconcrete" experience. Learning materials used during these experiences by the beginning learner should bear as much tangible similarity and resemblance to the original objects, events, persons, or places that they refer to as possible. The more advanced learner can deal with semiconcrete learning materials that tend toward intangible similarities or resemblances. The sophisticated learner can conceptualize abstractly because the series of funded learning experiences in the sophisticated learner's background has provided a basis for rich conceptual understanding.

Semiconcrete learning experiences and materials for art students are crucially important, owing to certain characteristics of the subject matter. Alphanumeric *and* pictographic images, words *and* pictures, ideas *and* icons are all important in the visual arts because each functions to clarify and instruct. They function differently from one another and, in the extreme, they are mutually independent. Certain kinds of pictorial concepts cannot be effectively expressed verbally, just as certain verbal concepts cannot be effectively expressed pictorially(4). The pervasive, personal, and recognizable attributes of an artwork, which allow us instant, tacit recognition and appreciation of a Matisse or a Mozart, a Still or an Ives, are displayed to us visually or aurally. They are, in J. Gibson's terms, "primary surrogates"(5). These are presented meanings of artworks available to the sophisticated learner and denied the naive learner. To move the naive learner toward such sophistication requires semiconcrete learning experiences and materials, so that primary surrogates, the presented meanings of artworks, are recognized and reacted to. These acts are basic to enjoying the arts and understanding aesthetic experiences(6).

Books and all forms of written, symbolic (abstract) materials are inadequate to the learning of presented meanings in pictorial communication. The visual arts are specifically manifested as pictorial imagery, and understanding the presented meanings of art objects must begin with empathic and educated viewing of objects. Visual concepts embedded in artworks are aspects of the iconic imagery that they present to the viewer. These presented concepts provide access to aesthetic realities (for the sophisticated student of the arts) that simply cannot be reached through verbal means. Visual images present veridical iconic communications to the viewer, and these must be experienced visually, concretely, as a foundation for their understanding. John Dewey pointed out, a long time ago, that it is fallacious to believe that what the imagery artists have created "can be translated into words with little if any esthetic loss"(7). There is some violation of the aesthetic integrity and some loss of intended iconic communication when a visual artwork is presented by words or any other media than the original. As anyone who has experienced the viewing of original artworks knows, vicarious experiences with the arts are shadows of reality.

Like all communication, visual imagery and its presented meanings are a mystery to those poorly acquainted with their fundamentals. Understanding and using visual communications with mastery and sophistication are as much learning tasks as understanding and using any other means of communication. There are stages of development and varying levels of learning to be achieved in these tasks. A cycle of learning experiences, based upon semiconcrete learning materials, is needed by the student of the arts in order to achieve conceptual growth and facility. These, in turn, are the basis for genuine aesthetic experience and sophisticated mastery of the concepts of art(8).

Two forms of semiconcrete learning materials for art education have been developed and used extensively, which are known as "kits and caboodles." There are many bases upon which the design of kits and caboodles is founded(9), but the primary aim is simply to provide semiconcrete learning materials that contribute to ultimate mastery of the visual, presented meanings of art objects. The conceptual realm that is presented in paintings, drawings, prints, sculpture, and all visual art forms are a major aspect of the subject matter of art(*10*).

A kit is a packaged collection of related materials designed to teach the user a predetermined content specific to the arts in conceptual, historical, critical, or aesthetic dimensions. Kits are assembled and created from related but diverse packageable materials. The relatedness of their diverse contents is their strength. A caboodle is a variation of a kit. Caboodles are packaged collections of related materials designed to provide the user experiences with content specific to the arts of conceptual, historical, critical, or aesthetic dimensions. The major difference between the two is their respective purposes. Kits are designed for specific instruction. Caboodles are designed for learning outcomes or learning experiences without predictable definition. For instance, a caboodle of many art reproductions on postcards, gathered together because the original objects were created during the 1950s, may teach many different outcomes. Only one of these may be "art of the 1950s." Because caboodles are one variation of a kit, in the following discussion "kit" will be used to refer to both types of materials unless otherwise specified.

Unlike textbooks or art curricula, kits may contain variable, adaptive, manipulable, alterable, nonsequential devices and images, and other visual, aural, and tactile materials in organized form. A kit or a caboodle, unlike a textbook, can be put together quickly and a new idea or event brought to the student almost as quickly as its artifacts become available. Kits that present local artists, regional and other recent exhibitions, local art projects, contents of local museums, and many similar themes that may never reach textbook publication (and if they do, it will be several years later) can be presented in the classroom as quickly as appropriate materials are assembled and packaged. A diverse collection of images that clarify a visual concept is easily brought together as a kit. Visual concepts that require diverse materials to exemplify the concept are most appropriately presented in the form of kits.

Great numbers of commercially available devices and materials can be used to support art learning and visual concept learning. Yet few are specifically designed for classrooms, and fewer still are available with specified correlation to specified art concepts or typical art education outcomes. Imaginative teachers can make these materials fit their instructional programs—though usually this requires alteration, regrouping, or additions to the available materials. Such alteration, regrouping, and creation of additions that increase the instructional value of the materials serve as a beginning for creating kits.

If we take sophisticated mastery of subject matter based upon developed adult understandings as the end point of art education, we must relate and judge all educational experiences and materials offered the student against that conception. This "yardstick" challenges many practices currently offered in art classrooms. Every experience offered students should be judged as to its validity in the world of art. Semiconcrete experiences and materials, reflecting valid art content, should be offered every student. These materials should lead the student toward the problems, practices, and solutions (products) of adult artists. It is in experiencing these that the learner's conceptual understandings may expand from the naive to the sophisticated. Kits and caboodles designed for this purpose are one means of enriching the art program in schools. They are not curricula per se. They may serve motivational, enrichment, or expansion needs of the teacher's program. They may also introduce to the student content and experiences that would otherwise not occur in the ongoing program. In this additive sense, kits and caboodles are learning resources much like library books or trips to museums. They offer students independent inquiry experiences. If well designed, use of the materials will contribute significantly to the student's education. It is this latter use, as additive content, that should direct the kit and caboodle designer.

1. *Art* is the subject matter.
2. Only *one* idea–icon–theme is presented.
3. Form should be *consistent* with content.
4. *Visual* materials should be used to present visual concepts.
5. *Verbal* materials should be used to present verbal concepts.
6. Kits and caboodles should be designed for *independent,* personal use by students.
7. The need for valid *critical, historical,* and *conceptual* content should mitigate against "production" or "media" themes.
8. Kits and caboodles should contain a variety of *touchables:* multi-sensory, manipulative materials.
9. Kits contain directions, study guides, and extension references.
10. Caboodles are self-contained, without study guides or reference lists.

    1. Art is the subject matter. An excellent art education kit introduces or teaches concepts that are viable in the field of art. These may be an artist, an artist's works, or selected works by an artist, a style, an iconic image, a visual theme, or any other art-related concept. Art concepts are not found in educational theory, child development theory, or typical art curricula. Art concepts are found in art criticism, art history, artists' writings, and, of course, in the defining characteristics of artists' works.

    2. Only one concept is the proper content for one kit. A kit may be used to present broad, inclusive themes, but only one theme or concept should be pursued by every piece contained in the kit. Every component, whether visual or verbal, should be singularly present and reinforce one organizing principle.

3. The form of a kit should be consistent with its contents. "Funk Art" as a theme or "M. C. Esher" as a theme dictate wholly different contents and exterior forms of the kit. It is inappropriate to present only "hands-off," expensive, coffee-table art books as study materials in art classes. Some kits may be designed to be consumed, just as students use up the manila paper or clay. Some kit themes may lend themselves to that, although most will not.

4. Visual materials should be used to present visual concepts. At the extreme, totally nontextual, totally iconic kits are most appropriate to the purposes of learning iconic concepts and recognizing presented meanings of artworks. This is an extreme, and the more sensible position is to minimize the verbal contents as much as possible. Visual concepts are best presented and developed through the examination of visual materials.

5. Verbal materials should be used to present basically verbal concepts. Surrealism, Dada, art manifestos, art criticism, and certain other art phenomena are distinguished more by their ideational base than by their visual manifestations. Such themes are best presented to students as collections of writings, photos of practitioners, and historical settings than by the insufficient or partial evidence their visual manifestations present.

6. Because learning and aesthetic responding are personal, individualized acts, kits should be created for individual use by students. Packages for teachers and for simultaneous use by large groups of students are misdirected. Kits for individualized learning are needed for students to use independently of the class or the teacher.

7. Additionally, because we are creating materials to fill learning needs not commonly met, materials for art production lessons are inappropriate. There is a plethora of production experiences based upon the use of art media available to art teachers. There is a dearth of materials designed to teach art concepts and visual understanding as classroom experiences. Therefore, kits should be used to present critical, historical, and conceptual content from the arts and to enrich aesthetic experiences for students.

8. Kits should contain "touchables." The kit should allow a manipulative, adaptive physical rearrangement and selective use of its contents by students. This physical contact and selective use are precisely the reasons why kits and caboodles best serve the learning model that underlies them.

9. Kits will contain directions to the student, study guides for the materials contained, and extensions such as related bibliographies, production experiences, or questions that require further experience with the content to be answered.

10. Caboodles, unlike kits, are self-contained. Their contents will fill all the above premises as appropriate except premise 9. Their use will, like reading a library book or visiting a museum exhibition, contribute nonaccountable experience and content to the student.

The preceding premises are a conceptual framework that the kit designer applies to the actual creation of such learning materials. Conceptualization of a kit, itself, will proceed in the following order:

1. Identify the "BIG IDEA," the possible organizer to be presented.
2. Analyze the organizer into component parts.
3. Identify a single theme as the actual organizer.
4. Justify the importance of this theme in the world of art.
5. Project all possible material contents you may want to include.
6. Identify application of possible contents to the theme.
7. Project actual contents to be used.
8. Describe the range of educational settings and uses intended.
9. Describe the subject matter or curriculum orientation to be served.
10. Project evaluation of the contents and their effectiveness.

Because these are "pencil-and-paper" steps, the kit designer can critique, then modify and improve the kit's instructional worth by applying the premises at each step.

Perhaps the most important and crucial step in the development of an instructional kit is the selection and defining of its organizer. More mistakes are made at this step than at any other. The organizer, whether a concept, icon, artist, style, or any other, must be weighed, first, as to its validity in the study of art. Second, it must be narrowed from a general idea to a practical, specific idea. Third, it must be conceived in practical terms of available components. Some examples of organizers that fail one or more of these tests include "Picasso" (too inclusive; narrow to one medium, one work, one period, or one decade of his life), "Line," "Color," "Shape," "Texture," or "Composition" (questionable validity as isolated content, too inclusive, physically impractical if comprehensive; these typical art education organizers should be avoided). These are examples cited to caution the designer of the need to critically question the content organizer chosen before proceeding further. The decisions made at this step will have more bearing on the educational worth of the ultimate kit than those made at any following step.

A further critique, after completing the preceding conceptualized model, may be applied by selecting the choices offered in the following sentences:

1. Designed for (a) individual or (b) group use.
2. Designed for (a) heuristic "discovery," or for (b) direct, straightforward presentation of content.
3. Contents present (a) introductory, (b) exploratory, or (c) summative content.
4. Kit presents (a) a single concept or (b) interrelated concepts.
5. Content is (a) timeless or (b) dated.
6. Kit (a) raises questions or (b) answers questions.
7. Organizer is presented primarily (a) visually or (b) verbally.

8. Presentation is (a) subjective or (b) objective.
9. Presentation is (a) expressive–poetic or (b) factual–precise.
10. Contents (a) may be used nonsequentially or (b) require necessary sequence.
11. (a) Kit–caboodle or (b) its contents are planned for (a) consumption by students or (b) retention by the teacher.

Each choice made in each of the preceding sentences will help direct the kit designer. Each choice reflects application of the premises offered earlier. Each should be examined critically and rationalized regarding consistency and integrity to the organizer, the "big idea," to be presented by the kit. Each bears heavily on the function intended, whether the materials created will be a kit or a caboodle.

If all the preceding have been followed, the resulting kits will be based validly on concepts derived from the arts, develop a single theme in depth, contain highly visual and minimally verbal content as appropriate, be designed for individual and independent use by students, and support the learning of conceptual content from the arts through physical manipulation of their contents.

The premises and steps are adaptable because the design of kits must allow for adaptation each time a new organizer is chosen. However, many patterns of content have emerged from the study of commercial resources and observation of student-created kits. Here are some models offered to exemplify, in more tangible terms, the ideas that have been presented.

An "artist" kit may take several forms. If the concept is the visual character of *his work,* the kit should contain as many images created by the artist as possible. If it is the visual character of one aspect of his work, the contents will be limited to that aspect only. Titles and dates of works may be included, but care should be taken that they do not compete with images; they should be on the reverse of images or separately catalogued. In addition, the kit should contain criticism of that work, preferably from reviews in major periodicals made available as reproductions of the original sources. The kit may also contain some of the artist's writing, his picture or portrait, and some reproductions of works by the artist's contemporaries, or possibly images that influenced his work.

Another, more exciting "artist" kit presents the artist himself. The theme *is* "Jackson Pollock" for instance. Now the kit designer has to select and present quite different contents. The purpose is to personalize— humanize—the artist as much as possible. Personal things are required as contents: snapshots of childhood, family, friends, the artist at work and at play, replicas of correspondence (preferably in the artist's handwriting), pictures of the artist's studio, a facsimile of his signature, a tape recording of the artist in interview (these may be reconstructed from the writings of an artist if he is no longer available for interview), perhaps a time-line of world events paralleling the artist's life. The kit will contain a few—but only a few—reproductions of his work. This type of kit displays an aspect of the arts rarely presented. How many of us know major artists in a personal, humanizing sense? This type of kit often helps students accept an artist whose works have been ignored or avoided in the past.

A major type of kit, usually a caboodle, is truly iconic. An image that recurs frequently in artworks, such as "the sun" or "the horse," is the theme. This type presents as many isolated images of that theme from as many sources as possible. The kit designer should deliberately avoid artist, source, date, or the attribution of any other historical data. The image repeated over and over again *is* the only critical content. "The English Sunrise"(*11*) is the title of a photographic essay that contains about 80 color photograph variations of an iconic image: a rising sun with radial beams emerging from the horizon. I bought a copy, shared it with my family, and from that day to this—over three years—we still point out an "English Sunrise" when we notice one on a fence or garage door or highway sign. This type of kit, the iconic image, is very effective in heightening visual awareness and attending. It forces, by its repetitiveness, conscious awareness of visual features that may have been ignored or attended to only lightly in the past. It calls attention to recurrent themes and icons and their constant redepiction and adaptation by artists.

A similarly constructed type of kit is based upon expressive themes that recur frequently in artworks. Death, loneliness or alienation, existentialism, love, the artist as social critic, the artist as art critic are a few such themes. There are obviously an infinity of possibilities. "The artist as critic" may be shown as a major artist's work that is obvious in its redepiction of another artist's work. Some examples are "David" by Magritte, "Alexandros of Antioch" by Dali, "Daumier" by Van Gogh, "Stuart" by Larry Rivers, "Monet" by Lichtenstein, and "Ingres" by Picasso. The world of art is replete with this phenomenon, and it portrays a fascinating visual concept when gathered together as paired images (the original and the "copy"). This particular concept raises many new questions for art students unfamiliar with the frequency with which it occurs in the arts.

Another visual concept that may be used as a kit theme is an artistic style, either of an artist or of a group of artists. "Pop" as a visual phenomenon may be presented through the works of Warhol, Wesselman, Lichtenstein, and others. "Pop" works in large quantity, isolated from non-Pop works by the same artists, present a visual manifestation of what "Pop" means as a visual concept. Once again, the nonvisual facts of artists' names, dates, size of works, locations, and all forms of noniconic data are best separately catalogued in this type of kit. Conversely, historical–cultural setting and background materials in the forms of magazine articles, criticisms, artist's writings, photo essays on "Pop" sources are all possible contents for this type of kit as enrichment of its visual content.

The preceding paragraphs describe only a few of the possible types of art content that kits and caboodles can present in the classroom. Their possible conceptual content is limited only by the knowledge and imagination of kit designers. Teachers with vision can expand the learning experiences offered in their classrooms through adaptation of commercial resources and the creation of kits of learning materials in support of their own class content and teaching purposes. They can offer their students visual experiences in support of visual concept learning. They can minimize vicarious, abstract classroom experiences and in some degree offer semiconcrete, veridical experiences in the arts and aesthetics. Such experiences enrich, expand, and strengthen the conceptual understandings achieved through classroom studio experiences. Conceptually strong, well-designed, and carefully constructed kits and caboodles that present important visual arts concepts to students can help them move from a naive to a sophisticated level of understanding of the concepts of art.

References

1. Arnheim, Rudolph. "Art and Humanism." *Art Education,* 24:7, October 1971.
2. Whitehead, Alfred N. *The Aims of Education.* New York: The Free Press, 1929.
3. Dale, Edgar, and John Belland. *A Guide to the Literature on Audio-Visual Education.* Stanford, Calif.: ERIC Clearing House on Media and Technology, September 1971.
4. Clark, Gilbert A. "Icons and Ideas for Aesthetic Education." *In* Ralph A. Smith (ed.), *Aesthetic Education Today: Problems and Prospects.* Columbus, Ohio: Ohio State University, 1973.
5. Gibson, James J. "A Theory of Pictorial Perception." *Audio-Visual Communication Review,* 2:1, Winter 1954.
6. Gombrich, Ernest H. "Visual Discovery Through Art." *Arts Magazine,* November 1975; and Broudy, Harry S. *Enlightened Cherishing.* Urbana, Ill.: University of Illinois Press, 1972.
7. Dewey, John. *Art as Experience.* New York: Minton, Balch and Company, 1934.
8. Broudy, Harry S. "The Structure of Knowledge in the Arts." *In* Ralph A. Smith (ed.), *Aesthetics and Criticism in Art Education.* Chicago: Rand McNally & Company, 1966.
9. Clark, Gilbert A. "Art Kits and Caboodles: Alternative Learning Materials for Education in the Arts." *Art Education,* 28:5, September 1975.
10. Clark, Gilbert A. "Art Is Not a Verb, Except Poetically." *Art Education,* 27:9, December 1974.
11. Rice, Brian, and Tony Evans. *The English Sunrise.* London: Mathews, Miller, Dunbar, 1972.

Operational Concepts

1. The learning of art must begin at tangible, concrete levels and progress, sequentially, to the more intangible abstract levels.

2. Between the concrete and the abstract lies a middle ground, a "semiconcrete" level of artistic understanding that must be dealt with through specific content and methodology.

3. Both words and pictures should be used in teaching the visual arts; each contributes to communication and clarification.

4. In art instruction, the teacher must seek (a) specified outcomes relating to artistic understanding and knowledge, and (b) unspecified outcomes relating to aesthetic appreciation, artistic preference, and affective response.

Implications

Clark's ideas parallel, in a number of ways, those advanced by Greer in the previous essays. Both authors are convinced that the art curriculum must be based on something more than finger-painting and handicrafts. In an intriguing distinction, Clark refers to "kits" that can be used to achieve prespecified objectives in art education, and "caboodles" that lend themselves to more subjective, less definable outcomes.

Kits, says Clark, should stress particular concepts derived from the arts, develop a single theme in depth, and use primarily visual rather than verbal presentation. Above all, he argues, the learning materials incorporated in such teaching units, whether kits or something else, must permit children to learn through the physical manipulation of the content.

What, perhaps, is of greatest significance in the author's construction is the differentiation between instruction that communicates art concepts and instruction that elicits aesthetic response. Taste and preference, in matters of art, obviously cannot be taught. Fundamental knowledge, on the other hand, can. The obvious implication, therefore, is that teachers—in any given lesson—should be clear about which of the two objectives is intended.

Carol D. Holden

The Arts in General Education: Aesthetic Education

A CURRICULUM DILEMMA

What is aesthetic education? Do children need aesthetic education? Do we need to teach it in the schools? If so, who should teach it? What arts should be included in the aesthetic education curriculum? Is there a framework for teaching and learning that addresses the problems of content selection, methodology, and evaluation in aesthetic education? The answers to these questions will provide a basis for understanding and a general orientation to aesthetic education, as well as give some general direction for the inclusion of the arts in the regular school day.

WHAT IS AESTHETIC EDUCATION?

The term "aesthetic" is usually defined to mean the "beautiful" and that usage implies a standard for excellence or a yardstick by which to measure other similar objects or events. This historical and traditional connotation still prevails, but in current usage the term has come to take on a larger meaning and to refer to qualities that are intrinsically interesting to our senses in terms of color, shape, sound, or texture, and/or which appeal to our sense of form in terms of balance, proportion, and composition. The basis for aesthetic education stems from the nature of aesthetic experience. This kind of experience is different from ordinary, practical, or rational experience, just as it is different from psychological or religious experience. By aesthetic education, we mean the deliberate intervention in the artistic life of the child in two distinct phases or modes, the impressive phase and the creative phase. A successful program of aesthetic education depends on a good balance and combination of these two phases of teaching and learning. The impressive phase develops skills of looking, listening, and discerning—the perceptual and contemplative facet of aesthetic education. In the creative phase, we encourage children to explore the artistic possibilities of various media by experimenting with and manipulating paint, movement, sounds, words, or clay. This is the active, participatory, "hands on" side in which children physically encounter the materials of the various arts.

THE NEED FOR AESTHETIC EDUCATION

Although there is a recent surge of interest in the left and right hemisphere functions of the brain and their accompanying modes of perception and expression, the left hemisphere, with its linear, analytical, discursive, and mathematical functions, dominates the instructional mode of the school. This, of course, characterized the rush of the fifties to "catch up" with the Russians by beefing up our science programs in schools. However, many educators and parents now realize that there is more to education than just the cognitive and/or replicative (left hemisphere) side of learning. We have been systematically ignoring an important aspect of children's lives and what makes people uniquely human—the imaginative, artistic, visual, and metaphoric side of knowing and education.

A possible side effect of this curriculum lopsidedness is that our children are "turned off" at increasingly lower grade levels in schools. Teachers complain that often children exhibit a strange, almost apathetic, attitude while in school. A phenomenon common only to the high schools a few years ago, we now sometimes find this malaise in the elementary school by the second or third grade. The characteristic mannerisms of this "institutional attitude" are listlessness, apathy, nonparticipation, and poor attention. This attitude or role serves the function of a mask, disguising the student's real identity and personality; feelings and genuine concern are not exhibited. Perhaps it is reasoned that, if one's true self is not revealed, one cannot get hurt or suffer while in school. In other words, the right hemisphere function is suppressed and the reward system of the school is geared toward that condition. If a child is not truly and fully involved in a task or in a situation, there is less pain in failure; but, paradoxically, there is less pleasure and pride in success. Lack of interest in learning may be at least partly attributable to this curriculum imbalance. As long as the replicative use of learning and the use of standardized tests to measure the outcomes of learning dominate school practice, the schools will continue to play the role of child sorter—winners and losers according to one-dimensional test scores.

TRADITIONAL APPROACHES TO ARTS PROGRAMS

We have had a strong tradition of the arts in the schools in America, especially in music, and often these programs have been excellent, the best in the world. The music education programs have traditionally been built around the performing group—the band, orchestra, and chorus—and by their very nature have been geared for the talented or gifted students. It is a paradox that what makes them excellent is what removes them from the rubric of general education. However, even these very strong performance-based programs are now finding themselves more and more on the fringe of the curriculum. The time allotted for the program is minimal and is often really outside the regular school day, with rehearsals and classes scheduled for the early morning or in the late afternoon outside the official school day. Even if there is time in the regular day for class instruction or rehearsals, the student is often forced to make an unhappy choice between the music offering and some other required or elective curriculum area. It is true that there are some "general" arts and music courses, but they are usually one- or two-semester courses in junior high school and are "appreciation" courses or survey courses. In high schools such courses are nearly all electives, with a small percentage of the students electing them. The performance programs concentrate on the acquisition of technical skills and the appreciation programs concentrate on cognitive skills; nowhere is there a concentration on skills of perception, interpretation, or creative expression.

Art education receives less specialized attention in the curricula of the public schools than does music education. According to Eisner(1), competence in the teaching of art at the elementary level in American schools is required by less than half the school systems, and art specialists are present in only 10 percent of the schools. When present, the specialists tend to be itinerant teachers, traveling from school to school meeting forty to fifty classes per week and often seeing each class as infrequently as once a month. As in music, arts education programs tend to concentrate on skill development and the production of art products and usually those that can be completed in one class period.

Criticism of these programs and these teachers almost seems unfair and unfeeling. Yet there has been criticism of the performance–production approach to arts education, and it often stems from the argument that developing technical skills does not develop aesthetic sensitivity. This is evident when scholars claim that the arts education programs in our schools produce technically adequate or superior students in art and music, but that these same students often lack basic understandings of the nature of their art(2). Also these same technically superior students are often not conversant in any other art area and may be aesthetically naive. Furthermore, there is a cyclical effect in having technical specialists teach the arts programs in the schools(3):

> Teacher-training institutions continue to train teachers-to-be as artists and performers who will also teach, and these young teachers go into the schools and are caught up in teaching practices that maintain music and art as single-track, narrowly conceived subjects.

This cycle leads to an early specialization, which of necessity defines the music and art programs in the secondary schools as courses for the gifted or talented. It is no surprise to discover that "nationally, some 80 or 90 percent of the students do not participate in art or music at all while they are in high school"(4).

It might be argued that the standard music and art programs in many of our schools are irrelevant to the aesthetic education of the child, partly due to the approach and partly due to the fact that at best the programs occupy a tiny fraction of the allotted school curriculum time. The skills of performing, the cognitive skills acquired in appreciation or survey courses, and even technical skills learned in theory courses just are not the ones we would hope to develop in our students in aesthetic education.

Classroom teachers are often frustrated because they realize that the arts are neglected in the race for improved test scores and cognitive development. They may want to include the arts in their teaching, but may feel inadequate to do the job. Sometimes this feeling of inadequacy or lack of confidence is objective; many classroom teachers have limited skills in teaching and performing in the arts. Classroom teachers' lack of confidence may stem partly from the image of the teacher as a performing artist; no doubt it is an intimidating image. However, would a classroom teacher show the same reluctance to teach the arts if we could outline another approach to teaching and learning that is not performance based and which is possible for the generalist teacher to undertake? While wary of promising anything dramatic, there is a framework for teaching and learning in aesthetic education that has been tried and found successful and satisfying for both students and teachers in elementary classrooms. This is the perceptual approach to aesthetic education based primarily on the work of Harry Broudy and others who tried the approach in many settings and at many levels. To understand this form of aesthetic education, one needs to make at least three basic assumptions about arts education as part of general education:

1. Schooling is deliberate intervention in the life of the student.
2. The goals of general education include the development of the aesthetic capacities of all the students, rather than the select few.
3. Aesthetic education is a dimension of value education in that art has extra-aesthetic functions and shapes values and actions as well as feelings through the power of the "aesthetic image."

Whether or not there is extracurricular arts education for some of the students is not central to this position. Therefore, if the argument from Broudy's philosophy that the cultivation of the students' aesthetic capacities is a defensible task for the school and is to be subsumed under the general education rubric, then some form of arts education other than the present performance models should be explored. What follows is a framework for the establishment of this two-sided approach to aesthetic education.

A PERCEPTUAL APPROACH TO AESTHETIC EDUCATION

According to some theorists, an experience may be an "aesthetic experience," as distinguished from other types of experience, if certain conditions are met.

1. The experience must be a perceptual one. There must be an "encounter between a person and a thing, object, or event.

2. The person must come to the encounter with an "aesthetic attitude." One cannot be distracted by personal or practical interests or the resulting experience will be less than fully aesthetic. Lack of a proper attitude may partly explain why sometimes an art experience is not really enjoyable, and teachers should have some sensitivity toward their students' "frame of mind." Doesn't it seem wrongheaded to continually use Friday afternoon or the day before a holiday for arts experiences in school? A viewer with an aesthetic attitude and a work of art, object, or event are two conditions necessary for aesthetic experience. What else seems to be necessary?

3. One must bring to the experience a well-developed imagination. Some artists have defined art as being good honest work plus imagination. The literal interpretation of art is just as mistaken as the literal interpretation of a joke. It takes imagination to perceive human traits or moods where they actually and logically do not exist. To see paint as looking agitated or calm takes imagination. Children are said to have fine imaginations; they regularly see human qualities in nonhuman things and events. They anthropomorphize animals and nature, which takes imagination. Unfortunately, this natural gift (right-hemisphere function) is educated out of children by the kind of world that reinforces practical and technical responses over the aesthetic; too often parents and teachers negatively reinforce a lively imagination rather than capitalize on it to promote creativity and aesthetic sensitivity.

4. Another component in aesthetic experience is the use of metaphorical language. Artists use metaphors to convey their meaning and as such are a source of new and imaginative images that make life vivid and interesting; these metaphorical images have aesthetic as well as extra-aesthetic value. Images affect our feelings, serve as models of behavior or values, and function socially as stereotypes. Seeing X as Y takes training in the use of metaphors.

5. The fifth condition required for an experience to be aesthetic is that the perceived expressive qualities must be properly located *in* the work of art or object of perception, rather than in the viscera or mind of the viewer. This is the principle of phenomenological objectivity, which is the key to understanding this view of aesthetic experience. The expressive mood or character qualities, whatever they are, must be perceived as being out there in the picture, film, dance, or music, not actually felt authentically by the

viewer. If the viewer experiences personally the expressive qualities of an artwork (e.g., *actually feels* angry, depressed, or fearful), the chances are he is having a psychological experience and probably not an aesthetic experience. Much current popular art contrives to get the viewer personally involved to the extent that one actually vicariously identifies with a character or situation and gets a "thrill" out of the experience. This type of experience eliminates much that is aesthetic from the encounter; it is not possible to maintain an authentic identification with the main character and still see the subtleties of the plot, the interplay of the characters, and nuances of the situation. Oddly enough, it takes more and more to engage the viewer in this psychological response, and producers often must resort to extreme portrayals and situations. Disasters must be gigantic or super-colossal to have any impact. Characters must be supremely evil to get our attention, and violence must be reduced to the most raw and brutal levels to affect us. The public seems to be caught up in an addiction syndrome in which everything must be more and more thrilling and exciting to attract attention.

Of course, this is partly what is wrong with popular art in any medium. Really good art has staying powers that the wildly exciting can never have. The work which puzzles and engages us over a long time is the art that stays with us and affects us most deeply. To the extent that schools capitulate to the popular arts and do not use works that engage the mind as well as the viscera, they will do little to raise the taste levels of the students or in any significant way contribute to their aesthetic education.

These five components of aesthetic experience offer teachers a structure for developing the aesthetic capacities and sensitivities of their students, and further make the whole process amenable to instruction, because it is couched in observable and perceptual terms rather than in terms of vague inner states and feelings. Being amenable to instruction implies a content or cognitive structure by means of which curriculum developers and teachers may organize materials and experiences for the students, and, further, that there is at least some means of evaluating this instruction. If we agree that it is the role of the school to develop the capacities of children in the aesthetic dimension of value education, how might a program be structured?

THE TWO PHASES OF AESTHETIC EDUCATION

A complete program of aesthetic education depends on incorporating two phases of teaching and learning: (1) the impressive and (2) the creative. Aesthetic education means instruction in the perception of, as well as the creation of, artistic objects and events. By unifying these two phases of arts education into a side-by-side, dual approach with commonalities in purpose and experience, the generalist teacher may be able to offer children a more

221

complete aesthetic education than is usually the case. Only by relating what is created and expressed to what is perceived and imagined can a program in the arts be called fully aesthetic.

The Impressive Phase

The impressive phase is primarily concerned with the acquisition of perceptual skills to further aesthetic experience. These skills can be broken down into four main categories: (1) the sensory, (2) the formal, (3) the technical, and (4) the expressive. These four perceptual dimensions of aesthetic experience need to be well defined for the sake of instruction and so that the generalist teacher can undertake the task of teaching.

The sensory dimension of aesthetic perception includes the discernment of those qualities that make the artwork interesting to our senses (e.g., the visual elements: colors, shapes, size, line; the tactile elements: texture and the "touch qualities" of a medium; the kinetic elements: gestures, movements; the aural elements: sounds in all their variety). If children are to become "enlightened perceivers," they must develop skills in grasping the subtle elements of an artwork or an object. When one has these skills, one has at least some "aesthetic literacy" or "media sense."

The formal dimension implies discernment of the structural or organizational properties of an artwork, that is, the ability to pick out the pattern or design in terms of composition—themes and variations, balance and symmetry, similarities and differences, proportion and relationships. Form is very important to the working artist or musician, and changes in form or composition can change the overall artistic idea or image. Form is what ties the work together and gives it the look of "unity" or harmony with itself or artistic "rightness."

The technical dimension implies sensitivity to the particular skill, technique, or craftsmanship of the artist in creating a work of art. Obviously, in some works this dimension is more easily perceived than in others. In some modern or avant-garde works, it is the fascination with technique itself that is of the utmost interest. Interest in technique prompts questions: how did he do it? what materials did he use? was it difficult to do? is it hard for the performer to execute? Notice the distinction between an artist who **executes** an artwork and one who performs the artwork of another or replicates the artwork; where does the artist leave off and performer begin? Children are often very curious about how the artist got certain effects, and this curiosity may lead to a deeper aesthetic interest; interest in technique and/or skill of execution may lead to a genuine appreciation of the art.

The expressive dimension of aesthetic perception is more complicated than the preceding aspects in that it is more ambiguous, elusive, and personalistic. Art seems to embody human expressive qualities, actually to take on human traits and feelings. We regularly assign human feelings and character traits to inanimate things and animals, and children do it more naturally than adults. As we grow older we think this is silly and childish, but as we lose this ability we lose an important way to know the world, that is, the nondiscursive, metaphorical mode of knowing and experiencing. There is no "correct" expressiveness to be perceived in art; teachers should avoid telling children just how he "ought" to see or hear anything. Every person brings to an aesthetic encounter his or her own personal background and history of experiences, associations, and imagination which color that experience. One purpose of aesthetic education is to enhance and enrich those associations and experiences so that the child tends to have fewer stereotyped responses to art, and instead has a very open, imaginative response to the images he sees. We might expect that as skills in perception develop the child will tend to become more demanding of the art around him. Obvious and stereotyped images will not be so satisfactory as they once were. Clearly, this reflects a shift in values, a change in taste toward "connoisseurship" (see Table 1).

People, including children, need a variety of images of possible lifestyles, forms of personhood, images of dignified work, images of helping and sharing, images of children growing up in a pluralistic society, images of a nation as a part of a complex world, and images of maintaining life on a very small planet. These are necessarily aesthetic images, which will appeal to our imagination and intellect as well as to our emotions. Only if the images offered are, of necessity, more creative, complex, and varied than the type usually presented by the popular media will there be choice enough to stimulate imaginative transformation and/or modeling. Therefore, if a teacher wants to truly develop aesthetic sensitivity in her students, she must go beyond the popular arts as a source of content for aesthetic education. Furthermore, as one becomes sensitive to the variety and subtlety in art and as one's perceptions become more refined, it is possible to begin to see the world around you in entirely different ways. People and places take on more individuality and character. The groups we may not have "really noticed" before come alive and are interesting, unique, and valuable. Popular art, especially television, tends to reinforce social stereotypes; serious art tends to break down these stereotypes and force us to see the unusual and individual in all the complexity and particularity of that experience.

The Creative Phase

The creative phase of aesthetic education includes the creating, experimenting, and experiencing involved in making an artistic or expressive form using the materials of a medium. Children need to manipulate the sensory elements of an art area and work with them toward solving the problems of form—balance, symmetry, proportion, and rhythm. To get a creation that looks or sounds complete and unified and works well in that

223

TABLE 1 Hierarchy of Values and Goals in Aesthetic Education (5)

	VALUES	GOALS	
Life or long term	Critical judgment	Develops authentic standards for justifying taste based on critical evaluation. Uses learnings interpretively and applicatively, as a critic	Distant or long term
	Connoisseurship or "enlightened cherishing"	Makes associative and interpretive use of school learnings in the aesthetic dimension of life	
	Aesthetic values high in personal value schemata	Exhibits behavior, makes choices, judgments, and criticisms based on aesthetic value system	
	Aesthetic experience is valued as a "special kind" of experience	Assumes aesthetic attitude; perceives aesthetic qualities and interprets expressive content imaginatively	
	The arts are valued for expressive properties; artistic activities merit approval and support	Perceives sensory, formal, technical, and expressive qualities in several art areas; expressive characteristics of various media are explored by creating, composing, or constructing aesthetic forms	
School or short term	Aesthetic concepts organize perception	A vocabulary for talking about art is developed; terminology, definitions, and aesthetic theory contribute; learnings are used replicatively; perception is directed toward artworks	Proximate or short term
	Art is a candidate for attention		

medium is the challenge of creating in art. For us in the general classroom, the process of creativity is much more important toward aesthetic development and aesthetic sensitivity than is the realization of some satisfactory product.

The aesthetic decision making that comes with solving formal problems and problems of manipulating a sensory element leads to a sophistication that merely following a pattern can never accomplish. A child must learn to control the steps of his own creative efforts; ultimately, he must learn to rely on his own sensitivity and critical judgment. Unfortunately, this development is thwarted in many art classes when children cannot seem to decide on their own how their creation looks, but rather depend on the teacher to tell them that it is beautiful or lovely. The teacher should provide guidance in setting up initial artistic problems for the children to solve, but the development of a critical eye and reliable judgment is much more important than satisfactorily meeting the requirements of an assignment. Aesthetic decisions made during the course of progress of the work are important, perhaps more important than the ultimate outcome of the work, for enhancing aesthetic literacy.

We would hope that children would begin to find satisfactory artistic outlets for their imaginative ideas through the creation of aesthetic images in one medium or another. It is important for the teacher to remember that not everyone is equally comfortable or equally "at home" in each medium. Some of us find the world of sound more satisfactory; others find working in words or some visual expression best. Many young children need the opportunity to express their creative energy in terms of movement or dance. The point is that in most elementary classrooms there is very little exploration in very many media. It is usually very limited, and this may be one factor that contributes to stifling creative activity on the part of children. It also supports the criticism that the present arts programs in schools are too narrow in terms of the media explored.

SUMMARY

Educators and scholars in the arts have argued that the traditional approaches to education in the arts (the preformance–production approach and the appreciation approach) have failed to develop the general student's aesthetic perception of works of serious art. For Broudy, this is a critical flaw; he perceives aesthetic education as a part of general education for all students, ideally from K–12, not for just a select or talented few on a part-time basis. If we accept the argument that there is an aesthetic dimension to value education and a philosophy of education in which the "good life" is the aim of general education, with attainment of this goal being aided by the development of innate human capacities through (1) self-determination, (2) self-realization, and (3) self-integration(6), it follows that to cultivate the innate aesthetic capacities or potential of all students is a defensible role of the school. Broudy argues that to be "good" a life must be controlled by the person living it; it must not be the result of accident, the pushes and pulls of desires, or uncritical and unthinking choice. It is reason and imagination that give a life verve and character. The need for "aesthetic images" to stimulate the imagination of what life might be, what life could be, or what life ought to be is the extra-aesthetic role of aesthetic education and the social function of the arts. Through enriching the imagic store or image inventory of an individual's mind through the associative and interpretive uses of learning (right-hemisphere functions), aesthetic education can serve the function of presenting alternative possibilities of feeling, action, or being.

It is encouraging to find that agencies such as the Central Midwestern Regional Educational Laboratory, Inc., the John D. Rockefeller 3rd Fund, and the Cleveland Area Arts Council are interested in the problem of teacher education, both preservice and in-service. Of course, there is a curriculum materials shortage and a state certification problem for teachers. A number of states are now beginning to formulate comprehensive state plans for arts-in-education programs that go far beyond the narrow and limited traditional approaches to the arts in schools. Perhaps that progress which is slower and which stems from local and state educational agencies is likely to be more permanent and far-reaching than change that is mandated by the federal government and financed by huge amounts of money, but seems to wither away when the federal impetus is over or when the next bandwagon movement makes its appearance. If this is true, the outlook for aesthetic education and a broadly based arts-in-education curriculum for general education is very hopeful.

References

1. Elliot W. Eisner, *Educating Artistic Vision* (New York: Macmillan Publishing Co., Inc., 1972), p. 17.
2. Stephen A. Phillips, "A Course Design for the Teaching of Certain Art Concepts in an Integrated Fine Arts Course for Secondary Schools—A Formulative Study" (unpublished Ph.D. dissertation, Rutgers State University, 1966).
3. Kathryn Bloom, "Development of Arts and Humanities Programs," in *Toward an Aesthetic Education* (MENC, 1971), p. 90.
4. Ibid.
5. Carol D. Holden, "A Theoretical Framework for the Preparation of Elementary Education Teachers in Aesthetic Education" (unpublished Ph.D. dissertation, University of Illinois, 1975), p. 135.
6. Harry S. Broudy, *Building a Philosophy of Education,* 2nd ed. (Englewood Cliffs, N. J.: Prentice-Hall, Inc., 1961), p. 38.

Operational Concepts

1. Traditional instruction in the fine arts has concentrated upon the development of technical and cognitive skills.

2. Too little attention has been given to artistic perception, interpretation, and creative expression.

3. Aesthetic education should be an essential component in the general education of all students.

4. Effective aesthetic education involves two distinct aspects of teaching and learning: the impressive (perceptual skills related to aesthetic experience), and the creative (experiences involving the production of artistic and expressive form).

5. Five specific dimension of aesthetic experience should be stressed in the classroom: (a) perceptual experience, (b) the cultivation of aesthetic attitudes, (c) the stimulation of imagination, (d) practice in the use of metaphorical language, and (e) direct experience with art objects.

Implications

It is obvious that the theoretical ideas of Holden contrast somewhat with the arguments of the two preceding *Handbook* selections on art education. Despite these disagreements, however, there is also a good deal of consensus. For the purposes of the practitioner, consequently, it seems clear that aesthetic education warrants greater attention than it has routinely received. Such education should emphasize both creative and appreciative activity, expose children to artistic metaphor, provide them with direct aesthetic experience, and help learners to distinguish between artistic taste and artistic understanding.

It should be noted that the decision to include three articles on art education was not capricious or accidental. To the extent that the the curricular future is predictable, the indications are that art education will take on renewed importance as we move toward the third millennium.

Music

Beth Landis
Polly Carder

The Music Curriculum in the United States

Much of the eclecticism of American music education stems from deep within the American society. Surely no national group in the world is more widely diverse in as many ways as are the people of the United States. From the beginning, the American population was composed of groups and individuals with strong and differing characteristics. The characteristics have blended and mellowed, yet they remain. A traveler must find very striking the differences in the English language as spoken by Americans in Alabama, Texas, Minnesota, Maine, and metropolitan New York. This is but one of the evidences of cultural differences derived from the roots of three hundred years ago. Preferences in literature and the arts are as strong in many places as language differences. A child on an Arizona Navajo reservation, a Mexican-American child of New Mexico, and a San Francisco Chinese-American child will not sing the same folk songs or respond to music in the same way as a child of rural Vermont or rural Iowa. Nor will their parents be likely to have the same aspirations for arts education of their children. While in the past, especially in some periods of our history, Americans observed their old-country traditions and customs privately in their homes and neighborhoods, their attitude today is different. They often do not care to melt entirely into the image of the mythical American, but rather, they cherish their heritage and require that educators do likewise.

For generations in Germany and Hungary it has been most natural for children to begin musical experience with old, traditional folk songs of the country. Early America had no such songs, and from the beginning American children sang folk songs from the British Isles and Europe. In a nation still comparatively young, a literature of its own folk songs has developed, but often the songs are patterned after or even are based on melodies, rhythms, and texts from other places and times. A song (such as "En Roulant Ma Boule") that for one child is an oddity may be second

Reprinted from Beth Landis and Polly Carder, *The Eclectic Curriculum in American Music Education* (Washington, D. C.: Music Educators National Conference, 1973); by permission.

nature for a child in another part of the country. These facts give American children a very different starting place from children of other countries and a great variety of starting places within their own country. Furthermore, the philosophy of American music educators embraces the point of view that there is an obligation to include all musics of the world as material for music education, from ancient Chinese *gagaku* and the Indian *raga* and *tala* to twentieth-century composed music. Added to the variety of ethnic, folk, and composed literature is the literature of American popular or youth music and jazz.

Environmental and cultural differences are only one of the factors that affect the building of curriculum. The individual mental and emotional makeup of children gives a music teacher a great deal of pleasure and it gives him also the challenge and necessity of finding many avenues of musical appeal. Closely related to this challenge is that of developing a program for students with highly diversified goals. For some, music will become a profession. The music teacher is constantly pressed to feel that his program will be a help and not a hindrance to the musically gifted. For most, music will be an enrichment. To be enriching in the student years and to prepare for enrichment in later life, musical experiences must be vital, genuine, deep in emotional response and intellectual thought. The gamut of goals, including those of the dilettante, casual performer, professional performer, casual listener, and serious listener are included in the goals of musician–teachers working in a nation that aspires to educate all its children in all branches of human experience.

Other differences affecting curriculum in music education are those of school organization, the learning environment, and professional resources. A program designed for an urban, year-round high school from which students go directly into jobs or technical schools may be different from that designed for a rural or suburban high school. A program for an ungraded elementary school or for an open school will be somewhat different from that of a traditional school. An elementary program taught by trained music teachers who work directly with the children may not be the same as the program taught by classroom teachers. In education that encompasses all these differences in culture, locale, individual learning, diversified goals, school organization, learning environments, and professional resources, only a highly diversified curriculum can possibly function. Certainly, the differences are more numerous and more marked in the United States than anywhere else, and a chief objective must continue to be development of a diversified eclectic curriculum.

From where, then, or what, is unity derived? Certainly, fragmented and scattered plans for teaching music never can be effective. A bit of something here, an experience in something else there, in a program without design or developmental possibilities, never will result in satisfaction or the continuing, consistent growth that is essential in music education. In common practice today, the musical elements, defined in various ways, are considered to be the substance for contemplation, consideration, and analysis. The elements sometimes are defined in the general terms rhythm, melody, and harmony. From observation of these, the studies of related constituents such as dynamics and form are developed. Recently the trend with music educators is to define the elements in many terms, rather than few—terms that are less generic, more specific, and more inclusive, such as sound sources, pitch, pulse, duration, texture, dynamics, timbre, and organization. These terms are, to a greater degree, free from preconceptions and traditional meanings. Consideration of *units of pitches,* rather than *melody,* for example, makes possible analysis of the serial, chromatic, atonal, and electronic sequences of tones as well as the diatonic sequences that the term melody has come to connote. The term *sound sources* rather than *instruments* and *voices* allows for consideration of the many spoken, electronic, and concrete sounds found in contemporary music. These constituent elements, being the content of all music, become, then, the basis for study of musical sound. Whether the sound is the Indonesian gamelan, a Beethoven string quartet, drumming tunes from Ruwanda, or the latest American rock—consideration, analysis, and comparison are possible in terms of the basic elements. It is from the approach through observation and study of these elements that unity in the American music curriculum is chiefly derived.

Another curriculum dimension is quite generally accepted in this country—that of the types of participation through which musical content is experienced. The three areas of experience are performing, analytical listening, and experiencing–improvising–composing. Although in many schools they are not given equal emphasis, most teachers recognize the validity and need for all three. Each area has its concomitant musical skills. Development of skill in music reading is a part of each.

PERFORMING

Singing and playing music always have been and probably will continue to be the heart of the music curriculum. A major goal of American education is that every child develop his singing voice and enjoy expression in singing. Much of the curriculum in which children learn basic musical content and musical symbols stems from folk and composed songs children sing. Relatively simple melody and percussion instruments are considered to be an important part of classroom equipment. Bells, xylophones, the recorder, harmonica, Melodica, guitar, Autoharp, tambourine, drums, maracas, and a variety of other percussion instruments are commonly played by children in the elementary classroom. Opportunity to learn to play an orchestral instrument in the elementary school is a unique feature of American music education. Children in the upper age levels usually are offered lessons as a part of free public education, and sometimes instruments are furnished. Skills learned in small instrumental classes are reinforced by those learned in the general classroom. Reciprocally, young instrumentalists often play harmony parts with class singing and the class observes instruments at close range. Body movement and dance are a type of performing experience in the classroom. Primary children often have their first and most significant relationship with music as they listen and move to sounds played by the teacher on the piano, a drum, or other instrument, or on recordings. As children become aware of the musical elements, their movement is refined as realization of the music and becomes in fact a performance of it.

ANALYTICAL LISTENING

Believing that children must know a great deal of music literature beyond what they can perform, a large proportion of the curriculum is based on recorded music children hear and analyze. More or less unique to American education is the point of view that even young children should hear the greatest literature and a broad variety of it. From the beginning of their education, children hear sections of standard symphonies, concertos, and sonatas, and vocal works, as well as ethnic, electronic, and many other types of contemporary music. The biggest and most complex sounds are considered appropriate for children's listening. It is believed that general aesthetic experience is valuable and that intellectual analysis follows rather than precedes this experience. Primary children may dance with music they hear, play simple instruments with it, or discuss the more obvious elements. Older children will be expected to notice more of the details and to learn relationships. They may play motives on instruments or sing them. They may analyze verbally or through movement. Experience with a large repertoire of many types of music of all eras and cultures is expected to accumulate as a part of elementary education.

EXPERIMENTING–IMPROVISING–COMPOSING

The most generally accepted theory of American music education today is that students should discover musical principles through their own exploration and manipulation of sound. Teachers attempt to provide an environment in which children may experiment singly and in small groups with instruments, sung and spoken words, and tape recorders. Projects are initiated through which children explore sound sources, develop original patterns of sound, and discover and apply compositional principles. Problems of notation are discovered as children devise symbols for the sounds in their compositions. Such projects are important in the study of musical elements and structures and they have important value in building attitude toward less creative experiences. A child who has developed his own theme and variations will have deeper interest in those of Beethoven. A child who has just engaged in a do-it-yourself project will be likely to give contented attention to less active music projects.

American music educators have one goal that permeates all others—that of making school music a joyous experience. Many educators, including administrators, depend upon the music experience to counteract what a contemporary writer calls the "joylessness of education." Most teachers feel that musical skills and knowledge of music cannot be well learned or applied except with pleasure. This is not to say that every moment of developing a skill will be enjoyed, but in an overall view of the experiences, enjoyment of musical sound and happiness in expression through music will prevail.

There never has been in all of history or anywhere else in the world a plan for public school music like that of present-day America. A much fuller curriculum is attempted than has been conceived in other times and places. Instrumental music is taught on a widespread basis. Every child is included in the aspiration of teachers. The fulfillment of such a plan is the enormous and often well-done job of American music educators. It is in this general plan that the principles of Dalcroze, Kodály, and Orff are being practiced in various degrees of adoption or adaptation.

Operational Concepts

1. Parents generally want their children to be familiar with the music of their ethnic and social backgrounds.

2. A music curriculum should serve multiple ends: the development of ability, the cultivation of knowledgeable appreciation, and the establishment of a basis for aesthetic satisfaction.

3. The structure of the music curriculum must fit the school organization and setting.

4. The intellectual analysis of music, although desirable, does not ensure increased aesthetic gratification.

5. Teachers should enable children, wherever possible, to discover musical principles by manipulating and exploring sounds.

Implications

The situation in music education parallels, almost directly, that in art education. More must be done to enrich the musical education of the nonperforming student who neither plays an instrument nor sings in a choral group. Most students, of course, receive some exposure to music during the primary and intermediate elementary grades, but involvement drops off sharply from the junior high upward.

Since we now acknowledge that the youth subculture has a preferred musical idiom of its own, it would be sensible to make greater educational use of the music adolescents enjoy. Not only does the best of contemporary music have artistic merits of its own, but since the song lyrics often reflect the social concerns and values of youth, there is educational benefit to their consideration. Not only can legitimate musical understanding be developed through the analysis of popular as well as classical music (particularly since the two are based on the same musical theory), but—at the same time—a continuity can be established between the students' in-school and out-of-school interests.

Also paralleling the situation in art, effort should be made to enlarge the learner's aesthetic understanding and familiarity with musical principles. A greater knowledge of the functions of melody, harmony, and rhythm, for example, would add much to the learner's musical sophistication. Students should also be encouraged to regard music as an authentic intellectual and emotional experience rather than as a kind of auditory thumb twiddling. Music education should demonstrate the capacity of music to enrich life.

And, perhaps of greatest importance, the regrettable tendency to use music (and other experimental courses) as a depository for students who have difficulty in the conventional academic curriculum should be interrupted.

Home Economics

J. Lloyd Trump
Delmas F. Miller

Home Economics

Many stories have been developed around the theme of a lifelong search for an ideal or a precious object that is ultimately found on the searcher's own doorstep. In curriculum studies, this is the story of home economics. Curriculum makers look constantly for subject matter related directly to the lives of pupils—subject matter that has practical application and will lead ultimately to a vocational pursuit. Home economics involves learning activities that meet these requirements, yet it is a field that has been received with something less than enthusiasm by administrators, parents, and pupils. In many instances, it has been a subject forced on all junior high school girls and relegated to the slow learners in the senior high school.

Parents often take a negative attitude toward home economics, although it is a subject that will be involved in the lives of all pupils who someday will be establishing their own homes. It is a subject that some parents would deny the right to be in the curriculum, contending that mothers should teach their daughters the art of homemaking in their own homes. There has been a sparse enrollment in home economics for many years. It is only recently that enrollment figures show some tendency to increase.

Home economics is an area of education that has as its major concern the total well-being of the family. Chaotic social conditions in many sections of the country have caused educational planners to reevaluate the responsibilities of the family. Home economics programs need to be restructured to accommodate mobile families with multiple parental obligations.

TITLE CHANGES AND DEVELOPMENT

A brief look at the history of the field of home economics reveals changing attitudes and objectives. At one time, the field was known as

Reprinted from J. Lloyd Trump and Delmas F. Miller, *Secondary School Curriculum Improvement, Challenges, Humanism, Accountability,* 2nd ed., © 1973; by permission of Allyn and Bacon, Inc.

"domestic science," probably because the title sounded scientific and imposing. In those days, the two main subjects were cooking and sewing, with pupils enrolled for cooking one semester and sewing, the next. The present title, "home economics," became associated with the subject as increased emphasis was placed on economics as applied to the home and family.

Home economics gained stature in 1917 with the passage of the Smith–Hughes Act, which allocated federal money for the support and development of home economics as a vocational subject. The use of the additional term "vocational home economics" began at this time. This legislation and others that came later were designed to emphasize the contribution of home economics education to the vocation of homemaking. This required the broadening of the field to include child care and guidance, family relationships, and home management. It also meant the inclusion of principles of other disciplines such as science, psychology, sociology, and economics.

A dualism exists in home economics curriculums of the secondary schools of today. A school will have either vocational home economics or nonvocational home economics. This is determined by whether or not the school receives federal funds for the support of the program. It is also marked by the certification of teachers to perform in either one type of program or the other. Federal legislation dealing with vocational home economics sets up definite time schedules for teachers that enable them to plan work with pupils in school that carries over into the activities of the home. Vocational teachers are hired on a twelve-month basis with fringe benefits including a paid vacation and travel allowance. This means that pupils are also enrolled in a twelve-month program. Although they do not report for daily classes during the summer months, they are expected to pursue home projects under the guidance and supervision of the teacher.

Critical Views

The field of home economics has its usual share of critics who would change the trend of things and limit developments. Some of these people contend that as it is now conceived, home economics is not a field at all, or at best it is entirely synthetic. They point to the fact that principles of science are involved in health and housekeeping practices, principles of psychology and sociology determine child care and family relationship, and principles of economics are basic to the whole structure of family finance. These critics propose to retain these learning principles in the setting of their own discipline and thus save valuable pupil time in already overcrowded curriculums.

Other critical groups are alarmed at the invasion of home economics into the sacred tenets of the home. They hold that marriage, child rearing, and family intimacies are too complicated for secondary youth to comprehend. They would have the school confine itself to the teaching of the fundamentals. These alarmists are never too specific as to what the fundamentals are.

Some critics of vocational home economics claim there is too much federal dictation in the programs. However, most administrators of schools that have the vocational programs work on the assumption that federal directives can be instrumental in the development of good learning situations. Recent surveys show many nonvocational programs with offerings broadened to include the same comprehensive activities as the vocational classes. (Heretofore these nonvocational programs have involved mostly cooking and sewing; and even after revision many of them have inherent limitations.)

Regardless of the critics, home economics is enjoying its best enrollment of pupils to date. Over 95 percent of all public secondary schools of the nation have classes in home economics. Close to 50 percent of all girls take one or more courses in the field. About 1 percent of the boys pursue the subject. There is little doubt that homemaking of some form or other will continue to be taught in the secondary schools.

Should Boys Enroll?

As has been noted above, boys constitute about 1 percent of the present enrollment in home economics. Some authorities contend that 25 percent of the boys in the school should be enrolled in any given year[1]. Occasionally schools will set up special programs for them. In other instances they will be enrolled in regular classes. A thought might be given to whether more boys should enroll.

A good case for the affirmative can be made when consideration is given to the changing conditions in family life. Where working wives are concerned, it is logical to expect the husband to assume part of the burden for homemaking. The expanding programs in home economics offer experiences needed by both boys and girls in such things as child care and guidance, family relationships, and home management. Some proponents of home economics for boys point to the vocational possibility in training to become chefs. This is a limited prospect, however, since most programs do not deal with preparation of large amounts of food. Such a program would interfere with more general objectives, and this type of training probably should be assigned to a regular vocational school. Either at the vocational school level or at the college level, programs are being developed for training men in food management for restaurants, hotels, college residence halls, etc. There are also vocational opportunities to specialize in textiles and clothing design. The pertinent question here is whether secondary school home economics courses should furnish the preparatory background for this specialized work.

The negative side of the question of whether home economics is a subject for boys is represented by the boys who enroll in classes as a "lark" or as an escape from more "difficult" subjects. They can become a nuisance and impede the progress of pupils with more serious purposes. Some authorities contend that boys would be better off in the behavioral sciences where they can secure adequate concepts of masculinity and better understanding of the need for emotional stability in their future wives. Whether more boys enroll in home economics or not, it is doubtful whether the subject will be functional and purposeful for any great number.

HOMEMAKING IN A CHANGING SOCIAL ORDER

In recent years the term "homemaking" has been used more and more in connection with home economics. Although there are numerous vocations in the field of home economics, such as home demonstration agents, home economists for utility companies, and several types of government positions, the chief vocational pursuit is homemaking. It furnishes a practical application of classroom teaching, and requires no on-the-job training. Everybody agrees it is important, and few can escape the ultimate need for its basic content. Homemaking in the modern social order is an inclusive process involving foods and nutrition, clothing selection and construction, child care and training, family relations and social graces, home furnishings and equipment, consumer education and money management, and the many problems related to family health.

The field of home economics, like most of the other subjects in the school curriculum, is bound to be affected by the changing social order in an automated, technological society. Those making curriculum decisions concerning home economics must be very conscious of the social forces that are shaping modern family living(2). If the subject is to be worth a prominent position in the curriculum of the comprehensive secondary school, it must earn this position through the vital contribution it makes in helping pupils face the complexity of modern living.

It is of little value to compare the modern home with the nostalgic image of a patriarchal father reading the Bible and conducting family prayers before an open fireplace. Those are days of another era. Home life today must be evaluated in terms of a changing social order. The home must be assessed as a changing social institution. What is viewed by some as the collapse of the home and family life is nothing more than necessary adaptations of the institution for survival in a culture now predominantly urban and technological rather than rural and agrarian. The employment of both father and mother outside the home calls for mutual responsibilty in homemaking, although women will necessarily continue to carry major responsibility for operation of the household and for the spiritual, intellectual, and aesthetic tone of the home. Any going back to the simple life is impossible. The job of the school is to teach people to live well in an urban culture in an imaginative and creative way(3).

As had been stated before, challenges in curriculum development in home economics are greatly increased by the complexity of American life.

An inflationary economy practically necessitates multiple wage earners in the lower- and middle-income families. A modern home in the $30,000 to $40,000 price range, soaring prices of all commodities, and increased economic tax burdens negate the possibility of economic survival with only one wage earner.

The homemaker–wage earner is a new image emerging in the home economics field. Curriculum adjustment within home economics programs and development of interdisciplinary courses related to modern family problems are resulting necessities. Statistics identify the working mother as 38 percent of all women who work out of the home, and women make up 35 percent of the labor force. Half of American mothers bear their last child at the age of 30, hence more than half of their lives remain for gainful employment. Care of children of working mothers is an acute problem. Surveys show 8 percent of children of working mothers are expected to take care of themselves while the mother is at work. Divorced, separated, and abandoned mothers create the problem of one-parent families. Six million children, nearly one in ten, are living in one-parent homes.

There is no doubt the secondary school home economics curriculum should include programs adjusted to the needs of prospective homemaker–wage earners. Content for such programs should emphasize human relationships applied to both family and job responsibilities. Principles of management, including decision making, goals, values, standards, and nature and use of resources should be included in content. Integrated subject matter should include budgeting and consumer education. Materials and activities from physical education that emphasize physical well-being through nutrition, recreation, and exercise should be included. Child care and child guidance has a special kind of identity in the program for the part-time mother. The dual role that women play today in homemaking and wage earning complicates and broadens the scope of home economics education.

Thus it may be seen that modern home and family life needs to be analyzed critically by curriculum planners in the field of home economics. The schools serve all social, economic, and cultural levels. If the teaching of homemaking is to be the responsibility of the secondary schools, and if this responsibility is to be met realistically, the homemaking curriculum needs all of the characteristics common to other secondary school fields, such as ability grouping, problem solving, content adjustment, and sensitivity to a changing technological order. Of particular concern to the homemaking field are such social factors as the mobility of people, crowded living conditions in urban life, stress of rapid change in employment conditions, necessity for living in diversity, and the need for a common value structure.

SUBJECT-MATTER ARRANGEMENT

The content and sequence of course work in home economics is of primary concern to curriculum planning. A survey of existing curriculums reveals two common patterns. One pattern shows a series of separate courses in sequence of relationships and difficulty. Such courses cover such topics as foods, clothing, home management, health and home nursing, family relationship, child development, and consumer buying. The second pattern has yearly courses designated as Homemaking I, II, III, and IV. Each year a series of topics is covered. Parts of these topics are repeated in succeeding years, but in increasing difficulty and application. The proponents of this plan contend that it provides for the establishment of interrelationships among the topics.

Two major problems are found in the home economics programs of many schools. The tendency is to require the subject in the junior high school for at least two of the three years. This tends to dull the eagerness of pupils to enroll in senior high school classes, which are usually elective. Senior high school teachers are critical of the fact that too much work of an advanced nature has been attempted in the junior high school, with the result that pupils either lose their zest for the subject or complain of forced repetition. This problem is likely to be present when programs are set up on a yearly basis labeled home economics I, II, III, and IV. It takes careful planning to avoid boring repetition in such programs. One of the hardest things to do is to control the degree of difficulty.

If the plan of a yearly series of topics or units is followed, placement and sequence might be made on this basis:

Junior high school

1. Nutrition and health
2. Personal care
3. Making friends
4. Room arrangements
5. Safety in the home
6. Care of young children
7. Care and construction of clothing

Senior high school

1. Clothing selection and construction
2. Food for the family
3. Child development
4. Home planning and furnishing
5. Home entertaining
6. Family relationships
7. Family finance
8. Home nursing

Research shows that these are the topics pupils, parents, and teachers consider important. Parents and pupils suggest certain emphases in these topics, such as more help in child training rather than child care, and more attention to moral and spiritual values in the home rather than skills of housekeeping.

PRESENT TRENDS IN THE FIELD

The best thinking among curriculum leaders in the field of home economics is consistent with curriculum development in other subject-matter areas. In meeting the needs of the wide variety of pupils found in a comprehensive school program, it is necessary to build curriculum content on basic concepts and generalizations. Results of extensive research and conference planning suggest five major divisions of content for home economics courses. These include:

1. Human development and the family
2. Home management and family economics
3. Food and nutrition
4. Housing
5. Textiles and clothing

The five major areas of content above are not suggested in any sequence or order. They are only means of identifying what constitutes the field. Arrangement, adjustment, and application of this content will differ from school to school. Learning should be established in problem-solving situations where the development of skills and the evaluation of experiences are major objectives. Independent study and clinical activities may be provided by study in depth of such subjects as personality development or family financial security. Special survey courses may be arranged for the college bound, for business education pupils, or for seniors who for some reason or other have never had the opportunity to take work in the field. Special school projects may be part of the program. They would include child care centers, clothing repair centers, and centers for social graces.

A closer look at the textile and clothing unit will illustrate a suggested approach. The skills necessary for the design and construction of clothing continue to be basic and necessary, as is an understanding of the values and uses of textiles. The major emphasis, however, is put on an understanding of the uses of textiles and clothing as a means through which roles in life may be identified and expressed.

Through problem-solving situations, pupils become acquainted with the basic values and purposes of clothing in communicating personality and desired impressions. An individual can reflect and express personal values through clothing. Certain consequences can result from clothing choices. Impressions can be striking or subtle. Values can be established or destroyed. The history of societies and civilization can be traced through clothing choices. Thus it may be seen that a knowledge of the uses of clothing can be of far greater impact than skill in design and construction. Fame and fortune may come to the limited few who design clothing; a certain satisfaction may be gained by those who construct their own clothing; but the responsibility for intelligent wearing of clothing is the problem of all.

According to Ruth P. Hughes, there are three trends in the home economics field of uppermost importance(4):

1. Awareness of sociological and psychological characteristics of students which have necessitated curricular changes. One change important enough to be noted as a separate trend is a greater emphasis on vocational education.
2. Careful analysis and appropriate use of empirical findings relevant to home economics education. Of particular importance is current work both in psychology of learning and sociology for the classroom. These require a research orientation among staff in home economics education.
3. A broader concept of teacher education to include not only the traditional preparation of secondary teachers but others whose mission is some form of innovative teaching.

The sociological and psychological changes in the characteristics of students affecting curricular changes relate to the so-called sexual revolution of today. The open warfare between the proponents and opponents of sex education courses in the schools has perplexing aspects for the experienced secondary school principal. In a previous era sex education was neither emphasized nor identified. Content areas in biology, health education, social studies, and home economics included units of material related to reproduction, child care, health hazards, and social implications of promiscuity. If queried, most principals could identify their sex education program, but they would be surprised at the question being put in such form.

The sex education controversy has implications for home economics education. Whether the sex education program aspects related to home economics are part of an integrated program of the school or continue as part of the home economics curriculum will vary according to the mores of different communities. The fact remains, however, that sex is a basic integral part of family life and as such is in the providence of responsibility of home economics education. The major task is in the restoration of the role of the family as the behavior-constraining and behavior-defining agency for youth. Readily available contraceptives, high physical mobility, and a consumer-oriented economy with its explicit approval of self-indulgence do not uncomplicate the problem. Possible solutions for the sex education problem as well as the many other problems in the home economics curriculum field will be found by teachers benefiting from broader concepts of teacher education emphasizing the use of empirical research and problem-solving techniques.

THE HOME ECONOMICS CURRICULUM
OF THE FUTURE

The vocational aspects of home economics undoubtedly will continue to be stressed. It is a field that fuses theory and practice. Surveys of future job opportunities for young people reveal two general types of employment. One will be in positions associated with technology and will require well-developed technological skills. The other will be in positions of service to people. Here, too, skill and training will be necessary for those who want to be in the best competitive positions. Home economics can contribute to the vocational preparation of pupils for both technological and service jobs either directly or indirectly. In the case of very capable pupils preparing for jobs of a technological nature, the role of home economics may be limited to the homemaking responsibilities of these pupils. This touches on the question of whether intellectually gifted pupils should enroll in home economics classes.

In the past, only a limited number of the very intelligent girls enrolled in home economics work. Yet 95 percent of American women marry and have an average of three children each. This means that regardless of training and job position, a girl is almost sure to be a mother and a homemaker. Therefore, it is reasonable to assume that part of her preparatory education should contribute to this ultimate responsibility. Some authorities lament the waste of womanpower in the present technological order. These authorities would load the secondary school preparation of capable girls with science, mathematics, and foreign languages. Psychologists maintain, however, that no school subject is markedly superior to another for "strengthening mental power," and the undeniable need for educating homemakers is merely avoided. The question that faces the planners of home economics curriculums is one of designing home economics classes that will challenge capable pupils. Instruction needs to reach the rich potential these pupils have both intellectually and artistically. This instruction should include concept development and critical thinking on a high level. It is the responsibility of the comprehensive secondary school to prepare pupils for the dual role of making valuable contributions both within and without the home.

The need for people in service occupations has developed rapidly with the urbanization of the population. People living within limited space and lacking opportunities to be self-sufficient need the services of many others. These service jobs have become more and more specialized, so that those who render the services must be trained. Whether the home economics curriculum should include vocational preparation for all service jobs is an open question that should be answered. Much of the content of home economics classes in the past has been applicable to the training for service jobs, but it has been homemaking oriented. A brief listing of some of the service jobs needs will illustrate this: child care services; clothing services—

244

dry cleaning, etc.; institutional work—hospitals, motels, hotels, etc.; housing and home furnishing—florists, gift shops, department stores, etc.; and specialized services such as companions to the elderly, and shopping guides.

If the home economics curriculum of the future is to fulfill its role in a comprehensive school, there is no doubt that adjustments must be made. Practically all girls, including the intellectually gifted, will be future home-makers. If all girls and a substantial number of boys enroll, instruction must be adjusted to ability, as in any other subject. Many of the pupils who will pursue service jobs are already in home economics classes. New content and training in new skills will be necessary to adequately prepare these pupils. Home economics programs face a new urgency in helping youth adjust and make discriminating use of available resources, both human and physical. The pupils must learn to make sensible decisions in order to gain maximum satisfaction and contribute significantly to the building of good homes and good communities.

References

1. Elizabeth J. Simpson, "Challenges in Curriculum Development in Home Economics," *Journal of Home Economics* (December 1968), pp. 767–773.
2. Marguerite C. Burk, "In Search of Answers About Family Economic Behavior," *Journal of Home Economics* (June 1966), pp. 440–444.
3. Mary Lee Hurt, *Current Developments in Vocational Home Economics Education* (Washington, D.C.: U.S. Department of Health, Education, and Welfare, 1970), pp. 1–21.
4. Ruth P. Hughes, "Trends in Home Economics Education," paper delivered at the West Virginia Home Economics Association Annual Meeting (February 1971).

Selected Reading

Brown, Marjorie, and Plihal, Jane. *Physical Home Environment and Psychological and Social Factors*. Minneapolis: Burgess Publishing Company, 1969.
     This is a good source for evaluation of the physical makeup of the home. It furnishes guides for establishment of experiences with manipulating sensory stimuli such as colors, sounds, physical arrangements, etc. It would be helpful for curriculum decisions in this phase of course content.
Fleck, Henrietta. *Toward Better Teaching of Home Economics*. New York: Macmillan Publishing Co., Inc., 1968.
     This book furnishes material for home economics education seeking answers for family living in relation to scientific and technological

245

developments, affluence and poverty, the population explosion, the growing role of government in family life, and the changing functions of the family that characterize contemporary American society. Special attention is given to new approaches in curriculum development.

HALL, OLIVE A., and PAOLUCCI, BEATRICE. *Teaching Home Economics.* New York: John Wiley & Sons, 1970.

This is the second edition of this popular textbook in the field of home economics. One of the new chapters gives special attention to deviates in the learning process, both retarded and accelerated. Both the affective and psychomotor domains are given analytical treatment.

KILANDER, FREDERICK H. *Sex Education in the Schools.* New York: Macmillan Publishing Co., Inc., 1970.

This volume is aimed at helping educators organize and conduct meaningful learning experiences in family life and sex education. Emphasis is on the acquisition of knowledge and the development of wholesome attitudes. Part One contains Chapters 1–13, dealing directly with family living aspects of sex education in the schools.

New Directions for Vocational Home Economics. Washington, D.C.: Report of a National Conference, American Home Economics Association, 1971.

Over four hundred home economists assembled for the purpose of finding what directions educators in vocational home economics should pursue. This report contains the major addresses given at the meeting. At least three of the addresses may furnish guideposts for the next decade.

SIMPSON, ELIZABETH JANE. *The Classification of Educational Objectives, Psychomotor Domain.* Washington, D.C.: U.S. Department of Health, Education, and Welfare, 1966.

This report is most influential on the development of a classification system for educational objectives, psychomotor domain in taxonomic form. The field of home economics is finding new directions from this report.

246

Operational Concepts

1. Home economics education should go beyond sewing and cooking to involve the student in a penetrating study of family life, parenting, and interpersonal relationships.

2. As vocational careers for women become more commonplace, it will be desirable for home economics curricula to deal with the integration of homemaking and vocational roles.

3. The educational benefits of home economics courses for boys, at least in the immediate future, seem minimal.

4. Since social readjustment is inevitable, homemaking education, to the extent possible, should base its instructional concepts on the probable future rather than on the past and the present.

5. The relationship of family and home to satisfying adulthood is germane to many areas of the curriculum. Thus, strong interconnections between homemaking education and other subject areas are desirable.

Implications

The major need in home economics education, seemingly, is that of extending content well beyond the traditional cooking and sewing. Much, to be sure, has been written in the literature about antiquated course structure, but practice still lags.

Recent societal trends suggest further that more attention must be given to the function and significance of family life. The conventional sequence of instruction should be broadened to include such matters as the relationship between family experiences and personality, masculine and feminine roles, the responsibilities of parenthood, family size, interpersonal communication, and so on.

What this implies, in turn, is that home economics education must be integrated more closely with other subjects in the curriculum. Because of the enormous social importance of a stable family unit, the social studies, language arts, and even science classes should be used to help students understand why no society has ever survived without a strong family structure.

In this same spirit, the objectives of homemaking education could be expanded to include life-coping skills in general. Imaginative new instructional programs might be devised that increase content relevance, offer more flexibility in catering to individual student interest, and permit a larger number of options with respect to alternative study topics.

Since people are likely to enjoy increasingly large amounts of leisure, the curriculum must also begin to touch upon the various ways in which this leisure can be used productively with respect to the ways in which human needs can be satisfied in a rewarding home environment. Like art, music, and other "nonacademic" subjects, home economics courses frequently are used as a convenient accommodation for students outside the college-preparatory curriculum. Given a more attractive and exciting body of content, it is safe to conjecture that college-bound students, too, might begin to regard such courses as worthwhile, and that the "custodial" aspects of home economics programs would diminish.

248

J. Lloyd Trump
Delmas F. Miller

Industrial Arts

Industrial arts programs run the gamut from almost complete obsolescence to sparkling modernity. The recent experience of a state university curriculum coordinator illustrates the point. He received an enthusiastic invitation from a young industrial arts teacher to visit his new shop. The coordinator was pleased to find the shop housed in a modern addition to the school sufficiently isolated from the main building to prevent noise problems. His enthusiasm cooled, however, as he approached the new shop area and sniffed the familiar odor of fresh sawdust. His suspicions were confirmed as he entered the shop proper. The commodious area was filled with woodworking tools and woodworking power machinery, and the neatly piled lumber rack was well stocked with new lumber.

The university visitor was discouraged to find such a limited concept of a modern industrial arts program. His main consolation came with the remembrance of shop programs in other parts of the state which provide high school pupils with experiences in metals, woods, plastics, graphic arts, application of electricity and electronics, application of design and drafting, and research in the production of industrial products. These shops represented the best in industrial arts programs.

Studies of curriculum guides for industrial arts in the various states reveal a diversity of programs. In some states it is difficult to find published materials. In other states there is an abundance of material dealing with drawing, woodworking, metal working, electricity, and radio. Far less attention is given to plastics, graphic arts, and power mechanics. Most of the curriculum guides concern themselves with the use of hand tools, the operation of machines, and related information concerning materials. It is difficult to find agreement on what should be taught. From a perusal of the available curriculum materials, it is reasonable to conclude that industrial arts in the hinterlands has not progressed very far from the concept of

Reprinted from J. Lloyd Trump and Delmas F. Miller, *Secondary School Curriculum Improvement, Challenges, Humanism, Accountability*, 2nd ed., © 1973; by permission of Allyn and Bacon, Inc.

teaching basic tools and machine processes. Too often, the making of the "take home project" is the ultimate objective. Most individual arts curriculums need reorganization, both in their concepts and in their objectives.

CHANGING CONCEPTS

While the term industrial arts is now in good usage by those connected with the field, and the laboratory for learning activities is properly labeled the industrial arts shop, this has not always been the case(1). The earliest term used in the field was manual training. Objectives were related to the development of skills in the use of hand tools, and woodworking was the major activity. Frequently, mechanical drawing was taught as a related subject. In some instances, courses in woodworking and mechanical drawing were given in alternate semesters; in other cases the courses were given during the same semester, on different days of the week. Enrollment in manual training was confined mostly to boys.

As increased technological knowledge brought new products and new industrial processes into everyday living, curriculum planners sought to incorporate this new information into the shop classes. There was a feeling that pupils needed a wider knowledge of materials and processes of industry. They also needed information on the use and maintenance of the many modern conveniences and labor-saving devices coming into the home. To cover this wider scope of activity, the term manual arts came into use. Learning activities in the manual arts shop included the use of plastics, graphic arts, textiles, bookbinding, etc.

The use of manual arts as a term to identify the field never gained wide usage, and it soon gave way to the current term, industrial arts. Programs of industrial arts have both technical and aesthetic aspects; many processes in the arts, such as ceramics, and different forms of crafts, such as weaving and leather working, are taught. The increased emphasis on a wide variety of activities in the industrial arts field soon identified it with the purposes of general education. Out of this grew the concept of the general shop.

Emphasis in industrial arts has never been on vocational education. Confusion sometimes arises over this matter. The vocational overtones in industrial arts are secondary. Vocational education demands specialization and depth preparation that are not stressed in the industrial arts shop. The primary objective is to give pupils a wide range of preparatory experiences that will lead to later vocational choice or avocational pursuits. The theory behind the general shop is that pupils with wide experiences in industrial processes will adjust to the rapidly changing demands of a technological order. It presupposes that the job training of today may not be usable tomorrow. Vocational specialization too early may be wasted, but purposeful, planned experiences in a wide variety of industrial processes can result in intelligent vocational choices as opportunities occur. Even if no vocational choice results, avocational skills learned in general shop may result in personal satisfaction and worthwhile leisure activities.

Industrial arts experiences are for both boys and girls. Both are involved in the technological culture. It is doubtful whether any great number of girls will enroll in shop classes, but there is no reason to assume that they lack aptitude for it or that their needs are not as great as boys. Women are engaged in all phases of industrial life. They also share equal responsibilities in homemaking and recreational pursuits. Perhaps more experimentation is necessary for discovering the feasibility of a commonality of experiences between industrial arts courses and home economics courses.

CURRICULUM OBJECTIVES

One of the earliest lists of industrial arts objectives is *The Standards of Attainment of Industrial Arts Teaching*(2), published by the American Vocational Association in 1934. Objectives emphasized the manipulative skills in the use of hand tools and the execution of simple basic operations. The list remained essentially the same through revisions in 1948 and 1953, with the exception of added objectives for health and safety. It was a good listing at the time it was made, and it still contains many of the fundamentals of a good industrial arts program, but it does not reflect adequately the needs of the modern industrial order.

A study of industrial arts objectives recently compiled by leaders in the field shows a definite effort to meet the needs of youth in a complex society. These objectives include emphasis on problem solving, design, and experimentation as facets of a more wholesome approach to learning through intelligently organized experiences that help orient the student in the realm of industrial and technological subject matter. The proper emphasis given to the manipulative activities continues to be an issue, but more stress is being placed on the correlation of science and mathematics and the relation of various industrial processes to lifelike situations.

The report of a U.S. Office of Education conference in 1960 includes four rather broad objectives(3). These objectives were the result of extensive surveying and summarizing of previously established objectives by recognized authorities in the field. They were meant to provide experience for the slow learner as well as the gifted and are worthy of careful analysis.

1. To develop in each student an insight and understanding of industry and its place in our culture: There is no doubt that this objective is ordinarily the responsibility of courses in economics, sociology, and physical sciences, but industrial arts can show both the theoretical and the functional aspects of the occupational and productive activities of society. Industry is a dominant element of the modern social order. The school shares a heavy responsibility for helping each student understand this industrial-

ization. Industrial arts can furnish basic training in skills, techniques, and information that will be of value for those who enter industry and the phases of business associated with industry. A desirable background also can be furnished for those who expect to go into advanced work in the various professional areas related to industry.

2. To discover and develop talent of students in the technical fields and applied sciences: The fulfillment of this objective would bring a new type of pupil to the industrial arts shop. The stigma of being a dumping ground for uninterested pupils of questionable ability would rapidly disappear. Pupils would be guided into industrial arts courses as a result of their identification with scientific and technological pursuits. Future technicians, engineers, and production workers would gain basic experiences suitable to their aptitudes and needs.

The discovery aspect of this objective is worth careful analysis. The academically capable pupil is often cloistered in abstract subject-matter areas where the premium is on storing knowledge rather than applying it to practical situations. Part of these pupils graduate from sceondary schools completely inept in the simplest of applications. Experience in industrial arts would not only aid in discovery of technical abilities, but would give confidence and satisfaction in use of such abilities.

3. To develop technical problem solving skills relative to materials and processes: Problem solving continues to be a cardinal process for learning. There is a concentration of emphasis on problem solving in most of the subject-matter fields that are undergoing significant change in content and teaching techniques. When properly directed in industrial arts, this approach leads to creative thinking, the application of principles of science and mathematics, and technological know-how. The use of tools and materials divorced from problem solving may be glorified busy work, and this does not satisfy basic needs of pupils, regardless of whether they are of high ability or low ability.

4. To develop in each student a measure of skill in the use of the common tools and machines: This is one of the oldest objectives in the industrial arts field and it still is fundamentally sound. The skilled use of tools is essential in the many phases of industrial arts. This skill needs to be developed beyond the mere manipulative phases of the use of tools and machines. It leads to a necessary understanding of industrial processes and gives the pupil an opportunity to develop his talents in technical fields. This ability is a means to an end in problem solving ability.

A recent visitor to the Argonne Laboratories in Chicago observed what appeared to be an ordinary workman soldering wires on an electrical panel board. It was on a Sunday afternoon and the laboratories were deserted except for the solitary workman. His appearance and the work he was doing gave credence to the belief that he was a technician called in to do a special job. The visitor was quite surprised to learn that he was observing one of the best physicists in the nation. Here was an example of a top-ranking scientist making use of manipulative skills in the world of experimentation.

The basic objectives of industrial arts programs should be concerned' with the contributions that can be made to general education. They must satisfy the ramifications of complex industrial experiences, as well as patterns of general civic and human relationships. Industrial arts experiences, if indeed they have progressed beyond the hand tool stage, need to be broadened beyond the materials and processes of modern industry to include unique patterns of human relations such as those involved in the delicate balance between labor and management.

INDUSTRIAL ARTS
IN THE COMPREHENSIVE SCHOOL

The role of industrial arts in the comprehensive school needs better delineation. For example, a basic concept of the comprehensive school is the proper balance of curriculum offerings to meet the needs of all pupils(4). The connotation of balance appears to mean that pupils should have experience in subjects contributing to the educational, vocational, and citizenship aspects of their lives. It is sometimes referred to as a balance between the academic and practical, or between the academic and the manipulative skills. Industrial arts represents a balancing subject in the curriculum as well as a subject that can exhibit balance within its own subject-matter area.

The industrial arts shop is unique as a facility for bringing together and synthesizing the various phases of a good educational program. Functional industrial arts should exploit this uniqueness and extend its benefits to all pupils. Those things that make specific contributions to all youth should be emphasized. Industrial arts has the subject matter and activities to challenge the more able pupils. Attention should be given to the establishment of special, high-level classes that will attract pupils interested in science and engineering. Extensive experience in dealing with the less capable certainly ought to aid in charting sound programs for their needs. A minimum program for all abilities is a good objective.

The increasing complexity of our industrialized society and the increasing amount of mechanization encountered everywhere makes it essential that industrial arts experiences be regarded as basic and fundamental for all youth. There is definite evidence of need for reorganizing industrial arts objectives and content around modern industrial development and basic problems of industry, incorporating the accepted objectives of the comprehensive school.

There is no doubt that industrial arts as a part of general education can provide profitable and valuable experiences to all pupils in the public schools(5). There are opportunities within its bounds to make positive contributions to the teaching of moral and civic responsibilities. It can also be an important adjunct to scientific research and experimentation.

There is a tendency to adjust industrial arts programs to provide more meaningful experiences for the college-bound pupil. This idea is commendable and has merit for those who plan to specialize in any form of engineering or highly developed industrial pursuit. However, the terminal pupil continues to deserve major emphasis in the industrial arts program.

The shop teacher would doubtless prefer to have pupils of average and above average intelligence, and if vocational objectives are to be fulfilled in areas of industrial management and technological skills, this is a worthy preference. The ability to conceive from abstract ideas, to bring to life on the drawing board and to execute a finished product from raw materials is the ultimate objective of every industrial arts teacher. This does not mean that industrial arts cannot fulfill worthy objectives for pupils of lesser academic ability. Research studies continue to show that academic proficiency as expressed by IQ and other mental measurements has no correlation with the success of students in subjects that are primarily of the manipulative type.

In addition to providing pupils with knowledge for hobby pursuits and home mechanics efficiencies, industrial arts is in the pleasant position of being able to offer knowledge, skills, and techniques that can be used directly and immediately in gainful employment. It might be argued that this is vocational education and perhaps would include all vocational aspects, but no experience that becomes basic for life's work can be divorced from vocational experiences. The need for draftsmen, mechanics, and technicians is ever present. Many skilled hands are needed between the drawing board and the launching pad.

It must be repeated, however, that industrial arts objectives are different from those of vocational education. The responsibility for preparing youth for job situations is the function of vocational education and should be identified as such. It is more important for pupils in industrial arts courses to learn of the complexities of American industrial culture and the resulting effects on the lives of people. The more technology and science expand, the more important it becomes for a person to understand industrial processes.

The Unit Shop and the General Shop

The unit shop represents one of the prize creations of curriculum planners in the industrial arts field. It has come to symbolize the best aspects of depth instruction in several industrial processes, since pupils gain enough information to understand these processes and to make decisions as to possible vocational pursuits. The wide variety of experiences usually offered by a unit shop program includes work with woods, plastics, metals, graphic arts, electricity, drafting, etc., and serve to introduce pupils to design, formation, and utility of materials. These experiences afford the pupils enough of a basic understanding of the uses of industrial materials for personal consumer practices or vocational choices in an area of specialization.

There are those who contend that the unit shop will gradually fade out of the industrial arts program. They believe future programs will not be divided into specific areas such as wood, plastics, and metals; content will deal more with principles and concepts of industrial procedures. Emphasis will be on application of mechanisms, methods of production, influence of automation on labor and economics, and creating new ideas and new products. These same authorities see innovations in teaching methods that will involve experimentation, research, and problem solving. Changes in content and method will necessitate revamping of industrial arts laboratories and classrooms. This probably means the unit shop will lose much of its identity.

The general shop represents another industrial arts innovation in curriculum planning. It differs from the unit shop in emphasis rather than organization. While the unit shop tends to stress depth instruction in sound industrial processes, the general shop covers in breadth more of the expanding field of industrial processes. Advocates of general shops give less emphasis to the preparation of pupils for particular industrial positions. They consider the general shop in keeping with the general education objectives of the comprehensive secondary school. Perhaps general shop concepts are better oriented with present curriculum trends.

CURRICULUM TRENDS

There is a problem in bridging the gap between philosophy and theory in the new industrial arts programs. There are detractors as well as advocates of plans that feature technology as the basic content ingredient and the increased use of classroom activity procedures at the expense of laboratory experiences. There are those who contend the tendency is to make programs with too many classroom activities and too few laboratory activities. The problem is to use industrial and technological processes as content and keep relevant learning activities in the laboratory. If industrial arts is to be a vital subject in the curriculum, ways must be found to coordinate laboratory experiences with all phases of the program.

Those who advocate increased use of classroom experiences in industrial arts programs point to the major responsibility the subject has for carrying out the aims of occupational education(6). These are classified as: (1) development of technological and industrial awareness, (2) encouragement for exploration of individual aptitudes, capabilities, interests, and characteristics, and (3) development of skills and habits of hand and mind.

Technology Approach

Although industrial arts has been a part of the secondary school curriculum for a long time, industrial arts educators continue to defend its legitimacy and struggle with semantics of identity. They continue to make statements such as "Industrial arts *is* a school subject and is important in the general education pattern of all students"(7). This same authority holds that industrial arts curriculum building concerns only content, that curriculum starts and ends with content. Outcomes are not part of curriculum, but merely describe what values are to be achieved from the study of subject matter. Neither are methods a part of curriculum design, only an explanation of how subject matter is taught.

In contrast to the above, another industrial arts educator explains curriculum as the medium through which the aims, purposes, and objectives of education are implemented and realized(8). He introduces the word "structure" (used interchangeably with the word "model") as the vehicle for establishing various content levels to meet changing knowledge requirements.

Despite differences in approach, there is a growing agreement among industrial arts educators that the dominant objective of industrial arts should be that of providing an understanding of American industry and an awareness of its changing technology. Programs using this as the basic objective are identified with a technology approach. In its simplest form this approach redefines the old objective of "a degree of skill" as an understanding of the necessity for skillful use of tools rather than skill in the use of tools. In more complex form technology as related to industrial arts is conceptualized as a study of man as the creator of technology incorporating the fundamental technical and cultural elements of the several areas of technology.

Paul DeVore proposes that an industrial arts curriculum based on the study of man and technology has the following characteristics(9):

1. Provides a better base from which to implement the purposes and objectives of general education;
2. Is not limited or isolated by geographical boundaries, thereby evidencing the true nature of disciplined inquiry;
3. Is concerned with man as the creator of technology regardless of national origin;
4. Provides a meaningful relation between technology and man's culture. Historical, anthropological, social and economic elements of the culture are important to the understanding of man's technology, and a knowledge of man's technology is vital to the understanding of any culture; and
5. Identifies a knowledge area meeting the criterion of a discipline in the truest sense of the term.

DeVore structures the organization for content in a technology-oriented industrial arts curriculum around three technical areas(*10*):

1. *Production:* providing goods and services of economic value for man's needs and wants. Instruction would center around tools, materials, processes, machines, and organization and management of procedures related to fabrication, processing, and constructive technology.
2. *Communication:* providing information dissemination, storage, retrieval, and use. Subject matter would be related to information about sensing, encoding, transmission, signaling, receiving, and decoding systems through the use of radiant energy and mechanical–chemical and electromechanical means.
3. *Transportation:* providing movement of man, materials, products, and services. Content would include information on propulsion, guidance, control, structural and suspension systems for the solution of problems related to terrestrial, marine, atmospheric, and space environments.

If the proposals for an industrial arts curriculum based on technology are incorporated into the comprehensive secondary school program, industrial arts will undoubtedly take on a new image. Its position in general education will be solidified and its integration with other subject-matter areas will be axiomatic. It will necessitate retraining of teachers and the opening of the industrial arts curriculum to the entire school.

Enterprise—Man and Technology

A new industrial arts program for secondary schools has been devised at Southern Illinois University. The program is entitled "Enterprise—Man and Technology." The students, either individually or in groups, decide on a certain enterprise to develop. The initiation, conduct, termination, and consequences of the enterprise are the responsibility of the student or groups of students. The program calls for laboratory experiences, homework, classroom activity, field trips, and a work cooperative.

Laboratory activities involve work experiences whereby students learn to integrate specialized work tasks with efficient production. They design a salable product or service, arrange to finance production of the same, design and prepare tools and fixtures, rent equipment, procure supplies, hire and train a work force, and produce a predetermined number of units or services. They arrange for distribution of products and evaluation of the results.

Homework in the enterprise consists mostly of readings agreed upon by student and teacher. The material relates to the enterprise involved and the broader aspects of technology. Homework assignments can also entail production planning and preparation for laboratory and classroom activities to follow.

The major portion of classroom activities is devoted to the study of a productive society. Classroom consideration of man's role in technology involves discussions related to the student's experiences in the laboratory. Topically, the major headings include planning, organization, control, and evaluation. The selected categories of technology are: electronics and instrumentation, visual communications, materials and processes, and energy conversion and power transmission. Resource people are involved and use is made of multimedia.

The Enterprise program makes extensive use of community resources. Planned visits are made to commercial, industrial, civic, and recreational facilities. Whenever possible, students are encouraged to make arrangements for on-the-job training relating to their enterprise. The proponents of the Enterprise idea believe that students encounter the fundamental problems of a technological society. They discover the kinds of competition that develop when technological and human innovations are put to work. They are brought face-to-face with the basic need for expertise in the world of work. Leadership in secondary education is turning to the community as a base resource for the curriculum. An important phase of the open school idea is its outward thrust.

Other Programs

Industrial arts curriculum planners may want to take a closer look at one of the following programs as described by Eugene R. Flug. Each program has some of the characteristics of the two programs previously described, although each program has specific features of its own(*11*).

Industrial Arts Curriculum Project: this project lists three main objectives: (1) to create an understanding of the concepts, principles, generalizations, problems, and strategies of industrial technology as a body of knowledge; (2) to develop an interest in and an appreciation for industry as an integral part of the economic system that provides industrial goods for human wants; (3) significant value for occupational, recreational, consumer, and sociocultural purposes.

The Partnership Vocational Education Project: students study the unity or wholeness of industry and explore underlying functions that relate to possible vocational choices. Stress is placed on information that shows the correlation of industrial–technical subjects with other academic areas.

Galaxy Plan for Career Preparation: the purpose is to bring activities of business, agriculture, home economics, vocational–technical education, and industrial arts closer together in order that students can explore career possibilities in the world of work.

Orchestrated Systems Approach: this approach aims at development of knowledge and competencies for understanding and participating in the production of goods and services that contribute to betterment of life in an industrialized society. Product-producing and servicing experience are features of this program.

More Use of Research

One of the most encouraging aspects of curriculum development in the industrial arts field is the amount of research going on and the availability of results for industrial arts teachers. There has been a substantial increase in the number of studies using good research techniques. These studies are based on sound analytical endeavors to identify, classify, and organize content and experiences of industrial arts students.

As is true in so many fields in education, a discouraging thing about research in industrial arts is the lack of consistent findings, particularly those dealing with techniques and modes of teaching. There is little experimental evidence to indicate comparative superiority of any teaching method for any specific subject matter or any group of learners. The number of variables influencing teaching effectiveness is apparently so great that researchers have not been able to isolate and identify these variables precisely enough to permit accurate description of "best" teaching metholology.

Regardless of outcomes, it is encouraging to find so much research and experimentation going on in the field. It is a harbinger of improved techniques for the future. At present the questionable quality of many of the instructional strategies no doubt contributes to the lack of consistency in the findings of methodology studies. The experience of curriculum workers indicates that several revisions based on large-scale field tests are required to produce quality instructional materials and methods(*12*).

THE FUTURE OF INDUSTRIAL ARTS

Industrial arts curriculum planners face a dilemma in deciding what direction programs should take. Involved are several pertinent questions. Will shop class teachers acquiesce to administrative pressures to make their special charge the less capable pupil who cannot make it in other areas of the curriculum? Will the shop idea be replaced by area program developments? Will industrial arts programs become theory-centered classes and primarily feeders to technical education?

Probably the best answers to the foregoing questions will be found in analyzing the stature industrial arts ought to maintain in a comprehensive school. Without doubt, the field has much to offer the slow learner and, especially, the handicapped. This is a responsibility that industrial arts teachers ought to capitalize on rather than reject as a thankless task. Second, industrial arts is made to order for the contributions that can be made to a technological social order where increasing demands are for purposeful leisure time pursuits. The great "do it yourself" mania that has swept over the nation has not come about by accident. These needs are genuine and they should be planned for in the education program of a comprehensive school. The industrial arts shop should be a laboratory for the development of purposeful industrial and leisure time skills. Finally, industrial arts teachers must be cognizant of the impact technology is making on American industry. The body of science, techniques, and skills related to industrial development must be constantly reviewed for the purpose of making proper adjustment in industrial arts programs so as to attract and retain pupils of ability commensurate with the increasing difficulty of such programs.

There is a strong possibility that industrial arts theorists will outdistance practical thinkers in the rush to bring sophistication to the field. It may appear to the practical-minded industrial arts teacher that his shop is to become a citadel for physical science and mathematics rather than a place where pupils use skilled hands to shape industrial products, as formerly conceived. And indeed, this may be true. There are those who see the industrial arts program of the future rich in applied science. Principles of physical science will be evident in a large percentage of problem-solving, project-making activities of the future shop.

Those who would bring greater sophistication to industrial arts see pupils involved in making telescopes and studying astronomy, learning the lapidary art from geological investigations, and engaging in a wide study of electronics involving the building and understanding of radio equipment, high-fidelity sound, and even satellite tracking. Such programs would forego the regular auto mechanics course and teach the broad field of power, its resources, its conversion and use. The industrial arts shops would be an extension of the science laboratory. Pupils would see meaning in scientific principles by associating phenomena with familiar products and daily operations.

Industrial arts can make a real contribution to the secondary comprehensive school program. The opportunity is present for the development of an industrial arts program that will be vital in the lives of secondary school youth. Courage and vision on the part of industrial arts leaders can open many new vistas in the field.

References

1. Marshall L. Schmitt and Dale W. Chismore, "Definitions for Industrial Arts," *Industrial Arts and Vocational Education* (March 1967), pp. 100–119.

2. American Vocational Association, Inc., Industrial Arts Division, *Standards of Attainment of Industrial Arts Teaching* (1934).

3. Office of Education, *Improving Industrial Arts Teaching* (Washington, D.C.: Government Printing Office, 1960), pp. 3–18.

4. William G. Floyd, "Industrial Arts: A New Approach," *Bulletin of the National Association of Secondary School Principals* (March 1967), pp. 24–31.

5. Roy W. Roberts, *Vocational and Practical Arts* (New York: Harper & Row, Publishers, 1971), pp. 16–47.

6. Leslie H. Cochran, *Innovative Programs in Industrial Arts* (Bloomington, Ill.: McKnight and McKnight Publishing Co., 1969).

7. Robert S. Seckendorf, "Where Should We Be Going in Industrial Arts?" *The Bulletin of the National Association of Secondary School Principals* (November 1969), pp. 98–107.

8. Paul W. DeVore, "Structure and Content Foundation for Curriculum Development" (Washington, D.C.: The American Industrial Arts Association, November 1970), p. 1.

9. Ibid., p. 2.

10. Ibid., p. 12.

11. Eugene R. Flug et al., "Roundtable: Comparing Programs in Industrial Arts," *Industrial Arts and Vocational Education* (January 1970), pp. 24–26.

12. Daniel L. Householder and Alan R. Suess, "Current Research in Industrial Arts Is Increasing," *Industrial Arts and Vocational Education* (September 1970), pp. 4–5.

Operational Concepts

1. The constitutional provisions regarding education deal with the overall consequences of educational experience, and not with the designated curriculum alone.

2. From a legal standpoint, distinctions must be made between instruction that is logically relevant (the incorporation of specific subject matter deemed useful) and psychologically relevant (the incorporation of ideas and methods that stimulate student interest).

3. In general, teachers' rights to determine teaching content and methods are protected by the First Amendent as long as (a) the resulting instruction is related to legitimate school objectives, (b) the instruction is not inappropriate to the age and maturity of the student, and (c) the instruction is not disruptive of school discipline.

4. In judging the educative consequences of curriculum, the courts consider both the explicit and the implicit effects of schooling.

5. Administrators responsible for determining the legality of instructional procedures should consider both the direct and indirect consequences of a student's school experience.

Implications

Industrial arts education, in common with other aspects of the instructional program, must anticipate the kind of reforms that will be mandated by a rapidly changing society. Although it is probable that an expanding technological era will not eliminate the pleasures associated with hand craftsmanship, the nature and techniques of the crafts themselves may alter.

The critical difficulty, in present programs of instruction, is that of achieving greater congruity between the intellectual concepts relating to industry and technology and direct, hands-on experience with tools, machines, and materials. What we most need, consequently, are new conceptions of industrial arts learning activities that better integrate (1) cognitive ideas, (2) manual dexterity, and (3) the affective gains that come from planning and exercising personal craftsmanship.

In a more general vein, there also would be an advantage to greater emphasis on the practical problems of home maintenance, on a more sharply focused treatment of the generalizations relating to technology and industrial production, and on a continuing effort to give students experience with materials other than the customary aggregation of wood, metal, and plastics.

As new instructional devices become available, the teaching potentials of game simulations and computer-assisted instruction, particularly in the cognitive aspects of the course content, will increase.

Lastly, as our conceptions of sex roles continue to be redefined, more girls probably will seek industrial arts experiences. Thus, as student participation broadens, the aesthetic aspects of leisure-time activities involving craftsmanship can be demonstrated more fully, and a closer linkage between industrial arts education and the general curriculum can be sought.

Physical Education

Dorothy L. Fornia

Signposts for the Seventies

Transformation—scientific, technological, economic, political, societal, and professional—characterizes contemporary society. The world is changing more rapidly today than at any other time in history. Change is omnipresent, societal values and traditions are being challenged, and professional educators find themselves embroiled in transition and turmoil.

Not only must educators be aware of ideas and processes unknown yesterday but they must also be prepared to meet situations which are unknown today. If progress is to occur, some educators must have this skill tomorrow; uncertainty regarding the future cannot justify facile evasion of difficult issues. Therefore, despite this period of questioning the basic moral and ethical values upon which society is predicated, of reorganization and evolution within the profession, an attempt has been made to ascertain professional consensus as a baseline from which to project physical education in the seventies.

If the ability to change course with the impingement of each new catalyst is requisite to professional survival, the nature of the implications inherent in the past course must be fully comprehended. Rarely are problems or issues resolved without critical analysis. Although this study may not clarify just where the changes will lead, the findings should provide some useful referents. Professionals of the seventies must demonstrate flexibility of thinking, breadth of experience, and ability to make rational judgments based on careful research and evaluation. Only by apprising themselves of the pertinent trends and complex facets of related issues can physical educators fulfill these professional expectations.

To identify the trends and issues most likely to influence the goals, priorities, and curricula of the seventies, opinion was solicited from leaders in all six geographical districts of the American Association for Health, Physical Education, and Recreation. In spring 1971, an opinionnaire was distributed to 476 representative faculty of both public and

Reprinted from Dorothy L. Fornia, "Signposts for the Seventies," *Journal of Health, Physical Education, and Recreation*, October 1972, pp. 33–36; by permission of the publisher.

private institutions of higher education in forty-eight states and Canada. Accumulated from 349 or 73 percent of the participants, data were analyzed according to percentage of responses. Although the sample did not include the total membership of any professional organization, participants do represent a characteristic cross-section of the National Collegiate Physical Education Association for Men, the National Association for Physical Education of College Women, and regional organizations. Consensus should be viewed as a synthesis of opinion of professionals, not as the official opinion of any professional organization.

REDEFINITION OF THE PROFESSION AND REASSESSMENT OF PURPOSES

Identification of a specific body of knowledge predicated on scientific facts which support the value of physical education was considered a major trend by 83 percent of 290 respondents. Inherent in the process are reassessment of purpose and curricular relevance with subsequent extension of the parameter of evaluation to programs at all levels. Based upon knowledge and experience of experts, evaluation of the degree to which student and professional goals and needs are met also lies within its purview. Increasing emphasis on sociopsychological goals, as opposed to those of fitness and exercise physiology, and acknowledgment of the importance of satisfaction of such needs as self-esteem, self-actualization, and peer acceptance have added impetus to this trend.

Although few would suggest that physical fitness should comprise an entire program, as one goal of a comprehensive program it may be appropriate. Justification for maintenance of physical fitness in the curricula include projected life expectancy of 120–150 years before the turn of the century, manipulation of the genetic code, development of plastic and metal organs and arteries, transplants, wonder drugs, and individually tailored diets.

On occasion, opinion regarding an appropriate title for the discipline has assumed the proportion of an issue. However, it is the nature of the discipline, the areas of concern unique to physical education, which merit attention during the process of redefinition and reassessment.

EMPHASIS ON STRONGER ACADEMIC BASE FOR PROFESSIONAL PREPARATION

Increasing support for a stronger academic base for professional preparation was perceived as an important trend by an even larger number of respondents, 396 or 85 percent. Curricular focus in professional physical education appears to be upon the interdisciplinary approach with commensurate decrease of emphasis on teaching methology. One exception has been implementation of internship specialization in various components of physical education. Content from psychology, sociology, philosophy, and history—as well as related concerns in health, climate, atmosphere, and movement problems—have become integral parts of the physical education curriculum.

While some respondents support closer identification with the aforementioned disciplines, others question student motivation for not enrolling in already established departments.

MORE SPECIALIZATION IN UNDERGRADUATE PROFESSIONAL PREPARATION

Undergraduate professional preparation has definitely moved toward specialization; 81 percent or 285 respondents identified this trend. Illustrations are specialization in research, sports, coaching, aquatics, physiotherapy, adaptive physical education, elementary–secondary education, and dance. Although dance was included in physical education as an activity, professional preparation in this specialty has dimensions in other departments, for example, fine arts.

Increasing emphasis on motor growth and development is evident throughout the undergraduate preparation, but the trend is most noticeable in preparation for elementary teaching. At the kindergarten and primary levels, orientation to body movement—including psychological, sociological, and physiological components—is the most common manifestation of the movement-sensory motor emphasis.

Respondents reinforced the traditional issue—theory as opposed to application, general practitioner as opposed to in-depth specialist. As old patterns and curricular rigidities disappear, the trend toward undergraduate specialization remains somewhat clouded.

DEVELOPMENT OF GRADUATE PROGRAMS INTO AREAS OF SPECIALIZATION

Development of programs reflecting the trend toward specificity of training and assignments in contrast to the generalistic approach is even more significant at the graduate level. Although most evident at the doctoral level, the trend is increasing in programs culminating in the master's degree and certification for instruction in public schools, according to 83 percent or 290 respondents. Respondents are aware of the proliferation of graduate programs designed to prepare candidates with specializations in perceptual motor behavior, biomechanics, exercise physiology, and philosophical–sociocultural aspects of the discipline, and some warned that too much specialization narrows the usefulness of the candidate. Open-end comments included the suggestion that master's degree candidates be allowed a specialist or generalist option, dependent upon their projected careers.

Both undergraduates and graduates should become more knowledgeable regarding current research data; respondents noted that highly sophisticated research conducted by physical educators, especially in biomechanics and exercise physiology, is gaining acceptance among researchers from other disciplines. Furthermore, interdisciplinary and college-community cooperation in research projects may reinforce this trend in the future.

The issue attendant to the widely acknowledged trend toward specialization is not whether it would occur but rather at what levels in the professional preparation and to what degree.

INTENSIFICATION OF ELEMENTARY PHYSICAL EDUCATION IN PUBLIC SCHOOLS

Public elementary schools have intensified their programs of physical education, according to 81 percent or 286 respondents. Program experimentation may have been influenced by increasing awareness by public school personnel of state and federal funding for disadvantaged and emotionally handicapped children. At no educational level is the cardinal personal–professional value of the individual personality considered of more consequence than in the elementary school. Because of this, the team approach appears to be increasing, an approach which utilizes the expertise of physician, nurse, psychologist, social worker, guidance counselor, and physical education teacher in the diagnosis, prescription, and possibly remediation requisite for effective physical education for each child. Clinical education has become a viable means of education and therapy of the handicapped. Furthermore, use of paraprofessionals has provided increased flexibility and educational alternatives.

Recent research exploring the relationship between motor performance and academic achievement has further increased interest in physical education activities at the kindergarten and primary levels. As a result, in many preschool, kindergarten, and primary grades physical education learning experiences are utilizing the cognitive domain as fully as the psychomotor. For example, multisensory thinking, movement exploration, perceptual-motor development, and strategies designed to encourage self-direction, self-discipline, problem-solving skills, and creativity through dance now characterize some of the more advanced elementary physical education programs.

Numerous new careers have become available as physical education has become part of preschool programs in a variety of settings—home, college, church, social agencies, and government subsidized programs such as Head Start and Community Action Projects. Undoubtedly, efforts of professional associations to affect legislation for elementary physical education have also made an impact on the trend toward intensification.

Any major shift in emphasis from traditional curricula facilitates emergence of related issues. The primary issue appears to focus on movement education vs. skill requirement. Respondents' open-end comments reflected strong support for movement education as one valuable teaching approach, not necessarily limited to the elementary level. It should not, however, be considered an end. While some supported movement exploration as appropriate through grade 3, they believed a shift in emphasis should occur in grades 4 through 6. Others commented that knowledgeable teachers will use movement education as a basis for skills—swimming, field hockey, volleyball, and gymnastics. Still others lamented the loss of the drive for skills and activities within the profession and the reliance on academic areas for communication with others. One is led to question whether or not the issue really exists or whether it is simply a breakdown in semantics and understanding.

MORE SUPPORT FOR ELECTIVE PHYSICAL EDUCATION AT SECONDARY AND COLLEGE–UNIVERSITY LEVELS

Increasing support for elective physical education and subsequent provision of greater breadth of activity designed to appeal to a wider spectrum of talent and aspiration was acknowledged by 85 percent or 297 respondents. The trend toward elective physical education is not limited to the collegiate level, and despite some authorities' preconceived ideas of personal and social values attributed to specific activities, curricula are being selected in accordance with needs and interests of individual students as early as junior high school. Early emphasis on life-long skills and coeducational activities is increasingly evident.

With implementation of elective physical education in secondary schools, necessity arises to analyze carefully the effects of flexible scheduling, use of paraprofessionals, and continual shifting of faculty and staff assignments. Student, faculty, and administrative opinion should be solicited to maintain viable programs. Within the context of elective physical education, some teaching techniques which may prove effective are totally individualized instruction, independent study, team teaching in coeducational classes, and extensive use of audiovisual aids including instructional television and videotaping.

At the collegiate level, implementation of elective physical education has resulted in few required experiences and a commensurate increase in coeducational intramural programs and construction of new facilities to service them. Innovative curricula will undoubtedly be another outgrowth of the trend. Collegiate program designers desirous of apprising themselves of some unique programs already in operation should investigate the offerings at San Jose State College, California; State University College at Brockport, New York; and University of Toledo, Ohio.

When a specific new interest is considered of sufficient magnitude to warrant inclusion in the physical education program, perhaps an elective pilot course should be offered for a trial period, retention to be determined on the basis of evaluation and continuing interest. An illustration is the current interest in self-defense courses for women. Consideration of the implications for elective physical education as a base for careers other than teaching might also be apropos.

As the elective trend and recreational focus increase, some respondents expressed concern for maintaining balance. Retrenchment of physical educators was perceived in remarks warning that inherent in implementation of elective physical education are dangers of loss of appeal and purpose, reduction of faculty and staff, and inadequate facilities.

Differences of opinion regarding the advisability of elective physical education seem to stem from divergence in proponents' focus on leisure time vs. skill. Opinion ranged from unqualified support to total disapproval. However, general consensus reflected acceptability of elective physical education only at the secondary and collegiate levels and contingent upon students' having had strong foundations. A Canadian respondent commented that an issue no longer exists there as elective programs are prevalent.

INCREASED EMPHASIS UPON INTERCOLLEGIATE COMPETITION FOR GIRLS AND WOMEN

Recognizing the trend toward increasing interscholastic and intercollegiate competition for girls and women, 77 percent or 276 respondents offered both guidelines and warnings. As this competition becomes more extensive, some respondents appear apprehensive that the "evils" established in some men's programs may plague women's competition. Specifically, female respondents cited as possible detriments recruitment procedures, athletic scholarships, and decreased concern for health and scholarship of skilled players.

Open-end responses indicated significant support for increasing intramurals which involve many, as opposed to interscholastic–intercollegiate competition which emphasizes the capability of the few. If the trend continues to gain momentum, respondents suggested that competition for women be retained within the administrative framework of women's physical education departments; that a variety of activities, including dance, be involved; and that no conscious attempt to emulate men's programs be made. To limit the detrimental effects of competition for girls and women, adherence to policies published by national and state organizations is recommended.

A significant number of respondents acknowledged that interscholastic–intercollegiate competition for boys and men has been overemphasized. In their concern for the public image of the physical educator, respondents warned against catering to students with high achievement levels, particularly those interested in varsity sports, to the neglect of those who are less skilled. Even at the elementary, junior high, and senior high levels, the total physical education program has suffered commensurate with the overemphasis on athletics.

Another problem related to this trend is the lack of sufficient professional preparation for coaching responsibilities among faculty with split assignments in English, history, and other disciplines. Just as female respondents warned against transmisssion of the "evils" in men's competition to newly emerging programs of women's competition, male respondents suggested means to ameliorate what many considered an overemphasis on interscholastic–intercollegiate competition. Some called for a return to "amateurism" and discontinuance of "big-time" sports programs completely. Others proposed inclusion of more recreational sports for after-college years, more motivational studies, and putting "fun" back into physical education; effective collegiate physical education programs should provide something of genuine interest for everyone. Although the problem of overemphasis has not yet reached major proportions, it is closely aligned with the issues ensuing from the trend toward division of athletic and physical education programs. And it is the sequence to the issues upon which attention of educators should be focused.

DIVISION BETWEEN ADMINISTRATION OF ATHLETICS AND PHYSICAL EDUCATION

An administrative division developing between athletic and physical education programs was noted by 71 percent or 265 respondents. Proponents of "academic" physical education placed high priority on differentiation between exhibition and entertainment in athletics and serious physical education. The credibility gap which exists between physical education and athletics is of serious concern as physical educators ponder whether or not questionable values demonstrated in the operation of some athletic programs and widely publicized conduct of athletes will denigrate physical education.

Few question the fact that the values of society are shifting. Perhaps educators cannot stop the shift; perhaps they should not try. But they must deal with change, they must view it in contemporary perspective, and they must meet the exigencies of the times. Identified as clamant issues in open-end comments were inequities in budget, overemphasis on competition, athletics as a money-making business, and maintenance of perspective. The trend toward division is not commanding, but issues regarding inequity are increasing.

Inequity is also the nucleus of an issue regarding merger of men's and women's departments of physical education. Respondents noted that in departments which have merged opportunities for women in administrative capacities, as well as their opportunities to teach theory courses, have decreased. In the opinions of some respondents, women physical educators also desire careers as administrators and specialists in aquatics, sports, dance —with equal status to men. Apparently they are not willing to be technicians who merely implement orders. In an age of "women's lib" uncompromising attitudes may be indicative of inner uncertainty rather than deep conviction and commitment. An implacable stand may be directed against an inner doubt rather than an outside assailant.

Issues appear to result from inequities existing between athletic and physical departments and unequal opportunities for women in combined departments of men's and women's physical education. No nexus seems to exist between the principle of combined vs. separate departments and these issues. With the granting of total autonomy and assumption of program accountability by an increasing number of schools of health, physical education, and recreation, consideration of means to resolve these inequities should be accelerated within the college community.

CONCLUSION

No aspect of contemporary life is untouched by the all-pervasive dynamics of change—personal, technological, and professional—for change is the aegis of today's society. No philosophy of curriculum, educational organization or procedure, technique of personnel management, or any other component of a discipline can be perceived as permanent. But change for the sake of change should not be invited. Certainly some traditional policies, attitudes, and values should be discarded, but others should be preserved. Physical educators, should not be content to lounge in the comfort of tradition; in areas of demonstrated need, they must seek change. Clues provided by public school teachers and college students must be acknowledged, the changing environment sensed, and commitment to action made.

To help students know themselves, their strengths and limitations; to help them achieve some degree of self-actualization; to offer self-discipline as an alternative to hedonism are challenging educational priorities for the 1970s. As theorists, physical educators must ascertain the margin of choice offered by the individual student and degree of fiscal adequacy in the institution, then clarify alternatives within that frame of reference. As educators, their success is dependent upon the ability to respond to demands for change. Rapidity with which change occurs may threaten those whose professional lives are attuned to a measured, less syncopated beat. The time span allowed in which to become accustomed to an emerging trend and develop a new pattern of response consistently shortens.

Innovation appears to be prerequisite to living in a contemporary society. However, only those innovations which will improve the program for all, not fragment it to please a few, should be implemented by physical educators.

In summary, many believe that the discipline of physical education should be perceived as a synergistic medium through which extensive professional and societal values can be affected. Among the ensuing implications are the beliefs that ghetto problems can be resolved, leisure time utilized more effectively, environment protected from pollution, potential social dropouts made productive members of society, and teacher education made really effective.

No immutable paradigm exists; there are myriad alternatives for the future. The success of the discipline in meeting the challenge of the 1970s may be determined by its capability to stress creative, self-fulfilling, heuristic goals reinforced by performance objectives; to acknowledge salient trends and issues and act in accordance with them; and to maintain curricular relevance through continuous evaluation.

Operational Concepts

1. The traditional physical education objectives of body fitness and regular exercise must be balanced with greater emphasis on humanistic concerns.

2. The cognitive aspects of physical well-being need increased curricular attention.

3. The physical education programs of the future should make provisions for movement education, self-defense activities, interscholastic competition for girls, and more noncompetitive athletic experiences for both sexes.

4. Recreational sports appropriate to leisure-time pursuits deserve greater curricular stress.

Implications

Reduced to their essence, the problems confronting physical education are principally those of improving the long-range effects of instruction. A majority of Americans do not yet prize the advantages of a strong and healthy body, the social preoccupation with spectator sports continues to outdistance the interest in personal physical activity, and far too little is accomplished in the way of developing atheletic skills that provide a pleasurable outlet for leisure time.

It is not the goals of physical education but rather the success with which they are reached that should concern us most. Physical education curriculum planners should direct their creative imagination toward the invention of new teaching ideas that aim at stimulating greater physical activity out of school, dramatize the pleasures of active involvement in recreation and sport, and strengthen student attitudes regarding the importance of a well-functioning body.

Aurelio Eugene Florio

Safety Education

Accidents are one of the most serious social and personal problems facing our nation. They rank fourth among the causes of all deaths and first among the causes of death in the age group from one to forty-four. Specific causes of accidental fatalities and injuries include motor vehicle accidents, fires, burns, drownings, poisonings, falls, and accidents with firearms. It is, therefore, most essential that young people become familiar with the hazards of modern living and learn how to live safely in their environment.

One of the best ways of combating the accident problem is a high-quality safety education program in the schools. Strong administrative leadership in such programs is essential for developing a safe school environment and ensuring that safety education is part of the total school program. Effective teaching by properly trained teachers is necessary to influence every student to protect himself and others from potential dangers in all circumstances and develop the proper habits, knowledge, skills, and, most important of all, attitudes for safety.

An effective safety education program conveys certain basic concepts to the student: (1) Accidents waste time, money, and life, but most of them can be avoided. (2) Accident prevention is not the task of a few people but the responsibility of many. (3) Safety enables the individual to enjoy adventure without the hazards of accidents. (4) Safety is related to physical and mental health and requires adjustment to the situation, not just perfunctory behavior. (5) There will be a reduction of accidents when man accepts greater responsibility for his acts, when he takes fewer foolish risks, and when there are more effective environmental controls. (6) In order to prevent accidents, it is necessary to know how they occur.

Guidelines for planning a safety program are provided in the Safety Charter for Children and Youth, developed by a joint committee representing seven departments of the National Education Association, the Society of State Directors for Health, Physical Education, and Recreation, and the National Safety Council.

Reprinted from Aurelio Eugene Florio, *The Encyclopedia of Education*, Vol. 8 (New York: Crowell-Collier Educational Corp., 1971), pp. 1–6; by permission.

INSTRUCTIONAL PATTERNS AND TECHNIQUES

The teaching methods used for safety education are governed by the ultimate objectives of the program. The primary objectives are to teach correct behavior and provide a wide variety of experiences which will enable the student to make wise decisions when the possibility of injury arises. There are three specific patterns of instruction that may be used: (1) direct teaching, (2) correlation, and (3) integration.

Direct teaching is used in two basic situations. First, it is used in courses concerned exclusively with safety, which, like history or chemistry, are distinct subjects in the curriculum. Second, it is used when a teacher of another subject—such as social service or health education—includes one or more units on safety in the regular course. The direct teaching method is most appropriate at the junior and senior high school levels, where subjects are compartmentalized.

Correlation involves the use of other curricular areas as vehicles for safety education. In the elementary grades, for example, where the teacher has the same pupils most of the day, it is possible to incorporate safety education into other areas.

Integration is a radical departure from the other two patterns. Instruction revolves around a central theme or objective and relates parts of the subject to the whole. Thus, all of the instruction supports a single purpose.

In many instances a combination of patterns of instruction may be used, or safety instruction may be centered around student organizations and activities—such as student safety councils, safety patrols, and student government.

The instructional techniques used in teaching other subjects can also apply to the teaching of safety. The traditional approaches of discussion, lecture–discussion, reading assignments, and demonstrations are often used. A problem-solving approach to discussion is particularly effective; this involves the presentation and analysis of a real problem which culminates in a conclusion or solution. Dramatizations (in the form of pantomines, playlets, role playing, and debates) and oral presentations by panels or individuals are useful techniques.

Various outside activities promote student interest and involvement. These include individual or class projects to compile information, collect objects, or construct materials and surveys and inspections of the school, home, or commnity, involving the scientific investigation and study of specific problems. The teacher can utilize the resources of the community by taking the class on a field trip or inviting an outside speaker to the school.

The choice of instructional techniques depends on various factors: the nature of the students; the teacher's personality, competence, and background; the time allotment; the materials available; and the administrative organization of the school.

Many instructional techniques can effectively use audiovisual materials. Fortunately, there are excellent audiovisual materials—such as films, slides, records, tape recordings—dealing with various aspects of accident prevention. Sources for these materials include national, state, and local educational agencies, college and university audiovisual departments, insurance companies, automobile manufacturers, and motor clubs. Audiovisual materials are usually provided at no cost to the school.

CONTENT

The basic areas which safety education should deal with are (1) traffic safety—for pedestrians, drivers, bicyclists, and motorcyclists, (2) safety in sports and recreation, (3) home safety, (4) disaster procedures, and (5) safe use of firearms and other equipment.

Traffic Safety

Traffic safety is an increasingly complex problem. Over half of the people in the United States are licensed drivers, and more than 3 million young people reach the driving age each year. There are 25 million bicyclists, 90 percent of whom are children. Because of the great number of motor vehicles on the streets and highways and the increasing traffic congestion in the cities, accidents involving pedestrians are becoming more frequent. Traffic accidents are the leading cause of death among children. For these reasons, traffic safety is obviously one of the most important concerns of safety education programs in the schools.

Education in traffic safety involves instruction not only in the proper use of the automobile but also in sound pedestrianism, bicycling, and motorcycling. Every student should be given the opportunity to develop the habits, skills, knowledge, and attitudes essential to the intelligent use of streets and highways.

Various studies of the pedestrian accident problem have illustrated that a sound education program can be effective in promoting pedestrian safety. A well-organized program requires the cooperation of the community, particularly law enforcers, traffic engineers, safety councils, and various public information media and provides learning experiences that lead to an understanding of safe pedestrian practices. A list of safe practices could serve as a starting point in developing a pedestrian education program. One such list is *Pedestrian's Rights and Duties Listed in the Model Traffic Ordinances* (National Committee . . . , 1968), a guide for sound pedestrianism that was developed over a period of years by the National Committee on Uniform Traffic Laws and Ordinances in Washington, D.C.

Formal instruction in traffic safety should be started the day a youngster begins school for the first time and should be integrated into or correlated with everyday learning activities in the elementary and junior high schools. At these levels the objective of traffic safety education should be to help reduce deaths and injuries from traffic accidents by developing in the student (1) a sense of responsibility for the safety of himself and others while going to and from school; (2) recognition and understanding of situations involving traffic hazards; (3) understanding and appreciation of the work of police officers, school traffic safety patrols, adult crossing guards, traffic engineers, and others concerned with safety, and recognition of the need to obey them; (4) understanding of the meaning and need for obeying various aids to safety along streets and highways—such as signs, signals, and road markings; (5) habitual use of the safest route to and from any area; and (6) understanding of the causes of traffic accidents and knowledge of what is being done to reduce them (Office of Superintendent of Public Instruction, 1963).

The particular traffic safety program in high schools is commonly called driver education. It is usually a separate course but can also be integrated with other subjects—such as health education or social and physical sciences.

The recommended high school driver education course is divided into two phases. The classroom phase consists of learning experiences centered on classroom instruction. The second phase, usually known as the laboratory or practice driving phase, provides actual driving experience on the streets and highways or on an established driving range, using a dual-control automobile.

The recommended minimum time allotment is thirty clock hours for the classroom phase and six hours for actual driving experience. The practice driving requirement can be partially fulfilled by the use of driving simulators and the driving range. Best results are obtained when the student is taught by a teacher who has met state certification and other requirements.

The increasing use of the bicycle as a means of economical transportation, recreation, and developing and maintaining physical fitness has added to the traffic safety problem. Bicycle accidents are annually responsible for a considerable number of deaths and injuries, particularly of young people. Since the great majority of bicycle riders are school-age children, the problem of bicycle safety should command the serious attention of students, parents, and schools. Teaching bicycle safety in the elementary schools would be an appropriate method of preventing accidents and also providing basic training for future motor vehicle operators.

Because the bicycle is considered a vehicle by state laws, it is necessary that bicycle riders abide by motor vehicle regulations. Nationwide statistics show that three of every four bicyclists injured in a bicycle–motor vehicle collision were violating some traffic law or safety practice, and one of five bicycles involved in accidents had some mechanical defect. Therefore, bicycle safety programs should be primarily concerned with teaching traffic laws, safety practices, and proper maintenance of the bicycle.

An effective bicycle safety program would assist in reducing accidents by helping students to (1) understand traffic regulations that apply to cycling; (2) develop habits, knowledge, attitudes, and skills conducive to safe cycling; (3) acquire knowledge necessary to maintain the bicycle in safe operating condition; and (4) acquire skills necessary to operate a bicycle on streets and highways at all times and under all conditions. Learning experiences should be provided whereby bicyclists can achieve these objectives. Useful resources for teachers include the publication *Model Traffic Ordinances,* which states the regulations for bicycles, and information provided by the Bicycle Institute of America and the National Education Association's Commission on Safety Education, which deals with selection and maintenance of bicycles and with correct techniques of riding.

The use of motorcycles for transportation, touring, and sport has reached a new peak in this country in recent years, and the number of motorcyclists is growing every year. This development has been accompanied by a sharp rise in accidents involving these vehicles. During the 1960s the number of motorcycle driver deaths increased from about 700 a year to more than 2,000.

Because the motorcycle appeals to younger people and because this group has the greatest number of deaths and injuries, these is undoubtedly a need for a systematic instructional program for beginning motorcyclists. Many motorcycle accidents seem to stem from the same causes as automobile accidents. Since all states now provide high school driver education programs for beginning automobile drivers, similar programs could be developed for motorcyclists. Because of the close relationship of motorcyclist to motorist and the need for mutual understanding, it is desirable to correlate motorcycle safety with regular driver education programs. Researchers at State University College at Oswego, New York, organized a meaningful program for motorcycle driver education and demonstrated that this program brings beneficial results (Dunn, 1967).

Areas which could be included in a motorcycle safety program are familiarization with the motorcycle laws and rules of the road, motorcycle operation (including instruction on controls, proper riding habits, and maintenance; skill exercises; and road tests in traffic), accidents and traffic hazards, and the psychology of motorcycle riding. Excellent teaching materials are available from the Motorcycle Scooter Allied Trades Association and from most motorcycle companies. Universal Underwriters Insurance Company provides an excellent guidebook for motorcycle driver education instructors.

Safety in Sports and Recreation

Various studies have shown that the majority of school accidents occur in the physical education or athletic programs. Obviously, this type of activity exposes students to more dangers than normal classroom activities. Nevertheless, safety education programs can do much to increase safe participation.

All too often a factor contributing to accidents, particularly at the elementary school level, is that many classroom teachers must teach physical education without adequate preparation and competence. Sometimes they do not even have the help of specially trained supervisors. Studies reveal that poor leadership is directly responsible for many accidents in athletics. A thoroughly competent recreation leader, coach, or instructor can minimize or eliminate most of the conditions that are likely to cause accidents.

Four basic requirements, understood and practiced by well-prepared and professionally trained leaders, will go a long way in providing safe participation: (1) understanding the hazards involved in each activity, (2) removing unnecessary hazards, (3) compensating for hazards which cannot be removed, and (4) creating no unnecessary hazards. Since no teacher or coach can watch every participant every minute, it is important that participants be made to follow these basic requirements and to understand the importance of developing individual responsibility for their own safety.

In recent years greater emphasis has been placed on the subject of safety in physical education by the American Association for Health, Physical Education, and Recreation. The association holds national conferences on accident prevention in physical education and athletics and has developed the textbook *Accident Prevention in Physical Education and Sports*. The National Safety Council and the American Medical Association have also demonstrated much interest in this area.

Another important reason for the schools' responsibility to provide instruction for safe participation in sports is that millions of people engage in sports and recreational activities outside of school. Since swimming and many other types of water activities are so popular, safety education programs should be concerned with swimming ability. Although the American Red Cross, YMCA, Boy Scouts, and other organizations have done a great deal in promoting and conducting education programs in water safety, drownings still rank high in accidental deaths, particularly among young people. There is an increasing number of drownings in backyard swimming pools, especially of youngsters under five years of age. Of the millions who frequent beaches each summer only a small percentage are skillful swimmers capable of handling themselves and others in the hazardous situations they may encounter.

There is unquestionably a need for expanded school programs in swimming safety. Every physical education program in the public schools should emphasize developing good swimming and diving ability: the schools must go beyond the point of teaching youngsters to swim only well enough to expose them to danger.

Boating is an increasingly popular water sport, enjoyed by approximately one-fourth of all U.S. citizens. Lack of proper training causes it to be a hazardous activity. Factors contributing to the dangers of boating are inexperience in boating, inability to handle oneself and others in a water emergency (often due to poor swimming and lifesaving abilities), unsafe or unsportsmanlike behavior, and unsafe condition of the boat (for instance, poor mechanical condition, overloading, or lack of life preservers).

The American Red Cross and the Coast Guard Auxiliary have aided immeasurably in reducing the deaths, accidents, and injuries that occur annually as a result of unsafe boating. However, boating education programs in the schools, minimum and maximum age limits for boaters, and required licensing of operators are still much needed.

Skin and scuba diving, water-skiing, and snow skiing also attract millions annually. The dangers of these sports are minimized if the participants are well trained by expert instructors. Organizations conducting these activities and manufacturers of equipment have developed rules and regulations for safe participation. These are useful for safety education programs in schools where many students participate in these activities.

Home Safety

Despite the feeling of security many people have in their own homes, the problem of home accidents is one of great magnitude. More than twice as many injuries occur each year in home accidents as in motor vehicle accidents, and accidents in the home account for nearly twice as many fatalities as do accidents at work.

An analysis of home accidents reveals that most are caused by human failings, environmental hazards, or a combination of both. Like many other accidents, home accidents result from inadequate knowledge, insufficient skill, and faulty attitudes. Therefore, any safety education program should attempt to overcome these inadequacies by helping students to recognize and understand the many hazards in and around the home, develop a sense of responsibility toward safeguarding themselves and others against the possibility of home accidents, gain skills required to perform household tasks safely, and acquire safe, orderly habits in all home activities.

Home safety instruction should start early in life, primarily as the responsibility of parents. But schools should continue this instruction by integrating or correlating home safety with other school subjects, by teaching specific home safety units in subject areas—such as home economics, health education, and vocational education.

It is also possible to combat home accidents through student organizations, service clubs, and health departments, and the various communications media (radio, television, newspapers, magazines, and motion pictures).

Disaster Procedure

Additional areas that should be given adequate time in a safety education program are preparations for civil defense emergencies and natural disasters such as tornadoes, floods, blizzards, explosions, hurricanes, and earthquakes.

Fire prevention and protection should be an integral part of any safety education program. Analysis reveals that destructive fires are fundamentally the result of carelessness or failure to understand and recognize fire hazards. Deaths, injuries, and property damage can be greatly reduced if people are taught proper methods of fire prevention.

Certain aspects of fire prevention can be taught in almost any academic course or extracurricular activity. Areas which should be considered are (1) the causes of fires—smoking, matches, electricity, heating units, explosive materials, rubbish and other flammable materials, lightning, and construction faults; (2) procedures to use when escaping from a fire; and (3) fire-fighting procedures, including use of fire extinguishers.

Since panic is often a cause of tragedy in school fires and other disasters, instruction and practice in how to behave in emergencies is necessary. Disaster drills of all types need to be organized and conducted frequently in schools, college and university dormitories, fraternity and sorority houses, and other types of housing facilities. Disaster procedures should be known by all school personnel, including new students, new teachers, and substitute teachers. It is the responsibility of the school administrator to establish, define, and assign fire drill responsibilities to certain staff members and see that all school personnel are thoroughly familiar with fire drill and fire prevention procedures.

Safe Use of Firearms and Equipment

Instructions in the proper use of firearms, explosives, and fireworks should also be included in safety education. The National Rifle Association of America in Washington, D.C., and the Shooting Arms and Ammunitions Manufacturing Institute in New York City provide excellent resource materials for these areas.

Another area which should be a component of the safety education programs in rural schools is the safe use of farm equipment. Since accidents in agriculture account for a considerable number of the deaths from industrial accidents, it is obvious that farmers must be trained in the proper use of equipment. Because the safety practices established for farming must be self-enforced, every farmer must fully understand the many hazards that surround him, the need for precautions, and the value of working safely. Education and training are the only feasible means of achieving this goal.

Coordination

Before a sound, comprehensive program of safety education can be achieved, all school personnel should be firmly convinced of the importance of such a program. The administrator should be thoroughly familiar with all school safety policies and codes and should see that they are strictly enforced. A concerned administrator may appoint a safety coordinator or supervisor, charged with administering and coordinating the school's safety policies, developing curricula, helping to improve instruction, establishing school and community relationships, and evaluating the program. Effective safety education programs and prudent enforcement of necessary safety precautions can help students to eliminate painful and costly accidents and can help boards of education, teachers, and school administrators to avoid liability suits for student injuries.

Selected Readings

DUNN, LEROY. 1967. "Teach Them to Ride." *Safety,* 3, no. 2:16–19.

National Committee on Uniform Traffic Laws and Ordinances. 1968. *Pedestrian's Rights and Duties Listed in the Model Traffic Ordinances,* Rev. ed. Washington, D.C., The Committee.

Office of Superintendent of Public Instruction. 1963. *The Challenge of Safety Education,* Circular Series A-128. Springfield, Ill., The Office.

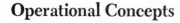

Operational Concepts

1. The principles of human safety can be taught both directly, in special teaching units, and indirectly through integration with other areas of the curriculum.

2. Effective programs of safety education should stress accident-prevention tactics related to firearms, traffic, recreation, home, and environmental disaster.

3. Safety education must go beyond exposure to procedures and techniques, and emphasize positive attitudes toward preventative behavior.

Implications

Safety education is based, chiefly, upon a knowledge of basic rules, a disposition toward prudent behavior, and an interest in self-protection. The high accident rate which still prevails, however, is simple testimony to the fact that the battle is far from won.

As we continue to struggle with an impossibly bloated agenda for schooling, time for specific instruction in safety education will become increasingly scant. What we must do, consequently, is encourage all teachers, at all levels, to stress the principles of safety whenever and wherever the classroom activities permit. What passes for common sense is not nearly as common as is sometimes assumed: students need constant reinforcement with respect to recognizing safety risks and using good judgment.

Nutrition Education

Earl P. Schubert

Nutrition Education: How Much Can or Should Our Schools Do?

On an Indian reservation in Tulalip, Washington, an elementary school principal and his wife, a registered nurse, have effectively minimized the ravages of "Indian" sores, rashes, and infection among school-aged children, improved the overall alertness and stamina of an elementary school population to an extraordinary degree, culminated the problem of the presence of underweight children in his school community, and increased his school's average daily attendance from under 80 percent four years ago to its present 98 percent.

How? By assuring each child two well-planned meals on a daily basis, providing dental and physical examinations on a regularly scheduled basis, and supplying health services when necessary. The entire school population, including teachers, participates in a carefully designed health program in grades K through 6. An expanded summer program gives continuity to what has been developed during the regular school year.

In the Mexican-American community of San Diego, Texas, where over 60 percent of the households has an income of less than $3,000 and low educational achievement, functional illiteracy, high infant mortality, and inadequate housing has characterized the county, a startling and almost unbelievable transition has taken place in its school system during the past six years.

Exclaiming emphatically to all within listening distance that "hungry children cannot learn, and that "if the Title I money was genuinely intended to relieve the school's most present educational problems, then health and nutrition most deserved these funds," the district's superintendent of schools has developed a health and nutrition program for all grade levels that could readily serve as a model for the nation. The Texas Nutrition Survey team, a part of the National Survey effort by the Department of Health, Education and Welfare, conducted one of its comprehensive clinics in San Diego. The data collected there were convincing, to

Reprinted from Earl P. Schubert, "Nutrition Education: How Much Can or Should Our Schools Do?" *Journal of Nutrition Education*, Vol. 2, No. 1, 1970, pp. 9–13; by permission of the publisher.

say the least. No school-aged child in San Diego had low or deficient hemoglobin levels. Only 6 percent were considered low or deficient in plasma vitamin A content, far below the state average. None were listed as low or deficient in serum vitamin C.

The survey director described the condition of their teeth as the best examined during the entire state survey. Subsequent analysis of these findings at the national level revealed them to be superior to those encountered in other state surveys. By using all types of funding from federal sources under which his health and nutrition program requirements qualify, by the efficient and imaginative use of state and local funding, and by working with local professional and service groups in helping needy youngsters and their families, an expansive feeding and health care program has been developed which has had a tremendous impact on the educational process. In addition, the program has been designed to carry over into the adult community, and malnutrition in any serious form is comparatively nonexistent in the immediate area. In the schools themselves, overall daily attendance has risen above 95 percent, school dropout rates have decreased to less than an average of 10 per year, discipline problems have become negligible, vandalism simply doesn't exist, and few grade failures due to lack of interest, ill health, or low stamina have been recorded.

FIFTY PERCENT GO TO COLLEGE

Probably most remarkable of all is that nearly 50 percent of the high school's graduates are being accepted into schools of higher learning. The spirit and dedication of the school system's faculty and staff is a remarkable thing to observe in this day of discontent and militancy in education.

In West Virginia, the state department of education through the mechanism of its Comprehensive Education Program has designed a Health-Nutritional Project geared toward the overall strengthening and upgrading of nutritional health education in the state's schools. State and local educators have strongly suggested a critical need to overhaul nutritional health instruction, practices, and services in assuming a leadership role in minimizing problems of malnutrition that exist in their state through a statewide nutrition education effort.

The project includes an assessment and evaluation of existing nutritional health activities, the coordination of ongoing programs at the state and county levels, curriculum development, in-service workshops for teachers, the conducting of Health-Nutritional institutes in cooperation with teacher preparation institutions, the collection and distribution of resource aids, and an ambitious plan to include parents and the community in the education process. A formal statement describing why this project is being proposed and supported reads, in part, that "Realizing that much of the nutritional health problem in West Virginia is caused by the lack of adequate education on this subject by both children and adults, the staff of the Department of Education has been searching for ways to improve this element of the educational program."

In Virginia, a teacher information brochure developed by the American Institute of Nutrition Council is being tested in selected high schools. An innovative and exciting science project which could conceivably influence the structure of secondary school science curricula, its instructional and laboratory program is centered around the topic "Nutrition as a Science in Everyday Life."

The Boards of Education in Hinds County, Mississippi, and Williamsburg and Lee Counties in South Carolina, have approved somewhat innovative use of their school buses in extending nutrition education and services to their communities. In Hinds County, school buses are used to take members of needy families to food distribution points, where formerly it was impossible for those people to obtain transportation. In Williamsburg and Lee Counties, a complete kitchen occupies the rear of vintage school buses, transforming them into mobile units for demonstration work in nutrition education. These mobile units travel from town to town, demonstrating how to prepare low-cost, well-balanced meals under the supervision of a trained nutritionist.

To the casual observer, these uses of school buses appear to be obviously appropriate. "After all, the school bus sits in somebody's back yard or driveway 21 hours a day, and it doesn't cost much to run." To the average school professional or school board member, however, this type of innovation in school bus usage is a gigantic step repleat with legal interpretations, insurance hang-ups, wage disputes, questions of responsibilities, and challenges to tradition.

TEXAS PROGRAMS

In the state of Texas, 20 regional education service centers have been established to serve the numerous independent school districts located within their regional sectors. Under the sponsorship of the Texas State Department of Education—known as the Texas Education Agency—and the Texas Medical Association, a Conference on Optimum School Health was held in San Antonio in July, 1969. School health teams were represented at the conference from all 20 regions.

The teams were made up of school board members, superintendents of schools, elementary and secondary principals, nutrition educators, school lunch supervisors, medical directors, school nurse supervisors, school health coordinators and teachers, PTA members, public health nurses, curriculum specialists, and other health and community related personnel. A major part of this conference was devoted to the improvement of nutritional health education and services in the schools of Texas. The Region XIII

Service Center, located in Austin, shortly thereafter embarked upon a project to develop a written plan describing a "Model Nutrition Program in a School Setting," and will incorporate the results of current research and established educational practice, using the findings of its own field testing which will have involved all features of a school–community nutrition program in a medium sized school system. The project has the strong support of the Texas Education Agency and can ultimately be used as a model throughout the state.

While efforts by educators such as those described here continue to be duplicated in ever increasing numbers in isolated localities throughout the nation, opposition to the school's role in accepting responsibility in the nutritional health of its school population still persists in many quarters. Even in the aforementioned programs, some parents, educators, health personnel, and political figures have been less than enthusiastic in endorsing this concept of public education's responsibility. Superintendent Bryan P. Taylor (San Diego, Texas) is confronted by some fellow educators on occasions with the statement that "the schools should not be in the food and health business." Principal Ron Smythe (Tulalip, Washington), still is admonished from time to time to "leave health and feeding where it belongs—with parents. If not parents, then the church."

A state legislator upon having this concept of a school's responsibility in a local community described to him, responded after much serious and sincere objective thought that "in the final analysis, this very well may smack of a welfare state philosophy. Is this what we want?"

A well-qualified public health official in all sympathy and candor quietly exclaimed "But the schools simply do not have the expertise to develop such an overall program in depth, and I must confess that many local health departments can offer little assistance if, indeed, a local health department exists."

However, the findings of H.E.W.'s authentic and much publicized National Nutrition Survey, along with those of smaller independent studies, not only are revealing the true status of malnutrition in the United States but are also giving impetus to the swelling nationwide demand that this problem be attacked forthwith by all appropriate agencies and groups regardless of old established traditions and operational practices. In the numerous reports submitted to the President by the panels participating in the White House Conference on Food, Nutrition and Health, the urgency of these progressive steps and the insistence that federal, state, and local governments strive immediately to cut bureaucratic red tape to meet the problem head on were manifested throughout the recommendations submitted.

PRIORITY RECOMMENDATIONS

In report after report, high on the list of priority recommendations emanating from many of the twenty-six panels were statements dealing with the necessity of delivering professional nutritional health information to the population through effective informational and educational programs. These recommendations ranked second only to those dealing directly with immediate food and food stamp distribution and related family income. The evidence appears to be that Americans today at all economic levels know pitifully little about sound eating habits, selection of food, food purchasing, and food preparation. The middle and higher income levels have the financial capacity of overcoming this handicap to some degree by mass purchasing. Our nation's poor and underprivileged, however, continue to suffer through malnourishment and its accompanying diseases. They have neither the funds to purchase food in proper quantities nor the knowledge of what food should be consumed to sustain health or how to prepare it if it were available. Yet, nutrition is related in some manner with every aspect of human health, growth, and development.

The plight of the hungry and the malnourished is compounded by this ignorance. The health status of the well-fed also is manifestly influenced by the same ignorance. Obesity in a wealthy suburban neighborhood can be just as much of a threat to good health as iodine or protein deficiency in the lower income areas.

Nutrition education, then, must necessarily loom large in overall planning to combat malnutrition in America. To continue to ignore or minimize this obvious fact is shutting one's eyes to the sad documentary of the evidence of serious health problems at all economic levels attributable to inadequate and oftentimes extremely harmful nutritional habits by our citizenry. In essence, the stamina, health, and productiveness of a significant segment of the nation's population in a land of plenty is seriously impeded by apathy and/or ignorance on the subject of nutritional health.

How can this problem be corrected and who is responsible for correcting it? Is anyone responsible?

We've all heard the same old story from time to time that you can't make people eat and drink what they don't want to eat and drink. This is true, and it is not proposed here that this be attempted. It just wouldn't work. As a matter of fact, it would rightfully be interpreted as an affrontery to individual freedom of choice and action. After all, if an individual wishes to endanger his own health and well being, voluntarily or otherwise, he can usually do so. We are witnessing this today in widespread overindulgence of alcohol, tobacco, and even drugs, while evidence of the dangers involved mount. It this good enough reason for leadership in a reasonible society to simply shrug the whole thing off? Of course not. Consequently a sustained nationwide effort by responsible agencies and institutions is, at last, now being made to inform the population of these dangers. Ignorance, rumors, and misinformation are being eliminated with enlightenment and facts. A healthier, stronger nation should ultimately emerge.

Earl P. Schubert

SCHOOLS A KEY FACTOR

The key factor in this whole national effort is the increased role that the public and private schools are taking through the updating and strengthening of curricula and instruction related to school health. Children from the early elementary grades through high school are increasingly being exposed to the truth concerning the adverse effect on the body of alcohol, tobacco, and drugs. A whole new generation in most areas of the country now has a chance to grow up with this knowledge and understanding, and the opportunity to decide accordingly. This, of course, will not eliminate the problem, but ignorance of the causes of the problem can no longer be pleaded as an excuse for indulgence, and the incidence of children innocently being led or tempted into indulgence is being increasingly minimized.

As the educational and informational effort in this direction mounts, shouldn't there be a similar effort in nutritional health, an area of human development no less significant to the population's well-being, and one which directly touches every citizen throughout his life on a daily basis?

The food industry and apropriate local, state and federal agencies, community groups, research organizations, and institutions of higher learning have a responsibility to inform and educate the public in matters related to nutritional health. Uniform laws need to be established for the fortification and enrichment of commonly used foods, and an explanation of these laws and their implications must be made known in laymen's terms to every citizen.

The tragic shortage of trained nutritionists at all levels places any planning effort of consequence in this direction at a distinct disadvantage. In addition, physicians having little or no formal training in nutrition oftentimes find their attempts to counsel patients in proper nutritional health practices inadequate and ineffective. It follows, then, that our medical schools must assume an increased responsibility in the training of professional personnel.

In all matters related to this national problem, a herculean effort is necessary to combat ignorance and confusion on a gigantic scale to say nothing of bringing about the simple recognition that, indeed, a nutritional health problem even exists in America. It will take time to highlight the problem sufficiently so that it is accepted as such. Even more time will be needed before apropriate groups will responsibly devise methods and techniques to attack it.

So, there appears to be little chance at this time of minimizing malnutrition through education in the near future on a scale that would effectively influence the nutritional habits of the average citizen in all walks of life. However, the obvious question arises pertaining to the nation's responsibility to our present school-aged population as to whether we should knowingly permit a whole new generation to grow up with

291

the same misinformation, confusion, and ignorance of nutritional health that characterizes their elders.

This is inexcusable in this age of scientific knowledge and extraordinary progress in communications.

Should not the nation's schools consider nutritional health as an intricate and necessary part of the optimum school health curriculum from Head Start through the twelfth grade and possibly into the community college program? This effort by the education sector appears to be the obvious channel into every American community offering the most direct, swift, and effective potential, and certainly one requiring a minimal financial drain on existing funds.

To anyone having a token understanding of the operation of a local school system, it shouldn't require too much imagination or vision to recognize that when you touch a child in matters relating to his health, growth, and development you touch the parent and, ultimately, the community. Imagine, for example, what the impact of a well-planned and coordinated local school–community project in nutritional health would have on that community, exploiting the specific characteristics of the community's professional, economic and social base. Here is really a meaningful proposal for a group like the PTA to tackle, working with the school administration and faculty, local physicians and dentists, health clinics, food merchants, community action groups, and service clubs. It could be approached in a number of other ways including initial leadership efforts coming from the school, the professional community, or a combination of both. This is an exciting concept to contemplate, and its potential in eradicating local health problems due to malnutrition is unlimited.

SCHOOL HEALTH PROGRAMS

Whether or not one believes that comprehensive school feeding programs and health services as described earlier should be a school responsibility—and there are legitimate and reasonable opposing arguments to this philosophy, it certainly should be agreed to by all concerned in education that a well-structured curriculum in health instruction is a traditional and educationally-acceptable part of the total school academic program. Much is being said and accomplished in reviewing and evaluating optimum school health programs in the schools. Most veteran teachers and administrators will candidly admit that this has been a neglected area of the academic program and is long overdue. It is held here, then, that nutrition education should be incorporated into this optimum school health curriculum on a serious, well-developed, and effective basis. Home economics teachers have been carrying the load for too many years and then only in the teaching of a usually small percentage of female students enrolled at the high school level. Some informed and inspired biology teachers will touch upon nutrition as a part of their study units. In some instances, an interested physical education teacher will include nutrition in a meaningful way in his or her health course. These teachers deserve the professional compliments they very rarely receive.

These efforts need to be expanded. Nutrition education must become a significant part of health instruction throughout the school child's academic experience beginning in the early grades. In literally thousands of communities across this land, the only opportunity in too many instances that a six- or seven-year-old has of learning something about the health care of his little body and what he should be eating all too often depends solely upon what the elementary teacher standing in front of him every day is able to teach him. His very mental and physical growth and development is directly influenced by this association. Yet, rare is the teachers' college that imparts minimum knowledge in nutrition to its teacher trainees, or a state education department that requires even one unit of nutrition education for teacher certification.

It should be clearly understood that this is emphatically not an attempt to indict education on this count nor should it be considered a negative reflection on a profession that has brought such extraordinary credit to our civilization. There are other agencies or professions having far more responsibility in this area of the nation's health. However, the die has been cast. Conclusive evidence now indicates that malnutrition is most certainly a serious health problem to our population at all economic levels and must be recognized as such.

SOLVING THE PROBLEM

Ignorance and misinformation are as much a cause of the problem as is any other factor. Education is one of the answers to solving it. The schools have a most important role to play in the enlightment of our youngest generation, with a carry over potential to their elders. The national problem will be compounded if this fact is not recognized, and worse still if it is ignored.

What can be done about it? For openers, let's look at these approaches:

1. State departments of education, with comparatively little funding required, can (a) study, evaluate, update, and upgrade health curriculum guides with particular attention being given to nutritional health education at all grade levels; (b) re-examine with teacher training institutions the certification requirements of teachers, particularly of teachers in the elementary grades and health-related subject areas in the secondary schools, as to their relativity to basic preparation in aspects of nutritional health; (c) assume a leadership role in highlighting and projecting the importance and significance of nutritional health education in school curricula, the necessity to strengthen instruction in this area, and the need to compile

and further develop updated materials and audiovisual aids; (d) to further train appropriate staff supervisory personnel on the department's staff or employ new personnel with adequate expertise in nutrition; and (e) take a leadership role in developing working relationships with health departments, medical and dental schools and associations, and other related professional groups, so that consultative assistance may be forthcoming on a cooperative and coordinated basis.

2. Local county, district, or city school systems—through their superintendent, supervisory and curriculum personnel, and school administrators —could take the leadership in evaluating, updating, and strengthening their total school health program from K through 12 by (a) giving impetus to improving the stature and credibility of health instruction as a major academic responsibility; (b) initiating, if necessary, and developing consultative and cooperative working relationships with appropriate professional health personnel and agencies; (c) creating an awareness of the importance of nutritional health education and improved services (school lunch, etc.) in the school communities; (d) providing in-service training in updated instructional methods and techniques in nutritional health, and the use of new materials and aids, to appropriate teaching personnel; (e) giving school lunch personnel the opportunity to participate in refresher courses or in-service workshops related to food selection, preparation, and serving, at the same time making the school cafeteria available for laboratory purposes; (f) encouraging innovative procedures in the enrollment of students in the home economic courses and supporting teachers of these courses in their efforts to expand the scope of instruction and course content; (g) considering new ways to include nutritional health units in family living and science courses, and incorporating aspects of food and agricultural awareness in courses such as geography (soil and topography), world history (food production characteristics of nations), and foreign languages (food and eating vocabularies); (h) projecting the role of the school health nurse where this has not been done, and establishing this position on a level commensurate with her professional experience and training; and (i) developing a community awareness of the significance and importance that the school is placing on the relationship between mental and physical development and proper nutritional health practices.

The above observations are made simply to describe a possible starting point in determining the direction that educational agencies could proceed in recognizing their potential in an overall national effort to ultimately bring about the culmination of malnutrition in their own communities due to ignorance and/or misinformation related to nutritional health. Unquestionably, many school systems are attempting these approaches and others of even more significant merit and potential. The very fact that in some areas of the nation, particularly where the National Nutrition Survey was conducted with the support and assistance of local school districts, educational agencies are recognizing the increased role they can play in further assuring the well-being of their school populations is the beginning of a breakthrough in attacking this serious problem. It should be clearly understood, however, that this is not an easy accomplishment. Increased community pressure is being exerted from all directions to upgrade and broaden more so-called academic subject matter opportunities for students. Budgeting must be earmarked for better salaries, increased school construction, expanded transportation, and equalization of educational opportunities through ever-widening comprehensive programming.

When boards of education and school administrators understand that their schools do, indeed, have a key role to play at this particular time in educating children in nutritional health and that this role is related not only to the growth and development of the children but also to the welfare and progress of their communities, we can expect that the challenge will be met irrespective of the time, effort, and expense involved.

Over the years, a sense of gratification and self-indulgence has lulled us into believing that serious malnutrition could not exist here. The fact is that it does exist on an unbelievable scale affecting millions of our fellow citizens. A continually uninformed and misled citizenry in such a vital area of personal health as nutrition would only compound the perplexing situation that exists and further weaken efforts to resolve it regardless of the size of a family's income and however crucial its importance. Time, of course, is the essence. There is much to do by responsible leadership in an overwhelming number and variety of establishments. The thought advanced here is that with understanding, concern, vision, and action, future generations of Americans need not be victims of ignorance in health matters pertaining to what the nutritional intake of their bodies should be, health matters vitally associated with mental and body development throughout their entire lives. Overdramatization? Unfortunately, the facts being uncovered prove differently.

The concepts and implication related to the teaching of nutrition education appear on pages 305 and 306.

Hazel Taylor Spitze

Innovation Techniques
for Teaching Nutrition

The classroom door was closed. As the principal walked down the hall, he heard excited sounds coming from the room.

"4-4-2-4," one student almost shouted.

"Aw, heck, you beat me," said another, "but I would probably have won in the next round. I have everything but one meat."

"Maybe I'd have won," said another. "I was missing only one vegetable."

His curiosity compelled him to open the door, and he saw an unusual sight. Students were really *enjoying* learning. They were excited about learning *nutrition*, a subject often considered dull by both teacher and students. Some of the students seemed to be teaching each other, while the teacher went about as a resource person to help where needed, to encourage, to challenge, to question.

Four students at one table were playing a card game, and two others were doing something with flash cards. But these flash cards were different; they had colored bar graphs on one side and the name of a food on the other. At another table, a group was playing a new kind of dominoes (with foods instead of dots), and two others were preparing a bulletin board titled, "How Do You Spend Your Calories?" Some were reading. One girl had the *Journal of the American Dietetic Association,* and another was reading a little paperback called *We Are What We Eat(1).* Two others were preparing an exhibit for the hall display case entitled, "The Building Blocks of Food."

The principal thought to himself, "I wonder how long it has been since this teacher sent me a 'discipline problem'."

The teacher observed the quizzical look on the principal's face and wondered if he were displeased with her noisy classroom. As soon as she could get free, she went over to him to add her explanations to those the students were giving for what he was observing there.

"Last summer," she began, "I went to this workshop in the teaching of nutrition at the University of Illinois . . . ."

Reprinted from Hazel Taylor Spitze, "Innovation Techniques for Teaching Nutrition," *Journal of Nutrition Education,* Vol. 2, No. 4, 1971, pp. 3–7; by permission of the publisher.

This article summarizes that four-week workshop held at the University of Illinois in 1970 and directed by the author and Dr. Esther L. Brown, nutritionist of the Department of Home Economics. A fuller account, with more details of techniques and photographs of visual aids, may be found in the *Illinois Teacher,* Vol. XIV, No. 1, September–October, 1970. Other issues of the *Illinois Teacher* which contain ideas for nutrition education include Vol. XI, No. 1; Vol. XIII, No. 2; Vol. XIII, No. 5; and Vol. XIV, No. 2(2).

As a point of departure in the workshop, we used the "Basic Conceptual Framework of Nutrition," developed by the Interagency Committee on Nutrition and accepted by The White House Conference on Food, Nutrition and Health as an adequate base for nutrition education. To arouse interest, we used a 160-item "test" which stimulated questions and discussion.

We classified teaching techniques, according to the principle of reality, as: (1) real life situations, (2) simulations of reality, and (3) abstractions from reality(2). Accepting the theory that the effectiveness of a technique increases as it approaches a real life situation, we strove to develop techniques which utilized reality or simulated reality as closely as possible.

The simplest, most basic concept in nutrition, i.e., *diet affects health,* is probably the most difficult to teach. Unless it is understood, other concepts may not seem important. We used a documentary film, "Hungry Angels," from Association Films, and the National Dairy Council film "How Hamburger Turns into You" as part of our effort to teach this concept. We also used slides of animal and human deficiency diseases and pantomines of deficiencies, the latter adding a touch of humor which was preserved on video tape for later use. Rat demonstrations can also be used to teach this concept.

Of course, the very best technique for teaching that diet affects various aspects of appearance and health is to work on the real problems of the students. If some of them change their eating habits, e.g., decide to start eating breakfast or stop consuming quantities of candy and pop and then experience a desired change in the way they feel or look, their testimonials will carry more weight than all the slides and simulations.

Two workshoppers created bulletin boards and displays which called attention to this most basic concept. A junior high teacher used cartoon figures to point out that food affects one's appearance, personality, growth, health, and vigor. A high school teacher showed high- and low-calorie snacks beneath a poster titled "What does your shape measure show?" with tape measures around the middle of a plumpish and a lithe, coquettish figure. The message that snacks made the difference was loud and clear.

The second basic idea, that foods vary in nutrient value, is much easier to teach and can be approached through an amazing variety of games and simulations.

Innovation Techniques for Teaching Nutrition

FIGURE 1 Cardboard Models Are Used in Game "Food Power"

Food Power

One example is a game called "Food Power" (Figure 1) suggested by another high school teacher, who set up a "cafeteria" using the cardboard food models of the National Dairy Council. Each student selected a breakfast on a tray and then, using the information on the back of the models, plotted the nutrient values in terms of percent of RDA on a chart containing columns for each of the eight most common nutrients. The process was repeated for lunch and for dinner, and the total values for the day were noted and compared with the needed 100 percent. Snacks could be included if desired.

When all calculations were finished, scores were allowed as follows *for each nutrient:*

PERCENT	RATING	POINTS
85–100	Excellent	3
70–84	Good	2
55–69	Fair	1
40–54	Poor	0
Below 39	Very poor	−1

If teams were formed, all members' scores were totaled to ascertain team winner.

During the course of the game, the teacher circulated, commented, asked questions, and did some one-to-one teaching. A summary discussion after the game stressed the content to be learned.

A junior high teacher made a set of "nutrition dominoes." Instead of dots, the dominoes had names of foods, and in order to match one domino to the next, a player had to attach foods that were rich (i.e., had at least 10 percent of the RDA) in the same nutrient. A player who made an error missed his next turn, and the winner for that round was the player who got rid of all his dominoes first. He scored one point for each domino still held by the other players.

Another project was an adaptation of a television program called "Will the Real Vitamin A Please Stand Up?" In addition to guessing which panel member was the real vitamin A, the players determined which nutrient the other panelists represented. Some members of the class served as advisers to the panelists when they needed help in answering players' questions since all questions had to be answered correctly. Others served as judges.

The Comparison Cards of the National Dairy Council were used as constant references displayed in the classroom and were sometimes involved in games or evaluations. Examples are shown in Figure 2 in which the name of the food was concealed and students chose, from five alternatives, which food was represented by this combination of nutrients. These can be used as "flash cards" in a similar way.

Simulations added spice and variety to classroom activity, too. A junior high teacher sponsored a press conference held by the United Nutrients. Members of the press corps queried the representatives of the various nutrients and wrote a "news story" for their own publication stressing the information which would be of most interest to their readers.

A teacher from an Air Force base in the Philippines created a corporation called Body, Inc., and had three students represent the personnel board to hire employees to fit its various needs. Job applicants represented individual foods, and in the job interview they explained what they could do for Body, Inc., and offered to work for a salary commensurate with the caloric value of one serving of that food. The total budget for Body, Inc., was a day's allotment of calories for one person.

In another simulation, suggested by a student teacher, a defendant was accused of malnutrition and tried in court. Students represented defendant, defendant's lawyer, prosecuting attorney, witnesses, jury, and judge. For this role play, the diet of the defendant should be presented in detail, and the jury should have time to calculate its nutritive value before pronouncing the verdict. If defendant is found guilty, the punishment is whatever deficiency symptoms would normally ensue from such a diet.

Also along the line of civic affairs was an "election" in which candidates represented nutrients running for the Board of Health. In the campaign speeches, each candidate stressed what he could do for improving or maintaining health; the rest of the students listened and cast their ballots for the most convincing speaker. A group of "election advisers," including the teacher, made sure that all candidates gave accurate information.

FIGURE 2 Students Match Nutrients with "Flash Cards" Representing Foods

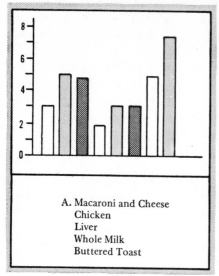

A. Macaroni and Cheese
   Chicken
   Liver
   Whole Milk
   Buttered Toast

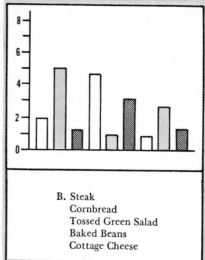

B. Steak
   Cornbread
   Tossed Green Salad
   Baked Beans
   Cottage Cheese

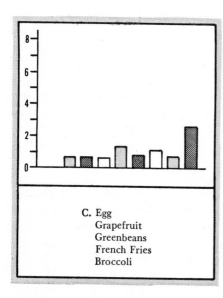

C. Egg
   Grapefruit
   Greenbeans
   French Fries
   Broccoli

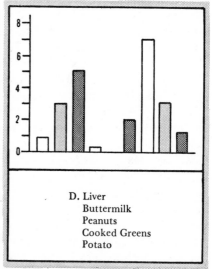

D. Liver
   Buttermilk
   Peanuts
   Cooked Greens
   Potato

Other workshoppers selected other concepts to stress and created games, visual aids, etc., to teach them. One made a deck of food cards and played a variation of rummy called "4-4-2-4." Another suggested "Nutrition Password," and one workshopper built a board fashioned after the television game "Concentration" and called it "Challenge."

In the game of "Challenge," numbered cards were hung on hooks (see Figure 3) each touching the next, and behind them another card with a picture or a word pertaining to nutrition. Players, alternating by teams,

FIGURE 3 "Challenge" Is like a TV Show

chose two numbers and those cards were removed. If the player could state a *nutritional* relationship between the items on the cards beneath, he scored a point for his team, and those cards were removed from the board, revealing still other cards which contained part of a nutrition cryptogram to be guessed at any time a player thought he knew the solution. Wrong guesses were penalized with negative scores of 2, and a right answer gave a bonus score of 5. If a player could not state a relationship when his chosen numbers were removed, the numbers were replaced. No pencils were allowed! One person served as leader of a summarizing discussion at the end.

The "building blocks of food" (see Figure 4) were made from reclosable boxes covered with self-adhesive plastic and letters which can be used in a variety of ways. At the present, we are working on some "inside information" about each nutrient to place in the boxes to serve as a reference in the classroom. The information will probably be typed on sheets of paper in four different colors, each representing different levels of difficulty

Figure 4 "Building Blocks of Food"

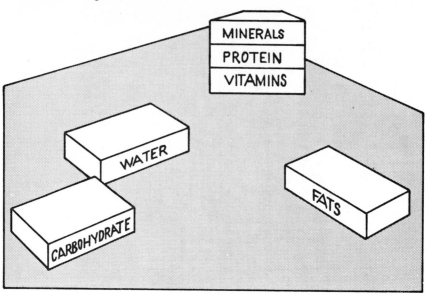

and technicality, so that students of different ability levels can be referred to the appropriate information. We think many students, especially the slower learners, will find this reference more interesting and usuable than a textbook, even though the information it contains is the same.

Some of the workshoppers prepared bulletin boards which asked good questions and provided opportunity for students to discover some answers. A high school teacher asked, "How do your snacks score?" and added three dimensional materials and charts to her bulletin board. Another asked, "How do you spend your calories?" To help students find answers to this latter question, we are presently developing some games—card games, board games, etc.—in which the information becomes impressive and the learning enjoyable.

Teaching techniques developed in an earlier workshop on consumer education at the University of Illinois may also be adapted for teaching nutrition. These ideas include a scavenger hunt, a football game with yards gained depending upon the difficulty of the questions the team answers, a guessing game, the in-basket technique, and stories used for teaching.

Graduate assistants and student teachers at the University of Illinois have also been actively engaged in developing teaching techniques for nutrition. One graduate assistant kept her students interested with a game called "Concentrition" (see Figure 5). The cognitive level reached while playing the game depends upon the questions. Simple recall or recognition types are easiest to construct, but questions requiring application,

FIGURE 5 Teams Play "Concentrition"

analysis, and synthesis are also possible, and the game can still move rapidly. More than three difficulty levels could be used.

To play the game, the class is randomly divided into teams who choose questions from the board and receive point values, as indicated on the board, for correct answers within a specified time limit. The winning team can be the first to reach a predetermined score or the one with the highest score within a predetermined time limit.

Another aid developed earlier was a variation of Tic-Tac-Toe in which each player chose, or was assigned, one of the common nutrients and, in turn, wrote with his X or O the name of a food rich in that nutrient, "rich" being defined as having at least 10 percent of the RDA for that nutrient in one serving. He had to be sure that his chosen food was *not* rich in the opponent's nutrient since the opponent could also use it if it were. The winner, of course, was the player who first obtained three X's or O's in a row.

One teaching assistant created a guessing game in which players received scores according to how many clues they required to guess a food or a nutrient. She is presently working on a simulation technique involving an insurance policy.

Another departmental assistant developed an independent learning package to teach principles involved in the concept of protein. It involves manipulable materials, pencil-and-paper tests with answer keys, case situations, etc., and can be used by a teacher with a class as well as by an independent learner.

The possibilities seem endless. Teaching and learning the science of nutrition can be the most exciting subject in the curriculum if the techniques lead students to *discover* the important intellectual relationships, or principles, involved. The content is certainly *relevant,* by anybody's definition. Improved teaching of nutrition could make a significant contribution to improved health and even to solving some of our more serious social problems. Well-nourished, healthy people learn faster, get along with their fellows better, and are more employable. The possible benefits seem worth more than the effort required. We at the University of Illinois hope that our work in nutrition education will inspire others to continue developing new ideas and to give greater emphasis to nutrition in the curriculum of home economics, health and physical education, biology, or wherever it can reasonably be taught in either elementary or secondary schools. We find it exciting, and anyone who drops in for a visit may find himself invited to sit down and play the latest game being developed. Our continuing efforts will be reported in future issues of the *Illinois Teacher.*

References

1. Spitze, H. T. and P. H. Rotz, *We Are What We Eat,* Steck Vaughn Company, Austin, Tex. 1966.
2. Spitze, H. T., *Choosing Techniques for Teaching and Learning,* Home Economics Education Association. National Education Association, Washington, D.C. 1970.

Operational Concepts

1. Americans, at all income levels, seem to have little knowledge of basic nutritional facts.

2. Malnutrition cannot be combatted without good programs of nutritional education.

3. Teacher preparatory programs must incorporate techniques for teaching nutritional values.

4. School administrators should endeavor to initiate improved school health programs.

5. State departments of education should reevaluate health curriculum guides and develop new materials as needed.

Implications

As in the case of safety education, health education, and physical fitness, the essence of teaching about nutrition lies in cultivating the student's instinct for self-conservation. In present instructional units much of the material seems unduly abstract. Because of our ultimate instructional objectives, student sophistication with respect to the chemical properties of say, carbohydrates, is less useful than a pragmatic knowledge of good dietary habits.

It would be desirable, therefore, to emphasize the dominant principles of good nutrition more directly. Students can investigate the negative effects of "junk" foods, become aware of the long-range consequences of poor nutrition, and, perhaps through case studies, become knowledgeable regarding the health breakdowns in middle and old age that are attributable to improper diet.

In many respects, the improvement of nutrition education depends largely upon the development of appropriate values. Students, in short, are more likely to violate health rules out of carelessness than out of ignorance. As a result, the great need is for instructional materials aimed at students' attitudinal predispositions.

Health Education

Carl E. Willgoose

The Secondary School Health Program

The American secondary school, somewhat like business, has certain cyclical characteristics. During these cycles, varying amounts of attention have been given to patterns of school organization, subject content within the curriculum, various interpretations of excellence in teaching method, and an education for the world of work. Historians have chronicled these cycles in terms of educational objectives and values. Education for healthful living has always been a part of this cyclical emphasis and deemphasis. Recently, such interest has increased and is more intense. The secondary schools of the nation have felt the impact of alcohol, drugs, tobacco, and sex problems. Moreover, difficulties in national and world politics, starvation, pollution, abortion, and other community-wide concerns have been so profoundly related to the physical and mental well-being of large numbers of young people that health education now appears to have a continuous claim on educational priorities.

Defining the Ends

Education is a process of changing behavior toward certain preconceived goals. The emphasis is on the *process*. It is not haphazard; it is orderly and planned. In keeping with the Latin root *educere,* it seeks to "lead forth" or "draw out" the latent or potential qualities in a person. In addition, education considers the whole man as he strives to fulfill some far-reaching purpose. Every subject matter area must ultimately do the same.

The school health program represents the combined effort of all school and community forces bearing upon the health of the school population. These forces are coordinated by school personnel and are channeled into three traditional divisions: health services, healthful school environment, and health education.

Reprinted from Carl E. Willgoose, *Health Teaching in Secondary Schools* (Philadelphia: W. B. Saunders Company, 1972), pp. 28–41; by permission.

Figure 1

Health services comprise the many procedures used to determine the health status of the student, to enlist his cooperation in health protection and maintenance, and to work with parents to correct defects and to prevent illness.

Healthful school environment refers to the total school setting—a wholesome location, a healthful school day, and the existence of teacher-pupil relationships that are safe, sanitary, and favorable to the optimum development of everyone.

Health education is the instructional program—the organization of learning experiences. It is a subject-matter area. More specifically, it is defined as the sum of one's experiences which favorably influence health attitudes and practices. It is an applied science that relates research findings to the lives of people by narrowing the gap between what is known and what is practiced. Moreover, it seeks understandings through a broad, multidimensional approach which frequently overlaps many other school subject areas.

The health effort will always be a multidisciplinary endeavor, for it is a study of what Whitehead describes as "life in all of its manifestations." Moreover, it cannot be approached in an isolated fashion. It requires direct attention in the classroom and the lunchroom as much as it does in the health office. This is because the topic of health is both subtle and dramatic, both obvious and hidden, and means many things to many people. Someone has said that "health is a crown on the well man's head that only the sick can see." From the Anglo-Saxon root, it means "hale," "sound," "whole," and is not simply an ideal state achieved through complete elimination of disease. What it is in reality is a modus vivendi enabling man to achieve a rewarding existence while he copes with an imperfect world.

The task of secondary education is to somehow infuse the means of health education with the values exposed in defining the ends. In the years ahead, health education must help students graduate from facts to feelings and from feelings to values. Goodlad makes his point very clear in writing about education programs in 1980(*1*):

The most important task for our schools during the next few years—and for many generations to come—is their daily practice and demonstration of those qualities of compassion, sensitivity, sound judgment, flexibility, adaptability, humanity, self-renewal—and many more that we have long claimed to be seeking in the human products of education.

Early writers on education—Spencer, Comenius, Rousseau, and others—were just as enthusiastic about values and determining the ends for healthful living as are some of the more recent educators. This is fully documented in several lists of educational aims and objectives that have been periodically prepared over the decades. Most of these goals were set forth in broad philosophical categories such as "life and health," "optimum organic health," "healthful living," "to live most and to serve best," and "self-realization." This was helpful in pointing to educational requirements, but it left the reader the task of relating the health objective to the needs of the times. However, in 1966 the American Association of School Administrators published *Imperatives in Education*, which sets forth in a descriptive and practical way the essential purposes of an education. Because the imperatives are relevant to the seventies and may be related to total health teaching, they are reproduced here(2).

- To make urban life rewarding and satisfying.
- To prepare people for the world of work.
- To discover and nurture creative talent.
- To strengthen the moral fabric of society.
- To deal constructively with psychological tensions.
- To keep democracy working.
- To make intelligent use of natural resources.
- To make the best use of leisure.
- To work with other peoples of the world for human betterment.

These imperatives reflect the changing times, set attainable goals, and call for an individual who is dynamically healthy, able to satisfy his own needs and to contribute his share to the welfare of society. The long-range goal of the health educator, therefore, is to prepare persons with the wherewithal to struggle toward the imperatives because they possess:

1. Optimum organic health and the vitality to meet emergencies.
2. Mental well-being to meet the stresses of modern life.
3. Adaptability to and social awareness of the requirements of group living.
4. Attitudes and values leading to optimum health behavior.
5. Moral and ethical qualities contributing to life in a democratic society.

FIGURE 2 Why Health Education? (Courtesy of the American Medical Association.)

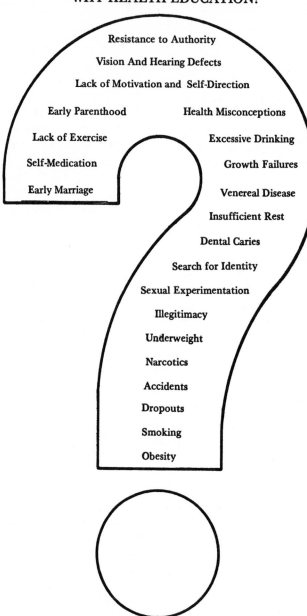

WHY HEALTH EDUCATION?

Resistance to Authority

Vision And Hearing Defects

Lack of Motivation and Self-Direction

Early Parenthood   Health Misconceptions

Lack of Exercise   Excessive Drinking

Self-Medication   Growth Failures

Early Marriage   Venereal Disease

Insufficient Rest

Dental Caries

Search for Identity

Sexual Experimentation

Illegitimacy

Underweight

Narcotics

Accidents

Dropouts

Smoking

Obesity

HISTORICAL PERSPECTIVE

If you have built castles in the air, your work need not be lost; that is where they should be. Now put the foundations under them.

Thoreau

To a large extent much of the early school health work was only a weak beginning. Few schools actually accomplished anything significant. It was indeed a case of building "castles in the air." However, in 1842, Horace Mann, editor of the *Massachusetts Common School Journal,* began to write about the need for "knowledge of laws of structure, growth, development and health of the body" as essential to intellectual and moral behavior. This was a new twist, for it meant that educators and humanists, and not just the biologists and dispensers of medicine, were studying health. It was a slow move from a period when scientists were looking at the living organism in terms of the material bases of life and organismic functions to an era of dealing with the experiences of whole men and women "responding in all their complexity to the stimuli and challenges of their total environment"(*3*).

This slow-to-start shift in viewpoint regarding the health function of the school gradually began to be noticed. Late in his life William Alcott, named by James F. Rogers as the "father of health education," wrote a health book for schoolchildren and stressed both health services and health instruction(*4*). By 1890 every state in the country had a law requiring instruction in the area of alcohol and narcotics. Much of this legislation was engineered by temperance societies unhappy over the increases in the use of alcohol and drugs.

By 1894 the Boston schools were starting regular medical examinations of schoolchildren. Chicago, New York, and Philadelphia followed. In 1909 the Metropolitan Life Insurance Company opened its health and welfare division to reduce preventable diseases and premature death through enlightenment of schoolchildren and the general public. Since that time this voluntary health agency has established an admirable record of having distributed about 21 billion pamphlets of health and safety and 15 billion health messages through the media carrying information on such timely topics as alcoholism, venereal disease, amphetamine abuse, and obesity.

The New York City Health Department established a bureau of health education in 1914. Although its main concern was public health, it had a favorable influence on school health practices in the city. Because of the work of official and voluntary health groups, numerous schools taught hygiene courses consisting chiefly of anatomy and physiology. Interest was further generated for health teaching at this time by the efforts of the National Tuberculosis Association (1916) and the newly formed American Child Hygiene Association (1918). Perhaps the biggest boost to school health education came in 1924 with the publication of *Health Education* by the Joint Committee on Health Problems in Education of the National Education Association and the American Medical Association, the oldest NEA committee in existence, established in 1911.

In 1922 Clair E. Turner, working with Mary Spencer in Malden, Massachusetts, set up a school health demonstration project which extended over a two-year period(5). An experimental group of children was compared with a control group relative to growth, health status, and health practices as a result of formal health instruction. The demonstration was widely publicized and caused a number of school personnel to explore the area of health teaching more seriously.

About 1911, nurses were hired in schools to help control communicable diseases. Later it was decided that they could be useful as first aiders—perhaps to lessen the liability of the schools. In the 1930s and 1940s the follow-up of defects was considered to be the chief concern of the nurse. Slowly her role developed into one of education and she evolved from the nurse to the nurse–teacher category.

Over the years the School Health Section of the American Public Health Association, the American School Health Association, and the American Association for Health, Physical Education and Recreation have done a great deal to promote the total school health program throughout the nation. This support, added to the activities of the World Health Organization, state education departments, and professional education agencies, has brought the topic of the health of schoolchildren into almost every community. Sensing this increased concern for health instruction, the Joint Committee of the National School Boards Association and the American Association of School Administrators in 1968 recommended a comprehensive program of health education in grades K through 12 to meet the health needs, interests, and problems of the school-age group and prepare them for their role as future citizens.

THE UNIFIED APPROACH AND PRESENT TRENDS

Perhaps the most significant part of the recommendations of the Joint Committee of the National School Boards Association and the American Association of School Administrators was the unmistakably clear call for a comprehensive school health program:

> Such a comprehensive approach should be supported by groups interested in a single health area because it assured an orderly and progressive consideration of the separate topics in the context of total health and, hence, offers more effective student exposure through the grades. It avoids "bandwagon" approaches, crash programs, and piecemeal efforts focused on one or a few topics that happen to be enjoying popularity or extensive press coverage at a particular time—an approach which on the basis of past experience has proved to be largely ineffective.

In 1969 the School Health Division of the American Association for Health, Physical Education and Recreation set forth a position paper stressing the need for a unified approach to health teaching. They too were aware of how easy it is to fragment health education into a number of unrelated parts. It was their recommendation, therefore, that the health instruction program be organized and scheduled to reflect proper scope and sequence through the years K–12, on a continuing basis; it should also emerge from curriculum development activities involving both school personnel and individuals from the voluntary and official health agencies.

Further support for the comprehensive school health program came early in 1970 from the National Congress of Parents and Teachers. This highly effective group also called for a specified time allotment, qualified teachers, an adequate budget, and a well-planned program of health instruction with appropriate progression. It seems reasonable to say that, unless this particular concern for a unified approach in the school health effort is actually carried out, the multiple implications of the topic will go unrecognized, and a full understanding of the meaning of human ecology will not occur.

Fortunately, much is happening in the seventies to encourage more effective school health services, a greater concern for healthful living within the school, and interesting health instruction. The experimental curriculum materials developed by the School Health Education Study have helped measurably(6). So have the courses of study and guides developed by numerous cities and towns.

In comparing the school health practices of several decades ago with those of the present, it is noticeable that a number of improvements have been made. Some noteworthy examples are summarized in Table 1.

TABLE 1 School Health Then and Now

PRESENT TRENDS	PAST PRACTICES
1. The function of the school health services department is concerned with every health-related factor in the school community—medical, dental, psychological, and environmental.	1. Health services activities were generally limited to the giving of physical examination and minor nursing duties.
2. Medical examinations of secondary school pupils are thorough and are given about every three years by either the family physician or the school physician. The follow-up of findings is a significant activity.	2. Medical examinations were given hastily on an annual basis, and with very poor organization for following up needy cases.
3. Teachers, nurses, physicians, and parents serve on health councils	3. There was very little effort made for teachers, parents, and medical

(continued)

313

Present Trends	Past Practices
designed to determine individual pupil weaknesses and provide health guidance.	personnel to solve health problems.
4. Teachers are better prepared to teach with a multidisciplinary and ecological approach to health education, and a willingness to go beyond the classroom for a continual in-service education.	4. No special ability was required to teach "health and hygiene"; sometimes taught by the physical education instructor as a rainy day program.
5. Concepts are stressed rather than bits and pieces of knowledge. At examination time facts are recalled by students as a means of supporting major concepts.	5. Health facts were dispensed rather formally and related essentially to the particulars of anatomy and physiology.
6. School nurses with a health education background act as resource personnel for classroom teachers, and assist with program planning.	6. The school nurse remained pretty much in the health services office— more as a clerk first-aider than an educator.
7. Self-appraisals, in which students evaluate their own health practices, are carried out and followed up with informal discussion groups.	7. Students seldom related the health topics to themselves in a personal way, especially through any wide discussion and appraisal.
8. Health textbooks and other teaching aids are designed to guide discussion, provoke ideas, and suggest pupil activities leading to understanding and decision making.	8. Textbooks tended to be straight health facts calling for more memorization activity than understanding and personal application.
9. Formal health education classes, which provide for a more in-depth treatment of topics and are more effective than integrated and correlated classes, are increasingly being taught in both small towns and large cities.	9. Health instruction, often haphazardly arranged, was frequently made a small part of such subjects as biology, science, home economics, physical education, and social studies.
10. Health education supervisors and consultants are employed to assist teachers in planning and teaching.	10. Supervisors were sometimes looked upon as quite unnecessary since they would do little actual classroom teaching themselves.
11. Health education receives near-equal or equal consideration with other subject areas in the curriculum.	11. Health education, if taught at all, was considered an "extra" or "fringe topic" in the school.
12. Standardized tests from reputable testing services are used to determine level of pupil knowledge and the extent to which it may be applied.	12. Knowledge tests, when employed at all, were used to measure knowledge of health facts only.

Present Trends	Past Practices
13. Attention is given to the mental and physical health of the teacher, since it frequently sets the tone of the classroom.	13. The health of the teacher was incidental to learning.
14. Curriculum development, with appropriate scope and sequence, is an almost common practice in alert communities, and leads to the construction of teacher guides and detailed courses of study.	14. The health "curriculum" was often carried in the head of one person, and not put down on paper with the help of school and community personnel.

A significant trend is the upgrading of legislation pertaining to school health and health education. This has occurred in a number of states, both large and small. An excellent example is the Revisions of the Commissioner's Regulations on Health Education for the State of New York, which became law in 1969 and was implemented in the fall of 1970.

Health (and safety) education in the secondary schools. The secondary school curriculum shall include health (and safety) education as a constant for all pupils. In addition to continued health guidance in the junior high school grades, provision shall also be made for (approved health and safety teaching either as a part of a broad science program or as) a separate one-half-year course (or its equivalent). Health (and safety) education shall be required for all pupils in the junior and senior high school grades and shall be taught by teachers (with approved preparation) holding a certificate to teach health. A member of each faculty with approved preparation shall be designated as health coordinator, in order that the entire faculty may cooperate in realizing the potential health-teaching values of the school program.

A final trend, which is barely in evidence, is the increasing attention being given to research in health instruction and health services. Numerous professionals in health education are today attempting to open boundless new horizons to human experience through research into methodology, aids, and behaviors. School health personnel conduct surveys and search for causes. Ultimately, every secondary school graduate should be able to determine his own course of action through a well-founded process of inquiry and decision making. Local research projects, preferably involving students, have a significant role to play in educating for health.

It might appear from the above "trends" that everything is indeed rosy and beautiful today in health education practice. Talks with teachers and administrators, coupled with personal observations, will pretty much convince one that a great deal remains to be accomplished. There is still a need for more supervisors of health instruction, more detailed curriculum guides, less student indifference, better facilities and teaching aids, increased parental support for programs and follow-up for children in need

315

of health services, vitally interested teachers, sufficient time for in-depth instruction, and flexible scheduling of health classes to permit wider discussion of prime issues.

ADMINISTRATIVE GUIDELINES

In an attempt to get away from "crash" programs and move toward solving some of the shortcomings related to health education, the California Association of School Administrators, the California School Boards Association, and the California Medical Association endorsed a set of administrative guidelines for health education in the California secondary schools(7). These guidelines were developed specifically to assist school boards and administrators in the critical review of their programs. They are an admirable contribution to the field, for they spell out in clearcut fashion just what is expected in order to have an adequate secondary school program of health education.

Programs

1. Health education should be identified as a separate subject in the school curriculum.
2. School districts have an obligation to make provisions for health education as an integral part of general education.
3. Health education should be planned sequential programs in grades kindergarten through 12; crash programs emphasizing special health topics should be avoided.
4. Adequate time and resources for health education should be provided.
5. Districts should be encouraged to explore innovative organizational patterns for instruction such as flexible scheduling in order to provide for effective health education.
6. Districts should also offer preschool and adult health education programs, if not otherwise available.

Curriculum

1. Curriculum development should focus on student achievement of desired behavioral objectives.
2. Relevant health concepts should be included at the most appropriate developmental levels of children and youth.
3. Health education should be responsive to the needs of students and the demands of society and should reflect current scientific knowledge.
4. The curriculum should focus on the positive aspects of health.
5. Students and the community should be involved in curriculum develop-

ment to insure the inclusion of instruction based on health needs, interests, and problems.

6. Districts should be encouraged to explore innovative and creative instructional methods which actively involve students in the achievement of established behavioral objectives such as small discussion groups, independent study, and team teaching.

Time

1. Health education should receive equal consideration with other subject areas in the curriculum.
2. Adequate time should be provided to achieve the established behavioral goals and program objectives.
3. Specific time allotment should be given to the treatment of health education in depth as well as recognizing it as an inherent portion of several other disciplines.
4. Time allotment will vary depending on individual and community needs.

Teachers

1. Health education in schools should be taught by an adequately prepared teacher with a demonstrated interest and aptitude in health education. Wherever possible, the teacher should have a specific preparation in health education, preferably a major or minor.
2. Desirable teacher qualities should include: ability to interact meaningfully and honestly with students, to act capably as a resource for students, and to be sensitive to individual differences and needs.
3. Districts should provide continuing programs of in-service teacher preparation in health education that should also reflect current scientific information.

Coordination

1. Responsibility for the development, coordination, and implementation of health education in the school district should be assigned to a specific person.
2. Districts should be encouraged to seek and utilize consultant services from county school offices, from medical and other sources.

Community

1. School districts should be responsive to and involve the community in planning, developing, and implementing programs in a variety of

ways, including the establishment of and/or the participation in school–community health councils.

2. Districts should never assume permanent acceptance of health education by the community but should constantly assess and revise the program in accordance with changing needs and attitudes.
3. Districts should enlist the help and support of community leaders.
4. Available community resources should be utilized to augment and enrich the instructional program.

Financing and Facilities

1. Sufficient financial support should be provided to insure adequate facilities, personnel, and instructional materials to achieve the established objectives.
2. School districts should seek resources which may be available from a wide variety of community agencies and organizations.

Evaluation

1. The program should be periodically evaluated in terms of effectiveness based on realistic and measurable criteria.
2. Pupils, teachers, parents, and others should be involved in the evaluation of the program at regular intervals in terms of relevance to pupils.

RELATIONSHIP OF HEALTH SERVICES TO HEALTH INSTRUCTION

The effectiveness of the health instruction program depends in part on the kinds of relationships that exist between a number of school functions and personnel. Obviously, there should be a close bond of feeling and communication between the physician, nurse, and others in the health services department and the health instructor. There are opportunities to tie in classroom happenings with health services activities. When, for example, medical examinations are given to appraise health status, and when screening examinations are conducted for height–weight–growth, teeth, hearing, seeing, and so forth, there is an excellent opportunity to involve junior high school students (who are especially aware of their appearance and rapid growth changes) in classroom discussion. A significant function of school health services is to help prevent and control disease. Another is to provide emergency service for injury or sudden sickness. These functions require a fair amount of attention to the total school environment—everything from the quality of specific facilities to the health of the teacher. From a teaching viewpoint it is just as important to know about hazardous buildings, grounds, and equipment as it is to know about the number of decayed or missing teeth among members of the freshman class. Defective stair rails, broken sidewalks, obstructed exits, slippery floors, and unsanitary lunchroom facilities are frequently being brought to the attention of health services personnel. Quite often the school physician knows a good deal about the effect of temperature, ventilation, and humidity on school performance. Moreover, he has his figures on accident statistics and may be conducting local research on how to reduce the incidence rate of accidents.

In some schools the school nurse is the only member of the health professions on the staff. She is a health specialist whose nursing skills are combined with a background in health and education. She acts as a consultant and helps plan and conduct health services as a positive learning experience which enhances formal health instruction. In some schools she teaches one or more classes. More and more she is being asked to participate in the design of the curriculum—a particularly significant activity in view of her traditional liaison with medicine, the home, and the community. In addition, her status is being upgraded in many schools. She is being freed from the band aid–clerical image which she projected, and cast in the role of supervisor of aides, helpers, and assistants who handle routine screening, first aid, reports, and records. In a number of schools this requires the use of paraprofessionals, who are carefully selected and trained.

The demand for fully trained nurse–teachers is growing, particularly as it becomes evident that the nurse is in the best position to tie together all parts of the school health program. Teachers require some prodding in order to take advantage of the numerous classroom opportunities both to observe and to instruct boys and girls along health lines. An active nurse gets around. In his study of school nurse services in several large cities, Jenne found a significant correlation between increased nurse–school contacts and the numbers of health observations made by teachers(8).

Another concern is research. Research carried on by health services has practical use in the instruction program. Big cities and a number of smaller towns study their school population in several ways. Evidence relative to health practices is frequently on hand from group surveys, interview, and case studies that may be used to make a health topic "real" in almost any location. What, for instance, do students know about school absences? How meaningful are these kinds of statistics? The Delaware School Health Study, for example, discovered that high absence is associated with having low grades, being over age for one's grade, having low socioeconomic status, coming from a broken home, and attending an urban school(9). Think of the several ways this information can be used in the classroom to make environmental or community health a vital topic.

In a number of states, particularly Colorado, California, and Wisconsin, the state medical societies have been very active in working with local health services personnel to improve health instruction in the schools. In Wisconsin, sex education, drug education, physical education, and the

319

FIGURE 3 Support for School–Community Cooperation

RESOLUTION NO. 5

Adopted by
Joint Committee on Health Problems in Education
National Education Association–American Medical Association
February 13–16, 1971

Coordination of School–Community Health Programs

Whereas,   The component parts of the health program for schools frequently are fragmented, and

Whereas,   The overall school health program is ineffective if there is no organizational structure to coordinate the component parts of a school health program with all phases of the school system, and

Whereas,   The solution of major child and youth health issues requires the concerted action by the entire community, including schools, therefore be it

Resolved,   That the component parts of a health program in a school system be coordinated by an advisory school health council consisting of representatives of the administration, instructional staff, students, parents, employees, and the health disciplines, and be it further

Resolved,   That local medical and dental societies, advisory school health councils, other educational related organizations, and all health related agencies be encouraged to work together through a community Health Council or Comprehensive Health Planning Council to coordinate efforts in solving health issues in school and communities.

---

certification of teachers for health were given a big boost by medical personnel vitally interested in school health. Another example of how local medical associations have worked through school health services to make a contribution to health education is found in the activities of the Los Angeles City Unified School District. Here, the cooperation with the Los Angeles County Medical Association has been noteworthy in improving health education programs at all teaching levels.

The need for greater cooperation between health services personnel and health teachers is evident. Such activity stands to make local health problems real to students and provide incentives for prevention. Preventing disease, accidents, and injury is a social issue in which school and community groups ultimately have to work together, perhaps under the leadership of the health instructor. George M. Wheatley, long known for his enlightening work on health observations of schoolchildren, makes the point that teachers for at least a quarter-century have been instructed to detect signs and symptoms of poor health and refer pupils to proper medical personnel. Moreover, most of those pupils reported do indeed have something wrong with them. Health observation, therefore, is an art in which all teachers should have some skill. Learning to be a good observer is important for every teacher in every classroom. For the health instructor it is even more important, for it relates to both teaching content (the "teachable moment") and the teaching method.

OTHER SCHOOL SUBJECTS AND HEALTH INSTRUCTION

The school health program would be incomplete if opportunities to tie in such subjects as home economics, science, physical education, social studies, and English with the formal teaching of health were overlooked. Such opportunities are more apt to be planned for when a health consultant or health supervisor has been employed. This kind of person is a leader. He is a coordinator of all loose ends that can be brought together to form an optimum health program. He helps teachers and other health personnel work together. He programs activities that are full of meaning to students because they are taught "as if you taught them a naught" through clever integration and correlation of learnings.

The day has long since passed when school health was limited to the health lecture and the periodic visit to the nurse's office. Every facet of instruction now bears on the health topic. Nowhere is this better illustrated than in the area of English when the teacher assigns such reading material as *Catcher in the Rye* and evokes a discussion which relates to learnings gathered in sex and family living education. Another example is the physiological nature of physical fitness (work capacity) and how it relates to coronary heart disease; it is of concern to health teachers and physical education instructors alike. The economics of our social system as it pertains directly to the health needs of the poor, race problems, the population explosion, and consumer welfare is another example of an area vital to the social sciences as well as to health education. There are many examples of these kinds of associations. They need more attention than they get. This is perhaps the chief reason why some health education programs are so barren and unrelated to the world in which students live. Moreover, the students are the first to say so, especially if they are asked.

SCHOOL AND COMMUNITY HEALTH ORGANIZATIONS

As indicated previously, there are numerous official and voluntary health organizations in the country today that are anxious to be of assistance in the school health program. Such groups are especially valuable at a time when the school is in the process of revising a course of study or preparing new curriculum materials. Those agencies having to do with

321

child health, vital statistics, nutrition, accident prevention, fire protection, consumer health, drug abuse, alcoholism, cancer, heart, mental health, air and water pollution, respiratory disorders, and the several other degenerative diseases of mankind all have a real interest in assisting school health specialists and teachers to be more effective. Not to call on them regularly for help is to have tunnel vision, and to miss an excellent opportunity to improve school relations with the public.

By bringing representatives of all health related agencies in a community together at the school, it is possible to achieve a balance in influence. That is, no one group will be quite so apt to unduly affect the program. It has happened in a number of instances that one or two well-organized health agencies that distribute a large number of appropriate teaching aids have been able to dominate the curriculum emphasis—particularly if their field relates to the so-called "hot" topics of alcohol, drugs, tobacco, or mental health. Needless to say, the planners of the comprehensive curriculum keep this in mind as they strive to use the expertise of all community groups and seek to achieve balance in the contributions from all contributors.

References

1. John I. Goodlad in *Designing Education for the Future,* No. 2, Edgar L. Morphet and Charles O. Ryan (New York: Citation Press, 1967), p. 47.

2. American Association of School Administrators, *Imperatives in Education* (Washington, D.C.: American Association of School Administrators, 1966).

3. René Dubos, *Man and His Environment,* Britannica Perspectives, Vol. 1 (New York: Encyclopaedia Britannica, Inc., 1968), p. 33.

4. For a full coverage of this early period see Richard K. Means, *A History of Health Education in the United States* (Philadelphia: Lea & Febiger, 1962), Chapters 2 and 4.

5. Clair E. Turner, "Malden Studies in Health Education and Growth," *American Journal of Public Health,* 18:1217–1230, 1928.

6. Elena M. Sliepcevich, "Health Education: A Conceptual Approach" (Washington, D.C.: School Health Education Study, 1965).

7. Harold J. Cornacchia, "Guidelines for Secondary School Health Education," *School Health Review,* 1:22–24, November, 1969. Copies are available from the California Association of School Administrators.

8. Frank H. Jenne, "Variations in Nursing Service Characteristics and Teachers' Health Observation Practices," *Journal of School Health,* 60:248–251, May, 1970.

9. Doris E. Roberts et al., "Epidemiologic Analysis in School Populations as a Basis for Change in School Nursing Practice," *American Journal of Public Health,* 59:2157–2167, December, 1969.

Operational Concepts

1. Ideally, health education should be a multidisciplinary endeavor.

2. Student indifference to health education remains a critical problem.

3. When instruction is properly organized, the concepts of sound health can be integrated, without academic detriment, throughout the curriculum.

4. Better collaboration between school health programs and public health agencies is highly desirable.

5. In the interests of a well-balanced program, care must be taken to avoid stressing some facets of the health program at the expense of other elements.

Implications

What holds true for safety and nutrition education is equally applicable to health education in general. The instructional objectives involve behavioral change that can only stem from knowledge and belief. There is a striking deficiency in the average high school graduate's understanding of common disease and physical pathology. Matters would be helped considerably if teachers were provided with good instructional materials that familiarized students with the known facts regarding heart disease, cancer, diabetes, and so on.

An additional task lies in combatting the remarkable willingness of people to take good health casually. Carelessness and unconcern are the prime contributors to self-inflicted body damage: it is these, therefore, which must be attacked in health education. Better attitudes, beliefs, and values—coupled with a broader grasp of basic medical information—constitute the critical goals.

To depend upon courses in health education alone would be to waste much of our opportunity. Teachers must strive, throughout the curriculum, to take advantage of classroom situations where good health practices can be conveyed.

Lee Richardson

Who's Afraid of Consumer Education?

If the statistics were collected to indicate the percentage of Americans over age 18 who had received consumer education, they would show nearly 100 percent had taken the course. Unfortunately, no one taught that course —it just happens that consumers have to learn to buy and consume in order to survive and function in the marketplace system that characterizes the American economy. Professors might call this means of learning something besides education, claim that the statistics concerning the percentage of graduates therefore showed 5 percent or less, and triumphantly dismiss the rest of this article.

That would be a pyrrhic victory because it admits that less than 5 percent of consumers are informed about goods and services. These are statistics of the past mistakes of a society which largely preaches free enterprise for sellers and practices too much *caveat emptor* for the people who pay the bills.

Bringing the professional educator to the task of informing consumers in light of the revelations of the modern-day consumer movement has been haphazard. It first requires the teaching of teachers, yet the record of the fifty states with a few exceptions has been poor in this regard. Too many teachers of teachers need to be taught first! All of this leads to the proposition that educators now would do well to reassess the nature of the needs for consumer education before charging ahead with instant solutions, pleas for funding, and personnel to apply the solutions. Educators who are not inspired about consumer needs should especially look at the first principles of consumer education for the 1970s and start working immediately to improve consumer welfare. This article offers a start.

DOES ANYONE KNOW HOW WE GOT HERE?

The role of classroom teachers in consumer education has a limited history. Specialized consumer education courses are an even less extensive

Reprinted from Lee Richardson, "Who's Afraid of Consumer Education?" *Illinois Education*, Vol. 61, No. 1, 1972, pp. 5–9, 39–40; by permission of the publisher.

subject for historians. The earlier pioneering efforts by home economists, personal finance specialists, family management teachers, business educators, economists, consumer economists, home management teachers, and many others have laid the groundwork for expansion by others who can consolidate the interdisciplinary facets of the consumer education field. American education has long stressed a general preparation for living, and as a result educators in traditional required subject areas such as mathematics, physical education, health, or English have made many informal contributions to the preparation of classroom students for the realities of being consumers. Textbooks written for the early prototype consumer-oriented courses merit a great debt from curriculum specialists, administrators, and teachers of today.

With the advent of the great wave of U.S. consumer awakening in the 1960s, consumer educators have received new incentives for expansion. The character of the movement offers much to the educational philosopher who wishes to upgrade his subject matter and methods to levels of relevance to the students of today, who will form the society of tomorrow. Several writers have attempted to describe the movement's goals and objectives in terms of the deepest personal strivings for self-fulfillment, but not with the same impact that a President of the United States can say them. In his Consumer Message to Congress, Feb. 25, 1971, President Nixon laid down a program and consumer education philosophy which is beginning to take shape at the federal level.

> Legislative remedies and improved enforcement procedures are powerful weapons in the fight for consumer justice. But as important as these are, they are only as effective as an aware and informed public make them. Consumer education is an integral part of consumer protection. It is vital if the consumer is to be able to make wise judgments in the marketplace. To enable him or her to do this will require a true educational process beginning in childhood and continuing on.
>
> The Office of the Special Assistant for Consumer Affairs has established guidelines for consumer education suggested for use at the elementary and high-school level. Those guidelines have been sent to every school system in the country, and their reception has been encouraging. I believe they mark an effective step toward developing an informed consumer. The office has also begun the development of suggested guidelines for adult and continuing education with particular emphasis on special socioeconomic groups and senior citizens.
>
> Now, in order to expand and lend assistance to consumer education activities across the nation, I am asking the secretary of health, education, and welfare, in coordination with my special assistant for consumer affairs, to work with the nation's education system to (1) promote the establishment of consumer education as a national educational concern; (2) provide technical assistance in the development of programs; (3) encourage teacher training in consumer education; and (4) solicit the use of all school and public libraries as consumer information centers.

I am also asking the secretary of health, education, and welfare, in co-ordination with my special assistant for consumer affairs, to develop and design programs for the most effective dissemination of consumer information, and particularly to explore the use of the mass media, including the Corporation for Public Broadcasting.

Under Public Law 92-318 signed by the President on June 23, 1972, the U.S. Office of Education has been charged to create the position of director for consumer education with broad authority to undertake research, foster curriculum development, and fund various projects. Twenty million dollars was authorized for the director's budget and the U.S. Office of Education is in the process of developing organization plans, actual funding levels, and policies.

Meanwhile, state departments of education, private groups, and the federal government have launched numerous projects which will ultimately weld together as consumer educators begin to discover each other on a nationwide basis. The *Guidelines for Consumer Education* by Illinois' Office of the Superintendent of Public Instruction is known as a nationwide model. The Office of Consumer Affairs has likewise received much comment and remarkable sales from the *Consumer Education Bibliography,* now in its revised edition, and the *Suggested Guidelines for Consumer Education, K–12* a general treatment of the field. Several recent grants from the U.S. Office of Education to develop consumer education materials, specific curricula, and a model program for the states are notable among the new initiatives.

With many educational interest groups and disciplines coming into the field with varied perspectives on the subject, consumer education is in the pioneer development stages. A lot of questions are unresolved and many mistakes are being made. Mistakes are an important indication that learning is taking place, unless they are repeated. Some teachers and administrators have much enthusiasm about this subject today, which raises the challenge to constantly review what is being done and where all the activity is leading. That challenge should appropriately be met now.

DOES ANYONE KNOW WHERE TO GO FROM HERE?

Consumer educators should have little interest in history although it may prevent repetition of mistakes and save the trouble of again figuring out why education is being done the way it is. The road map is clearer because guidelines and other aids are now published, but every professional teacher and administrator realizes the real struggles occur and puzzles arise when translating general guides into school system and pupil specifics. Low-income adults in a rural setting have different requirements in terms of education than do Spanish-speaking city children. The classroom, the available media, the educational institutions, and administrative policies of school systems all offer challenges for various types of educators who must cope with the problems at different levels.

The following principles of consumer education do not offer the complete answers to quality education, but should raise some needed questions about what teachers and administrators are doing and planning. We educators tend too often to overorganize our thoughts—it's our academic training perhaps, but this list of suggestions tends to go in the opposite direction by pointing out the highlights only.

DO ADMINISTRATORS THINK THIS ABOUT CONSUMER EDUCATION?

Those who plan and direct educational programs hopefully have the same goals and philosophy as do teachers. Their role in educational systems varies, however, and the following principles should apply primarily to the larger over-all questions of administration. Those who lecture, write, produce materials, and directly contact students in multiple varieties of ways may also wish to evaluate administration in terms of some principles with which they might agree.

Consumer Education Isn't a Classroom Subject

A system of information and training should be envisioned for meeting the needs of buyers, homemakers, and all household members. The consumer should receive training in general concepts, techniques, and methods of decision-making in some organized manner of presentation. This step is quite complex, and formal classroom training for youth and adult groups is a critical component for U.S. consumers. A second problem is the need for information to enable consumers to evaluate specific choices at a given time and place. Evaluating 8000 supermarket items is not done solely with general concepts, sans data, any more than the untrained consumer can be expected magically to deal with the overwhelming information available to him in the choice process. Consumers won't buy foods with appropriate consideration for their nutritional needs unless they know both the proper concepts of nutrition *and* also have data available that objectively tell them the nutritional worth of their market choices.

Educators certainly have not saturated the needs of consumers for the kinds of conceptual information best obtainable in the classroom. A balanced approach recognizes the fact that most education (concepts plus information) for consumers will come through personal experience, informal education from other individuals, advertising, and the mass media, and such an approach will utilize the classroom as only one component of the educational system of a community, a state, or the nation.

While conceptually this is an acceptable principle, our educational institutions are not geared yet to deal with a subject that has such profound implications that it is a lifetime educational process. Classroom educators, the mass media, and the advertising industry, for example, are not normally thought of as having important mutual responsibilities in educating America's consumers. Clearly, they do.

Consumer Education New—Not Old Hat

The natural tendency of logical professional persons is to try to classify every new thought in terms of old ones. There are those who believe consumer education is a means of fraud prevention. Others see it as a sector of economics. Many disciplines claim that it belongs to them, and administrators view it as a subject to be slotted into one of the existing traditional departments whether it might be business education, home economics, vocational education, or even social welfare. If any of these attempts at classifying were valid, consumer education would not be the difficult subject that it is.

Consumer Education Makes Economic Waves

If everyone today receives the idea that old behavior should be replaced by new behavior, then that idea is radical and will change our tomorrow. If consumer education succeeds in presenting new ideas to people, they will change their patterns of consumption. This may create market opportunities for progressive businesses and destroy sales of companies dependent on ignorant consumers. Purchases of dangerous glass doors might decline, hypoallergenic cosmetics might increase in the market, and private label aspirins might become as preferred as nationally advertised brands. All of these changes would likely be gradual, but the ideas imparted by educators could be viewed as competition for business firms, trade associations, and other economic interest groups.

Given these outcomes and possible frictions, the consumer educator should be made especially aware of the importance of the work being undertaken. Failure to lead people to understand some of their misconceptions is a much greater error than creating friction that may occassionally accompany needed changes in consumers' behavior.

Business Will Support Consumer Education

In view of the preceding, this principle appears contradictory. Businessmen have shown, however, that they believe informed consumers are good customers. The progressive business firm normally is the first to introduce new benefits to consumers—such as the credit card, the money-back guarantee, the consumer relations specialist, the hotline for service, and the easy-open package. These firms seek new ways to serve and they are rewarded by the good image, the repeat sale, and the loyal customer. Sensing new trends in our society, many modern businesses see a real opportunity to serve the increased desires of consumers for better information. Unit pricing, open dating, ingredient labeling, home economics departments, home service representatives, and many other manifestations of the business response to educational need in recent years can be cited.

The immediate value of business to consumer education is support of new programs in specialized areas such as nutrition (food companies), credit education (financial institutions), and similar curricular changes in the public schools. Businesses also may provide speakers and resource persons of immense value. Independent auto mechanics, for example, have interesting views on automobile manufacturers' quality controls. Professional business people generally offer objective advice when the educator screens them well and advises them of their role in the educational process. Some business-produced materials, including promotional literature, can be utilized. In any program involving business groups, however, it is necessary for educators to be keenly aware of possible attempts by some to utilize the educational system for sales and public relations purposes of disputable worth. Realize, too, that student consumers may place a great deal of credibility in implicit educator endorsements of business materials and that the businessman working in education is often quite expert and persuasive.

Consumers Being Badly Educated

Inadequate, erroneous, incomplete, or even misleading, the information and concepts used by consumers to make choices are used out of necessity. Consumers spend their money on automobiles, vacuum cleaners, asparagus, chewing gum, and insecticides based on what they know rather than what educators think they should know. As a consequence, the problems of teachers who teach adults include trying to change old habits and behavior patterns—trying to convince a cola drinker to try fruit juices or a lazy homeowner to undertake some simple do-it-yourself home maintenance.

Consumers are all too frequently old dogs resisting new tricks. Family living patterns, the aspirations of individuals and households, even dreams are wrapped up in consumer behavior. Those who propose to unravel the mysterious individual life styles and the pressures upon 210 million Americans to help them improve and alter their behavior will not lack challenges.

Consumer Education Has No Constituency

The consumer interest in this country is fragmented and no single organization has yet grown to the size necessary to represent the broad interests of all consumers in the field of consumer education. Representation requires power and power is needed in terms of employees, active members, and financial resources. It may be that academic groups such as the American Council on Consumer Interests will grow to the point where one or more of them can successfully represent the needs of consumer education to legislators and agencies, but this is not yet true. As a result, there are administrators in state departments of education and university education departments who are not even aware of the needs for a higher priority for consumer education. This neglect represents professional failure and the only solution is an extra effort to impress the need upon them. The best candidates for informal membership in the exclusive club charged with promoting consumer education are other educators and consumer organizations.

Consumer Education Belongs in Social Programs

Wherever people are provided with income or a chance to earn income, an opportunity exists to assist them in wisely spending that new income. Particularly in situations where individuals and households are able to increase their income significantly, they are in need of advice to help them adjust to this new circumstance. They will be entering the market for new types of purchases never before available to them and their mistakes may seriously affect their standard of living. Consumer mistakes waste this new income. Likewise, consumers whose economic circumstances are jolted by unemployment are often financially and psychologically unprepared to adjust to their dismal new circumstances.

Some of the specific programs of federal and state government that warrant consideration for consumer education components include unemployment compensation, economic development projects, manpower training, welfare and family assistance, social security, housing, and urban redevelopment projects. Persons who have been institutionalized for any of a variety of reasons for an extensive period often are in desperate need of ideas to help them cope with their return to normal consumer life. Long-term residents of corrective institutions require training on such basics as the availability of family health care services, the value of the dollar, and the cost of small loans—or their resulting economic desperation may lead them to violate the law again to improve their finances.

Consumer Education Involves 210 Million

Reaching the general public involves reaching people in a tremendous variety of circumstances. The nuclear family at home is not the only consumption point in the United States. Consider the varieties of media, curricula, and information needed to assist the following specialized groups:

1. Students at college on a minimum budget.
2. Tourists seeking facilities in unfamiliar communities.
3. Persons on the verge of bankruptcy.
4. Newly hired employees with increased incomes and a new community and social environment.
5. Newlyweds.
6. Divorcees with children.
7. Credit union members.
8. Foreign students with language difficulties.
9. Military personnel in strange domestic or foreign environments.
10. Newly retired couples with reduced incomes.
11. Elderly widowers on social security.
12. Residents of Indian reservations.

Federal Government Won't Underwrite All Programs

It would solve a lot of problems if it did. The fact is that the vast bulk of federal aid to education which can be used under various conditions for consumer programs is administered through state departments of education. Current consumer education programs receiving federal monies are usually classified as innovative or demonstration projects. Three thousand cities and counties and fifty states are not going to receive federal monies to undertake basic consumer education programs in the public schools on the ruse that they are all pilot programs. Permanent funding will have to come from local and state initiative and money unless federal policies drastically change. Educators and consumer groups who are advised to "go to Washington" to obtain money since the state or locality's budget is "fully committed" may also inquire whether those commitments were made with a full understanding of the needs for consumer education in the near and long-term future.

Mandatory Consumer Education Is False Issue

Administrators' reactions to enthusiastic appeals for a mandatory consumer education course for every student in the public school system have not always been as enthusiastic as in the Illinois experience. There are many claimants seeking a portion of the students' time and only a limited quantity of that time is available for division. If a few of the basic concepts of consumer education are appreciated, then the issue is really a matter of *how* to implement it into a school system. Consider the following from *Suggested Guidelines for Consumer Education, Grades K–12:*

> There are generally considered to be four possible methods of implementation. They are not mutually exclusive and all four may be used simultaneously. They are: Individual Teacher Approach, which focuses on the

development of a course of study taught by one educator; Team Approach, which suggests combining the expertise of several teachers for teaching a single course; Interdisciplinary Approach, which stresses the opportunities for incorporating consumer education into all courses in varying degrees of sophistication; and System Approach, which involves the entire school system as well as the community and the parents.

The question is a matter of how to begin in order eventually to achieve a system approach.

DO TEACHERS THINK THIS ABOUT CONSUMER EDUCATION?

Teachers and writers constitute the consumer contact points where knowledge is imparted. Teachers will be in a variety of different situations in and out of classrooms as they meet the needs of consumers. Many of the outstanding examples of success in consumer education come from teachers who may be reaching 30 or 100 students at a time, but whose impact per student is literally magnificent. Entering into consumer education for the first time in their careers, often with inadequate preparation or training in the subject matter, spirited and innovative teachers often manage well under these handicaps.

Consumer Education Must Be Based on Behavioral Research

The technician views his work as offering ways and means for people to reach given goals and objectives. Many teachers likewise prefer to avoid challenging opinions, beliefs, values, and attitudes of students in an effort to be neutral in allowing each student to achieve his own type of self-fulfillment. That approach is harmful to students in consumer education because it tends to freeze the status quo of economic aspirations as formed by unwitting students under the persuasive influences of advertising, selling, and old wives' tales. In specific terms the teacher needs to ask whether a traditional diet is the result of culture, religion, or just bad habits. A student's desire to own his own house for reasons of a deep-seated personal preference for private property needs to be respected, but that same student should be exposed to the other consequences and costs of a decision to own rather than rent. Status symbols are psychologically significant purchases, but the student should compare high-cost automobiles to his other needs for life insurance, savings, health care, and family recreation.

Consumer Education Challenges Values

Consumer education will change values best by leading people to understand the consequences of their choices. It will not succeed, on the other hand, by standardizing the answers to recommend that all individuals change and follow the same pattern of behavior.

Cultural, group, and individual patterns of behavior represent the results of many different inherited and environmental influences. Consumer educators must recognize that they cannot expect all students to drive economy cars, eat soya flour, or choose the giant economy-size package. In fact there will be some consumers who forget to brush their teeth, are too busy to change the oil in their cars, or insist on cola drinks for breakfast. Some won't like the taste of liver, others will wear nothing but blue denim clothes, and others won't ride in an airplane. People are too human, perhaps.

If People Change, Consumer Education Is Working

All educators must be evaluated in terms of some perceptible influence they have on the lives of pupils. The fact that teachers present materials or that students memorize them does not mean that lives are any different. Ultimately, the sales of some products should rise and others should fall. The mix of products and services consumed by individuals should change. The amount of effort spent buying and that spent not buying should be altered. More people may make their own clothes and others may roll their own cigarettes. Time spent in museums and numbers of bird watchers could even be affected. Whatever the basis of evaluations may ultimately be, the teacher should look for evidence of it to reevaluate teaching methods, subject matter, and efforts expanded.

Basic Concepts As Yet Undeveloped

Some of the fundamental consumer questions are not yet answerable. Some of the answers available for other questions are quite complex. The subject matter of consumer education is often difficult for theorists and exceedingly difficult to explain to many audiences.

What clothes should I wear? Should I rent an apartment or buy a house? How do I choose a life insurance policy? What is the food value of cane sugar? How can I get my deposit back? Should I buy products only on the basis of the lowest unit price? To begin to answer such questions convincingly and meet the implicit personal needs behind each of them requires a good deal of work with the questioner.

Many analytical questions do not yet have answers. There is no generally accepted formula to compare the value of benefits from two standard whole life insurance policies. There is dispute over minimum nutritional requirements of adults, children, pregnant women, and all other people. The impact of statutory interest rate limitations—such as 10 percent on the availability of consumer credit—is not easy to predict. A teacher gains humility dealing with subjects that should, but don't, lend themselves to direct answers.

Consumer Education Growing from Bottom Up

Indicative of administrative insensitivity to an increasingly evident trend is the fact that consumer education in public schools is so far primarily progressing through the efforts of individual teachers. Numerous teachers have taken it upon themselves, sometimes with no administrative support, to introduce new consumer courses or new materials into existing courses. Many of these teachers are home economists.

One elementary teacher supplied students with a food allowance which was to be spent in a store to accumulate food for one day. Some of the six- and seven-year-old students who bought only candy and cookies quickly learned how important wise planning for meals was to the family.

A group of teachers encouraged students to report consumer news in a school paper, which covered school store overcharges as well as mislabeled cans of mixed nuts (too many peanuts—too few cashews).

A teacher taught his business management students the hidden consumer consequences of their future management decisions implementing certain advertising campaigns, cutting cost corners at the expense of quality, failing to warn customers to practice safety precautions, etc.

A teacher provided a local consumer organization with the results of a survey of prices in local supermarkets. The survey's publication gave students the satisfaction of seeing many people benefit from their consumer research work.

Consumer Education Should Include Consumer Advocacy

A complete study of the problem leads to the conclusion that certain legal, social, and economic changes would enable consumers to function much more satisfactorily. Teachers should seek opportunities to identify serious consumer frauds, such as certain multilevel marketing schemes in need of legal action. Teachers need to recognize the value of alternative methods to corporate enterprise including credit unions, mutual insurance companies, mutual savings and loan associations, cooperatives, and buying clubs. The need for voluntary business reform actions in such fields as advertising ethics, special services to disadvantaged consumers such as the physically handicapped or low-income families, or improved consumer complaint handling should be faced squarely by the teacher.

Consumers need a concept of responsibility as citizens. Participation in voluntary consumer organizations should be encouraged. Consumer representation in regulatory proceedings, activity in the political arena, and activity in the legislative process should be encouraged, lest politics be left to the politicians alone.

Consumer Education Is Immediately Relevant

Everyone is a consumer and has had much experience in consumption if not in buying. Past consumer problems of students offer teachers a base of common understandings upon which to launch further learning and exploration of new ideas. The interest of students in the potential practicality of the material is a great advantage to the teacher. The teacher soon learns which subjects are most successful as examples. Can a 15-year-old boy be motivated by a discussion of automobiles? Can a new mother become interested in infant nutrition? Does the sun rise in the East?

Consumer Education Is Good Protection

Education can prevent many common forms of current consumer problems. The informed consumer should avoid some of the deceptive snares laid by certain salesmen and merchants. The properly prepared individual will avoid dangerous toys, select the protein-rich foods, and check out the reputation of the plumber before calling him.

According to economic theory and good sense, the bargaining equality of buyer and seller should lead to a more efficient marketplace. Such conditions should reduce the need for regulations to protect one party against the other's superior information and bargaining position.

Consumer Education Solves Social Problems

Many other individual and social problems are interwoven with consumer issues. Assistance for women which resolves the difficulties they have in obtaining credit extends the rights of women in the society. Likewise solutions to problems of low-income buyers help alleviate poverty. Efficient use of products not only saves money, but conserves natural resources and preserves ecological balance.

SUMMARY

Consumer education is poised on the edge of a period of true growth and maturation as a discipline and a significant branch of education. It has elements that distinguish it from traditional disciplines, yet educators are not prepared in significant numbers to bring about that growth. A serious effort to understand the nature of the problems and opportunities of the field at this point will give consumer education the chance it needs to begin serving basic needs of America's 210 million consumers.

The Consumer Educator's Essential Library

1. *Consumer Education Bibliography,* Second Edition. Order from Superintendent of Documents, U.S. Government Printing Office, Washington, D.C. 20402. $1. (Developed by The Office of Consumer Affairs, Consumer Education Division.)

2. *Developing a Resource Center in Consumer Education: An Annotated Bibliography,* E. Thomas Garman, Floyd L. Crank, and Julienne V. Cochran. July, 1971. Northern Illinois University, Business Education Department, Wirtz 323, DeKalb, Il. 60115. $2. (Excellent materials identified.)

3. *Consumer Product Information.* Consumer Product Information Coordinating Center. Free from congressmen. (Quarterly updated list of Federal Consumer Materials.)

4. *Suggested Guidelines for Consumer Education, Grades K–12.* Order from Superintendent of Documents, U.S. Government Printing Office, Washington, D.C. 20402. 65 cents. (Developed by the Office of Consumer Affairs, Consumer Education Division.)

5. *Teaching Consumer Education and Financial Planning.* Council for Family Financial Education, Twin Towers, Silver Spring, Md. 20910. $6. (Quite complete.)

6. *Guide to Federal Consumer Services.* Order from Superintendent of Documents, U.S. Government Printing Office, Washington, D.C. 20402. (Developed by Office of Consumer Affairs to analyze federal programs and information.)

7. *Economics for Consumers,* Sixth Edition, Leland J. Gordon and Stewart M. Lee. Van Nostrand-Reinhold Co., 450 West 33rd Street, New York, N.Y. 10001. (One of the college-level standards.)

8. *The Consumer in American Society: Personal and Family Finance,* Fourth. Edition, Arch W. Troelstrup. McGraw-Hill Book Co., Princeton-Hightstown Road, Box 404, Hightstown, N.J. 08520. (One of the college-level standards.)

9. *The Consumer and His Dollars,* David Schoenfeld and Arthur A. Natella. Oceana Publications, Inc., Dobbs Ferry, N.Y. (One of the textbook standards.)

10. *Personal Finance.* Third edition, Maurice A. Unger and Harold A. Wolf. Allyn and Bacon, Inc., 470 Atlantic Avenue, Boston, Mass. 02210. (One of the college-level standards.)

11. *The Dark Side of the Marketplace,* Sen. Warren G. Magnuson and Jean Carper. Consumers Union Edition available at 256 Washington Street, Mt. Vernon, N.Y. 10550. (A modern classic of the consumers' plight.)

12. *The Poor Pay More,* David Caplovitz. The Free Press, New York. (A modern classic of the low-income consumers' problems.)

Key Periodicals

1. *Money* (New from Time, Inc.) .

2. *Changing Times,* 1729 H Street NW, Washington, D.C. 20006.

3. *Consumer Reports,* Consumers Union, 256 Washington Street, Mt. Vernon, N.Y. 10550.

4. *Consumer News*, Superintendent of Documents, U.S. Government Printing Office, Washington, D.C. 20402.

State and Local Resource Materials

1. Bulletins of state and local government consumers offices.
2. Newsletters of voluntary consumer groups.
3. *State Consumer Action—'71*. Superintendent of Documents, U.S. Government Printing Office, Washington, D.C. 20402. (Summary of state activities in all consumer fields developed by Office of Consumer Affairs.)

Operational Concepts

1. Present consumer practices leave much to be desired.

2. Programs of consumer education must be tailored to the specific life interests of particular kinds of students; correspondingly, teachers must be familiarized with these interests through in-service education activities.

3. Students should learn choice-making skills that relate to their present and future purchasing habits.

4. Consumer education is inseparable from values education.

5. The quality of consumer education is heavily dependent upon teacher commitment to consumer advocacy.

Implications

The basic objectives of consumer education have to do with helping students to become more intelligent consumers during adulthood. As things now stand, consumer judgment frequently is overshadowed by the lures of salesmanship. It suffices to say, hence, that the potency of the consumer education curriculum must be bolstered not only with respect to buying skill, but also with respect to value judgments regarding the material necessities of life.

On another front, however, a new dimension of consumer education has emerged. With the growth of consumer advocacy groups, the schools are being called upon to instill a greater concern for consumer rights. New instructional procedures and materials are thus needed. Students should be encouraged to take a larger interest in consumer affairs and to become more knowledgeable regarding the principles of fair business practice. The methods through which malpractice is perpetuated must be better understood; and, generally, students must learn that protection of consumer rights depends, in large measure, upon an informed citizenry that refuses to be victimized. If, as has been widely suggested, students can acquire a greater part of their education through involvement in community affairs, the implications for strengthening consumer education through active, firsthand experience are obvious.

Frank M. Hewett
Steven R. Forness

Current Issues in Special Education

By way of introduction to this discussion, we will first examine a phenomenon with special relevance to both historical and current problems in the field. The phenomenon is dissonance; it occurs when our experience in the real world does not match up with our previously held beliefs and expectations.

LABELING AND CATEGORIZATION

The question of pinning diagnostic labels on exceptional learners and assigning them to categories is one of the most overlooked issues in special education. A number of the clichés that have emanated from it include: "medical rather than educational-model based," "self-fulfilling prophecies," and "hardening of the categories." Even though the issue is an old one and "Down with labeling and categorization" is a familiar battle cry of special educators, complete elimination of labeling practices is apt to create dissonance in the field.

Although it has become increasingly apparent that such practices do a disservice to our exceptional learners in many ways, let us look at two major pitfalls that may await us if traditional labeling is abandoned totally. First, we have the communication problem in building the bridge from the other side. Our earlier position was that special education should consider turning the tables on the disability labeling practices of extra-educational disciplines that often assume primary responsibility for diagnosis and evaluation and that we should describe learning and behavior problems first in educationally relevant terms. This would support abandonment of traditional labeling and categorizing.

Yet bridge building is a two-way enterprise, and even though the most pressing need may be for special education to take a long overdue initiative, we must still recognize the importance of maintaining meaningful com-

Reprinted from Frank M. Hewett with Steven R. Forness, *Education of Exceptional Learners,* © 1974; by permission of Allyn and Bacon, Inc., Boston.

munication and interaction with the physicians, neurologists, pediatricians, psychologists, social workers, and other professionals standing by to contribute to the welfare and understanding of the exceptional learner. These individuals will continue, at least for a while, to translate their efforts into diagnostic labels, particularly with those children who manifest physical and sensory-based problems. A complete refusal on the part of the special educator to continue to communicate in terms of such labels might seriously disrupt our important interdisciplinary working relationships. Here we have dissonance reflected. We would like to free all exceptional learners from the negative effects of labels, but in the process we could create a problem that might limit our overall effectiveness to help them.

The author has observed, however, an interesting trend away from traditional psychiatric labeling in the Neuropsychiatric Institute on the campus of the University of California, Los Angeles. Here, children and adolescents with serious emotional and behavior problems are hospitalized for limited periods of time for intensive study and evaluation. In the early 1960s, it was not uncommon for complex labels such as childhood schizophrenia or neurotic depressive reaction to be given these individuals during the course of their stay in the hospital. In 1971, such labels had all but disappeared; the majority of diagnoses fell into the broad categories, adjustment reaction of childhood or adjustment reaction of adolescence. Thus, in other disciplines concerned with exceptional individuals, the labeling practices of the past are also currently undergoing scrutiny and alteration.

The second problem area is related and has to do with communication and maintenance of traditional working relationships with others outside the field of special education. Programs to educate exceptional learners cost money, and this money comes from federal, state, and local community support. In the past, we have presented our case to legislators utilizing the concept of handicapping conditions among school-age children to obtain funds. Utilization of this concept inevitably relies on reference to traditional labels and categories. Whether we like to admit it or not, such an approach facilitates a simple, direct, and meaningful communication with these individuals and carries with it an emotional appeal. Some people may deplore advocating emotionality in gaining support for educational programs for exceptional learners; but the author contends it can be a valuable means of calling attention to the needs of these children and that in actuality it represents a fact of life.

In this regard, the author recalls a situation in which a legislative body was to be approached regarding the allocation of funds to help children with serious reading disabilities. On the one hand, the special educators who were formulating the request could describe the children as having difficulty in learning to read and as needing special help to catch up. If this were done, there was a good chance the officials representing a layman's point of view regarding education might shift focus to the educational system that had failed to teach these children to read and negatively

342

react to continued demands by the field of education for help with its problems. On the other hand, these special educators could describe the children as victims of specific developmental dyslexia, an affliction with a suspected neurological basis suffered by 2 to 5 percent of school-age children in the United States. Now the focus is clearly on a handicapped child who is designated by a specific label and category; the impact and emotional appeal vary considerably. It was the latter plan that was followed in this case, and the request for special funds was readily granted. Here we have another example of dissonance. The category of dyslexia may adversely affect the teacher's expectations in working with a child and constitute one of the most questionable labels we ever apply to a child, yet it serves its purpose well in obtaining support for special education.

This example illustrates the complexities involved in any such "out with the old, in with the new" maneuver in special education. Labels and categories are not desirable, yet they may be inevitable for certain communication and funding purposes. The way out of this dissonant situation is clear-cut: learn to live with traditional labels in the extraeducational domain but replace them with educationally useful and relevant descriptive terms once the child crosses the classroom threshold. This has been a theme throughout this text; little more needs to be said here regarding the author's position. In the next chapter, a public school model for dealing with the three dissonant issues described here will further illustrate alternatives to the traditional labeling and categorization approach.

Despite the current hue and cry about labeling (much of it centered on the mentally retarded and emotionally disturbed), special education has some examples to its credit of building the bridge from the other side, or replacing reliance on medically based labels with a functional educational approach. One of the most notable examples began in the 1930s and concerns the visually handicapped. In 1935, the Social Security Act required a legal definition of blindness so that eligibility for federal aid could be determined. For this reason, a definition based on visual acuity was adopted for both the blind and partially seeing. This definition was presented in Chapter 2 and individuals were classified according to it as a result of ophthalmic measurement.

Those children who functioned according to the definition as "legally blind" were candidates for braille instruction and those functioning as "partially seeing" children as being able to learn to read print. But the classification based on ophthalmic measurement did not hold up in practice. When viewed in purely educational terms, that is in terms of actual ability to read print, large numbers of so-called legally blind children were found to have residual vision that enabled them to read print. Therefore, the ophthalmic measurement utilized as a basis for assigning legal labels of blind and partially seeing was not wholly adequate for educational purposes. A far more useful classification reflecting an operational approach has emerged. Partially seeing children are those who can learn to read print, and blind children are those who cannot learn print but who need instruction in braille. Thus, the shift from a medical measurement to an educational operation has resulted in a major step forward in resolving the labeling dilemma with the visually handicapped. In a somewhat similar fashion the label learning disabilities has replaced earlier categories of brain damage and neurological impairment, moving us a bit closer to relating what we call a child to what we do with him in the classroom. We still have a long way to go with such categories as emotionally disturbed, mentally retarded, and socially and economically disadvantaged, but we have made a beginning.

Of particular note is a project which has grown out of a concern of the U.S. Department of Health, Education, and Welfare. The Project on Classification of Exceptional Children (Hobbs, 1973) is being guided by a distinguished group of physicians, psychiatrists, special educators, sociologists, lawyers, administrators of national, state, and community agencies and programs for the handicapped, and parents of exceptional children. The project will culminate in a report to the Secretary of Health, Education, and Welfare covering (1) theoretical issues of classification and labeling, (2) the adequacy of classification systems, (3) labeling in institutions, (4) consumer perspectives on labeling, (5) public policy issues, and (6) recommendations for policies. On the basis of this comprehensive look at the entire labeling process, it is hoped positive action will occur on the part of government agencies and professional associations to correct inequalities in our present classification system across all areas of the handicapped.

SPECIAL CLASS PLACEMENT VERSUS REGULAR CLASS INTEGRATION

Historically, as exceptional learners were identified and schools were assigned responsibility for educating them, the special school or class model was seen as the logical approach to follow. Children with physical and sensory handicaps were among the first to receive special school assignment; by the late 1800s, unruly boys and mentally retarded children were assigned to special day classes in a few large cities. The only alternative for most of these children was exclusion from school, since their learning and behavior problems markedly interfered with meeting the expectations of a regular class program.

Even though the issue of special class placement versus regular class integration concerns each type of exceptional learner, most current attention has been directed toward the mildly retarded and the emotionally disturbed and the child with a learning disability. Simply stated, the issue is concerned with the optimal instructional setting for helping exceptional learners receive the maximum benefits of an education. Should they be isolated and taught full time as special children? Or should they be placed in the mainstream of the regular classroom and educated there? For some of our exceptional learners, the issue has been dealt with for a longer period of time, and in many cases a workable solution involving both special and regular education has been found. The visually handicapped child may spend long periods in a regular class and receive outside resource help with assignments and instruction in braille. The hearing handicapped child who is provided with amplification by means of a hearing aid may also be a candidate for regular class programs for much of his school day, although outside resource help in language and speech training may be provided. Many physically handicapped children can work well in regular class programs if physical facilities are conducive to their moving about (e.g., ramps instead of stairs for wheelchairs). Speech handicapped children who receive speech therapy on a scheduled basis are usually assigned full time to a regular classroom. Educational provisions for gifted children often involve participation in a combination enrichment and regular class program. The disadvantaged child presents a separate problem in relation to this issue. Many so-called regular classes in large urban cities are filled with children with learning and behavior problems who need special educational approaches, and as such the regular class *is* the special class. In other situations, these children may be classified as emotionally diturbed, learning disabled, or even mentally retarded and assigned special class placement according to these categories.

Most research that focuses on the special class versus regular class integration issue concerns the mildly retarded, and questions regarding efficacy of either placement have centered on social adjustment, problems in level of self-esteem, and academic achievement. Bruininks and Rynders have examined the positions that have emerged from such research studies and have provided an interesting if dissonance-producing picture of where things stand. To begin with, the controversy surrounding the special class for retarded children is not new. In 1896, when the first special class for the retarded opened in Providence, Rhode Island, a newspaper columnist in that city composed a sarcastic report entitled, "The Fool Class." Binet and Simon, who developed the first widely accepted intelligence test, challenged special class placement in 1905 by stating, "To be a member of a special class can never be a mark of distinction, and such as do not merit it, must be spared the record."

The 1960s brought forth a number of research studies and position papers also challenging the use of the special class with the mentally retarded. MacMillan, in reviewing many of the studies, concluded "the child can't win," since some evidence has been presented suggesting he suffers in a special class and other evidence reported that he suffers in a regular class, thus setting the stage for dissonance in the field. The validity of these research efforts is a major consideration since sampling bias, lack of control of preplacement experiences, and questionable criterion measurements were frequently found to be limitations. The predicament of the "child who can't win" is highlighted by the conclusion of a number of special educators who have written regarding this issue. Perhaps most notable was the position paper of Dunn, which indicted special education for imposing special class placement on the mildly retarded with minimal justification, for including large numbers of disadvantaged children in such classes, and for failure to develop viable options. Other writers who have expressed viewpoints related to this issue are Johnson, Christophos and Renz, Kidd, and Lilly. Bruininks and Rynders have summarized some of the positions taken by these authors, and Forness has illustrated how even regular education must share the blame for the problems in special class placement.

To begin, we can conclude from some research studies that mentally retarded children placed in regular classrooms are rejected by their more able peers, thus supporting special class placement. But evidence also exists that the special class isolates the retarded child from normal social experiences, thereby restricting his opportunities for learning interpersonal skills. The mentally retarded child placed in a regular classroom may suffer from loss of self-esteem because of his inability to cope with demands and expectations that are a part of that program. The same child in a special class, however, is apt to suffer loss of self-esteem because of the stigma of being isolated and rejected by other children. Even though we may support special class placement for the retarded on the basis that homogeneous grouping by ability level leads to more effective learning, there is little evidence to support such grouping as providing the optimal learning situation for either normal or retarded children. We may also assume that a special class designed to deal specifically with the major learning problems of the retarded will constitute a superior educational setting for him, but we also must face the fact that such settings clearly place the responsibility for academic failure on the child rather than on schools and teachers. A smaller class offering individualized instruction would seem to guarantee that better academic learning would take place, but studies show the retarded often make as much or more academic progress in the regular classroom as they do in the special classroom. In defense of the special class, we can take the position that such classes should not be held responsible for mistakes in diagnosis and placement. The mere existence of the special class, however, encourages misplacement of many children, particularly those from minority groups.

The theme of dissonance is evident throughout the statements made in the preceding paragraph. Once again we are faced with the unenviable position of not being able to deal directly with the issue on an either–or basis. The solutions must lie somewhere in the middle, for it is highly improbable that a full swing of the pendulum and total abandonment of the special class concept will serve the cause of education of the exceptional learner.

There are some children with special learning and behavior problems who can never be in school if they are not separated from the regular class

346

program. Certain severely disturbed and retarded children are a case in point here. There are other children with learning and behavior problems who are not candidates for full-time placement in the regular classroom and if that is the only option, they will fail to receive the education appropriate for them. Among these groups would be representatives from every category of exceptional learners. Then there are children with learning and behavior problems who may well profit most from full-time placement in the regular classroom, provided there is an individualized curriculum and a teacher knowledgeable and understanding in relation to their problems and willing to accommodate their uniqueness in the program.

Forness has stated that the special versus regular class issue may lapse into irrelevance for two reasons. First, class action lawsuits initiated on behalf of plaintiffs from low income or minority backgrounds who allegedly have been placed in special classes for the retarded in inordinate numbers have forced discontinuation of special class placement as a single option in a number of instances. Thus, the courts have had and probably will continue to have a direct influence in modifying special education practices. Cohen and De Young have prepared a comprehensive report on the role of litigation in affecting educational programs for exceptional learners. Under such influences, special education will never be able to wait until all the evidence is in regarding the efficacy of special versus regular class placement. We must act now and create a range of placement options that more adequately meet the educational needs of exceptional children in the nation. Secondly, Forness challenges the notion that the mildly retarded constitute a homogeneous group. He sees the singular option of the special class as creating an either–or situation for retarded children, one that falsely assumes that mental retardation is an all or none phenomenon. Such a situation, in fact, places the burden of proof for retardation squarely on the child in that he must prove to us by repeated failures that he is retarded enough to be eligible for special class placement.

In dealing with the special class placement versus regular class integration issue, we must plan for all types of children, and indeed movement in this direction is occurring in the field. Bruininks and Rynders summarize some of the options in personnel roles, instructional resources, and adminstrative placements that are emerging. The range in personnel roles to aid the mildly retarded is being extended to include paraprofessionals to support the regular class teacher, resource learning specialists to provide consultation, special education resource teachers offering part-time help, and full-time special class teachers for some children. Administrative placements may range from nongraded, open school plans through regular class placement with various supporting outside services to the special class part or full time to homebound instruction, and residual school placement. Thus, the solution to the dissonant special versus regular class issue is to be found in extending the range of resources available in the school and community on both a creative and practical level. The logic of this approach is obvious and sound; yet such an extension of resources makes many demands on both special and regular educators that will take time to meet effectively.

IMPACT OF CHANGES IN SPECIAL EDUCATION ON REGULAR EDUCATION

Discussions of opening the door of the special class and integrating some exceptional learners into the regular classroom often fail to consider how open the regular classroom door might be and just how ready, willing, and able the regular classroom teacher is to include such children. Regardless of how intensive the individualized work with children with learning and behavior problems is in a special class setting or how it is focused on preparing the child for survival and success in the regular classroom, if there is a lack of understanding or acceptance on the part of the regular teacher once the child arrives, we have hardly improved the present state of affairs.

Hewett, Quay, Taylor, and Watson have explored the opinions of regular classroom teachers regarding the effects of having mildly retarded, emotionally disturbed, and learning disabled children integrated in their classrooms. An "Information Survey" was developed, which asked regular teachers to respond on a five-point scale (from "strongly agree" to "strongly disagree") to statements related to placement of these exceptional learners in their program. The statements focused on behavior and learning problems that might be presented by the children themselves (e.g., "The behavior of an emotionally disturbed child will be disruptive in a regular classroom"); the effect of these problems on the rest of the class (e.g., "The presence of an educable mentally retarded child will adversely affect the motivation to learn of normal children in the regular classroom"); the academic learning potential of the exceptional learners (e.g., "If properly taught, an emotionally disturbed child will learn reading as well as the normal child"); and the additional problems that might be faced by the teacher if such children were integrated (e.g., "Teaching the educable mentally retarded child will require at least weekly consultation with the school psychologist"). Three hundred regular elementary teachers were given the survey. An extensive range of responses was obtained. A comparison of the top 25 percent of the most knowledgeable and positive responses with the bottom 25 percent of the least knowledgeable and positive responses revealed that many of the statements significantly differentiated the teachers in the sample. Even though this survey was developed as a means of measuring changes in regular class teachers' opinions after actually working with exceptional learners in their classrooms and participating in in-service training programs, this standardization data provided interesting evidence regarding the widely discrepant positions that regular class teachers hold regarding the inclusion of exceptional learners in the regular classroom. This is an important problem area that must be dealt with if we are effectively to resolve the special versus regular class issue.

In the author's experience, regular classroom teachers do vary in terms of their range of tolerance for behavorial and academic differences among children in their classrooms. There is no way of describing the typical regular classroom into which we may be placing an exceptional learner. Each classroom will be unique as each teacher is unique. If we are going to move toward increased integration we will have to help regular teachers broaden their ranges of tolerance for behavioral and academic differences, increase their effectiveness with individualized instruction, and effect an appropriate teacher–child match-up with respect to placing a given exceptional learner in a classroom so that he falls within the existing ranges of tolerance of a given teacher.

One approach to accomplishing the first task might be increased emphasis and course work in teacher preparation programs on individual differences among children in general and among exceptional learners specifically. Such programs leading to certification seldom stress these areas, although some expectations can be found across the country. A major increase in this regard would probably be difficult to implement because of the slowness with which curricular change occurs in college and university programs. The author is reminded of a survey of the credentialing standards of the fifty states with respect to courses in reading instruction required for an elementary teaching certificate. Until the early 1960s, more states required course work in music and art areas than in basic reading instruction. If our teacher preparation programs have been that slow in incorporating required coursework in such a critical and basic area as reading instruction, it is highly doubtful that we can effect an overnight increase in required study in areas related to the problems of exceptional learners.

The more realistic approach is probably on an in-service level. That is, we may not have the time to wait until major changes are brought about in teacher training programs; we need to consider ways to communicate directly with the regular teacher working in the field at the present time.

To bring about more direct communication between special and regular education, special educators must work as hard to decrease the specialness and separatist orientation as regular education must work to increase its ranges of tolerance for behavior and learning differences and effectiveness in individualizing instruction. During the 1960s, when the field of special education was rapidly going through infancy, childhood, adolescence, and moving toward maturity, we may have overemphasized a specialized identity. Reliance on labels and categories played a large part in shaping such an identity. The point was reached at which teachers with specialized credentials in one area of exceptionality often were reluctant to include children with problems falling outside their specialized area of preparation in their classrooms. Assigning a blind child to a teacher of the blind in a school district was fine, but if this child was also mentally retarded or emotionally disturbed, serious questions might be raised about the appropriateness of such a placement with the teacher. Obviously, special educators have become far too special when categorical boundaries are rigidly established for programs. Such boundaries are also a serious deterrent to establishing more meaningful and direct communication with regular educators. Part III of this text was devoted to an attempt to reorient special education away from specialized, categorical boundaries for communication and practice and toward generalized areas of learning competence that cut across these boundaries. Hopefully, this reorientation will positively contribute to improving communication between special and regular educators.

Despite in-service training and improved communication efforts, can we really hope to enlist the regular class teacher's support and increased acceptance of exceptional learners in regular classrooms? A positive answer appears doubtful when we consider some provisions often included in contacts drawn up by teacher organizations for negotiation with school districts. Such provisions may call for complete control to be given regular teachers over who is kept in or who is referred out of the classroom. Children whose behavior falls outside the teacher's range of tolerance can be referred out to the principal on a permanent basis. Although such teacher organization demands do not exist on a nationwide basis, they suggest that many regular teachers are more ready to remove problem children from their classrooms than they are to accept additional children with learning and behavior problems.

In this regard, it is the author's contention that two basic points must be stressed when communicating with regular educators about establishing a closer working relationship between special and regular education. The first point is this: *no matter how many children with learning and behavior problems we remove from your classroom, when the state and district quotas are filled you are still going to find children with problems left for you to teach.* The second point is closely related: *most of what special education is all about concerns extending good teaching practices so that more children receive the benefit of an education. As special and regular education achieve a closer working relationship, we can anticipate better quality education for all children in our schools.*

We have briefly examined three contemporary issues in the field of special education and the dissonant state each of them places us in. Labeling and categorization is undesirable but perhaps necessary at some levels in our total efforts to provide resources for exceptional learners. Special class placement as a single option is inadequate, but elimination of all special classes will deny educational opportunities for some children with learning and behavior problems. Special education has come of age building on its specialness, but the time has come to alter our identity somewhat if an effective working relationship is to be developed with regular education. The pendulum must swing from established positions, but not full arc.

As the field of special education contemplates the issues before it, we find legislative activity across the nation also reflecting major changes in provisions for the education of exceptional learners. Some of this activity has been brought about by lawsuits directed against state departments of education and local school districts by individual parents and organizations of parents of handicapped children. The State–Federal Information Clearinghouse for Exceptional children, a project of the Council for Exceptional Children and part of a project supported by the Bureau of Education, U.S. Office of Education, has summarized five current trends in state legislation that are related to the education of exceptional learners. Briefly stated, these trends are:

1. Mandatory laws for guaranteeing that all handicapped children will receive the benefits of an education. In the past, a permissive structure in some states allowed considerable flexibility for local districts to operate within when it came to accepting responsibility for certain types of exceptional learners. About thirty-five states now have some form of mandation and others are considering it.
2. Consideration of cultural and ethnic differences in identification and placement of children in special education programs. Keeping parents informed of identification and placement practices as well as state laws governing such practices is also receiving attention.
3. Creation of laws to provide early education programs for both handicapped and nonhandicapped children.
4. Alteration of definitions of handicapped conditions so that certain types of children are not excluded.
5. Increase in comprehensive services such as transportation facilities for handicapped children. Also, laws have created regionally based programs in areas where local school districts alone cannot provide good programs for certain types of handicapped children.

In California an attempt is underway to translate these trends into a practical framework through which special education will be delivered to all children according to their needs. The *Master Plan for Special Education* of the California State Department of Education is a unique and comprehensive document that is being reviewed by educators at all levels. If approved, it will ultimately serve as a philosophical and practical framework for pertinent legislation. The plan calls for a series of options to serve every child "with exceptional needs" and affirms not only that regular education be more responsive to individual needs of exceptional children but also that special education must take the responsibility for showing how this can be done and for helping regular classroom teachers to do so.

Operational Concepts

1. The "labeling" of handicapped students has advantages and disadvantages; nonetheless, present classification systems are inadequate in that they frequently stereotype the special education child unfairly.

2. Mentally retarded children, placed in regular classes, tend to be rejected by their more able peers.

3. Placement of mentally retarded children in special classes tends to result in harmful isolation.

4. New placement procedures and provisions, eliminating present inadequacies, are badly needed.

5. To accomplish desirable integration with regular classes, teachers must be helped through special in-service activities to increase their tolerance for the culturally different child.

Implications

The central implication to be drawn from current theoretical thought on special education is that, as new reforms and improvements are tested, the primary aim should be that of providing the special education child with as normal an educational experience as possible.

To achieve this end, parents, students, and teachers alike must be helped to overcome discomfort in the presence of students with handicaps. In addition, the educator's conception of what handicapped children can accomplish must be enlarged. Self-fulfilling prophecies invariably occur in special education: where too little is expected, too little is gained.

Substantial good might accrue, as well, from experimental programs in which normal children, matched on a one-to-one basis, are teamed with handicapped children—both as an experiment in peer tutoring and as direct experience in altruistic behavior.

Continuing Education

Alan B. Knox

Higher Education and Lifelong Learning

CONTINUING HIGHER EDUCATION

Lifelong learning has become a fundamental theme of our rapidly changing society (Faure et al., 1972). The foundations have been laid during the past century as various sponsors of continuing education for adults have provided expanding opportunities for adults to study part-time by participating in such activities as evening courses, extension workshops, and correspondence study (Knox, 1969b). As more adults have participated and as more mention of continuing education of adults has occurred in the mass media, the idea and practice of lifelong learning have become a visible and accepted aspect of adulthood.

Best estimates indicate that last year more than 30 million American adults engaged in continuing education sponsored by almost every type of institution and organization in our society (Johnstone and Rivera, 1965). Over the years, most of this continuing education occurred at the margin of the sponsoring institutions. In recent years, continuing education activities have become more central functions of many organizations and institutions such as schools and colleges, employers and labor unions, churches, and professional associations.

The purpose of this essay is to illustrate some of the emerging relationships between institutions of higher education and adults engaged in life-long learning. Because resulting continuing education activities have been quite varied, it is difficult to generalize from the diverse and unique learning episodes that have occurred. Variability has been associated with sponsoring institution (major university, four-year college, community college), contributions of cosponsors (school system as employer, professional association), type of format and setting (media, evening course, organizational development), methods of learning (reading, listening to presentation, observation of innovative practices, participation in discussion), and

Reprinted from Alan B. Knox, "Higher Education and Lifelong Learning," *Journal of Research and Development in Education*, Vol. 7, No. 4, 1974; by permission of the publisher.

characteristics of participants (aides, teachers, counselors, administrators). For this paper the focus will be on school teachers and administrators as participants in continuing education activities, and on universities as sponsoring institutions.

A crucial ingredient in lifelong learning is that the adult learner assumes a major responsibility for continuing his or her own education (Houle, 1972; Tough, 1967, 1971). This is especially so for persons engaged in professional occupations. Although there are variations in the extent of self-directedness by the adult learner, and in the approaches that are used, both the adult learner and the sponsoring institution have important contributions to make. The following fictional examples illustrate ways in which universities can facilitate the efforts of school teachers and administrators to continue their education.

IN-SERVICE EDUCATION OF TEACHERS

Take the example of Ellen Mellon. During her fourth year as a high school social studies teacher, Ellen began to feel more comfortable in her role as teacher. She had become familiar with the methods and materials that she typically used, and she now related fairly well with most of her students. Having survived her initial teaching years, Ellen was ready to explore ways in which her teaching could become a more exciting experience for herself and for her students. As she discussed this concern with some of the other social studies teachers, several agreed that they too would like to try something new. A few weeks later at lunch, Ellen mentioned her interest in curricular innovation to the local director of public school adult education and asked him for suggestions about ways that she and the other interested teachers might best proceed. As they talked about problems of curricular innovation, they agreed that general reading of professional literature, participating in in-service meetings by the school system, and attending university extension courses did not provide sufficient focus and depth for Ellen's purpose. Then the adult education director mentioned that at a recent meeting of the local adult education council the director of continuing education at the hospital had described peer review procedures that they were using to increase profession competence and improve patient care (Knox, 1974). This casual comment launched Ellen on an unusual and profitable lifelong learning experience.

A conversation with the hospital director of continuing education provided Ellen with a description of peer review procedures and with the suggestion that she contact one of the staff members in the university division of continuing education and public service who had assisted with the planning of the hospital peer review. In response to Ellen's request, a continuing education program administrator at the university sent materials on peer review as a vehicle for staff development, along with a reprint of a chapter on self-directed education of professionals (Knox, 1974).

Ellen discussed what she had found out about peer review as a vehicle for continuing education in other professional fields with other social studies teachers, including the social studies curriculum coordinator for the school system. As a result, a committee was set up with Ellen as chairman to conduct a modest peer review and to report the results to all the social studies teachers in the school system. At that point Ellen contacted the continuing education program administrator at the university for advice on how best to proceed. He indicated that he was familiar with peer review procedures in other professional fields and that a faculty member in the College of Education was interested in exploring ways to adapt 'peer review procedures for secondary school teachers. The program administrator suggested that the education professor work with Ellen's committee on a field service arrangement, to assist them in planning, conducting, and evaluating the modest peer review.

During the following few months, Ellen and her committee, with the assistance of the education professor, conducted a peer review which included the following activities.

1. *The committee decided that it would be necessary to focus the review on one aspect of practice at a time.* Otherwise they would be unable to conduct it along with their regular teaching responsibilities. They decided to focus on practices that were important to most social studies teachers, on practices that the teachers themselves could readily modify, and on practices that would likely be perceived by the teachers as moving them in desirable career directions. The education professor urged the committee to focus on a few objectives at the outset. The selected aspect of practice was the use of simulation materials as a way of helping high school students to better understand complex social phenomena such as small group behavior, community decision making, and international relations.

2. *The committee prepared a guide that social studies teachers could use to describe their plans for and use of simulation materials in teaching.* The education professor provided some examples of guides that had been used in the preparation of descriptions of other practices. The resulting guide had the following sections:

   a. Concept or social process that the students should better understand as a result of using the simulation materials.

   b. Identification of the specific simulation materials that were planned, such as a decision-making game, a computer-based simulation, or materials for conducting a role play.

   c. Description of the number and background of the intended students.

d. Copy of the teacher's lesson plan for use of the simulation, including teacher preparation, intended student and teacher activities when using the simulation, and evaluation plan.

e. Record of the way in which the teacher and students actually spent their time during the simulation, including both the use of simulation materials and discussion of the experience.

f. Evidence of outcomes or results of the simulation experience, such as achievement test scores, summary of student opinionnaire forms, and ratings by teacher or observer.

3. *The committee agreed upon criterion performance.* This was perhaps the most difficult but educative task that confronted the committee. The purpose was to describe an attainable ideal or standard against which to judge or compare the actual performance of the social studies teachers who participated in the peer review. The committee decided that the main way to define criterion performance should be to select a few high school social studies teachers who had the reputation of being outstandingly effective in the use of simulation materials, and to arrange for them to use the guide to describe their use of simulation. The education professor agreed to help locate some outstanding teachers in similar schools who might cooperate, and to work with several of his graduate students, who were enrolled in a practicum, to assemble and summarize the ways in which the outstanding practitioners used simulation. The committee then agreed upon the common characteristics of outstanding performance which constituted an attainable ideal or standard.

4. *Next the committee prepared an overview of the peer review procedures they were proposing and discussed this proposal with the teachers they hoped would participate in the review.* This inclusion of the teachers who would participate in the review in its planning was deemed an important way to focus the effort on their experience and concerns, to increase their commitment to use the results, and to minimize concern about external interference in professional activities. Fortunately, many of the social studies teachers were interested in participating in the peer review regarding simulation and a plan of action was decided upon.

5. *During the subsequent month or so, the participating teachers prepared case descriptions of their use of simulation, using the committee's guide for organizing the case description.* The education professor and his graduate students assisted the committee in the preparation of a summary that identified the ways in which the participating teachers typically used simulation. Upon request of some of the participating teachers, one of the graduate students observed some classroom sessions in which simulation materials were used.

6. *The committee then compared the actual performance of the partici-*

*pating teachers regarding use of simulation with the criterion perform-
ance of outstanding practitioners to identify the gap to be narrowed by
continuing education.* The committee could use the summary information for all participating teachers as the basis for recommendations
regarding group activities to focus on shared gaps. The case descriptions
prepared by each teacher could be returned along with the description
of common characteristics of outstanding performance. This would enable the individual teacher to reflect on his or her specific practices in
the use of simulation and to identify specific changes to be tried. Ellen
noted that teachers who participated in the review process were more
likely to accept a gap as something to do something about and to have
some ideas about what to do about it than a comparable teacher who
merely had a deficiency pointed out to him or her.

As Ellen and her committee discussed the results of their modest peer
review, they came to the following conclusions.

1. It entailed more time and effort than they had anticipated.

2. The experience, however, was more professionally beneficial for the
   time spent than most in-service training activities in which they had
   engaged.

3. The professor of education proved to be a valuable resource for the
   committee because of his familiarity with relevant practices, people, and
   materials elsewhere, and the assistance that he and his students provided.

4. The teacher's behaviors for closing the gap between typical and outstanding performance in the use of simulation could be translated
   directly into objectives for continuing education.

5. The participating teachers were more interested in participating in the
   peer review process and subsequent continuing education activity because they could see the direct benefits for the students and for their
   own satisfaction from the teaching–learning transaction.

6. The peer review could be conducted periodically to evaluate the impact
   of related continuing education activities.

7. The education professor was well prepared to plan and conduct a workshop on simulation for a larger number of interested social studies
   teachers in the region.

As Ellen reflected on the results of the peer review experience, she
concluded that she had received an additional personal benefit. She had
begun the project in a search for something new. In the process she discovered ways to relate action problems and decisions that she confronted
in teaching more closely to the knowledge resources in her school system
and in the university. "I wonder," she mused, "why both my preservice
and in-service education in the past couldn't have placed more emphasis on
relating knowledge and action?"

INCREASING ADMINISTRATIVE COMPETENCE

The relation between action and knowledge can also be illustrated by the example of Ed Deane. Ed had recently become director of continuing education in a community college after twenty-five years of teaching. During his first year as an administrator he concentrated on becoming familiar with operational procedures, such as arranging for people to teach evening courses, preparing brochures to publicize the program, and filling out the seemingly endless progression of forms for such purposes as budgets, ordering supplies, reporting, and getting people paid.

As he started his second year as director, Ed began to think more about his clientele. He had become interested in the continuing education of adults because of his concern about the educationally less advantaged. As he got to know other directors of continuing education in the state, he discovered that many of them also shared his missionary zeal. However, when Ed examined a summary of the characteristics of participants in his continuing education program, he concluded that he was serving a predominantly middle-class clientele.

Ed had about decided that his major goal for the coming year was to try to broaden his clientele when he received a brochure from the university which announced a workshop on marketing of continuing education. That clinched it. He registered for the workshop, which was organized in three segments. The first segment was a three-day residential session held at the university's continuing education center. This initial segment consisted of reading, presentations, and discussion on topics such as contining education clientele analysis, social stratification, life-style, influences on decisions by adults to participate in educative activity, and the relative effectiveness of various communication channels in reaching various target populations. The middle segment was the subsequent two-month period during which the workshop participants were to develop a plan for a continuing education marketing effort as they worked along in the context of their own institution. The final segment consisted of a concluding two-day workshop which focused on an assessment of the plans that were prepared and an exploration of ways to implement them effectively. When the university program administrator confirmed Ed's registration, he sent along a two-page orientation statement, which suggested that Ed make a preliminary analysis of an action problem related to marketing of continuing education, in preparation for participation in the initial workshop. Ed pulled together some thoughts and materials regarding broadening his clientele. His personal program of continuing education was underway.

Some weeks after the concluding workshop, Ed listed for a colleague the following major activities in which he had engaged.

1. *Decided upon encouraging undereducated adults to participate in continuing education as the action problem on which he wanted to*

focus. His growing concern about broadening his clientele, his reading of the two-page workshop orientation statement, and his preliminary analysis of his current practices related to marketing each helped Ed to clarify his expectations when he entered the initial workshop.

2. *Recognized relevant organized knowledge.* During the initial workshop, as Ed read, listened, and discussed, he gained a better understanding of the topics related to continuing education, communications, sociology, and marketing that were most relevant to broadening his clientele.

3. *Retrieved pertinent ideas from various sources.* The initial workshop included some time periods during which Ed was engaged in trying to locate and understand ideas pertinent to marketing of continuing education. Toward the end of that workshop, the participants reviewed the various sources of relevant knowledge they had utilized before and during the workshop. The list included:

   a. Pertinent information stored in his own memory.
   b. Records in his own office.
   c. Relevant sections of books and journals in the library.
   d. Resource persons with competence related to marketing of services.
   e. Reports from modest research or evaluation studies which he and other practitioners conducted to obtain organized knowledge directly applicable to their own setting.

4. *Explored implications from the organized knowledge for his specific situation.* When he returned from the initial workshop, Ed discussed implications from practice with people with whom he worked in community-college continuing education.

5. *Redefined the problem.* Before the initial workshop, Ed conceptualized the problem mainly in terms of motivational deficiences of non-participants. After the workshop, the emphasis shifted to ways to reduce barriers to participation, which the community college staff could more readily influence. He was also able to define the problem more specifically in relation to his own situation.

6. *Specified alternative solutions.* In the process of reading and discussing and becoming more familiar with the experience of his colleagues regarding marketing of continuing education, Ed became familiar with a variety of approaches to broadening his clientele. Some approaches were quite standard and widespread, such as the use of mass media and cosponsorship. Other approaches, such as the use of vestibule activities as feeders to his program, were unusual.

7. *Considered the advantages and disadvantages of the alternative solutions.* Mainly from what he learned from the experience of other practitioners through reading of case studies and discussion with them

in their own setting, Ed was able to weigh the relative advantages and disadvantages of the several marketing approaches that appeared to be most appropriate to his situation.

8. *Selected a course of action.* Ed decided on an approach that seemed best. In arriving at his decision he talked with those with whom he would work to implement the plan, so that he would have the benefit of their thinking and commitment.

9. *Developed a plan.* In preparation for the second workshop, Ed prepared a marketing plan that he intended to put into action.

10. *Considered criteria of success.* In the process of evolving a marketing plan, Ed again turned to organized knowledge, especially reports on similar projects and findings from research and evaluation studies, for information to use in judging the relative success of his effort to broaden his clientele. The criteria were useful in selecting a course of action, in developing a detailed plan, and in evaluating his marketing effort as it proceeded.

The example of Ed Deane illustrates the way in which a professional can alternate between action problems and knowledge resources as he increases his competence, and the way in which a university can facilitate his lifelong learning activities.

MENTOR ROLE

Many adults such as Ellen and Ed are discovering that if they are to become all that they want to be they must find more effective ways to link action and knowledge. Educators work with knowledge as well as with things and people. The most successful professionals have developed a repertoire of effective strategies for alternating between action problems and knowledge resources (Knox, 1974). Thinking and feeling and doing continually intermingle as the adult seeks to maintain and enhance his selfhood, to find direction and fulfillment, to cope with the demands and constraints that confront him, to achieve understanding and mastery, to develop more creative and humane relationships with other people, and to become a fully functioning person (Rogers, 1969).

When adults enter a continuing education activity, they typically do so for several fairly specific reasons. Many are trying to educate themselves, to find answers to their questions, and to formulate more useful questions. They engage in learning in order to improve their ability to know and feel and act (Knox, 1968). Those who successfully help adults to learn have a respect for their growth strivings and have ways to facilitate the process. The process of facilitating learning is basically the same whether the learner is somebody else or oneself (Tough, 1967). The process of planning and guiding adult learning is termed the mentor role. Persons who effectively serve as facilitators of learning are able to perform well in the main components of the mentor role.

A better understanding of the mentor role should result in a more insightful identification of the major decisions to be made and a more effective approach to doing so. Most of these decisions cluster around five components of the mentor role, which deal with learners, setting, objectives, activities, and evaluation (Knox, 1974). They are not steps but components whose interrelationships must be considered, and the planning or improvement of a continuing education program can begin with any component and proceed to relationships with each of the other components until all have been taken into account. Decisions regarding all these components occur during both the planning and the conducting of educational programs and attention should be given to them throughout the process (Houle, 1972). These components of the mentor role apply when someone is planning and conducting a learning episode for himself, for another indiviual, or for and with a group of adults.

Learner Characteristics

An adult is more likely to change if a gap is identified between his or her actual present behavior and a changed behavior that seems more desirable. The behavior may be knowledge, skill, attitude, or actual performance. It may be understanding group dynamics, being able to use questions effectively in group discussion, appreciating the performance of a skillful discussion leader, or performing well as a discussion leader. One way to specify desirable behavior is to define it as an attainable ideal as personified by people who perform it very well. The master teacher serves as a role model for the student teacher. The excellent performance of outstanding practitioners can be compared with that of the potential learner to identfy the gaps. This comparison serves two purposes. One is as a basis for the selection of educational objectives and learning activities to help close some of the major gaps. The second purpose is to encourage the potential learner to become committed to narrowing the gap by a change in his behavior. Familiarity with the performance of an experienced administrator may inspire a staff member to commence graduate study. Someone who wants to facilitate adult learning can help to appraise educational needs by assisting the learner to understand the rationale, to use the procedures, and to recognize attainable standards of excellence to compare with his actual present performance. This component of the mentor role contributes especially to the setting of objectives. Background information about adults as learners, typical needs, and dynamics of learning can sensitize those who facilitate learning to ways in which their help is most likely to be effective (Knox, 1968).

Awareness of Setting

A learning episode for an adult typically occurs within a societal context that also influences his performance of his major roles in family, work, and community. A second component of the mentor role is becoming aware of the major influences in the setting and harnessing some of them so as to increase the likelihood of personal growth and change. A school system in which innovation is encouraged and improved performance is rewarded provides great impetus for continuing education of the staff. There are three types of contextual influences on continuing education that the learner should be helped to recognize and use. One type of influence is the set of criteria against which the effectiveness of continuing education is judged. Examples include increased professional effectiveness, improved student achievement, greater participation in professional activities, or closer relations between school and community. The learner can use these criteria as reference points for short-term goals and assessment of progress. Another type is the set of positive influences and resources that encourage participation in continuing education. Examples include a favorable image of continuing education, encouragement by the school administrators, and available educational materials and facilities. The learner can use these sources of encouragement as aids to progress and boons to motivation (Rogers, 1971). A third type is the set of negative influences that serve as barriers to participation. Examples include competing activities, high costs, fear of failure, and an overwhelming welter of possible objectives. The learner is more likely to offset these negative influences if he recognizes them (Knox, 1968).

Setting Objectives

The adult typically confronts far more gaps to be narrowed by continuing education than he can attend to. Priorities must be set, if only by default. The third component of the mentor role is the selection of objectives upon which to focus continuing education activities. The selection process includes a review of sources of objectives and a listing of the major objectives that might be attended to. Sources of objectives include analysis of their own role performance, opinions of peers, consideration of current personal and social issues, and recommendations of experts. The selection of objectives in which to invest time and attention typically takes into account the desirability of closing the gap and the feasibility of doing so, even with assistance. Ellen decided that more effective use of simulation had the highest priority as an educational objective at the current stage of her career. Someone who helps to facilitate the learning of another adult confronts the additional task of achieving a satisfactory match between his own expectations and those of the learner. Although a facilitator of learning may have a greater understanding of that which is to be learned, the expectations of the facilitator should not be imposed on the adult learner. Instead, the early part of each learning episode should be devoted to objective setting. A typical procedure is agenda building for the session. In the process of agenda building, consensus is achieved. When there is substantial agreement and objectives are straightforward, the objective setting phase may take but a few minutes. Up to one third of the available time can be devoted to objective setting and still accomplish more learning achievement than when objectives are inadequately understood and agreed upon.

Learning Activities

The most evident component of the mentor role deals with the learning activities themselves. Learning occurs mainly as a result of an interaction of individuals with new information or experiences. This interaction typically takes the form of activities such as reading, listening, writing, discussing, and viewing. These activities have been developed singly and in combination in dozens and dozens of learning methods (Rogers, 1971). This component of the mentor role consists of the selection and organization of learning activities to achieve the educational objectives and to fit the learning style of the individual learner. Some learning activities are more likely to enable the learner to develop a competent level of performance and the commitment that results in a "refreezing" of new habit patterns and subsequent utilization of the new area of performance. These types of learning activities usually include opportunities for the learner to practice the new area of performance in settings similar to actual performance. Examples include role playing and case analysis. The main criterion for the selection and organization of learning activities is the achievement of the specific educational objectives that were selected as of high priority. This fitting of activities to objectives should take into account both the content that is being learned and the behavior of the learner that is to be changed. Another criterion is the fit between learning activities and the learner's preferences and style of learning. Some adults strongly prefer to encounter a highly structured presentation by an acknowledged authority, such as a recorded lecture on a tape cassette. Some other adults strongly prefer a less structured way of exploring the same content, such as an informal discussion with knowledgeable peers. If each is able to use materials and activities that fit his preferences, it is likely that his motivation and the learning outcomes will be greater.

Evaluation

The remaining component of the mentor role is the process by which persons associated with the educational activity make judgments about effectiveness based on evidence in ways that encourage use of the conclusions to improve the educational activity (Knox, 1969a). These judgments are made by the learner himself and by those who try to facilitate his efforts. The main type of judgment is a comparison between expectations and performance. Did the social studies teacher learn as much about simulation as she expected to? There are several aspects of the educational activity that might be the focus of evaluation. Was the scope of the educational objectives regarding marketing too broad, too narrow, or just about right? Did the gaps that were identified turn out to be among those with the highest priority? Were the learning activities planned so that they fit well with other commitments and personal preferences? Were the benefits of the continuing education activity worth the investment of time, money, and effort?

In many continuing education programs sponsored by institutions of higher education, the decisions regarding components of the mentor role are made by professors. When a professor teaches an extramural course, he typically discusses the course plan with the participants and modifies it somewhat as it proceeds. For many university workshops, the planning committee is composed of professors, representatives of participants, and a continuing education program administrator. The foregoing examples of Ellen Mellon and Ed Deane illustrate ways to shift greater responsibility for the mentor role to the adult learners. In these instances, university personnel helped the participants to recognize the components of the mentor role and to make decisions where they were ready to do so, and the professors provided supplementary assistance where needed. With this approach, the professor's emphasis shifted from presenting information to facilitating learning.

CONTRIBUTIONS OF HIGHER EDUCATION INSTITUTIONS

Institutions of higher education can use various methods to facilitate lifelong learning. Most university graduates are familiar with standard continuing education methods such as extramural courses, correspondence study, and residential workshops. Some of the less familiar methods entail linkage between the university and either individual self-directed learners or organizations with which the adults are associated (Havelock, 1970). Examples of these organizations include schools, PTA's, colleges, and professional associations. The means by which linkage is established are also varied. They include such activities as publication, research, evaluation, training, consultation, and collaboration. Each of these methods provides a way of linking knowledge-producing systems with knowledge-using systems. The most effective linkage mechanisms appear to be those that facilitate and support the information-seeking activities of the adult users. Listed below are some specific examples of ways in which institutions of higher education can facilitate lifelong learning.

1. *Provide standards of excellent performance.* Many professionals lack clear standards or attainable ideals against which to compare and judge their own performance. Regarding continuing education, such standards serve as criteria for appraising needs and for evaluating program results. University personnel who serve as linkage agents for continuing education can assist by identifying outstanding practitioners, preparing case studies of effective practices, and disseminating reports of pertinent research and evaluation studies.

2. *Describe need-appraisal procedures.* An accurate estimate of educational needs is crucial to effective continuing education program development. However, there are few standard need-appraisal procedures. University personnel can facilitate lifelong learning of adults by providing a rationale for continuing education need appraisal, by producing forms for the collection of data about educational needs, and by conducting need-appraisal studies.

3. *Suggest criteria for the selection of objectives.* Most adults, especially those in professional occupations, become overwhelmed by the many educational objectives they could profitably pursue. University personnel can facilitate continuing education by suggesting some criteria that can be used to select a few educational objectives on which to concentrate. A procedure such as peer review provides the basis for selection by identifying the proportion of those served by a professional worker who are affected by a practice, the extent to which they are affected, and how much can be done to improve the practice. It is also useful to assist the adult learner to consider a possible educational objective in relation to his likely career directions.

4. *Increase familiarity with the range of continuing education activities.* Most adults are aware of only a small portion of the relevant and available continuing education activities. University personnel can help to make continuing education opportunities more accessible in several ways. One is to work with various sponsors to prepare combined listings of continuing education activities. Another is to develop retrieval procedures, such as computer searches or indexes, to readily identify activities that are appropriate for an adult who seeks assistance. A third way is to backstop counselors in many settings who provide educational counseling for adults.

5. *Develop self-administered evaluation materials.* The preparation of effective evaluation instruments requires much expertise and effort. However, once effective evaluation materials are developed they can be readily used and adapted in various ways. University personnel can facilitate lifelong learning by developing materials such as self-assess-

ment inventories and sets of illustrative program-evaluation forms. Normative information regarding the performance of various categories of persons on the instruments allows the individual who uses them to interpret his performance or that of his group.

Institutions of higher education can contribute to lifelong learning in several ways in addition to sponsorship of continuing education programs for adults. One way is to help people throughout our society to better understand how central lifelong learning is to contemporary life. Colleges and universities can lead the way in demonstrating that continuing education is the fifth freedom upon which other freedoms are based (Knox, 1972). All institutions are coming to realize that they have a continuing education function and that together they are creating an educative community that provides the incentives, resources, and rewards for individual adults to continue to learn and grow.

A second contribution of higher education institutions to lifelong learning occurs as a result of the inclusion of continuing education practices as part of preparatory education. The concern for relevance and coordination of education is worldwide. Lifelong learning was the central theme of the report by a recent UNESCO commission on education (Faure et al., 1972). As institutions of higher education expand nontraditional study opportunities and external degrees, the beneficiaries include full-time college students of the usual college age (Houle, 1973). College students who learn to perform many tasks of the mentor role for themselves are more likely to become effective lifelong learners. Those who become teachers can assist children and youth to become more self-directed in their learning throughout life.

Higher education institutions contribute to lifelong learning in a third way. About a hundred American unversities now have graduate programs that prepare people to develop and administer continuing education programs for adults. In addition to master's degree and doctoral programs, many of these universities also conduct noncredit workshops for teachers and administrators in the field, and some universities conduct pertinent research and evaluation studies (Knox, 1973).

A fourth contribution is the provision of assistance to other sponsors of adult and continuing education. This assistance takes the form of inservice education of staff, research and evaluation studies, consultation, and collaboration on demonstration projects. Some cooperation occurs at the local level informally and through adult education councils, and some occurs at state and national levels through professional associations and federally supported projects.

A fifth way in which institutions of higher education contribute to lifelong learning is the development of models, rationales, and materials that facilitate lifelong self-directed education. As more and more adults become used to performing much of the mentor role for themselves and for others, ours will become truly a learning society. In this process, one of the greatest contributions that any sponsor of continuing education can make is to assist learners to increase their repertoire of effective strategies for alternating between action problems and knowledge resources.

References

FAURE, E., ET AL. (1972). *Learning to Be: The World of Education Today and Tomorrow*. Paris: UNESCO; London: George G. Harrap & Co. Ltd.

HAVELOCK, R. G. (1970). *A Guide to Innovation in Education*. Ann Arbor, Mich.: University of Michigan, ISR, CRUSK.

HOULE, C. O. (1972). *The Design of Education*. San Francisco: Jossey–Bass, Inc.

———. (1973). *The External Degree*. San Francisco: Jossey–Bass, Inc.

JOHNSTONE, J. W. C., and RIVERA, R. J. (1965). *Volunteers for Learning*. Chicago: Aldine Publishing Co.

KNOX, A. B. (1968). "Interests and Adult Education," *Journal of Learning Disabilities*, Vol. 1, No. 4.

———. (1969a). "Continuous Program Evaluation," Chapter 18 in *Administration of Continuing Education*. Washington, D.C.: National Association for Public School Adult Education, pp. 368–391.

———. (1969b). "Extension Education," *Encyclopedia of Educational Research*, 4th ed. New York: Macmillan Publishing Co., Inc., pp. 481–487.

———. (1972). "Achieving the Fifth Freedom," *Adult Leadership*, September, 21:100–104.

———. (1973). *Development of Adult Education Graduate Programs*. Washington, D.C.: Adult Education Association of the U.S.A., 64pp.

———. (1974). "Life Long Self-Directed Education," Chapter 2 in Blakely, R., *Fostering the Growing Need to Know*. Washington, D.C.: Government Printing Office.

ROGERS, C. R. (1969). *Freedom to Learn*. Columbus, Ohio: Charles E. Merrill Publishing Company.

ROGERS, J. (1971). *Adults Learning*. Harmondsworth, Middlesex, England: Penguin Books Ltd.

TOUGH, A. M. (1967). *Learning Without a Teacher*, Educational Research Series No. 3. Toronto: Ontario Institute for Studies in Education. (See also Tough, *The Adult's Learning Projects*, Educational Research Series. Toronto: Ontario Institute for Studies in Education, 1971.)

Operational Concepts

1. Adult learners, as autonomous persons, must assume responsibility for their own continuing education.

2. Effective continuing education programs are goal oriented, aim at specific objectives, and develop new competencies and understanding.

3. Adult learning is facilitated when the margin between actual competence and desired competence is clear to the learner.

4. Motivation to grow is enhanced when the individual's work organization rewards professional growth.

5. The use of a "mentor" is helpful in setting professional improvement priorities; and, as universities expand continuing education, the mentor is useful in personalizing independent study.

Implications

The rapidly developing field of adult and continuing education yields five basic implications. First, the public school must work zealously to nurture an interest, among its clients, in lifelong education. Second, through learning games, interactive instructional television, and similar devices for promoting home-based learning, the value of activities in which parent and children learn together must be seriously explored. Third, secondary school students must become aware of the probability that they will find it desirable and necessary to participate in adult and continuing education programs throughout the course of their lives. Fourth, extensive research must go into the development of collaborative teaching programs among education, business, and industry so that educational opportunities outside the school are greatly enlarged. In this last connection, it would also be useful to test arrangements wherein businesses and industries are encouraged to engage in such collaborations through government incentives and subsidies. Fifth, access to adult education opportunities in the university must be greatly expanded.

Section 2 Current Movements

As any other institution charged with serving the public good, education is subject to popular movements—to periodic shifts in focus and emphasis that attract widespread attention. Changes in the curriculum occur not only because of ideological transitions, new research discoveries, and fundamental alterations in the social fabric, but also because the human penchant for searching out something new, and possibly better, is endemic to the species.

The curricular movements described in the essays that follow span a continuum of time: as some trends ascend in popularity, others are in the process of losing their currency. Fashions and fads, alas, are not restricted to clothing and cosmetics alone. In an effort to keep pace with societal shifts, education, religion, government, and other institutions adapt and readapt to changing circumstances. The new programs characterizing these adjustments, however, are absorbed into practice at varying rates and, as a consequence, the early adopters of new ideas are in retreat from an innovation at precisely the same time when late adopters are considering its introduction. Furthermore, the permanence of an innovation is not entirely attributable to its intrinsic merits: dollar costs, difficulty of installation, consumer bias, and a spate of other factors invariably influence a movement's staying power. What should be recognized, therefore, is that modifications in instruction are not always completely rational, and that the mechanisms for introducing and sustaining educational change are often as important as the substance of the change itself.

The producers of instructional materials have long known that quality does not necessarily guarantee consumer interest. The response accorded a typical innovation can, in fact, range from complete lack of interest to wild infatuation. Bilingual education, to cite a case in point, has won considerable favor in some school districts but is ignored elsewhere, even in locations serving non-English-speaking children. It is precisely this unpredictable ebb and flow among movements that, over time, settles into a kind of natural balance and creates a semblance of stability in curricular evolution.

In this connection, the instructional controversies of the recent past have, once again, made it abundantly plain that, whatever else they do, the schools must be responsive to societal expectations. Indeed, it may well be that the conspicuous lack of definitive reform in schooling during the last half-century is primarily a result of the incompatibility between public expectations and the reform policies advocated by theorists. Forecasts regarding the social future, for example, suggest that larger amounts of leisure time and a dwindling supply of material artifacts will make the aesthetic side of our lives a good deal more important than in the past. Be this as it may, the introduction of new curricula emphasizing aesthetic education will progress slowly—if at all—until such programs are perceived as valuable by students and parents. One of the profession's vital needs, therefore, is to develop methods by which the mass communication media can be used to educate the public about education, and to help it rethink learning priorities. The need is sufficiently pressing, in fact, that it may well become a new specialization in curriculum leadership.

However the priorities are defined, it is highly unlikely that the citizenry will back away from its traditional expectations regarding college and vocational preparation. Most people believe that, as an integral part of their responsibility, the schools must equip their clients to "make it" in the social order. A curriculum that fails to meet this imperative—to facilitate entry into a job or an institution of higher education—is almost certain to have little more than a half-life. In sum, radical change in the schools cannot occur until corresponding change has transpired in societal values. Curriculum designers, however tempted, dare not seek to socialize for a world that does not exist.

Public agreement as to educational purpose, moreover, is not easily won. In the typical community, one routinely finds parents who prefer a formed approach to basic education as well as those who prize informal learning. Similarly, some opt for the development of vocational skill, while others want college entrance requirements emphasized, and so on. In seeking to accommodate these diverse interests, administrators tend to find eclecticism preferable to the risks of parental antagonism. They strive, consequently, to forestall criticism, to incorporate a bit of what each faction regards as important. As a result, the typical curriculum is an irresolute mélange that takes its definitive shape from the particular values of the individual doing the teaching. One of the major thrusts of future curriculum research, in fact, probably will focus on learning more about how the attitudes and beliefs of teachers influence what goes on in the classroom.

Parental concern for their children's postschool survival is, perhaps, largely responsible for the declining interest in open and informal education programs. It is not so much that parents question the virtues of these movements, but rather that they fear that the aims will interfere with the mastery of orthodox objectives. The child whose school hours have been devoted to humanistic experiences, for example, probably will not "know" as much standard detail upon graduation as the one who has subsisted on a steady diet of inductive drill. Moreover, since both university admission officers and employers discriminate on the basis of academic achievement rather than humanistic attributes, the student matriculating from an experimental curriculum may, in conventional competition, fall short of his peers who have been specifically groomed for academic entrance tests or the requirements of the marketplace. The recent fall in Scholastic Achievement Test scores (a possible consequence of reduced curricular structure and rigidity) has therefore provoked widespread alarm among parents. The odds are good, consequently, that the present period of neoconservatism will be extended, and that, as in progressive movements of former times, a promising and perhaps more virtuous curriculum will have been indicted without fair trial.

Another impetus to public conservatism regarding education emanates from the contemporary societal plight. Rising amounts of crime, governmental violations of public trust, seemingly irresolvable economic difficulties, and similar problems have produced a general sense of malaise, prompting many adults to assume naively that old-fashioned education will regenerate old-fashioned social stability. There is, of course, little basis for such presumptions, but the public will is not likely to be denied, and most schools will have little choice but to make at least a partial retreat to things past.

Beyond the liabilities imposed by consumer pressures, the curriculum also suffers from inept and clumsy changeover processes. Here, too, a new kind of specialization may be in the offing. It has now become clear, for example, that curriculum change must be managed with considerable skill and care. The failure of new programs often stems not from flaws inherent in the attempted innovations, but rather from faulty intro-duction techniques, inadequate preparations, and so on. As educational movements develop, a kind of vogue materializes and schools may sometimes rush into a new venture without adequate involvement of teachers, students, and parents. A useful innovation is thus abused, disappointing consequences accrue, and potentially valuable changes are prematurely abandoned.

Yet, for all these vicissitudes, several new movements are likely in the time immediately ahead: a renewed stress, for example, on citizenship education is likely; moral education will be given proportionately greater attention; the pendulum will swing even further in the direction of basic education; and enlarged programs in early childhood education will become increasingly commonplace.

These predictable trends aside, the prognosis for other aspects of the curriculum is somewhat conjectural. Although a grounaswell of interest in community-based education has arisen, its possibilities remain largely untested. There is little doubt, from a theoretical point of view, that students can acquire useful education through direct community experience and service, but the logistical problems are enormous. First, the society's willingness to make revolutionary changes in school and work laws remains largely unknown; second, a massive commitment, over an extended period of time, would be necessary before the long-range consequences of such programs could be assessed; and third, the budgetary factors are exceedingly uncertain.

Judging from the current state of the economy, it can perhaps no longer be assumed that the nation is able to afford the best of all possible educational systems. The facts seem to suggest that a major quest in future curriculum design will center upon procedures for delivering the same amount of learning at a reduced cost, or more learning for the same cost. It may be, then, that compromises of many sorts will need to be made. In any event, it seems probable that future curriculum developers will find it necessary to rethink the optimal arrangements through which the school's obligations can best be discharged.

It is to be hoped, therefore, that in the realignments and rebalancing that are to ensue, we can find cures for some of our curricular ills and initiate further improvements without losing the benefits attached to the movements described in the pages that follow.

Louis Rubin

Open Education: A Short Critique

It is possible that more confusion has evolved around the phenomenon known as "open education" than any other movement in recent educational history. Not only has open education been confused with "free schools," humanistic education, and alternative schools, but its basic spirit has been interpreted—and misinterpreted—in an endless variety of often contradictory ways. And, beyond all this, we have repeatedly failed to distinguish between "open classrooms" as learning environments characterized by large amounts of unencumbered space and "open classrooms" characterized by a particular conception of teaching and learning. The net result is that the movement has been victimized by an extraordinary amount of misuse and abuse. What schools must now do, consequently, is clarify the true nature of open education and acquaint teachers, in easily understood terms, with the essential ingredients in its recipe.

The basic ideology is rooted in the notion that children have a natural interest and desire in learning. Thus, when there is a conducive environment, and when the learning structure does not inhibit individuality, good education invariably will occur. What we have come to call relevance, as a result, is built into the fundamental philosophy itself; the curriculum, in short, is derived almost entirely from student interests and needs. There is no prescribed, predetermined, course of study, and lesson plans—when they exist at all—are sufficiently flexible that they can be altered whenever circumstances warrant. Given this great commitment to children's learning appetites, it is to be expected that in a healthy open education program children are happy, contented, and richly stimulated.

The critical distinctions between open and traditional education are that the goals are different, their means of attainment vary, and different outputs are yielded by each. A traditional program, for example, requires that a prescribed course of study be followed, leaving little leeway for accommodation to individual student interests. Its chief virtue, therefore,

Reprinted from Louis Rubin, *Curriculum Development: A Study Guide for Educational Administrators* (Fort Lauderdale, Fla.: Nova University Press, 1973), pp. 138–141; by permission.

is that we can determine in advance, to a very sizable extent, what the child will and will not learn. But in an open education climate precisely the opposite condition prevails; since the child's own intellectual interests serve as the educational point of departure, predetermined objectives must defer to individual whim, and specified learning outcomes cannot be guaranteed. One can, in a traditional program, specify that, say, the child will learn the principle of gravity; in an open system, on the other hand, no such specification is possible. The child's learning pursuits may bypass the subject of gravity and, instead, take him deep into the mysteries of, say, photosynthesis.

It follows logically, then, that because of these and other differences, the role of the teacher, too, must vary. Whereas in the traditional program teaching is closely affiliated with didactic pedagogy, through which the teacher dictates the child's course of learning, in an open educational setting the teaching seeks to facilitate and stimulate in whatever direction the learner's curiosity goes.

In fairness, it must be acknowledged that the proponents of open education have sometimes built their case upon a straw man. Traditional education—although formalized and structured—need not be depressing nor debilitating of the learner's spirit. In point of fact, there is abundant reason to believe that some learners thrive better in a traditional setting than in an open one. To wit, children sometimes find a lack of structure uncomfortable and large doses of freedom anxiety provoking. Similarly, provisions for the affective components of education, for the emotional feelings of students, can be made in both a traditional and an open format. As a result, one cannot in good conscience claim that an unstructured, open, curriculum is necessarily more "humanistic" than a structured, traditional, one.

Nor, to extend the point further, can one claim that an open curriculum automatically teaches the child to think more than a traditional one, or that multi-age grouping cannot exist in either situation, or that prescribed programs of instruction must, inevitably, prohibit individualization. Put another way, a large number of benefits habitually claimed by champions of one approach or the other can, in reality, be used with equal effectiveness in both.

There is nothing to prevent us from mixing both open and traditional procedures in the same classroom. Considering the breadth and diversity of contemporary curricula, there unquestionably is room for child-centered learning in the social studies, language arts, and sciences, as well as for prescriptive learning in fundamental skills. A teacher, for example, could organize a generally open learning environment and, simultaneously, provide traditional exercises and drills in arithmetic, reading, and so on. Where this is the case, it is likely that the child will master as many arithmetic and reading skills as in most other programs. Where, on the other hand, circumstances are left to chance and proven learning exercises are not imposed, the level of achievement is unpredictable. It is perhaps for this reason that the wiser proponents of open education have frequently forewarned us to start small and work carefully in making the transition from the old to the new.

Finally, it is particularly important to reinforce two other well-known arguments. First, the implications of the open education movement for teacher retraining are more deep-seated than may at first be apparent. The concept of openness makes special demands not only upon the teacher's techniques and skills, but, even more basically, upon a fundamental sense of role. Indeed, it may well be that many able teachers, by virtue of their personality and value orientation, are not suited to an unstructured learning situation. Some teachers, in brief, are more comfortable with systematic behavior, and some have an ingrained philosophical aversion to total pupil independence. Even more importantly, because of the enormous array of individual learning activities that must go on in the authentic open classroom, the teacher's workload is considerably more taxing than in the traditional milieu. Moreover, the teacher must be blessed with a high tolerance for ambiguity and pupil independence as well as a knack for spontaneous planning. Where such aptitudes are scant, the classroom benefits of openness are diminished proportionately.

Most presently certified teachers were trained to function in a traditional rather than an unstructured context. Consequently, a considerable amount of reorientation may need to preface successful teacher performance in the open classroom. This retraining must encompass a new set of trade tricks and a deep-seated grasp of what open education means, of the goals it can serve, and of the constraints it must respect.

Second, there is the ubiquitous problem of public acceptance. In view of the mounting concern regarding the adequacy of the nation's school system (whether the criticisms are valid or invalid), and despite the fact that our schools may be far better than the public imagines, in pursuing programs of open education it would be folly to ignore parental expectations. If a good many parents do not prize flexibility, relevance, and child-centered curricula—preferring, instead, traditional programs that equip their children to master a prescribed course of study and, thus, to gain admittance to convential universities or the work world—open education programs will breed an intensely dissatisfied constituency. Should this occur, the public's confidence in its school system will dwindle even further. An indispensable obligation, therefore, is attached to the expansion of the open education movement: through a variety of communication devices, the public-at-large must be made aware of the underlying rationale, and parents must be helped to understand that open and traditional curricula are different vintages, aimed at different goals, and yielding different advantages. Parent, child, and teacher, hence, must together collaborate in making responsible choices.

All the foregoing is not to say that the movement is without virtue. Its basic emphasis on trust, its abiding respect for the child, its presumption that children have a natural desire to learn which easily is destroyed by authoritarian mandate, its dedication to individuality in learning style and taste, its rejection of conformity for the sake of conformity, drudgery for the sake of discipline, and drill for the sake of repetition, its non-threatening environment, its preoccupation with a wide diversity of learning materials, and its conception of the teacher as facilitator rather than as dictator or inquisitor—all are welcome relief from the pedagogical sins of the past. In the best of such classrooms, children are remarkably motivated and content, and schooling becomes both pleasurable and productive. In the words of two of its foremost champions(*1*):

> Open Education is a way of thinking about children and learning. It is characterized by openness and trust; by spatial openness of doors and rooms; by openness of time to release and serve children, not to constrain, prescribe and master them. The curriculum is open to significant choice by adults and children as a function of the needs and interests of each child at each moment. Open Education is characterized by an openness of self. Persons are openly sensitive to and supportive of others—not closed off by anxiety, threat, custom and role. Administrators are open to initiatives on the part of teachers; teachers are open to the possibilities inherent in children; children are open to the possibilities inherent in other children, in materials, in themselves.
>
> In short, Open Education implies an environment in which the possibilities for exploration and learning of self and of the world are unobstructed.

The ultimate questions, however, are, first, whether such education provides children with all the requirements for postschool success, and, second, whether it enables children to cope with societal expectation. For if open education is a conception ahead of its time—one which the social system is not yet ready to absorb—the schools may face a difficult paradox. Should this be the case, balance, integration, and compromise will prove to be more desirable than arbitrary choice. In the immediate future, then, open education's greatest contribution may lie in its impetus to remediate some of traditional education's more serious faults, rather than in its force as a distinct alternative.

Reference

1. ROLAND BARTH and CHARLES RATHBONE, "Informal Education—The Open School: A Way of Thinking About Children, Learning, Knowledge," *Center Forum*, July 1969.

Operational Concepts

1. In the authentic open classroom, the curriculum is generated from students' interests and needs.

2. Open and nonopen curricula differ in goals, in learning processes, in teaching methodologies, and in ultimate outcomes.

3. Many useful teaching techniques heretofore associated with only the open or only the traditional curriculum could be used interchangeably with equal success.

4. Teaching roles, however, differ markedly in open and nonopen classes.

5. Public acceptance of open education depends upon the extent to which parents are willing to affirm its ends and, correspondingly, to forego the more conventional expectations associated with traditional curricula.

Implications

In all probability, neither the open nor the nonopen curriculum alone will satisfy current educational demands. An amalgam of some sort is more likely to serve our immediate purposes. Fortuitously, an integration of the two does not present serious problems. In keeping with the particular instructional objectives at hand, teachers can shift from one mode to the other; classroom lessons can utilize both structured and unstructured activities; and, given reasonable pedagogical adeptness, the interests of students can be capitalized upon either extemporaneously or through an established course of study.

Even though many pedagogical techniques are appropriate to both open and nonopen curricula, each curriculum also imposes its own special teaching requirements. Therefore, staff development programs should help teachers to acquire discrete methods with which to achieve both prescriptive (subject-centered) and nonprescriptive (open) goals. Similarly, evaluation and assessment procedures must also fit the particular objectives that prevail.

Recent trends suggest that, given proper orientation, parents have little difficulty in recognizing the particular merits of each approach and little objection to their fusion. In sum, not much is to be gained by arguments over the respective merits of the two philosophies; instead, attention should be focused on the ultimate quality of the learning that occurs and on the competencies manifested by students.

Gene Stanford
Albert Roark

Schools Without Walls

An encouraging educational trend in recent years has been the establishment of a number of experimental programs that utilize the community as the classroom. Perhaps the best known of these is the Philadelphia Parkway Program. According to John Bremer, the project's director:

> There is no school house, there is no separate building; school is not a place but an activity, a process. We are, indeed, a school without walls. Where do the students learn? In the city. Where in the city? Anywhere and everywhere. If students are to learn about television, they cannot do this apart from the studios and locations in which television is produced. So we use television studios and we use radio stations, and we use the museums, social service organizations, and we use the business community. The Philadelphia city government departments assist us—the Police Department, and the District Attorney's office to name only two. Parents help us. A large number of people help us and we are grateful. Everyone has a stake in education, everyone has a right and a duty to be involved, to participate. The community helps us in a great variety of ways; by providing us with meeting space, with resources, with instructors, even with total programs. And without the community's help we cannot do our job.

The Parkway Program was established as a four-year high school experience. It derived its students from previously existing schools in the city, who were chosen by lottery. Other programs "without walls" have been incorporated as alternatives *within* a preexisting high school. Below are excerpts from a description of Lexington (Massachusetts) High School's "Education Without Walls" program, which was established to serve volunteers from the regular school program:

> Some people would rather start their own business than read about management and marketing. Some people would rather be teachers' aides in a Boston school than read *Up the Down Staircase*. Some people would rather

Reprinted from Gene Stanford and Albert Roark, *Human Interaction in Education*, © 1974; by permission of Allyn and Bacon, Inc., Boston.

make a film than watch one. Some people would rather read Eldridge Cleaver than Charles Dickens. Some people would rather find out what makes a criminal tick than study crime statistics. Some people would rather find out what makes themselves tick than serve detention. Some people find that their high school experiences are not meaningful. They have developed interests and needs that simply are not met in the traditional school curriculum. It was in recognition of these people that the Education Without Walls Program was devised.

What Is "Without Walls" Education? Education is a total experience. The confines of the classroom and the limits of the academic disciplines are artificial. Man's natural curiosity cannot be contained within a school building. The community—indeed, the whole world—should be man's classroom. It is on this conception of education that Lexington's Education Without Walls Program is based.

How Was the Education Without Walls Program Created? The framework of the Program was developed in a summer workshop in 1968. Participants included: high school teachers, students, administrators, and consultants from the local businesses and the community. During the school year 1968–1969, Education Without Walls began to take more definite shape, as teachers and students met frequently to discuss the Program. The specific form of Education Without Walls was refined in a summer workshop in 1969.

Whom Is the Education Without Walls Program for? Approximately 100 seniors have volunteered for the Education Without Walls Program for the school year 1969–1970. Next year, the Program will be expanded to include juniors as well as seniors. Eventually, the Program will be open to all high school students. In Education Without Walls are students of widely varied backgrounds, interests, "ability levels," aspirations, attitudes and needs. There is no "typical" EWOW student.

How Will "EWOW" Meet the Diverse Needs of ALL of Its Students? *In the morning*—Mondays are devoted to a course designed to meet the universal desire of people to understand themselves. Students' own problems and questions form the basis for this Social Relations Course. A variety of interdisciplinary elective courses, based on the expressed interests of participating students, is offered on Tuesday through Friday. Students may also initiate their own individualized course, working with a teacher or a resource person from the community.

What are some of the elective courses being offered?

Film-making	The Black Man Revolts
City and Suburb	Science for Decision Making
Freud and the Boys	Sociology
The Criminal Mind	How to Use Your Money
Oceanography	The Psychology of Violence
American Music	Prisons, Jails and Reformatories
Managing a Small Business	Communist Theory

In the afternoon—Students may work at an occupation that will help to prepare them for a career. They may volunteer for service experiences in Lexington or in nearby communities or pursue independent research projects. Students may take courses offered in the High School outside of the Education Without Walls Program. They may observe or study occupations that interest them.

What will some of the students be doing in the afternoon?

Managing a Gas Station	Taking Flying Lessons
Studying a Foreign Language	Opening a Boutique
Elementary Teacher Aide	Research in Science Museum

How Will Students in the Education Without Walls Program Be Evaluated? Students and staff members will agree on a contract—a statement of the student's goals for his Education Without Walls experience. The student's performance will be assessed according to his achievement of the goals to which he has agreed. Students will receive a written evaluation, as well as letter grades, for the morning elective course. Each student will receive a written evaluation of his overall performance in the Program on the combined observations of his teachers, his consultants and his employer.

Other high schools have offered modified "without walls" programs on a smaller scale—often only to seniors. The Cultural Enrichment Program at Horton Watkins High School in suburban St. Louis allows a senior (who is able to complete graduation requirements before his final semester) to work on a project away from the school. A more elaborate program is the Senior Seminar at Denver's East High School. Here are excerpts from a description of the program that appeared in the annual report of the Colorado Outward Bound School:

For 93 seniors at Denver's East High School, the last semester of their senior year was unlike anything they had experienced before—in school or out. It began with two weeks on a remote stretch of beach on the Gulf of California in Mexico. With 8 teachers they sailed, hiked in the desert, climbed a high peak and each spent two very personal days alone—the sun, the ocean and the sea birds their only companions.

This was the unique beginning of a program called the Senior Seminar, designed to proved that learning is not restricted to the classroom, that experience is an effective and impressive teacher. The students were selected from volunteers to accurately reflect the student body of East. They were a mixture of middle class and ghetto, high achievers and dropouts.

Returning to Denver from their two weeks in Mexico, the students discovered that the entire city was to be their classroom and the people who worked and lived in that city their teachers. They studied Power and Politics by going to the State Legislature to participate in the actual business of running a state. They talked to lawmakers and lobbyists, to leaders of minority groups. They discovered first-hand how the democratic process works.

In the Urban Design module, another of the eight areas of investigation open to students, they collected trash with city sanitation crews, visited Urban Renewal construction sites, talked with city planners and explored the challenges that face a growing city. "City problems like pollution never bothered me before," wrote one student. "Seminar turned me on to the fact that they are my problems too, and I better do something about them before it is too late."

Additional modules—Hispano Culture, Space Technology and Man, Urban Arts—exposed the students to the diverse personality of the city.

"My Indian mother couldn't speak English, but we communicated with each other through the children. I never will forget them. I learned so much from them," was one girl's reaction to her week-long live-in with a Navajo family in the Southwest. Students became a part of their Indian families for the week, chopping wood, tending sheep and growing through their experiences. They followed up the live-in with a brief study of Indian anthropology at Prescott College in Arizona, and the very abrupt challenge of rock climbing and high rappel.

Floating the Yampa and Green Rivers of northwestern Colorado provided the culminating experience of the Seminar. Over the eons the rivers have carved from the land a geologic textbook of staggering proportions. Indian storage caves and petroglyphs gave a feeling of the timelessness of this ancient land. More recent history included stories of Spanish missionaries and explorers, and the outlaws Butch Cassidy and the Sundance Kid, who travelled through this remote and inaccessible region. Paleontology came to life in the Dinosaur Quarry, where the fossilized skeletons of long-extinct animals are being painstakingly excavated.

The experience of negotiating awsome rapids in the seven-man rubber rafts gave the greatest challenge. It was an exercise in group decision making and discipline. A mistake in the planning or the execution of a route through the rapids meant an overturned raft and an unexpected swim in the cold rough water.

Statistics provide some insights into the success of the Seminar. It had a dropout rate of 2.2 percent, compared with 11.5 percent for the remainder of the Senior class at East. The program, while not designed specifically for potential dropouts, had 25 low achieving, poorly motivated "target" students. By the end of the Seminar, 17 of these 25 had applied and been accepted at colleges.

But what of the human effects—the statistically immeasurable results of this intensive five months of living and learning together? One student summed up: "The mountains, ocean, beach, solo, live-in, river, dancing, acting, plastic furniture, environmental disasters, city—these are only classifications and the minutest part of the experience. Each module gave new thoughts and ideas, each opened a new world to explore." Another wrote: "I've gotten closer than ever before to people in a learning situation. I've discovered new depths in feeling and understanding people. And I've learned a lot about life and myself. It's going to be that way—learning and growing —for the rest of my life."

And finally: "The Seminar has meant more to me than anything I've ever done in my life. I'm really sorry it's all over. But I'm also happy, because I've reached a point in my life where I understand a lot more things and now I feel I know where I'm going—and have the strength and determination to get there."

ONE SCHOOL'S APPROACH: CHERRY CREEK'S OFF-CAMPUS PROGRAMS

We feel that we can best convey the possibilities for activities outside the classroom by describing the way one school district has made off-campus projects an integral part of its educational program.

The program we are going to describe is unique in that—to the best of our knowledge—it represents the first time a school district has *required* off-campus experiences for high school graduation (except, of course, in those schools-without-walls such as the Parkway Program, in which the total school program is based on interaction with the community). Other districts with programs that take students into the community have seen these experiences merely as frosting on the cake (as implied by the name itself of the Cultural Enrichment Program at Horton Watkins High School, which we mentioned earlier). Or, they have made the experiences into elective courses, such as East High School's Senior Seminar, which at least carries course credit. But the Board of Education of the Cherry Creek School District, serving an upper-middle-class suburb of Denver, considered out-of-school experiences so important that they passed Board of Education Policy #5127, which requires an "off-campus activity experience, i.e., work, exchange, outward bound, camp participation or a service activity experience. . . ." The policy, based on a rationale developed by Pino and Armistead, will first affect the graduating classes of 1975. In the meantime, other students are free to participate in the programs voluntarily and for credit.

According to Albert R. Thompson, Director of Off-Campus Programs, Cherry Creek High School offers experiences of four basic types, which students can utilize to meet the new graduation requirement: teaching, service, exchange, or paid work or unpaid career exploration. We will describe each of these areas in detail.

Teaching

At the present time there are two ways a high school student at Cherry Creek can gain some direct experience with the role of teacher: the Mutually Aided Learning Project (MAL) and the Students Assisting Teachers Program (SAT). In the former, the high school student has eight subject areas—math, computers, sciences, fine arts, social studies, industrial arts, English and French—in which he or she can work with elementary school children. In charge of each subject area is one high school teacher. During the first few weeks of the MAL program, these teachers instruct the students in the use of the instructional material and techniques that they will use. After several training sessions, the high school students begin to work at the elementary school.

385

Under the supervision of one or two elementary teachers, high school students work with small groups of children, one hour a day, three days a week. Mondays and Fridays are generally reserved for lesson planning, conferences with elementary or high school teachers and further training. MAL is a regularly scheduled course that meets at specific and constant times each day. The "Learning Assistants," as the high school students are called, receive one hour per week of in-service training in their specific subject matter area from high school teachers and are observed on-the-job by a high school teacher at least once a week. To qualify, students must be either juniors or seniors, must have the approval of their parents and school counselor, and must submit an application to and be interviewed by one of the high school teachers involved or the project director. They receive one-half unit of credit per semester, which counts toward graduation.

The SAT program has the same requirements as those for the MAL program, except that freshmen and sophomores are also accepted. Unlike the MAL Learning Assistants, SAT participants are not responsible for the instruction of any specific group of children but instead act as teachers' aides. They help the teacher with a mutually agreed upon combination of instructional, clerical and custodial tasks, spending at least four hours per week in the elementary or junior high school they have been assigned to. SAT is an independently scheduled course that is put into the student's unscheduled or "free" time. The participants receive one hour of pre-service orientation from the program coordinator and receive no in-service training in a specific subject matter area. Once per semester they are observed on-the-job by the program coordinator. Like the MAL Learning Assistants, they receive one-half unit of credit for each semester's participation. High school students are strongly encouraged to take SAT before taking MAL, but that is not required.

Service

The second type of program through which students can meet Cherry Creek's requirement of an off-campus experience is nonpaid service activity. The Educational Participation in Communities (EPIC) Program seeks to involve students, faculty and parents in activities that encourage them to be actively concerned about other people. Students are trained to work in cooperation with existing agencies in the Denver metropolitan area, such as Head Start, Interfaith Task Force, Denver elementary schools, Ridge Home, Tri-County Health Department, Denver Museum of Natural History and others. Students are assigned to teams composed of fifteen to twenty students, one faculty member and interested parents. Each student must work at his assignment regularly, attend feedback sessions and operate upon the format established by the team of which he is a part. Unstructured or after-school time is used for the on-the-job experiences, involving at least four hours per week including feedback sessions. Students in grades nine to twelve can participate, if their application is approved by the program coordinator after being signed by the students' parents. For satisfactory completion of the course, one-half unit of credit is awarded.

Exchanges

Students in grades ten to twelve at Cherry Creek, who have the permission of their parents and approval of their teachers, can participate in one of a wide number of exchange programs—visits by Cherry Creek students to other high schools in Colorado or across the nation, with a return visit to Cherry Creek by students from the other school. Most exchanges last for one full week, but some may take only one day and others may run for as long as three weeks. The main purpose of the exchange program is to develop better human relations between Cherry Creek students and high school students from other communities that are significantly different in one or more respects from the socially homogeneous suburb that Cherry Creek High School serves.

Through advance discussions, rap sessions during exchanges and reports to the exchange class upon their return, participants expand their ability to relate to new people and situations, some of which are profoundly different from what the students have known before. A variety of schools are included to help Cherry Creek students appreciate and enjoy the personal touch of the small rural school, to expose them to the excitement and challenge of a school with a high percentage of students from minority groups, or to give them an opportunity to experience the educational style of independent, nonpublic schools. Exchanges have been arranged with, or are pending with, the following schools among others: Carthage (Missouri) High School, Craig (Alaska) High School, St. Louis High School in Hawaii, East High School in Denver, Evanston Township (Illinois) High School, John Marshall High School in Oklahoma City, Aspen (Colorado) High School and Ringstead (Iowa) High School.

Participants must pay their own travel expenses and school lunch costs when visiting another school, but are provided free room and board in the home of a student from the school they are visiting. In order to meet his or her off-campus activity experience requirement, a student must visit another school for a minimum of five days and host a student who is visiting Cherry Creek for an additional five days or more.

Work and Career Exploration

A fourth approach to meeting the requirement for off-campus experience allows the student to work part-time at a job related to his career interests. Some jobs are paid; others constitute volunteer work. The current offerings in this area at Cherry Creek are almost limitless: Cooperative Office Education, Distributive Education, Related Careers in Human Resources, Child Management Specialist, Cosmetology, Nurse's Assistant and Hospital Orderly, Health Careers, Cooperative Career Development Program, Medical Careers, Engineering Chemistry and Physics Careers. In addition, students may also meet the requirement by taking one of the following courses and arranging to work part-time at a job related to the course content: Commercial Art, Workshop in Precious Metals, Woodworking II, Cabinet Making, Advanced Metals II, Electronics III, Vocational Auto Mechanics, Engineering Drawing, Mechanical Drawing, Vocational Agriculture II and III, Ornamental Vocational Horticulture II, Major Appliance Repair II, Data Processing IV and Graphic Arts II.

Other Programs

Cherry Creek High School also offers a number of special programs which give students direct experience in the world outside the classroom:

Mexican Culture Exchange Tour

Students spend two weeks during spring vacation touring historical, cultural and educational points of interest in Mexico under the guidance of teacher-chaperons. Preparation beforehand is required, and includes extensive readings in the Spanish language and five hours of lectures and group meetings.

Introduction to Community Service and Social Studies Field Techniques

This three-week summer course offers students a chance to become totally involved—on a twenty-four-hour-per-day, seven-day-a-week basis— in the multicultural life style of a rural community (near Cortez, Colorado) composed of Ute Indians, Spanish-speaking and Anglo-Americans. Students learn about the region through studying its ecology, geology, biology, history and culture, and through involvement in community service activities such as tutoring Head-Start children, excavating ancient Indian dwellings or serving as a cataloger in the Four Corners Museum.

Human and Nonhuman Ecology

This program involves participants in an interdisciplinary study of the natural and human environment, untilizing the Denver metropolitan area for a three-day study of urban ecology and then moving to the isolated setting of Pingree Park in the Roosevelt National Forest for an additional seven days. Sioux Indian students from Pine Ridge, South Dakota, also participate, and help the other participants learn about Indian culture through studying their crafts, cooking, beliefs and total life study. The program is staffed by a team of Cherry Creek High School counselors and teachers from the science, social studies, art, English and mathematics departments.

Find Out

This program provides an opportunity for students to explore a subject they are interested in while using educational methods other than the traditional classroom approach. In most cases, students involve themselves in experiences outside the school. One week is devoted to this alternative program, and every student at Cherry Creek is eligible to participate, but participation is not mandatory. School is in session for those who don't wish to take part.

The major responsibility for planning a given activity is left to the student. He first arranges to meet with groups of other students and faculty with similar interests to see if projects can be combined into group experiences. But a student may elect to work individually. He then fills out an "intent form" explaining the educational value of the proposed activity and giving a brief description of it. A screening committee considers the intent forms and either approves or disapproves them. Those groups or individuals with approved intent forms must then submit a formal proposal, which goes through a second screening committee. Those groups whose proposals are approved can then begin to make plans for their activity. Limitations on Find Out activities include the following: Students must spend the equivalent of one week of school engaged in the activity, they must have parental permission, they must have faculty sponsorship and they must undertake all of the expenses themselves. The proposed activity must be within the law and cannot expose the participants or the district to legal action. It must also be an educational experience that is beneficial to the student and can be shared with others and thus benefit them.

A total of 1,074 students participated in Find Out the first year it was offered. Their activities can be categorized as follows: Career Exploration (such as working with schools or hospitals, or visiting businesses), Independent or Small Group Activity (including learning to fly a plane, doing library or laboratory research, producing a film or play), Trips (including visits to colleges and universities, other schools in Colorado, the state penitentiary and reform school, Chicago (via train), Mexico and Hawaii), Outdoor Experiences (including winter survival techniques) and Large Group Experiences (including a crash course in jewelry making and a study of the court and criminal systems). Students' projects carried titles such as the following: "Weaving Lessons," "What Does It Take to Get an Airplane into the Air?" "Observing Procedures in a Veterinary Clinic," "Working with Denver Police Department," "Creating Toys and Games for Porter Hospital," "Working and Researching Project in Pre-Columbian Section in Denver Art Museum" and "Studying in Isolation and Solitude."

Operational Concepts

1. Schools should experiment with a variety of nontraditional curricula, since traditional subject matter may have limited utility in equipping students with essential life skills, and since other learning experiences in the social community may be equally or more useful.

2. The psychological usefulness of "learning contracts" is as yet unclear; studies are needed to determine whether such agreements genuinely help to increase student commitment, responsibility, and autonomy.

3. Experimentation with "learning contracts" should be restricted to authentic educational activities. For example, experiences such as "a day alone with the sun, ocean, and seabirds as companions" may have merit but they are not educational, at least in the present pragmatic usage of the term.

4. Although some schools have, with appreciable success, permitted students to engage in various activities (community service, paid and unpaid work experience, and the tutoring of other students) in lieu of traditional course of study, the central issue is not whether these experiences are profitable or educational, but whether they constitute the most useful expenditure of the learner's time.

390

Implications

   The motives underlying experimental curricula are clearly defensible. One could argue, in fact, that even more imaginative experiments might be tried here and there. Despite the usefulness of the experimentations, however, the ultimate potential of the ideas remains unknown. Risks are certainly inherent. Will those who control access to the vocations regard unconventional education as useful? Can the society's need for an informed citizenry be satisfied by any learning activity that is pleasing to the learner? Is a knowledge of, say, history as useless as we are sometimes led to believe? Should there be any distinction between what we regard as an authentic educational experience and other useful, but non-educational, experiences? Until these questions are answered—and until it is clear that the public is willing to accept substantial departures from tradition, at least some caution would seem prudent.

   In the upper grades of the secondary school, the usual courses of instruction have limited appeal for some students. To overcome this problem, schools have sought to try out other activities that students might find a good deal more attractive. From a theoretical point of view, therefore, the question is: should schools teach whatever students enjoy so as to maintain their holding power, or would it be better to deliver a body of essential knowledge and, at the same time, seek to enhance its student appeal?

   Our dilemma, clearly, is that the ancient disputes regarding the practical knowledge of greatest value must again be debated in a contemporary context. The conclusions we reach, moreover, must reflect a number of considerations: student expectations, basic conceptions of what constitutes an educated person, and the requirements for a satisfying life once schooldays have come to an end.

Community Involvement

Merle B. Karnes
R. Reid Zehrbach

Flexibility in Getting Parents
Involved in the School

How many times have you gone to parent teacher association meetings for the handicapped only to find that the teachers outnumber the parents? How often have you said, "We teachers care more about the handicapped children than their parents; look, they don't even come to the meetings." When you stopped to analyze the poor attendance, were you able to get beyond blaming the weather, the night of the week, the presence of younger children in the home, or the parents' lack of interest?

Did you ever put yourself in the role of a parent and imagine what he is thinking? For example, he may say to himself:

> The teachers don't understand my problem. The speaker at the meeting talked about bed wetting. My kid doesn't wet the bed. I need help with getting my kid to talk better. Why do teachers set up lectures for me? Why don't they show me how to help my child, let me practice doing it, and tell me when I'm doing it right?

Reflection about the kinds of people who attend parent meetings reveals that there is one type of parent—individuals who are more outgoing, are reasonably comfortable in social situations, and find support in being with other people—who typically attend the meeting. Other parents you'll undoubtedly be able to identify at a meeting are those who come to the first meeting to get acquainted with their child's teacher, but once their interest is satisfied no longer feel a need to return. The question remains, "Who are the other types of individuals who never show up at a parent meeting?" A few may come to parent teacher conferences because they know they will get to talk personally and privately with their child's teacher. They come because they will receive the courtesy of an individual approach and not face the strain involved in social settings. This still leaves a large number of individuals who do not come to school because they have to

Reprinted from Merle B. Karnes and R. Reid Zehrbach, "Flexibility in Getting Parents Involved in the School," *Teaching Exceptional Children,* Vol. 5, No. 1, 1972, pp. 8–19; by permission of the publisher.

work, fear the teacher will tell them bad news, feel the teacher has nothing to offer them, find it too painful to talk about their handicapped child, or have had poor past experiences with teachers or authority figures in the school.

One interpretation of the above observations is that parents of the handicapped are first of all parents and, thus, have feelings similar to those of any parent about his child. In other words, parents of the handicapped have needs, hopes, desires, wants, and frustrations like any other parents. One cannot treat all parents alike any more than one can treat all handicapped children alike. To involve parents in the process of educating their handicapped child, one must utilize a variety of techniques, activities, and approaches designed to meet their individual needs.

PARENT NEEDS VARY

The goals of parent involvement will be almost as varied as the number of parents in the program. Some parents will need to be involved because they need to learn new ways to teach their child in the intellectual or cognitive areas. Other parents will need to learn how to foster their child's social and emotional development. Other parents may need the emotional support derived from the teacher and other parents of handicapped children; still others may need to gain information as to where to seek answers to or help with problems such as legal rights of the handicapped, technical schools for training the handicapped, tax deductions specific to the handicapped.

The success of a parental involvement program is contingent upon:

1. The attitude of the professional—there must be a positive attitude which connotes that parents have a contribution to make to the growth of their child.
2. The recognition that there is more than one way to involve parents— parents have individual needs that must be recognized to help them select the best way to involve themselves in the educational program of their child at a given time.
3. The belief that each parent is capable of growth—the amount of growth of parents will vary. The extent to which a parent progresses is dependent upon the degree to which the teacher changes, expands, and increases the breadth and depth of activities in the parent involvement program.

During the remainder of this article an attempt will be made to describe a variety of new and tried techniques for involving parents, taking into consideration the needs of parents and the activities that are consonant with these needs. The first three approaches that will be discussed are the more traditional ones: (1) group meetings with a speaker, (2) small group discussion meetings, and (3) individual conferences. These approaches will be related to specific parental needs rather than assuming that they meet the needs of all parents if they would just participate. Guidelines are delineated for obtaining maximum benefit from each approach.

LARGE GROUP MEETINGS OFFER GENERAL KNOWLEDGE

Typically, group meetings are designed to provide information quickly and easily to relatively large groups of people. Ordinarily, the information tends to be general and limited to a given topic. An outside speaker makes a presentation which often uses semitechnical vocabulary that confuses more than clarifies concepts for the audience. Typically, the topic is chosen by the professionals and is judged to be what the parents need to hear. A question period usually follows the speech, and as a general rule there is little audience participation. Refreshments are served at the close of the meeting in order to generate more informal interactions.

In general, the advantages of large group meetings are that a timid individual can sit quietly and listen without feeling ill at ease and out of place. The professional is often able, especially if experienced, to select topics that are relevant and critical but of which the parent is not aware. Likewise, the professional is able in many instances to identify competent speakers who present their material in an interesting manner.

The disadvantages of group meetings are that all of the individual needs of the parents cannot be met. The very shy individual is reluctant to ask questions in a group or in any way call attention to himself. Further, he is likely not to attend in the first place. Those who have had unpleasant experiences associated with school attendence will avoid such encounters with school personnel by staying away. Some who are reluctant to face their problems will excuse their inattendance by saying to themselves, "There will be so many there, I won't be missed anyway."

The astute teacher will, then, be able to determine those parents that respond positively to the large group approach by observing those who come and remain throughout the refreshment period. She will also realize that those who do not remain for the informal part of the meeting may be responding to pressures at home to leave early or to feelings of social insecurity in the less structured environment.

Parent Involvement and Timing Make for Success

One of the goals of the teacher is to maximize the value of group meetings for those who are ready to attend. The authors, through direct

394

experiences in working with parents of the handicapped, have found that the most successful meetings are characterized by:

1. Parent involvement in the selection of topics, speakers, and date and hour of meeting.
2. Meetings scheduled no more often than once monthly.
3. Notification of the meeting through the use of several media (written flyers or notes, telephone calls through a parent network, newspaper notices, radio announcements).
4. Timing. There should be an initial notice at least a month in advance and followup reminders four and seven days prior to the meeting.
5. Dynamic speakers and use of visual aids.
6. Arrangements for baby sitting at the site of the meeting.
7. Car pools or other transportation arrangements.
8. Involving parents in committee work to support the group.
9. A friendly, but not imposing, atmosphere increases the likelihood of parents returning to future meetings.
10. Avoidance of the solicitation of funds at the meeting.

Following the group meeting, the teacher should record the names of those in attendance and any pertinent observations or remarks made by parents that can enable the teacher to gain more insight into the needs of individual parents. Following the above, the teacher should become better able to guide the parents into activities that match their individual needs. The teacher should not assume that the parents who were not at the meeting were disinterested in their child and unwilling to become involved with the school. Rather, she should begin to gather information from all available sources that will help her plan to reach nonattending parents through a new or different approach.

SMALL GROUP MEETINGS GET TO SPECIFICS

The next approach the teacher might use is small group meetings in which an attempt is made to bring together four to seven parents who have similar needs, e.g., parents whose children are retarded in language. Typically such groups are held either at school or in the home of a parent or the teacher at a time that is most convenient for all concerned. The social structure is more informal and the opportunities for interaction are greater than in the larger group. The small group setting lends itself to the consideration of more socially and emotionally laden content than the larger group. The somewhat reticent person may gain confidence and feel more free in this less imposing setting. This is particularly true when the meeting is held outside the confines of the school, usually in the home of a parent.

Disadvantages may occur if groups form cliques so that other interested parents find it difficult to be accepted in a closely knit group. Another disadvantage is that the small group approach is time consuming for the teacher. It is also difficult to obtain highly qualified outside speakers, since one is reluctant to take the time of a busy person to speak to such a small group.

Individual Needs and Concerns Important

Some of the characteristics that enhance the success and assure the attendance at small group meetings are:

1. Frequent meetings, usually as often as once weekly.
2. Related or interrelated topics chosen by the parents.
3. Responsibilities rotated for planning and conducting meetings.
4. Articles, books, and cassette tapes, reviewed during the week, as the basis for meetings.
5. Careful attention given to the individual needs of the group—social, emotional, and intellectual.
6. Content of the meeting challenging, yet on a level where comprehension and assimilation are possible for all participants.
7. Social amenities such as dress and language compatible with the group needs.
8. A relaxed but goal oriented atmosphere.
9. Teacher participation but not in dominant or condescending manner. A first name basis for interacting may be appropriate for one locale and inappropriate for another.
10. Small group setting which may offer an opportunity to plan ways of helping new parents or reluctant participants to become involved in activities suited to their needs. Focusing the group on this kind of problem enhances its cohesiveness.
11. Meetings held for definite, predetermined periods of time, usually not exceeding two hours.
12. A teacher who is alert to the growth and development of the group members so that an individual who progresses to the point where he has outgrown one group can be encouraged to shift to a more appropriate group.
13. Group goals geared to meet the individual needs of members of the group.
14. A teacher who is sensitive to the need for changes and provides neces-

sary support and guidance. The teacher should view such changes as growth.

Information on pertinent materials emerging during the meeting should be recorded by the teacher following the meeting.

INDIVIDUAL CONFERENCES
PERMIT FLEXIBILITY

Once the teacher has organized, with the help of interested parents, the large and small group meetings, it will become obvious that she is still not meeting the needs of all parents. She may well plan to meet with individual parents who may be part of a large or a small group or both but who have needs that are not being met in a group. In addition, she will be able to identify and meet with those parents who have not, for a number of reasons, become involved in the large or small group meetings.

One of the basic characteristics of a conference is its inherent flexibility in terms of time, place, and content. Conferences can be held before school, during a lunch hour, after school, or in the evening or weekends depending upon the availability of the parent and teacher. The content can be very specific and highly confidential. The parent can be more comfortable in discussing some materials than he would be in a group setting, and there can be more interaction. The language of the teacher can be more closely geared to the cognitive level of the individual parent rather than geared to the average of a group.

The success of individual conferences will be enhanced by:

1. Making the parent feel comfortable and accepted.
2. Being highly sensitive to individual needs and responding in ways to assure that needs are met.
3. Maintaining an objective yet warm relationship.
4. Avoiding the promotion of dependent, or too close, personal relationship.
5. Keeping the discussion focused on material relevant to the well-being of the handicapped child and avoiding the elicitation of irrelevant material the teacher is not professionally trained to handle. Teachers should not try to play the role of a therapist.
6. Referring complex cases to another staff member or through another staff member to an outside agency. For example, discussion of marital problems is outside the teacher's realm of training. The social worker may be the person to encourage a referral to outside the school.
7. Discussing parent conferences with the appropriate school staff members—principal, psychologist, social worker—to help maintain objec-

tivity and to increase skills in involving parents meaningfully in the education of their child.

8. Initiating conferences on a prescheduled and preplanned basis. A teacher should not just drop in on a parent unannounced.

9. Establishing a specific time limit for each conference. Short conferences occurring more frequently are more productive than prolonged conferences widely spaced.

10. Keeping records of each conference. Notes should be recorded as soon after a conference as possible. These notes should be carefully reviewed and considered when planning the next conference.

11. Establishing continuity of materials covered during conferences. At the close of a conference it is desirable to summarize and to jointly plan for the next conference. The parent should feel at the close of the conference that something specific was accomplished and that future plans have been established.

TEACHING THROUGH PARENTS

In addition to large and small group meetings and individual conferences, there are a variety of activities for involving parents that have come to the forefront in recent years. These activities tend to cluster into three categories: (1) promotion of specific selective changes in parental behavior through *direct* approaches, (2) promotion of knowledge and attitudinal changes through *indirect* approaches, and (3) expansion of professional services through the involvement of parents.

Parents Can Become Behavior Modifiers

One of the most important changes in programs for parents stems from the work of the behavior modification group who have developed a variety of related procedures for helping parents learn how to make specific changes in their own and their child's behaviors. The basic thrust of this approach requires the parent to specify exactly which child behaviors are his concern, gather data to record the frequency of such behavior, develop a specific procedure for changing the child's behavior, and then note the degree of change in the child's behavior. Implementation of this procedure requires that the teacher first learn the new techniques. Then the teacher must train the parent to use the technique. This technique typically requires rewarding the child's positive behavior and ignoring his negative behavior. Rewards can take a variety of forms from M&Ms to verbal praise, from listening to records to trips to the beach.

Parents who can profit most from this approach would appear to be those who are fairly stable, can be consistent, and have a strong need to

398

bring about positive change in their child's behavior. Further, the behavior that needs to be changed will likely occur with reasonable frequency.

An advantage of this approach is that is it flexible enough to be used in the classroom, at home, or in the community. Once the parent has learned the approach and is convinced that is can be used successfully, it can then be used to modify or change other behaviors of the child. One disadvantage of this approach is that initially parents find it hard to reward the positive behavior and ignore the negative behavior they wish to extinguish. Parents tend to be reluctant to believe the approach will work. In addition, ignoring a selected behavior of a child in the home may create problems for other family members. Since the principles work, *misapplication* can lead to negative results just as appropriate application can lead to positive results.

Programed Material Teaches Specific Skills

Another approach that is emerging is the use of packages of programed material through which parents receive specific instruction on how to teach specific skills or knowledge. This approach may be found in 16 mm film presentations, in multimedia types of presentations, and in pamphlets. The differentiating characteristic between these materials and others is the specificity with which it attacks a particular problem. For example, a film may be on an exact procedure for teaching a child to put on his clothes rather than on the general topic of self-help.

The strength of such an approach is that a parent can learn the procedure quickly, the procedure will likely be successful, and the parent will know in advance exactly what he is to learn. The weakness is essentially the obverse, that is, a parent who does not need that particular skill will tune out or not show up for the viewing of the film or he may show up for one film and not return for others. As is true in all parental involvement activities, the needs of the child and his parents must be matched with the activity. Individualization to meet parental needs is a must. Where possible, the teacher should plan her overall program so that a parent has access to the specific film or other material that he needs when he needs it. It is highly desirable, when finances permit, for equipment and materials to be made available to parents to check out and use at home. When such is possible, not only one parent but both parents, siblings, relatives, and even neighbors may benefit from the use of the materials.

Teacher Demonstrations Followed by Parent Practice

Demonstrations with the handicapped child, conducted by teachers or by other parents in the school setting or at home, have proven fruitful. Such demonstrations focus on the development of specific skills followed by the actual practice of the parent with his child. One often overlooked activity is teaching the parent how to read a book to his child. During the demonstration the teacher will likely need to point out to the parent how to hold the book, how to direct the child's attention to specific pictures, how to ask questions, and how to reinforce a child for appropriate responses. Other skills which may be taught are identifying objects with the sounds the objects make, learning specific meanings of prepositions, and sorting objects according to specific colors, shapes, or sizes.

Specific Lesson Plans Speed Parent Learning

The use of a specific lesson plan written for parents may enhance the speed with which the parent learns the technique or skill. Specific lesson plans often can be used by parents without further demonstration, especially if the plans provide information regarding objectives, materials to be used, and step by step procedures for using them. Once parents become proficient in learning new skills through lesson plans, they will be able to readily reinforce in the home skills taught in school.

Lesson plans can be written by parateachers, parents, and volunteers after being taught how to write them by teachers. Lesson plans must be clear, concise, easy to follow, and must make use of easily obtainable materials (see Figure 1).

FIGURE 1 Sample Lesson Plan: *Shape Lotto*

This activity will help the child:
1. Learn the names of basic geometric shapes.
2. Match shapes that are the same.
3. See form in his environment.

You will need:
1. Three pieces of stiff paper or cardboard—about 12" × 16".
2. Ruler, scissors, crayons.
3. Large envelope.

To make the Shape Lotto:
1. Using a black crayon and ruler, divide one piece of cardboard into eight equal spaces. Draw a shape in each space, following the diagram.

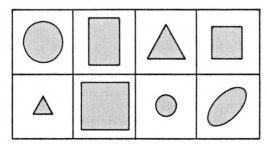

This is the game card.
2. Draw the same shapes on each of the other two pieces of cardboard. Cut them out. These are the individual shape pieces used in playing the game. There should be sixteen pieces.

Emphasize these words:
1. Shape.
2. Circle.
3. Square.
4. Triangle.
5. Rectangle.
6. Oval.

To use the Shape Lotto:

The First Day: Place the game card on a table in front of your child. "Look at all the shapes." Point out each shape, helping your child trace it with his finger. Talk about each one as he traces it: "This shape goes around and around. See how this shape has corners." Ask your child to repeat the word "shape." Then, referring to one set of the individual shapes, say, "All of these shapes have names. Let's talk about their names." Hold up a circle. "This shape is a circle. Say circle with me. Now feel the circle. Can you find a circle just like this one on the game board? Put this one on top of it." Repeat this procedure until each shape has been named and placed on the game board. Then say, "Now, let's put the game back in the envelope. First, give me the circles." Ask for each shape by name, helping your child find the right one.

The Second Day: Let your child hold the game board. Review the shape names. "Yesterday we talked about the names of these shapes. Let's see if you remember them. Show me the circle. Say, 'This is a circle.' Now, find the square." Repeat this procedure for all of the shapes. Give your child time to find the right shape but be ready to help him if he is not sure. After each shape has been named, give him both sets of individual shapes. "I will watch while you play the game. Put these shapes where they belong on the game board." Show your child what you mean by selecting one of the shapes and placing it on top of the matching shape on the game board. Encourage your child to name the shapes as he works.

The Third Day: Place one set of individual shapes in front of your child; help him name them. "Let's play a new game with the shapes. First, you choose a shape; then we'll look all around the house to see how many things we can find that have the same shape." Repeat the game with the remaining shapes.

The Fourth Day: Place one set of individual shapes in front of your child and ask him to name them as you point to each one. Collect the shapes. "Let's play a guessing game with the shapes." Have your child put his hands behind his back. Put a shape in his hands and ask him to identify the shape by feeling it. After he has guessed the names of the shapes, lay them in a row on the table. "Look carefully at the shapes because in a minute I will take one away and you will have to tell me which one is missing." Ask your child to hide his eyes while you remove a shape. Repeat this activity with several other shapes.

The Fifth Day: Place both sets of shapes in a pile in front of the child. "The shapes are all mixed up. Can you find all the shapes that are the same and put them together?" Show your child what you mean by finding all the circles and putting them in a group. Then put them back with the other shapes. "Now you do it by yourself." As soon as your child finishes, ask him to name the groups of shapes.

Other ways you can help your child:
1. Point out shapes in the environment: plates, glasses, knobs, and clocks are circles; windows and tables are squares; doors are rectangles.
2. Help your child make designs from the shapes.

3. Help him draw and cut out shapes.
4. Let him find shapes in picture magazines.

Parents Acquire Skills in the Classroom Setting

Teaching in the classroom can be a direct approach for helping the parent acquire competencies in teaching other children or his own. The professional teacher can train the parent to teach certain skills through workshops which include demonstrations, use of audiovisual aids, a critique of the teaching of others, and the direct implementation of a carefully written lesson plan. By training the parent to teach in the school setting, the teacher can anticipate that the parent will transfer to the home environment some of his knowledge about stimulating the growth of the handicapped child. The way the teacher differentiates between viewing teaching in the classroom as a direct attempt to influence a parent's behavior rather than an indirect approach or as an extension of herself is based on the goal the teacher holds for the parent. To be classified as direct intervention, the teacher's greatest concern should be for creating change in the parent's behavior as quickly and efficiently as possible.

The direct approaches used to promote changes in parental behaviors and to elicit appropriate behaviors in children reviewed here do not require the transfer of general knowledge to a specific situation. These approaches give specific assistance in dealing with the teaching of specific skills. This does not imply, however, that what is learned in one situation cannot be transferred to another. The parent gets immediate feedback and reinforcement when his efforts are successful. A disadvantage is that since the instruction is specific, the parent may have difficulty generalizing to similar problems. By planning a series of activities, the teacher may be able to develop a broad range of skills in the parent which may then promote a more generalized approach to problems.

Classroom Provides Indirect Learning Situation

Among the techniques categorized as indirect approaches for involving parents in an educational program for the handicapped is the previously mentioned teaching in the classroom. In this instance, parent with useful knowledge and skills such as talents in art, music, crafts would be encouraged to participate in the classroom program for the alleged purpose of helping the classroom teacher; however, the purpose of the teacher is to teach the parent, indirectly, those skills and knowledge she would like the parent to learn. This approach is most useful for those parents who resist acknowledging their child's handicaps, yet who can be challenged and allowed to save face by using the parent's strength to help train a weakness. One of the important attitudes of the professional teacher should be that she conveys to the parent confidence that the parent has something important to offer in the classroom and subtly encourages development in areas of weakness.

Parents Teach Each Other

Another activity is to have one parent who has demonstrated a good teaching skill reinforce this skill by helping another parent acquire the skill. The above can be accomplished by having one parent go to the home of another and demonstrate a skill with that parent's child. The visited parent should then actually practice with his child under the guidance of the skilled parent. Another activity is to have a parent develop teaching plans and interpret the plans to another parent who can implement the plan with his child.

Cassette Tapes Convenient for Listening

In recent years, cassette tapes prepared by professionals, or in some cases by parents themselves, serve as ueful tools in conveying knowledge and developing attitudes among parents. This approach is felt to be indirect since the parent has to assimilate what he hears and apply it to his own situation. One advantage of using cassette tapes is that a parent can listen to the tape when it is convenient without disrupting household tasks. The tape can be repeated as many times as the parent feels the need. In addition, the approach is inexpensive. Some parents may own a cassette while other parents may need to borrow the equipment from the school.

Cassette tapes can be on any topic—"Sibling Relationship with the Handicapped Child," "Use of Reinforcement Procedures to Shape Behavior," "Handling the Problem of Masturbation," "Promoting Expressive Language." Such tapes also lend themselves readily to stimulating group discussions. Because this approach is somewhat unique it holds the attention of parents and encourages interaction. Another advantage of the individuals making tapes is that, in reading and thinking about a problem, the person learns a great deal himself. The very fact it is one of the group revealing his thinking makes it particularly interesting to the others. To enhance the quality of the tapes for group presentation, a small, inexpensive portable speaker can be obtained and easily plugged into most recorders.

Field Trips and Newsletter Nurture Enthusiasm

Taking a field trip to another program to search out new ideas by observing how other parents are contributing to an educational program for handicapped children can be a very worthwhile experience. Such parents usually come back to their own programs with a fresh outlook and renewed enthusiasm. Sometimes they return thinking that the parents in their program are doing a very good job; however, a field trip usually spurs them on to put forth greater efforts because of the acquisition of new and different ideas.

Publication of a newsletter is another way parents can be involved in a program. The act of collecting, integrating, and preparing ideas, experiences, and techniques for publication can be greatly beneficial to those individuals preparing the publication and, of course, provides a service to the readers—other parents or family members. Parents, like any other persons, like to see their names in print. When their names are printed because they have made some positive contribution, it is even more meaningful. Further, news about a handicapped child can often be stated positively so the parents can feel good about the reported progress of their child.

Parents Encourage Community Support

To obtain support for their programs, parents can make presentations at community meetings, write articles for newspapers, be interviewed on the radio or a television program, make presentations to government bodies. Such activities often prove challenging to fathers, hence this is one way they can be indirectly involved in the program.

Advisory boards with parent representation have become almost universal. Parents on such boards receive indirect training because they are required to consider and make decisions on the total program and thus on their handicapped child.

PARENT INVOLVEMENT INCREASES AVAILABLE SERVICES

Once a parent has become involved in a program and has learned many useful skills, his continued involvement can best be viewed as extending the skills of the professionals rather than enhancing his own skills. A parent will benefit from the following activities because they reinforce through practice the knowledge, attitudes, and skills he has developed. The most obvious activity that extends a professional's service is teaching in the classroom. With young children especially, a high adult–child ratio for handicapped children is a must. The progress of the handicapped child is dependent in no small measure on the degree of adult–child interaction. The services of a trained parent can greatly multiply the effectiveness of a professional teacher.

Likewise, parents can serve as aides to nurses, social workers, psychologists, and coordinators of parents and volunteers. Here again, the needs and talents of each parent must be studied carefully. Not all parents are ready or have the potential to serve as aides to the above mentioned professionals. They must first have the necessary personal qualities and then they must be specifically trained by professionals. Often the training can be started by assigning them to a specific, simple task and then by increasing the scope and complexity of responsibilities as they, the parents, become more proficient.

Some parents find it exceedingly difficult to develop the interpersonal relationships that make it possible for them to work with adults. Such parents, however, are often able to do routine tasks such as keeping records, maintaining a toy lending library or parent book library, or checking out equipment to parents. Repair and maintenance of equipment is a needed service which many fathers are able to supply. Making instructional materials for the classroom or the lending library is still another way parents can contribute.

The professionals should keep in mind that anything a parent can do to contribute to the educational program of the handicapped children will release her energies for developing an improved program.

Selected Readings

BADGER, E. D. A mother's training program—The road to a purposeful existence. *Children,* 1971, *18*(5), 168–173.

BECKER, W. C. *Parents are teachers in child management programs.* Champaign, Ill.: Research Press, 1971.

BROPHY, J. E. Mothers as teachers of their own preschool children: The influence of socioeconomic status and task structure on teaching specificity. *Child Development,* 1970, *41*(1), 79–97.

BURNEY, V. K. Home visitation and parent involvement. *Today's Education,* 1971, *60*(7), 10–11.

DeROSIS, H. A. A primary preventive program with parent groups in public schools. *Journal of School Health,* 1969, *39*(2), 102–109.

EMMRICH, W. The parental role, a functional-cognitive approach. *Monograph of the Society for Research in Child Development,* 1969, *34*(8), 1–71.

FRAIBERG, S. Intervention in infancy: A program for blind infants. *Journal of the American Academy of Child Psychiatry,* 1971, *10*(3), 381–405.

FREDERICKS, H. D. Parents educate their trainable children. *Mental Retardation,* 1971, *9*(3), 24–26.

FRESHOUR, F. W. Beginning reading: Parents can help. *Reading Teacher,* 1972, *25*(6), 513–516.

FUDALA, J. B. Utilization of parents in a speech correction program. *Exceptional Children,* 1972, *38*(5), 407–412.

GALLOWAY, C., and GALLOWAY, K. C. Parent classes in precise behavior management. *Teaching Exceptional Children,* 1971, *3*(3), 240–243.

GOLDSTEIN, S. B., and LANYON, R. I. Parent clinicians in the language training of an autistic child. *Journal of Speech and Hearing Disorders,* 1971, *36*(4), 552–560.

GOMBERG, A. W. Can disadvantaged parents motivate children for reading? *Record,* 1970, *71*(3), 451–454.

GORDON, I. J. *Baby learning through baby play: A parent's guide for the first two years.* New York: St. Martin's Press, 1970.

GORDON, I. J. Parent involvement in early childhood education. *National Elementary Principal,* 1971, *51*(1), 26–30.

GORDON, I. J. Early child stimulation through parent education. *International Journal of Early Childhood,* 1971, *3*(1), 26–36.

GRAY, S. W. Home visiting programs for parents of young children. *Peabody Journal of Education,* 1971, *48*(2), 106–111.

HARMER, W. R. To what extent should parents be involved in language programs for linguistically different learners. *Elementary English,* 1970, *47*(7), 940–943.

HELLMUTH, J. (ed.) *Disadvantaged Child.* Vol. 2. Seattle: Weikart, D. P., and Lambie, D. Z., 1967.

HERSEN, M. J. Behavior modification approach to a school phobia case. *Journal of Clinical Psychology,* 1970, *26* (1), 128–132.

HERSTEIN, R. Mother-child workshops. *School Arts Magazine,* 1970, *69*(7), 18–19.

JOHNSON, B. Taping parent opinion. *Instructor,* 1970, *79*(7), 144–145.

JOHNSON, J. M. Using parents as contingency managers. *Psychological Reports,* 1971, *28*(3), 703–710.

JONES, E. Involving parents in children's learning. *Childhood Education,* 1970, *47*(3), 126–130.

KARNES, M. B., STUDLEY, W. M., WRIGHT, W. R., and HODGINS, A. S. An approach for working with mothers of disadvantaged preschool children. *Merrill-Palmer Quarterly,* 1968, *14*, 174–184.

KARNES, M. B., TESKA, J. A., HODGINS, A. S., and BADGER, E.D. Educational intervention at home by mothers of disadvantaged infants. *Child Development,* 1970, *41*, 925–935.

KATZ, D. A home-made curriculum. *Volta Review,* 1971, *73*(5), 273–277.

KEMP, C. J. Family treatment within the milieu of a residential treatment center. *Child Welfare,* 1971, *50*(4), 229–235.

KUNREUTHER, S. C. A preschool exchange: Black mothers speak and a white teacher listens. *Children,* 1970, *17*(3), 91–96.

LUTERMAN, D. M. A parent-oriented nursery program for preschool deaf children —A followup study. *Volta Review,* 1971, *73*(2), 106–112.

McGEENEY, P. *Parents are welcome.* New York: Humanities Press, 1969.

NEWMAN, S. *Guidelines to parent-teacher cooperation in early childhood education.* New York: Book Lab, 1971.

NIEDERMEYER, F. C. Parents in the reading program. *Reading Teacher,* 1970, *23*(8), 717–721.

NEIDERMEYER, F. C. Parents teach kindergarten reading at home. *Elementary School Journal,* 1970, *70*(8), 438–445.

OREM, R. (ed.) *Montessori for the disadvantaged.* New York: Rietz, D., and Rietz, R., 1967.

PAINTER, G. *Teach your baby.* New York: Simon and Schuster, 1971.

PETERSON, B. G. School readiness training at home: A case study. *California Personnel and Guidance Association Journal,* 1970–1971, *3*(2), 66–68.

PICKARTS, E. *Parent education; toward parental competence.* New York: Appleton-Century-Crofts, 1971.

PICKARTS, E. M., and McCANDLESS, E. B. The parent's role in education. *Journal of Secondary Education,* 1969, *44*(5), 231–236.

PIEPER, A. M. Parent and child centers—Impetus, implementation, in-depth view. *Young Children,* 1970, *26*(2), 70–76.

POWELL, F. Parents should know about reading skills. *Reading Teacher,* 1970, *23*(8), 738–740.

RADIN, N., and WEIKART, D. A home teaching program for disadvantaged preschool children. *Journal of Special Education,* 1967, *1*(2), 183–190.

RAPPAPORT, J. Advocacy and accountability in consultation to the poor. *Mental Hygiene,* 1972, *56*(1), 39–47.

ROBERSON, D. J. Parents and teachers: Partners in the teaching of reading. *Reading Teacher,* 1970, *23*(8), 722–726.

RYBACK, D. Sub-professional behavior modification and the development of token-reinforcement systems in increasing academic motivation and achievement. *Child Study Journal,* 1970–1971, *1*(2), 52–68.

SAXE, R. W. An unstudied problem: Parent visiting. *Education Forum,* 1969, *33*(2), 241–245.

SCHAEFER, E. S. Children under three—Finding ways to stimulate development. *Children,* 1969, *16*(2), 59–61.

SLATER, B. R. Parent involvement in perceptual training at the kindergarten level. *Academic Therapy Quarterly,* 1971–1972, 7(2), 149–154.

SMITH, M. B. To educate children effectively we must involve parents. *Instructor,* 1970, *80*(1), 119–121.

SULLIVAN, H. J., and LABEAUNE, C. Parents: Summer reading teachers. *Elementary School Journal,* 1971, *71*(5), 279–285.

SWIFT, M. S. Training poverty mothers in communication skills. *Reading Teacher,* 1970, *23*(4), 360–367.

TANNER, D., and TANNER, L. N. Parent education and cultural inheritance. *School and Society,* 1971, *99*(2330), 21, 24.

TEHMISIAN, J. A., and McREYNOLDS, W. T. Use of parents as behavioral engineers in the treatment of a school phobic girl. *Journal of Counseling Psychology,* 1971, *18*(3), 225–228.

VALETT, R. E. *Modifying children's behavior: A guide for parents and professionals.* Palo Alto, Calif.: Fearon Publishers, 1969.

VITO, P. Parents as partners. *Urban Review,* 1971, *5*(2), 35–40.

WADSWORTH, H. G., and WADSWORTH, J. B. A problem of involvement with parents of mildly retarded children. *Family Coordinator,* 1971, *20*(3), 141–147.

WARTENBERG, A. A parent-teacher speaks. *Reading Teacher,* 1970, *23*(8), 748–750.

WILLIE, L. Moms are a must. *American Education,* 1970, *6*(3), 25–29.

WILLMON, B. J. Reading readiness as influenced by parent participation in Head Start programs. *International Reading Association Conference Proceedings,* 1968, *13,* 617–622.

WILLMON, B. J. Parent participation as a factor in the effectiveness of Head Start programs. *Journal of Educational Research,* 1969, *62*(9), 406–410.

WILSON, A. L. Parent education in a public school program of speech therapy. *Journal of Speech and Hearing Disorders,* 1971, *36*(4), 499–505.

WITTES, G., and RADIN, N. Two approaches to group work with parents in a compensatory preschool program. *Social Work,* 1971, *16,* 42–50.

WOLMAN, T., and LEVENSON, D. Parent-school partnership in pre-kindergarten. *Teachers College Record,* 1968, *69,* 421–431.

Operational Concepts

1. The education of handicapped children is measurably improved when parents are involved.

2. To maximize the benefits of parental involvement, it is important to respect the special concerns of the particular parents.

3. When due allowance is made for the concerns and interests of parents, it frequently is possible to teach them to teach their children.

4. Studies indicate that behavior modification techniques are useful in assisting parents to work with their children.

5. Under favorable conditions, parents can reinforce school-taught skills in the home.

Implications

Logic suggests that what is true with respect to the teaching potential of handicapped childrens' parents probably is true of parents in general. It may be that the parents of the handicapped are less inclined to trust the entire educational development of their children to the school. But if these parents can be persuaded to take an active interest in the educational progress of their children, considerable benefit accrues.

We have long assumed that most parents are either incapable of, or not interested in, perpetuating their children's formal education outside the school. The assumption has been prompted, seemingly, by the belief that once parents support schools with taxes, they have fulfilled their obligations with respect to their children's educational needs. As the relationship between home experience and educational achievement becomes more apparent, however, and as parents become more aware of their capacity to facilitate learning, as technology creates more leisure time, and as efforts to devise effective home learning games and activities continue, it is likely that more and more parents can be persuaded to assist in their children's formal and informal education. What all this suggests, then, is that steps should be taken to alleviate our lack of knowledge regarding optimal ways of coordinating home and school learning.

Alternative Schools

Louis Rubin

Alternative Schools

Throughout the history of schools, people periodically have become disenchanted with either their character or their output. When such dissatisfaction reaches a sizeable proportion, new movements invariably arise. In some instances, these movements become full-fledged evolutions and the practice of schooling is altered. In other instances, they fail to stand the test of popular appeal and in due time disintegrate. At the height of a movement, however, it is exceedingly difficult to predict which of these two ends eventually will transpire. One can only observe the sometimes fascinating development of the movement, seeking to understand the social forces that created the impetus.

Such is the case with alternative schools. The name, self-evidently, denotes a deliberate departure from tradition. Thus, in a way of speaking, any nontraditional school represents a legitimate alternative. But, since the various departures from convention now underway differ in style, spirit, and purpose, the name "alternative" is sometimes misleading. Despite this fact, however, there is a kind of central tendency that characterizes many of the experiments that now are being tried.

Most, for example, exist in urban settings. They are somewhat smaller than their public school counterparts, tend to attract a cross-section of ethnic groups, and tend to enroll students from different levels of the social strata.

The essence of the alternative school philosophy, moreover, follows a recurrent theme: students should play an active part in making decisions about their educational affairs; constraining rules regarding standards, behavior, and educational process should be loosened; individuality in learning style is to be respected; opportunity for self-expression must be a definitive feature of the curriculum design; and heavy emphasis should be given to developing the student's capacity to make decisions for himself. In short, alternative schools place maximum emphasis upon stu-

Reprinted from Louis Rubin, *Curriculum Development: A Study Guide for Educational Administrators* (Ft. Lauderdale, Fla.: Nova University Press, 1973), pp. 180–184; by permission.

410

dent self-direction, and delimit bureaucratic intervention as much as possible.

The formal classroom structure, figuratively and literally, is interrupted. Education is either taken beyond the walls—or the walls are taken out entirely. Film-making is as likely to be studied as, say, algebra. The relationship between student and teacher is a good deal more informal and often more congenial; close, even intimate, relationships between the two are not uncommon. And, there is larger and more general attention to children's emotional involvements.

The alternative schools, in a sense, are exercises in participant democracy. Their protagonists generally envision a school in which:

1. Mutual trust and understanding underline the interaction between students and staff.
2. Students from different cultural backgrounds are deliberately integrated so as to enrich the social mix.
3. The special interests of individual students are nurtured with great care.
4. Student independence in action and thought is prized.
5. The total community serves as the environment for learning.
6. Students are encouraged not only to take gratification in their own social backgrounds, but also to understand and respect other cultural strains in the society.
7. Decisions affecting the group are made by the group and thus there is a cooperative give-and-take among parents, teachers, and students.
8. Basic skills (reading, arithmetic, and writing) are to be mastered through as realistic life-experiences as possible.
9. The rigid compartmentalization of children according to age is avoided.
10. Much of the curriculum deals with the political and social processes through which people organize their affairs.
11. The traditional system of grading is either eliminated or substantially modified.
12. Students are largely responsible for setting the course of their own learning activities.
13. Natural (unstructured) learning takes precedence over artificial curricular impositions.
14. Considerable attention is given to the student's emotional security.
15. The personal interests, concerns, and aspirations of the individual child are the significant elements in curriculum design.
16. Social and personal conflicts are brought to the fore, clarified, and resolved through role encounters.
17. Process is usually more important than content.

18. The evaluation of learning is somewhat intuitive and the criteria go far beyond skill attainment.
19. Teachers and students alike are at liberty to pursue their own goals.
20. The range of personal freedom, for all concerned, is far greater than in traditional schools.

These objectives are, to be sure, impressive and exemplary. They have their greatest appeal, obviously, for students and parents who despair of the worst features in conventional schools. Hence, alternative schools seek to provide massive relief from bureaucratic impedimenta, and from the conformity demanded by monolithic systems.

Such schools, moreover, require teachers who not only embrace the underlying philosophy, but who, in addition, have a much broader repertory of skills. Even so, participant democracy is as difficult in a school as anywhere else, and frequently the ambitions of the alternative schools are defeated by human limitations. In the August 1972 issue of the *Harvard Educational Review*, for example, the administration of a particularly well conceived alternative school summed up the teaching difficulties as follows:

1. Staff members had a close relationship with students, were willing to listen to students' gripes about the program, and were often sensitive in reaching to and even anticipating students' needs.
2. The staff felt ultimately responsible for the success of the program; we felt that if it failed, its demise would be perceived as our responsibility, not the students'.
3. Unexpectedly, the excellence and creativity of the staff worked against student involvement. Tentative student ideas were often pale in comparison to teachers' well-developed ideas that grew out of long experience and analysis.
4. However much a staff member was consciously committed to student involvement, his or her past life experience as a teacher and earlier as a student had cast students in a submissive role. Especially when harried and overworked, staff tended to revert to old role definitions.
5. Some staff members were ambivalent about the desirability of student involvement in decision making and unsure of its limits. They communicated this ambivalence, often in subtle ways, by their actions in the decision-making process.
6. Teachers had superior skills in the process of bureaucratic decision making compared with students. This competence acted as a constant pressure (of which we were generally not aware) that consolidated the staff role in decision making vis-à-vis the students.
7. Even when students were present in staff meetings, staff shaped the event. We were always there, and we knew past history of which students were unaware:

412

Teacher: Do you know what's going on?

Student: No, I wasn't here when you discussed it last week.

Teacher: See, that's one of our biggest problems. We'll never get anything done if it always goes on like this.

8. The staff itself encountered formidable problems in becoming an effective body for making and carrying out decisions. We had had limited experience in working in this capacity in previous teaching assignments. Personality clashes sometimes obscured issues; an initial rejection of procedural rules allowed discussions to wander aimlessly; those present at meetings were often unclear as to when a decision had been reached; those absent were not always informed about decisions; responsibility was often not clearly assigned for carrying out a decision. When decisions required widespread cooperation of students and staff, staff members were hesitant to confront individuals who violated agreements(*1*).

The writers also make clear some pervasive problems which must be clarified through additional research:

1. Varying perception of school goals by staff and students.
2. Contradictions between specific practices designed to achieve conflicting goals—for example, freedom in the choice of courses that allows students who can't read to avoid all reading-related activities.
3. The success or failure of specific practices—for example, the fate of a campaign to get students to try to actively change learning experiences with which they are dissatisfied, rather than cutting out on them.
4. Adequacy of specific practices in achieving school goals—for example, the relationship between group counseling of students and the capacity of student groups to make and carry out group decisions(*2*).

In the poorest of the alternative schools, it may be that the cure is worse than the disease. And in the best, it is entirely possible that a new conception of educational purpose will make its mark. Everything depends, as we saw earlier, on the goals we take to be most important. We can devise a school that views student autonomy, self-direction, and freedom as its highest ideals; we can devise one that attempts to indoctrinate the learner into his social system; or we can seek a reasonable compromise between the two. For, if nothing else, the alternative schools have dramatized many of the traditional system's most devastating weaknesses. The schools of today are far better than those of the past. But they also are a long way from ideal. Upon occasion, we still subject children to hopeless boredom, alienate their natural curiosity, abuse their self-esteem, and so on.

As social institutions, schools perform a multiplicity of functions. They provide custodial care, taking children off the streets, and out from under the feet of their parents; they sort children into various occupational mainstreams; they provide a vast complement of practitioners with a vocation;

and they educate children. It is the last of these functions that most pre-occupies the defenders of alternative schools. Put another way, they regard education as natural rather than manipulated growth.

Within the general rubric, there are a number of variations on a theme. Some experiments, for example, are known as "free schools," some as "new schools," and some as "open schools." Despite the differences in nomen-clature, all share a common rejection of the traditional school's pattern: routine evaluation, competitiveness, grouping by ability, large classes, a predetermined course of study, and teacher control. It is interesting to note, in this connection, that some parents are moving to geographical areas served by open schools, and others—having experienced them—are re-versing the process and moving to homes in areas where traditional schools still prevail. At the present time, there are approximately 400–500 alterna-tive schools scattered throughout the nation. The bulk can be found in California, Massachusetts, and New York. Some are full-time residential schools, some involve parent–teacher cooperatives, some are best described as community elementary schools. A few are close replications of A. S. Neil's *Summerhill*, whereas others bear little resemblance to this celebrated prototype. And, for the high-school drop-out, a spate of street academies have developed in the neighborhoods of poverty-stricken minorities. In virtually all, however, the hallmark of the curriculum is an abiding faith in the benefits of freedom, and a strong conviction that regimentation and constraint hinder intellectual and emotional development.

The evidence is not yet in. Indeed, we may need to wait until the present alternative school children reach adulthood in order to appraise the blessings of the movement. But, for the time being, it is safe to say that the movement is not without its significance, its advocates, and its critics.

References

1. Moore, Donald R., et al. "Strengthening Alternative High Schools," *Harvard Educational Review*, 42(3), August 1972, pp. 321–322.
2. Ibid., p. 340.

ADDENDUM BY THE AUTHOR TO *ALTERNATIVE SCHOOLS*

The critical purpose of an alternative school, self-evidently, is to give students greater choice. Logic would suggest that no single school, howso-ever eclectic its organization, can hope to accommodate all students with equal effectiveness. Alternative schools, when they provide students with options, therefore fulfill a valuable function. Nonetheless, it is important to remember that—given this purpose—alternative is synonymous with difference rather than with open, structured, streetfront, ethnic, or any other specific movement. To assume that the alternative school is aimed at a specific set of educational goals would be to deny the very point of its existence.

Instead, although some alternative schools are known as nontraditional, free, multicultural, or continuation schools, the label alternative can properly be applied to any school with a program structure different from that which generally prevails. Put another way, the concept of alternative does not preclude an academic or humanistic curriculum, a practical or theoretical orientation, a rigid or permissive behavior code, or anything else. Rather, it permits the creation of any kind of school that is tailored to the interests and needs of its clients.

At bottom, the dominant thrust of an alternative school is to somehow be more responsive to its clients. It is this goal of responsiveness that, above all, must determine the alternative school's philosophy, operation, and objectives. Similarly, an alternative school cannot be evaluated according to the same criteria as a conventional one; it must be judged by the extent to which it achieves the purposes for which it was created.

Finally, beyond the obvious considerations of management, organization, and cost, it is important to remember that alternative schools—like the standard ones that they replace—must equip their students to cope with whatever educational and social requirements they will face after leaving the school, and ultimately to enter the societal mainstream successfully.

Operational Concepts

1. The dominant purpose of the alternative school movement is to extend the range of pupil options while increasing the educational system's responsiveness to students.

2. Most alternative schools tend to emphasize unstructured curricula, informal learning methods, and greater student freedom, but the concept of alternative education is not limited to any particular educational philosophy.

3. However laudable an alternative school's intentions, worthwhile objectives do not compensate for poorly conceived programs, lack of cohesion, insufficient teacher guidance, and other organizational weaknesses.

4. Any school program, whether conventional or alternative, must be evaluated according to its particular purpose and intent.

5. Since all schools bear a fundamental obligation for the socialization of the young, alternative schools, whatever their design, must still equip students to function successfully in a variety of social contexts once they have left the school.

Implications

All things considered, the society probably needs more rather than fewer educational alternatives. Much will be lost, however, if the alternatives are restricted to a narrow range of different ideological conceptions. Dramatic innovations are possible in curriculum content, instructional methods, the architecture of the educational environment, and so on.

There is, moreover, nothing in the theory of alternative education to prevent districts from offering a variety of options *within* a school: since the essential objective is to accommodate the individual child's nature to the fullest extent possible, it is the availability of choice rather than physical location that is crucial.

Perhaps the most sensible point of departure in seeking alternative programs lies in accurately identifying the interests and needs of students. In short, alternatives are desirable whenever an existing program, in one way or another, is not adequately responsive to the learner's requirements.

Yet, as the issues raised on many of the *Handbook's* pages demonstrate, the extent to which children's interests and preferences should be indulged remains a point of disagreement. Few would doubt that the educational system should enable the individual to follow his or her natural bent, to learn whatever seems useful, and to explore the personal paths of intellectual curiosity, but most observers also would agree that schools must fulfill a few inalienable obligations. Children, for example, must learn to read, to count, and to communicate effectively with others. To an extent, then, the freedom of alternative schools is constrained by the responsibility to social expectation.

The organization of schooling creates its own definitive climate, and life in school goes on in a relatively artificial environment. Even so, schooling is an apprenticeship in the social interaction that will follow. Accordingly, if the milieu of the alternative school deviates too sharply from the conventions that prevail in the larger social system, students may be faced with an inevitable—and sometimes difficult—readjustment. In sum, alternative education should not be construed as absolute license to abdicate the basic obligations associated with public education and to deviate at will.

Schools of the Future

Edward J. Meade, Jr.

Models for Reforming Education in the City

As one who has had a good many years of experience in deciding whether or not to fund school projects of all kinds, I have come to feel that to speak of models (or, if you prefer, "beacons," "lighthouses," or "pilot projects") for reforming urban education is both presumptuous and over-simplified.

Of course, the very word "model" implies that a tested structure and substance are to be duplicated. And we all know the refrain of reformers proposing an innovative project, "Well, if the model works in the city, it will work anywhere." But I worry about the attitude which impels school people to invest expensively in either developing new model programs or copying another city's model without a deep sense of the dynamics and realities of different contexts. Rather, we should think of urban school reform not in terms of casting out the old and replacing it with the new, but in terms of what works and what doesn't work and for what purposes.

What are the basic conditions which give rise to the search for models of schools in today's urban society? Schools are institutions rooted in *stability;* in modern urban settings they coexist with pressures of *change* and *diversity;* the confrontation between stability and change produces conflict. To resolve that conflict schools must have the capacity to assess their work regularly and be prepared to recycle content, teaching methods, or organizational structures that are obsolete for a generation living in a fast-moving urban culture. As preparatory agencies, schools are a contradiction in terms if they do not help youngsters learn how to function in a changing society.

In fairness to our children we ought to try to take stock of the prodigious contrast between the pace and preoccupations of the times when those of us near or over forty grew up and the temper of today's scene, then ponder the rate of change we can expect between now and the year 2000.

Around World War II, our time and space horizons were still long. Cross-country travel was still a matter of several days' train ride. Radio was

Reprinted from Edward J. Meade, Jr., "Models for Reforming Education in the City," Ford Foundation Reprints, 1973; by permission of the Ford Foundation.

418

our only electronic means of mass communication. Commercial air travel and television had not collapsed distances. Computers were still only embryonic brain children of scientists. Office copying machines were virtually nonexistent. Delay, prohibitive expense, and a human intermediary attended a long distance telephone call. The most advanced ground weapons were tanks. Urban growth was just beginning to accelerate. Our awareness of social justice and cultural diversity was not aroused.

Today we live in a predominantly urban environment, with a consciousness of worldwide perspective and a sense of limitless technological potentials. Our urban surroundings cause us to work, live, and travel in close proximity to large numbers of our fellow man. Advances in transportation and communications technologies have stepped up the pace of our work, and increased its flow. With the proliferation of new jobs has come ease of mobility; job changes are now regarded as essential to both satisfaction and growth. Today, racial, economic, and cultural disparities press for even greater attention. Our new communications media also have come to be instruments for making insistent a wider and deeper range of value-laden problems than many of us care to know about. Not only may we no longer ignore the rightful claims of racial and other minorities and women to unapologetic expression of their identities and fair economic reward, but we also must turn our minds more to the claims of our grandchildren and unborn generations for a physical and social environment fit to live in.

Man, a highly adaptable animal, has taken in stride the evolution of modern urban stress and change. But we have not come to terms with it. Nor do our schools help youngsters come to terms with it. Yet I say that without pessimism. The same imperatives that are reorienting other social institutions—the judical system, the political process, the family unit, the business firm—also are wearing away schools' resistance to change.

For all their trappings of modernity schools still try to hold out as bastions of stability. Indeed there is a sense in which they ought to offer a safe and nurturing environment in which young roots can grow. But stability in terms of preserving past attitudes and trivial knowledge is not conducive to healthy growth.

Consider the ways the formal education system contributes to the perpetuation of a stable character for schools. A whole system of training, accreditation, tenure, and remuneration has geared teachers and administrators to lifelong commitment to a hierarchy of roles, as perceived when they were in training. The basic content of school programs is conceded to be stable over time; although other subjects have been introduced, the heart of every school program still is reading, writing, arithmetic, science, history, geography, and civics. Even the order of presenting content is subject to little interference.

So there is weighty evidence of the school's natural tendency to stand as a stable institution amid a tempestuous sea of change. One may argue, "Ah, but ships at sea rely on the lighthouse's firm beam for safety." I agree, but they look to that lighthouse for *guidance* in navigating rough and strange waters, not for *shelter*.

That is my scenario of conflict: a restless, changing, mobile society in our cities and, withstanding the currents around them, relatively stable, slow-changing education systems. While a little conflict and tension can be useful, I believe the strains in urban areas and urban schools are well past creative friction and have almost reached the point of blinding despair.

CLARIFYING STABILITY AND CHANGE

As Americans, we are inclined to want a clean answer—a yes or a no, a go or a no-go. We prefer sharp and clear alternatives. Should we therefore insist that changing society adapt to the stable school? Or should we ask the school to adapt to the society? That question answers itself. An older and wiser acquaintance, a school superintendent, once answered it by reminding his audience of who pays the bills.

But as much as we have been exercised over the conflict between stability and change, we have done little to clarify what needs to remain stable in schools and what ought to be changed. Instead, almost by default we have evolved two models for urban education, neither of which is satisfactory for children, or society, or educators.

The first is the "add-on" model. It started back in the 1950s as work in our cities became more specialized and new courses and programs were added on to correspond to occupational distinctions. For example, courses in art alone did not suffice; we atomized the field into separate, special purpose concentrations—classical art, modern art, commercial art, graphic art, advertising art. In the 1960s, as we began to relinquish the historical melting-pot view and consciously admitted our society's cultural diversity, city schools responded with still more programs. At first they consisted of more dollars and more people to deal with more diverse people, interests, and backgrounds. Educators and policy makers though that by simply overwhelming those economic and cultural differences with remedial "compensatory" programs aimed at assisting kids to fit the schools, school and society could proceed in their comfortable patterns, unchallenged. These programs assumed that the corpus of our schools was in good health but many so-called disadvantaged kids were not.

Later, the "add-on" model became more sophisticated. It started legitimizing subject areas different from the stable fare of the school. Suddenly, and with the considerable assistance of an awakened federal government, we added on programs having their own identity and integrity —bilingual education, minority studies, media studies.

Still, with all of the add-ons the school stayed very much the same. True, it had more from which to choose, but the educators make the choices, not the student-client. The pros were sure they knew all that was good for school kids.

Eventually educators began to concede, however reluctantly, that perhaps the school alone could not deliver all that was expected of it. They decided that schooling needed to spread out—a little at least beyond the schoolhouse itself. They allowed that the surrounding community could be an educational resource of value. Thus emerged the newly popular model—the "spread-out."

THE "SPREAD-OUT" MODEL

With or without direction from teachers, kids found themselves free to piece together their own educational program from places and people in the world outside the stable school walls—from factories, banks, museums, offices, even from the streets. "Relevance" was the rationale. The meaning of old labels such as work–study took on fresh luster. Exemplars of this "spread-out" model—the Parkway Program (sometimes known as a "school without walls") and the "community as a school"—quickly multiplied in the urban areas. Underlying even this movement, however, is still the assumption that such activities are only for the more restless students, ancillary, possibly only short-term, complements to the stable and secure school we know.

These two school reform models, created by default, have failed to resolve the conflict between the spirit of stability and the imperative of change, and we still remain unclear in our sense of what the schools need to preserve and what they need to change.

The primary stable role of any school is helping children learn how to learn. Educators will have failed if they do not assist children to master how to learn things,-and to manage learning for themselves. Teaching them to know specific things is hardly education; educating children is to lead them to knowledge of the world and self.

To my way of thinking, therefore, there is a need for stability in our schools in the sense of giving children structured and expanding experiences in learning keyed to the realities of the times. Attuning that structure and those experiences to changing times may well mean, however, that many of the traditional features of educational systems must be realigned.

Another part of the schools' proper stability is its role as a haven for the youngster as he ferrets out his values, his interests, his potentials, his responsibilities, his person. It seems to me that the school, especially in urban centers where change is rapid and more often unplanned than deliberate, needs to offer a stable ground where children may test and be tested without having to suffer the hardships of failure or the added responsibilities of success. It must afford a climate of support for critical self-assessment, where the outcomes of youthful experimenting feed further

421

positive growth and development without the full and sometimes severe penalties that may attend risk taking in the reality of job place, the family, the community, and the society at large. In short, schools should provide an internship for life.

But the *means* whereby the system assures stability for these basic functions, however, can be ever-changing. There is no need to hold stable the places, procedures, processes, programs, or people that serve learning. Injustice is done by holding on to traditions and practices that deny children fuller opportunities to learn. School people, their citizen supporters, and friendly critics and goads, need to evaluate continuously every facet of school life, from curriculum to schedules to teacher training. Is the way schools are doing things now in keeping with work and life styles outside the school? In an era of liberation, in what ways does our educational system perpetuate mindless, regimented action? What practices reflect sheer anachronisms?

Consider a few examples of changes that can be made:

First, school buildings and facilities need not be constructed to last forever, or even for a generation or two. Maybe we should consider such items consumables that depreciate over limited time spans, just as do factories, office buildings, homes, and equipment. The forms of learning will change, and our facilities need either to be adaptable to such changes or be replaceable. Also, the location of schools, especially city schools, may over time become removed from where the children are. School and educational facilities are to serve, not to be served.

Second, school rules and regulations need to be in touch with the realities of life in the greater society. Procedures need to be efficient in terms of helping children learn, not in terms of managerial convenience or to gratify some antiquated dictum of ancient bookkeepers. The criterion for assessing all procedures and changes is, "Will it help children learn?" For example, the routine for processing books and consumable materials can be redirected to the reason for such supplies—that of facilitating learning, not of insuring long life for the goods. Also, pupil records that document trivial incidents of growing up and a child's track record of consuming short-lived academic knowledge are less meaningful to anyone concerned with learning than would be systematic collection of more reliable data about the child's development—his circumstances, his learning styles, his interests, his abilities. Systems of marking and grades—artificial arbitrary measures that reveal little if anything of a child's learning—are ripe for scrapping in favor of more thoughtful assessments of the individual and his competition with himself, not artificial competition with others of different strengths and weaknesses. Because learning proceeds in erratic spurts inconsistent with any imposed time frame, semester and class periods may be no more realistic modules for learning than an agrarian-based school year. Organizational structures—grade levels, and how we divide the system into elementary, middle, and secondary schools—are administrative conveniences and nothing more. Then there are the rules of conduct: How does one explain hall passes for students close to or already of voting age? How do such demeaning control tactics contribute to learning, to self-development, and responsibility?

Third, the processes of instruction need to be as up to date as knowledge about learning and as instructional technology. If learning can be more effectively and efficiently stimulated by the computer, the television set, and the overhead projector, as their use outside the school implies, should not their usefulness in formal schooling be admitted? If various systems of instruction all seem to work for at least some, then all must be available so that differences in learning styles can be accommodated and fulfilled. There is nothing sacred about any one instructional orthodoxy.

Fourth, the programs, courses, or content for learning need thorough review and freshening. It is easy to forget why something was put in the curriculum, but because it is there it continues to be taught for its own sake. The goal in teaching any subject area is for the child to learn its fundamentals and its context—not all its content. The content, by and large, is the vehicle for building skills and understanding about mathematics, science, literature, and the like. The basic elements are still available for learning whether in the guise of Shakespeare, *Silas Marner,* Willy Loman, or Holden Caulfield, whether in book format or film.

Finally, let's consider the people, the educators, and those of us who think of ourselves as committed partners in education. In our professional endeavors are we readily flexible, open to new thinking? Some occupations demand that quality; education, alas, seems to reinforce the opposite—a reverence for past wisdom at the expense of welcoming thought. More often than not we change jobs rather than ourselves, and teachers are no exception, tenure notwithstanding. No school expects its faculty and staff to remain intact for a long period of time. Mobility is commonplace. Therefore, any school needs to create within itself ways and means to accommodate personnel changes without damage to children. Equally important, the school must insure continuing reeducation of its personnel to meet the changing needs of children and society. Professionals too need recycling and renewal. Helping learners is a demanding and tiring role, and no educator who cares can afford to fall into the safe rut of doing as he has always done nor let his colleagues do likewise.

Thus the entire support system, the whole panoply of people and patterns that make up schooling, deserves and needs evaluation. This task is a heavy burden for our schools, and they are ill prepared and unwilling to initiate without the imperatives of crisis or public urging.

In fact the task implies fashioning a model capable of "rolling reform." But I hesitate to propose that such a model be truly formalized in new, add-on mechanisms. Rather, the rudiments of a model for adapting our schools to change should be infused throughout the educational system—in the training centers, administrative echelons, policy-making bodies, and school people themselves. These rudiments are both a questioning of basic purpose and an attitude of self-renewal. The parent and the citizen participant in educational affairs can help forge this model for urban education by steadily accenting for the practitioners the criterion, "Does it help children learn?" The rest of us must continue to push in our own ways for policies and practices system-wide to keep learning rather than teaching, learning rather than administering, the focal point of school reform.

Our quest for a genuinely useful model for reform of urban education is best found in ourselves, in all of us who have some measure of responsibility for schooling in the city. It calls for a self-critical responsiveness to change, a sensitivity to the stress of time and the pulse of urban vitality. It holds constant the goal of helping people, mainly the young, to learn with dignity and humanity in ways that they, in turn, can best serve themselves and the urban society.

In 1874 Benjamin Disraeli said, "Upon the education of the people, the fate of the country depends." Many years later, H. G. Wells in his *Outline of History*, casting his thoughts to the future, observed that "human history becomes more and more a race between education and catastrophy." Those of us who live in and care for the city know especially well the truth of these statements.

RELATED FORD FOUNDATION ACTIVITIES

For several years efforts to improve urban education, including examples of the "add-on" and "spread-out" models referred to in the preceding address, have been assisted by the Foundation. Several grants have been made for experimental alternative schools that show promise of offering more responsive and flexible education systems. In most of these experiments, there is a large measure of parental and community involvement and a greater sensitivity by schools to the needs of the individual student.

Philadelphia's Parkway School, for example, is an experimental "school without walls" that uses more than a dozen neighboring cultural, scientific, and business institutions as its classrooms. Partly as a result of Parkway's success, the Philadelphia school system is now sponsoring more than fifty alternative education programs and maintains a special office to help them. "The City as School," a Brooklyn, New York, public high school, gives students the chance to learn in such diverse settings as museums, government agencies, and private businesses. Students also share with teachers the responsibilities for decision making and teaching.

In Syracuse, New York, an experimental off-campus program is encouraging high school dropouts to resume study by drawing on the learning resources of the entire community. Faculty advisors help students from a five-county area plan study programs that lead to a high school diploma.

A grant to the New York City Board of Education helped establish within one troubled high school sixteen minischools, each of which is closely attuned to student interests and ability. The program subdivides the curriculum into a wide variety of interest and vocational areas. Some students continue to take courses that prepare them for college; others concentrate on electronic, automotive, and aerospace studies; still others choose the performing and creative arts and urban affairs, or a program that combines work with study.

Public schools in Berkeley, California, also offer students a choice among several distinct styles of learning. One option enables selected high school students to supplement their courses with work in the community. Another option is a minischool within the high school, where several hundred students participate in decision making with staff and parents and devote half their time to traditional subjects, the remainder to community-oriented projects.

In New York City's East Harlem, students, parents, the Board of Education, and the Foundation-assisted Committee for a Comprehensive Education drew up the plans for Park East High School. Park East combines vocational and academic subjects both in the classroom and in other city resources.

In addition to working within the public school system, The Foundation has also supported several independent schools, created especially by parents to serve children in low-income areas. The Federation of Boston Community Schools, one of whose three "free schools" closed this year, was successful in motivating students who had difficulty learning in the public schools. Harlem Prep, which was recently incorporated into the New York City public school system, was established in 1967 to give high school dropouts another chance, and nearly all of its 500 graduates have gone on to college.

Community involvement is an important ingredient of the Tutorial Community Project in the Los Angeles city public schools, begun six years ago as a vehicle for older children to tutor younger children, both learning in the process. Because staff, teachers, pupils, and parents all help plan and conduct day-to-day learning activities, the program has developed into a community effort toward change. With Foundation assistance the project has expanded to five schools(1).

Because alternative education models now are developing nationwide through a variety of means and many are being incorporated into public school systems around the country, the Foundation is shifting its support to other areas, such as staff development projects that help train teachers on-the-job to work more effectively in a variety of alternative and conventional educational settings. A review of the Foundation's assistance to the development of alternative educational programs will be published later this year and will be available on request.

During the 1960s the Foundation granted more than $30 million for the Comprehensive School Improvement Program (CSIP), one of the largest privately supported efforts to improve education in the public schools(2). Projects in twenty-five suburban, rural, and urban schools adopted such innovations as team teaching, programmed instruction, flexible scheduling and space arrangements, audiovisual technology, independent study, nongraded programs, and school and university partnerships for new curricula and teaching methods.

In addition to assisting the above "add-on" and "spread-out" models, the Foundation has also sought to help improve urban education in other ways, for example, by supporting (1) inservice training for teachers and other instructional personnel in such cities as Washington, Boston, and New York; (2) research on learning and teaching (Rockefeller University); (3) improved educational planning and management through projects in Los Angeles, Boston, and New York City; (4) public school finance reform (e.g., the Syracuse University Research Corporation study on federal aid to education and its impact on cities); and (5) educational television programming for children ("Sesame Street" and "The Electric Company").

References

1. *Tommorrow We'll See What Happens,* a Ford Foundation film about the Tutorial Community Project, is available for purchase or rental from Phoenix Films, Inc., 470 Park Avenue South, New York, N.Y. 10016.
2. "A Foundation Goes to School," a report on CSIP, is available on request.

Operational Concepts

1. The search for universally applicable programs of school improvement that can be effectively used across the national spectrum has been largely fruitless. Educational environments vary so greatly that we must, instead, search out specific solutions for specific situations.

2. Much of the substantive content in the traditional subjects now being taught is obsolete; updating is essential.

3. In guiding the educational development of the young, schools have made too little use of personal information about the individual student; the accumulation, interpretation, and utilization of such data should be emphasized in subsequent reforms.

4. In recent times, the curriculum has suffered from a dangerous tendency toward excess. The solutions to education's problems do not lie in the endless imposition of new subjects or new topics to be studied. Despite the potential advantages in developing occupational skills, the efforts to expand education into the community at large pose serious organizational and theoretical problems.

5. Education's recent past has been characterized by a period of extreme stress and tension. A period of comparative stability—wherein problems and possible solutions are subjected to thoughtful reexamination—is now necessary.

Implications

Public institutions, particularly those immersed in long tradition, are not easily altered. Education, after an early history of relative changelessness, has gone through, in recent years, an era of dramatic upheaval. The widespread demand for innovation undoubtedly served to diminish public resistance to change, but we now find ourselves in a period of confusion. Reaching out to an ever-increasing array of goals, we perhaps have forgotten that the essential function of the school is to help children learn. What we now need, therefore, is to assess the net consequences of a frenetic decade of transition.

It is not uncommon, as humans seek to readjust their social institutions, for temporary periods of confusion to occur. Such seems to be the case at the moment, for a good deal of uncertainty is evident: should the schools eliminate competitiveness? Do dollar constraints mitigate against better education, or will society support the best system that can be devised? Can lasting values be taught? Can the learning handicaps with which some children enter school be overcome? Can deleterious out-of-school experiences be counteracted in a humanistic school? These and a host of other issues have given rise to sustained debate, political confrontation, and outright factionalism.

It now seems clear that, although schools can serve many masters and fulfill many purposes, they cannot do all things equally well or at the same time. As a result, we are now faced with philosophical questions of choice and priority. It is professionals and laymen together, then, who must begin to sort out major and minor goals. Until there is reasonable agreement as to the schools' primary purpose, arguments over the ways and means for accomplishing particular ends are likely to have little point.

Arden D. Grotelueschen
Dennis D. Gooler

Evaluation in Curriculum Development

Evaluation means different things to different people. For example, it is judging the worth of a program (Scriven, 1967). It is describing a program as fully as possible (Stake, 1967). It is documenting how well program objectives are met (Tyler, 1942). It is providing useful information to decision makers (Stufflebeam, 1969). It is all of these, and combinations of these, and more things besides. The characteristic common to each of these perceptions of evaluation is a focus on what has been done or what is presently being done.

We propose that evaluation also be applied to things not yet done. The perceptions of evaluation suggested above are not inappropriate to our proposal. But in this paper we will argue, as Moynihan (1970, p. 14) did, for "evaluation in advance." To do so, we feel, requires a more-than-usual reliance upon judgmental data.

FUNCTIONS OF PLANNING

Planning, viewed as an aspect of curriculum development, serves four basic functions. Planning results in the identification of potential curriculum *goals*. Goals of some kind exist even if systematic planning is not carried out. However, planning seeks to sharpen goals. Goals may be stated in broad terms (students will become good citizens), or they may be stated specifically and behaviorally (the seventh-grade student will be able to identify four reference books). Planning enables the program manager (and his staff) to select particular goals, from a universe of possible goals, that seem appropriate for his curriculum. "Good" planning also attends to changing goals as the curriculum is implemented.

Reprinted from Arden D. Grotelueschen and Dennis D. Gooler, *Curriculum Theory Network* (Ontario: Ontario Institute for Studies in Education, 1972), pp. 7–21; by permission. An earlier version of this paper was read at a symposium of the American Education Research Association Meeting, New York, February 1971.

Planning should assist the program director or curriculum developer in defining alternative *means* for reaching potential goals. Too often we make decisions based on very limited knowledge of our alternatives. If we wish to instruct children in the values of our society, we should consider the alternative means. Reading literature produced by our predecessors and contemporaries is an alternative. Attending to the mass media is another. But are there others? Can we make use of technology? Should more emphasis be given to the education of the parents of these children? How else can we reach this goal? To be sure, the planning process must include feasibilty checks, but wise planning necessitates that we have an array of alternatives before us.

Just as planning should identify and define alternative means-to-ends, so should planning define some possible *consequences* of selecting each alternative. A common practice is to choose an alternative, implement it, and then analyze the consequences of that choice. We can no longer enjoy the luxury of this procedure. In terms of cost alone (not merely the dollars and cents), we need to be as fully aware as possible of the consequences of our actions before we act. The plan implies identifying consequences, even though this is not a simple task. We think evaluation could be especially relevant to this problem.

Planning has a direct bearing on the *allocation of resources*. As alternative actions are considered, the resources required to implement each alternative must be considered also. What would it cost to use computer-assisted instruction? What resources will be needed to accomplish a certain goal? New resources may be desired. Planning leads to a more efficient and effective allocation of resources, as systematic planning minimizes haphazard expenditures of funds and personnel.

FUNCTIONS OF EVALUATION IN PLANNING AND CURRICULUM DEVELOPMENT

Traditionally, evaluation has sought to determine the extent to which students in a program achieve goals set for that program. In our view of evaluation and planning, evaluation is broader than this. It should be pointed out here that the traditional use of evaluation remains an important component in the planning process. Description of goals and assessments of attempts to achieve those goals are necessary. Needs assessment is, in part, a measure of the discrepancy between desired outcomes and things as they are. To determine the discrepancy, we need somehow to measure things as they are. We contend, however, that evaluation has tended to emphasize too heavily a preciseness of measurement of present and past events, and in so doing has forfeited possibilities of more futuristic thought. We believe evaluation can play a wider role in planning and curriculum development.

Too often, goals of a curriculum are regarded as constants. Those who look at a curriculum tend to consider ways implementation could be changed, not whether the goals of the curriculum are appropriate(*1*). We contend that goals should be examined—their quality and their appropriateness ought to be assessed—before they are implemented. This idea is not new; Scriven (1967), for example, made a strong argument for the examination of goals. Evaluation can seek to develop criteria for goal inclusion, to examine the relationships among goals, and, even more basically, to discover what people mean when they propose a certain goal.

Not only should evaluation consider the quality and appropriateness of stated (or implicit) goals, but evaluation ought to delineate alternative goals. A goal of the local school might be to get parents to the school. Might an alternative goal be to get the school to the parents? What we are striving to accomplish through our curriculum might be considered in relation to possible achievements through different curricula with different goals. What are our alternatives? Is there a pool of goals from which we can select?

A discussion of goals will often eventuate in a discussion of priorities. Which goals are most important? Given that we cannot accomplish all things with our limited resources, how do we determine the goals to pursue? In curriculum development and program planning, the question of goal priority is critical.

What do different groups with interests in a particular curriculum think goals for that curriculum should be? Do students have different priorities from teachers? What of parents and community members? What are their educational priorities? Do priorities change over time? Are our curricula sensitive to the priorities of those involved in these curricula?

In an earlier paper (Gooler and Grotelueschen, 1971), we encouraged, as have others, the curriculum developer to consider various "audiences." We think curriculum developers should be held accountable for (to report, explain, or justify) decisions they make. The question of educational priorities is related to how a group or individual will consider program accountability.

Any educational program or curriculum tends to touch a variety of people, in a variety of ways, at a variety of times. These various groups can be viewed as audiences who come with various biases and demands, public and private concerns, and motives of assorted legitimacies. Each of these "pockets of persuasion" may serve its notice of accountability to the program planner or administrator. The parent has some expectations as to what his child should be able to do. The taxpayer sees much money being spent in the school, and wonders if that money is being used most efficiently. Eighth graders wonder if they will be able to compete in high school. The amount of "clout" these audiences possess in serving that notice is not at question here; the reality of their existence is. The manner in which the planner must account for the program will differ according to who is raising the questions, what those questions are, and when they are raised.

We suggest that the curriculum developer spend part of his time identifying audiences, "pockets of potential persuasion." Furthermore, it is not enough to merely acknowledge the existence of different audiences. Judgments made by these audiences about the goals selected for a program should be considered by the administrator in his decision making. The administrator, or the developer, may be able to uncover (not by second guessing but by direct inquiry) the questions these groups will be asking, the claims they will be making, the axes they seem to want to grind. Armed with that information, the administrator or developer can determine what kinds of data should be ready for use in response to potential questions. Perhaps more important, the data can be used as developmental input; it can exert an influence on what is developed. Program planners cannot follow suggestions made by all audiences, nor should they. Suggestions may be in direct opposition to each other. However, by considering possible suggestions and possible demands, the administrator can determine, before the fact, what the consequences of not attending to a particular suggestion or group might be. He need not yield only to those who speak the loudest; he may not follow the demands of audiences. He does need to know what people want and think, if only to know better how he is to report, explain, or justify what he intends to do and how he intends to do it.

In addition to examining goals, we would argue that evaluation should seek to identify alternative *means* for accomplishing the goals a curriculum program includes. This is not an easy task. The identification and structuring of alternative means-to-ends have been hindered by our preoccupation with attempts to get precise measurement of what has already happened. Such attempts require large commitments of time and resources, and consequently little effort is expended on considering alternative ways of doing things.

A role of evaluation in planning might well be to gather approximations of what has previously happened, and to identify alternative means-to-ends based on those approximations. Planning does not and cannot wait until all evidence is in. Plans for next year's programs are laid before this year has expired. Traditional evaluation or research data has come in too late and has been too narrowly conceived to be of much use to the planner. Evaluators must learn how to approximate conditions and outcomes. They must also learn to gather judgments from potential curriculum constituents. From these approximations and judgments—approximations of what has been or is and judgments of what ought to be—will grow plans for the future.

When we offer alternative means to given ends, we are obliged to project possible consequences of selecting those alternatives:

If you utilize these means, you might reasonably expect these consequences. For example, if we use program X in the twelfth grade, your children will probably be more interested in vocational placement, but will

432

emerge caring less about the fine arts. In addition you may need to expect to retrain many of your teachers. If you stress critical thinking, you may have students less willing to accept things as they are.

We would opt for less effort expended in obtaining precise measurement, and more effort toward structuring alternatives for the future. We recognize a trade-off: mistakes may occur if we do not know why something done previously worked or did not work. We are in danger of repeating mistakes if we only approximate the past in attempts to study the future. Wardrop (1971) suggests that an important concern of educational evaluation is explanation—the determination of the most probable cause of a phenomenon. We contend, however, that explanation is extremely time consuming, and that decisions about future programs may need to be made before explanation is complete.

The apparent broadness with which we view the function of evaluation in planning may cause some of our colleagues to feel we have been talking about something other than evaluation. Is the structuring of alternative goals and means and consequences a measurement of student outcomes, or an assessment of the worth of something, or a collection of useful information for the decision maker? Perhaps not. Perhaps "evaluation" is not the most appropriate term for the procedures and purposes we are proposing.

In the next section of this paper, we will suggest how some of these ideas might be operationalized. We will stress the importance of ascertaining alternative goals and means. Further, we will suggest procedures for determining priorities among potential goals and means. Finally, the inclusion of these data into curriculum development will be discussed.

THE IMPORTANCE OF ALTERNATIVES

. . . it is a tale,
Told by an idiot, full of sound and fury,
Signifying nothing.

Macbeth, Act V, Scene V

There are many such tales. And most of us fear that our ideas may be so described. Those involved with curriculum development must be prepared to risk this Shakespearean evaluation of their ideas. They must also be willing to examine alternatives to what is presently being done.

One role of evaluation in the planning of a curriculum program is to describe the goals that different constituents think should be included, as well as the variety of goals seen as desirable by people not directly involved in a development effort. Evaluation is not obliged to derive consensus. Divergence may be highly desirable: we think it is essential. It is also important to describe how goals were derived and the characteristics of the people making goal statements.

It is easy to view our society and our curricula from a narrow perspective, and it is possible to remain comfortable with that view if we are never forced to consider alternatives to the traditionally held goals. We have argued that change is constantly accelerating. Our perception of the world as we have always viewed it may not be a valid perception of the world that now is. We think the individual who considers many goals may be more likely to examine what he is now doing in terms of what he could be doing, than an individual not confronted with these alternative goals.

Perhaps even more important is the process of habitually scrutinizing alternative goals. This involves a continual examination of goals, programs, and society.

Ziegler (1969) has suggested that planning is the traditional method of attempting to impose some order on the future. The future may be similar to the past in many ways. The future is not the past, however. Given the present and probable future rate of change, it is more and more unlikely that the future will be a replication of the past. The alternative goals we delineate must be indicative of *what is* and *what will be* as opposed to *what was*. We are suggesting that less emphasis in planning should be on the past.

GOALS AND PRIORITIES

Goals have been held, discussed, and debated since the beginning of man. They exist at many levels. There are personal goals, professional goals, and goals held to be "for the good of society." Goals range from the highly general (to lead a productive life) to the highly specific (the student will be able to name the presidents). We have been urging developers to consider a wide variety of possible goals. The array of possibilities should reflect the specific and the general, as well as the insiders' and the outsiders' views. And the goals must be stated in such a way that their intent is clear to the people who will judge them.

What should be included in a curriculum? A response to this question implies priorities. How do we structure a curriculum when it must operate under constraints, making impossible the pursuit of some of those goals we recognize as good and useful? Priorities are the assignment of relative worth to two or more functions or ideas. Priorities imply choice.

Priorities are formulated and operationalized constantly. We do it every day. Mostly implicitly. Sometimes explicitly. We decide to go to the store, as opposed to staying home. We select a particular television program. We choose certain foods. But we are urging the education planner to make more explicit the implicit. We are asking that people think about priorities. In the next section, we will describe how information about goal priorities might be collected and used.

Arden D. Grotelueschen and Dennis D. Gooler

PROFILES OF GOAL PRIORITIES

A number of techniques may be used to collect information about the priority various people (or groups) assign to possible goals of a curriculum. Some of these techniques will be illustrated below.

Sorting

Downey (1960) used a technique called the Q-sort to determine how sixteen educational goals were rated by a variety of people.

Using this method, the investigator asks the respondent to sort a series of possible goals into categories according to perceived importance of each goal. The respondent is allowed to put only a certain number of goal statements into each category. If there were sixteen goals, as Downey had, the categories would be as in Figure 1. Each box represents one goal statement. Thus, the respondent must choose one goal as most important, two goals as next important, and so forth.

The average ranking assigned to each goal by the group of people being questioned can be computed. On the basis of these rankings, the entire group of goal statements can be ranked for each group of people. The results may be plotted as a profile. Another way to present the information would be simply to list the goals according to average ranking.

Rating

Respondents might be asked to rate a particular goal on a continuum of importance. Consider Figure 2 as an example of a format for asking about the importance of possible goals of an overall secondary school curriculum.

FIGURE 1

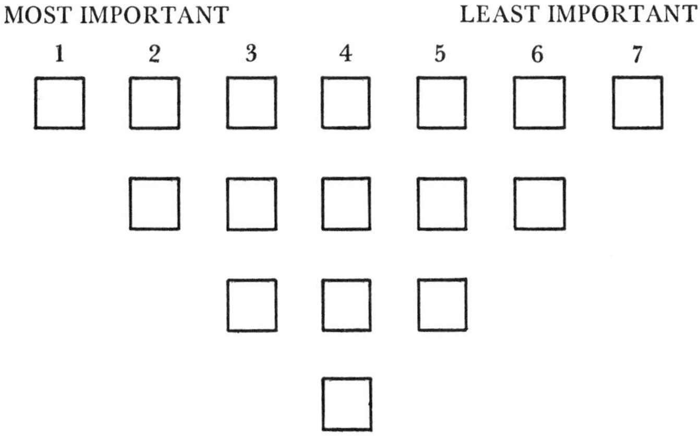

MOST IMPORTANT   LEAST IMPORTANT

435

FIGURE 2

	Carefully avoid pursuing	Consider relatively unimportant	Consider relatively important	Consider extremely important
To provide the student with training and placement in the vocation of his choice.				
To foster the development of the student as an enlightened consumer.				
To foster in the student emotional stability and good mental health.				

– – – – – – Students

——————— Parents

A mean rating could be calculated for each of the goals and a profile drawn for a particular group or individual. These ratings could also be plotted for various groups as shown above.

Individuals might be asked to rate the importance of various content areas in the total school curriculum. Gooler (1971) asked forty-four secondary school teachers to rate these content areas, according to how things now are and how things ought to be. The results are shown in Figure 3. The same technique could be applied to more specific objectives for a particular curriculum.

The investigator may wish to note those goals consistently rated as very important, and those goals people feel should not be pursued in a given curriculum. Frequently, he will choose to compare the profiles of various groups.

Allocation of Resources

It is possible that an individual confronted with ten or seventeen or sixty-two goals for a curriculum program might rate all of the goals as "very important." In the rating technique outlined above the respondent is not forced to rank goals, as he was in the Q-sort exercise.

Resources are finite, however. No curriculum program can accomplish everything. One way to gain some insight into what people think is important is to ask them to allocate these finite resources among goals.

One way of allocating resources is to ask people what percentage of the total amount of money available for implementing a given curriculum

436

FIGURE 3 Profile of Mean Ratings of Perceived Importance of Courses and Content Areas by Secondary School Teachers

SUBJECTS (courses, content areas, activities)	This subject:			
	avoid	relatively unimportant	somewhat important	extremely important
Science				
Morality: what is right and wrong				
Language arts (English)				
Afro-American studies				
Interpersonal relations				
Social studies				
Athletics and physical education				
Music and art				
Family life and sex education				
Spelling				
Reading				
Mathematics				
Home economics or vocational education				

———————— Perception of present state

— — — — — Perception of what should be

should be allocated to pursuing each of a number of goals. The respondent might also be asked how he would allocate time. Those goals receiving greater amounts of time or money resources would be considered more important than goals receiving fewer resources.

Suppose an individual were given a series of goals potentially appropriate for a proposed curriculum in a certain community. The individual might be asked to respond to an item such as the following:

> Resources, both time and money, are often not as plenteous as we would like them to be. Educators try to pursue as many goals as they can with the time and money available. Suppose the school were required to cut back drastically on its curriculum. What educational goals are most important for the school, if they are not able to pursue all of them? Below, list the number of the goal that best completes each statement.

> If the community had enough resources to pursue:
> | | |
> |---|---|
> | 1 goal, it should pursue | Goal_____ |
> | 2 goals, it should pursue the previous goal and | Goal_____ |
> | 3 goals, it should pursue the previous goals and | Goal_____ |
> | 4 goals, it should pursue the previous goals and | Goal_____ |

The strength of resource allocation as an indicator of priorities lies with familiarity most people have with some kind of resource allocation. Most of us have to decide how we will spend our time and/or our money, and we have learned some things about manipulating both kinds of resources(2).

Two points should be made concerning the brief description of methods we have outlined for collecting priority information. First, the usefulness of priority information will be largely dependent on the quality and quantity of the goal statements people are asked to respond to. If respondents do not have many alternatives to choose from, the investigator may not obtain as complete a picture of what people think is important.

Second, we feel that the most complete representation of what people think is important may include a look at priorities from several perspectives. An individual may order a set of goals one way when asked to talk about those goals in terms of importance; he may order those same goals differently when asked to allocate resources. No one ordering may be more or less accurate than another. Rather each is different. It is important to look at the differences as well as the commonalities.

USING PRIORITY INFORMATION IN CURRICULUM DEVELOPMENT AND EVALUATION

Our brief discussion has been, at best, suggestive of ways of collecting information about goal priorities. But how is the information to be used once it has been collected?

A study of priorities will reveal concerns and disagreement among various groups of people as to what education ought to be doing. The curriculum developer can use this information in several ways. First, he may plan curricula that will attend to those things people think are important. Second, where he detects disagreements he may plan ways to lessen that disagreement. He may need to supply additional information to the disagreeing groups. He also might enlist the aid of advocates to clarify particular curriculum goals.

At best, knowledge of where disagreements may occur will enable the developer to lay a careful basis for the implementation of a curriculum so that its goals might be achieved. At worst, the developer will know where he might expect resistance. To be sure, the information obtained about goal priorities allows the developer to seek means for actively reflecting or obtaining program support.

We have said that evaluation too often looks exclusively at the past. It is possible to collect judgments about the worth of possible curriculum goals before those goals are actually implemented. We can manipulate situations or constraints, and can monitor how people will order these goals given different constraints. The situations or constraints we utilize may reflect our best understanding of what the future will look like. If people are told that additional resources might be available, how will they order their education goals? And will that ordering be different if, instead, there is actually a decrease in available resources? Which are rated important in each of these situations?

Knowledge of goal priorities held by various kinds of people does not tell the developer how a curriculum is to be made operational. Knowledge of goal priorities has been emphasized in this paper as a useful means of determining what goals people feel ought to be pursued. Similarly, knowledge of priorities might be useful in determining possible means for obtaining curriculum goals.

People may hold the same goals but disagree as to the best means of achieving them(3). The "experts" may regard particular means as the most pedagogically sound; others involved in the curriculum program, however, may find those means unacceptable. The developer may then wish to consider information about means priorities.

Techniques similar to those used in determining goal priorities might be used. The developer may want to consider means according to an "acceptable" or "unacceptable" dichotomy. He may simply ask people whether a particular means to an end is acceptable to them. Again, the "experts" may say that, of these acceptable means, A is more appropriate than B or C. Such a distinction, however, may be too fine for most groups with which the developer might deal.

CONCLUSION

We may be guilty of confusing, rather than clarifying, the issue of curriculum development. We have sought to establish a case for considering priorities as an important aspect of development. We have argued that it is important to consider a variety of goals for any program. We have suggested, and only briefly, how information about priorities might be collected, and how that information might be used by the developer.

If the developer is to do what we have suggested, he will make some trade-offs. To study priorities takes time and money and effort. What are the payoffs for education? We are not sure yet. We speculate that there are payoffs. Most important, we think, the study of what goals and means people feel ought to be pursued may orient planning toward the future rather than toward the past.

Notes

1. Much of the discussion about program operation has assumed goals to be need based. (See, for example, Stufflebeam's 1969 discussion of context evaluation.) We contend that goals may also be preference based. That is, certain goals may be desired by various groups of individuals.
2. See Gooler (1971) and Wilder (1968) for more detailed examples of priority data collection.
3. The Phi Delta Kappa Report has suggested that input evaluation should result in an analysis of alternative procedural designs in terms of potential costs and benefits. In addition, we argue, the analysis may need to include statements of how acceptable various means-to-ends are to various kinds of people.

References

DOWNEY, LAWRENCE W. *The Task of Public Education: The Perception of People.* Chicago: Midwest Administration Center, University of Chicago, 1960.

GOOLER, DENNIS D. "Strategies for Obtaining Clarification of Priorities in Education." Unpublished Ph.D. dissertation, University of Illinois, 1971.

——, and GROTELUESCHEN, A. D. "Accountability in Curriculum Evaluation." *Curriculum Theory Network,* 7 (September 1971), 27–34.

MOYNIHAN, DANIEL P. Counselor's Statement. *Toward Balanced Growth: Quantity and Quality.* Washington, D.C.: Government Printing Office, 1970, pp. 3–15.

SCRIVEN, MICHAEL. "The Methodology of Evaluation." *Perspectives of Curriculum Evaluation,* R. E. Stake. Chicago: Rand McNally, 1967.

STAKE, ROBERT E. "The Countenance of Educational Evaluation." *Teachers College Record,* 68 (1967), 523–540.

STUFFLEBEAM, DANIEL E. "Evaluation as Enlightenment for Decision Making." *Improving Educational Assessment and an Inventory of Measures of Affective Behavior.* Washington, D.C.: Association for Supervision and Curriculum Development, 1969.

TYLER, RALPH W. "General Statement on Evaluation." *Journal of Educational Research* (March 1942), 492–501.

440

WARDROP, JAMES L. "Determining 'Most Probable' Causes: A Call for Re-Examining Evaluation Methodology." Paper read at American Educational Research Association Meeting, New York, 1971.

WILDER, DAVID, et al. *Actual and Perceived Consensus on Educational Goals Between School and Community.* New York: Bureau of Applied Social Research, Columbia University, 1968.

ZIEGLER, WARREN. "Some Notes on How Educational Planning in the United States Looks at the Future. Part I." *Notes on the Future of Education,* 1 (1969), 2–4.

Operational Concepts

1. Different special-interest groups within the society have different curricular expectations.

2. Multiple curricula are therefore necessary if the school is to be responsive to these differing expectations.

3. The critical aspects of curriculum development occur when significant, long-range decisions are made.

4. Curriculum development should be sensitive to the differing aspirations of various constituencies.

5. It is unlikely that a theoretically "ideal" curriculum would be acceptable to all special-interest groups. Therefore, curriculum design is essentially a matter of compromise.

Implications

Curriculum theorists have always faced a sensitive dilemma: different special-interest groups within the subculture invariably are concerned about specific aspects of the curriculum, but their concerns vary: what is critical to one group is seen as trivial by another. The probability of incurring consumer dissatisfaction is high, particularly when curriculum designers are unaware of the particular wishes of a given special-interest group. To prevent such unawareness—and thus unresponsiveness—an effort must be made to carefully monitor public expectations.

Practitioners sometimes forget that evaluation serves a multiplicity of purposes: it can be used, for example, both to facilitate the determination of objectives and to assess the extent to which they have been realized. Similarly, ascertaining parental beliefs regarding schooling is an important function of evaluation, which properly should precede curriculum development.

Once the educational objectives of various special-interest groups are known, conflicts and contradictions often become apparent. The curriculum designer must then (1) devise different programs that satisfy different expectations, (2) seek to achieve some sort of consensus among the disparate expectations, or (3) install whatever program seems best, irrespective of client preferences.

Although we can, with reasonable ease, create alternative instructional units in response to various demands, we presently lack an effective organization for simultaneously offering a large number of diverse programs. Experiments are needed to help overcome this deficiency as well as to refine the processes through which public expectations are identified and clarified.

Joseph Featherstone

Measuring What Schools Achieve

Throughout the 1960s an organization called the International Association for the Evaluation of Educational Research (IEA) surveyed the
achievement of school children in some twenty-two countries in mathematics and other conventional academic subjects(1). The results of many of
these surveys are now being published, and recently a conference at Harvard
met to discuss what they mean. With cross-national samples involving over
250,000 schoolchildren, the IEA researchers used the same sort of statistical
procedures as those employed for the British Plowden Report, *Children
and Their Primary Schools;* by the sociologist James Coleman in his report,
Equality of Educational Opportunity; and by Christopher Jencks and his
colleagues in their book *Inequality.* The data add an interesting international dimension to the long and often muddled debate over the relative
effects of home background and schooling on children's achievement test
scores.

On the whole, the IEA studies tend to confirm earlier findings: Social
class and family background seem more important than schooling in accounting for differences in children's achievement test scores. There's
one major qualification, however: Schooling seems to be more important in
some subjects than in others. Both the Coleman and the Plowden reports
dealt with tests for verbal and mathematical ability; the IEA surveys show
significant school influence in science, literature, and second language
teaching. In the case of literature particularly, the survey suggests that
schoolchildren pick up very distinctive approaches to discussing literary
works. Those in Chile, England, and New Zealand take an interest in
matters of pure form; those in Belgium, Finland, and the United States
talk about themes and content; those in Italy take an essentially historical
approach. We don't know why. Nonetheless, the literature survey suggests
that responses to literature—and presumably to other parts of the curriculum not tested by these surveys—may indeed be learned, and that the
learning may well be the result of different sorts of school experiences.

Reprinted from Joseph Featherstone, "Measuring What Schools Achieve," *Phi Delta
Kappan,* March 1974, pp. 448–450; by permission of the publisher.

This would scarcely be an astonishing revelation were it not for the heated current arguments over what schools can do. The IEA data suggest that in certain kinds of subjects schools do indeed make a big difference.

The most dramatic fact in the IEA surveys is the huge gap in achievement scores between children in the wealthy, developed nations and children in poor, developing nations. Differences in reading scores among affluent nations are not great, whereas reading scores in three developing nations —Chile, India, and Iran—are so low that 14-year-old students seem almost illiterate by comparison. In discussions at Harvard of the educational plight of the poor nations, two points were stressed. The first was their need to build up some kind of educational *system*. In developed nations a wide array of formal and informal educational institutions have existed for three or four generations, and egalitarian social policy has slowly—with some glaring exceptions—narrowed the range of differences between schools. This very systematization poses a new set of problems: standardization, bureaucracy, overly rigid professionalization. Poor countries do not share this affluent malaise. A rural school in Chile may have no books at all, and so the problem is not how well or how soon children learn to read but whether they will ever learn.

A second point made at the Harvard conference was that however great the need for system, it is an open question whether the models of schooling developed in the industrial West are appropriate for developing nations. No developing nation has thus far established an advanced educational system without exacerbating class and caste divisions, and without according brain work a higher status than hand work. This problem was debated in Bolshevik Russia in the 1920s; it is a pressing issue in China and many other poor countries today. Ivan Illich and other proponents of deschooling and of a Tolstoyan nostalgia for rural life are right when they warn developing nations not to adopt educational institutions that are ill-suited to the needs of a majority of their people. And yet our countercultural assaults on schools and reading have a shallow and elitist ring; there is something unedifying about the spectacle of the jaded and overeducated rich preaching deschooling to poor nations hungry for education. Representatives from poor countries at the Harvard conference noted that literacy and numeracy are coming to be reckoned as fundamental human rights, and although warnings about an overelaborated educational edifice are well taken, the problem remains: how to equip students in developing nations with practical, functional skills such as the ability to read a newspaper, political pamphlet, or tractor repair manual.

In economically advanced societies, the tests of 14-year-olds showed Japan, Hungary, and Australia first, second, and third in science. (The pitfalls of cross-cultural research were revealed when a Japanese gentleman politely pointed out that the IEA survey overlooked the fact that Japanese secondary school students attend school six days a week; after momentary consternation, it was decided that this probably did not alter the results significantly.) In reading comprehension for 14-year-olds, New Zealand and Italy were first and second, with the United States, Finland, French Belgium, and Scotland all tied for third. (Some innovation-happy Americans were startled when a man from New Zealand suggested that one reason for his nation's high reading scores was the lack of abrupt changes of content and direction in New Zealand reading programs.) The United States ranked fifth in science; in literature its 14-year-olds scored second.

Now, achievement tests are a limited art form. Each culture has distinct educational aims; all cultures want much more for their children than a narrow range of skills that can be measured by achievement tests. Mass cross-cultural survey data probably should be taken with a pinch of salt. For one thing, the tests ignore important differences within each nation's educational system—most notably the proportion of students at a given age who remain in school to be tested. (The tests were given to 10-year-olds, 14-year-olds, and students in the last year of secondary school.) Also some observers accuse the tests of a Western bias, and it is true that students in poor nations are not as test-wise as the examination-ridden children of affluent societies. Few children in developing nations have ever even had the dubious pleasure of facing a multiple choice test on which the IEA surveys largely rely.

One illustration of why simple comparisons of test scores in a "cognitive Olympics" don't mean much arises from considering the US position in the science survey. Those who remember educational debates in this country in the fifties will recall that Admiral Hyman Rickover and others used to argue that the highly selective, elitist science education in European secondary schools was far superior to the science education of American students in our more or less comprehensive high schools. Now it turns out that the admiral and other critics were wrong. More students in secondary schools does not mean worse, although the results look wretched enough at first glance: The mean science scores of American students are lower than those for any other developed nation. However, it makes no sense to compare the performance of average high school graduates in comprehensive secondary school systems like America and Japan with the selected students who sit for *baccalauréat* in France, because the American and Japanese students constitute a majority, whereas the French students are a minority. If instead of comparing all science students you instead look at the performance of the best, the highest-scoring 1, 5, and 9 percent, you discover that they score about the same as their top European counterparts. Thus in the United States, which graduates over 70 percent of its students from high school, the scores of top science students come close to those of the best students in selective European education systems graduating fewer than 20 percent of their students. The IEA data suggest that the performance of more able students is not hurt when masses of students are given access to comprehensive schooling. Traditionally those who argue for elite systems measure the quality of the surviving few; those who favor more comprehensive education focus on the quality of education given to all. Within the sharp limits of the conventional terms of achievement tests, the IEA scores are mildly reassuring on the first point for American educators, who, if they are candid, will confess that they have not squarely faced the second.

One other aspect of the science study is of interest: the clear advantage of boys in science across the board and across the world. Boys everywhere are more interested in science and do better on the tests. The gap widens as students grow older. Differences are most marked in physics and slightest in biology. The IEA science report hints here and there at innate sexual differences, but most of the scholars at the Harvard conference preferred the simpler hypothesis of sexual bias. (In reading comprehension and literature, girls did better than boys.) What has now been documented on an international scale is the degree to which much of science learning is a male preserve.

Because of the political situation within their own country, Americans at the conference were particularly concerned about the public response to this sort of research. One point that keeps getting blurred in American debates is that the research that has been done does not show that schools make no difference. What it does show is that by certain crude measures schools are very similar to one another.

We should not confuse discussions of the effects of schooling (about which we know very little) with research on the effects of differences between schools in a roughly uniform educational system.

As matters stand, the effects of schools on achievement tests are much alike—though their effects on the daily lives of the children who attend them may vary enormously. But matters may not stand still. Schools could change their ways of teaching, or—more plausibly in the current political climate—budget cuts and declining support for education might create significant differences between the schools that are adequately supported and those that are starved. The authors of *Inequality* speculated that if schools were shut down—or, presumably, if schools for the poor were to deteriorate markedly—what they call the "cognitive gap" between rich and poor and black and white would be far greater than it is now.

All the school research so far leaves unexplained a great deal of the variation in students' test scores. You may call whatever explains the leftover variation "social character," "as yet unmeasured characteristics of students, teachers, and schools," "luck," or perhaps even "love," as Lewis Carroll's Duchess might put it. Whatever you call it, it is a mystery to the researchers. Complex methodological issues lurk like carp beneath most statements about schools. Critics of the IEA surveys argue that the methods used inflate home effects and minimize school effects, a criticism that the economist Samuel Bowles and others have made of the Coleman Report and similar research. There was repeated questioning at the Harvard conference whether mass surveys of schooling have not reached the limits

447

of their usefulness, and persistent complaints that particular research paradigms are too limited, covering over fundamental uncertainties with a misleading layer of numerical precision. Some educators argued that the IEA surveys' reliance on standardized achievement tests runs counter to a growing international trend promoting individuality, diversity, active learning, and a variety of styles of thinking among students. Educators in many countries are beginning to see education as lifelong, not as steps up an achievement ladder. Although the IEA data contained noncognitive items on student attitudes, a number of scholars were also critical of a basic neglect of values. There is certainly a need to look at education from perspectives of people not normally part of the research and policy system: children, teachers, parents, poor people. There was surprising agreement at the conference that the various goals different nations have for their schools are far too broad and complex to be settled by the crudities of mass testing.

This subdued emphasis on complexities—the sense of how little is actually known—is probably the most important thing for the public, policy makers, and practitioners to realize. By itself this ignorance constitutes a good argument for further research, research in a variety of modes. Yet many educational practitioners are coming to feel the same way about research as the exasperated student who, after taking yet another IEA test, wrote, "The money for this would have been better spent sending woolens to Africa." But as the process of framing educational policy becomes more self-conscious, the kind of research that is available and how it gets reported is important. The Plowden Report, for example, presented the British public with important quantitative research on the limits of schooling, along with qualitative material on classroom practice and educational philosophy that was of direct benefit to British practitioners. This combination is unheard of in this country, where educational discussions often manage to avoid the problems of practitioners altogether. It would be foolish pragmatism in our present state of basic ignorance to insist that all or even most educational research directly helps children and teachers, but it is not hoping too much that some of it will, and that some researchers will be willing to spend at least as much time working with teachers and children as Konrad Lorenz spends with his ducklings.

Part of the current animus against social science on schools is the age-old desire to kill the messenger who brings unwelcome news. To the degree that these sorts of studies check the traditional American faith in the boundless power of schooling to effect fundamental social change, they perform a valuable service. For the dark side of the coin of our utopian faith is the despair that sets in when schools do not do the impossible. In this despairing mood, educators tend to exaggerate the baleful impact of research, forgetting the primacy of the political climate. Much of recent American writing on the effects of schooling was intended as a critique of liberal sentimentality about the power of schooling, on the part of scholars who imagined that liberals would continue to dominate educational policy; the research reads strangely in an era when policy is in the hands of conservatives intent on dismantling the social services. It is, however, not the research itself, but the *Zeitgeist* that is mainly responsible for how particular findings get interpreted, emphasized, and acted upon. Arthur Jensen is, so to speak, always waiting in the wings, because the debate between conservative hereditarians and liberal environmentalists is perennial. It is only a political climate of despair and retreat from social commitment that puts the spotlight on him.

Meanwhile, in its endless concern for its schools, the American public might keep in mind two points made by one participant trying to sum up the IEA findings and other similar research. Home background is the best predictor of children's achievement scores, and yet the older students in school do successively better on the tests than the younger ones. The first point suggests the limits on the differences schools make; the second indicates that they may make a measurable difference on achievement test scores, as well as in more important, less readily measurable realms. Knee-deep in computer printout, and profoundly divided on many of the research issues, the scholars are still far from having resolved this key ambiguity.

Reference

1. See page 358, January, 1974, *Phi Delta Kappan.*

Operational Concepts

1. Social class and family background tend to exert a greater influence on student achievement than instructional method.

2. Recent allegations to the contrary, schools do influence the life patterns of students.

3. Although good schools everywhere tend to be somewhat similar, there is a substantial disparity in the academic achievement of children in affluent, developed nations as opposed to those in poor, under-developed ones.

4. Many of the important effects schools have on their students remain largely untestable.

5. Despite the great volume of research that has been done, much about schooling remains an enigma. Hence, further exploration is needed.

Implications

A journalist rather than an educator, Featherstone brings a unique point of view to the controversy surrounding the causes of educational success and failure. He observes that government control of education has now passed from the liberals to the conservatives, and goes on to argue that society has always expected too much from its schools. He also suggests, in commenting upon the comparative educational achievement of children in twenty-two countries, that "achievement tests are a limited art form." Much goes on in schools that is not yet fully understood. He contends, consequently, that although much of educational research has not seemed particularly powerful, it does not follow that further efforts will be without benefits. As educators, we perhaps owe Featherstone a massive debt for his efforts to persuade the public that no form of social science research can deliver instant cures or miracle-producing solutions. The functional meaning of his observations, presumably, is that, mindful of our shortcomings, we must persevere in our tasks, seeking greater competence and better curricula.

Early Childhood Education

Marilyn Segal

Curriculum in Infancy

As educators become more and more frustrated with the results of compensatory education, they are turning their attention to the infancy period and the effects of early training on later academic achievement. Two lines of investigation have sparked this recent interest. First, evidence from many sources suggests that infancy is a critical period for both cognitive and affective development. Second, a sizable amount of research points to significant differences between the middle SES parent and the lower SES parent in several dimensions of parent behavior. The advocates of infancy programs are convinced that if they can pinpoint the kinds of early experience that differentiate the lower and middle SES infant and can provide the lower SES infant with these kinds of experiences at the appropriate point in time, the differential in later achievement between these two groups of children will be reduced.

The case for infant intervention is built on a variety of research findings. Animal studies produce evidence of critical learning periods in the course of development in which deprivation effects are irreversible (Mason, 1970; Held, 1965; Bronfenbrenner, 1972). Studies of infants brought up in fosterhomes and in institutions (Skeels and Harris, 1943; Skodak, 1939; Skeels and Dye, 1939; Skodak and Skeels, 1972) reflect the effect of early environment on cognitive functioning. Longitudinal studies relate child-rearing practices to later personality and cognitive variables (Schaeffer, 1972). Experimental studies demonstrate behavioral changes in infants in response to controlled stimulation (Bijou and Baer, 1965). Intervention studies demonstrate significant changes in IQ levels between experimental and control groups that hold up over time (Karnes et al., 1970; Gordon, 1973; Weikart and Lambie, 1970).

An impressive array of research studies, too, can be summoned up to demonstrate significant differences between middle and lower SES child-rearing practices. Studies of language development show that the lower SES parent spends less time talking with his child and is less apt to use expansion as a technique for teaching language than the middle SES parent

(Bee and Bronfenbrenner, 1972). Also, according to Jerome Kagan (1970), the lower SES parent vocalizes less, maintains less eye contact during conversations, and makes fewer attempts to keep the child busy than the middle SES parent. Willerman et al. (1972), in a study conducted at the Massachusetts Lying-In Hospital, indicate that the long-term effect of a particular adverse experience during infancy is strongly dependent on SES.

There is then considerable support in the literature for the position that critical learning takes place in the early years of life and that the child-rearing practices in the average middle class home are substantially different from practices in the lower SES home.

This research has created a surge of interest in infant stimulation programs and has inspired speculation on several key issues that have a direct bearing on the structure and curriculum of these infancy programs. These issues include philosophic arguments on goals, values, and responsibilities; psychological arguments on learning and motivational variables; and practical arguments involving the "nuts and bolts" of infancy programs and infancy curriculums.

THEORETICAL ISSUES

The two theoretical issues that probably give rise to the greatest divergence of opinion are (1) what should the underlying purpose of an infancy program be, and (2) what persons or agencies should be responsible for the initiation of infancy programs?

What Is the Purpose of an Infancy Program?

Although the original interest in infancy programs stemmed from the concern among educators that Headstart began too late to have a significant effect on the academic achievement of the disadvantaged child, advocates of infancy programs have not limited their objectives to effecting academic achievement. In an interview study with parents, Gordon (1973) found that the majority of parents were interested in having a child that "could make it." This concern with coping behavior rather than academic achievement is characteristic of educators as well as parents and has had an impact on infancy program development. It would seem obvious that the goals of infancy programs tend to reflect the values of the culture in which the program develops. In a typical Israelian kibbutz, for instance, independence and competency are major goals of the infancy program. In Russia, in a government-sponsored crèche, the infant curriculum stresses programmed stimulation and communal living. Nurses are given an exact schedule to follow, and every infant is programmed on a daily basis according to a carefully delineated curriculum plan. As soon as an infant is old enough to be aware of the presence of other children, he is placed in a playpen with five or six other infants and is taught to share his toys (Bronfenbrenner, 1970).

In America, the underlying goals of an infancy program follow no uniform pattern. Some programs hold academic achievement as their primary goal. Others stress competency, coping behaviors, or the development of curiosity. Still other infancy programs are set up as day-care centers developed to serve the needs of the working mothers. In these programs, the primary goal is to keep the baby safe and healthy while the mother maintains her job.

Who Should Initiate Infancy Programs?

A second theoretical issue concerns the assignment of responsibility for the development of the infancy program. This issue is not unrelated to the first. If the primary goal of an infancy program is to narrow the achievement gap between children in the middle and lower SES groups, the responsibility for developing infancy programs lies within the educational community. If, on the other hand, the major purpose of the program is to free a mother to work, the social agencies within the community might be charged with the responsibility of initiating infancy programs.

PSYCHOLOGICAL ISSUES

Psychological issues as well as theoretical ones assume prime importance as infancy programs are developed. These issues include the following: (1) how does a child learn, (2) should an infancy program teach parents or children, (3) what should be taught to the infant or parent, (4) at what age should the teaching begin, and (5) where should an infancy program be taught?

How Does a Child Learn?

The question of how a child learns is a fundamental issue directly involving the developmental model that a programmer adopts. Although there are divergent positions even on categorizations of theoretical models, the classification of the developmental positions into four major schools is fairly typical. McCandless et al. (1973) label these four schools as follows:

1. The humanistic theory.
2. The behavioristic theory.
3. The cognitive developmental theory of Jean Piaget.
4. The dynamic or psychoanalytic theory.

454

The humanistic point of view holds as a central tenet the uniqueness and the "humanness" of each individual and the intrinsic quality of human motivation. A child is not a powerless robot reacting to the external forces that shape his destiny, but a self-propelled actor programming his own activity and shaping his own growth. He is "the master of his fate" and the "captain of his soul." He is capable of intent, of making rational decisions, and of purposefully planning for his future. He is curious and creative and is excited by the new and the novel. Development is a continual unidirectional process leading to self-actualization. The humanistically oriented program helps to provide for each infant a safe and comfortable environment that fosters creative development.

The second point of view, "behaviorism," as its name implies, is concerned with the learning capacity of the individual. Learning is thought of as a function of the properties of the stimulus and the previous history and present state of the organism. The behaviorist, in developing an infancy program, is primarily concerned with the conditions of learning, and attempts to engineer an environment that promotes and reinforces cognitive growth and development along with prosocial behavior.

The cognitive developmentalists, in the tradition of Piaget, believe that intelligence is developed as a result of the interplay of experience and biological readiness. Between age 0–2 the child is in a sensorimotor reflexive stage of development where he knows the world by the actions he performs upon it. This sensorimotor stage is further divided into six sequenced substages, each characterized by typical action patterns that reflect the infant's level of functioning. As long as the infant has opportunities to practice the schemas he has learned and to develop new schemas in response to new events, development takes place at a normal rate. An infant program should promote development by providing appropriate stimulation at the infant's point of readiness.

The psychoanalytic school is concerned primarily with emotional adjustments and the effects of interpersonal relationships on psychosocial development. Development is conceptualized as a progression through age-related stages, with a particular sexual conflict associated with each stage. Because parents play a vital role in helping their children overcome these basic conflicts, a day-care situation that takes an infant away from the parent creates anxiety and frustration, and is considered a threat to mental health. The psychoanalytic school is supportive of an infancy program only if it preserves and fosters the infant–parent bond.

Should an Infancy Program Teach Parents or Infants?

Although psychologists might agree that the goal of an infancy program is to enhance the development of the infant, there are two quite different positions as to the means of achieving this goal. In some infant programs the "client" is the infant. In other programs the parent is thought of as the client. The rationale to support a program aimed at parents is twofold.

1. The parent is the central figure in the baby's world and teaching can be effective only if the parent is the teacher.
2. What makes a difference in the way an infant develops is not the kinds of toys he plays with or the kinds of games he plays but the whole climate in which he is reared.

Schaeffer (1970) suggests a compromise approach between the parent-as-client and the infant-as-client positions. Schaeffer suggests a four-stage model for the early education of the child:

1. The development by the parent of the positive attachment to the child.
2. The development by the child of a positive relationship with the parent.
3. The mutual enjoyment in an activity or exploration of an object.
4. The development of autonomy and inner motivation on the part of the child.

The task of the "teacher" is to work with both the infant and the parent to bring this progression into being.

What Should Be Taught to the Infant or Parent?

Whether the objective of an infancy program is to teach babies directly or to teach parents to teach their babies, the question of curriculum arises. The type of curriculum that is advocated for a program reflects the underlying theoretical position of the curriculum designer or consumer.

The psychoanalytically oriented infancy curriculum is an outgrowth of the Freudian position, which asserts that trauma and frustration in infancy lead to adult pathology. The focus of the psychoanalytic curriculum is on the responsiveness of the caretaker to the needs of the infant and the interaction patterns that emerge from this responsiveness. The overall objective of the curriculum is to foster healthy development by engendering a sense of basic trust. The demonstration Project in Group Care for Infants in Greensboro, North Carolina (Evans and Saia, 1972), and the Frank Porter Graham Child Development Center in Chapel Hill, North Carolina (Weber, 1970), attempt to generate this kind of supportive environment.

A second and quite different type of curriculum is a direct outgrowth of the behaviorist or social learning viewpoint. Here the emphasis is placed on the provision of early and adequate stimulation, with positive reinforcement of appropriate responses. Attention is given to the interaction of child and caretaker and the reinforcing effect of infant responses such as smiling and quieting on the nurturant behaviors of the caretaker. The

Crispus Attucks Children's Center in Boston is behavioristically oriented. The program is highly structured, with academic achievement the primary objective (Evans and Saia, 1972).

The writings of Piaget on infancy provide the theoretical basis of still another type of infant curriculum. According to Piaget, every infant goes through an invariant sequence of sensorimotor substages. The newborn infant is equipped with a bundle of reflexes or wired-in responses. As he uses these built-in reflexes, he learns to make discriminations and to recognize familiar things and people. Piaget describes this as the development of "schema." Through the interaction of maturation and experience, the infant coordinates these schema and develops primitive notions of time, space, and causality. During this period, too, the infant develops object constancy; he recognizes that objects continue to exist even when he can't see or feel them. A Piagetian based curriculum depends on the caretaker's awareness of stage related developmental sequences. By identifying the developmental stage an infant is in, the caretaker can arrange conditions that permit practice of already acquired schema, and provide opportunities for new learning to take place. The Ypsilanti Carnegie Infancy Education Project, developed by Weikart and Lambie (1969), the Infant Toddler Learning Program developed by Badger (1970), and the Children's Center at Syracuse, New York, directed by Lolly (1973) are built on Piagetian models.

A fourth type of infancy curriculum is derived from research on SES variables and seeks to emulate the middle-class home environment. The rationale is that differences in achievement related to SES do not appear until the second year of life. Therefore, educators postulate, these differences could be caused by differences in the teaching style and behavior of the mother. According to Kagan (1970), middle-class mothers engage in more face-to-face talking with their infants and use more varied, complex, and expanded language than lower SES mothers. Also, a middle-class mother is more apt to play peek-a-boo with "theme and variations," to allow grasping and clinging, to model nonimpulsive behavior, and to respond consistently to the infant's overtures.

Laboratory studies in infancy provide still another source of infant curricula. Infants are observed in controlled situations to determine the qualities of visual stimuli that influence fixation time, thresholds of response, and reactions to social stimulation. These data are then transformed by the curriculum writer into a prescription for structuring an ideal environment. Playtentials, an infant toy program designed by Burton White, is inspired by laboratory experiments.

The final and probably most common method for developing an infant curriculum is to design a sequence of activities that match the infant's age. Painter (1971) provides a daily activity program that outlines activities to stimulate seeing, hearing, feeling, imitation, speech, spatial relationships, and self-awareness of cause and effect. Segner (1970), from the John F. Kennedy Child Development Center, bases her curriculum on the Bayley Scales of Infant Development, and the Revised Yale Developmental Schedule. Many of the activities suggested at each age level correspond to test items on the developmental tests.

A final kind of curriculum is essentially eclectic. Behavioral objectives are classified in broad categories like motor, cognitive, and language. Suggested activities are selected on a pragmatic basis to provide opportunities for practice in each of these categories. Ira Gordon's program is essentially an eclectic model.

At What Age Should the Teaching Begin?

There is a general consensus that SES-related differences in performance on developmental scales do not appear until the fourteenth month of life. There are several explanations given for the SES-related divergency in developmental scores.

1. Genetic differences in capacity to operate symbols are manifested for the first time when a child learns a language.
2. Items on developmental scales prior to fourteen months measure motor functions rather than cognitive functioning. At the fourteen-month level, the items tap cognitive functions, so that innate differences begin to show.
3. During the first year of life, the infant is learning to learn. If an infant has experienced a healthy developmental climate during the first year of life, he will have developed the potential to learn. The potential will be expressed in measurable behavior during the second year of life.
4. Differences in teaching style of middle and lower SES parents have an effect on language learning. The lower SES child performs less well on a developmental test during the second year because he has had less opportunity to learn language.

The first two positions are usually not acceptable to advocates of an infancy program. Those who support the third hypothesis believe that an infancy program should begin in the first months of life when the infant is learning to learn. They suggest that the curiosity and investigatory characteristics fostered in the first year enhance the infant's ability to learn from experience in the second year. Those who support the fourth hypothesis are more likely to suggest that intervention should begin around the fourteenth month when language learning takes place. They believe that an enriched language experience at the critical age for language development can overcome the problem of a cumulative deficit.

Where Should an Infancy Program Be Taught?

The question of where an infant curriculum should be taught is answered both on pragmatic and theoretical bases. Where a program is set up to serve a working mother, it is based in a center for pragmatic reasons. Some programs, on the other hand, are center based for ideological reasons. The kibbutz in Israel and the crèche in the Soviet Union are expressions of the theoretical position that infants can best be served outside of home and family.

Home-based programs are built on quite a different set of assumptions:

1. The role of parent as educator is important for both parent and child.
2. Attachment behavior and stranger anxiety reach a peak during the first year of life, and the infant who is taken away from the parent at a critical period may enter into an acute depression that would traumatize him for life.
3. The most important learning is home based.
4. The real benefits of a home-based program are derived from the parents' increased awareness of and responsiveness to infant's needs.

Prototype Programs

Because of the relative newness of the infant stimulation programs, many of the controversial issues involving structure, content, timing, and type of delivery system have not been experimentally investigated. It is possible, however, to identify some prototype programs that express different positions on controversial issues.

One of the best known of the home-based programs is the Ypsilanti Carnegie Infant Education project. This project was established in 1968 and funded as a home-care program by the Carnegie Corporation. The basic objective of the program is to prepare a family for learning through scheduled home visits by classroom teachers. The home teacher works with both parents and infant, modeling appropriate activities and capitalizing on teaching opportunities provided by spontaneous play. Although flexibility is a major tenet of the program, some curriculum guidelines have been set up.

1. The teacher, using the Piagetian description of the sensorimotor stage, must give the parent information about infant development.
2. The curriculum must be adjustable.
3. The teacher must have room to express her own creativity.
4. The curriculum must provide criteria for assessing the program.
5. Teacher must help parent to recognize cumulative behaviors that build up to the developmental milestones.

Although a statistical study of the first nine months of the program showed no significant differences between treatment and control groups, positive changes in the affecting domain were noted by the examiners (Weikart and Lambie, 1969).

The Home Learning Center Approach to Early Stimulation developed by Ira J. Gordon of the University of Florida is another experimental home-based infancy program. It differs from the Ypsilanti approach in that non-professionals are used as the key educators of parent and child. Longitudinal data from the study indicate significant gains in intellectual performance for the experimental group. According to Gordon (1973),

> current results indicate that a home visit program only using paraprofessionals as home visitors on a once-a-week basis in the first two years of life, and continued home visits combined with a small group setting for four hours a week during the third year of life, leads to (a) improved intellectual performance of the children as a function of time and age of entry in the program, and (b) positive attitudes and behaviors of mothers toward their children. Of special significance is the performance at age 5 of those who were in the program for only nine months, when they were three to twelve months of age. Further, consistency as well as length of time in the program is important.

The Family Development Research Program, in Syracuse, New York, although essentially a center-based program, incorporates some of the features of a home-based program. Parents enter the program during pregnancy, and are visited at home on a weekly basis by a staff of paraprofessionals. Visiting staff provide the parents-to-be with information on nutrition and child care, and help with family problems as they emerge. At six months old, the infants are brought into the center, where the ratio of caretaker to child is four to one. The caretaker follows an infant curriculum based on the theories of Erikson and Piaget. The first longitudinal cognitive data on the project include Binet IQ scores at thirty-six months for children's center children, low education controls, and high education contrasts. Children's center children scored significantly higher than the low education controls (a mean score of 111.2 compared to a mean score of 98.4), whereas the high education contrast group scored significantly higher than the center group (mean 125). According to Lolly, these results negate Jensen's hypothesis that intervention programs will do little to change the IQ of children who are not operating at a low cognitive level (Lolly, 1973).

The Nova University Play and Learn Program (Segal, 1973) presents an alternative to both the home-based and the center-based infancy program models. Nova's program uses commercial television as its major vehicle of parent communication. A series of nine programs, "To Reach A Child," has been developed to cover the first year of life. These programs provide information on child development and demonstrate age-appropriate toys and activities. A manual that accompanies the program expands on the information provided in the shows and includes directions for making the toys that are demonstrated. The program is still in the developmental stage and results are not available as yet.

CONCLUSION

Although the infancy programs that have emerged in recent years are diversified in format, focus, and theoretical orientation, several convergencies can be identified:

1. There is general consensus that an intervention program for lower SES infants should be initiated before the age when SES differences are observable.
2. Parent involvement is a critical element in an infancy program whether it is home or center based.
3. Infants in the first year of life require interaction with a caretaker on a one-to-one basis.
4. The effect of an infancy program can only be assessed on a longitudinal basis.
5. An infancy program has the potential of producing change in the parents as well as the infants, and these changes can be affective as well as cognitive.

A final question that we may want to ask about infancy programs concerns expectations for the future. Does the current interest in infancy programs represent a fad or a trend? Are the school systems going to become increasingly involved in infancy programs? Will infancy programs have a positive influence on home–school relationships? Will the initiation of infancy programs for lower SES and high-risk infants help to equalize educational opportunity and reverse the cumulative deficit hypothesis? Hopefully, as the findings of current studies are reported, some answers to these questions will be forthcoming.

References

BADGER, E. *Project Advisor*. Mt. Carmel, Ill.: Mt. Carmel Parent and Child Center, 1970.

BEE, H. L., and BRONFENBRENNER, U. *Influences on Human Development*. Hinsdale, Ill.: Dryden Press, 1972.

BIJOU, S. W., and BAER, D. M. *Child Development II—Universal Stage of Infancy*. New York: Meredith Corp., 1965.

BRONFENBRENNER, U. *Two Worlds of Childhood*. New York: Russell Sage Foundation, 1970.

———. *Influences on Human Development*. Hinsdale, Ill.: Dryden Press, 1972.

EVANS, E. B., and SAIA, G. E. *Day Care for Infants*. Boston: Beacon Press, 1972.

GORDON, I. J. *The Florida Parent Education, Early Intervention Projects: A Longitudinal Look*. Detroit: Merrill-Palmer Conference on Research and Teaching of Infant Development, 1973.

HELD, R. Plasticity in Sensory Motor Systems. *Scientific American*, 1965, *213*, 84–94.

KAGAN, J. In Denneberg, V. H. (ed.), *Education of the Infant and Young Child*. New York: Academic Press, 1970.

KARNES, M. B., TESKA, J. H., HODGINS, A. S., and BADGER, E. D. Educational Intervention at Home by Mothers of Disadvantaged Infants. *Child Development*, 1970, *41*, 925–935.

LOLLY, J. R. *The Family Development Research Program Progress Report—College for Human Development*. Syracuse, N.Y.: Syracuse University, 1973.

MASON, W. A. In Denneberg, V. H. (ed.), *Education of the Infant and Young Child*. New York: Academic Press, 1970.

McCANDLESS, B. R., EVANS, E. B., and ELLIS, D. *Children and Youth Psychosocial Development*. Hinsdale, Ill.: Dryden Press, 1973.

PAINTER, G. *Teach Your Baby*. New York: Simon and Schuster, 1971.

SCHAEFFER, E. S. Towards a Revolution in Education. A Perspective from Child Development Research. *The National Elementary Principal*, 1972, *551*, 17.

———. In Denneberg, V. H. (ed.), *Education of the Infant and Young Child*. New York: Academic Press, 1970.

SEGAL, M. *To Reach a Child*. Fort Lauderdale, Fla.: Nova University, 1973.

SEGNER, L. *Ways to Help Babies Grow and Learn: Activities for Infant Education*. Denver, Colo.: University of Colorado Medical Center, 1970.

SKEELS, H. M., and DYE, H. B. A Study of the Effects of Differential Stimulation on Mentally Retarded Children. *Proceedings of the American Association on Mental Deficiency*, 1939, *44*, 114–136.

———, and HARRIS, I. Children with Inferior Social Histories—Their Mental Development in Adoptive Homes. *Journal of Genetic Psychology*, 1943, *72*, 283–294.

SKODAK, M. *Children in Foster Homes*. University of Iowa Studies Child Welfare, 1939, *165*(1), 16.

———, and SKEELS, H. M. In Bronfenbrenner, U. (ed.), *Influences on Human Development*. Hinsdale, Ill.: Dryden Press, 1972.

WEBER, E. *Early Childhood Education, Perspectives on Change*. Worthington, Ohio: Charles Jones Publishing Company, 1970.

WEIKART, D. P., and LAMBIE, D. *Ypsilanti–Carnegie Infant Education Project*. Ypsilanti, Mich.: Department of Research and Development, Ypsilanti Public Schools, 1969.

———, and LAMBIE, D. In Denneberg, V. H. (ed.), *Education of the Infant and Young Child*. New York: Academic Press, 1970.

WILLERMAN, L., et al. In Bronfenbrenner, U. (ed.), *Influences on Human Development*. Hinsdale, Ill.: Dryden Press, 1972.

Operational Concepts

1. Research data suggest that preschool educational intervention produces worthwhile cognitive and affective improvements in children from lower socioeconomic groups.

2. Parental involvement is of critical importance in preschool educational intervention, irrespective of whether the "infancy-education" program is home-based or not.

3. Infancy-education programs may deal with a number of objectives, including preparation for later academic learning, language development, and stimulation of curiosity.

4. In the absence of infancy-education program or similar intervening experiences, children with lower socioeconomic backgrounds may enter school with serious learning handicaps.

5. The issue of whether preschool educational intervention is more effective when parents are instructed in how to teach their own children or when the children are taught directly remains largely unresolved.

Implications

Infancy-education programs are a relatively new phenomenon that has recently attracted widespread interest. Although there seems to be little question that the programs yield measurable benefits, a number of peripheral issues must still be considered. Is it the school's task, for example, to work with children whatever their "natural" state at age five, or is it to begin their public education at the earliest point where benefit can be derived? Even more fundamentally, should the school attempt to neutralize socioeconomic differences at all?

Does the school, since infancy-education programs seem to have greatest impact away from the home, have moral justification for taking preschool children from their natural home environment merely for the purpose of improving their learning capabilities? And, if one concludes that it does, since it is economically more efficient to have trained specialists work directly with the children, do other factors mitigate against depriving parents of their acculturing role? Finally, in view of the ubiquitous charge that schools already undertake far more than they should, would it be both more practical and more humane to eradicate the social inequities that create economically disadvantaged families in the first place? Would it not be more sensible, in short, to attack the root problem rather than the symptoms?

Until these issues are resolved, and until more is known about the long-range consequences of various early-childhood-education endeavors, educators probably are best advised to follow developments in the field with close attention—but to delay wide-scale activity until more evidence is in.

Bilingual–Bicultural Education

Henry T. Trueba

Bilingual–Bicultural Education: An Overview

Instruction in language other than English (in German, French, and Spanish) has existed in the United States, both in private and public schools, since the late eighteenth century. The German–English schools, for example, existed from the early nineteenth until the early twentieth century. During this century, Chinese, French, Poles, Slovaks, Japanese, and other linguistic groups used their own language as a vehicle of instruction (Andersson and Boyer, 1970:17–21). However, it was not until the 1960s that bilingual education in response to political pressures exerted by minority groups gained national momentum in the legislature.

RECENT DEVELOPMENT

In 1963, Dade County in Florida and, in 1964, Webb County and the City of San Antonio, Texas, launched bilingual programs that had significant national impact. Subsequently, many other programs were started in public schools in Texas, California, Arizona, New Mexico, and other states, with large numbers of non-English-speaking children.

Bilingual education legislation was introduced in the U.S. House of Representatives (Congressional Record, 1973:H.R. 9840) by James Schewer from New York, on May 10, 1967. This bill was modified and presented as an amendment to the Elementary and Secondary Education Act, Title VII, and finally passed in Congress on January 2, 1968. It was sponsored by numerous senators from New Jersey, Pennsylvania, Massachusetts, Florida, Texas, Ohio, Illinois, Arizona, Indiana, New York, Washington, California, Maine, and Hawaii, among other states. Bilingual education was defined by the U.S. Office of Education (USOE) as the use of two languages, one of which is English, as media of instruction for the same student population, in a well-organized program that encompasses part or all of the curriculum, and includes the history and culture associated with the student's mother tongue. This interpretation has been reaffirmed in the amendment of October 9, 1973, presented by Senators Cranston, Kennedy, and Montoya:

> Comprehensive Bilingual Education Amendments Act of 1973 . . . declares it the policy of the United States that bilingual educational methods and techniques shall be encouraged and developed in recognition of the special educational needs of children of "limited English-speaking ability" . . . Sets an expanded definition for "program of bilingual education" adding studies in the native language of the child; directs the study of the history and culture of the United States; allows the participation of bilingual children in regular classes . . .; provides the voluntary enrollment of children whose language is English; and provides individualized instruction (Congressional Record, 1973:S 18814).

Bilingual education was seen by the legislators as an application of the Equal Educational Opportunities Act, which in Section 201, Title II, stated that equal educational opportunity should not be denied to an individual on account of color, national origin, or by failure of an educational institution to overcome language barriers that impede equal participation of students (Congressional Record, 1973:S 18810).

It was estimated in October of 1973 that approximately 5 million children whose native tongue is other than English, about 10 percent of the 51.5 million enrolled in public and private schools (see Table 1), are not equipped to receive instruction in English (Congressional Record, 1973:S 18807). To force such children of Spanish, Chinese, Japanese, Italian, Eskimo, German, or any of the other fifty linguistic backgrounds to start formal learning in English often results in practical illiteracy, both in English and the mother tongue, and in serious psychological problems. In a country that has been from its foundations multicultural, the need to maintain and develop other languages and cultures has encountered resistance on the part of ill-informed educators and politicians who aim at a speedy and total assimilation of all children to the misconceived notion of a monoculture America. The recent emphasis on bilingual education is not totally altruistic. Bilingual education is seen as a means to curtail truancy, crime, and discontent in ethnic minorities. What is bilingual–bicultural education in the United States today really like, and what should it be? These questions are crucial to assess the meaning and significance of this revolutionary movement in education.

Impact of Existing Programs

We do not know what criteria are used to identify children eligible for bilingual education. Judging from other surveys and estimates, for example those made in the state of Illinois, we suspect that the figures are rather conservative. It is quite significant that in Illinois Spanish-speaking

TABLE 1 Approximate Number of School-Aged Children in the United States Needing Bilingual Education

ETHNIC-LANGUAGE GROUP	APPROXIMATE NUMBER
Mexican-American	3,100,000
Puerto Rican	800,000
Other Spanish-speaking	380,000
French-speaking	350,000
American Indian (including Eskimo)	180,000
Portuguese	60,000
Chinese	40,000
Japanese	20,000
Russian	8,000
Chamorro	7,500
Other	10,000
Major States	
California	800,000
Texas	650,000
New York	350,000
New Mexico	100,000
Illinois	70,000
Colorado	60,000
Arizona	50,000
Total in the United States	5,000,000

SOURCE: Albar Pena's estimate used by M. M. Swanson, "Bilingual Education: The National Perspective," 1973:8.

children alone number 4,280, that is, 80.5 percent of all children of limited English-speaking ability, and that the states of California, Texas, New Mexico, and Arizona account for 1.6 million (32 percent) of the total number of children in that situation. (For an approximate ethnic distribution of school-aged children in federally funded programs, see Table 2; for the geographical distribution of programs and level of funding per state, see Table 3.)

Ninety percent of the existing programs are for Spanish-speaking children; the remaining 10 percent is distributed among French, Chinese, Portuguese, Japanese, Russian, Italian, and thirteen Indian languages: Navajo, Chamorro, Yuk, Pomo, Ute, Passamaquoddy, Crow, Northern Cheyenne, Cree, Zuni, Kereson, Choctaw, and Cherokee, among others.

To compound the problem of minimum impact on the target populations, studies done by Gaarder (1970) and Kjolseth (1972) suggest a great deal of disparity between aims and means, as well as the lack of proper cultural component in most programs. A significant change in the traditional low esteem and unclear self-identity of children in those programs

TABLE 2 Approximate Number of School-Aged Children in the United States
Enrolled in the Title VII Bilingual Programs for 1972–1973

ETHNIC-LANGUAGE GROUP	APPROXIMATE NUMBER
Mexican-American	70,913
Puerto Rican	14,179
Other Spanish-speaking	6,046
French-speaking	2,095
American Indian (including Eskimo)	2,180
Portuguese	567
Chinese	639
Chamorro	240
Multilingual	2,897
Major States	
California	27,184
Texas	34,991
New York	10,238
New Mexico	5,449
Illinois	1,372
Colorado	2,212
Arizona	3,017
Total in the United States	100,391

SOURCE: Compiled from information listed in *Guide to Title VII ESEA Bilingual–Bicultural Projects in the United States*, 1972–1973, ESEA. Austin, Tex.: Dissemination Center for Bilingual–Bicultural Education, 1973.

remains to be documented. At best some programs are trying to emphasize equal proficiency in the two languages, although not enough familiarity with both cultures. Obviously, the need for an in-depth research to assess the impact of existing programs is urgent. According to Fishman, bilingual education in the United States suffers from "three serious lacks: a lack of funds (Title VII is pitifully starved), a lack of personnel (there is almost no optimally trained personnel in this field), and a lack of evaluated programs (curricula, material, methods)" (Fishman, 1970:1).

Civil Rights Commission Reports, such as those for the Southwest Mexican American (1971–1973), have provided abundant information on the precarious condition of minority students in all school levels and demonstrate the tragic failure of the American educational system, its ethnocentric, racist, and irresponsible neglect of millions of children whose only sin was to be culturally different. The Civil Rights Commission Report of 1971 concluded that

minority students in the southwest—Mexican Americans, blacks, American Indians—do not obtain the benefits of public education at a rate equal to

TABLE 3 Title VII, ESEA, FY 1973: Number of Programs and Funds by State in Ranking Order, and Percent of Nationwide Enrollment of Spanish-Speaking

NUMBER OF PROGRAMS FOR ALL LANGUAGE GROUPS	STATE	FUNDS	% OF NATIONWIDE ENROLLMENT OF SPANISH-SPEAKING
62	California	$8,965,659	30.4
41	Texas	6,651,869	24.4
26	New York	4,358,128	13.7
12	New Mexico	1,085,625	4.6
3	Florida	918,000	3.3
7	Colorado	876,122	3.2
4	New Jersey	870,828	3.1
2	Pennsylvania	611,678	0.7
4	Illinois	591,929	3.6
4	Michigan	488,400	1.3
7	Massachusetts	463,387	0.7
3	Connecticut	406,750	0.9
9	Arizona	330,356	3.8
2	Washington	267,943	0.7
2	Indiana	247,193	0.6
4	Louisiana	189,038	0.2[a]
1	Wisconsin	178,713	0.4
1	Ohio	118,904	0.8
1	Idaho	100,000	0.2
1	Virgin Islands	100,000	—[a]
1	Puerto Rico	88,000	—[a]
2	Rhode Island	85,000	—[a,b]
1	Oregon	3,583	0.3

[a] Bilingual programs other than English–Spanish.
[b] Puerto Rico is experimenting with bilingual programs with returnees from the continent who can't speak Spanish.

SOURCE: For FY 1973 funding: A Report to the Assistant for Spanish Speaking Americans, U.S. Department of Health, Education, and Welfare, October 1972. For population: *Directory of Public Elementary and Secondary Schools in Selected Districts*, Fall 1972, U.S. Department of Health, Education, and Welfare, Office for Civil Rights, Table IV, p. x. *Bilingual Education in Illinois. A Status Report*, by Isidro Lucas, Ph.D., 1974.

that of their Anglo classmates. . . . Without exception, minority students achieve at a lower rate than Anglos: Their school holding power is lower; their repetition of grades is more frequent, their overageness is more prevalent; and they participate in extracurricular activities to a lesser degree than their Anglo counterparts . . . (U.S. Commission on Civil Rights, 1971, pp. 41–42).

In 1968, for example, of the 290,000 Mexican Americans enrolled in grades 1–6 in Texas public schools, it was estimated that 140,000 would never receive a high school diploma (ibid.).

In spite of the obvious shortcomings and the limited number of the existing bilingual education programs, we can today, based on the clear success of some programs, look at bilingual education as one of the possible solutions to the educational problems of some minorities. For many Chicanos in the Southwest, bilingual education represents the most important enterprise and most sincere effort to change the American educational system and make it more sensitive to the needs of non-English-speaking children, as well as an opportunity to build up personal pride, distinct self-identity, and to lay the foundations for a fuller participation in the socio-economic blessings of this country (Trueba, 1974:8–10).

The Future of Bilingual Education in the United States

Whether or not bilingual education will in fact respond to the expectations of ethnic groups, remains to be seen. Much of the success will undoubtedly depend on legislative support and available funds. Up to the last months of 1973, only twelve states had legislation of any kind on bilingual education: Connecticut, Louisiana, New York, Pennsylvania, Rhode Island, Texas, Alaska, California, Illinois, Massachusetts, Maine, and New Mexico; and only the latter six states had explicit laws providing for bilingual education (Congressional Record, 1973:S 18807–S 18810). Recently a few other states have introduced and/or passed bills on bilingual education. The fact is that bilingual education depends by and large on federal funds. Meanwhile, in those states where bilingual education has been allowed, encouraged, or mandated, the task of preparing personnel, adapting curriculum materials, and establishing sound criteria for evaluation is gigantic.

Bilingual–bicultural education is, by its own nature, a multidisciplinary field that must draw from psychology, sociology, anthropology, pedagogy, and linguistics, among other disciplines. In the modern socioeconomic context of the United States' political struggle for equal educational opportunies, bilingual–bicultural education is not primarily a linguistic problem. The languages of culturally different children have been rejected by American educators not because they have certain structural, syntactic, or semantic features, but because they are intimately related to the culture that such languages transfer and perpetuate from generation to generation. Ethnic groups, as they grow in numbers and demand recognition, have become clearly a threat to American educators who fail to see the multicultural nature of American society.

Bilingual–bicultural education as a multidisciplinary and cross-cultural field has nourished on linguistics and on the social sciences. It is useful to view bilingual education as an international phenomenon, but

470

we must not forget that in this country it responds to a set of specific political and economic pressures in a unique historical context. As Mackey states, "One of the pawns in the politics of local minorities has been the question of bilingual schooling. This is a question which often arouses bitter conflicts" (Mackey, 1970:64). Thus, the meaning of bilingual–bicultural education corresponds to the expectations of the various peoples involved in it, which differ from country to country.

There is indeed much we can learn from technical developments and research done abroad but we have to adapt them to the United States. Most of the pioneers in this field, such as Andersson and Boyer (1970), Lambert (1955, 1956, 1961, 1967), Fishman (1952, 1964, 1965, 1966, 1970), Mackey (1952, 1953, 1962, 1965, 1967, 1968, 1970), and others, have had extensive experience with bilingualism outside of the United States. Subsequently, other distinguished linguists, educators, modern language professors, and social scientists have rushed to study, plan, organize, and make policy on bilingual education in this country. Thus the field reflects a variety of theoretical and practical orientations. Second-language acquisition, the teaching of English as a second language, language interference, testing of language skills and general achievement, degree of assimilation to American society, attitudinal change, motivation, recruiting, training and retraining of personnel for bilingual programs, curriculum evaluation and development, program organization and administration, and federal and state legislation on bilingual education are, among many others, the concerns of scholars and practitioners involved in bilingual education. Undergraduate and graduate programs have been established all over the country; and most recently, a doctoral program was begun at the University of Illinois, Urbana. Institutes for bilingual education, dissemination centers, bilingual education services of all kinds, and other agencies are aiming at the rapid and effective organization and operation of bilingual–bicultural education programs. Unfortunately, we do not have as yet a fully documented case of programs studied in depth, diachronically, which describes and measures the impact of such programs on the children as well as in the community involved.

The USOE appropriated $45 million for bilingual programs in FY 1973, $85 million in 1975, $97 million in 1976, and $115 million in 1977. Certainly one critical area of concern to many educators and politicians is the preparation of personnel to staff new programs and the retraining of some of the staff already working in the existing programs.

TEACHER TRAINING

A recent meeting of fifty national specialists on bilingual–bicultural education was held in Chicago on September 26 and 27, 1974, under the auspices of the Illinois Board of Higher Education, to study the training and certification of teachers in the state. Their recommendations regarding requirements for bilingual teachers can be summarized as follows:

> Bilingual teachers must, therefore, demonstrate evidence of the following skills, knowledge, and competences and experiences:
>
> 1. Adequate communication skills: aural–oral comprehension, as well as reading, speaking and writing knowledge of the target and dominant languages. It is also desirable that these teachers have basic knowledge of general and comparative linguistics.
> 2. Methodological and technical knowledge to teach in the bilingual setting, mainly in the teaching of reading both in the target and dominant language.
> 3. Clinical experience or fieldwork in the bilingual setting.
> 4. Familiarity with the historical, philosophical and theoretical development of bilingual education cross-culturally.
> 5. Understanding of the culture of the target population, both in its contemporary features in the United States, as well as in the country of origin of the children's parents. Also understanding of the cultures and history of the United States.

At the present time, the organization of undergraduate programs leading to certification should not emphasize an increase in the time for teacher preparation, but rather the reorganization of the curriculum to provide relevant knowledge and skills for the task in the bilingual setting, without jeopardizing normal training to function effectively in the regular monolingual setting. The need for flexibility in undergraduate as well as graduate programs cannot be stressed enough. Each institution contemplating the idea of starting a graduate program in bilingual–bicultural education should carefully survey its own resources and limitations, and then design highly individualized programs that would capitalize on institutional resources, as well as on the students' academic and personal experiences. The symbiotic relationship between undergraduate and graduate programs, between the research orientation of the graduate programs and the actual needs of children and staff in existing programs, cannot be overemphasized. Research efforts should focus on the urgent problem of testing language skills of children for placement at the point of entry; on testing of subject matter achievement in the native and second languages; on curricular development, funding and administration of programs, goal design and evaluation; teaching techniques, mental and psychological development of children, language maintenance, and other areas of immediate application. Bilingualism had been systematically studied only by linguists. Unfortunately, there is no adequate system of classification and measurement of bilingualism, although excellent initial research has been done by Mackey (1952:142–147). As Dell Hymes pointed out a decade ago, if we see linguistic theory as the theory of the nature of language (not solely a theory of what linguists do), and if linguistic theory must play a crucial role in the study of cognition and cultural behavior, then the interdependence of linguistics with other disciplines will be recognized. One of the most important tasks of the social sciences today is to build what has been called the "ethnography of communication," the systematic description of the differential role of languages and of speech behavior in socialization, personality structure, social interaction, beliefs, and cultural values (Hymes, 1964:11–12).

CONCERNS AND CONCLUSIONS

Bilingual–bicultural education programs have been in existence for a decade in some parts of the country. Long-range planning and orientation will depend on careful and complete studies of those programs with the longest and most successful record. We need to know the changes in the home environment of children attending the program, the changes in the community's linguistic behavior, its socioeconomic and educational upgrading, and its support for bilingual education and actual involvement in the program; we need to assess the progress of children in their bilingual and biliterate skills, their reading, writing, and oral–aural comprehension in both the target and dominant languages; we must study the emotional impact of the program for the personal identity of the children. Then we must identify the formal features in those "successful" programs and compare them with the features of other less successful programs in order to be able to generalize about the characteristics of a good program, a good bilingual teacher, good teaching techniques in bilingual settings, a good curriculum, etc.

There are numerous unresolved questions about bilingual–bicultural education. The trend of coverting monolinguals in the mother tongue into monolinguals in English will perhaps continue for many years (Trueba, 1974:14). But this fact cannot be interpreted as an ipso facto renunciation of personal identity. Early socialization patterns, family life-style, solidarity in the face of similar oppression, emotional and psychological communication patterns will find new symbolic expressions in the second language; thus, world view, self-identity, and active participation in community affairs will continue also to give ethnic groups the cultural support that they need to survive. If the long-range goal of bilingual–bicultural education cannot be achieved, what will be the future of ethnic groups in this country? Some scholars would like to hypothesize that assimilation is enhanced by the failure of bilingual programs. This position remains to be documented.

Perhaps one of the most revolutionary philosophical developments of American education in this century is precisely the philosophy underlying bilingual education; for it looks at the educational process in its broader perspective intimately related to the home cultural environment, it recognizes equal status and respect for all languages and cultures, and it stresses the legitimacy, desirability, and expediency of adapting the school to the needs of culturally different children with their own learning styles, values, and cultural heritage.

It is rather unfortunate that funding policies, as well as educational mandates, have confined bilingual–bicultural education to the boundaries of the schools, and thus have, in fact, undermined the dynamics and the potentiality of the family and the community, which should be the center for bilingual–bicultural activities. Home and community, if they are supported by state and federal legislation and by the local schools, will have a better chance to survive culturally, to defend their most valued right to their language and culture. Otherwise, they will continue to struggle for cultural, economic, and social survival in the face of societal pressure demanding rapid assimilation to the Anglo way of life, ultimately causing much personal waste and confusion.

References

ANDERSSON, THEODORE, and MILDRED BOYER. *Bilingual Schooling in the United States,* 2 Vols. Washington, D.C.: Government Printing Office, 1970.

Congressional Record. *Proceedings and Debates of the 93rd Congress.* First Session, Vol. 119, No. 150, Tuesday Oct. 9, 1973. Washington, D.C.: Government Printing Office, 1973.

Dissemination Center for Bilingual–Bicultural Education. *Guide to Title VII ESEA Bilingual–Bicultural Projects in the United States: 1972–1973.* Austin, Tex., 1973.

FISHMAN, JOSHUA A. "Degree of Bilingualism in a Yiddish School and Leisure Time Activities," *Journal of Social Psychology,* 36:155–165, 1952.

———. "Language Maintenance and Language Shift as a Field of Inquiry: A Definition of the Field and Suggestions for Its Further Development," *Linguistics,* 9:32–70, 1964.

———. "The Status and Prospects of Bilingualism in the United States," *The Modern Language Journal,* 49, No. 3:143–155, 1965.

———. *Language Loyalty in the U.S.* New York: Humanities Press, 1966.

———. "Bilingual Education in Sociolinguistic Perspective," paper presented at the TESOL Meetings of March 20–29, 1970, San Francisco.

———, et al. *Bilingualism in the Barrio.* Bloomington, Ind.: Indiana University Press, 1971.

GAARDER, A. BRUCE. "The First Seventy-Six Bilingual Education Projects," in J. E. Alatis (ed.), *Monograph Series on Languages and Linguistics. 21st Annual Round Table,* No. 23. Washington, D.C.: Georgetown University Press, 1970, pp. 163–178.

HYMES, DELL. "Directions in (Ethno-) Linguistic Theory," *American Anthropologist,* Special Publication, Part 2, Col. 66, No. 3:6–56, 1964.

KJOLSETH, ROLF. "Bilingual Education Programs in the United States: For Assimilation or Pluralism?" in B. Spolsky (ed.), *The Language Education of Minority Children*. Rowley, Mass.: Newbury House, 1972, pp. 94–121.

LAMBERT, WALLACE E. "Measurement of the Linguistic Dominance of Bilinguals," *Journal of Abnormal and Social Psychology*, 50, No. 2:197–200, 1955.

———. "Developmental Aspects of Second-Language Acquisition," *Journal of Social Psychology*, 43:83–104, 1956.

———. "Behavioral Evidence for Contrasting Norms of Bilingualism," in Michael Zarechnak (ed.), *Monograph Series on Languages and Linguistics No. 14:* 73–80, 1961.

———. "A Social Psychology of Bilingualism," *Journal of Social Issues*, 23, No. 2: 91–109, 1967.

LUCAS, ISIDRO. *Bilingual Education in Illinois: A Status Report*. Chicago: Office of the Governor, 1974.

MACKEY, WILLIAM F. "Bilingualism and Education," *Revue Trimestrielle Pédagogie-Orientation*, 6:135–147, 1952.

———. "Bilingualism and Linguistic Structure," *Culture*, 14:143–149, 1953.

———. "The Description and Measurement of Bilingualism/Description et Mesure du Bilinguisme," *The Linguistic Reporter*, 9, No. 6:1–2, 1962.

———. "Bilingual Interference: Its Analysis and Measurement," *Journal of Communication*, 15, No. 4:239–249, 1965.

———. *Language Teaching Analysis*. Bloomington, Ind.: Indiana University Press, 1967.

———. "The Typology, Classification and Analysis of Language Tests," *Language Learning*, Special Issue No. 3:163–166, 1968.

———. "A Typology of Bilingual Education," in T. Andersson and M. Boyer (eds.), *Bilingual Schooling in the United States*, 2 vols. Washington, D.C.: Government Printing Office, Vol. 2, pp. 63–81.

SWANSON, MARIA M. "Bilingual Education: The National Perspective," reprinted from *ACTFL Review*, Vol. 5 (no page nos.), n.d.

TRUEBA, HENRY T. "Bilingual–Bicultural Education for Chicanos in the Southwest," *Council on Anthropology and Education Quarterly*, 5, No. 3:8–15, 1974.

U.S. Commission on Civil Rights. Mexican American Educational Series. Report I: *Ethnic Isolation of Mexican Americans in the Public Schools of the Southwest*, 1971.

———. Report II: *The Unfinished Education*, 1971.

———. Report III: *The Excluded Student: Educational Practices Affecting Mexican Americans in the Southwest*, 1972.

———. Report IV: *Mexican American Education in Texas: A Function of Wealth*, 1972.

———. Report V: *Teachers and Students: Differences in Teacher Interaction with Mexican American and Anglo Students*. Washington, D.C.: Government Printing Office, 1973.

Operational Concepts

1. In a multicultural society, people often have a strong desire to sustain and reaffirm their ethnic heritage.

2. Large numbers of minority children leave school with less education than their majority counterparts.

3. Bilingual education can facilitate learning among non-English-speaking students.

4. Present programs in bilingual education are not likely to improve without extensive attention to teacher training.

Implications

The major advantage of bilingual education, presumably, is to make it easier for non-English-speaking children to participate in the educational process. Since school itself is regarded as a form of acculturation, instruction carried on in the child's mother language should permit acculturation to occur more efficiently. Although bilingual education may increase the child's sense of personal identity and diminish negative feelings of "being different," these benefits are secondary to the benefits derived from the primary objective of improving learning.

Bicultural education, on the other hand, is aimed at a rather different objective: here, the intent is to familiarize the child with a personal cultural heritage and to sustain pride in ethnic identity. It is important to note, however, that the terms bicultural and countercultural connote distinct differences; that is, the purpose of bicultural education is not to substitute ethnic values for those associated with the host culture, but, rather, to emphasize both.

It can scarcely be doubted that present educational practice has serious deficiencies in the case of minority children. Improvements are badly needed, particularly with respect to developing teaching methods that will produce better learning achievement, enhance motivation and involvement, and increase holding power. Toward this end, bilingual instruction is certainly desirable. Such instruction, nonetheless, should not mitigate against the child's opportunity to learn (1) effective English skills and (2) the prevailing culture. Both are essential to successful participation in the social mainstream.

Values

Richard L. Gorsuch

Moral Education from a Psychological View of Man as an Ethical Being

Most educators are aware of the fact that educational processes may teach ethical values. Part of such teaching may be deliberate but, in the contemporary educational process, it is likely that most teaching of values is accidental. It occurs through subtle interactions between the student and his teacher, classmates, and materials. It may even arise from the examples a lecturer uses. Through all of these sources, the student receives data which implicitly communicate the values of the originator or editor of that input.

But awareness of the possibility is not equivalent to a constructive approach to helping each child develop and live an appropriate ethical system. This arises from the fact that educators may respond in a variety of more or less adequate ways to the challenge of value education.

The possibilities before educators include four distinctly different conceptualizations of the educator's role in the critical and moral development of his students. Others could be added to the list, but these will suffice to illustrate the range of options.

First, the educator may ignore values. He pays no attention to them in the hope they will cause no problem. This approach may arise because the educator assumes values are formed elsewhere and are none of his business.

A second approach is to attempt to minimize the role of the educator in the process of the pupil's ethical and moral development. This differs from ignoring values because the educator does assume that he can influence them. The principal concern is to leave the child's values unaltered. If the student enters the class on the first day with value X, then he must leave on the last day with value X. It is usually referred to as "respect."

A third approach is to hold that education should allow the student to choose his own values. In this paradigm, the role of education is to prepare the student to make his own value choices. At the point of the actual

Reprinted from Richard L. Gorsuch, "Moral Education from a Psychological View of Man as an Ethical Being," *The Educational Forum*, Vol. 37, No. 2, 1973, pp. 169–178; by permission of the publisher.

choice, the educator's sole task is to create an atmosphere for free choice.

Deciding explicitly to teach one particular value system is a fourth option. In this approach, a standard of values is adopted and the educator moves the student toward the standard as rapidly as possible. While research such as that of Hartshorne and May(*1*) has found traditional programs of indoctrination to be ineffective, recent breakthroughs in psychology suggest that more successful programs could be established in the near future.

Each of the above positions, however, implies an untenable view of the ethical nature of man. They are all incompatible with the facts as American psychology knows them. They are therefore unacceptable to the thinking educator.

Ignoring values assumes that man is fundamentally a nonvaluing, nonethical being. While such a theory might have been tenable in the days of unchallenged logical positivism, it has never been good psychology. Man has always functioned as an evaluating creature and has judged the world around him in good–bad categories(*2*). Indeed, Rokeach(*3*) even suggests that the long dominance of attitudes in social psychology is being replaced by the concept of values.

Ignoring values actually turns out to be the teaching of unexamined values in an unexamined way. As with any haphazard procedure, the results may come as a surprise and shock to the educator himself. The approach becomes especially problematic when the educational system is confronted by those who are in opposition to the ethics which it is unknowingly teaching.

Minimizing the impact of education on values implies that a man can be divided into compartments. Into a select number of these compartments are placed the products of education. Into other compartments, carefully separated from the former by double bulkheads, are installed the person's values. But values and moral judgment are too central for this to occur. They are a powerful solvent, that, in time, dissolves the most carefully built barriers. How can a student study the history of World War II without facing ethical questions of the deepest sort? How could Galileo have claimed that his studies would have no effect on the value systems of future generations? Minimizing the impact of values in the educational process would result in an educationally sterile situation.

Man's values interact with his whole approach to reality. It is for this reason that Berelson and Steiner(*4*) conclude their review of the findings of scientific studies of man with the conclusion that man's whole approach to reality is filtered through his needs and values. Even his judgment of the diameter of a coin may be influenced by such considerations. Man's values cannot be compartmentalized without so altering man that we would no longer recognize him as our kin.

Educating the student so that he is truly free to choose his own values, the third approach, assumes that the educator can detach himself from his own filters sufficiently to recognize when the choice is free. However, such "recognition" invariably has its own implicit norms since it is seen through the educator's own value filters. If too many students, for example, choose the instructor's position, he would probably shift his approach until more students were demonstrating their "freedom" by rejecting his values. This may mean that he has taught and reinforced another value system. Who can tell? Deciding that a choice is "free" is a relative matter and can be considered to be a function of one's own values.

The freedom of choice approach also assumes that the educator can remove all implicit and explicit social influences that he might have on the student at his time of choice. But the other major conclusion that Berelson and Steiner draw from their overview is that man is a social creature, highly influenced in the most subtle ways by his fellow man. Recent research has shown that a man cannot even run rats through mazes without unintentionally influencing them to run in accordance with his expectations(5). With the greater possibilities of influence when man deals with man, can anyone seriously claim that he can establish an educational program that leaves the student truly free to choose his own values?

The value teaching approach is a straightforward one. It has a reasonable theory of students as ethical creatures since it acknowledges the importance of values and the educator's possible impact on them. It is, however, prone to assume that the educator is of a higher species than the student. He can decide the values for all from his position on Mt. Olympus. Unfortunately, the clouds prevent the educator from seeing that he is only on a nearby hill instead. Any educational theory of value instruction must take into account the fact that even the best of educators are fallible when it comes to ethical decisions.

The very fact that these positions fail because they lack a scientific viable theory of man as an ethical being suggests a possible approach to the problem. Given contemporary evidence on the nature of man as an ethical creature, what are the implications for education? To pursue this question, we shall briefly note some findings in psychology concerning the nature and development of ethical man, and then discuss their implications. While this approach will give us a framework for reflection, it must be remembered that science has not yet scaled Mt. Olympus. Indeed, psychology would be delighted to awake one morning and discover itself on a foothill near Mt. Sinai.

A CURRENT PSYCHOLOGICAL PERSPECTIVE

When we turn to psychology for statements about the nature of ethical man, we would ideally like a notion of what the truly ethical man is like. Psychological data might enable us to identify the values the ethical man holds as compared to the values held by ordinary men.

Some would argue that psychology cannot perform this task. It can only describe the present and analyze processes of change, but that it cannot say any part of the present is good or that one change is better than another. This position means that psychologists can only work from a culturally or philosophically given definition of the truly ethical man. Given such a definition, so the reasoning goes, psychology can investigate other characteristics associated with strong character, where ethical men are found, and how moral and ethical development occurs. It could hardly pit the ethical man against the ordinary man since the results would only be tautological.

This writer is sympathetic towards such a position. Psychologizing one's own values by calling the psychologist's ideal man the "mentally healthy" person or the "mature" individual has been a dangerous practice. It is dangerous because it implies the psychologist's (or psychiatrist's) credentials allow him to usurp the role of the moral philosopher. The tragedy is that these psychologists seldom realize they are out of their field. An even greater tragedy is that some educators fail to question this abuse of professional status.

While sympathetic with these arguments, this writer feels that they are not the whole story. The psychologist is a member of the society and as such has a mandate to reflect on that society within the range of his expertise.

The answer to the question of whether or not psychology can identify the ethical man is a qualified yes; it can if it makes reasonable assumptions and opens these for reflection by others. Indeed, considerable progress may be achieved by accepting only a few simple propositions. This writer sees no moral or philosophical problem in making such assumptions; the moral problem occurs when psychologists suggest that their role as psychologists means no one else can challenge their assumptions or refuse to examine the implications of their data in the light of commonly held positions.

My basic assumption shall be this: *we are concerned with the kind of ethical principles found in mature individuals of our society rather than in children.* Maturity is not used here as a way of indirectly introducing my set of values but is operationally defined in terms of growth curves. If one finds a function related to ethics increasing across the years of childhood but leveling off in the adult years, then we shall assume that the state which is characteristic of the adult years is better than that found in children. Whether or not any such functions exist in contemporary Western man is an empirical question.

The major area of research on the growth of ethic maturity is that of moral judgment. Investigators such as Piaget(6), Peck and Havighurst(7), Kohlberg(8), and Bull(9) have all felt they could identify systematic shifts in the nature of moral judgments across the years in the Western culture. While the division of the ages into stages vary somewhat, they agree on the basic sequence. The child typically proceeds from a self-centered, amoral state to an expedient, situationally oriented state, then to an other person orientation, and finally to an autonomous position. Kohlberg's(*10*) version of the stages is given in Table 1.

The central concern of the stage approach is the extent to which the child's reasoning processes are mature. Does he approach moral judgments from an amoral or principled position? The exact decision reached is not a determinant of the stage of moral judgment of the child.

Since stage theorists have reached a point of reasonable agreement on the ethical nature of the mature individual, a more detailed examination of such a person is warranted. The tentative evidence from an examination of stage 6 thinking is that their guiding value is that of justice(*11*). They treasure each individual person and insist that all people be accorded the respect that is their inalienable right. Since each person is of equal value, one person's rights do not exceed those of another. Therefore, each and every person must be treated more than equally, that is, with justice. The person at a high stage of moral development knows that he too is to be accorded the same rights and privileges as any other person, and no more.

It appears likely that this basic position can be expressed in other functionally equivalent terms. One example is the principle of love. As Fletcher(*12*) notes, it is quite similar to that of justice, although it could be suggested that love has an even greater concern for the other person than justice alone.

TABLE 1 Kohlberg's Stage Sequence

Preschool	0. *Amoral.* Child responds in terms of specific conditioning in specific situations. He does not appear to comprehend the ethical question.
	1. *Fearful–Dependent.* The child's major concern is with the possible punishment following any transgression. He considers issues only from his point of view and defers to superior power or prestige.
	2. *Opportunistic.* This is the naively egoistic orientation of the unenlightened hedonist. Right action is that which benefits the actor. He responds to sanctions in situations but not to moral principles.
	3. *Conformist: Person Oriented.* The person's concern is with approval, and with pleasing and helping others. The concern is often generalized so that conformity to stereo-typical images of the majority's opinion occurs.
	4. *Conformist: Rule Oriented.* Essentially, the "other person" of stage 3 is replaced by an authoritative source of rules and regulations. These are often interpreted legalistically.
Mature Young Adult	5, 6. *Principled Autonomy.* Recognizing the relativity of authority systems, the stage 5 person has a social contact/social utility approach to ethical issues. The stage 6 person appeals to principles of choice stressing logical universality and consistency, with values of justice, mutual respect, and trust dominating his decisions.

What happens when stage 6 individuals come into conflict? In part, such situations are resolved by the laws of the society. Ideally, the laws are an attempt to guarantee equitable treatment of all so that no individual and no minority or majority unjustly imposes its will on others.

Unfortunately, the data supporting this highest stage are relatively meager. Too few of these people occur! Even in samples of young adults, fewer than 10 percent are clearly at this stage(13). Cross-cultural evidence is likewise meager since less technologically developed cultures have even fewer stage 6 people. Of course, it is hard to conceive of any human society that did not function with some degree of fairness and justice.

Bull's(14) research on the development of principled concern for the value of another's life presents a case of a value following a growth curve. His results show that seven to nine-year-old children have a basically amoral view of life. During the early adolescent years, a radical shift occurs. By the age of 15, most have an autonomous concern for the value of life. This finding provides further content as to the basic values that should be taught by schools.

In normal times, educators can move beyond the basic value of justice and the worth of human life to less abstract values. This is because education takes place within a particular society and each society is based on an extended set of values. Sherif and Sherif(15) report data that underscore this point. Regardless of the socioeconomic status of adolescent boys and regardless of ethnic background—WASP, Latin-American, etc.—the terminal values expressed were the same.

Since discussions and news media concentrate on where our values diverge, it is sometimes surprising to see how great the convergence on basic values is within our culture. In a part of our research, we have used open-ended techniques to solicit the value categories used by children in different subcultures. While there were some minor differences, both lower-class black and middle-class white children, for example, used the same basic categories. They were all concerned with being kind towards others, good manners, academic achievement, etc.(16). Variations within subcultures within the United States do exist but do not seem very great, a conclusion shared by others who have investigated this problem(17). In normal times, it appears that mature individuals of our modern culture do hold to quite similar basic values, although they may diverge greatly in their other attitudes.

Since education is the process of teaching the accumulated wisdom of a society to the next generation, it has an obvious mandate to communicate the basic values. Psychology, sociology, and cultural anthropology can contribute by making these basic values more important, but I suspect that most educators already have a reasonable grasp of them.

But are these normal times? There is real question as to whether or not the unity of ultimate values found by, for example, the Sherifs still exists. Either a vocal section of present youth object to the basic values or they feel the present structures are not maximizing them to a significant degree.

Evidence that basic values of college students are relatively unchanged is provided in another of our studies(18). In comparing 1969 college students' ethical judgments to those of college students in 1929, 1939, 1949, and 1958, it is obvious that little change has occurred overall. This is particularly true with the values basic to society, such as those surrounding dishonest interpersonal relations or crimes against the person. Only in the area of premarital sex and religion has any noticeable change occurred. The general trend suggests that the second position, i.e., that youth feel the present society is not maximizing its values, is more tenable than that those values basic to society have shifted. The Sherifs did, it should be noted, find differences between adolescent groups in the degree to which they were able to achieve the common goals.

However, the probable uniformity in the ethical thought and values produced by mature individuals does not mean that there is one answer to every moral dilemma. Each situation requires the application of the principles within a particular historical context, and the answer is partially a function of one's views of the situation. Given the extent to which man's factual evaluations are influenced by his own predispositions, any person needs to take his own judgments with more than a grain of salt. Regardless of whether the group is majority or minority, establishment or antiestablishment, it is bound to be looking at reality through distorted glasses. This leads to the high probability that even the most ethical man will occasionally disagree with other equally ethical men. And it means that giving a student pat answers—e.g., "You should never lie"—is generally inappropriate.

From a psychological perspective of ethical man, it is apparent that education has an important role. It must communicate to the child and youth those values that are characteristic of the mature man in Western technological society. And it must help endow the next generation with the personal characteristics needed to manifest the values themselves and to create the conditions under which others can manifest them. Psychological research is already sufficiently advanced to give some clues regarding the nature of the product education should be producing.

SOME IMPLICATIONS FOR CONTEMPORARY EDUCATION

The above is a basis for a contemporary view of ethical man in the modern Western world. The results are sketchy due to the limits of space in a paper such as this and the tentativeness of the research. While extensive, detailed conclusions for education may not be warranted, some

484

implications for educational practice can be drawn from the facts given above as they interact with our knowledge of how ethical development occurs.

The first implication is the necessity of alerting educators to this area. Many gross violations of good teaching principles occur due to ignorance or lack of concern. For example, it is altogether too apparent that teachers often communicate by using an appropriate level of reasoning. When high school students, normally at stages 3 and 4, are given stage 2 arguments for not cheating, e.g., "you might get caught," it is no wonder that they turn elsewhere for ethical guidance.

A second implication is that educators need to turn to psychology for information on how values such as justice develop. While this research is far from definitive, it has progressed to the point where some tentative conclusions can be drawn(19). In addition, the research is quite encouraging. For example, Rokeach(20) has recently reported that pointing out the inconsistency of valuing freedom without also valuing equality leads to a significantly increased rate of joining the NAACP *a full year later,* in an experimental group as compared to a control group. This isn't bad for only five minutes of Socratic teaching. It does suggest that modern psychology may be helpful in shaping programs of moral development and that ethics can be related to behavior as well.

Psychology's major conclusion on improving the maturity of ethical judgment is that the experiences which a child has can either lead to moral development or fixate him at a particular level. He adapts to what his world is like. Thus it come as no surprise that Haan, Smith, and Block conclude that youth still at Kohlberg's opportunistic or hedonistic stage come from families that "did not seem to encourage their children to develop a sense of responsibility and autonomy"(21). Youth at both conformity stages, however, "describe their parents as relating to them in a manner consistent with the strategies generally recommended by social learning theory for the development of morality"(22). The higher stages viewed their parents as entering into moral dilemmas in a more involved way; decisions were less black and white and differences of views were obvious. This latter setting provides for an adaptation requiring the youth to utilize his own internal principles.

The learning of ethics and moral behavior does present some unique differences from learning in other areas. For example, Turiel(23) found dissonance in moral judgments to be somewhat unidirectional, that is, to be more powerful in one direction than in another. When a child is presented with arguments both for and against a course of action in a moral dilemma, the effect depends on the level of the argument. If it is slightly more mature than the level the child normally uses, he is is more likely to accept it than if it is slightly less mature than his level, a result also found by Le Furgy and Woloshin(24). This means that open discussion of a moral issue by a peer group tends to shift the less mature child towards the more mature one rather than vice versa, if the more mature position is spelled out. In this sense, teaching students how to reason on moral issues is more like teaching them how to solve mathematic problems than teaching them a set of facts they are to parrot. The more ethical approach is recognized as better by the student without someone having to label it as better.

Many occasions for directed peer discussions of ethical issues occur spontaneously, and the teacher needs to take advantage of them. Every classroom has incidents of a moral nature. Usually these are resolved in an authoritarian manner by the teacher. What a pity! These are ideal situations for the entire class to enter into a mutually beneficial learning session. In high schools almost all such problems could be given to the student body with the young people making the decisions under adult guidance. The argument that they would be too harsh on each other is an open admission that they have not learned to be just, and underscores the necessity of a moral development program throughout all grades. The fact that it might be argued against because it takes more time than the present authoritarian approach points to our lack of concern with the moral and ethical development of our children. With the soaring rate of juvenile delinquency, should we not be spending more time in this area?

The involvement of the school peer group would reduce one current problem of major importance: the negative effects of the peer group. As Bronfenbrenner(25) has empirically confirmed, the American peer group is one which encourages deviance from adult norms. If U.S. youth are asked whether or not they would go along with their peers in a deviating situation, they say they would. Even more important, they answer this way much *more* often if they know all their classmates will see their answers than if no one but the investigator will see them. This seems to apply at all levels, even with the "nicest" groups of pro-school, upper-middle class girls. In many other countries, the results are different. Their youth are *less* likely to go along with a deviation, if they know the broader peer group will learn of their actions. The difference is probably the basis of the higher rate of vandalism and other such gang activities in our country. Involving the peer group in the school's decision-making process on ethical problems would do much to reverse this trend since they would see the actions of their peers in that broader perspective on which our society is based.

The involvement of adults in such a system would neeed to vary depending on the level of maturity of the students. At the youngest ages, it would be heavily adult dominated. But by the time the students had spent ten years in a system where they are given progressively more ethical training and responsibility, they would probably fulfill these functions as well or better than the average present teacher.

A derivative advantage of involving both students and teachers in the consideration of the moral issues within the school itself is the modeling effects that would occur. Students would hear the arguments of their teachers and learn therefrom. Perhaps even more important is the fact that an individual teacher would not always get his way, thus giving a model for behavior when one loses. Learning to deal justly with the minority when one is in the majority and to deal justly with the majority when one is in the minority are both important in the process of moral and ethical development.

CONCLUDING COMMENTS

From a contemporary theory of man as an ethical being, it is apparent that education will affect the moral and ethical development of children regardless of whether or not we want it to. The proper paradigm to be adopted by educators must seek to build upon this fact so that education helps rather than retards the student's character development. The present lack of utilizing the peer group suggests that the current system has been established with little concern for the important variables of moral development.

The proper educational paradigm must be a composite one. In a pluralistic society, it is true that the minor variations in value systems need to be respected and the student left relatively free to come to his own conclusions. However, students do need to be encouraged to value justice, life, fairness in dealing with other people, and the other basic values of Western culture. The teaching of these values and of the necessary skills to practice them are well within both the educator's mandate and the range of possibilities that can be actualized.

References

1. Hugh Hartshorne, Mark A. May, and others, "Testing the knowledge of right and wrong," *Religious Education Association,* Monograph 1, 1927; Hugh Hartshorne and Mark A. May, *Studies in the Nature of Character, Vol. I: Studies in Deceit* (New York: Macmillan, 1928); Hugh Hartshorne, Mark A. May, and J. B. Maller, *Studies in the Nature of Character, Vol. II: Studies in Service and Self-Control* (New York: Macmillan, 1929); Hugh Hartshorne, Mark A. May, and Frank K. Shuttleworth, *Studies in the Nature of Character, Vol. III: Studies in the Organization of Character* (New York: Macmillan, 1930).

2. For example, Charles E. Osgood, George J. Suci, and Percy H. Tannenbaum, *The Measurement of Meaning* (Urbana: University of Illinois Press, 1957); also W. T. Norman, "Towards an adequate taxonomy of personality ratings," *Journal of Abnormal and Social Psychology,* 66:574–583 (1963).

3. Milton Rokeach, *Beliefs, Attitudes, and Values* (San Francisco: Jossey-Bass, Inc., 1968), p. 157.

4. Bernard Berelson and Gary A. Steiner, *Human Behavior; an Inventory of Scientific Findings* (New York: Harcourt Brace Jovanovich, Inc., 1964), pp. 662 ff.

5. R. Rosenthal, *Experimenter Effects in Behavior Research* (New York: Appleton-Century-Crofts, 1966).

6. Jean Piaget, *The Moral Judgment of the Child* (New York: The Free Press, 1965; original edition, 1932).

7. Robert F. Peck and Robert J. Havighurst, *The Psychology of Character Development* (New York: John Wiley & Sons, Inc., 1960).

8. Lawrence Kohlberg, "A cognitive developmental approach to socialization," in D. A. Goslin (ed.), *Handbook of Socialization Theory and Research* (Chicago: Rand McNally, 1969).

9. Norman J. Bull, *Moral Judgment from Childhood to Adolescence* (Beverly Hills, Calif.: Sage Publications, 1969), Chapter 4.

10. Kohlberg, op. cit.

11. Ibid.

12. Joseph Fletcher, *Situation Ethics: The New Morality* (Philadelphia: The Westminster Press, 1966), Chapter 5.

13. Norma Haan, Brewster Smith, and Jeanne Block, "Moral reasoning of young adults: Political-social behavior, family background, and personality correlates," *Journal of Personality and Social Psychology,* 10(3):183–201 (1968).

14. Bull, op. cit.

15. M. Sherif and C. W. Sherif, *Reference Groups: Exploration into the Conformity and Deviation of Adolescents* (New York: Harper & Row, 1964).

16. Richard Gorsuch and Ruth Smith, "Naturally occurring value categories in children." Paper presented at the Southeastern Psychological Association, 1970.

17. Melvin Kohn, *Class and Conformity* (Homewood, Ill.: The Dorsey Press, 1969); Sherif & Sherif, op. cit.

18. Richard Gorsuch and William Daly, "Changes in ethical judgments of college students: 1958 to 1969," *American Psychological Convention Proceedings,* 1970.

19. For more detailed consideration of procedures cf. Urie Bronfenbrenner, *Two Worlds of Childhood, U.S. & U.S.S.R.* (New York: Russell Sage Foundation, 1970); Lawrence Kohlberg, "The Stages of Moral Development as a Basis for Moral Education" in C. M. Beck et al. (eds.), *Moral Education* (Toronto: University of Toronto Press, 1971); Louis E. Raths et al., *Values and Teaching* (Columbus, Ohio: Charles E. Merrill Publishers, 1966).

20. Milton Rokeach, "Long range behavioral effects of experimental changes in values." Presented at the Joint Peabody-Vanderbilt Colloquium, April 16, 1970.

21. Haan, Smith, and Block, op. cit., p. 196.

22. Ibid., p. 194.

23. Elliot Turiel, "An experimental test of the sequentiality of developmental

488

stages in the child's moral judgments," *Journal of Personality and Social Psychology*, 3:611–618 (1966).

24. William G. Le Furgy and Gerald W. Woloshin, "Immediate and long-term effects of experimentally induced social influence in the modification of adolescents' moral judgments," *Journal of Personality and Social Psychology*, 12(2):104–110 (June, 1969).

25. Bronfenbrenner, op. cit.

Operational Concepts

1. The values shaped by the child's overall educational experience are of profound curricular importance.

2. The incidental aspects of curriculum—stemming from human interactions among students and teachers—also influence the child's values, both directly and indirectly.

3. It is essential, in organizing a curriculum for moral education, to recognize the powerful impact exerted by the learner's peer groups.

4. Although the teaching of values can be assigned to a particular segment of the curriculum, it should also be a universal concern among all teachers.

5. In guiding the moral education of children, teachers must be aware that the reasoning processes through which children form values are as significant as the values themselves.

Implications

Whatever the subject matter, it is imperative that curricula provide students with ample opportunity to explore the significant moral issues of the time. In considering these issues, the learners should be encouraged to analyze ongoing social problems, to debate alternative solutions to the problems, to speculate about the possible consequences of each solution, and to reach conclusions regarding appropriate human conduct. Once these conclusions have been reached, it is of great importance that they be compared against other, widely endorsed perceptions of moral behavior. Such comparison are useful in developing (1) a tolerance for cultural diversity, (2) a sense of moral pluralism, and (3) an open mind.

Irrespective of whether the study of values occurs randomly or as part of the planned course structure, instruction and learning should be carried on to the largest possible extent in group contexts. Moreover, since moral issues lend themselves to reasoning, and since reasoning is an acquired skill, the classroom consideration of ethical behavior should be approached cognitively.

Finally, the teacher's task in guiding the moral education of children is exceedingly delicate; not only is considerable pedagogical finesse required, but effective teaching requires a substantial knowledge base. Hence, considerable in-service training should be devoted to the mastery of appropriate teaching techniques, to different conceptions of human ethics, and to techniques through which moral development can be integrated with the overall instructional program.

Robert J. Snavely

Values Education: A Moral Dilemma

There exists a country where truth, justice, and equality are considered cornerstones of its national creed. Yet, this country contains numerous examples of racial strife, apparent differentiation in the application of its legal code, and national leaders are prompted to resign because of alleged improprieties in office.

The youth of this nation are said to be alienated from the professed cultural norms and values. These alienated youth have been known to use various forms of drugs, study and practice the occult, and participate in a variety of mystical and transcendental activities. All these behaviors have been a part of a search for values or some framework to guide normative choices, according to some of the "intellectuals" of this society.

Rapid and sweeping changes are another characteristic of this country. Some sociologists claim that in earlier times there was a consensus concerning core values and their meaning. But, as technology developed, the citizenry was perplexed by a variety of alternatives competing with existing norms, causing an erosion of this consensus. These sociologists, along with a significant percentage of the populace, claim that the lack of consensus concerning basic values is responsible for the various social ills of the society, including the alienation of its youth.

Should this society's schools engage in the teaching of values? Why?

The schools of a society have traditionally been charged with passing on the culture of that society. Implicit in this charge is some degree of consensus concerning the salient goals and values of the society. Stanley contends that our society no longer possesses such a consensus, a fact which he feels is responsible for the "dilemma of education"(*1*). What values should the schools dispense and examine? What criteria should educators use to select the basic values? Which definition of justice or freedom should be applied to our social problems? to the students' demands for a more democratic school setting?

The increased pluralism of our society has prompted some educators, especially those involved with the social studies, to stress decision making(*2*). Engle and others have pointed out that facts and values are two

492

critical components of decisions. One considers revelant facts via the process of rational inquiry, and his values give those facts positive or negative valence(3). It is these ratings, based on value criteria, that may cause individuals to make different decisions from a common pool of facts. Because of the critical role played by values in decision making, a strong case can be made for including the study of values in educational programs designed to develop skilled decision makers.

The history of values instruction reveals a prescriptive stance toward values. The McGuffy readers are noted for their moralistic maxims. Citizenship training during the forties and fifties emphasized the inculcation of democratic ideals and anticommunist training. As social studies education moved in the direction of reflective thinking and inquiry(4), which included the examination of "closed areas"(5) and pressing social problems(6), the rational examination of values that support conflicting views became more prevalent.

Educators commonly employ one or more of the following strategies when dealing with values in the classroom:

1. Discounting the school's responsibility or right to teach and examine values.
2. Indoctrination of "core values."
3. Helping students become aware of their values and clarifying the meaning of personal values(7).
4. Discussions of moral dilemmas designed to expose the student to moral reasoning one or more stages above his present level of moral development, thereby stimulating movement to a higher level of moral reasoning(8).

The first strategy, placing values beyond the legitimate realm of schooling, is supported by moral relativism and freedom of choice. Moral relativism, as seen by those who feel values education should not be a part of the public school curriculum, places all values on an equal footing (i.e., one person's moral beliefs are as good as another's). Since one cannot prove one value superior to another, it is strictly a matter of preference, like choosing your favorite flavor at an ice cream parlor.

Another consideration of some who take a negative view of values education deals with the separation of religious teachings and schooling. This argument loses some of its credence as those concerned with values education shift their goals from teaching specific value conclusions toward programs that enhance the student's ability to evaluate and form normative choices.

If all values are equal and we have a commitment to individual freedom, then the schools leave themselves open for criticism when they teach specific values. Thus, those who see values education as instruction in a specific set of values see it as an infringement on the parents' right to

493

select the values their children should embrace. Since most parents cannot select the school or teacher for their child, and since schooling is required by law, the school should honor the parents' right of free choice and leave value training to the home and church.

A major criticism of the strategy of avoidance is that it severely limits student inquiry. If developing competent decision-making skills is a goal of education and if, as Coombs and others have pointed out, values play a significant role in normative decision-making(9), some form of values education seems in order. Students should not be asked to limit their inquiries to the empirical, factual dimensions of rational decision making. The values that give personal meaning to empirical data should also be examined.

The second strategy, indoctrination of "core values," seems to have special appeal during periods of rapid change and social unrest. The uncertainty of the moment is blamed on a retreat from basic values, rather than on a change in the social environment that developed and supported these once stable values. Whereas justice and equality are still components of the American creed, legislation, court decisions, and changing life-styles have produced a variety of definitions for this creed. Thus, the plea for a return to the core values of the past may mean a return to an outmoded moral code.

Closely akin to the indoctrination scheme for values instruction is a faith in "modeling" as a technique for moral development. "Morals are caught, not taught," is the motto of this group. Teachers are to exhibit the epitome of moral action, thus giving their students a proper model to emulate.

The modeling notion of values education meets a number of obstacles in a pluralistic society, especially a society with an instantaneous communications network. This society provides all its members, including schoolchildren, with a plethora of contradictory behavior models and moral codes. This social diversity presents an untenable atmosphere for a teacher interested in providing a proper model. Which values should he use as a pattern for his behavior? Which special-interest group, racial or political majority, minority, or religious persuasion should guide the teacher's ethical actions? Or should he choose the best each group has to offer, thereby alienating all groups? Value modeling is the domain of all who act. Unless individuals develop criteria for evaluating the morass of models available, there can be no rational choices among competing value models.

There is yet another problem with indoctrination as a means of forming behavior; it doesn't work. The Hartshorne and May studies of the late twenties, Brogden's study of sixth-grade boys, the work of Havighurst and Taba, and more recently, Byron and Walbek's research concerning views of charity and charitable behavior among children, all have failed to show that knowledge or moral rules or being able to explain what one ought to do has a significant correlation to moral behavior(10). Piaget's work examining children's moral judgments indicates two moralities, one of constraint and one of mutual respect(*11*).

> There exist at least two extreme types of rules and of authority—rules due to unilateral respect, and rules due to mutual respect. . . . These two types of rules lead to opposite results. The rule of constraint, which is bound up with unilateral respect, is regarded as sacred and produces in the child's mind feelings that are analogous to those which characterize the compulsory conformity of primitive communities. But this rule of constraint remains external to the child's spirit and does not lead to as effective an obedience as the adult would wish. Rules due to mutual agreement and cooperation, on the contrary, take root inside the child's mind and result in an effective observance in the measure in which they are incorporated in an autonomous will(*12*).

His research indicates a rationale for providing students with opportunities to examine social interactions and relations as mechanisms for developing rules of mutual agreement and the understandings that lead to these rules.

> It is absurd and even immoral to wish to impose upon a child a fully worked out system of discipline when the social life of children amongst themselves is sufficiently developed to give rise to a discipline infinitely nearer to that inner submission which is the mark of adult morality (*13*).

According to Piaget, it is counterproductive to give young people a digested moral code. It is better to let them work it out for themselves, with proper guidance as indicated by the child's development, if our goal includes having the child internalize any moral code.

The proponents of value clarification escape charges of indoctrination and proselytism by stressing a methodology that encourages students to freely choose and act on personal values in light of the consequences of these choices. Raths includes the following components in his "process of valuing"(*14*):

Choosing:	1. freely
	2. from alternatives
	3. after thoughtful consideration of the consequences of each alternative
Prizing:	4. cherishing, being happy with the choice
	5. willing to affirm the choice publicly
Acting:	6. doing something with the choice
	7. repeatedly, in some pattern of life

These seven aspects of the valuing process are designed to guide the student through his search for values, as he attempts to select a cadre of values capable of directing normative decisions.

Values clarification has been attacked for its relativistic or neutral stance with regard to specific value choices(*15*). In this method the primary considerations for evaluating student's values are the following:

1. Were the values choosen freely with a conscious view of the conse quences?
2. Does the student consistently act in accordance with his stated values?

The Raths process does not emphasize the need to develop value principles that could be used to justify the comparative worth of one value over another. In the values model developed by Coombs and Muex, value principles are one of the end products when significant value objects are examined(*16*).

Scriven addresses the problem of assessing consequences(*17*):

> *The great majority* of value disputes can be settled by empirical investi- gation and logical analysis. The educational task is to push back the frontiers of analysis as far as possible.

He feels value conflicts occur primarily because individuals have differing views concerning the possible consequences of a decision or action, rather than competing values themselves causing the disagreement. There is a dearth of ability to seek evidence to support purported consequences, rules of evidence are absent, while criteria for maintaining the relevance of cer- tain data and discounting others are frequently missing in discussions sur- rounding value disputes. Scriven feels these skills are requisite to the rational settlement of most value conflicts.

Discussions surrounding the desirability of population control illus- trate the need for investigation and analysis skills. These sample questions must be answered if this question is to be dealt with in a reaonable manner:

1. How much can the world's food supply be increased?
2. What is our current rate of natural resource consumption? What will this rate be five, ten, and fifty years from now if our present rate of population growth continues?
3. How does the quality of life contrast between countries with low birth rates and countries with high birth rates?
4. How will individual freedoms be affected by large-scale birth control programs? By the absence of these programs?

Answering questions of this genre requires some sophistication in defining, seeking facts, and verifying of conflicting claims. These skills can only be developed as students are given increased opportunities to examine norma- tive issues(*18*):

> [Moral] effort, like every other form of behavior, requires time to ripen, and its primitive forms, though very different from the final product which

496

alone receives the sanction of adult morality, may well be indispensable to the normal development of the individual. It is therefore not wasting a child's time to let him acquire by himself the habit of work and inner discipline. In the moral as in intellectual domain we really possess only what we have conquered ourselves.

The elaborate strategies developed by Coombs and Muex(19) can assist students in moving from primitive value investigations to a more encompassing, rational process of normative inquiry. Their process includes collecting relevant data, rating the data on the basis of value criteria, testing possible choices, and developing value principles. A unique feature of this model is the link between facts and values, which occurs during the rating procedure. Also, the four tests of a value judgment [new cases, subsumption, role exchange, and universal consequences(20)] force the student to rigorously evaluate the consequences of his judgment.

Kohlberg's work, growing out of his study of Piaget's efforts, has had a tremendous effect on the values education movement. Kohlberg believes that moral development occurs in a fixed sequence of stages, paralleling the cognitive developmental stages described by Piaget, and that these stages have a consistent sequence across cultures(21):

> According to Kohlberg, the aim of moral education is . . . the stepwise stimulation of development toward more mature moral judgment and reasoning, to culminate in a clear understanding of the universal principles of justice(22).

He defines moral principles as(23)

> universal modes of choosing which we wish all men to apply to all situations and which represent morally self-justifying reasons for action. . . . Moral principles are not specific rules for guiding action, but are modes of making judgments and decisions.

Movement toward higher stages is desirable, because each new stage encompasses a stance that expands the application of justice. Higher-order moral reasoning allows one to reflectively process more data concerning the moral dilemma and arrive at a decision that provides justice for a broader spectrum of those affected by the decision.

The stimulation of moral growth occurs through the discussion of genuine moral conflicts in a milieu that displays moral reasoning one stage above the child's current level(24). The teachers' task is to help the child(25):

1. Focus on genuine moral conflicts.
2. Think about the reasoning he uses in solving such conflicts.
3. See inconsistencies in his way of thinking.

4. Find means of resolving such inconsistencies and inadequacies . . . if the child is challenged so as to perceive the contradictions in his own thinking, he will try to generate new and better solutions to moral problems. Thus, teachers' discussions must be provocative and must deal with important issues in order to facilitate the child's experience of genuine conflict . . . the teacher must focus on the reasoning used in the children's moral judgments, rather than on the content of their moral choice . . . it is necessary to introduce a sense of contradiction and discrepancy by discussing the reasoning itself.

It is the moral reasoning that supports a value judgment, not the judgment itself, which is the substance of Kohlberg's methodology.

The valuing process decribed by Raths and the strategies developed by Coombs and Muex could prove useful in challenging students' existing moral reasoning and the formation of a subsequent synthesis from alternative modes. The examination of freely chosen alternatives, assessing factual data, and the process of evaluating possible conclusions through role exchange or the test of universal consequences, could prove to be valuable tools in dealing with the inadequacies and inconsistencies of one's moral reasoning.

Although the work of Kohlberg has been a boon to moral education, translating Kohlbergian principles into instructional programs has not been easy(26). Studies describing and evaluating programs based on moral development have not conclusively demonstrated the feasibility of this approach to values education in the classroom. Most of the preliminary work has been done with small groups of students or under conditions unlike most classroom environments. Classroom teachers may have difficulty assessing each child's developmental stage and preparing moral arguments that illustrate three, or more, stages of moral reasoning, as the Kohlberg stimulation process requires. For example, in the Blatt studies(27), the assessment of student levels was done through rather involved, individual interviews, and the moral dilemmas were carefully developed. Also, the researcher had time to develop and assess statements at various levels of moral reasoning. Few classroom teachers work under similar conditions.

Fenton is revising the Holt social studies materials to include more work with moral dilemmas(28). This revised curriculum is an attempt at integrating the ideas of Kohlberg into specific subject area curriculum. A part of this revision process will include in-service training to assist teachers in becoming familiar with the goals and procedures of moral development.

CONCLUSION

It seems readily apparent that values education should be a part of schooling. To expel values from the classroom is to unduly limit the scope of inquiry and decision making. Values are an inexorable ingredient in decisions of consequence.

To shy away from dealing with values to avoid indoctrination indicates a limited view concerning the goals of values education. It is not specific value conclusions or beliefs that are taught, but rather a process of examining the moral point of view, i.e., the valuative components of a given situation. Kohlberg states(29):

> Moral education should not be aimed at teaching some specific set of morals but should be concerned with developing the organizational structures by which one analyzes, interprets and makes decisions about social problems.

The processes of values clarification can assist young people in developing an awareness of their present values and the implications of these values. These techniques can be used to maximize the facility of the individual's existing moral reasoning. The value clarification procedures are also helpful in reconciling inconsistencies in moral reasoning and the application of moral principles.

The stimulation of moral development, as described by Kohlberg, is a valid goal of education. Few people question the desirability of moving children toward the level of abstract operational thought in cognitive thinking. This goal is desirable because it gives the student increased abilities to manipulate cognitive data. Higher-stage moral reasoning can have the same positive effect with regard to normative data.

The discussion and evaluation of values should be an integral part of school curricula. Values education should not be reserved for Friday afternoon discussions or only dealt with during "current events." Most important questions have moral implications, and alternative solutions frequently are applications of differing value stances. Equipping students to deal with present and future realities is one goal of education. Values and value conflicts are an undeniable part of human reality. Because of this fact it is imperative that educational curricula provide repeated and varied opportunities for children to study and develop values.

References

1. William O. Stanley, *Education and Social Integration*. New York: Columbia Teachers College Press, 1953, pp. 118–136.
2. Shirley Engle, "Decision Making: The Heart of Social Studies Instruction," *Social Education*, Vol. 24, pp. 301–304+, Nov. 1960.
3. Lawrence E. Metcalf (ed.), *Values Education: Rationale, Strategies, and Procedures*. Washington, D.C.: National Council on Social Studies, 1971, pp. 13–19.

4. Frederick R. Smith and C. Benjamin Cox, *New Strategies and Curriculum in Social Studies.* Chicago: Rand McNally, 1969, pp. 40–59, 113–152.

5. Maurice P. Hunt and Lawrence E. Metcalf, *Teaching High School Social Studies.* New York: Harper & Row, 1968, pp. 275–449.

6. Fred M. Newmann and Donald W. Oliver, *Clarifying Public Controversy.* Boston: Little, Brown and Company, 1970.

7. Louis E. Raths, Merrill Harmin, and Sidney B. Simon, *Values in Teaching.* Columbus, Ohio: Charles E. Merrill, 1966.

8. Lawrence Kohlberg and Elliot Turiel, "Moral Development and Moral Education," in *Psychology and Educational Practice,* Gerald S. Lesser (ed.). Glenview, Ill.: Scott, Foresman, 1971, pp. 410–465.

9. Jerrold R. Coombs, "Objectives of Value Analysis," in *Values Education: Rationale, Strategies, and Procedures,* Lawrence E. Metcalf (ed.). Washington, D.C.: National Council on Social Studies, 1971, pp. 1–28.

10. Dorothy C. Adkins, Frank D. Payne, and J. Michael O'Malley, "Moral Development," in *Review of Research in Education,* Vol. 2, T. Kerlinger (ed.). Itasca, Ill.: F. E. Peacock Publishers, 1974, p. 109.

11. Jean Piaget, *The Moral Judgment of the Child.* New York: The Free Press, 1965.

12. Ibid., p. 362.

13. Ibid., p. 404.

14. Raths et al., op. cit., pp. 28–30.

15. Kohlberg and Turiel, op. cit., pp. 417–420.

16. Metcalf, op. cit., pp. 1–119.

17. Michael Scriven, "Values in the Curriculum," in *Readings for Social Studies in Elementary Education,* 3rd ed., John Jarolimek and Huber M. Walsh (eds.). New York: Macmillan Publishing Co., Inc., 1974, pp. 244, 245.

18. Piaget, op. cit., pp. 365, 366.

19. Metcalf, op. cit., pp. 29–166.

20. Ibid., pp. 54–61.

21. Kohlberg and Turiel, op. cit., pp. 429–439.

22. Ibid., p. 447.

23. Ibid., p. 447.

24. Ibid., pp. 447–456.

25. Ibid., pp. 454, 455.

26. James R. Rest, "Values Education: A Review of 'Kohlbergian' Programs," *Review of Educational Research,* Vol. 44, No. 2, pp. 241–259.

27. Ibid., pp. 246–255.

28. Edwin Fenton, "The New, 'New Social Studies'," speech delivered at Midwest Regional Convention of NCSS, Milwaukee, Wisc., Apr. 26, 1974.

29. Rest, op. cit., p. 442.

Operational Concepts

1. The social decisions of individuals are influenced by the facts at their command and the values that they hold.

2. Indoctrination, as a means of teaching values, can be counter-productive.

3. Students should be given greater opportunity to examine the social dilemmas of the time, and to analyze the related moral issues.

4. The curriculum should teach children the processes of moral reasoning rather than a catechism of selected values.

5. The development of sound values involves affective as well as cognitive considerations.

Implications

Considerable disagreement exists regarding (1) the school's responsibility in the teaching of values, and (2) the techniques by which values—if they are a school responsibility—should be taught. It is widely acknowledged that values among people differ, but there is also relatively widespread agreement that some values, such as modesty, integrity, and loyalty, are universally regarded as desirable.

Little, seemingly, will be gained by endless debates over the appropriateness of moral education. The schools are better advised to seek effective instructional procedures through which ethical behavior and morality can be examined.

Whatever the instructional method, it seems clear that values education should be based upon (1) the examination of commonplace moral issues, (2) the analysis of personal values and beliefs, (3) an oportunity to consider the comparative advantages and disadvantages of alternative values, and (4) experience in selecting, internalizing, and acting out particular values.

These objectives cannot be accomplished without further refinements in methodology and corresponding programs of teacher orientation. It is comparatively easy for most teachers to preach gospels, but the evidence makes it clear that students do not internalize values in accordance with teacher directions. Hence, professional orientation programs should enable teachers to integrate moral reasoning with a variety of subject matter, to guide learners through a systematic analysis of value options, and, ultimately, to assist them to develop a lasting commitment to the beliefs that they adopt.

Louis Rubin

The Human in the System

In America, success in school is closely linked with vocational opportunity and, in turn, with material affluence during adulthood. Whether a boy is destined to fill gas tanks or debate in a courtroom is in large measure determined by the number of years he spends in school. What is learned, how much is learned, and the amount of emotional scar tissue that is accumulated in the process all are secondary; the object of the game is to acquire the degrees which are the price of admission to well-paid occupations and the "good life." That much of the money which ultimately rewards success in school may, in time, be spent on psychiatrists, pills, and various other forms of anxiety control does not seem to be important. Nor is the possibility that a man who fills gas tanks may lead a thoroughly satisfying life, and a lawyer may be a desperately unhappy person, of any consequence. In our way of things it generally is considered better to be rich than poor—and if affluence alone mattered, it probably would be.

Because of the tie between schooling and earning power, the expectations of parents regarding the education of their children are largely conditioned by the social ethos, and their standards for judging the quality of schools are clearly drawn. In the eyes of parents, completing school (irrespective of whatever it is that is completed) is crucial. Thus, good schools are recognized as ones which enable their students to go further in the educational hierarchy, and bad schools are ones which do not. Consider for example, that although drop-outs sometimes are happier after they leave school, their parents invariably are disappointed.

The use of the school system as a control valve for entry into desirable vocations, coupled with the aspirations parents have for their children, results in a great emphasis on acquiring information and passing tests in the classroom—on cognitive instruction. It is scarcely surprising, therefore, that most teachers are predominantly interested in the kind of learning that can be measured on standardized tests for a teacher's reputation and

Reprinted from Louis Rubin, "The Human in the System," *The California Elementary Administrator*, December 1970, pp. 43–49; by permission of the publisher.

esteem depend upon equipping students to score well on such tests. Reducing a child's anxiety or enhancing his self-concept, on the other hand, do not carry much of a reputational payoff. In the typical classroom, resultingly, the cognitive goals are the chief thing and the stage is set for drill, repetition, and occasionally, the mastery of test taking for emotional repression.

Children, however, are not so made. Whereas the teacher strives for knowledge of book, the child strives for knowledge of self. Whereas the teacher—at the day's end—counts the number of pages covered, the child counts his good and bad experiences. Whereas the teacher worries about intellectual gains, the child worries about emotional losses. There is, in short, a fundamental conflict of interest between teacher and pupil in the schoolroom. One is driven by the god of cognition and the other by the god of affect. What students are after, in other words, is a feeling of personal adequacy. They want to be liked by their teacher, accepted by their peers, and applauded by their parents; they want, in sum, *to be winners rather than losers*. So, when kids do learn, it is not so much because they prize the subject matter, but because they fear the loss of the success symbols which are withheld when they do not learn.

The consequences of all this are of course often disastrous. Even with the winners—with children who successfully perform the required cognitive tricks—a great opportunity is lost. Instead of using cognitive insight as a springboard to emotional growth, instead of searching out a sane balance between feelings and facts, teachers settle for half-best. And for the losers, school becomes an intensely destructive experience. It breeds a familiarity with failure and a growing sense of impotence: once the student falls far enough behind, there is little hope of ever catching up. We have produced, through all this, a vast number of children who hate school, who doubt their capacities, and who, for the remainder of their lives, may be defeated by a defective self-concept.

THE NEW SCENE?

Currently, a radical answer to this problem is reflected in the spate of "new schools" which recently have arisen. Much about them is commendable and, in instances, they well may point the way for the "old schools." Although these counter-school movements vary from place to place, most of the schools take humaneness and freedom as their cardinal principles. Emotional support is a first order of business, there often is a sensitive effort to avoid needless trauma, and the child is free to pursue his own interests. The learning environment (at least in the best of the lot) is clearly more therapeutic than in the majority of regular schools. But with respect to the other side of the educational obligation, the expansion of intellect, their effectiveness is becoming increasingly questionable. If the children of the free schools do not learn something of man's accumulated wisdom, if they cannot add a column of figures properly, they too will fail both themselves and their society. They may not, for example, forever be able to resist the temptations of good jobs and affluence. And, as their tutors hope, if they are to become agents of social reform during their adulthood, a well-informed mind will surely not be a disadvantage. Put another way, in their present shape, the new schools may be a different kind of excess rather than an authentic alternative.

Social institutions, the school among them, must of necessity undergo constant readjustments. Not only does the nature of the human predicament shift from time to time, technical capabilities grow increasingly sophisticated, and the society periodically displays a willingness to deal anew with pervasive problems from the past which have remained unresolved. Schools, consequently, will always be faced with the need to deal with their own weaknesses, for howsoever good their quality, the changing social scene will continue to make realignments necessary. The present time is no exception to this historical condition. Although today's schools are better than any which have existed before, they suffer nevertheless from a variety of infirmities, some of which could not have been foreseen a generation ago. Parts of the curriculum have become archaic; teaching—once an authentic helping profession—has in cases reduced itself to uninspired routine; a growing bureaucracy has found it increasingly difficult to be responsive to the diverse demands of a pluralistic public; and, crucially, the system itself has been unable to adjust rapidly enough to the extraordinary character of the current youth generation. Definitively different from any previous generation, a subculture unto itself, youth has found it both more important and more difficult to gratify psychological needs. It is thus more vulnerable to, and more fearful of, the pain and emasculation which accompany sustained anxiety. It is perhaps for this reason that the young are so profoundly interested in their own emotional lives.

The natural linkage between emotion and intellect is hardly a new idea. Its importance has long been acknowledged in the literature. Consider, for example, these words of Prescott, written fully thirty-two years ago:

> Schools must help children to understand the nature of social conflicts, to recognize the rights of others in the struggle for security, to tolerate reasonable social experimentation aimed at ameliorating suffering and insecurity, and to accept personal responsibilities and a share in the burden of caring for the unfortunate and underprivileged. These seem to be essential elements of educational policy necessary to social integration.
>
> Schools also have a different function varying from individual to individual. They must seek the personal adjustment of children who are thwarted or insecure under immediate conditions. They must help some to develop fortitude to endure that which simply cannot be changed. They must guide individual adolescents into socially useful forms of self-realization and

assist them in the discovery of means for rich and satisfying experience. . . . Schools must be reorganized to avoid being, themselves, the cause of frustration, or loss of status, of realizable ambitions, of deep resentment against social authority, of repeated humiliation. To accomplish their differential aims, the schools often must stand as a buffer between the child and some social processes. They must be of definite assistance to children who are misunderstood, exploited, incompetent, or underprivileged. This is no easy task. The social order itself is greatly confused and the future is quite obscure.(1)

THE RITUAL OF POLARIZING

The end destination, therefore, is a point on which there is widespread agreement; *it is the question of route that is open to dispute.* My own conviction is that the answer lies in cultivating what is most simply described as a wise and humane teacher—one sensitive to the connective tissue between mind and spirit. We must indeed be accountable, to ourselves and the social order; machines and instructional systems, to be sure, do have their place; but it is the humane teacher who best can negotiate the delicate compromise between the free school, where a child can spend his days kicking a can or throwing pebbles, and the establishment school, where often a child must put aside feeling, imagination, and creativity in order to survive.

It is not a mere middle-of-the-road policy that is argued for here. Rather, it is for a conception of learning which respects the inseparability of rational thought and emotional experience. A skillful teacher can draw forth the psychological overtones of an intellectual problem and, conversely, the intellectual insights which illuminate and clarify an emotional hang-up. Such a teacher is neither compelled to make use of blind walks, nude encounter groups, and other faithless rites—nor to seek educational salvation in the memorization of a list of the world's largest rivers. The cultivation of such wise and humane teachers and the construction of a school system which permits them to survive are together the twin challenges we face.

As the movement to reform education mounts, a major controversy has been kindled. The roots of the dispute lie in the long-standing conflict between utilitarianism and humanism. Whenever the question of changing human behavior arises, the morality and efficacy of manipulation soon become critical issues. Maturation—the psychological and intellectual torque of human growth—is, in essence, the transitional process between a nurturing environment and self-sufficiency. Are we therefore to trust in the sanative benefits of healthy experience, or are we to place our faith in scientific precision and assume that human behavior—because it is predictable—can be shaped and controlled by calculated intervention?

There are no sure answers, save for the fact that each position offers advantages and disadvantages. Human behavior *is* lawful. No action is without its cause. And the causes—the energizing forces which govern our conduct—rarely are simplistic. They are, instead, a complicated mix of perception, attitude, belief, value, and identity. Because reward and punishment are powerful incentives, they can indeed be used to regulate human action. If we wish, we can tame the spirit of leaders (and followers) as effectively as we train dogs and parrots. The question is, however, whether such training is ethical or permanent, and whether it destroys something that is peculiarly human.

MANIPULATION VERSUS SELF-DIRECTION

If we resist the temptation to manipulate people's behavior, we can also stimulate change through the psychodynamics of self-evaluation. By making it possible for an individual to increase his awareness, to gain new insights which enlarge his sense of options, we unleash the human capacity to resolve problems creatively. Such creative freedom is the seminal element of growth, for in authentic growth each man is responsible only to himself.

The difference between self-directed growth and other-directed conditioning is therefore clear. Both spawn behavioral change, but in the former impulse stems from the desire and will to become more adequate, and in the latter it stems from the bribe of reward or the threat of punishment.

We can program people as surely as we program machines and obtain machine-like precision, but in so doing, we also will obtain machine-like insensitivity and rigidity. Machines, even magnificent ones, must be readjusted again and again as circumstances require. The free human spirit, in contrast, is self-adjusting.

We look to our leaders for the vision of something better, and for the strength and imagination to take us from where we are to where we should be. Thus, the control of one's destiny is the indispensable precondition of leadership. But the purpose of programming is to impose constraints, while the purpose of leadership is to shatter them. One therefore destroys the other.

I do not mean by these warnings to imply that the science of behaviorism is without merit. The careful observation and recording of behavior need not interfere with imagination, free thought, and the expression of feelings. Once observed, however, we often attribute cause to the wrong stimulus. For example, the child may find the behavior itself intrinsically more satisfying than the nickel which is offered as a reward. It is also true, of course, that every teacher seeks to influence the behavior of the children in her charge, and that the children, like their adult counterparts, respond to the reinforcements which follow their actions. If we wish pupils to learn a particular behavior, it would be senseless to deny the laws of operant conditioning. Unless great care is taken, however, we may unintentionally teach, as well, some bad emotions, and we may find that the child's inalienable right to teacher affection has been subverted into the bribery of a conditional payoff. The pitfalls rather than the potency of the behavioristic method should give us pause.

ON TARGET

To return to the opening theme, then, four predominant needs provide a setting in which to consider the use of instructional systems: *first,* the need to conceive of schooling, not as a period of vocational preparation, but as a stream of events which cut deeply into the child's experiential record, leaving permanent markings; *second,* the need to conjoin intellectual development with the regular psychological exercise that builds strong emotional muscle; *third,* the need to invent alternative approaches to learning, borrowing all that is wholesome from the new experimental schools; and *fourth,* the need to capitalize as often as possible upon self-directed growth, progressively lessening reliance upon manipulative conditioning.

Good learning systems ensure that pupils reach predetermined objectives which lead to change in behavior. As such, they are immensely valuable. Properly engineered systems aim at a clearly defined target, marshal the most powerful resources available, make due allowances for the situational constraints in which the learning is to be accomplished, and provide a means for ascertaining whether the goal has been reached. Construed in this way, a learning system benefits equally the third-grade teacher who wants her students to learn elementary computational skills and the superintendent who wants to decrease drug consumption among high school students. Good systems, in short, increase the precision and efficiency of expended energy.

The wise administrator, therefore, does well to harness systems theory to his task. It should be remembered, however, that *an incomplete system is no system at all.* A teaching program, a computer, an evaluation scheme, a technique for individualizing instruction—all are but pieces of a potential whole. Only when they are integrated, when in concert they constitute a skillfully organized set of procedures that produce a specified end, do they create a legitimate system. The abiding danger, self-evidently, is that if any of the essential components are left out or misused, the worth of the system is destroyed. Systems, by definition, cannot be used piecemeal. And it is also clear that even a potent system, in and of itself, is no guarantee of educational quality. A good system, deployed toward a bad end, is a double tragedy; for when this is the case an undesirable goal is accomplished with spectacular proficiency. It is insufficient, consequently, to think of the system alone; system and objective must be judged in a body.

Learning is a natural whole, the parts of which support one another in some inexplicable way. Disciplined and systematic study, the freeflow of imagination, and the search for the inner peace of emotional stability are branches of the same tree. All feed the school's highest ambition: the enrichment of the person's life so that joy, satisfaction, and meaning transcend what is simply existence. To cut off one branch in favor of another would be to commit the fatal error.

Let us by all means put our instructional systems to good use. So too can we exploit what psychologists have learned about behaviorial change. But let us, at the same time, guard against mindless authoritarianism, against the destruction of independent thought, and against the substitution of habit and routine for the inward freedom that so easily is lost.

Reference

1. Daniel A. Prescott, "Emotion and the Educative Process," American Council on Education: Washington, D.C., 1938.

Operational Concepts

1. Because of prevailing parental attitudes, schools place dominant emphasis upon the cognitive achievement of students. Students, on the other hand, are a good deal more concerned with their affective responses to school.

2. Schools, as a general rule, lack an effective methodology for dealing with the affective domain and for teaching the skills of emotional control.

3. Life success—in its broadest dimensions—probably depends more upon the individual's emotional well-being than upon an acquired stockpile of knowledge.

4. The curriculum must be realigned so that a better balance between cognition and affect is achieved.

Implications

   The tensions of school frequently spawn in children various kinds of emotional trauma: stressful interpersonal relationships, fear of teacher disapproval, threat of competition, test anxiety, and other psychological strains that are disruptive to children's emotional well-being. To the extent that circumstances permit, teachers should be sensitive to these dangers and use preventative tactics to overcome them. In addition, whereever cognitive and affective lessons can be linked, learners should have an opportunity to become more familiar with their own emotional nature. Such familiarity is the beginning step in a learning process that assists individuals to manage their emotional impediments more effectively.

Affective Education

Louis Rubin

Curriculum, Affect, and Humanism

Gold and silver, precious metals in themselves, are next to useless when—as a substitute for plastic—they are employed in the wrong ways. So it is with the movements known as affective and humanistic education. Inspired by an enlightened conception of what human fulfillment can mean, rich in potential, embodying psyche and spirit as well as mind, the movements give promise of liberating education from the shackles of too narrow vision and no-longer-viable tradition. Yet, like other valuable inventions, if their benefits are to be captured, they must be harnessed properly, organized, and used with sensitive intelligence.

It would be well, in considering their potential, to begin with a clarification of terms, for few educational ideas have been as subject to confusion and misinterpretation as have the notions of humanistic and affective teaching. In the sense that I intend them here, affect has to do with emotion and feeling. Affective education, therefore, is concerned with emotional states, with the antecedent conditions giving rise to the feelings these emotional states evoke, and with the consequent behavior the feelings themselves generate. To speak of an affective curriculum, then, is to speak of skills through which people can cope with the inevitable emotional impediments in life, with anger, anxiety, frustration, and the dark moods of despair.

A humanistic curriculum, in contrast, may have affective overtones, or even incorporate a substantial program of affective education, but it nonetheless represents an entirely different curricular philosophy. In the true humanistic school, traditional content is subordinate to the child's nature and interests, the processes of feeling become as important as those of thought, personal ethos and private experience are viewed as *the* significant subject matter, and classical values, rather than passed on whole, are to be examined, appraised, interpreted, and altered to fit the individual's purpose and circumstance.

Reprinted from Louis Rubin, "Curriculum, Affect, and Humanism," *Educational Leadership*, Vol. 32, No. 1, 1974, pp. 10–13; by permission of the publisher.

HUMANISTIC AND AFFECTIVE DIFFERENCES

The common ground between humanistic and affective education lies in the methods of the humanistic psychologists wherein inner concerns and personal experience serve as the material for improving affective adaptation. Thus, we could, without undue difficulty, add a component of affective education to the conventional curriculum and, if we wished, teach it prescriptively. To fuse the humanistic and the conventional curricula, however, would necessiate considerable compromise because·the two, at least in a technical sense, are basically antithetical.

Several other points must also be clarified before the case I wish to make can be argued. Psychologists speak of positive (desirable) and negative (undesirable) affect. Satisfaction with a task ably performed, for example, creates positive affect and anxiety over anticipated failure produces negative affect. One acts to *achieve* positive feelings and to *prevent* negative ones. Hence, although, philosophically, pleasure might be defined as the absense of pain, affective education must of necessity be directed toward the mastery of two related but different sets of skills: those aimed at preventing disabling emotion, and those aimed at nurturing the feelings of contentment.

There is, moreover, a special bit of confusion over the distinctions between humanistic education and a humane school. What we mean by a humane school, at bottom, is one in which negative affect regarding the school is minimized. A humane school, in other words, neither bores nor brutalizes; its activities please rather than displease its clients, and the compulsory time spent there is sensed as pleasant rather than unpleasant. A humanistic school, in contrast, is one in which the dominant instructional emphasis is on self rather than on subject. It follows, therefore, that the artist teacher might well teach, say, Babylonian history, in so humane a fashion that positive affect toward school was kindled in the students and, conversely, the bumbling teacher might teach, say, self-awareness, so clumsily that negative affect was induced.

Finally, to touch upon one additional source of communication chaos, the term "feeling," too, poses a problem. For affective educators it tends to function as an adjective, describing emotional states such as sadness or loneliness; for humanistic educators it is more likely to function as a verb, designating a particular way of achieving insight. We can learn through feeling as well as through reasoning. Thus, aesthetic experience, sensing, and the art of feeling itself, humanists contend, have a legitimate place in the curricular galaxy.

I have not meant, in these preliminary remarks, to engage in theoretical quibblings or to pick nits over definitional terms. It would not be dismaying, or even surprising, if some of my professional colleagues saw fit to dispute the meanings I have assigned. My primary purpose has been that of identifying what seem to be the basic thrusts of affective and humanistic education so that the succeeding commentary on instructional legitimacy and teaching method is reasonably clear. It is implication not terminology that concerns us most.

COGNITION, AFFECT, AND HUMANISM

What, then, can be said about the virtues, first, of affective education and, second, of humanistic education?

To begin with, the evidence suggests that the largest part of affective education must be cognitive in nature. Emotional responses to situations, whether good or bad, stem from the interplay of (1) our perception of our needs, (2) the circumstances in which we find ourselves, and (3) our attitudes regarding appropriate behavior in these situations. Cognition, in short, provides the connective tissue between stimuli and affective response. Put another way, our perception of a situation is cognitive, our interpretation of its meaning is cognitive, and our choice of responsive action is cognitive. Or, in Piaget's words: "affectivity is nothing without intelligence. Intelligence furnishes affect with its means and clarifies its ends."

Perception, attitude, belief, and choice constitute the cornerstones of affective education. These, therefore, must serve as the nexus of cognitive exercises designed to improve the child's adaptation to emotional crises. It is not stress, but the way we cope with stress, which in the main determines whether or not we will be defeated by our emotional shortcomings. In essence, cognition and affect function in tandem. Cognition (belief and perception) is a dominant force in shaping attitudes, and attitudes—because they, as Allport said, "determine for each individual what he will see and hear, what he will think and what he will do," play a vital role in controlling our emotional responses to our life situations. Attitudes are intimately bound up with affective states precisely because our needs, our expectations, and our desires—as well as the emotions set loose when these are facilitated or impeded, all are heavily influenced by what we value and believe. Our attitudes, in sum, virtually make us what we are.

The relationship between cognition and affect, then, is further deepened by our personal conceptions of our needs. Beyond the fixed primary needs (essential to the maintenance of life), the secondary needs (essential to wholesome self-concept and a feeling of well-being) are influenced by our beliefs. Beliefs (values) and attitudes (predispositions to behave in certain ways) are therefore manifestations of what we consider significant in life. Individuality in emotional education therefore is ordained by the uniqueness of the organism's nature and circumstance.

It is thus plain that authentic affective education cannot consist of artificial efforts to induce one kind of counterfeit feeling or another, or of meaningless charades, or of hopeless searches for never-ending euphoria.

514

It must instead concern itself with the learner's attitudes toward himself, his life, and his purpose; with his perception and interpretation of the social scenes in which he finds himself; and with the tactics he uses to counteract and inhibit unpleasant emotion. And, importantly, it must acknowledge its own limitations: educators are not psychiatrists; long-standing affective habits are not easily altered; and, self-awareness—howsoever useful—does not negate the need for skill in reading and numbers.

WHAT ARE SCHOOLS FOR?

The fundamental issues surrounding humanistic education follow logically. From the standpoint of the curriculum designer the critical question is: shall we abandon the present instructional program and replace it with a humanistic one; reject, out-of-hand, the humanistic philosophy; or work for a balanced compromise? The dilemma, self-evidently, is more ideological than operational. Have the society and human aspirations so changed that the old no longer is serviceable or, rather, are we merely in the midst of an ebb and flow cycle in social evolution? Or, even more basically, is it time to redefine what schools are for?

One can scarcely deny that the present curriculum is far from adequate. There is little concern for the individual as a person; preoccupation with thought tends to obliterate feeling; the significance of personal ethos, personal knowledge, and personal experience is largely ignored; and, worse, the realization of human potential is left mainly to chance.

Each of us is impelled by a profound desire to function successfully—to exploit our talents, to do what we do well, and so to earn esteem among our peers. For if we are not considered worthy by those whose opinions we value; if we do not have a secure sense of belonging to and being accepted by the social groups in which we find ourselves; if we cannot both give and receive affection—it is almost impossible either to think well of ourselves or to be content with our lives. It is hardly surprising, therefore, that when schooling is measured on the yardstick of these needs, the prevailing program of instruction is found wanting.

Learning remains more passive than active, reason drowns feeling, values are passed on second-hand, aesthetic education is seriously undervalued, and often life in school scars permanently the child's own sense of adequacy and worth. It should not be so.

Hence, the following propositions seem reasonable.

With regard to the school environment: (1) school experiences may produce disabling emotions; (2) disabling emotions may diminish learning; and (3) teaching can so be organized that negative affect toward school is minimized.

With regard to affective education: (4) schools cannot prevent the traumatic events in the out-of-school milieu which spawn emotional difficulties; (5) therapy is the business of therapists, not school people; but (6) vulnerability to emotional problems can be reduced by classroom experiences which (a) sharpen perceptual accuracy with regard to people and events, (b) familiarize students with constructive responses to emotion-laden situations, and (c) promote the cumulative development of healthy, personally satisfying attitudes, beliefs, and values; and (7) such experiences can in most instances be integrated with the formal lessons in history, literature, science, language, and virtually everywhere else in the curriculum.

With repsect to humanistic education: (8) wherever possible the learner must be encouraged to look inward as well as outward; (9) knowledge of self must be seen as important as knowledge of world; (10) the relationship between freedom and responsibility—between autonomy and commitment to the public good—must be made more clear; (11) self-expression must benefit from higher priority; (12) the significance of the self, interacting with others, must be studied more closely; (13) the wisdom buried in the humanities must be brought to bear upon the mounting tide of helplessness, hopelessness, and resignation among the young; (14) values must be reexamined; yet (15) public expectation cannot be slighted; the realities of the social system cannot be disregarded; the benefits of man's hard-won enlightenment cannot be denied; and, importantly, we must remember that—whatever the turmoil afflicting adults—schools are for children.

Operational Concepts

1. Affective education is concerned primarily with the child's emotional well-being.

2. Humanistic education, in contrast, centers upon the child's personal experience and personal response to life situations.

3. An individual's emotional reactions to life situations are strongly influenced by his related perceptions, beliefs, and knowledge; affect and cognition, consequently, are essential components of humanistic education.

4. The comparative advantages of a curriculum that is humanistic, as opposed to one that is subject-centered, depend upon one's belief regarding the purpose of education.

5. The evidence seems to suggest that typical curricula are presently somewhat out of balance, in that affective and humanistic elements often are slighted because of excessive preoccupation with factual information.

Implications

It is doubtful that humanistic education, at least in its pure form, will replace traditional subject-centered instruction. Considerable advantage would accrue, however, if more humanistic philosophy were incorporated into the curriculum. Toward this end, greater emphasis should be placed upon the child's knowledge of self, upon the ways in which past experience are perceived, and upon healthy ways of coping with negative emotion. It should also be recognized that a study of the humanities does not necessarily make one humane, and that the goals of affective education normally must be accomplished through cognitive activity.

An equally important dimension of humanistic education involves the enhancement of students' altruistic impulses and their commitment to human welfare generally. In particular, learners must understand that the "good life" does not depend upon the material alone, that the constructive use of one's talents is essential to personal well-being, and that in the time ahead humans will become increasingly interdependent.

Finally, curriculum designers should repeatedly remind themselves that public expectations regarding basic education and essential knowledge cannot be disregarded—whether the expectations are valid or not.

Program Planning and Budgetary Systems

Walter J. Foley   Ralph A. Van Dusseldorp
Duane E. Richardson

Program Planning and Budgeting Systems

Program planning and budgeting systems (PPBS) have gained much acclaim since being introduced to the Defense Department by Secretary Robert S. McNamara. Then President L. B. Johnson asked each cabinet member to immediately begin to introduce this new and revolutionary system of planning and programming the budgeting throughout the vast federal government. He felt that this tool of modern management would help to bring about ". . . the full promise of a finer life to every American at the lowest possible cost . . ."(1).

These sentiments by the then president of the United States have continued to be heard through all branches of government, and they are continuing to have a great deal of impact upon the budgeting practice in education as well.

WHAT IS PPBS?(2)

PPBS is in many ways more a decision-mking process than it is an operations research tool. PPBS utilizes the mathematical analysis of operations research in the decision process, but PPBS is not a tool that can be applied to a specific problem situation. In this sense, it is more of a planning tool than a specific problem–solution-oriented tool.

Good educational managers have been using many of the elements of PPBS for years, but few, if any, have applied all segments. The purpose of this paper is to provide an understanding of PPBS concepts. For detailed operational guidelines, additional study will be necessary. An introductory bibliography is included at the end of the paper for this purpose.

Before a school district can attempt to implement PPBS, there should be a commitment to the system on the part of the superintendent. This is necessary because PPBS is designed to aid the person who ultimately makes the decisions, or at least is held accountable for decisions; without the superintendent's commitment to the implementation of PPBS, any attempt by others on his staff to implement the system will probably be wasted. PPBS is not designed to replace the intuitive and experimental judgment of the superintendent, but rather to sharpen his decision making by making available data in other forms and formats than is typically possible through traditional budgeting documents.

The superintendent must be willing to clarify his own philosophy of education and value structure and, based upon these, determine the kinds and quality of data needed for effective decision making. This is necessary as the format of the PPBS is based upon the tasks of the educational system. He must be willing to structure the budget in relation to goals and programs, and then it is expected that new channels of communication will probably be necessary if change is to take place through the implementation of PPBS. Traditionally, the budgeting process has been carried out by central office personnel. Building principals have been involved occasionally; department chairmen, sometimes; teachers, almost never. Several committees (or action groups) are recommended to implement PPBS. The strategy for involvement should involve the establishment of a Central Planning Group. The composition of this group will be unique to each school district, depending upon the degree of centralization desired for planning. Some theorists feel strategic planning should be done by the central administrative staff. If total staff involvement is considered important, however, representation from all levels of the organization is necessary. For effective working relationships, this group should be limited to from seven to fifteen members. They should be responsible for assessing district needs; recommending district objectives; recommending district program structure; forecasting long-range projections of proposed program alternatives; studying resource allocation, projecting long-range cost effectiveness of the proposed program alternatives; and coordinating other groups. It is possible to become involved in all of these areas at once, but since the ongoing school program demands staff time, it is probable that only one area can be attacked at the onset. A prime target for first consideration in the implementation of PPBS is the program structure. The advantage to this approach is the necessary teamwork required by curriculum personnel and business officials at the outset. Note, budgetary documentation should not be considered first. Once the Central Planning Group has determined and recommended the district objectives and program structure to be used, specialist groups for each program should be formed. These are ad hoc groups having one specific function—that is, to establish and recommend to the Central Planning Group district objectives for specific programs. Members of these groups should be teachers and curriculum specialists in the program area being analyzed for implementation. Each group should be given specific deadline dates for submitting its recommendations. These groups may continue to exist beyond these deadline dates for refining objectives and the development of specific instructional objectives.

Walter J. Foley, Duane E. Richardson, and Ralph A. Van Dusseldorp

A Budget Committee, another specialized group, can be organized and can begin functioning when the program focus has been established by the Central Planning Group and has been adopted by the school district board. *The preparation of budget documents is one of the key elements of PPBS.* These must reflect the educational goals, objectives, methods, and resources of the school district. The preparation of these documents necessitates a close working relationship among all members of the staff. The Budget Committee might be composed of members of the district business office, the accounting staff, and the professional staff. Once district objectives for specific programs are adopted, the Building Planning and Programming groups should be formed. These groups need to be formed wherever the district program is implemented as an activity for students. They should be composed of people appointed by the building principal or director who has "expertise" in the programs. The duties of these groups are to write curricular or support objectives, establish criteria for evaluation, and recommend alternative ways of reaching district objectives within individual programs.

It appears most districts initiating program budgeting have adapted it to the present traditional school district organizational structure. Educators may be forewarned that the traditional structure harbors potential problems for the implementation of PPBS and the use of these concepts may reveal many possibilities for operational reorganization. How do you develop a program structure for the school district? Theoretically, the district program structure should be developed from the goals, the policies, and the district objectives that have been derived after lengthy study and discussion by many people. In actual practice, this may not be feasible. It may be more appropriate to analyze the present system and from this analysis construct a program structure that most nearly reflects the ongoing system. This analysis will allow explication of district goals and policy objectives and may possibly suggest the redesign of the program structure.

The components of a program structure can be seen as:

- Interface
- Program
- Program subcategories
- Base elements

INTERFACE

By definition, an interface is a document that relates a subsystem to a larger system. Legally, a school district is a subdivision of the state, and hence, part of a larger system. If, for instance, the state has certain educational objectives, an interface document might be necessary. It is not basically a component of the program structure and may or may not be necessary. The requirement of specific educational attainment by the state would impose certain constraints on the design of a program structure within an individual school district and would make mandatory careful study of state requirements before a district program structure were designed. Program structure may be affected by external demands for data, and the construction of an interface document may be a necessity to assure meeting these demands.

PROGRAM

Technically, a program is a major district endeavor oriented to the district objectives and defined in terms of actions required to achieve an output objective. Many variations of program structures are found in districts implementing PPBS. Examples of these program structures are:

1. Elementary, Junior High, Secondary, Community Services, and Support.
2. Instruction; Instruction, Support; Instruction, Exceptional; Community Services; and Support.
3. Kindergarten and Lower Elementary, Middle School, Secondary, Special Programs, Community Services, and Support and Technical Services.
4. Language Arts, Mathematics and Science, Humanities, Fine Arts, Health and Physical Education, Vocational, Special Programs, Community Services, and Support.
5. Consumer satisfaction, personal safety, economic satisfaction and employment opportunities, satisfactory leisure time activities, transportation, satisfactory home and community environment, learning, and general administration and support.

The list is almost inexhaustible and will differ with each school that implements PPBS.

PROGRAM SUBCATEGORIES

A program must be divided into subdivisions. For example, if one of the programs is High School, the program subcategories could be: English, Mathematics, and Science, Vocational, etc.

BASE ELEMENT

Program subcategories, then, are divided into units where the actual service is provided to the students. Following the example, the base element could be English IV.

Walter J. Foley, Duane E. Richardson, and Ralph A. Van Dusseldorp

HISTORICAL ANALYSIS

One of the initial responsibilities of the Budget Committee, after the Central Planning Group establishes the program structure, is to use past data to analyze the costs of the programs. This process is called "Historical Analysis." It is particularly recommended that this analysis include the immediately past fiscal year and be projected to include the current fiscal year. This analysis may identify some major problem areas that call for immediate decision making.

This analysis is accomplished by assigning costs on a program basis, inventorying expenditures in the different program areas, and assigning these costs to the different program categories.

DISTRICT GOALS AND PHILOSOPHY

A written statement of educational philosophy exists in most school districts. Theoretically, the goals of the district will be adapted from this statement of philosophy.

A number of schools in the nation are adopting, as goals, the nine "Imperatives in Education" as prepared by the American Association of School Administrators in 1966(3). They are to:

1. Make urban life rewarding and satisfying.
2. Prepare people for the world of work.
3. Discover and nurture creative talent.
4. Strengthen the moral fabric of society.
5. Deal constructively with psychological tension.
6. Keep democracy working.
7. Make intelligent uses of natural resources.
8. Make the best use of leisure time.
9. Work with other people for human betterment.

A number of school districts in the Southwest are adopting versions of the "Texas Goals for Education"(4). These usually include:

1. Knowledge and intellectual discipline.
2. Econmic competencies.
3. Civic and social responsibilities.
4. Cultural appreciations.
5. Moral and ethical values.
6. Self-realization.

Each district must adapt, create, and adopt a statement of goals. It is imperative in the development of a PPBS system that the goals adopted must be capable of transformation into objectives. The objectives, in turn, must be capable of hierarchical arrangement.

DISTRICT POLICY, PROGRAM, AND CURRICULUM OBJECTIVES

Objective setting must focus on the educational philosophy and the general goals of the school district, as well as upon the target population.

Four categories of objectives are prepared for the establishment of a hierarchy of objectives. These four are:

1. Policy objectives.
2. Program objectives.
3. Curriculum objectives.
4. Instructional objectives.

Some districts utilize only three types of objectives by fusing curriculum and instructional objectives.

Policy objectives are derived from the values and/or policy decisions of higher level organizations, which in turn derive them from their perceptions of the values of the sponsoring society. These are normally issued as a written statement by the superintendent and are based upon the necessity of the district to attain the broad educational goals. They give rise to rules and regulations, superintendent's directives, and the bylaws of the school board.

Program objectives are derived from policy objectives. They propose competencies or improved competencies for a program or its constituents. They also include the intended location of resources and efforts. There are three types of program objectives:

1. District performance objectives are statements proposing the improved state of some aspect of district performance, or they may be an intent statement describing how well some aspect of the district will perform some function at some future time.
2. Program element performance objectives are statements proposing the performance of an element of a larger organization. A program element performance objective might also be an intent statement describing how well some function will be performed at some future time.
3. Learner benefit objectives propose the improved state of the typical learner that will result from the functioning of programs and from the district as a whole.

Curricular objectives are derived from program objectives and include sets of learning outcomes stated in behavioral terms.

Instructional objectives are derived from curricular objectives and include a statement or learner product in the explicit behavioral form that is expected from the influence of instruction.

Each objective contains five components:

1. Outcome statement (an aid to the movement of the district towards an output orientation).
2. Condition statement (how the objective is to be evaluated).
3. Criterion statement (standards of acceptable performance).
4. Rationale statement.
5. Modifier statement.

Management by objectives requires a definition of objectives. The forgoing is basically the configuration and definition of *one* hierarchy of objectives. The adoption of this objective definition is not meant to be definitive, but could be as a guide in considering the objective approach.

Some important criteria for objectives are:

1. Is the objective, generally speaking, a guide to action?
2. Can it facilitate decision making in a school district?
3. Does it relate to the goals and broader objectives of the district?
4. Can progress toward the attainment of the objective be measured and effectiveness be determined?

DEVELOPMENT OF PROGRAM FINANCIAL PLAN AND PROGRAM MEMORANDA

Each building principal or unit administrator should develop a Program Financial Plan (PFP). This document, arising from data forwarded to him by classroom teachers, will assist in his construction of the Program Memorandum (defined later). Accompanied by this latter document, it will in turn be forwarded to the Central Planning Group, the superintendent, and the board.

Each level PFP document should include the following broad categories of information for each program:

1. A breakdown of costs by development, implementation, and operation.
2. Costs for the fiscal year for which the program is being planned with projections for at least five years.
3. Identification of objectives being met by the program.
4. Estimations of the effectiveness of the program.
5. Identification of the number of students to be served.
6. A description of evaluative procedures for the program.

The Program Memorandum (PM) presents to the Central Planning Group, the superintendent, and the board program recommendations within the framework of program objectives complete with an identification of the alternatives and recommendations for decisions. In the event of school district administrative decentralization, these documents would, of necessity, be channeled through the intermediary office.

The PFP should show specifically at least three alternatives for each program being developed for future implementation. If a program is experimental or demonstrative, it should clearly identify this fact. From the building level the PM will include the recommended alternative feature only, and persons wishing to consider other alternative procedures at a later date must refer to the PFP. The PM, then, presents the analysis of the PFP to the decision-maker for his consideration.

PROGRAM-BUDGETING CALENDAR

After the establishment of the documents and the data flow system, the district administrators should develop the budgetary planning cycle. This cycle should be of at least eighteen months duration. Events that should be completed for each program to be analyzed include:

1. Established objectives.
2. Develop base element alternatives.
3. Develop program subcategory alternatives.
4. Develop program alternatives.
5. Estimate costs for different alternatives.
6. Estimate total resources available.
7. Determine staffing patterns.
8. Submit budget to the board.
9. Adopt budget for next fiscal year.
10. Modify programs according to resource allocations after budget is operational.

SELECTION OF PROGRAM AREAS FOR DEVELOPMENT

Most program structures presently designed consist in five to ten major programs. To analyze and develop in-depth alternatives for all of these programs within one year is a major undertaking and probably is not advisable. The development of a calendar for program development over a five-year period seems more realistic. Thus, areas of immediate thrust need to be decided. One criterion for the selection of program thrusts dictates that a program that has first call on the resources of a district should be developed first. The program having the least call on the resources should be developed last.

Once a program is developed, it should operate for a five-year period of time allowing the evaluatory system to modify procedures as necessary. Prior to the terminal date of the program, planning should be reinstituted for an additional five-year period.

EVALUATION PROCESS DEVELOPMENT

In PPBS there are two major concerns:

1. The projection of estimated costs and effectiveness.
2. Actual costs and the evaluation of effectiveness.

The determination of costs of individual programs is a relatively simple task for the business officials. It will not be discussed further in this section.

Effectiveness is ascertained through the evaluation process and, basically, answers the question of how well a program has met its objectives. Evaluation is a procedure of collecting pertinent information about program outcomes. This information is fed back into the system to facilitate decision making.

Evaluation, then, must meet many criteria. It must:

1. Facilitate self-evaluation.
2. Encompass every objective established for the program.
3. Facilitate learning and teaching.
4. Produce records appropriate to the purposes for which records are kept.
5. Provide continuing feedback for larger questions of educational policy.

Evaluation is usually considered to have four components. These are:

1. Input: the state of the recipients of the program at the time of entry.
2. Process: what actually occurred in the program to the students, staff, methods, time, supplies, materials, equipment, and facilities.
3. Output: the state of the recipients upon the completion of the program.
4. Input–output: the difference between the outcome and the antecedent.

The validity of the evaluation rests upon the establishment of effective objectives and measurements of attainment. It should be noted that evaluation will be only a crude process in its initial stages. Hopefully, sophistication in the use of PPBS will improve evaluation.

DATA PROCESSING

A data processing system should be developed to include all factors in PPBS. The computer capabilities needed for the computerization of data in PPBS must be sufficient to generate the current fiscal year and five-year projections of program costs, as well as the impact of program decisions on these projected budgetary costs for specific programs. They must also include grids for evaluation data, as well as accounting capabilities. A most important function to the computer is storing projection information from year to year, updating only those data that change but allowing the generation of new projections with comparative ease.

ASSIGNMENT OF COSTS

A program-oriented budget should include within each program as many of the estimated costs as practicable. The most ambitious data system proponents argue that all school costs can, and should be, assigned to the various programs that fulfill the purposes for which a school is operated. Such cost allocations are possible. However, they are not essential to PPBS. Indeed, an attempt to deal exhaustively with the proration of costs may consume the time and energy needed for proper planning, programming, and budgeting.

For example, little purpose is served by prorating facilities operation and maintenance costs among the various instructional programs. The building will likely be maintained, heated, and lighted whether reading, Spanish, or democratic living is being taught. Although identification of Facilities Operation and Maintenance as a program is recommended, the cost of new facilities, as well as the cost of maintaining and operating those facilities, must be considered when conducting a PPBS study of proposed new programs, alternative methods of satisfying program objectives, or the proposed discontinuance of existing programs. For example, a proposed new swimming pool has financial implications far beyond the original cost of the pool. A PPBS study should answer these functions:

1. What are the measurable objectives to be satisfied through the use of the new pool?
2. What students will be served?
3. What other program might satisfy the needs of these students and the objectives of the program?
4. What alternative programs should be considered?
5. What measurable objectives could be met through each alternative program?
6. What students will be served by each alternative program?
7. What is the one-time cost (usually a facility cost) for each of the programs?
8. What are the direct personnel costs for each of the programs?
9. What are the costs for each of the programs?

528

Heating?
Lighting?
Travel?
Specific operations (such as filtering plant)?
Custodial?
Special services (such as laundry)?

While it is recommended that no attempt be made to assign all school costs to the instructional programs, it is recommended that all costs uniquely identifiable and attributable to a program be assigned accordingly. At the present time, many schools are accounting for their expenditures under mandated financial systems that fail to accommodate such cost assignments. A number of states are studying this problem and hope to modify their coding structures to accommodate PPBS. The U.S. Office of Education, in the summer of 1969, contracted for a revision of the *Financial Accounting Manual Handbook II*. It seems axiomatic that the revision will not only accommodate, but will encourage, PPBS.

In the meantime, subsidiary accounting to accommodate PPBS may be adopted as needed.

POLICY IMPLEMENTATION

No matter what factors might inhibit adoption of PPBS, no superintendent should recommend a new program or a new aproach to meeting existing program objectives without employing the concepts of PPBS.

For example, suppose a superintendent is faced with the problem of burgeoning enrollments in driver education. The high school principal has recommended the development of a multiple-car off-street driving range to avoid having to hire additional teaching personnel. Assuming that driver education is mandated by state law, there is no question about its competing with other programs for the educational dollar. Nevertheless, it should be exposed to the rigors of the PPBS techniques to optimize the return on the dollars spent, particularly before investing in a multiple-car off-street driving range.

A chronology of the PPBS study might be as follows:

1. State measurable objectives: the superintendent sought the help of your staff, professional literature, insurance companies, and university personnel in deciding upon the following objectives:

   a. The course should be an elective course open to all youth of the district who meet the age requirements and who have not previously completed a course in driver education.

   b. All students satisfactorily completing the course should meet all requirements for a driver's license in this state.

   c. At least 70 percent of those students completing the course should achieve a score in the "good range" on the Aaron–Strasser Driver Performance Test.

   d. At least 90 percent of the students completing the course should achieve a score of average or above on the Aaron–Strasser Driver Performance Test.

   e. Pupils should be capable of skilfully executing the following fundamentals exercise.

     (1) Parallel parking.

     (2) Angle parking.

     (3) Driveway turnabout.

     (4) Lane change.

     (5) Backing.

     (6) Garage parking.

     (7) Hill parking.

   f. All students who complete the course should score a minimum of 75 percent on the "Road Check" film test (Aetna series) or on the "Let's Review" film test (Allstate series).

   g. Students should have knowledge and simulated experience that will enable them to successfully cope with emergency situations. Competence in this area should be demonstrated by a minimum score of 75 percent on the "Driving Emergencies" film test (Allstate).

   h. Five-year follow-up studies should reveal a significantly below-average incidence of moving traffic violations for graduates of this course.

   i. Five-year follow-up studies should reveal a significantly below-average incidence of reportable accidents for graduates of this course.

2. Assign priorities: all of the objectives listed are reasonable and appropriate. The superintendent elected to retain them all and give them equal status. (The *assignment* of priorities is more applicable to situations in which several new programs are competing for the same available financial resources.)

3. Determine alternative plans to meet the objectives: it was noted that the classroom phase of a driver education program in this state is fixed by law at a minimum of thirty clock hours. This time allotment may be exceeded, but a careful study of the course content. the opinion of the driver education staff, and the statements made by the University Safety Personnel and the leading insurance companies all indicate that thirty hours of classroom instruction is appropriate no matter what laboratory method is selected for teaching the driving skills. The study revealed three distinct plans for teaching the laboratory phase (driving skills phase) of driver education.

Walter J. Foley, Duane E. Richardson, and Ralph A. Van Dusseldorp

Plan A

The plan being utilized in school at the present time consists of six hours behind-the-wheel dual-control driving instruction. Students typically observe other students drive for twelve hours, but this procedure is employed as a scheduling convenience and has little, if any, educational value in itself.

Plan B

Plan A is followed, but the time requirement is reduced from six to three hours. The other three hours are replaced by twelve hours of training on a driving simulator.

Plan C

The driving simulator is utilized in exactly the same manner as Plan B. Six hours of multiple-car off-street driving range experience can be substituted for all but one hour of behind-the-wheel dual-control driving instruction. The superintendent proposes to utilize the full six hours of driving range instruction. Due to the initial cost of Plan C and its newness to the state, the superintendent felt it appropriate to be a bit cautious or conservative.

4. Assign dollar values to each of the alternative plans: the direct cost of each of the three plans for teaching driver education involves the number of teachers needed, the salary per teacher, fringe benefits per teacher, and supplies. Plan B has an additional direct cost for driving simulators and a room to use them in. Plan C has still another direct cost—acquiring four acres of land and developing a multiple-car off-street driving range. Data for past years can be used to calculate the estimated future costs of plan A. Costs of plan B and plan C also can be determined from existing data files in conjunction with projected costs of simulators and the driving range. The cost of providing, maintaining, and operating the plant, equipment, and supplies is estimated to be the same for all three plans. Projections of driver education enrollments, class size, teachers required for each of the three plans, average teacher salaries and fringe benefits can be determined through sophisticated use of data systems, or they can be calculated through pencil and paper calculations. The "one-time" costs need to be estimated. Usually these estimates are made independent of existing data files. Frequently architects, equipment supplies, contractors, or real estate agents provide some of the needed data. After all of the data have been determined, they should be displayed in a logical format similar to that shown in Table 1.

5. Select a plan for implementation: it should be pointed out the decision reached concerning which plan to adopt will not necessarily be the least costly nor the most costly. It should, however, optimize the return on the educational dollar over a period of years. In the illustration, the evidence suports the adoption of plan B.

6. Use the plan you have selected: once a plan has been selected, it should be implemented as planned.

TABLE 1 Projected Cost of Teaching Driver Education Using Three Alternative Plans

FISCAL YEAR	1971–72	1972–73	1973–74	1974–75	1975–76
Est. driver enrollment	318	327	346	351	365
Base salary est.	7,500	7,800	8,100	8,500	8,700
Avg. teacher salary	10,500	11,232	12,150	13,260	13,920
Avg. teacher fringe benefit	1,810	1,915	2,330	2,650	2,838
Avg. teacher cost	12,310	13,147	14,480	15,910	16,758
PLAN A					
No. teachers needed	3.0	3.0	3.2	3.2	3.4
Teacher cost	36,930	39,441	46,336	50,912	56,977
One-time cost	0	0	0	0	0
Other cost	9,555	9,920	11,420	11,570	12,056
Total cost	46,485	49,361	57,756	62,482	69,033
PLAN B					
No. teachers needed	2.0	2.2	2.2	2.2	2.4
Teacher cost	24,620	28,923	31,856	35,002	40,219
One-time cost	40,300	—	—	—	—
Other cost	9,555	9,920	11,420	11,570	12,056
Total cost	74,475	38,843	43,276	46,572	52,275
PLAN C					
No. teachers needed	1.4	1.6	1.6	1.6	1.6
Teacher cost	17,234	21,035	23,168	25,456	26,813
One-time cost	220,800	—	—	—	—
Other cost	9,555	9,920	11,420	11,570	12,056
Total cost	247,589	30,955	34,588	37,026	38,869
COST DIFFERENCES					
B − A	27,990	−10,518	−14,480	−15,910	−16,758
Cum B − A	27,990	17,472	2,992	−12,918	−29,676
C − A	201,104	−18,406	−23,168	−25,456	−30,164
Cum C − A	201,104	182,688	159,530	134,074	103,910
C − B	173,114	−7,888	−8,688	−9,546	−13,406
Cum C − B	173,114	165,226	156,538	146,992	133,586

7. Review the objectives and evaluate the extent to which you are meeting them: a review of the objectives of any educational plan is always wise. It is no less timely with a PPBS application. PPBS objectives are measurable, and the extent to which they are being fulfilled should be determined.

8. Keep searching for more efficient alternative plans: again, this step in PPBS seems self-evident. There is a danger, however, that decisions based on careful studies may be blindly—and perhaps unjustifiably—pursued against the light of later truth.

Will PPBS increase demands made upon administrators' time? The answer is definitely affirmative. The amount of extra time required will depend upon the size of the district, the nature of the staff and schools, and the skill of the administrators. Some districts may need to employ additional professional personnel (i.e., a PPBS coordinator) or clerical assistance. Other districts may need to spend some additional money for computer services. A few districts may need only redirect the efforts of existing staff and resources to implement PPBS.

A PPBS system should not be considered a responsibility of business management personnel. However, they should provide technical and support services. This is not to suggest a diminished role for the business management personnel. The kinds of information they will need to provide in support of the system will be more demanding than most budgeting systems used previously. It does suggest, however, that the programs and program elements that are developed are the responsibility of those charged with fulfilling the philosophy, policies, and goals of the district.

Outside consultants from such agencies as state departments of education, colleges, and universities may be contracted to give guidance and support to the coordinator. They probably will recommend that a critical study be made of other districts implementing PPBS. It also may be helpful to use these consultants in conducting a general staff orientation covering such topics as:

1. An overview of PPBS leading to an understanding of the rationale for its implementation.
2. Development of the planning organization.
3. Development of district program structure.
4. Development of management by objectives.
5. Planning for informational flow.
6. Development of understanding of the analytical capabilities of PPBS.
7. Development and understanding of other managerial tools, i.e., data processing, budgetary documents, mathematical and sociological devices.

One of the crucial tasks for the coordinator is to gain cooperation of staff involved in curriculum development and business matters of the school district. In brief, the duties of the coordinator seem to be to:

1. Keep abreast of the developments and research in PPBS.
2. Weld a cooperative effort to provide for and direct the in-service education for the central office staff, as well as the various school staffs and other employees who will be involved in PPBS.
3. Act as an advisor and consultant to the administrative officers and teachers throughout the district.
4. Design and coordinate the various committees working on objectives and programs.

Important throughout the planning and implementation of PPBS is the involvement of people at all levels in the educational organization.

In summary, PPBS does not fall in the descriptive category of operation research as presented in other sections of this book. PPBS does provide a framework for structuring school programs and accounting systems to facilitate long-range planning and evaluation. PPBS allows adminstrators to do "opportunity planning" rather than planning to solve problems. This means acting instead of reacting and causing things to happen rather than waiting for them to happen.

References

1. David Novick (ed.), *Programming Budgeting, Program Analysis and the Federal Budget* (Cambridge, Mass.: Harvard University Press, 1967), pp. xi, xvi.
2. Special credit should be given to Ronald Harper of Northwest Regional Education Laboratory and J. Patrick Westcott of Washington State University for their contribution to this chapter. Many of the ideas presented here are a result of a study they conducted for the state of Washington.
3. American Association of School Administrators, *Imperatives in Education* (Washington, D.C., 1966).
4. Texas State Education Agency, *Texas Goals for Education* (Austin, Tex., 1968).

Suggested Readings

Administrative Technology and the School Executive, American Association of School Administrators. Washington, D.C., 1969.
General Design for an Education Planning–Programming–Budgeting System. Prepared by Government Studies Center, Fels Institute of Local and State Government, University of Pennsylvania, June 28, 1968, p. 35.

Walter J. Foley, Duane E. Richardson, and Ralph A. Van Dusseldorp

GIBBS, WESLEY F. "Program Budgeting Filters Down to Education." *Nation's Schools* 81, no. 5 (1968).

HARTLEY, HARRY J. *Educational Planning–Programming–Budgeting, A Systems Approach.* Englewood Cliffs, N.J.: Prentice-Hall, Inc., 1968.

HIRSCH, WERNER Z., ELBERT W. SEGELHORST, and MORTON J. MARCUS. *Spillover of Public Education Costs and Benefits,* Institute of Government and Public Affairs. University of California, Los Angeles, Calif., August, 1964.

Imperatives in Education. American Association of School Administrators, Washington, D.C., 1966.

KERSHAW, J. A., and R. N. MCKEAN. *Systems Analysis and Education.* Santa Monica, Calif.: The RAND Corporation, 1959.

KNORR, OWEN A., ed. *Long-Range Planning in Higher Education.* Boulder, Colo.: Western Interstate Commission for Higher Education, April, 1965.

NOVICK, DAVID. *Efficiency and Economy in Government Through New Budgeting and Accounting Procedures.* Santa Monica, Calif.: The RAND Corporation, February, 1954.

NOVICK, DAVID, ed. *Program Budgeting, Program Analysis and the Federal Budget.* Cambridge, Mass.: Harvard University Press, 1967.

Planning–Programming–Budgeting System in the New York City Public School System. PPBS Staff, Stanford Research Institute, June, 1967.

SMITHIES, ARTHUR. *A Conceptual Framework for the Program Budget.* Santa Monica, Calif.: The RAND Corporation, September, 1964.

Texas Goals for Education. Texas State Education Agency, Austin, Tex., 1968.

Operational Concepts

1. PPBS is a planning tool rather than a problem-solving tool.

2. Operations research, the genitor of PPBS, serves essentially to facilitate administrative decision making.

3. The ultimate worth of a school's program depends not upon the procedures used for planning and budgeting alone, but also upon the program's educational goals. In this regard, PPBS does not identify goals; rather, it helps in managing their accomplishment.

4. Goals, policies, methods, objectives, and resources are key factors in budgeting decisions and, hence, key factors in using PPBS strategies.

5. The use of PPBS techniques requires that policies and goals be translated into specific instructional objectives.

6. The dominant benefits of program planning and budgeting techniques lie in their capacity to help the administrator measure instructional effectiveness against cost.

Implications

PPBS tactics have undeniable virtues. Logically, maneuvers that allow the administrator to anticipate probable gains against probable cost, and eventually to determine cost effectiveness, are not to be dismissed lightly. Yet, it is important to remember that the ultimate benefits of program budgeting depend upon the objectives toward which they are directed. Moreover, the calculation of cost–benefit ratios does not mitigate, in and of itself, against any particular educational philosophy or goal. Program budgeting offers precisely the same potential to all curricula; its methods, for example, can be deployed in humanistic programs as well as in traditional ones. Although the attainment of some educational objectives is more easily verified than the attainment of others, wherever the net degree of change can be approximated, even in general terms, program budgeting principles can be invoked.

Despite these advantages, however, a word of warning is in order. Efficiency may not be everything; that is, some objectives, even though impossible to accomplish with a high degree of economic efficiency, may be of sufficient importance to pursue whatever their cost. As a case in point, to argue that worthy citizenship should be eliminated as an educational goal because it cannot be achieved with striking efficiency would be patently absurd. It behooves the administrator to recognize, therefore, that many curricular objectives, although difficult to measure, may need to be sustained, if only as articles of faith.

Systems Engineering

Louis Rubin

Systems Engineering and the Curriculum

It is somewhat paradoxical that the two innovations in greatest currency and perhaps of greatest potential would seem—on the surface—to be contradictory; yet, the specificity and precision of systems planning and the implicit openness and flexibility of humanistic education need not, necessarily, conflict with one another.

Most of the things that go on in the world transpire according to some sort of system. Just as the human body functions as a system, involving a series of subsystems which ensure that blood will be delivered, nervous impulses carried, and so on, all organized human endeavors make use of a pattern of activities designed to realize a specified outcome.

Stated most simply, the systems approach to education consists of four sequential steps: (1) determining the specific end results desired, (2) determining what sequence of activities is most likely to achieve these results, (3) initiating the activities, and (4) determining whether the specified results have in fact been achieved. Systems of these sorts require careful attention to precise detail; in particular, not only must the end goals be defined, but the subgoals on which the end goals depend also must be specified. If we wish that the child be able to read (end goal), we cannot efficiently reach this objective without first identifying the prerequisite skills essential to competent reading—vowel sounds, letter recognition, phonetics, and so on (subgoals).

It is for this reason that behaviorial objectives are a vital part of systems planning, for without a specific goal in mind, learning activities cannot be selected with any accuracy. Similarly, assessment criteria are equally important; we cannot evaluate a system designed to teach children to read if we do not have some reference point by which to determine whether the child's reading ability is satisfactory or unsatisfactory. Thus, in planning a system of reading instruction, we would specify the goal (ability to read), specify the desired level of competence (a reading rate of 400

Reprinted from Louis Rubin, "Systems Engineering and the Curriculum," *Curriculum Development: A Study Guide for Educational Administrators,* © 1973; by permission of Nova University Press, Fort Lauderdale, Fla.

words per minute, using a standard eighth grade level material, with a comprehension of 90 percent or more), and then seek to determine, as closely as possible, the specific subskills that are required. We might plan, for example, phonics exercises, word recognition games, eye-span training, and vocabulary drill. At this point, we will have fulfilled two of the four essential steps: the identification of a specific objective, and the selection of activities intended to achieve the objectives. Moving on to step 3, we might test the system by planning an instructional program for a group of students; in short, we would test the activities we had selected. Finally, moving on to step 4, we would check the students to see how well they read.

Suppose that we discovered, however, that most of the students did not meet the criteria we set; their reading ability, in other words, was less than we had hoped to achieve. It would then become necessary to discover the underlying cause: we might have selected the wrong training activities, or perhaps the activities were appropriate but the instruction was inadequate, or the activities may have been appropriate and the instruction good, but the children lacked adequate incentive. We would look to our evaluative procedures in order to determine what was what. On the basis of this evaluation, we would then be in a position to make the necessary modification. The systems engineering movement, in essence, represents an effort to pursue such systematic planning and evaluation throughout the curriculum; wherever a behavioral objective is specified, an appropriate system is designed.

Many names have been applied to the process described above. The most generic is probably PPBS (planning–programming–budgeting system). Other titles include systems analysis, and—where the objective has to do with determining dollar cost—systems budgeting, benefit–cost analysis, and program budgeting. Whatever the nomenclature, however, each of these engineering models represents a relatively scientific method of making curriculum decisions. But, of even greater importance, each system also permits the school administrator to calculate the cost of instruction, system by system, and, in consequence, to assign a dollar-effectiveness value to each portion of the program. For example, in the reading program referred to above, by adding together the cost of teacher salaries, instructional materials, housing, and other related costs, the administrator can determine how much money he must spend on the program. This, in turn, allows him to compare the costs and benefits of one program with those of another. Presumably, if all other considerations are equal, program budgeting should result in less waste and greater efficiency.

Let us look, for a moment, somewhat more closely at the differences between traditional budgeting methods and program budgeting. In the traditional method, an administrator might decide, say, that he would spend—on the sixth-grade class—X number of dollars for supplies, equipment, and personnel. He assumes that useful instruction will take place, and thus makes no attempt to determine how much money is spent on reading, arithmetic, or folk dancing. With a program budgeting approach, in contrast, he is able to project how much each facet of the program will cost, and he thus budgets a particular amount for reading, arithmetic, and folk dancing. He is able, in short, to control the investment of dollars, allocating his resources in terms of their priority and economic efficiency. Note, however, that to do this he must deal in quantifiable terms. He cannot, for instance, merely budget a sum of money to teach spelling. Rather, he must specify that his objective is to achieve a year's progress on a standardized spelling test with thirty-five children and calculate his costs accordingly.

It is still too early to determine whether PPBS and other systems procedures can be made to work profitably on any large scale. Thus far, the evidence is mixed and theorists are divided. Consider, for example, the following summary by Joseph McGivney(1):

> While this writer believes that PPBS, or program budgeting, represents improvements over the more traditional methods, he does not believe that it has been (or will be) the basis for a "revolution" in management, or that it provides policy makers with "full knowledge of expected accomplishments" of alternative programs, so that policy makers can better decide. Moreover, as was shown, the new approaches are built upon assumptions about the nature of the policy process that are difficult to support on theoretical or empirical grounds. Furthermore, the methodology associated with the new rationality has shown to be less than completely objective with regard to showing a decision maker expected accomplishments of alternative programs.
>
> On balance, however, the new rationality in budgeting and planning represents a marked improvement over traditional budgeting, because (1) it calls for the establishment of objectives in quantifiable terms; (2) it calls for the consideration of all costs and benefits; and (3) it requires an analysis of the objectives and alternatives over an adequate time horizon. Therefore, it requires decision makers (and their systems analysts) to think through programs and their alternatives in output terms. In fact, its greatest contribution may be in stimulating *the asking of policy questions.* To the extent that the new "systems" approaches stimulate decision makers (and their staff) to think through the programs and objectives in a systematic, efficient way, they will have aided in the process of improving resource allocation decisions.

Now, for another viewpoint, consider this argument by Kraft and Latta(2):

> It is our prediction that by 1975 systems analysis will have become a well-polished technique or approach contributing greatly to solving educational problems and to planning in education. It is also our prediction that specialists in this field will become more numerous and that most school districts will have one or more such specialists in their employ. Salaries for these specialists can be expected to range between $30,000 and $40,000 per annum. Administrators will become more like managers in the true sense of the word.

Schools of the future, staffed with systems specialists, will operate much more like corporate enterprises. These future schools will be maximizing some objective functions while at the same time minimizing their costs. It is conceivable that the specialist of the future will be referred to as an educational planner; and systems analysis will simply be one of his techniques or approaches to solving problems in education.

All in all, the principles of systems engineering will undoubtedly have some effect on educational planning. The stakes are too high, the dollar resources too limited for its benefits to be ignored.

But what of the humanistic elements of education? Do they conflict with the systems approach? The answer, obviously, depends upon the objectives that are selected. If, as a case in point, schools restrict themselves to goals that can be measured in terms of behavioral performance, most humanistic objectives will be eliminated since they are exceedingly difficult, if not impossible, to assess with instruments now available. But it is entirely possible that we will develop new devices with which to evaluate humanistic education, and there is nothing to prevent us from using a systems approach with some—but not all—educational objectives. There is no reason, in other words, why schools cannot invoke behavioral goals in skill and substantive areas and, at the same time, pay some attention to the child's emotional well-being and inner development. Indeed, a quality curriculum should perhaps do precisely that.

References

1. Joseph McGivney, "The New Systems Approaches to Resource Allocation Decisions: A Second Look," *Educational Technology,* 1969, 9(12), pp. 31–34.
2. Richard H. Kraft and Raymond F. Latta, "Systems Engineering Techniques: Embarrassment or Opportunity for Today's Education?" *Educational Technology,* 1969, 9(9), pp. 26–30.

Operational Concepts

1. Systematic planning and budgeting have demonstrable advantages.

2. Systematic procedures can be used to determine instructional efficiency, dollar efficiency, or both.

3. Systematic planning and humanistic education are not necessarily antithetical.

4. Some humanistic objectives cannot be subjected to systematic planning, but in a balanced curriculum where both cognitive and affective goals exist, systematic planning and analysis should be used wherever appropriate.

Implications

One of the most destructive aspects of curriculum planning lies in the tendency to polarize and to assume that alternatives are always contradictory. At the present moment, for example, practitioners sometimes assume that a commitment to humanism negates the use of behavioristic-oriented methods. The dichotomy is contrived and counterfeit since both have their time and place.

A similar situation exists with regard to the presumed contradiction between systems engineering and affective education. Rather than succumb to an either/or fallacy, schools should utilize behavioral objectives and systems planning wherever fitting and, in instances involving humanistic goals, seek other types of evaluative evidence. Recorded observations among participants, the solicitation of individual reactions, and many other forms of indirect evidence can be used in judging the effects of humanistic activities. Different tactics, in short, are suitable for different purposes, and eclecticism in curriculum design offers a multitude of benefits.

Grouping

William H. Schubert

Grouping: Practices, Controversies, and Beyond

> PARENT JONES: *So many adverse effects come from grouping children together according to so-called similarities that I don't see why it is continued.*
> PARENT SMITH: *I disagree. If schools don't place children in groups according to similarities, individual needs won't be met.*
> EDUCATOR: *Is there no way out of this dilemma?*

These comments are, as is well known by the experienced educator, illustrative of a controversy that has raged for decades, a controversy for which a solution may be currently emerging. The question of grouping has roughly aligned itself in two camps, i.e., those who favor homogeneous grouping and those who favor heterogeneous grouping. *Homogeneous grouping* is the grouping of students relative to certain similarities; educationally, the criteria have been predominately chronological and/or mental age of students, and more recently some combination of evaluations of mental, emotional, physical, achievement, and social competencies and potential. *Heterogeneous grouping* refers to organization of students—usually of similar chronological age—without intentional regard for other similarities. It is largely the exaggeration of opposing viewpoints that has caused the problem to long remain unresolved. A constructive look at the history of grouping practices and controversies will indicate directions that lead beyond partisan positions toward a more flexible personalization of instruction.

BRIEF HISTORY OF GROUPING

Being certainly no new problem for educators, grouping has an interesting history, which merits review prior to further discussion of the topic. At first, most children were taught individually by their parents; the more wealthy hired private tutors. Eventually, schools were begun in which all the children of an area were taught in a group. Elementary

544

schools functioned without children being taught in particular classes (the little red schoolhouse); students were neither passed nor failed at the end of the year. In the early 1800s the advent of the graded reader by McGuffy stimulated the growth of graded classrooms(*10*, p. 27). Educators soon came to the realization that children possessed individual differences in learning rates; therefore, various schemes were devised to promote more adequate education designed to meet individual needs.

The Pueblo Plan of 1888 exemplifies the numerous plans that consisted of unique policies for promotion, graded requirements, and ability groups. It was an effort to individualize instruction and permit organization in smaller groups on a homogeneous ability basis(*15*, p. 53). However, not much attention was given the individual in public education until the twentieth century. "If they didn't make the grade, they dropped back, dropped out, or were put out," was the philosophy applied to the individual (*7*, p. 14). Neubauer listed several new experimental plans introduced at the beginning of the twentieth century: a platoon method by which pupils received instruction in the fundamental subjects in one group and had a chance for special study in a second group; a plan especially for individual progress and promotion; a plan by which the tasks were set and the pupil worked on his own, only occasionally checking with the teacher; a plan whereby the pupil was placed in a group with intelligence tests as the only criterion; and a plan composed of teams of teachers(*15*, pp. 54–55). It can be readily seen how many of today's methods have evolved from these older plans.

The first attempt to create homogeneous grouping on an ability basis was introduced in Detroit under the leadership of Charles S. Berry in 1920; it was known as the XYZ plan(*15*, p. 55). By 1926, homogeneous grouping became widely practiced, but in 1934 the trend moved toward heterogeneous grouping(*10*, p. 27). From that time until now a tremendous conflict has flourished between advocates of homogeneous and heterogeneous grouping. From 1935 to 1950, the concerns of educators changed from favoring rigid ability grouping to emphasizing grouping patterns that sought the development of a more well-rounded child, an attempt to consider the whole personality in its social context(*10*, p. 30). Today, in spite of research evidence against it(*6, 8, 19*), ability grouping remains widely practiced. Let us look at some of the arguments on both sides of the issue, keeping in mind that the primary objective of both sides is to provide for individual student needs.

CURRENT CONTROVERSIES

Proponents of heterogeneous grouping give several reasons to support their views. It is well known that students learn from association within their group; therefore, the dull and average students could benefit scholastically from the bright students in a heterogeneous class. Being with students in several subject areas, the teacher has opportunity to know each student quite well, and can be better qualified to plan educational experiences that provide for individual needs. Here it is assumed that children grouped heterogeneously have this advantage more frequently, because homogeneous grouping often entails different groupings for different subjects. Heterogeneous grouping also provides opportunity for individual instruction with a minimum of organizational mechanics and pupil movement, two "evils" inherent in homogeneous grouping. Warner pointed out that, over our country as a whole, homogeneous grouping has been abandoned because the unfavorable emotional effects it produced more than offset benefits from adjusting subject matter to mental ability (*24*, p. 52). Strang illustrated this point by the comment of a child who experienced homogeneous grouping(*20*, p. 29):

> As one child said, "The teacher calls our groups
> the Reds, Whites, and Blues, but she might as well
> call us Fruits, Vegetables, and Nuts."

Grouping homogeneously creates numerous administrative problems, especially those of tedious grouping and regrouping. It also brings frequent adverse relationships among faculty members, because some faculty members usually feel that someone else got an easier load. A well-qualified teacher may appreciate an advanced or average section, but a dull group is often considered more difficult to teach. A less capable teacher may assume that, since a class is grouped homogeneously, there is no need to provide for individual differences. The latter could hardly be more erroneous.

It is also relatively common that the assignment of youngsters is overly influenced by the socioeconomic status of their family(*21*, p. 128). Heterogeneous grouping provides experiences in living with a cross section of humanity such as people are faced with during the remainder of their lives. Without it the student is robbed, as some believe, of part of his due educational experience.

How can an intelligent discussion be maintained if all students of a group are dull? Dissenters to homogeneous ability grouping frequently ask this question. They further contend that in an advanced homogeneously grouped section each bright student does not get an opportunity to lead a discussion. Tillman emphasized this by saying that "pupils who are academically damaged most severely by homogeneous grouping are those in the lower half of the high group"(*21*, p. 128). How, then, can the proponents of homogeneous grouping respond to these criticisms? Some light might be shed on this dilemma by a 1968 National Education Association study which pointed out that the placement of children in groups is usually done according to academic achievement, IQ, and reading achievement, but the consequences of such grouping are often evaluated relative to achievement, attitude, and personality(*6*, p. 164). Hence, proponents of homogeneous grouping could contend that objectives should be set in terms of the criteria for placement, and that evaluations should be made relative to the objectives.

Ross presented a poem that would meet favor with most of those who oppose homogeneous grouping; it points out that homogeneous grouping has made provision for all but the average range(*18*, p. 477):

> Johnny Jones has lost a leg,
> Fanny's deaf and dumb,
> Marie has epileptic fits.
> Tom's eyes are on the bum.
> Sadie stutters when she talks,
> Mabel has T.B.
> Morris is a splendid case
> Of imbecility,
> Billy Brown's a truant,
> And Harold is a thief,
> Teddy's parents gave him dope
> And so he came to grief.
> Gwendoline's a millionaire,
> Gerald is a fool;
> So everyone of these darned kids
> Goes to a special school.
> They've especially nice teachers,
> And special things to wear,
> And special time to play in,
> And a special kind of air.
> They've special lunches right in school.
> While I—it makes me wild!
> I haven't any specialties,
> I'm just a normal child.

Homogeneous grouping has beneficial qualities, and many persons believe it is the best method to reach each student's individual needs. It is generally favored because of the ability and achievement differences among children who have spent the same number of years in school. It makes it easier to adapt special methods and materials to challenge the bright student and help the dull student. In numerous cases mental and social traits have been shown to increase in bright students as a result of homogeneous grouping(*18*, p. 474). A high consensus of viewpoints of those who advocate homogeneous grouping favors the idea that groups should always remain flexible so that each child can be moved from one group to another according to his particular needs. Continuous evaluation is necessary on the part of all involved, especially the students, if such grouping is to be successful.

Proponents of homogeneous grouping believe that, because one tends to work with and associate with those of similar intellectual and social status, homogeneous grouping would better exemplify life than heterogeneous grouping. It is further felt that slow students who are grouped together are allowed to progress at their own rates, and that this lessens the chances that they will hate school and feel inferior. Torrance reported that homogeneous groups in three Minneapolis elementary schools showed little evidence of social strain and possessed few problems in entering class discussions(22, p. 139).

In general, advocates of homogeneous ability grouping believe that failure is decreased and response is increased among slow students. They believe that the bright group, normally having a tendency to loaf, would have its interests held when work is at its level. Teachers can handle large homogeneous groups—especially of bright and average students—easier than large heterogeneous ones. Grouping is thought to lessen instructional cost, since more students can use the same type of materials. Mehl's studies point out that results are generally improved when homogeneous grouping is intelligently employed(14, p. 432). Most advocates of homogeneous grouping would admit that complete homogeneity cannot be obtained, because of the extremely wide range of human variables. As Goodlad and Anderson put it(9, p. 20):

> To search for a teaching Utopia where homogeneous grouping will solve all of the problems . . . is to search for a will-o-the-wisp.

Agreeing with this, proponents of homogeneous grouping believe that putting together at least some educationally significant similarities will benefit education.

While noting advantages and disadvantages in each of the extreme positions, the reader has no doubt also noticed ambiguity, prejudice, faulty reasoning, poorly substantiated reasoning, lack of organization and continuity, and even blatant contradiction in the arguments on both sides of the issue. Attempts have currently been made to move beyond the homogeneous–heterogeneous partisanship by evolving other types of grouping practices that have as their goal to provide more fully for individual needs. Let us now look at a sampling of such schemes in light of their provision for individual needs.

NEWER GROUPING PRACTICES

Today, grouping practices are being devised with the hope of meeting the needs of the whole child as well as developing scholarship. Attempts to meet such needs have resulted in the newer grouping plans that have bloomed in recent years. Some of these are worth mentioning for the purpose of both providing perspective and for generating ideas for implementation. The reader is encouraged to notice tendencies toward homogeneous and heterogeneous grouping in the organizational patterns described below. The reader is also encouraged to notice how each grouping plan is an attempt to provide for individual needs.

1. *Nongraded grouping:* Students who fall within a certain broad age range are helped to progress through prescribed curriculum to the extent that capacity allows. Usually a large number of hierarchies are established for teaching children who have progressed to various levels.

2. *Multigrade or multiage grouping:* Children of three or more grade levels or age levels are grouped together (sometimes in a self-contained classroom, sometimes in other settings). The intent is to provide students with the benefits of a family-type atmosphere, which holds potential for peers providing assistance to one another.

3. *Team learning:* Students of the same or different grade levels are encouraged to pursue tasks as a team, emphasizing cooperation, mutual assistance, and the achieving of consensus.

4. *Interest grouping:* Grouping is based on student interest either by providing options among content for student selection or options among teachers who offer different topics at the same time, or allowing student groups to evolve around different interest areas. The rationale is that students who are interested will find relevance in their learning, and that such relevance might then be geared into other channels that enhance further learning.

5. *Trump plan:* This plan establishes a program whereby students are involved in a scheduled large group activity, small group activity, and independent study. Opportunity is thereby provided for several types of learning styles(23).

6. *Self-contained classroom:* Students are homogeneously or heterogeneously assigned to a room with one teacher. Teachers are felt to have the advantage of knowing and providing for student needs and interests more fully.

7. *Departmentalization:* Students move to different teachers for each subject. This approach is believed to provide for greater expertise in the several subject fields.

8. *Dual-progress plan:* This is an attempt to provide a combination of subject- and interest-oriented approaches. Academic subjects are pursued during one-half of the day; interest areas are developed during the second half(12, pp. 127–128).

9. *Contract grouping:* Students are grouped according to the manner in which they choose or accomplish learning tasks that they have agreed

to pursue. (This is not to be confused with "performance contracting," i.e., agreements made by business and industry to accomplish certain learning tasks in specified periods of time.)

10. *Minicourses:* Part or all of the curriculum is composed of a number of short courses to be pursued. In some cases students are able to select courses from a range of options. The intent is to expose students to a wide range of areas without allowing a topic to go beyond the student's attention span.

11. *Student-formulated curricula:* Students of an entire school, or a smaller group within a school, are allowed to devise their own curriculum. The rationale is that considerable learning will accrue from the decision-making processes, as well as from pursuit of the actual studies selected.

12. *Grouping among schools:* Several school systems have begun to offer alternative schools within their own district, which would provide for choice on the part of parents and students relative to particular beliefs, persuasions, and orientations. The possible advent of the voucher system (granting a certificate to parents that represents tax dollars to be spent for the education of their children in any of the alternative educational systems available) could provide for educational diversity of unrealized magnitude.

The experienced educator will no doubt be aware of the fact that each approach described holds considerable potential for providing for individual needs of certain students under certain circumstances. The fact that no single grouping practice is a panacea has long been realized by perceptive administrators, supervisors, and teachers. After surveying the research on grouping, Shores concluded that ". . . if we group, we must regroup often; and whether we group or not is of much less concern than whether we care for the differences within each group"(*19,* p. 172).

BEYOND: AND CONCOMITANT PROBLEMS

There is a movement, not overtly radical, but very significant, to provide for individual differences in the spirit of Shores's admonition. The movement resides under different titles, but might well be described as a "flexible-personalized" type of instruction, a style of teaching which stems from the assumption that no one mode of organization can best serve the needs of all students. It stems from the idea that planned heterogeneity in some situations is as important as planned homogeneity in others. In addition, as Esposito pointed out, both approaches often fail to provide frequent teacher–pupil contacts, flexibility in the use of the environment, opportunity for students to work and plan in a variety of educational situations, and opportunity for teachers to pool expertise in an effort to meet individual needs more fully(*6,* pp. 173–174). The attempt to meet these and other needs more fully requires rigorous study of what student needs, in fact, are. It requires an awareness of alternatives at local levels that many are unwilling to acquire. It requires teachers with time-consuming dedication, indefatigable effort and patience, and the desire to develop abilities to deal with students as persons. It requires the development of desirable incentives for teachers to extend such efforts. Finally, it requires comprehensive assessments and continuous revision. Such problems as these can only be given embryonic answers by suggesting increased adherence to what seems to be a growing dedication to flexible-personalized instruction.

Implicit in such dedication is a felt need for a change of emphasis in the spirit of Parker and Rubin, from viewing grouping patterns as fixed entities to viewing them as continuous processes of tailoring the patterns to meet the changng needs of persons and groups. The particular type of grouping to be used should be determined by the evaluated exigencies of each situation. This is not a call for a "do whatever you feel like" atmosphere devoid of overt structure, discipline, and organization. It is a suggestion that it is possible and necessary to flexibly group and regroup within the framework of any overt group setting established by a school district. Grouping within the parameters of a larger grouping scheme offers a very real possibility for the artistic principal, teacher, or supervisor to pursue, a possibility that could provide for individual similarities and differences necessitating overt alterations of school policy. The words of Thomas D. Baily seem appropriate here(2, p. 7). "In education as in everything else we cannot do today's job with yesterday's tools and be in business tomorrow." As previously implied by this writer, the homogeneous–heterogeneous argument itself is one of yesterday's tools. In *Reconstruction in Philosophy,* John Dewey, perhaps the greatest of our educational prophets, admonished thinkers to transcend the age-old obsession with dualism (either/or arguments)(4). Columnist Sidney J. Harris suggested that this dualistic fallacy cannot be transcended by mere recourse to the archaic pseudosolution of middle-road compromise. He further suggested that we hold the multifarious alternatives in a sort of "dynamic tension," i.e., a readiness for action relative to continually changing situations. In each situation encountered the possibilities on the line of tension should be shifted to meet current needs(11). This means that alternative grouping practices should be kept in mind, while additional variations are generated. Techniques deemed most appropriate for each situation should be applied. Such a process implies continuous situational assessment. The need to move beyond the semisolution of establishing one or another grouping pattern is now greater than ever; this attitude was expressed well by Alfred North Whitehead when he wrote(5, p. 94):

> Our rate of progress is such that the individual will be called upon to face novel situations which find no parallel in the past. The fixed person for

fixed duties who in older societies was a godsend, in the future will be a public danger.

This necessitates the spirit of "action-inquiry," the essence of Dewey's philosophy as emphasized in *Democracy and Education*(3). Implicit in the concept of action inquiry, as I interpret it, is a mandate to cease searching for all-inclusive panaceas for solving *general* problems (problems that seldom, if ever, exist in reality). We should begin to place increased emphasis on action guided by artistic inquiry that determines the possibility most useful as a basis for subsequent action in specific situations.

The spirit of action-inquiry can be stimulated from the apex of the power structure in schools, but specific mandates cannot be provided for dealing with each new situation a teacher encounters. If learning is to be enhanced through grouping, it cannot be done by establishing a general policy for *either* heterogeneous *or* homogeneous grouping. It requires teachers who are willing and able to continually study, work, and evaluate together, i.e., to activate Dewey's idea of action-inquiry. It is the essence of creative action-inquiry in educational leadership that is needed to inspire a significant move beyond current approaches to grouping, toward grouping that flows to meet the changing needs of students as persons.

References

1. Barker, R. G. *Ecological Psychology: Concepts and Methods for Studying the Environment of Human Behavior.* Stanford, Calif.: Stanford University Press, 1968.
2. Brinkman, Albert R. "Now It's the Ungraded School," *Education Digest,* 27:5–7, October, 1961.
3. Dewey, John. *Democracy and Education.* New York: The Free Press, 1916.
4. Dewey, John. *Reconstruction in Philosophy.* Boston: Beacon Press, 1920.
5. Elsbree, Willard S., and others. *Elementary School Administration and Supervision.* New York: American Book Company, 1967.
6. Esposito, Dominick. "Homogeneous and Heterogeneous Ability Grouping: Principal Findings and Implications for Evaluating and Designing More Effective Educational Environments," *Review of Educational Research,* Vol. 43, No. 2, Spring, 1973.
7. Essex, Martin. "How Good is Ability Grouping?" *National Parent Teacher,* 54:14–16, September, 1959.
8. Findlay, W. G., and Bryan, M. M. *Ability Grouping: 1970, Status, Impact and Alternatives.* Athens, Ga.: Center for Educational Improvement, University of Georgia.
9. Goodlad, John I., and Anderson, Robert. *The Nongraded Elementary School.* New York: Harcourt Brace Jovanovich, 1959.
10. Hammond, Sarah Lou. "Grouping Practices," *The Delta Kappa Gamma Bulletin,* 28:25–31, Fall, 1961.

11. Harris, Sidney J. "The Dilemma of Modern Man," lecture presented at Manchester College, North Manchester, Ind., 1964.

12. Lavatelli, Celia S., Moore, Walter J., and Kaltsounis, Theodore. *Elementary School Curriculum.* New York: Holt, Rinehart and Winston, 1972.

13. Manning, Duane. *A Humanistic Curriculum.* New York: Harper & Row, 1971.

14. Mehl, Marie A., et al. *Teaching in Elementary School.* New York: The Ronald Press, 1958.

15. Neubauer, Dorothy. "Toward Improved School Organization," *Elementary School Organization,* 41:50–128, December, 1961.

16. Parker, Cecil, and Rubin, Louis J. *Process as Content: Curriculum Design and the Application of Knowledge.* Chicago: Rand McNally, 1966.

17. Robinson, Helen M. (ed.) *Reading Instruction in Various Patterns of Grouping* (Chicago Conference). Chicago: University of Chicago Press, 1959.

18. Ross, C. C. *Measurement in Today's Schools.* Englewood Cliffs, N.J.: Prentice-Hall, 1942.

19. Shores, J. Harlan. "What Does the Research Say About Ability Grouping by Classes?" *Illinois Education,* December, 1964, pp. 169–172.

20. Strang, Ruth, and Lindquist, Donald. *The Administrator and the Improvement of Reading.* New York: Appleton-Century-Crofts, 1960.

21. Tillman, Rodney. "Is Ability Grouping Taking?" *The Nation's Schools,* 13:128, April, 1964.

22. Torrance, Paul E. "Can Grouping Control Social Stress in Creative Activities?" *The Elementary School Journal,* 63:139–145, April, 1964.

23. Trump, J. Lloyd, and Baynham, Dorsey. *Focus on Change: Guide to Better Schools.* Chicago: Rand McNally, 1961.

24. Warner, Ruby H. *Elementary School Teaching Practices.* Washington, D.C.: Center for Applied Research in Education, 1962.

Operational Concepts

1. Controversy concerning the relative advantages of homogeneous and heterogeneous grouping still exists. Both approaches tend to suffer from inadequate student–teacher contact, too narrow use of the learning environment, insufficient attention to cooperative student planning, and limited opportunity for teachers to collaborate.

2. Recent developments in grouping procedures have sought to amalgamate the major advantages of both homogeneous and heterogeneous procedures in order to enhance the individualization of instruction.

3. As a general rule, the efficient classroom is characterized by a variety of grouping techniques rather than by exclusive reliance on any one procedure.

Implications

The dominant conclusion to be derived from the writer's analysis is that arguments regarding the comparative advantages of homogeneous and heterogeneous grouping are largely useless. Both systems, under appropriate conditions, have a place and can be used to good advantage. The selection of a grouping mechanism should be governed by the particular situation that prevails at the particular time. No grouping procedure is ideal under all conditions. Hence, logic would suggest that teachers ought to be adept in the use of various grouping techniques and able to shift from one to another as the occasion warrants.

Lyn S. Martin
Barbara N. Pavan

Current Research on Open Space, Nongrading, Vertical Grouping, and Team Teaching

In the late sixties and early seventies, a number of educational innovations were tried in classrooms across the United States. Among the best known are nongradedness, team teaching, vertical or heterogeneous grouping of students, and the use of open space school building design. While there is no definitive evidence concerning their effectiveness, there *is* a growing body of research that practitioners may find valuable as they attempt to assess the value of these approaches.

As you read the research summaries that follow, certain limitations should be kept in mind. Terms are often loosely defined in the research literature. The word selected to describe a particular classroom or school innovation may be deceptive. It may not describe actual classroom practices at all, or it may apply to only a limited aspect of the innovation. Moreover, there is no universal formula either for implementing or evaluating innovations, and there is little consistency in research designs used for assessment. Assessing the validity of many studies is almost impossible because one cannot be sure that the innovation under scrutiny is the only dependent variable. Findings are seldom generalizable, because they are affected in unknowable ways by variations in teachers, children, curriculum objectives, and the organization of the space and activities. Finally, long-term effects of innovations have seldom been thoroughly researched.

Despite these problems, and despite the fact that research support for many educational innovations is scanty, there is a growing body of knowledge in the areas of child development, perceptual and developmental psychology, learning theory, social science, and education, with important implications for persons considering educational change.

In each research report reviewed below, an attempt was made to discover whether the researcher used valid methods in examining the questions he addressed (internal validity). If he did, we then asked whether the results were consistent with findings in other studies of the same

Reprinted from Lyn S. Martin and Barbara N. Pavan, "Current Research on Open Space, Nongrading, Vertical Grouping, and Team Teaching," *Phi Delta Kappan*, January 1976, pp. 310–315; by permission of the publisher.

phenomena (external validity). The most persuasive studies, naturally, were those demonstrating both types of validity and those characterized by larger samples, more replications, better designs, and greater numbers of controls for intervening variables. It must be remembered, however, that no research in education ever actually "proves" anything. We can only say that a number of valid studies yielding similar findings can add to our confidence about the findings. In general, then, what follows is not unquestioned "truth," but an attempt to drive meaningful conclusions from relevant literature.

OPEN SPACE

Open education classrooms and open space schools have often been erroneously equated in the United States. In most of the literature, open space refers to an architectural arrangement which may or may not be conducive to open education. Generally, the open space concept evolved out of a recognition that a young child's need to move about and interact with people and environment is strong. It offers a more natural way for children to learn.

"Architecturally open" characterizes a type of building designed to permit more children and teachers to share space in some way. A large open space may be used by different groups for all of their activities, or there may be separate rooms with an adjacent common space (a large room, corridor, etc.). To quote F. A. Brunetti's (1970) definition of the open plan, "the open space school is composed of instruction areas without interior walls, ranging in size from two to over thirty equivalent classrooms."

Poor conceptualization of teacher roles and program goals has led to many problems in open space classrooms (Deibel, 1972). Because of the corrosion of descriptive terms and program outcomes, few consistent benefits of the innovation can be seen. Several studies report no differences in organizational climate between open space and conventional schools (Warner, 1970; Jaworowicz, 1972; Holmquist, 1972; Leroy, 1973), a good indication that few real differences in approach were operating among teachers and administrators. These studies suggest that the open space school design, by itself, does not alter patterns of social interaction between teachers and the principal or produce perceptions of organizational climate differing from those found in schools of traditional design.

More positive attitudes and increased feelings of professionalism among the teachers in open space schools have been noted (Mills, 1972; Wren, 1972). However, these results may be attributable to the Hawthorne effect. Brunetti (1970) concluded that a high degree of colleague interaction and cooperative task performance was brought about by reducing the physical and organizational isolation of teachers in the open schools. However, J. B. Warner (1970) did not find significant differences between open area and self-contained classroom teachers on a number of organizational and attitudinal variables.

In other comparative studies, overall differences observed in achievement, self-concept, attitude, and personality of the students were small (Burnham, 1971; Jeffreys, 1971; Laforge, 1972; McCallum, 1972; Townsend, 1971; Warner, 1970). Some affective advantages for open space programs were noted in some of the literature, however. Risk-taking behaviors were found to be more apparent in the open space schools (Anifant, 1972), and this behavior has been linked with high creativity in children (Cropley, 1970). J. S. Jeffreys (1971) found that more individualized and small-group work, as well as more after-school activity, took place among children in the open schools, and E. A. M. Lueders-Salmon (1972) found open space classes to be more active. This may be one advantage of the increased space—that children are more free to move about and work together without bothering others, thus freeing the teacher for individual work with students.

Individualization has been a prime motivation for a move to open space. However, R. F. Deibel's (1972) study indicated that this goal is not being realized. Nevertheless, children in the open area classrooms seem to want and to achieve more autonomy from teachers and also to be more concerned with their teachers' "fairness" than children in self-contained classrooms (Myers, 1971).

Studies conflict regarding self-concept and attitudes of pupils in open space versus traditional classrooms. N. L. Heimgartner (1972) noted that open space students demonstrate greater identification with the group and increased self-esteem, while the self-contained comparison classroom children demonstrated a loss. S. J. P. Wren (1972), examining affective factors, also obtained results which favored the open area over the self-contained classrooms. He concluded that the open area situation does not create anxiety among children. Two other researchers (Beckley, 1973; Beals, 1972) also found more positive attitudes toward school and self in the open space school. However, J. W. Sackett (1971) found that the self-concept mean score in the open space schools he studied was significantly lower than for either a self-contained or departmentalized school. Moreover, H. E. Laforge (1972) found that the open space design of a school building did not significantly affect students when the total personality of the individual is considered. He did note, however, that the open space students were more "tender-minded" and sensitive to the needs of others than the comparison students.

Findings on cognitive achievement also conflict. C. K. Killough (1971) found that after pupils remained in the open space program for at least two years their mean achievement gains were significantly better during the third year, and for the total three-year period, than were those of their counterparts in another type of program and facility. They also achieved significantly better as they moved into a traditional junior high program.

However, J. B. Warner (1970) found no significant differences between open space and self-contained classroom students on standardized achievement measures; and lower achievement gains for open space students were noted by Sackett (1971) and Townsend (1971).

In a comprehensive study of many variables, F. L. Read (1973) found no differences between open space and self-contained schools in pupil achievement, attitude of pupils and staff, or educational practices within environments.

W. C. Kaelin's (1970) research seems to concur with other findings in the area. He concluded that (1) areas of disagreement among teachers and administrators working in open space schools will probably continue until a definitive philosophy is determined and accepted by all; (2) teachers' interpretations of individualization of instruction continue to emphasize academic learning; (3) administrators should be taking more active leadership roles in helping teachers resolve organizational problems; and (4) open areas sometimes mask abuses, such as overcrowding, which would be easier to detect in conventional school settings.

The studies as a whole do not find that open space school organization promotes any real differences in learning and teaching outcomes. Innovative programs of all types can exist within old buildings originally intended for traditional classrooms, and it seems evident that changes in architecture do not, *in and of themselves,* make a great difference.

NONGRADING

The concept of nongrading evolved from an acceptance of the notion that there is no such thing as a total class of students at one level of learning. J. L. Tewksbury's (1967) description of a nongraded program says:

> In a fully graded plan, all children in a given grade are expected to do the same work in a year's time, while in a nongraded program each child works at the level in each subject for which he is ready. Three ways of implementing a nongraded program are: (1) provide multilevel instruction in a self-contained, heterogeneous classroom, (2) assign children to self-contained classes according to performance levels, and (3) regroup a large aggregate of children from time to time to form classes that work at different levels under different teachers.

This definition implies that children are instructed at their own ability levels and may proceed at their own pace. Also implied in most nongraded approaches is that the teacher retains responsibility for content selection and that a standardized curriculum sequence is required for all children. While it may be that some nongraded programs have progressed to providing experiences appropriate to each child's present level of development, potential, interest, etc., most of them have so far achieved individualization in only one respect: Pupils proceed through the same materials in pretty much the same way, but they do so at their own rate.

Studies of nongraded programs have shown positive achievement results. Generally, students in nongraded programs have been doing as well as or better than their peers in the graded programs—usually better, according to several comparative studies (Bowman, 1971; Brody, 1970; Chalfant, 1972; Gumpper, 1971; Killough, 1971; Morse, 1972; Remacle, 1971; Ward, 1970; Wilt, 1971). In all cases where students were matched for IQ, the nongraded achievement scores were significantly higher. In a comprehensive review of research on nongrading from 1968 to 1973, B. N. Pavan (1973) concluded that there should no longer be concern that placing students in nongraded programs will be detrimental to their academic achievement. In general, nongraded groups perform as well as, and often better than, graded groups on tests designed for the graded schools.

It is probably safe to conclude from these studies that nongraded programs can enhance academic achievement and foster positive attitudes among children. Again, it must be remembered, as H. J. Wilt (1971) concludes, that "no single organizational change can hope to solve the needs of learners in a mass, heterogeneous society."

HETEROGENEOUS GROUPING

Homogeneous grouping refers to the organization of children on the basis of student similarity on one or more specific characteristics. The criterion for this classification may be age, sex, IQ, achievement, or a combination of these and other variables. Alternatively, heterogeneous groupings include a diverse mixture of children who differ on one or more variables. This innovation results from the hypothesis that, in many subjects, varied levels of maturity and experience may contribute more to the learning process, and that interaction of varied age groups may contribute to social growth and understanding as well as to academic growth.

The usual arguments for heterogeneous grouping include: (1) Homogeneous grouping is undemocratic and affects the self-concept of all children adversely by placing a stigma on those in lower groups, while giving other children an inflated sense of their own worth; (2) most life experiences do not occur in homogeneous settings, and students must learn to work with a wide range of people; (3) students of lesser ability may profit by learning with those of greater ability; (4) heterogeneity allows different patterns of abilities and needs to emerge within a group of children; and (5) homogeneous ability grouping may segregate children along SES and ethnic, as well as ability, lines.

The studies dealing with vertical grouping basically indicate affective (i.e., noncognitive) advantages for students. Grouping by ability has been found to increase competition among students (Morse, 1972) and decrease motivation (Zweibelson, 1967)—interesting findings in light of the common belief that competition *increases* motivation. On the other hand, there are *positive* research findings on heterogeneous grouping of students across abilities and ages. Improvements in self-concept have been noted (Junell, 1971), as well as improved attitudes toward school and schoolwork (Mycock, 1967; Junell, 1971; Samuels, 1969). These results may be related to the wider range of learning possibilities in a varied group of children, as well as to a reduction in anxiety and pressure to conform to a homogeneous group.

When advantaged and disadvantaged children were compared in socially mixed and socially segregated classes, results indicated that the disadvantaged children in mixed classes showed gains over the segregated classes in task persistence, verbal skills, and self-concepts, while their aggressive and dependent behavior decreased (Roger, 1969).

One study found that young, nervous, or immature children experience less admission stress in the mixed-age classroom (Mycock, 1967). They socialize more readily, and with a wider range of children. In addition, more roles are available as models due to the maturity and ability differences present in the classroom. Mycock concluded that all of these factors promote better emotional stability and security among young children, an important factor in early learning and attitude toward school. This study also concluded that children in a family group developed better work attitudes and had a closer, warmer relationship with their teacher.

Older (junior high) children have expressed a preference for heterogeneous grouping (Samuels, 1969), and their improved attitudes toward school seem to be a result of their widened opportunity for student–student interrelationships (Zweibelson, 1967).

A review of studies on heterogeneous and homogeneous grouping from 1920–1970 (Findley and Bryan, 1971) suggests that, in the area of scholastic achievement, there is little to clarify the issue of which form of organization results in better instruction. Data reported by D. Esposito (1971) indicate that, irrespective of organization, whether heterogeneous or homogeneous, the essential pattern of instruction and achievement in the teaching–learning process did not differ in self-contained elementary classrooms. The Junell (1971) study concluded that any age-grouping pattern per se seems to be "little more than a means of setting parameters to peer group influences." Junell found that vertically grouped children placed together for six years formed attitudes and values that were different and more positive than those formed by children grouped according to chronological age. He concluded that when grouping patterns give children of *all* ability levels broader scope for achievement, children improve academic performance and attitudes toward school as well.

561

In summary, then, cognitive outcomes appear to be the same in varied grouping arrangements, but there is evidence of social, affective, and maturational advantages in the vertical or heterogeneous arrangement. It must be kept in mind, however, that in cases where homogeneous or heterogeneous grouping is related to differential outcomes, the curriculum has often undergone substantial modification of teaching methods, material, and other variables which affect the teaching–learning process.

TEAM TEACHING

Teams of teachers working together in many ways constitute another frequently adopted innovation of the last ten years. Educators have become more aware of the variations in the knowledge, competence, and skills of teachers. The personal styles and value systems of teachers, combined with these professional variations, influence their teaching styles, which in turn affect the general atmosphere of the learning setting as well as how and what the students learn.

J. T. Shaplin and H. F. Olds (quoted by G. W. Bassett, 1970) give the following definition: "Team teaching is a type of instructional organization, involving teaching personnel and the students assigned to them, in which two or more teachers are given responsibility, working together, for all or a significant part of the instruction of the same group of students." C. O. Olsen (1968) defines team teaching as an "instructional situation where two or more teachers, possessing complementary teaching skills, cooperatively plan and implement the instruction for a single group of students, using flexible grouping to meet the particular needs of the students."

Advantages of team teaching are generally considered to be: (1) Children are taught by more than one teacher and exposed to the strengths of different teachers; (2) teachers are brought together to see other types of teaching; and (3) a more flexible approach to teaching is possible.

Research indicates that teachers who engage in team teaching must be able to work together harmoniously toward common objectives (Coleman, 1973). They must be able to share space and students, giving up traditional notions of "rights" to particular students or classrooms (Seyfarth, 1973; Traut, 1971).

It has been found that preparation is a vital component of effective team teaching (Gaskell and Sheridan, 1968; Funaro, 1969; Deibel, 1972; Traut, 1971). It also appears that successful teams have worked together to develop their own programs (Davis, 1966; Funaro, 1969; Engman, 1973; Olsen, 1968).

L. Engman's (1973) research revealed that team teaching has most often failed because of personality clashes, the inability of most teachers to integrate their material, and a lack of planning time.

H. C. Traut's (1971) conclusions were largely negative: (1) Team teaching did not assure that cooperative planning would occur either with other teachers or with students; (2) team teaching did not assure that instructional styles would change; and (3) there was no evidence that schools attempted to identify the most capable teachers for team tasks. This study calls into question some of the assumptions about what actually happens in team teaching situations, suggesting that, again, changes were made without clear goals or understanding of the nature and purpose of the change.

Other notable research findings on teachers in teams indicate that teachers on leaderless teams tend to be more satisfied than teachers on teams with formal leadership (Arikado and Musella, 1973), though *students* tend to prefer a team in which the leader is clearly indicated (Bowering and Splaine, 1974). J. Ables (1972) found that the greater the agreement between the belief systems of teachers on a team, the higher the morale. G. F. Foley (1971) discovered a positive relation between the leadership behavior of team leaders and the morale of team members. Teachers have been found to be generally positive about teaming, due to the greater variety of activities that can go on at the same time and the atmosphere of creativity which can exist (Meiskin, 1968).

Although the child in the team teaching situation seems to have been relatively neglected in the literature, several studies directly refer to him in some way. M. Bair and R. G. Woodward (1964) reviewed the research on team teaching and concluded that there were no significant differences in the academic achievement of team-taught children and children taught by individual teachers. The impact of teaming on the *teachers* was generally positive, they said. They also found that team teachers willingly work longer hours.

L. Wilder's (1969) research revealed that a team-taught class benefited from the talents and abilities of more than one teacher. The arrangement made possible a more flexible grouping of pupils according to the purpose of the lesson.

J. A. Burchyett (1972) found no significant difference between the academic achievement of children in a nongraded, multiage, team-taught school and the achievement of similar children in a self-contained classroom. Children in the experimental school excelled in creative thinking and general motivation, however.

C. J. McCallum (1972), studying the problems of children in a team-taught class and a conventional class, found no differences in the types of problems children experienced, the duration and depth of the problems, or who helped with the problems.

Positive results were found by Lueders-Salmon (1972), who concluded that teams of teachers working together in an open area classroom had more active classrooms. S. Samuels (1969) also found that students of junior high age *preferred* team teaching, while D. C. Bowering and J. E.

Splaine (1974) revealed that students perceived team teaching as being more effective; they felt that teachers were able to establish rapport in a team-teaching structure as readily as they could in a traditional approach.

Research in this area is not very comprehensive, nor are the results definitive. It would appear, however, that planning, understanding of program goals, and cooperation are essential to the successful implementation of team teaching. While specific advantages in achievement have not been demonstrated, students and teachers alike have expressed positive attitudes toward the innovation. Once again, results have to be interpreted cautiously, because of the wide range of variables which prevent isolation of teaching mode as the only difference between classrooms compared in the research.

Clearly, much remains to be done. Long-term evaluation is lacking in all areas, and definitive answers are still not available in many areas.

It does appear, however, that innovations such as open space schools, nongradedness, vertical grouping, and team teaching do not, either alone or in combination, result in detrimental effects on cognitive *or* affective outcomes. Overall, the research to date indicates that such innovations, when properly interpreted and implemented, may be a step toward educational improvement and are, in any case, valid alternatives to the traditional mode of teaching.

References

ABLES, J. "The Relationship of Congruence of Belief Systems and Morale Within Teacher Teams." Ph.D. diss., State University of New York at Buffalo, 1972. (*Dissertation Abstracts International*, 32, 6022A)

ANIFANT, D. C. "Risk-Taking Behavior in Children Experiencing Open Space and Traditional School Environments." (*Dissertation Abstracts International*, 1972, 33, 2491A)

ARIKADO, M. S., and D. F. MUSELLA. "Status Variables Related to Team Teacher Satisfaction in the Open Plan School." Paper presented at the annual meeting of the American Educational Research Association, New Orleans, 1973. (Available in ERIC as EDO76562)

BAIR, M., and R. G. WOODWARD. *Team Teaching in Action.* Boston: Houghton Mifflin, 1964.

BASSETT, G. W. *Innovation in Primary Education.* London: Wiley-Interscience, 1970.

BEALS, J. P. "An Investigation of Emotive Perception Among Students in Open Space and Conventional Learning Environments." Ph.D. diss., University of Tennessee, 1972. (*Dissertation Abstracts International*, 33, 5955A)

BECKLEY, L. L. "Comparative Study of Elementary School Student Attitudes Toward School and Self in Open Concept and Self-Containing Environments." Ph.D. diss., Purdue University, 1973. (*Dissertation Abstracts International*, 1973, 34, 206A)

BOWERING, D. J., and J. E. SPLAINE. "Team Teaching: Student Perceptions of Two Contrasting Models." Reprint of paper presented at the Association for Educational Communications and Technology convention, March, 1974. (Available in ERIC as EDO86240)

BOWMAN, B. L. "A Comparison of Pupil Achievement and Attitude in a Graded School with Pupil Achievement and Attitude in a Nongraded School—1968–69, 1969–70 School Years." (*Dissertation Abstracts International,* 1971, 32, 660A)

BRODY, E. B. "Achievement of First- and Second-Year Pupils in Graded and Non-graded Classrooms." *Elementary School Journal,* 1970, 71, pp. 391–94.

BRUNETTI, F. A., JR. "The Teacher in the Authority Structure of the Elementary School: A Study of Open Space and Self-Contained Classroom Schools." Ph.D. diss., Stanford University, 1970. (*Dissertation Abstracts International,* 31, 4405A)

BURCHYETT, J. A. "A Comparison of the Effects of Nongraded, Multi-age, Team Teaching versus the Modified Self-Contained Classroom at the Elementary School Level." Ph.D. diss., Michigan State University, 1972. (*Dissertation Abstracts International,* 33, 5998A)

BURNHAM, B. "Achievement of Grade-One Pupils in Open Plan and Architecturally Conventional Schools." York County Board of Education Report, Aurora, N.Y., 1971. (Appeared in *Growth Points,* 1971)

CHALFANT, L. S. "A Three-Year Comparative Study Between Students in a Graded and a Nongraded Secondary School." Ph.D. diss., Utah State University, 1972. (*Dissertation Abstracts International,* 33, 3178A)

COLEMAN, C. H., and I. BUDAHL. "Necessary Ingredients for Good Team Teaching." *NASSP Bulletin,* January, 1973, pp. 41–46.

CROPLEY, A. J., and E. FEURING. "Training Creativity in Young Children." *Developmental Psychology,* 1971, 4, p. 105.

DAVIS, R. J., JR. "Teacher Assessment of Team Teaching." *Science Teacher,* December, 1966.

DEIBEL, R. F. "An Investigation of Factors in Creating and Utilizing Open Space Elementary Schools." Ph.D. diss., Ohio State University, 1971. (*Dissertation Abstracts International,* 1972, 32, 6261A)

ENGMAN, L. *Team Teaching Will Work.* ERIC Document Reprints, 1973, ED885374.

ESPOSITO, D. "Homogeneous and Heterogeneous Ability Grouping: Principal Findings and Implications for Evaluating and Designing More Effective Educational Environments." *Review of Educational Research,* 43 (2), pp. 163–179.

Evaluation of Selected Components of: A Supplementary Center for Early Childhood Education. Title III: Englewood Board of Education. Washington, D.C.: Department of Health, Education, and Welfare, Office of Education, 1968.

FINDLEY, W. G., and M. M. BRYAN. *Ability Grouping, 1970: Status, Impact, and Alternatives.* Athens, Ga.: Center for Educational Improvement, University of Georgia, 1971.

FOLEY, G. F. "A Study on the Relationships Between Team Leaders' Leadership Behavior and the Morale and Effectiveness of Their Team Members." Ph.D. diss., State University of New York at Buffalo, 1971. (*Dissertation Abstracts International,* 32, 2944A)

FUNARO, G. J. "Team Teaching: The Danger and the Promise." *Clearing House,* March, 1969.

GASKELL, W., and J. SHERIDAN. "Team Teaching and the Social Studies in the Elementary School." *Elementary School Journal,* February, 1968.

GUMPPER, D. C., et al. *Nongraded Elementary Education: Individualized Learning, Teacher Leadership, Student Responsibility.* University Park, Pa.: Pennsylvania State University, 1971. (Available in ERIC as ED057440)

HEIMGARTNER, N. L. "A Comparative Study of Self-Concept and Open Spaces versus Self-Contained Classroom." Ph.D. diss., University of Northern Colorado, Greeley, 1972. (Available in ERIC as ED069389)

HOLMQUIST, A. L. "A Study of the Organizational Climate of Twelve Elementary Schools in the Albuquerque Public School System; Each Having Architecturally Open and Architecturally Closed Classrooms." Ph.D. diss., University of New Mexico, 1972. (*Dissertation Abstracts International,* 33, 5472A)

JAWOROWICZ, E. H. "Open Space School Design as a Situational Determinant of Organizational Climate and Principal Leader Behavior." Ph.D. diss., Wayne State University, 1972. (*Dissertation Abstracts International,* 33, 2028A)

JEFFREYS, J. S. "An Investigation of the Effects of Innovative Educational Practices on Pupil-Centeredness of Observed Behaviors and on Learner Outcome Variables." (*Dissertation Abstracts International,* 1971, 31, 5766A)

JUNELL, J. S. "An Analysis of the Effects of Multigrading on a Number of Noncognitive Variables." (*Dissertation Abstracts International,* 1971, 32, 94A)

KAELIN, W. C. "Open Space Schools: Advantages and Disadvantages as Perceived by Teachers and Principals in Selected Open Space Schools." Ph.D. diss., Florida State University, 1970. (*Dissertation Abstracts International,* 31, 4384A)

KILLOUGH, C. K. "An Analysis of the Longitudinal Effects that a Nongraded Elementary Program, Conducted in an Open Space School, Had on the Cognitive Achievement of Pupils." Ph.D. diss., University of Houston, 1971. (Available in ERIC as ED067726. *Dissertation Abstracts International,* 32, 3614A)

LAFORGE, H. E. "The Effect of the Open Space Design of an Elementary School upon Personality Characteristics of Students." Ph.D. diss., University of Houston, 1972. (*Dissertation Abstracts International,* 33, 1365A)

LEROY, J. M. "Classroom Climate and Student Perceptions: An Exploratory Study of Third-Grade Classrooms in Selected Open Space and Self-Contained Schools." Ph.D. diss., University of Wisconsin, 1973. (*Dissertation Abstracts International,* 34, 568A)

LEWIS, D. K. "A Continuous Progress, Individualized Educational System as Compared to a Conventional Curriculum and Instructional Educational System: A Study of Teacher Morale." (*Dissertation Abstracts International,* 1973, 33, 4743A)

LORTON, L. "Reorganizing for Learning at McKinley School—An Experiment in Multi-unit Instruction." Paper presented at the American Educational Research Association annual meeting, New Orleans, La., 1973. (Available in ERIC as ED075911)

LUEDERS-SALMON, E. A. M. "Team Teaching and the 'Active' Classroom: A Comparative Study of the Impact of Team-Teaching Schools on Classroom 'Activity'." Ph.D. diss., Stanford University, 1972 (*Dissertation Abstracts International,* 32, 6686A)

McCallum, C. J. "Children's Problems as Perceived by Children and Teachers in Open Space, Team-Teaching, and Traditional Elementary Schools." Ph.D. diss., University of Colorado, 1972. (*Dissertation Abstracts International, 32,* 6764A)

McLoughlin, W. P. "Continuous Pupil Progress in the Nongraded School: Hope or Hoax?" *Elementary School Journal,* 1970, 71, pp. 90–96.

Meiskin, M. "Cooperative Teaching in the Elementary School." *Education,* April–May, 1968.

Mills, F. M. "A Comparison of Teacher Performance and Attitudes of Teachers Performing Independently in Self-Contained Classrooms and Teachers Performing Cooperatively in Open Instructional Areas." Ph.D. diss., Arizona State University, 1972. (*Dissertation Abstracts International, 33,* 2038A)

Morse, P. S. *A Survey of Selected, Public, Elementary Open Classrooms in New York State, Final Report.* New York: Rochester University and Washington, D.C.: National Center for Educational Research and Development, 1972. (Available in ERIC as ED067747)

Mycock, M. "A Comparison of Vertical Grouping and Horizontal Grouping in the Infant School." *British Journal of Educational Psychology,* 1967, 37, pp. 133–36.

Myers, R. E. "Comparison of the Perceptions of Elementary School Children in Open Area and Self-Contained Classrooms in British Colombia." *Journal of Research and Development in Education,* 1971, 4, pp. 100–106.

Olsen, C. O. "Team Teaching in the Elementary School." *Education,* April–May, 1968.

Pavan, B. N. "Good News: Research on the Nongraded Elementary School." *Elementary School Journal,* March, 1973, pp. 333–42.

Read, F. L. "Initial Evaluation of the Development and Effectiveness of Open Space Elementary Schools." Ph.D. diss., United States International University, 1973. (*Dissertation Abstracts International, 33,* 3221A)

Remacle, L. F. "A Comparative Study of the Differences in Attitudes, Self-Concept, and Achievement of Children in Graded and Nongraded Elementary Schools." Ph.D. diss., University of South Dakota, 1971. (*Dissertation Abstracts International, 31,* 5948A)

Roger, R. P. *Heterogeneous Versus Homogeneous Social Class Grouping of Preschool Children in Head Start Classrooms.* Detroit: Merrill-Palmer Institute and East Lansing, Mich.: Michigan State University, Head Start Evaluation and Research Center, 1969. (Available in ERIC as ED045176)

Sackett, J. W. "A Comparison of Self-Concept and Achievement of Sixth-Grade Students in an Open Space School, Self-Contained School, and Departmentalized School." Ph.D. diss., University of Iowa, 1971. (*Dissertation Abstracts International, 32,* 2372A)

Samuels, S., et al. *The Influence of Team Teaching and Flexible Grouping on Attitudes of Junior High School Students. Final Report.* Albany: New York State Experimental and Innovative Programs, New York State Board of Education, Division of Research, 1969.

Seyfarth, J. I., and R. I. Canady. "Team Teaching: Indicators of Expectations and Sources of Satisfaction." *Clearing House,* March, 1973, pp. 420–22.

Tewksbury, J. L. "The Meaning of Nongrading" and "The Nongraded Movement in Perspective." Chapters 1 and 2 in *Nongrading in the Elementary School.*

Columbus, Ohio: Merrill's International Education Series, Merrill Books, Inc., 1967.

TOWNSEND, J. W. "A Comparison of Teacher Style and Pupil Attitude and Achievement in Contrasting Schools: Open Space, Departmentalized, and Self-Contained." Ph.D. diss., University of Kansas, 1971. (*Dissertation Abstracts International,* 32, 5679A)

TRAUT, H. C. "An In-Depth Study of Six United States History Classes Utilizing Team Teaching." Ph.D. diss., Ball State University, 1971. (*Dissertation Abstracts International,* 32, 845A)

WARD, D. N. "An Evaluation of a Nongraded School Program in Grades One and Two." (*Dissertation Abstracts International,* 1970, 31, 2786A)

WARNER, J. B. "A Comparison of Students' and Teachers' Performances in an Open Area Facility and in Self-Contained Classrooms." Ph.D. diss., University of Houston, 1970. (*Dissertation Abstracts International,* 31, 3851A)

WILDER, L. and R. K. JUNG. "A Team-Teaching Approach to Student Teaching." *Peabody Journal of Education,* September, 1969.

WILT, H. J. "A Comparison of Student Attitudes Toward School, Academic Achievement, Internal Structures, and Procedures: The Nongraded School Versus the Graded School." Ph.D. diss., University of Missouri, 1971. (*Dissertation Abstracts International,* 31, 5105A)

WREN, S. J. P. "A Comparison of Affective Factors Between Contained Classrooms and Open Area Classrooms." Ph.D. diss., University of Houston, 1972. (*Dissertation Abstracts International,* 33, 1397A)

ZWEIBELSON, I. *Student Attitudes and Motivation in Relation to Ability Grouping.* ERIC Document Reprints, ED011673, 1967.

Operational Concepts

1. Studies on open-space school organization do not show significant differences in academic achievement when compared with traditional classrooms.

2. Most nongraded programs increase the individualization of instruction with respect to rate but not with respect to content; pupils generally learn the same subject matter, in essentially the same way, but at their own pace.

3. Nongraded programs often enhance motivation and foster positive attitudes toward schooling.

4. Although heterogeneous grouping does not seem to increase scholastic achievement, there is evidence of some social and developmental advantage.

Implications

Innovations involving open space, vertical grouping, team teaching, and nongraded sequences do not, either alone or in combination, appear to have detrimental effects on either cognitive or affective outcomes. Used in circumstances that are appropriate for the learners and teachers involved, and properly implemented, such innovations seem to constitute a legitimate improvement over traditional arrangements, and a valid alternative to conventional modes of teaching. As in all other instructional structures, however, it is the quality of the teaching and learning that goes on—not the organizational scheme—that governs learner achievement.

It would seem, consequently, that in the further development of open space, team teaching, nongrading, and similar mechanisms, we must make an effort to exploit their potential and at the same time ensure that they accommodate the nature of the student and generate instruction that is well designed and efficacious.

When all is said and done, the classroom organization is probably of less consequence than the quality of the teaching. This fact, of course, does not mean that organization is unimportant, or that some students and teachers will not function better in one plan than in another. What it means, rather, is that no classroom organization will compensate for poor teaching: method and form are both crucial.

Bela H. Banathy
David W. Johnson

Cooperative Group Interaction Skills Curriculum: The Common Core of Vocational and Career Education

Goal directed cooperative behavior is essential to the successful functioning of the individual in societal groups and particularly in economic organizations. At the present time, however, formal education does not encompass the specific skills and attitudes that are necessary to develop such behavior. In this paper, therefore, we will discuss the rationale for, and the implications of, teaching cooperative group interaction skills in schools; we will propose that the learning of such skills should be the core of vocational and career education; and we will outline some key characteristics for a cooperative group interaction skills curriculum (CGISC).

This presentation is based on studies conducted by the authors; the paper is divided into four parts: rationale, implications for education, a cooperative group interaction skills curriculum (CGISC) as the core of vocational and career education, and some key characteristics of a CGISC.

RATIONALE

Our rationale for proposing a cooperative group interaction skills curriculum for schools is based on a general proposition that we derived from a series of specific propositions. These propositions are explicated below.

The General Proposition

There is a need in schools for a curriculum that focuses on the specific skills and attitudes necessary for the successful functioning of individuals in societal groups and particularly in economic organizations.

The individual in our *society* is faced with increasing demands for competent performance as a member—and often as a leader—of groups. Many young people have problems adjusting to, and working effectively in, the various groups encountered during and after formal education.

571

Such groups include the family as well as various peer and study groups—for example, recreational, political, fellowship, interest-related, and community-oriented groups.

When a person enters the world of economic organization, he needs to possess two sets of competencies. The first set is comprised of technical competencies, which enable him to perform the activities he is to carry out while functioning in a career. To be an electronic engineer or an electromechanical technician, for example, one must possess a certain set of technical skills. The second set is comprised of those competencies which enable him to work in concert with others(1). Since technical skills are of no use if they cannot be applied in cooperative efforts with other persons, the interpersonal and group skills needed for cooperating with fellow employees are most important. A person's career—finding, maintaining, and advancing in employment—depends a great deal upon his command of group interaction skills, that is, his ability to work cooperatively with other people. Persons who cannot communicate, build meaningful relationships, or manage conflicts constructively are not selected for retention and promotion within economic organizations.

The proposition that *both* technical *and* cooperative skills need to be emphasized in vocational and career education programs is derived from an understanding that, although our economic system is based upon the cooperative nature of humans, the socialization processes by which cooperative skills and attitudes are learned are rapidly changing. The influence of the family in the socialization process is rapidly decreasing, and, therefore, the need for educational programs that emphasize socialization is increasing.

Specific Propositions

The overall proposition introduced above was derived from the following set of specific propositions:

1. *The basis for our economic system (and all social systems) is cooperation.* Our economic system, all human social systems, and all interpersonal relationships exist on a foundation of cooperation. *Cooperation* can be defined as the coordinated, interdependent effort to accomplish mutually desired goals. Several noted scholars have taken the position that cooperation is a biological, ecological, anthropological, economic, sociological, and psychological necessity for humans. There is a deep human need to respond to others and to operate jointly with them toward achieving mutual goals. Human society and biology are constructed so that cooperation has always been absolutely necessary for the survival of every individual member of our species. There is no aspect of human experience more important than cooperation with others.

The quality of life in our society—in terms of material well-being and personal happiness—depends in large part on the success of economic organizations and the maintenance of the cooperative network of exchange of products and services. Our economic system is based upon a cooperative division of labor in which different organizations specialize in different activities. Within each organization, furthermore, there is a cooperation-based division of labor in which persons specialize and contribute their efforts to achieve specific goals. *The success of each economic organization, therefore, depends upon the cooperative skills and attitudes of its members.* If persons are unwilling or unable to cooperate, the economic organization of which they are members will be unsuccessful in achieving its goals or maintaining its effectiveness.

2. Besides being an absolute necessity for effective work, *cooperative relationships with fellow employees are the major source of motivation, satisfaction, and happiness on the job.* Persons enjoy their work more, accomplish more, are more motivated, and have more positive attitudes toward work when they are in cooperative relationships on the job.

3. *The meaning of work is based upon being part of a cooperative effort with other people.* The relationships a person builds on the job, and in his private life, greatly affect the meaning he derives from his work. An individual will take more pride in his work when other people recognize that his work contributes to the quality of their lives and, consequently, give him recognition for that work. Such recognition and support are strongest in cooperative relationships.

4. *Cooperative efforts in small groups are being emphasized more frequently in economic organizations.* Large industrial organizations are trying new, small-group structures. Automobile companies have constituted "teams" responsible for the entire assembly of a car, for example. In order to improve morale, decrease alienation, and increase production, the use of small groups is increasing in our economic organizations.

5. *The family is no longer an effective agent in imparting cooperative skills and attitudes.* Traditionally, the responsibility for socialization of children and work has been in the family. The family has been regarded as the central agent controlling the individual's personal and social growth. Profound changes in our society, however, are rapidly transforming the family, and the direction of change is toward increasing disorganization. The power of family life as an agent of socialization is diminishing. An increase in alienation in young people is resulting. This is reflected in their growing feelings of disinterest, disconnectedness, and even hostility toward the people and activities in their environment. Researching the documents of several noted developmental psychologists has led us to make the following observations.

1. The structure of the family is changing radically so that interaction between children and parenting adults is decreasing rapidly.
2. Developments of recent decades isolate children not only from parents but also from people in general.

573

3. Children are being isolated from the world of work. Many children have only a vague notion of their parent's job and have had little or no opportunity to observe an adult fully engaged in his work.

4. Family disorganization is a major developmental antecedent to behaviorial disorders and social pathology.

5. The rates of youthful drug abuse, runaways, school dropouts, suicide, delinquency, vandalism, and violence are all rising dramatically.

IMPLICATIONS FOR EDUCATION

The observations above have lead us to conclude that the school is the logical social system to increase systematically the socialization of cooperative skills and attitudes. The decline of the family as a socializing institution focuses attention upon the degree to which schools are successful in socializing children. The demise of the family, the increased time students spend in school, the use of education as certification for job opportunities, and other similar forces have resulted in the school becoming a major arena for socialization. When a person finishes school he is, ideally, a knowledgeable, skilled, healthy member of society who will enter an economic organization, family, community, and society with the technical skills and attitudes needed to contribute to their effectiveness. *Knowledge and technical skills, however, are of no use if the person cannot apply them in cooperative interaction with others.* No matter how knowledgeable or skilled a person may be in the technical aspects of his job, he will not be able to establish a productive career or maintain employment if he is unable to communicate and work with others, if he is unwilling to participate in economic activities and help share with others, or if he over-competes with or isolates himself from others.

In spite of the obvious educational imperative explained above, there is a marked absence of curricula aimed at the socialization of cooperative skills and attitudes in schools. There is a cliché that young people today are often inadequately prepared by their schooling for the world of work and careers. This statement is usually an indictment of the failure of public schools to provide the practical skills needed to enter particular jobs and professions. There is, however, another dimension to this "unpreparedness": the absence of curricular opportunities to familiarize and develop students in the skills, understanding, and attitudes needed to function in cooperative situations. *It takes years to acquire the skills and attitudes required for effective cooperative efforts; therefore, the school is in the best position to provide a substantial contribution to the development of such skills and attitudes.*

An emphasis in curricula on cooperative skills and attitudes is needed also for successful learning within the school. The time seems right for this new curriculum emphasis, for schools are changing. The assembly-line, mass-production approach to education based upon an earlier, more stratified, social structure has become more open and fluid. The typical organization of the classroom—bolted-down desks arranged in rows—has also changed. There is an increasing, widespread use of cooperative learning methods involving small groups, project teams, team learning, clustering of students, peer teaching, and special interest groupings. The success of these cooperative instructional and learning methods, however, clearly depends on the staff's and student's competence to work cooperatively in small groups.

A COOPERATIVE GROUP INTERACTION SKILLS CURRICULUM (CGISC) AS THE COMMON CORE OF CAREER AND VOCATIONAL EDUCATION

The propositions introduced above lead to the conclusion that:

1. Cooperative group interaction skills curricula lie at the base of youth's acculturation and socialization into society.
2. CGISC prepares youth to assume roles of responsible and competent participation in any task-oriented group, both in and out of school.
3. CGISC facilitates the acquisition of the knowledge, skills, and attitudes that are prerequisities to effective performance in the world of work and careers.

Therefore, CGISC should become part of the program of the school, because *preparing persons for job and career entry must include the development of cooperative attitudes and skills.*

The transition from school to the world of work and careers can be filled with confusion and conflict. Perhaps many of the initial failures of young people in adapting to the real world result from a lack of understanding of the cooperative relationships that operate in work settings, as well as a failure to exercise the appropriate behaviors for both leadership and membership situations in specific jobs. Since vocational education has traditionally helped youth prepare for job entry, and career education is now extending this preparation to all levels of education, it is appropriate to look to vocational and career education curricula for training in interpersonal and group interaction skills and competencies in cooperation. Making personal and social adjustments is a concomitant part of preparing for and entering any new situation, whether in school or in any social or economic organization. This should begin in schools before adult behavioral patterns have been established. *Cooperative group skills interaction curricula can therefore be considered the common core of vocational and career education. The design, development, and diffusion of such curricula has a significance second to none in implementing educational priorities.*

SOME KEY CHARACTERISTICS OF A CGISC

The following is a set of salient characteristics of a cooperative group interaction skills curriculum.

1. An interaction skills curriculum, a clearly defined domain of the program of the school, should have its own set of goals and objectives, content, learning experiences, and assessment means and methods.
2. It should be integrated with other domains of the school's program, such as the cognitive, technical, and life skills, the attitudinal domain, and the information–knowledge base.
3. If the program of the school is structured in subject matters, it should be fused with those.
4. CGISC should be implemented from the very first day of school on, throughout all levels, with special emphasis placed on it whenever career and vocational education is introduced.
5. The longitudinal scheme for this curriculum is the spiral model, revisiting the skill areas but expending the skill and its application, learning in more depth and at a higher level of competence.
6. Being a skills curriculum domain, it should be introduced through problem exposure, implemented as skill learning, and practiced through skill application.
7. It should be presented in the functional context of in- and out-of-school, real-life situations, in situations and tasks that are relevant and meaningful to the learner.

SUMMARY

In this paper, we presented a rationale for the learning of cooperative group interaction skills and attitudes in schools; we proposed such learning as the core of vocational and career education, and outlined some key characteristics of a cooperative group interaction skills curriculum.

Note

1. A set of cooperative group interaction competencies might include the following: knowing the characteristics and resources of the group and using group resources; planning and working with others in accomplishing joint tasks;

576

evaluating task accomplishment and group performance; communicating effectively with each other; building and maintaining emphatic relationships with others and motivating others; resolving conflict situations; sharing and assuming leadership functions; setting examples and representing the group; and acquiring attitudes and sensitivities related to performing in groups as described above.

Operational Concepts

1. Cooperative, goal-directed behavior is essential to the successful functioning of the individual in social groups.

2. Group interaction skills should constitute a specific teaching objective in the curriculum.

3. The ability to interact successfully with others is an essential objective of socialization and should therefore be stressed in citizenship education.

Implications

The authors argue convincingly that our existing social and economic system is heavily dependent upon human cooperation, and that the attitudes and skills leading to effective cooperation are therefore of great importance. The schools—because of their presumed basic responsibility for socialization—must, consequently, stress the development of cooperative behavior throughout the instructional program.

Banathy and Johnson further contend that inasmuch as the family is no longer an effective agent in teaching cooperative skills, corresponding adjustments must be made in school programs. Such adjustment, in fact, might help reverse the current tide of dangerous deterioration in family stability. Some, of course, will question whether schools ought to take on additional responsibilities, and others will argue that the skills of cooperation are already being taught. There is much to suggest, nonetheless, that the deliberate introduction of specific teaching techniques and materials, directed toward the systematic development of cooperative behavior, would be of considerable benefit throughout the curriculum, irrespective of whether these skills are used to complement or enhance existing classroom activity, or whether they are incorporated into the formal or the informal aspects of classroom life.

Louis Rubin

Section 3 INSTRUCTIONAL METHODOLOGY

The extensive efforts during the first half of the 1970s to improve instruction have once again made it plain that both method and content are integral parts of the curriculum. Whether schools use an "open" or a traditional format, employ individualized or group techniques, organize in graded or ungraded patterns, emphasize small or large classes, utilize team or solo teaching, deploy homogeneous or heterogeneous staffing— all these variables influence how well or how poorly English, arithmetic, and geography will be learned.

Pedagogical techniques have an equally profound effect on other matters of curricular importance: they affect the degree to which students will find school interesting or boring, the learning successes or failures they will encounter, the self-concepts that develop as a consequence of these successes and failures, the kind of interpersonal relationships that evolve, and so on. Instructional methods, in short, are both a means to a curricular end and an end in themselves.

Opinions regarding the importance of instructional method vary considerably. There are those who insist that the careful selection of an effective methodology is the critical factor in teaching; and there are others who claim, instead, that one workable method is about as good as another. Some argue that, since the affective aspects of education are at least as important as the cognitive, the selection of teaching activities should be based primarily upon what nurtures the child's personal sense of well-being; and others contend that it is not the instructional technique but the way the technique is used that matters most.

The effects of one variable can, of course, neutralize those of another: a good teaching method, for example, will yield disappointing results if the learning material is too difficult or the student too lethargic. But to assume that choice of teaching method is completely inconsequential would be to deny logic. A proper diet does not mitigate against an ear infection: however, one does not argue that since people may be afflicted by earaches, they might as well eat indiscriminately. It would be equally irrational to contend that, since some children lack motivation, any teaching method will do.

Much of the difficulty in placing method in a comprehensible perspective stems from our inability to decipher the intricacies of pedagogy. To wit, we have not as yet discovered an error-proof way of determining which teaching techniques are best suited to a particular subject, a particular teacher, or a particular student. An even more complex problem lies in the subtle interrelationships between teaching methods and instructional purposes. If one wishes, for example, to teach a body of significant facts regarding, say, the Korean War, a didactic presentation of information followed by testing and correcting activities would be sensible. If, on the other hand, one wished to encourage students to reflect upon the social impact of the Korean War, a number of other, more analytic, teaching techniques would be preferable. But, if one wished instead to use the Korean War as a device for increasing students' adeptness in acquiring and interpreting factual evidence, a heuristic approach to inquiry learning would be indicated.

Good teachers, as administrators have long known, obtain good results in many different ways. Poor teachers, in contrast, are unable to produce much of worth with any method. Yet it can scarcely be disputed that some methods must be better than others. Requiring a student to memorize the date on which President Franklin D. Roosevelt's children were born would be nonsensical, just as total reliance upon inquiry, as a teaching tool, would be highly inefficient. To contend, then, that the choice of a fitting and appropriate instructional procedure is of no importance is to deny the fundamental concept of quality. Whether or not a method *works,* in short, is not the prime issue; rather, the critical question is: Which method *works best?* Options for attaining an educational objective always exist, but it clearly is desirable to select the particular option offering maximum advantage.

The prevailing scene, and the prevailing trends, are a reflection of our uncertainty. Teaching toward specified objectives, for example, remains an issue in dispute; in most school districts some attempt is made to assess student achievement on criterion-referenced tests, but critics still contend that many educational aims cannot be measured. In contrast to the practices of the early 1950s and 1960s, process teaching is taken more seriously and teachers generally seek to develop cognitive skills as well as to cover prescribed content, but it is not uncommon to find instructional programs wherein children memorize right answers. Controversy over the importance of method is far from over.

More recently, a concerted effort to find a middle ground between structure and nonstructure, between prescribed and discretionary classroom procedures, has materialized. If, as has been said, the primary benefit of radicalism is to push conservatism a bit farther along the continuum, one may conclude that the radical position has prompted useful modifications in the way schools organize for instruction.

The hopeless quest for a universal method—appropriate for every teacher and every student—has gradually been abandoned in favor of procedures that fit better with the natural workstyle of the teacher. Moreover, attempts are being made to equip teachers with a repertory of methods so that, in a given instructional situation, some degree of flexibility is possible. Faced with incontrovertible evidence that no instructional method can be counted upon to produce predictable results, theorists have turned to more eclectic patterns of lesson design. How something is taught can, of course, be as important as what is taught; but the "how" depends both upon the practitioner's range of technique and intuitive judgment as to what is likely to work best.

Teaching in the future will be influenced to some degree by the research and development activities currently under way. At a recent convocation of the American Educational Research Association, for example, a number of eminent researchers debated the comparative rationality and irrationality of ongoing curriculum experimentation, as well as the strengths and weaknesses of present research endeavors.

Michael Scriven, for example, believes that excessive preoccupation with the methods of science has made educational experimentation somewhat counter-productive. Benjamin Bloom, on the other hand, contends that research has been relatively effective in generating new conceptions but comparatively ineffective in facilitating their implementation. Similarly, Ralph Tyler suggests that research must strive for greater potency by concentrating its efforts in places where a major breakthrough seems near; John Carroll argues that the research agendas have been far too disjointed and fragmented; Gene Glass faults the research fraternity for its inability to integrate experimental evidence into a cohesive set of meaningful generalizations; and David Krathwohl is convinced that experimentation and development have both suffered from the egoism of researchers who have led practitioners astray by promising too much. To these criticisms I would add my own suspicion that an unfortunate and unnecessary breech has developed between theory and practice largely because researchers have given too little attention to the problems practitioners view as critical, and because they have, in the main, been reluctant participants in the practical application of their research conclusions.

Senseless debates continue to rage over competency-based training (senseless if only because specific competencies do not eliminate the need for general artistry, and general artistry does not do away with the need for basic competencies); the champions of affective and humanistic education engage in endless and mindless quarrels with the proponents of purely cognitive curricula; existing stockpiles of research data are disregarded because of the difficulties attached to making them operational; and, as Scriven points out, educational researchers and developers have not been adequately trained in (1) judging the usefulness of particular research and development efforts, (2) evaluating the long-range cost benefits of these efforts, or (3) evaluating their practical utility.

Tyler has also observed that the relationship between research and development in teaching methodology, and elsewhere, is muddled. The purpose of research, he says, is to enlarge our understanding of phenomena affecting teaching and learning. The purpose of development, in contrast, is to design instructional programs that accomplish desired ends under existing constraints. In a good many instances, these disjunct objectives have been allowed to overlap and dilute one another. He is convinced, as well, that educational research and development have not taken advantage of the substantial knowledge base in disciplines outside education, and that educational researchers have been somewhat remiss in not studying significant school-related social problems.

Yet, these entanglements notwithstanding, an emerging configuration of curriculum and instruction is clearly discernible. Career education, for all its amorphous character and nebulous methodology, has gained considerable popularity among both the citizenry and the profession. The effort to provide students with marketable vocational skills has obvious appeal, and career education therefore is likely to claim a respectable amount of attention. The viability of its purposes, however, remains somewhat uncertain. Aside from the fact that many experts believe that vocational skills can be more effectively and more economically acquired in on-the-job apprenticeship programs, a balanced general education might, in the long run, prove more serviceable than premature occupational training. Some observers, but by no means all, predict that most of the new career education programs will ultimately prove ineffectual. The protagonists of career education, on the other hand, remain exceedingly optimistic about its potential.

It is this sort of predictive inconsistency, and the impossibility of resolving the uncertainties without actual test cases, that accounts for our tendency to bet, in some instances, on the wrong innovative horse. James Coleman's recent research data, for example, show that the overall consequence of court-mandated school integration has been generally deleterious: busing programs have failed to realize their intent, the public has been antagonized, massive resentment has been bred, and, all things considered, Coleman estimates that the integration effort has lost rather than gained ground.

Almost the exact reverse, however, obtains in the case of early childhood education programs. In a comprehensive study of their effects, Harvard's Sheldon White has concluded that the programs neither increase intelligence, enhance cognitive skills, nor improve later academic achievement. They seem, nonetheless, to be as popular with parents as integration is unpopular. As a consequence, the evidence regarding their *academic* utility notwithstanding—early childhood education undoubtedly is destined for bigger or better things.

A renaissance of interest in moral–ethical education is probable; partly out of the fear that malfeasance in high places may have seriously diminished the young's faith in their government, and partly out of mounting concern over what seems to be progressive societal disintegration (drug abuse, large-scale divorce, inflation, unemployment, and the declining stability of the family unit), instructional development activity in citizenship education is rising markedly. Considerable attention, therefore, is apt to be focused upon teaching methods which can be used to encourage prosocial behavior and promote rational values.

The linkage among goals, methods, and content is strong. Thus, value education, early childhood education, and career education each require teaching techniques that are particularly suited to the objectives at hand. Although most methods can, of course, be used in teaching a variety of subject matter, they are not, as a general rule, used in exactly the same way. Teachers, for example, ask questions to test student recall, to clarify, to prompt a new frame of reference, to focus attention on the illogic of an incorrect answer, and so on. In view of these strong connections between teaching methods and teaching objectives, the curricular thrusts of the moment are likely to have direct bearing on future methodological research.

Four of these thrusts, in particular, are likely to claim increasing amounts of research and development energy. The first, an outgrowth of Bloom's work on mastery learning, relates to the use of time as an instructional variable. By altering the amount of time and the degree of intensity given to an educational objective, it may be possible to better the learning achievement of students. Bloom's current work, enlarging upon previous constructions by Carroll, is oriented in this direction. Should his results provide cause for optimism, corresponding developmental efforts will almost certainly follow.

In a potential second thrust, a new generation of alternative schools, more controlled and prudent than many of the earlier models, may also lead to subsequent developmental activity. The alternative school movement of the 1960s, championed in the main by antitraditionalists, was associated with an exploration of radical concepts. The experiments of the late 1970s, on the other hand, are likely to occur under the aegis of more conventional theorists. Two related but distinct patterns may emerge: the trial testing of different kinds of schools and different instructional procedures for accomplishing the same educational goal; and the trial testing of new programs and techniques designed to accomplish very different goals that are more congruent with the aspirations of various subgroups within the society.

A third thrust will stem from the need to distinguish, if we possibly can, what is learned in the school from what is learned elsewhere. If, indeed, television does teach as much as some observers allege, the odds are good that, in time to come, variations of, say, Sesame Street linked to particular subject matter and particular age groups may well be put to a test. Similarly, the potential for teaching through cable circuitry, the possibilities of interactive instructional television, and the benefits of "hands-on" learning through community service may all be subjected to feasibility assessments.

The fourth of the potential new thrusts involves a renewed emphasis upon the long-sought but elusive effort to truly individualize instruction. Aside from the various developmental projects now under way, researchers are continuing their exploration of devices for making the school environment more adaptive: computer-assisted instruction, although far from trouble-free, is beginning to show a bit more promise; work on an aptitude-treatment intervention technology continues; extensive basic research on children's cognitive learning styles is ongoing; and theory building for instruction that strikes a reasonable balance between socially essential knowledge and student-relevant knowledge in all probability will be sustained for a considerable period of time. We have, in sum, come a long way from the point, not too far back, when we were content to deal with individuality merely by composing elegant hymnals to its virtue.

In the essays that follow, a number of instructional methodologies are analyzed and described. Although the writings vary in vintage, and although some of the techniques are more commonplace than others, the selections have been based mainly upon current interest in the particular method and upon the appropriateness of the essay for the *Handbook*.

Robert J. Kibler   David T. Miles
Larry L. Barker

The Influence of Behavioral Objectives
in Education

Behavioral Objectives and Students

Research concerned with the transfer of learning indicates that students generally do not apply learned skills or knowledge to practical situations unless the teacher specifically demonstrates the application. The popular phrase in academic circles which reflects this body of research is "teach for transfer." The teacher attempting to implement this strategy makes desired behaviors explicit and specifies the variety of conditions under which the behaviors or skills may be applied after they have been adequately learned. When behavioral objectives are given directly to students, the exact behaviors desired and the conditions under which the behaviors are to be exhibited are specified. By being given behavioral objectives, students do not have to guess what is expected of them in the learning setting. Learners may spend their time acquiring behaviors specified by the teacher rather than attempting to infer what the teacher expects of them.

Some recent research has demonstrated that when students are given a list of specific behavioral objectives for a course, they tend to perform better on objective examinations than when they are not aware of specific course objectives (Miles, Kibler, and Pettigrew, 1967). It stands to reason that if students know what is expected of them, they will expend less random energy studying unimportant material and concentrate on learning important skills.

One final value of giving behavioral objectives to students is intangible yet very important. It is the sense of security a student experiences when he knows what specifically is expected from him in a course and the conditions under which he will be expected to exhibit his competencies. Psychologists suggest that generalized fears cause greater emotional anxiety than specific well-defined fears. Behavioral objectives can help students understand specific requirements of a course and also reduce the amount of generalized anxiety about course requirements.

Behavioral Objectives and Teachers

The value of behavioral objectives to the teacher is dependent, of course, upon the level of instruction, the subject matter of the course, the nature of the school system, and countless other variables related to the instructional environment. However, there appear to be at least two values of objectives (for teachers) which remain constant in most teaching situations. First, objectives prompt teachers to determine the most significant aspect of subject matter to be learned. At the college level, students often joke that a specific course (e.g., Advanced Theories of Learning) is, in reality, a course in Professor X. In other words, the professor makes no attempt to define critical elements of subject matter related to the course but only talks about theories of learning of interest to him. In rare situations a course in Professor X may be desirable and useful, but from a curriculum viewpoint such a course creates a void of information in a student's educational background which might be important in the future. If teachers discipline themselves to analyze the content of specific courses for which they are responsible, the problem of majoring on minors or dwelling on unimportant issues will become less critical. It should be emphasized at this point that this value of objectives is not held universally by all educators.

A second value of objectives to teachers is their aid in establishing criteria for the measurement of classroom achievement. Most teachers have had the experience of teaching a unit in a course and then spending long torturous hours attempting to devise ways of measuring what the students have learned. Teachers often find that had they approached the subject matter in a slightly different manner or modified instructional strategies, the measure of classroom achievement could have been greatly simplified and improved (i.e., made more reliable and valid). Behavioral objectives require teachers to specify criteria for acceptable behaviors and determine in advance how acceptable performance will be measured. Thus measurement in the classroom may be improved.

A side effect of these two values for teachers is similar to that experienced by students. The teacher who is confident (1) that the subject matter being presented is of prime importance and (2) that measurement of achievement is efficient and appropriate to course goals, is more secure in his position and, consequently, is usually more satisfied with his professional contribution.

Behavioral Objectives and Administrators

Behavioral objectives are important at two levels of administration. The administrator responsible for designing and coordinating curricula (in conjunction with the instructional staff) relies on behavioral objectives to insure that content and subject matter are covered adequately and that there are minimal overlaps between courses, especially within related areas. The use of behavioral objectives also promotes consistency and a thread of continuity among related courses. Continuity is especially important in a series of courses where there is an introductory section followed by an intermediate or advanced section.

When the administrator is supervisor and teacher–evaluator, behavioral objectives help him in a different way. The objectives (1) suggest the degree of progress desired at a point in the course in light of the predetermined sequence of units and (2) help determine if teachers are pursuing adequately the goals of the course. When the behavioral objectives are developed by the teacher, they give the supervising administrator insight into the teacher's philosophy and course goals. This freedom to develop individual objectives is more prevalent at higher levels of instruction.

Behavioral Objectives and School Boards

One of the persistent problems in education is to obtain adequate funds for the maintenance of a quality educational program. *School board* refers to the group of citizens who control funds in an educational setting. In the college context the term *board of trustees* or perhaps the *committee on education* would be substituted for the term *school board*.

In order to defend an existing budget or demonstrate the need for increased funds, administrators and teachers often are required to describe the existing educational program or some proposed addition to the curriculum. It is difficult to provide the board with a verbal or verbal–pictorial representation of the learning situation as it really exists, because board members are often far removed from the classroom. However, when a school system requires behavioral objectives for courses, it is possible to demostrate the content of courses in objective form to a school board and thus demonstrate, more concretely than might otherwise be possible, precisely what learning achievements occur in a given classroom on a given day. This concrete representation of the educational program often may have some communicative or persuasive value to a school board. Thus, behavioral objectives may help educate and persuade those persons in charge of educational funds.

Behavioral Objectives and Parents

The parent is often neglected as a participant in the educational process. However, parents are becoming increasingly concerned about the quality of education in the school and are, therefore, becoming more involved with their children's educational growth and classroom problems. When students are given behavioral objectives, the parents may also elect to study them and determine what behaviors are expected of their child during the school year. Although we are unaware of the existence of such a practice, we feel that a procedure of periodically sending home a list of the actual objectives achieved by a student would be a marked improvement over the grade report card procedure commonly used. Parents could, thereby, gauge the progress of their child at intervals during the year to help insure that proper levels of achievement are being maintained. It is, of course, desirable that parents confer with teachers as well as with their children about educational achievement, but the presence of behavioral objectives can serve to make parents more familiar with the child's desired growth and, in some instances, indicate areas where the child needs special help outside of the classroom.

Parents may be overly concerned about minor points in the curriculum which were stressed when they were in school. The specification of *major* objectives can help parents emphasize and reinforce the goals being sought by the teacher and can alleviate tendencies on the part of some parents to stress relatively unimportant concepts to their children.

THE ENVIRONMENT OF THE SCHOOL AND THE USE OF BEHAVIORAL OBJECTIVES

The educational environment in a classroom or within departments of a university can influence profoundly the value and use of behavioral objectives. In the homogeneous classroom or in the college class primarily composed of majors in a given discipline, the objectives will probably be more valuable and realistic in light of the criteria specified for measuring desired achievement. When heterogeneous classes exist and when college courses include students with a variety of interests and major areas of study, the specification of performance criteria is often unrealistic for students at extreme ends of the achievement continuum. Therefore, the objectives should be flexible when possible and primarily serve as a guide rather than as a straightjacket for the teacher. The teacher should analyze the socioeconomic and educational structure of students in a class and determine whether or not a set of rigid behavioral objectives would be desirable and useful. This reemphasizes a point which has been made earlier—that objectives must be tailored to individual needs. A set of blanket objectives could do more harm than good in some classes or types of educational programs.

A second environmental variable which relates to the success of the behavioral objective is the attitude of the school system toward educational innovations. In a school system that encourages creative education, the objectives can serve to standardize content matter across modes of instruction, insuring that subject matter is not omitted or distorted as a result of the new teaching strategy. Behavioral objectives appear to be more valuable in an educational environment where creativity and innovation is encouraged. Behavioral objectives are also useful in an educational system which is static, but their value there is in curriculum standardization rather than in maintaining consistency across a wide variety of instructional strategies.

A school system's standards also affect the use of behavioral objectives. When academic standards are emphasized and measured, objectives can provide assessments of educational progress and eliminate much subjectivity and guesswork in evaluation of teachers' and students' performance. In systems that have relaxed standards and do not attempt to evaluate teachers or students, objectives have less value.

In conclusion, the educational environment plays an important role in determining whether objectives can be profitable, desirable, and useful. Objectives must be geared to a given teacher and class in the context of a particular school system in order to be of maximum value.

Operational Concepts

1. The establishment of behavioral objectives helps to clarify instructional purpose.

2. A clear understanding of intended objectives increases the student's sense of security.

3. The use of behavioral objectives requires teachers to discriminate among instructional priorities.

4. Clearly defined behavioral objectives provide a sound basis for the evaluation of instruction.

5. Consistently implemented throughout a school, behavioral objectives tend to increase instructional consistency.

Implications

Much senseless debate has raged over the advantages and disadvantages of behavioral objectives. There is no rational basis for denying that teaching, in many forms of instruction, should be directed toward specified objectives. This is not to say, obviously, that all classroom activity must, at all times, be restricted to goals that can be assessed behaviorally. To repeat an earlier point, many educational aims do not lend themselves either to exact measurement or to precise definition. It seems reasonable to assume, therefore, that (1) behavioral objectives have a legitimate place in the curriculum, (2) all learning outcomes cannot be expressed as behaviorally stated goals, and (3) such goals should therefore be used wherever appropriate.

James D. Raths

Teaching Without Specific Objectives

A central issue in the curriculum field is the dilemma, perhaps over-simplified, between *discipline* and *freedom*. Lawrence S. Kubie stated it most clearly(*1*):

> To put the question even more specifically, the educator must ask, "How can I equip the child with the facts and the tools which he will need in life, without interfering with the freedom with which he will be able to use them after he has acquired them?" We have learned that both input-overload through the excessive use of grill and drill, and input-underload through excessive permissiveness, may tumble the learner into the same abyss of paralysis and ignorance.

The aim of this paper is to argue that by accepting the basic assumption that the *primary* purpose of schooling is to change the behavior of students in specific predetermined ways, schools are only making the problem defined by Kubie more acute. In addition, this paper asserts that activities may be justified for inclusion in the curriculum on grounds other than those based on the efficacy of the activity for specifically changing the behaviors of students. It is also proposed that schools, while accepting a minimum number of training responsibilities, should take as their *major* purpose one of involving students in activities which have no preset objectives, but which meet other specified criteria.

TEACHING FOR BEHAVIORAL OBJECTIVES

Regardless of the underlying bases on which curricula are selected for inclusion in a program, a major problem is that of justifying the activities children are asked to experience. Clearly, the selection process always involves subjective and value-rated judgments.

Reprinted from James D. Raths, "Teaching Without Specific Objectives," *Educational Leadership*, Vol. 28, No. 7, 1971, pp. 714–720; by permission of the publisher.

Consider the junior high school teacher of science in his efforts to defend the behavioral objectives of his program. He may argue that a particular objective is justified on the grounds that it is related to student success in senior high school; that the objective has traditionally been taught as a part of the curriculum; that it reflects the behavior of scientists and as such is important to his students; or, more simply, that the objective is "in the book." None of these justifications, either singly or collectively, seems especially convincing.

The problem is seen most clearly in the affective domain. Lay persons and professionals alike have long asked, "What values should be taught?" Krathwohl, Bloom, and Masia(2) have argued that one reason which partially accounts for the erosion of affective objectives in our schools is that teachers hesitate to impose values on their students through the lever of giving grades. On the other hand, teachers seem to feel that manipulating students in the cognitive domain is ethical. For instance, a science teacher may want his students to acquire behaviors associated with the scientific method. Manifestly, there is no one scientific method, just as there is no one view of justice, yet teachers seem to feel no compunction about "forcing" students to learn the scientific method they have in mind while shying away from teaching one view of justice.

It is important in terms of the central thesis of this paper to consider the long range implications a teacher and his students must accept once it has been decided that all students are to acquire a specific instructional objective. The teacher's task becomes at once difficult and tedious. He must inform his students of the objective to which they are expected to aspire; he must convince them of the relevance of this objective to their lives; he must give students the opportunity to practice the behavior being taught; he must diagnose individual difficulties encountered by members of his group; he must make prescriptions of assignments based on his diagnoses and repeat the cycle again and again. Needless to say, this "method" of instruction has proved itself effective, if not provocative. It is the training paradigm perfected during both World Wars and utilized extensively in the armed forces and in industry to prepare persons for specific responsibilities.

It is the rare teacher who implements this procedure with the precision implied by the foregoing description. Few teachers have the energy, the knowledge important for making diagnoses, the memory needed to recall prescriptions, or the feedback capabilities of a computer. The ultimate training program is the research-based IPI model used experimentally in a few schools throughout the country. This observation is not meant to fault teachers as a group but merely to observe that in terms of the ways schools are organized, for example, teacher–student ratios, availability of special technical assistance, etc., only the most gifted and dedicated teachers can offer an effective training procedure to students. So instead of a rigorous training paradigm, most students are presented with "grill and drill" techniques, as cited by Kubie, repetitious to some and meaningless to others. Yet even if all programs could be set up on the basis of behavioral objectives and even if strict training paradigms could be established to meet the objectives, who could argue that such a program would be other than tedious and ultimately stultifying? This last comment applies both to the students and to the teacher. Usually, teaching for objectives is dull work. Most of the student responses are familiar ones and are anticipated by a teacher who is fully aware of the range of possible problems students might meet in acquiring the behavior. Hopefully, both teachers and students aspire to something other than this.

TEACHING WITHOUT SPECIFIC OBJECTIVES

To suggest that teachers plan programs without specific instructional objectives seems to fly in the face of many sacred beliefs—those dealing with progress, efficiency, success, and even rationality. On the other hand, such a proposal evidently does not fly in the face of current practices. Much to the distress of empiricists(3, 4), teachers do from time to time invite children to participate in activities for which specific behavioral objectives are rarely preset. Examples of some of these activities include taking field trips, acting in dramatic presentations, having free periods in school, participating in school governments, putting out a class newspaper, and many others. While teachers evidently hope that students, as individuals, will acquire learnings from these activities, the learnings are generally not preset nor are they imposed on all the children in the class.

Instead, teachers may intend that these activities will provide students with some of the skills they will need in life, either through the direct experience they undergo in the classroom in carrying out the activity or through subsequent follow-up activities. In addition, teachers learn to expect that some children will become bored with any single activity—whatever it is. This response can be found in most classrooms at any one time and teachers simply make plans to involve those students suffering from momentary ennui in other provocative activities later in the day or week.

While carrying out a program composed of such activities, a teacher must perform many important and difficult tasks, but the functions seem less perfunctory and more challenging than those carried out under the training regimen described previously. A teacher must listen to the comments and questions of his students with the intent of clarifying their views and perceptions; he must encourage students to reflect upon their experiences through writings, poetry, drawings, and discussions; he must react to their responses in ways that suggest individual activities students may consider in following up on their experiences. In these ways, teachers provide an environment that is sufficiently evocative to encourage children to become informed and capable, but in individual ways that would be difficult to anticipate either in the central offices of a board of education or in the test construction laboratories located at Palo Alto or Iowa City.

CRITERIA FOR WORTHWHILE ACTIVITIES

If we accept the argument that the major focus of our schools should be away from activities designed to bring about specific behavioral changes in students, then on what basis can activities be justified for inclusion in the curricula of our schools? This section advances some criteria for identifying activities that seem to have some inherent worth. The criteria set down here for identifying worthwhile activities are not advanced to convince anyone of their wisdom as a set or individually, but merely to suggest value statements that might be used to justify the selection of particular activities in a curriculum.

The value statements are couched in terms that can best be used in the following manner. As a teacher contemplates an activity for his classroom, each of the value statements may suggest ways the activity might be altered. For instance, if a teacher were to consider an assignment which requires students to write a report on Brazil, he might revise his assignment to include one or more of the value dimensions suggested by the criteria. With all other things being equal, the revised assignment would be considered, according to these criteria, more worthwhile than the original one.

A relevant question to raise at this point is, "Worthwhile for whom?" The answer necessarily is for the child and for society. While there can be no empirical support for this response, neither can any other activity or behavioral objective be justified through data.

1. *All other things being equal, one activity is more worthwhile than another if it permits children to make informed choices in carrying out the activity and to reflect on the consequences of their choices.*

An activity that requires children to select topics for study, resources for use, or media for the display of ideas, after some exploration of alternatives, is more worthwhile than one that provides children with no opportunities or another that gives choices at rather mundane levels, for example, a choice of now or this afternoon, or using a pen or pencil.

2. *All other things being equal, one activity is more worthwhile than another if it assigns to students active roles in the learning situation rather than passive ones.*

An activity that channels students' energies into such roles as panel members, researchers, orators, observers, reporters, interviewers, actors, surveyors, performers, role players, or participants in simulation exercises such as games is more worthwhile than one which assigns students to tasks such as listening in class to the teacher, filling out a ditto sheet, responding to a drill session, or participating in a routine teacher-led discussion.

3. *All other things being equal, one activity is more worthwhile than another if it asks students to engage in inquiry into ideas, applications of intellectual processes, or current problems, either personal or social.*

An activity that directs children to become acquainted with ideas that transcend traditional curricular areas, ideas such as truth, beauty, worth, justice, or self-worth; one that focuses children on intellectual processes such as testing hypotheses, identifying assumptions, or creating original pieces of work which communicate personal ideas or emotions; or one that raises questions about current social problems such as pollution, war and peace, or of personal human relations is more worthwhile than one that is directed toward places (Mexico or Africa), objects (birds or simple machines), or persons (Columbus or Shakespeare).

4. *All other things being equal, one activity is more worthwhile than another if it involves children with realia.*

An activity that encourages children to touch, handle, apply, manipulate, examine, and collect real objects, materials, and artifacts either in the classroom or on field trips is more worthwhile than one that involves children in the use of pictures, models, or narrative accounts.

5. *All other things being equal, one activity is more worthwhile than another if completion of the activity may be accomplished successfully by children at several different levels of ability.*

An activity that can be completed successfully by children of diverse interests and intellectual backgrounds is more worthwhile than one which specifies in rigid terms only one successful outcome of the activity. Examples of the former are thinking assignments such as imagining, comparing, classifying, or summarizing, all of which allow youngsters to operate on their own levels without imposing a single standard on the outcomes.

6. *All other things being equal, one activity is more worthwhile than another if it asks students to examine* in a new setting *an idea, an application of an intellectual process, or a current problem which has been previously studied.*

An activity that builds on previous student work by directing a focus into *novel* locations, *new* subject matter areas, or *different* contexts is more worthwhile than one that is completely unrelated to the previous work of the students. (This position is an example of one that is impossible to build into every activity presented to students. Obviously a balance is needed between new areas of study and those which are related to previous work. Value dimension number six asserts the need for some continuity in a program.)

7. *All other things being equal, one activity is more worthwhile than another if it requires students to examine topics or issues that citizens in our society do not normally examine—and that are typically ignored by the major communication media in the nation.*

An activity that deals with matters of sex, religion, war and peace, the profit motive, treatment of minorities, the workings of the courts, the responsiveness of local governments to the needs of the people, the social responsibilities of public corporations, foreign influences in American media, social class, and similar issues is more worthwhile than an activity which deals with mundane "school topics" such as quadratic equations or short stories—topics usually considered safe and traditional.

8. *All other things being equal, one activity is more worthwhile than another if it involves students and faculty members in "risk" taking— not a risk of life or limb, but a risk of success or failure.*

Activities that may receive criticism from supervisors and parents on the basis of "what's usually done," that may fail because of unforeseen events or conditions, are more worthwhile than activities that are relatively risk free—using approaches which are condoned openly by the community and the school administration and which have served teachers well in the past.

9. *All other things being equal, one activity is more worthwhile than another if it requires students to rewrite, rehearse, and polish their initial efforts.*

Rather than having students perceive assignments as "tasks to complete," activities should provide time and opportunity for students to revise their themes in the light of criticism, rehearse a play in front of an audience, or practice an interviewing technique to be used in a project so that they will begin to see the value of doing a task well. Activities that communicate to students that their efforts are approximations of perfect work—and that efforts can be made to improve their work—are more worthwhile than ones that merely suggest that once an assignment is completed the first time, it is finished.

10. *All other things being equal, one activity is more worthwhile than another if it involves students in the application and mastery of meaningful rules, standards, or disciplines.*

Using standards derived from students as well as authorities, panel discussions can be disciplined by procedures; reporting of data can be disciplined by considerations of control; essays can be regulated by considerations of style and syntax. Activities which foster a sense of meaningful discipline, either imposed or chosen by the children themselves, are more worthwhile than ones that ignore the need for the application of meaningful rules or standards.

11. *All other things being equal, one activity is more worthwhile than another if it gives students a chance to share the planning, the carrying out of a plan, or the results of an activity with others.*

One facet of the current trends in individualizing instruction found in some programs is that of minimizing the chance for children to work in groups and to learn the problems inherent in any situation that calls for individual desires to yield at times to group requirements. An activity that asks children to play a role in sharing responsibilities with others is more worthwhile than one which limits such opportunity.

12. *All other things being equal, one activity is more worthwhile than another if it is relevant to the expressed purposes of the students.*

While a prizing of children's purposes might well be protected by the value dimension previously expressed, of providing choices for children, it is important enough to stress in a value dimension of its own. As students are invited to express their own interests and to define problems in which they feel a personal involvement, and as the activities of the curriculum reflect those interests, the ensuing activity will be more worthwhile than one that is based on attributions of interests and concerns made by teachers.

Obviously, not all of the value components identified in this section can be built into a single activity. Also, not all the values listed deserve the same amount of emphasis in terms of time within a given program. For example, some assignments involving "risk" may be titillating for students and teachers, but a program which has more than a few activities reflecting the "risk" value would probably be out of balance. Finally, the list above is not exhaustive. It is meant to illustrate values that might be used in defining a program of worthwhile activities. The value criteria are merely working hypotheses at this time, subject to analysis if not empirical testing. Others are encouraged to develop their own set of criteria.

CAVEAT

It must be emphasized that all teachers, whether working at the first grade level or in graduate school, generally need to do some teaching for objectives as well as some teaching without specific objectives. Whitehead has suggested that in terms of the rhythm of education, many more of the tasks assigned to younger children should be justified on non-instrumental values, while those assigned at the upper levels might reasonably contain more performance-related activities(5).

EVALUATION

All of the foregoing is not to suggest that school programs need not be evaluated. As in the past, those activities which are justified in terms of the objectives they are designed to meet can be evaluated through criterion-referenced achievement tests. Other procedures need to be developed to describe school programs in terms of the characteristics of the activities which comprise the programs. The following procedure might serve as a way of communicating information about a given course or program which would be meaningful to administrators and parents.

Assume that a teacher accepted as the major values of his program those previously identified in this paper. (Presumably, this procedure could be used for any set of values.) He could periodically describe his program using a chart similar to the one presented in Table 1. The chart could be completed according to the following ground rules:

Column 1: This column would simply number the activity for purposes of identification.

Column 2: This notation would place the activity in the sequence of activities carried out during the reporting period.

Column 3: This entry would be another way of labeling the topics under study for purposes of identification.

Column 4: The number of students who successfully completed the activity would be entered here to communicate the extent to which all students in the class were involved with the activity.

Column 5: To give emphasis to the centrality of the activity to the scope of the course, the estimation of the average number of hours students spent on the activity would be entered in this column.

Column 6: In this column, teachers would check those components of the activity which in their eyes serve to justify it in their program. In the example entered in the table, the teacher has justified an activity, not in terms of what students can do on finishing it that they could not do before, but on the grounds that it gave students a chance to make a choice (no. 1); involved them in active roles (no. 2); included experiences with realia (no. 4); provided various levels of achievement which could be judged as successful (no. 5); and required students to apply meaningful standards to their work (no. 10).

If each line of every teacher's log were punched on a computer card, a program could easily be written which would yield output describing the percentage of time spent on each activity, and the number of children

TABLE 1 Teacher's Log

Subject: _____ Teacher's Name: _____ Unit: _____ Dates: From _____ To _____					
(1)	(2)	(3)	(4)	(5)	(6)
Activity number	Dates	Title of activity	Number of students completing activity	Estimated number of hours of participation per student	Justified by criteria (Check those relevant) 1 2 3 4 5 6 7 8 9 10 11 12
1	Jan. 6	Experiment with electricity	15	2	x x x x x

601

who were involved with programs under each value dimension. At present, no generalizations are available which could be used to rate definitively a given course description as adequate or inadequate, based on these data. Nevertheless, if a science program profile indicated that almost no time was spent with students in active roles, if students were almost never involved with realia, and if students had few opportunities to apply meaningful rules or standards to their work, then a person sharing the values espoused in this paper would have serious reservations about the quality of that particular science program.

In summary, the argument has been presented that an activity can be justified in terms other than those associated with its instrumental value for changing the behavior of students. In addition, this paper has presented a set of criteria for identifying worthwhile activities, proposed a modest procedure for describing programs in terms of those criteria, and issued an invitation for others to present alternative criteria. Most of all, it has asked that some concern be directed toward the quality of opportunities for experiences offered through our schools.

References

1. Lawrence S. Kubie, M.D., D.Sc. "Research on Protecting Preconscious Functions in Education." (n.d.) Mimeo, p. 4. Also see this paper in: A. Harry Passow, editor. *Nurturing Individual Potential.* Washington, D.C.: Association for Supervision and Curriculum Development, 1964, pp. 28–42.

2. D. R. Krathwohl, B. S. Bloom, and B. B. Masia. *Taxonomy of Educational Objectives Handbook II: Affective Domain.* New York: David McKay Company, Inc., 1964, p. 16.

3. W. James Popham. *The Teacher–Empiricist.* Los Angeles: Aegeus Press, 1965.

4. Henry H. Walbesser. *Constructing Behavioral Objectives.* College Park, Md.: Bureau of Educational Research and Field Services, University of Maryland, 1970.

5. A. N. Whitehead. *The Aims of Education.* New York: Mentor Books, 1929, pp. 27ff.

Operational Concepts

1. An excessive preoccupation with behavioral objectives may inhibit other desirable learning experiences.

2. Learning programs based entirely upon behavioral objectives can become unduly tedious and prohibit instructional spontaneity.

3. A number of benefits obtain when teachers and students jointly set educational objectives.

4. A healthy curriculum makes at least some provision for learning that is directly related to the individual student's interests.

5. If the structure of the curriculum is limited to conventional content deemed essential by society, an important aspect of education becomes impossible: namely, students are denied the opportunity to explore other intellectual ideas of worth that are omitted in the ordinary course of study.

Implications

Raths's statement, the second in a triad of essays dealing with behavioral objectives, serves to round out the disparate viewpoints on the topic. Like some of the other writers, he sees virtue in behavioral objectives and presumably would oppose their complete elimination; however, he fears that the behavioral paradigm alone does not allow room for other dimensions of education's mission.

He suggests, for example, that a defensible curriculum must provide students with a degree of personal choice, permit their active involvement in the planning of goals, allow a reasonable amount of unstructured exposure to reality, and, in general, offer direct experience in coping with life's requirements.

Putting the various arguments in perspective, then, we are left with the conclusion that behavioral objectives are valuable and desirable attributes of a curriculum, but that they are, nonetheless, insufficient unto themselves. They must be selected with intelligence, used prudently, and care must be taken to guard against their inherent dangers. But, above all, teachers must have the freedom to strive toward other kinds of objectives that cannot always be prescribed in advance or evaluated in quantitative terms.

W. James Popham

Objectives '72

When Sergio Mendes and his highly successful musical group Brasil '66 decided a few months ago to change their name to Brasil '77, they admitted that their prime motive was to maintain an up-to-date image. Mendes and his promoters recognized that potential record purchasers of the seventies might view recordings from a sixties group as more worthy of historical veneration than purchase.

In the field of education there is a comparable danger that when one considers the topic of instructional objectives images may arise which were more appropriate for the 1960s than for today. Instructional objectives '72 are not instructional objectives '62. And the educator who, basing his decision on an outdated notion of objectives, judges the relevance of instructional objectives to his current concerns will likely make the wrong decision. In the following paragraphs an effort will be made to inspect some of the more recent wrinkles in the rapidly changing countenance of instructional objectives. By considering a potpourri of contemporary conceptions and uses of instructional objectives, today's educator will, we hope, remain *au courant*.

THE FUROR SUBSIDES

In the early and mid-sixties there was a goodly amount of excitement about instructional objectives, particularly *behavioral* objectives. America's educators had located a new tool for their instruction kit—that is, objectives stated in terms of learner postinstruction behavior—and many teachers were truly enthralled by the new toy. During that period there were enough "how-to-write-'em" workshops to stuff a horse. With a few exceptions, horse-stuffing might have been a more beneficial pursuit. This was the era of drum pounding, and (speaking as a former drum pounder) many

Reprinted from W. James Popham, "Objectives '72," *Phi Delta Kappan,* March 1972, pp. 432–435; by permission of the publisher.

zealots viewed behavioral objectives as the first step on a stairway to educational paradise.

We'll never know whether the remarkable display of interest in behavioral objectives was due to (1) the activities of programmed instructional enthusiasts (who universally employed behavioral objectives), (2) the impact of Robert Mager's little self-instruction book(1) on how to state objectives (which could be completed in forty-five minutes, hence was praiseworthy on brevity grounds alone), (3) the markedly increased sales of the *Taxonomies of Educational Objectives*(2) (which may have made professors Bloom, Krathwohl, et al. regret their nonroyalty contracts with the publishers), or (4) the insistence of many U.S. Office of Education officials that instructional project proposals had to include behavioral objectives (which proposal writers often did, but project staffs often forgot).

Whatever the causes, many of our nation's educators became behavioral objectives enthusiasts. Everywhere one turned, a speaker was expounding the raptures of behavioral goals. The professional literature abounded with articles on objectives. A flood of books and filmstrips told how to state objectives behaviorally. "Behavioral" and "objectives" were, without challenge, the most persistent educational buzz words of the mid-sixties.

But much of the agitation about instructional objectives has abated. No longer behaving like newlyweds, educators and objectives are learning how to live with each other on a more permanent post-honeymoon basis. It will be interesting to see whether in this instance familiarity breeds contempt or contentment.

THE CONTROVERSY LINGERS

Most knowledgeable proponents of explicit instructional objectives have veered away from using the phrase *behavioral objectives,* for they recognize that some educators erroneously equate the adjective "behavioral" with a mechanistic, dehumanized form of behaviorism. What most objectives enthusiasts want is only *charity regarding instructional intentions,* not a stipulation of the strategy (such as behaviorism) used to accomplish those intentions. Thus, because such phrases create less misdirected resistance, expressions similar to "performance objectives," "measurable objectives," or "operational objectives" are often employed these days.

Some educators use the terms *objectives, goals, aims, intents,* etc., interchangeably. Others use the terms differently, depending on the level of generality involved. For instance, *goal* is used by some to convey a broader instructional intention, while *objective* is reserved for more limited classroom instruction. Anyone involved in a discussion of these topics had best seek early clarification of the way the terms are being employed.

But irrespective of the particular phrase employed to depict precise instructional objectives, there are still a number of people who, individually or collectively, find fault with such goals. Some critics(3) deal with particular technical issues such as the nature of the logical connections between the goal which is sought and the pupil behaviors which are used to indicate whether the goal has been realized. In a similar vein, other writers(4) raise questions regarding the optimal level of generality at which objectives should be explicated—that is, how can objectives be both precise enough to communicate unambiguously and broad enough to avoid the thousands of objectives which would surely follow if each objective equaled a single test item. These forms of criticism are useful to those educators who would work with measurable instructional objectives, for the problems identified must be solved, at least partially, to increase the educational utility of objectives. And even in the enlightened seventies it must be noted that there are a number of technical problems regarding the uses of instructional objectives which have not yet been satisfactorily resolved, the generality-level dilemma being a good illustration.

But there are other types of critics. Anointing themselves as Defenders of the Faith, these people view proponents of performance objectives as minions of an unseen force commissioned to destroy our currently laudable educational enterprise(5). These critics engage in all the classic forms of nonrational debate, either deliberately erecting straw men or displaying remarkable misinformation regarding current thinking on the topic of instructional objectives.

Certainly, there are abuses of instructional objectives. These are usually perpetrated by administrators who, having read Mager's little volume on objectives, feel themselves blessed with instant expertise and thus institute a free-wheeling objectives circus in their schools. Surely, there are too many examples of trivial behavioral objectives which, albeit measurable, no clear-thinking educator should ever pursue. Clearly, there are too few illustrations of really high-level cognitive goals or important affective goals. But these are rectifiable deficiencies. Those critics who wish to chuck the whole notion of measurable objectives because of such deficits would probably have rejected forever all antibiotics because some early versions of these medications were less than perfect.

One hopes that groups such as the National Council of Teachers of English, who two years ago at their national convention passed a resolution rejecting behavioral objectives almost *in toto,* will reappraise their stance. While teachers in fields such as English do find it difficult to frame some of their more important intentions in a form which permits subsequent assessment, they should not be excused from the task. Nor should they be applauded when they cast behavioral objectives proponents in the Arthurian role of the wicked knight. It is devilishly hard to assess many of the more profound goals of education. But if we can make some progress toward doing so, then we shall surely reap dividends for education and the learners it should serve.

OBJECTIVES DEPOSITORIES

One development that seems to be catching on in educational circles is the establishment of objectives bank agencies or test item depositories(6). These organizations collect large numbers of objectives and/or measuring instruments, thereafter making them available so that educators may select those materials of particular use in a local educational setting. The heavy demand for materials distributed by such agencies as the Instructional Objectives Exchange(7) suggests that American educators are finding these sorts of support materials useful.

There are some, critics of precise objectives, who find the provision of "ready-made" objectives particularly reprehensible. These individuals(8) contend that it is demeaning for teachers to select their objectives from an extant pool of goals. Teachers, they argue, should personally devise their own statements of objectives. This form of carping, it strikes me, is akin to asking a surgeon to manufacture his own surgical instruments. If I am about to undergo an appendectomy, I would prefer that the scalpel to be used had been professionally prepared by a surgical instrument manufacturer instead of pounded out in my doctor's toolshed. For that is precisely what objectives depositories are attempting to provide—*tools* for instructional designers and evaluators. The statements of objectives and pools of test items can be used, modified, or rejected by educators, depending on the suitability of the tools for a given instructional situation. To reject the provision of such tools is to yearn for the pre-hand-axe society of primitive man.

ACCOUNTABILITY EQUALS OBJECTIVES?

For some educators, the notion of explicit instructional objectives is inextricably tied up with the recent concern about educational accountability. They hear accountability enthusiasts attempting to devise educational monitoring systems which are anchored to behavioral objectives. They see PPBS devotees conjure up cost-effectiveness schemes in which precise objectives play a pivotal role. Thus they quite naturally assume that if you buy precise objectives you've also paid your first installment on the entire PPBS-accountability syndrome.

It is true that measurable instructional objectives can be highly useful in implementing schemes to satisfy the current quest for educational accountability; yet, to organize one's instructional thinking around precise goal statements in no way commits an instructor to the whole PPBS routine. In general, there is undoubtedly a positive correlation between educators' proclivities to employ measurable objectives and their inclinations to adopt an accountability stance. Nevertheless, a teacher who wishes to employ measurable objectives can do so while eschewing all the trappings of accountability.

OBJECTIVES AND TEACHER EVALUATION

In part because of the general movement toward accountability, we are beginning to see measurable objectives employed in procedures designed to assess a teacher's instructional skill. In several states—for example, California, Florida, and Colorado—there is considerable activity at the state legislative level to devise schemes for evaluating the quality of the state's educational enterprise in terms of specific instructional goals.

In their recently concluded 1971 legislative session, California lawmakers enacted a statewide system of teacher evaluation in which each school district in the state must set up a systematic teacher appraisal system. Local districts have certain options regarding the final form of the evaluation scheme, but the new legislation stipulates that "standards of expected student progress in each area of study" be established by all districts. Many California educators are interpreting this to mean that local districts must adopt precise instructional goals stated in terms of learner behavior. Further, the new law requires that each teacher's competence be assessed (probationary teachers annually, nonprobationary teachers biennially) "as it relates to the established standards." Quite clearly, instructional objectives will play a central role in the attempts to implement the new California teacher evaluation law(9).

Another teacher evaluation approach of considerable potential involves the use of short-term teaching performance tests as a vehicle for assessing one's instructional proficiency. A teaching performance test consists of determining a teacher's ability to accomplish a prespecified instructional objective with a small group of randomly assigned learners. By controlling the ability of learners (through both randomization and statistical adjustments) and keeping constant the instructional task (that is, the objective to be achieved), it is possible to discriminate among teachers with respect to this particular instructional skill—the ability to bring about prespecified behavior changes in learners. At least one firm(10) is now providing a limited service to evaluate teachers according to their skill with respect to teaching performance tests and, perhaps more importantly, is providing teaching improvement kits designed to enhance teachers' skills on this type of instructional task. We can readily foresee the more frequent use of such measurement strategies, whereby teachers will be judged, at least in part, by their ability to aid their pupils to achieve both cognitive and affective instructional goals.

OBJECTIVES PLUS MEASURES

Most classroom teachers can recount stories of an earlier era when their principal asked them to write out a list of educational objectives—typically broad goals at the platitude plateau—which were dutifully prepared, then placed in the desk drawer to be trotted forth only on PTA or back-to-school nights. Such goal statements rarely, if ever, made any difference in what went on in the classroom. But these, of course, were nonbehavioral goals that were really not supposed to affect practice, only offer solace to the public. Now, however, we find educators falling into the same trap with behavioral objectives. They believe that merely by having teachers gin up a flock of performance objectives a moribund instructional operation will be magically transformed into pedagogical grandeur. It doesn't happen that way.

A well-stated instructional objective communicates an educator's aspiration for his learners. To assess the degree to which the objective has been achieved, we need measures based on the objectives. By providing the measures—and this certainly includes more than pencil-and-paper tests—we can make it easier for teachers to find out whether the objective has been attained. And we have to make it *easy* for teachers to live the good pedagogical life. Some religious conservatives erect hurdle after hurdle which their brethren must leap on the way to the good life. The prudent pastor makes it simple, not difficult, to live the righteous life.

Objectives with related measures can make a ton of difference in our schools. Teachers are generally well-intentioned and conscientious human beings. They want what's best for their pupils. If they discover their goals are not being achieved via current instructional strategies, they'll probably try something different. But if they only have objectives without measures of those objectives, the odds are that they'll never find out how well their children are really doing. We desperately need more measures to match our objectives. Behavioral objectives *sans* measures offer only modest instructional advantages; behavioral objectives *with* measures can yield dramatic dividends.

NEEDS ASSESSMENT ENTERPRISES

As more educators are becoming familiar with measurable instructional objectives, they are finding more uses for them, as with most new tools. One application of explicit objectives which seems particularly noteworthy involves their use in systematically deciding on the goals of an educational system, e.g., district or statewide. Stimulated largely by requirements of ESEA Title III programs which demand the conduct of an educational needs assessment in which local educational deficiencies are identified, several educators are carrying out their needs assessments by

610

using measurable objectives. More specifically, they are either generating sets of measurable objectives or selecting them from objectives depositories, then having different clienteles, such as community representatives or students, rank the objectives in terms of their suitability for inclusion in the curriculum.

Because the use of measurable objectives reduces the ambiguity associated with statements of educational intentions, noneducators are better able to comprehend and thereby judge the importance of alternative instructional goals. By averaging the rankings of representative groups, the educational decision maker soon acquires a more enlightened estimate of the curriculum preferences of his school system's constituents.

In view of strong drives throughout the nation for legitimate community involvement in the schools, many astute school people will see the use of objective-based needs assessments as a reasonable vehicle for allowing appropriate groups to express their educational preferences. We can anticipate increased usage of objectives in this fashion.

OBJECTIVES AND EVALUATION

Some educators mistakenly believe that in order to conduct a defensible evaluation of an educational enterprise one must judge the degree to which the program's instructional objectives have been achieved. Michael Scriven, perhaps America's foremost evaluation theorist, has recently argued(*11*) for *goal-free evaluation* in which one attends to the outcomes of an instructional sequence without any consideration whatsoever of what was intended by the instructional planners. After all, it is not the instructional designers' rhetoric to which we should attend, but to the results their designs produce. Scriven's suggestions pertain to the role of an independent evaluator who might be unduly constrained in his attention to consequences if he becomes too familiar with an instructional project's goals.

This does not suggest that an evaluation cannot be carried out in terms of project objectives, but if a *goal-based evaluation* strategy is used, then the evaluator should be certain to (1) make an assessment of the worth of the original objectives and (2) carefully search for unanticipated side effects of the instruction not encompassed by the original goal statements. As Scriven puts it, objectives may be essential for instructional planning but not necessary for certain models of educational evaluation.

ALL OR NOTHING AT ALL?

Some classroom teachers who might otherwise organize a proportion of their instruction around measurable objectives have been so intimidated by behavioral objectives zealots demanding "measurability for each objective" that they reject the entire objectives bit. It is easy to see how those people who are enamoured of rational instructional planning can get carried away in their enthusiasm for measurability. After all, if a teacher can't tell whether a goal has been achieved, how can the teacher decide whether an instructional sequence is helping or harming the pupils' achievement of the goal? Interestingly enough, most educational goals can be operationalized so that we can tease out indicators of the degree to which they have been attained. Even for long-range goals we can usually find proximate predictors which, albeit less than perfect, can give us a rough fix on the degree to which the instruction is successful.

However, many busy classroom teachers do not possess the time, or perhaps the ingenuity, to carve out measurable indicators of some of their more elusive educational goals. These teachers, I believe, can be permitted to devote a certain portion of their instruction to the pursuit of highly important goals which, although unmeasurable by a given teacher, are so intrinsically praiseworthy that they merit the risk. The remainder of the teacher's instruction, however, should be organized around goals which are clear, hence clearly assessable.

MESSING WITH MISCELLANY

In an effort to keep the reader current with respect to instructional objectives. I have attempted to skitter through a potpourri of contemporary issues regarding objectives. To me the term "potpourri" has always referred to some sort of a miscellaneous collection. I made a last-minute dictionary check as I wrote this final paragraph and discovered that Webster offers a comparable interpretation—except that the *literal* definition of potpourri is a "rotten pot." The reader will have to decide whether the foregoing potpourri is literal, nonliteral, or merely illiterate.

References

1. Robert Mager. *Preparing Instructional Objectives.* San Francisco: Fearon Publishers, 1962.
2. B. S. Bloom et al., *Taxonomy of Educational Objectives, Handbook I: Cognitive Domain.* New York: David McKay, 1956; D. R. Krathwohl et al., *Taxonomy of Educational Objectives, Handbook II: Affective Domain.* New York: David McKay, 1964.
3. See Philip G. Smith's essay in this issue, p. 429.
4. For example, see E. L. Baker. *Defining Content for Objectives.* Vimcet Associates, P.O. Box 24714, Los Angeles, Calif. 90024.

5. For example, see Hans P. Guth's recent tirade in *The English Journal*, "The Monkey on the Bicycle: Behavioral Objectives and the Teaching of English," September, 1970, pp. 785–92. But don't pass up Peter W. Airasian's dissection of Guth's position in a later issue of that journal ("Behavioral Objectives and the Teaching of English," April, 1971, pp. 495–99).

6. The Laboratory of Educational Research at the University of Colorado, Boulder, for example, is setting up a pool of measures in the affective domain under Gene V. Glass's leadership.

7. Distribution statistics, Instructional Objectives Exchange, Box 24095, Los Angeles, Calif. 90024.

8. For example, see Deborah Ruth, "Behavioral Objectives: A Ratomorphic View of Man," a paper presented at the NCTE Annual Convention, Las Vegas, Nev., November, 1971.

9. A discussion of the new California teacher evaluation law is available; see W. J. Popham, *Designing Teacher Evaluation Systems.* Los Angeles: Instructional Objectives Exchange, 1971 ($1.25 per copy).

10. Instructional Appraisal Services, 105 Christopher Circle, Ithaca, N.Y., 14850; or Box 24821, Los Angeles, Calif. 90024.

11. Michael Scriven, "Goal-Free Evaluation," an informal working paper for the Institute of Education, November, 1971.

Operational Concepts

1. Some educational aims are difficult to either express or assess as precise measurable outcomes; these aims, consequently, must either be evaluated on some other basis or accepted as articles of faith.

2. The quality of instructional objectives determines, to a large extent, the quality of the ensuing education.

3. As new institutional goals are adopted which reflect continuing social evolution, corresponding new instructional objectives must be devised.

4. Since the pursuit of any one instructional objective could lead to unwarranted excesses, curricular imbalance, and other deleterious consequences, appropriate regulating devices are needed to ensure instructional equilibrium.

5. It is essential to continue the search for new affective and cognitive objectives which will extend the curriculum beyond its present limitations.

6. Curriculum assessment should include those aspects of learning that cannot be either taught or measured according to exact prescriptions.

614

Implications

Popham helps to further clarify some of the fuzziness associated with the objectives movement. *Behavioral objectives,* he says, are "objectives stated in terms of the learner's postinstruction behavior." *Instructional objectives,* on the other hand, deal with teaching intentions; they describe the desired outcomes of instruction. *Measurable objectives,* finally, are used to designate both instructional objectives and the specific measures that determine the extent to which they have been achieved.

It is also apparent, from Popham's observations, that the behavioral objective has been both abused and misused, and has not yet reached the stage of a fine art. In short, a poor measurable objective, badly conceived, may do more harm than good. Similarly, if the objective deals with the trivial rather than the significant, the resulting benefits are also likely to be trivial.

The essay constituted a reinforcement of earlier arguments: instructional objectives are valuable and deserve a large portion of the curriculum designer's attention. To the extent that a substantial amount of the educational enterprise is directed toward specific ends, identifying these ends and the devices through which their accomplishment may be assessed are matters of considerable importance. This is not to say, however, that all instructional effort must be directed toward measurable objectives, or that all evaluation must deal with such objectives.

What can be deduced from Popham's propositions, as well, is that the assessment of student achievement must consist of far more than paper-and-pencil tests. It would be exceedingly shortsighted, he also contends, to ignore potentially harmful side effects resulting from behaviorally oriented instruction, and to forget that careful judgments must be made regarding the quality of established objectives.

Simulation and Games

Jack E. Cousins

Simulations and Simulation Games

A MATTER OF DEFINITION

The terms "simulations," "simulation games" and "educational games" are used in a variety of ways by various authorities. Despite varying usages, there does seem to be considerable agreement in the literature about simulations. The definitions developed here are not intended to be universally acceptable and are offered only to add clarity to this discussion.

According to William Nesbitt(1), "simulation is a selective representation of reality, containing only those elements of reality that the designer deems relevant to his purpose." Another way of defining simulations is to say that they are models or sets of submodels which replicate some phenomenon of the real world. In other words, simulations are attempts to take a part or parts of physical and/or social situations and reduce them in size and complexity so that essential elements can be recreated in classroom settings for educational purposes. Clark Abt, who uses the term "game" when discussing simulations, says that when a game is reduced to its formal essence it "is an activity among two or more independent decision makers seeking to achieve their objectives in some limiting context"(2). These activities or models of reality contain only those elements which are considered essential for learning to occur and which are essential in order to establish the limiting context about which Abt has written.

The use of games seems to grow out of the very natural ways in which children learn about the world. It is not unusual to see several children about six years of age pretending to be adults. If one observes carefully, it is readily apparent that these children are role-playing adult problems. This play is not aimless. It is really, to some degree, preparation for the roles children will assume in due time. Even though they may be incorrect, these children play adult roles as they (the children) perceive them.

A six-year-old boy, for example, assumes the role of father who has just entered the house after a day at his work. He indicates he is angry

Reprinted from Jack E. Cousins, "Simulations and Simulation Games," in *Human Interaction in Education,* © 1974; by permission of Allyn and Bacon, Inc., Boston.

616

since the boss gave him some extra work to do. The "father" shouts at the "mother" and sends his "son" to his room for leaving his toys in the living room. Play? To be certain, but on the other hand, based on a child's observation of the real world. These children are, in a very natural way, preparing for the adult world. Perhaps educators can take this natural tendency and, rather than engaging in negative situations, help youth role-play the adult world as it could be. Unfortunately, this natural tendency to learn by playing seems to be lost by the time most children are firmly into their adolescent years. Is this natural, or does the adult world (including the schools) cause children to abandon play as a means of learning? Abt puts it this way(3):

> The world of the child and the young adolescent, like that of primitive man, is a dynamic world, full of emotion, imagination and physical action. Yet the opportunities for students' expressive action in the schools have yielded to strong pressures from adults for emphasis on abstraction; when students have tried to relate abstract thoughts to concrete action, adults have frequently felt their need for action and participation in a world which has become increasingly specialized and in which action has come to be the province of specified occupational groups.

Simulation seems to offer educators rich opportunities to regain the natural tendency to learn by enjoyable involvement.

There are other classroom activities which are more appropriately called by the simple term, *game*. For example, chess is simply a game, as opposed to a simulation game, since there is little (if any) attempt to seriously recreate any part of reality. To be certain, a player could gain some insight into medieval society, but chess for the most part remains only an intriguing game of strategy. "Propaganda," an activity designed to help students analyze various categories of persuasive statements, is also a desirable classroom game, but it is not a simulation game.

Actually, it is really not important whether one calls an activity a game, a simulation or a simulation game. But it is important to recognize that the various activities do accomplish different things as far as educational gain is concerned. All do, however, have one characteristic in common, and that is they involve students in an interactive way; they provide students with opportunities to be dynamic, emotional and imaginative in very desirable ways. This characteristic is probably more important than concerns for informational cognitive gains.

One other simulation-type activity that must be mentioned here is role playing. Although this has been thoroughly discussed in the preceding chapter, I mention it here since role playing is a very important component in most simulations. Further, there are role-playing materials which also contain many elements of simulation, but which are not intended to be careful models of reality. *Hang-Up* is an activity in which participants role play members of various racial groups. They are placed in certain social situations that, because of certain personal hang-ups (assigned with the roles), cause persons to become upset or frustrated. As these situations are presented, participants silently act out their "hang-ups" while the others in the group attempt to guess what they are. This activity is not an attempt to create an accurate model of reality, even though it is clearly recognized that such "hang-ups" do occur to people in similar situations. *Hang-Up* is intended to get people to openly discuss real hang-ups they have about persons of different racial, ethnic or social groups. One will often see such activities referred to as simulations, but in a rather technical sense they are role-playing activities. There are differences in these activities, but unless one wishes to be a purist about terminology, the identifiers are not as important as the contributions they make to education.

At this point, perhaps it would be helpful to summarize what has been a rather lengthy statement of definition. Activities generally identified by the word "simulation" actually represent a variety of related learning strategies. In a rather strict sense, *simulations* are models of reality simplified for classroom use. Such models usually require that participants assume the identity of another person. The models further require that the role-playing person solve some problem or reach some decision using information provided in the model itself. In another sense, simulation activities are often carried out in a gamelike atmosphere.

Other activities which, to a small degree, are based on reality and are intended to serve as initiators of group interaction, are not simulations. These are most often called *role-playing materials*. Perhaps the most convenient way to deal with these various terms is to simply call all such activities simulation games or learning games, and leave the technical terminology to researchers and developers. For the purposes of this chapter, we are concerned about materials that enable students to become actively involved in situations in which they interact with other students, with their own minds and with teachers. Throughout the remainder of this chapter the reader will probably notice that terms are used without consideration for consistency.

REASONS FOR USING SIMULATIONS

Generally, one cannot state that students learn more cognitive content of a traditional nature from simulation games than they do from conventional practices. On the other hand, students do seem to learn as much. And, as will be elaborated later, they do so with enthusiasm. Although these generalizations are supported by most of the research that has been reported to date, there have been a few exceptions which suggest that simulation may be more efficient as a means of teaching factual knowledge.

Baker, reporting a study he conducted with a pre-Civil War simulation, stated(4):

> The sum total of the evidence presented in this paper, on learning and on attitude change, seems rather clear; the traditional method of teaching American history to the above-average child in junior high school may be the most effective way. The simulation technique, which represents a break from currently accepted classroom procedures, is a potentially more efficient means of communicating historical facts, concepts, and attitudes to children at this age level.

Another study reported by Fletcher supports the conclusions reached by Baker. Fletcher stated that, "if the teacher encourages the students to plan, so as to make effective use of the information which the games provide, the result is a substantial increase in the knowledge gained by the students"(5). A very interesting finding in this same study indicated that, although general ability was related to the learning of facts and concepts, it (general ability) was not significantly related to learning of games strategies.

Thus, teachers who are using simulations can be certain that these activities do teach as much information as traditional approaches. They might also find that games do teach information more effectively.

"If games don't teach more, why should teachers upset the normal activities by incorporating them into the classroom situations?" is a question one hears quite often. This question is often accompanied with reasoning which goes as follows: "School is serious business and since games are enjoyable there seems to be little reason to use them in school." Abt, commenting about such thinking, stated(6):

> We reject the somewhat Calvinistic notion that serious and virtuous activities cannot be "fun." If an activity having good educational results can offer, in addition, immediate emotional satisfaction to the participants, it is an ideal instructional method, motivating and rewarding learning as well as facilitating it.

Boocock and Schild support this position, but caution that some teachers may justify using games simply because it is assumed that games provide for "morale-building relaxation" from the serious business of learning(7). An important point in all this is that simulations do provide for a relaxed atmosphere, but one in which learning does occur.

It has been consistently found that simulations motivate students. Both bright and average students are motivated by participating in these activities. Games *involve* students and it is seriously suggested that this involvement, especially when students enjoy the interaction with each other, is solid justification for using them. Further, it is suggested that the involvement of students is good reason for gaming even if traditional content goals are not reached. Rejected here is the idea that games are fine for the slow students, but a waste of time for the brighter ones. Evidence cited by Abt and Baker indicates that such reasoning is not sound. I contend that participation and involvement are in themselves justification enough for using simulations, and that this holds for all students. Boocock and Schild support this position(*8*):

> It is unquestionably true that games can generate great interest and involvement (although it is still an open question under what conditions this interest transfers to the study of related subject matter by other methods). But we also believe that games in themselves teach, that the players learn from their very participation in the game.

What do games teach other than cognitive content? First, games seem to help students suffering from negative self-concepts develop more positive ideas about themselves. Apparently this phenomenon grows out of the fact that all students, regardless of ability, can participate in the simulation activities. Games, according to Clarice Stoll, are "social democratizers"(*9*). They demonstrate that each individual possesses special abilities which are all too often unknown to traditional teachers. Successful players who may be among the bright or very average often present pleasant surprises. Self-concept, probably the strongest determiner of success, both in school and in life out of school, is slowly evolved out of daily experiences. Students who have endless successions of failures in school develop negative ideas about self and about school. Games provide alternatives to these unrewarding school experiences. It has been noted that students normally identified as slow can, and do, participate in games on equal footing with bright classmates. It has also been observed that "slow" students inductively learn very complex processes and use them consistently throughout the simulation(*10*). Such successful experiences can help change negative ideas about self to more positive ones.

Emerging evidence indicates that simulations can also cause one's attitude toward others to change. Wishing to know if the game *Ghetto* would result in changes of attitude toward the poor, Samuel A. Livingston(*11*) used the activity in an all-boy Roman Catholic school in Baltimore. He reported that the finding with the greatest statistical significance was that students' attitudes toward the poor were more favorable after the activity then they were before it. It is interesting to note that this shift occurred even though there did not appear to be any increase in factual information relative to the poor. Livingston suggests that shifts in attitude are a product of an intense involvement, although vicarious, in the role of some person facing very different life problems.

Without citing other evidence, it appears quite clear that participation in simulation does effect attitude change. It is further noted that attitude change is definitely related to the interaction and involvement which occurs when simulations are used. And, to repeat, students enjoy the activities.

What are the educational outcomes from simulations? Three major results have been presented in this chapter. First, students engaging in simulations will learn as much as students taught by traditional approaches. Furthermore, it can now be stated that there is some evidence, although slight at this time, which indicates that students can remember more information from simulations, especially over longer periods of time. The second important contribution is that gaming is highly motivational. Games motivate students with all ranges of abilities, not just the slow reader or culturally deprived. Third, games appear to be very valuable in effecting attitude change toward other ethnic or racial groups and toward little understood domains in society such as politics. The most important result is that students become involved in interaction with one another; even if the other three results were minimal, simulation would be desirable simply as a source of constructive interaction.

SUGGESTIONS FOR USING SIMULATIONS

Simulation is not the usual type of teaching strategy in which the teacher occupies center stage and dominates the action. Teachers must make some adjustments in order to get maximum educational benefit from the utilization of simulations.

First of all, no simulation game should ever be used without the teacher being thoroughly acquainted with the structure, procedures, roles and class organization necessary for conducting the game. Judith Gillespie suggests that teachers should ask the following questions about a simulation before using it(*12*):

1. Is the game interesting?
2. Is the game workable in a classroom situation?
3. Does the game have a sound knowledge base?
4. What is the central problem to be explored?
5. What choices are there for players?
6. What are the rules?
7. How is the game organized?
8. What summary activities are suggested?

Having decided to use a game, teachers should not hesitate to change the guidelines in the manual. Use your imagination! If you wish to adapt the simulation to meet some unique educational goals, do it. Furthermore, don't be afraid to interrupt the game if you feel there is a need for informational input, or a question that should be faced. Students find it quite easy to change from a role they are playing to their own identity without losing the continuity of the game.

Another suggestion is that teachers should not overprepare students for simulation action. Provide only enough advance organization to initiate the activity. Certainly one should present the intended goals of the activity, but if this is overdone, there is a good chance that students will be "turned off" by their teacher's preparatory lecture. Students can inductively figure out many of the rules as the activity progresses. Supply additional rules and information as needs arise during the simulation itself.

The teacher's role in some simulations is quite well defined. If this is the case, play your role but don't interfere with the students any more than you must, and if you don't have a clearly defined role, be as unobtrusive as possible. This does not mean that teachers should abandon their responsibility, but it does mean that they should be wise enough not to be too noticeable during the actual simulation.

After the game is completed, the teacher should conduct a definite analysis of the simulation; otherwise, the educational gains may be lost. The intentions of the simulation, what students think they have learned and how they feel about the game and themselves should be thoroughly analyzed. "A game without discussion 's of virtually no educational value"(13). Discussions should focus on the ways students played their roles, whether information was learned, whether attitudes have changed and how students feel about the game and its relevancy. Extensive discussions about clever ways of winning should be minimal, but discussion about why certain strategies were more effective is legitimate. To be brief, students who have just completed a simulation should be given ample opportunity to share with each other and with their teacher the experiences they have just had.

Any experienced teacher knows that motivation is difficult to develop with many classes. Since each student learns different things in simulation exercises, teachers should *never, never* administer a common test to be used in determining grades. Certainly, one might wish to collect data about the information students learned, but it should be very clear to students that this data is not to be used in determining grades. If students feel they are being graded, there is a good chance they will come to see simulations as one more trick teachers play on them, and the motivation and enjoyment will quickly disappear. While simulations are in progress teachers can make observations which should provide much evaluative information. The following questions are suggested as guidelines:

1. Are students enthusiastic?
2. Are bright, slow and average students participating?
3. Do students readily learn the processes necessary to participate in the activity?
4. Are students using information provided in the game, and seeking additional information upon which to base decisions?

5. Does the game seem to contribute to the overall study of the subject matter?

6. Is the interaction conducive to helping students become thoroughly acquainted with each other?

7. If appropriate, does the game seem to help initiate attitude changes?

References

1. William Nesbitt. *Simulation games for the social studies classroom* (New York: The Foreign Policy Association, 1971).

2. Clark C. Abt. *Serious games* (New York: Viking, 1970).

3. Ibid.

4. Eugene H. Baker. A pre-civil war simulation for teaching American history, in Sarene E. Boocock and E. O. Schild (eds.), *Simulation games in learning* (Beverly Hills, Calif.: Sage, 1968).

5. Jerry L. Fletcher. Evaluation of learning in two social studies simulation games, in *Simulation & Games,* September, 1971, 259–286.

6. Abt, *Serious games.*

7. Sarene E. Boocock and E. O. Schild (eds.), *Simulation games in learning* (Beverly Hills, Calif.: Sage, 1968).

8. Ibid.

9. Clarice Stoll. Games students play, *Media and Methods,* October, 1970, 37–44.

10. Boocock and Schild, *Simulation games in learning.*

11. Samuel A. Livingston. Simulation games and attitude change: attitudes toward the poor, The Johns Hopkins University, April, 1970; ERIC ED 039 151.

12. Judith A. Gillespie. Analyzing and evaluating classroom games, *Social Education,* January, 1972, 33–34, 94.

13. Stoll, Games students play.

Operational Concepts

1. Simulations are representations, or models, of phenomena that exist in the real world.

2. There is some evidence to indicate that, with certain types of subject matter, students learn as much through simulated games as through more conventional instructional techniques.

3. The use of instructional games seems to yield substantial benefits in terms of student motivation.

4. Games can serve as a useful stimulus to attitudinal change, particularly with regard to minority ethnic, racial, and political groups.

5. It is essential, in the use of simulation games, to involve the student in postgame analysis so as to reinforce the associated cognitive insights.

Implications

During the recent past, broad claims have been made regarding the educational benefits of simulation games, but despite claims to the contrary, the evidence is not yet firm. There is, for example, considerable variation in the extent to which teachers are willing to use simulation games for instructional purposes. An attractive game has the obvious virtue of appealing to students, and some intellectual insights are no doubt provoked, but questions remain as to whether the particular game offers the best possibility for developing the particular insight. Furthermore, since students vary both in their interest in games and their ability to profit from them, it is difficult to generalize.

It seems reasonable to conclude, consequently, that the use of games should neither be rejected out of hand nor relied upon excessively. Where they are used to promote instructional objectives, various conditions should be observed: game guidelines must be altered to fit circumstances; the simulations should be accompanied by other, parallel, learning activities; and whenever the use of a game is under consideration, the teacher must make a careful judgment as to whether the ends justify the means.

Educational Technology

Arthur Coladarci

The Application of Technology to the Educational Process

During much of the 1960s there was much interest in the application of communication media for education. The inconclusive and expensive nature of such experiments has prompted educators to closely examine the skills and knowledge necessary for introducing educational technology effectively into educational programs. Coladarci's examination of these concerns, and evidence from projects in the LDCs, prompts him to be both cautious and optimistic. It is clear that traditional, even marginally improved and expanded schooling, cannot ameliorate the problems of education, but with the highly reliable and sophisticated new communications and instructional systems that are being acquired by the LDCs, it is obvious that educators have an opportunity to push further experimentation and application.

In many school systems educators take a narrow view of educational technology and see it in terms of its threat to their own dominance over the learning environment. Where media are being utilized, they are used almost exclusively to supplement instructional or presentational functions. As such, they represent a significant input to the teaching process—such as the use of film to reinforce a concept or a picture to clarify a situation. Film projectors, television, and video-taping, overhead projectors and audio-cassettes have greatly expanded teaching–learning possibilities in learning situations. Unfortunately, such media have been accepted in name but often not in application. In contrast to this narrow view, is the description of the Ivory Coast program which indicates new or expanded uses for hardware and their ability to reach a wider and more diverse teacher–student clientele.

In some innovative teacher training programs, media are now being used in a broader array of educational activities. These range from the use of video-taped vignettes of real school situations for diagnostic purposes to computerized or programmed modules for self-instruction and video-taping of teaching performances for subsequent self-analysis. Ridden's description

Reprinted from Arthur Coladarci, "Technology, Teaching, and Sanity," *Teacher Education*, 1973, pp. 42-50; by permission of International Council on Education for Teaching, Washington, D.C.

of the microteaching program at the University of Nairobi represents successful ways that media can be utilized in EPP.

Certainly the São Carlos Program indicates how media can be incorporated into, and utilized throughout, teacher preparation programs. Educational technology represents that which is a direct result of systematically carrying out and evaluating the total process of learning and teaching in terms of certain highly specific and defined goals and objectives.

TECHNOLOGY, TEACHING, AND SANITY

"Things are in the saddle and ride the back of mankind," wrote the American poet, Emerson, in 1846, and a large proportion of contemporary educators in diverse tongues cry "Amen and Alas!" as they try to avoid or escape from the cold electronic clutches of modern instructional technology. This paper is addressed to such educators—to their disquietude and their long winter of discontent with "the things of learning," to use a recent engaging nomenclature(1). However, lest these few sentences and my tribal membership mislead you, I must warn that I come not as a protecting and comforting knight-errant but to point a stern, reproving finger at those who teach and those who teach teachers.

Educational Technology Is Booming

During the past two decades we have witnessed gigantic developments in the development and application of electronic instrumentalities for learning, together with the "software" accouterments(2). The rate of this development has increased exponentially through the present and can easily be projected to continue undiminished into the foreseeable future. Major funding and sponsoring agencies (e.g., the United States Agency for International Development, UNESCO, the United Nations Development Program, the World Bank) have included instructional technology in their major agenda. Many countries have instituted or are instituting national ETV systems, among them two particularly interesting ones on the African continent—Ivory Coast and Niger. A spate of literature and specialized journals in instructional technology has emerged in all major languages. Well-funded research in this general field has been carried out and continues in universities, centers and institutes around the globe. The vocabulary and grammar of education are heavily infused with the terms, metaphors and logics of engineering, electronics and mechanics(3).

But

The foregoing comprise a sample of phenomena suggesting that instructional technology is clearly among us, large and hyperactive, is presumed to be helpful and represents a considerable investment of capital, time, energy, intelligence—and sometimes passionate commitment. And, yet, as one observer notes(4):

> The claims that education technology would serve as a catalytic agent for overall educational reform—upgrading the quality of instruction, reforming curriculum, reaching large numbers of students, equalizing educational opportunity and reducing unit costs of instruction—with few exceptions have not materialized. School systems and educational opportunity . . . remain essentially the same. There has been some expansion and incremental reform, but few fundamental changes in the philosophy, structure, content and outcomes of schooling.

Or, again, in the language of James Koerner(5):

> In the 1950s predictions were widely and confidently made that education by 1970 or 1975 would be revolutionized by technology—that is, by the new technologies of communications that are generally lumped under the name "educational technology." Leaders and so-called futurists from the knowledge industry, from government, from education, and, I regret to say, from foundations joined in these rosy prognostications. Lately this enthusiasm has given way to embarrassment and disenchantment, as many a corporation has found its Edsel in educational technology. The metaphor is imperfect. The Edsel at least ran; the public just wasn't buying. Educational technology to date cannot be said even to "run."

Clearly, there appears to be a contradiction between claims and performance and an extensive gap between promise and achievement. Two executives of the Ford Foundation, which has supported and plans to continue its support to instructional technology, wrote earlier this year that "[d]espite the depth of feeling that [instructional technology] evokes and its increasing prominence, the field is enshrouded in vague definitions, hazy purposes and murky evaluation"(6). The ETV analyses conducted by Carnoy, an economist specializing in educational development, indicate that, in both cost–benefit and cost-effectiveness terms, it is difficult to define the results of most programs thus far and among his findings is the following: ". . . the cost of ETV schooling is much higher per pupil than classroom teacher schooling, and the performance of pupils is not significantly or consistently better when teachers are simply retrained to use more effective curricula(7). Teacher retraining costs are usually a small fraction of the cost of operating an ETV system"(8).

What is wrong? Why has a huge mountain labored so hard to produce only a few mice? The diagnoses are many—some of them relevant, others probably self-serving rationalizations. It is charged, for example, that teachers are not adequate to these electronic gifts from heaven. This may be true, but I am mindful of what the humorist, James Thurber, once said: "A word to the wise is not sufficient if it doesn't make any sense." Some feel that the difficulties arise from meanly motivated promoters of the hardware, who pursue their mission with fanatic zeal. There probably are too many such salesmen, who fit nicely the definition of a fanatic as one who does what he knows the Lord would do if given all the facts of the case. Another diagnosis is that both educators and technologists have been more fascinated with the medium than with the message. And so on through a long series of suspicions.

Of the relevant criticisms, let me briefly mention only two, which I select because they pertain centrally to the argument I wish to make about the classroom teacher's role in all of this: (1) While the hardware of instructional technology may be universally relevant and exportable, the content and process (i.e., "the software") is not; yet a substantial number of early ventures in educational technology (and some even now) involve content and processes defined by persons in Culture-X for application on persons in Culture-Y. This surely is a losing game. (2) The second diagnosis is not unrelated to the first. It is what Robert Locke calls "the cart-before-the-horse approach" to instructional technology: "instead of concentrating so single-mindedly on *products* for sale to schools, we should concern ourselves with the *processes* by which skills and knowledge are acquired"(*9*). In another place, he joined with Engler to add that "very little . . . analysis . . . had been in terms of how well [technology] can be adapted to an instructional strategy that takes into account the differences in learning style and rate(*10*).

The two criticisms, then, are that technology in education often has been an irrelevant intrusion, addressing instructional purposes other than those entertained by a particular school and with assumptions about learners that do not fit the particular learner characteristics confronted by the technology in a given time and place. These deficiencies are remediable; they are not inherent limitations of the medium—as is witnessed by the developmental work of Wilbur Schramm and the research efforts of Patrick Suppes, to mention only people at my own institution with well-earned international reputations in this field.

Nonetheless, despite increased pedagogical piety and prayer, a critical *lacuna* remains—the intelligent participation of the teacher. I now turn to the gravamen of my concern and to the stern reproving finger promised in my initial comments.

Nostra Maxima Culpa!

My thesis is simple—perhaps arrogantly so: (1) Since the effectiveness of instructional technology is a function of its ability to engage specific intended schooling outcomes in specific contexts and with specific learner background and process characteristics, the teacher (who resides in and arbiters these specificities) must be centrally involved. (2) On the other hand, teachers generally tend to have somewhat the same mindlessness about the teaching–learning process as the "technologists" whom they decry, suspect, criticize and fear. If I am somewhat correct on the second statement (which is frankly exaggerated), the difficulties with instructional technology are merely a microcosm of a fundamental and continuing deficiency in our profession.

We are told that teachers resist engagement with the new technologies, that they fear and are threatened by them, that they see in them a dissolution of the "essence of professional being"(11). I interpret that this "resistance" and "hostility" of teachers often is generated out of the inadequacy of their frames of reference for the act of teaching. As a particularly perceptive instructional technologist notes, "[t]he reason so little instructional technology is used in education today is that its visible faults always end up being compared with the teacher's invisible virtues"(12). Without an explicit, defensible frame of reference, any instrumentality will be seen as wanting and as an unwelcome intrusion. Those of use who teach or who prepare teachers have culpability and responsibility.

A Path to Secular Salvation: Teaching as Hypothesis Making

Having pointed the finger of criticism, I am under moral obligation to be constructive. What frame of reference is required to the intelligent conduct of an educative act? The answer comes with the question: *any* frame of reference that is explicit, rational, critical and reasonably exhaustive of the phenomenon called "teaching." Immodestly, and for what it is worth, I suggest one that I have described earlier and elsewhere(13). I find it useful. Whether others do or not is less important than that it may clarify my concern and prompt the development of alternative satisfying paradigms for teaching—whether the teacher is a warm-blooded human or an impersonal bit of hardware–software. I offer, then, a paradigm for what I call "a normative conception of the educative act." It is frankly a description of what *should be* rather than *what is* characteristic of teaching behavior. As I said earlier, it is simple—much too simple for this audience, but I ask for your tolerant patience while I sketch it out. While I shall make little or no reference to educational technology in what immediately follows, please bear in mind that I consider the absence of this (or an alternative) rational frame of reference precisely what is most difficult—in producing the effective application of technology to instruction.

Any frame of reference involves some stipulations and assumptions. In this case two must be made explicit: a distinction and a controlling asumption. My controlling assumption is the logical principle that empirical predictions can have only *probable* validity—they cannot be statements of certainty. While that assumption may be tolerable to all, you probably will not share the next stipulation—in which case you will simply have to go off and develop you own frame of reference based on the formulation you prefer. I refer to the distinction between "teaching" and "learning," terms and processes so often confused and confounded in educational discussion as to make constructive thinking most difficult. The distinction is between what is *intended to be learned* and what *is in fact learned*. Both phenomena occur in any educational enterprise, but the first (the intentions) are the starting point—or so I assume. That is to say, "teaching" is an *intentional* act; someone's intentions are involved. Clearly, as Cremin notes:

> What is taught is not always what is desired, and vice versa; what is taught is not always what is learned, and vice versa. Moreover, there are almost always unintended consequences in education; indeed, they are frequently more significant than the intended consequences. Hence, educational transactions are often marked by profound irony (John Calam noted one such irony in *Parsons and Pedagogues*. The Society for the Propagation of the Gospel in Foreign Parts mounted a massive educational effort to hold the American colonists to kind and church, and thereby spread literacy at precisely the time the colonists were being inundated with a literature of revolution)(*14*).

My assumptions, then, are that the educative act, whether mediated by a person or a machine, must be seen as an intentional act and of a probabilistic nature—the latter point I will elaborate later.

I conceptualize this educational act as comprising four simultaneous dimensions, all of which must be present conscionably at any instant in time if teaching is to be effective.

The Purposes Dimension

The first dimension of the educative act is suggested by the stipulation that the educative act is intentional and, more specifically, that it is assumed to be instrumental in generating desirable changes in the behavior of the learner. By definition, therefore, a *sine qua non* in any professional action of the teacher is a conscious awareness of what he considers these desirable expectations to be. Or, to put this in more familiar language, the responsible educator is always acting in terms of educational purposes that he considers worthy.

But desirability is not the only requirement for the purposes dimension; the educator's awareness of the desired expectations must also be clear. The necessity for clarity and the difficulty of achieving it are frequently underestimated. You can satisfy yourself on this point by examining the educational objectives, written or verbalized, held by a teacher at any grade level in a local school. The odds are that you will find the statements highly generalized and ambiguous in nature—statements which, to rephrase Gilbert and Sullivan, "say nothing in particular but say it very well." Considerable clarity is needed to illuminate effectively the specific decisions, judgments and procedures comprising education. Such clarity is not achieved easily and is found only rarely. Its absence seriously precludes the rationality of the educative act. Some of the greatest failures of

631

modern educational technology occur because clear and agreed upon purposes have not been set forth(*15*).

The Procedures Dimension

Another salient dimension of the act of educating encompasses the actions performed by the educator to bring about the changes in his pupil that his purpose proposes. That is, this dimension comprises the procedures the educator undertakes, expecting that they will result in the desired learning. What are they? The answer is fairly obvious in some cases: for instance, planning lessons, assigning homework, selecting curriculum materials and grouping pupils for instruction. Others, such as smiling—or frowning—at a pupil's response, planning the new school building and sending periodic reports to parents, may be less obvious. All these, however, are rational decisions deliberately made in light of anticipated changes in the behavior of the learner.

Such an orientation is far from representative of the way in which teachers actually behave. Many educators, as distinguished from our ideal one, see no necessary relation between some of their procedures and the purposes dimension. It is this very discontinuity between procedures and purposes that obscures the relevance of research and suggests the need for the kind of conception of the educative act that we are now elaborating.

Thus far, then, we have identified two logical dimensions of the educative act: the kinds of changes desired in pupils, the purposes dimension; and the instrumentalities introduced by the educator to bring about these changes, the procedures dimension. At this point our ideal teacher would verbalize any given moment of teaching thus: "I use this procedure because it will help the pupil change in these directions." However, our hypothetical relationship is not yet clear. Something is missing—the justification for assuming that the particular procedure will result in the desired learning.

The Information Dimension

Why does the educator use some procedures and not others when he is attempting to bring about a particular kind of change in the behavior of a learner? We can quickly dismiss random selection as an explanation for this choice, since such an explanation would be psychologically naive. Presumably, rather, the educator uses a particular procedure because information on hand leads him to conclude that it may be effective in generating the particular behavior changes he desires. The body of the information that generates dimension varies a great deal in kind. It includes, for instance, the teacher's recollections of his previous experiences with educational methods, reports of the professional experiences of other educators, generalizations produced in behavioral and biological sciences, recommendations of experts and implications of a particular theory of human behavior. The information also varies with respect to level of specificity. On the one hand, it includes propositions about learners and learning in general, and, on the other hand, it also involves highly particularized observations about the specific characteristics and idiosyncrasies of a given pupil, school and community. All these generalizations, experiences and data used by an educator to justify an educational procedure constitute the information dimension of the educative act.

With the addition of this third dimension, our ideal teacher would verbalize any given moment of teaching in a somewhat different way: "This information (information dimension) suggests that this procedure (procedures dimension) will lead to the achievement of these purposes (purposes dimension)." Although this formulation of the act of teaching goes beyond the recipe approach, it is not yet a professionally responsible one. Before the conception becomes intelligent, it must be cast in terms of a crucial characteristic of the information dimension. At this point we turn to what is the defining core of our conception of the educative act.

How certain can the educator be that his procedure will result in the particular behavior change for which he hopes? The answer to this question may be intuitively obvious: The educator cannot be certain that his procedure will be effective. But why? An immediate explanation lies in the present status of our knowledge in the behavioral sciences. As I noted earlier, present knowledge about learning and the conditions that produce learning is far from adequate. However, there is another and much more basic reason for this uncertainty in the educative act—the assumption that prediction has only probable rather than certain validity. This assumption, which stipulates an important qualification regarding the nature of the information dimension, permits us to conceptualize the educative act as an act of inquiry.

The problem can be stated as one involving the phenomenon of prediction. The purposes dimension of the educative act—that is, the behavior changes desired, refers to events that have not yet occurred. The educator, at any moment of the educative act, is attempting to bring about behavior not present in the learner. He is predicting that his procedures will produce the desired changes in the pupil. Now, what can we say about the validity of predictions? As was noted before, although we sometimes can speak with certainty regarding something that *has* occurred, logically we can only talk about the possibility of the future occurrence of an event.

Furthermore, the information dimension in the educative act consists mostly of statements of probability. Even the very best research in psychology, for instance, does not purport to tell a particular teacher, in a particular situation, with particular purposes in mind, what will happen with his particular learner; it is the teacher's task to make an inference about the probability of its truth in the specific situation. If this is so, what can we say about educational procedures? Clearly, if the information dimension consists of probability statements, and if the teacher is attempting to predict for a future situation, the conclusions drawn by him regarding the best methods for achieving his purposes are themselves probability statements.

Statements about teaching procedures must, therefore, be thought of as predictions of probable value and probable effect. The educator's operations are hypotheses and, like any hypotheses, have to be tested in the crucible of experience; they cannot be assumed to be valid. The value of any operation is not fully known until we determine the extent to which it actually is associated with accomplishing the specific purposes to which it is assumed to be relevant. Furthermore, a particular educational procedure retains this hypothetical character even if it has been demonstrated to be effective for other persons and in earlier situations. In effect, then, any educational decision or procedure, at the moment of application, must be viewed with tentativeness. Although the procedure, at that point, is an empirical hypothesis—that is, it predicts something will happen—the results are not yet known. The degree of confidence that the educator can invest in this procedural hypothesis attests to the clarity of his educational purposes, the reliability of the information used and the adequacy of the inductive and deductive logic he used to connect the two.

With this understanding, our ideal teacher now would revise his verbal description of his conduct at any given professional moment in this manner: "On the basis of this information, I hypothesize that this procedure will lead to the achievement of these behavior changes."

The Measurement and Evaluation Dimension

Given the hypothetical nature of the educative act, the final dimensions of our conception emerge necessarily. If we accept the argument that educational methods are to be thought of as hypotheses, we are obliged to assess the degree to which these hypotheses are good ones—that is, whether the methods result in the behavior changes expected. The rigorous testing of hypotheses is frequently a complex procedure and may require knowledge and time usually not available to the educator in a classroom or administrative office. However, the responsibility for initial and provisional evaluation of these educational hypotheses can be assumed consciously by any educator. He may determine the degree to which the hypothesized behavior changes manifest themselves in the behavior of pupils. If the expected and hoped-for changes are found to follow the procedures used, the educator has no immediate reason to reject the procedures, although (and this is an important caveat) he should not conclude that the changes occurred because of the operations he performed. If, on the other hand, the expected changes do not occur, or do not occur in the degree anticipated, he may conclude that the hypothesized procedure was inadequate under the given conditions. He then reexamines the logical process by which he formed the hypothesis, including the question of whether he had sufficient relevant data at the time, and formulates a new hypothesis.

The educator who does not assume this responsibility for evaluating the adequacy of his own procedures is left with no national basis for modifying his procedures or for knowing that he should modify them. The alternative is to rely on dogma, authority or luck. Such uncritical reliance, however, is markedly incongruent with membership in any profession.

Assessing educational hypotheses involves two identifiable operations: first, determining the status of the learner with respect to the behavior change in question and, second, evaluating the adequacy of this status. The first is the operation of observation and measurement; the second, the operation of evaluation. To state these operations in another way, the first is concerned with what change has taken place in the learner, and the second asks whether the change is consistent with the directions specified in teaching objectives and in sufficient degree. The distinction may help to make clear an important implication of our paradigm of the educative act: The basic professional relevance of measuring school achievement is that the data produced enable the educator to evaluate his own procedures and to modify them, if necessary. This is not the usual stance taken by educators. Unfortunately, too many of them see the measurement of achievement and the evaluation of this achievement as relevant only to the obligations of judging the pupil and informing the pupil, his parents and the school records of this judgment.

A careful study of the foregoing discussion will show that the educative act can be thought of as comprising an uninterrupted cycle of inquiry. The educator, with a clear awareness of the behavior changes desired and the most reliable information available, hypothesizes some procedures that are probably effective in producing the behavior changes. These procedures are put into effect; the behavior changes in the pupil associated with, and following the use of, these procedures are noted and compared with the changes expected; if the expected behavior change does not occur or occurs in insufficient degree, new hypotheses are generated, using all available data, including the new information produced by the measurement and evaluation operations; these new hypotheses are put into effect—and so on, without end. Those of you who are now familiar with Michael Scriven's distinction between summative and formative evaluation will recognize the latter in what I have just said.

So What?

What has my little model to do with technology, teaching and sanity? I suspect that you have inferred the answer already. In order to stay professionally sane, one must think of the technology of instruction as belonging in the procedures dimension of the educative act. It is an instrumentality of the educators' intentions and, as such, must be rationalized in terms of the educators' purposes, utilized in terms of local learner characteristics and evaluated in terms of the degree to which the intended learnings occur. However, such is not typically the case, and I attribute the current low effectiveness of technology to the absence of an *educative* rationale in its use. Those who promote, install and operate these technologies are often to blame for a serious naiveté about teaching and learning. But more culpable are the teacher trainers who prepare teachers inadequately. Unless teachers are helped to develop a rational conception of teaching, which makes them *participants* in the process of developing and evaluating professional knowledge, technology (whether television or book) will continue to be a loser in any cost–benefit analyses—and schools will continue to be at the mercy of the latest glib promoter of the latest electronic gadget.

Notes and References

1. James W. Armsey and Norman C. Dahl. *An Inquiry into the Uses of Instructional Technology*. New York: The Ford Foundation, 1973.

2. I am mindful of the current confusion in definitions of instructional technology many of which (happily, in my view) do not restrict themselves to "electronic." Although the technology can include everything from Abacus (through Book) to Zenith, it appears that pedagogical anxiety and resistance surface particularly with reference to those that carry arcane and esoteric impulses and currents—principally television, the computer, and their mutant offspring.

3. The initials for computer-assisted instruction (CAI) rapidly became a proper noun in educational conversation. During a recent visit in Spain, I found that it has also become a transitive and intransitive verb.

4. Robert F. Arnove. Bloomington, Ind.: School of Education, Indiana University, 1973 (unpublished paper).

5. James Koerner. "Educational Technology: Does It Have Any Future in the Classroom?" *Saturday Review of Education* (May, 1973), p. 43.

6. David E. Bell and Harold Howe II. "Introduction," *An Inquiry into the Uses of Instructional Technology*. Op. cit. (note 1), p. ix.

7. Martin Carnoy. "The Economic Costs and Returns to Educational Television." Palo Alto, Calif.: Stanford School of Education, Stanford University, 1973 (unpublished paper).

8. Ibid.

9. Robert W. Locke. "Has the American Education Industry Lost Its Nerve?" *Journal of Educational Technology*, Vol. 1, No. 2 (May, 1970), p. 112.

10. Robert W. Locke and David Engler. "Instructional Technology: The Capabilities of Industry to Solve Educational Problems," *To Improve Learning*, Vol. II. New York and London: R. R. Bowker Company, 1971, p. 916.

11. David Berkman. "The Learning Industry and ETV," *Educational Broadcasting Review*, Vol. V, No. 3 (June, 1971), p. 24.

12. Hugh Beckwith. "Innovations in Industry Likely to Affect Instructional

Technology During the Next Ten Years," *To Improve Learning.* Op. cit. (note 10), p. 851.

13. Arthur Coladarci. "The Teacher as Hypothesis-Maker," *California Journal for Instructional Improvement,* No. 2 (Spring, 1959), pp. 3–6; Arthur Coladarci, "The Relevance of Psychology to Education," *Foundations of Education.* New York: John Wiley & Sons, 1963, pp. 388–410.

14. Lawrence A. Cremin. "Notes Toward a Theory of Education," *Notes on Education.* New York: Institute of Philosophy and Politics of Education, Teachers College, Columbia University, June, 1973, p. 5.

15. Armsey and Dahl. *An Inquiry into the Uses of Instructional Technology.* Op. cit., p. 7.

Operational Concepts

1. Educational technology is likely to make an increasing number of learning aids available to the classroom teacher.

2. The usefulness of technology to education depends, in large measure, upon the ways in which it is deployed by the teachers; its methodologies and functions, therefore, must be clearly understood by them.

3. To be effective, the technological apparatus used in the classroom must fit both the instructor's purposes and the students' learning style.

4. The present limited ability of educators to make effective use of technology stems from the absence of an educative rationale for its use.

5. In developing a rationale for the use of technological aids, care must be taken to ensure that both means and ends are appropriate, and to provide for an adequate assessment of results.

Implications

The most obvious implication of Coladarci's postulations is that technologists and learning specialists must conjoin in developing an educative rationale for the use of technology. Before this rationale can be relied upon, however, it must be extensively tested and refined in a number of different contexts. Until such a rationale with demonstrable validity is brought into existence, the danger remains high that technology will continue to be misused, abused, or ignored.

A second implication is equally clear: if a period of experimentation proves that advanced technology can be harnessed successfully in classroom instruction, teachers must be helped to master the intricacies of its management through extensive training programs.

Research in computer-assisted instruction suggests that children who have been taught through the use of computer terminals from the early grades onward become more comfortable with their use and exploit their potential more fully and more easily than do the adults who teach them. It may well be, therefore, that the technological revolution in education will need to span a generation, or even two, of students before it truly comes into its own.

Edward A. Sullivan

Medical, Biological, and Chemical Methods of Shaping the Mind

Much research has been done recently to find out what can be done medically, biologically, and chemically to aid the learning process. Some of this research is examined here.

Dr. José M. R. Delgado(1) of the Yale University School of Medicine has pioneered in the field of electrical stimulation of the brain (ESB). He has been able to establish direct nonsensory communication between a computer and the brain of a chimpanzee and demonstrate that behavior can be influenced by remote radio command. He has also pioneered in the use of electrode implantation for the diagnosis and treatment of epilepsy, schizophrenia, and excessive anxiety. Delgado has predicted that within a few years we will be able to construct a model of our own mental functions through a knowledge of genetics and the cerebral mechanisms which underlie our behavior. He has also predicted that at some time in the near future we will be able to use cerebral pacemakers to treat Parkinson's disease, fear, and violent behavior by direct stimulation of the brain.

To demonstrate his ability to use ESB to control violent behavior, Delgado entered a bull ring in Spain in which the bull had electrodes implanted in its brain. As the bull charged, Delgado activated a radio transmitter. The signal affected an inhibitory area of the brain, causing the bull to halt its charge at Delgado. By pushing another button on the transmitter, he caused the bull to turn and walk away. Although this demonstration of ESB raised questions about the possibility of remote-controlled behavior, Delgado stated that ESB merely sets off a train of programmed events: biochemical, thermal, enzymatic, and electrical. He further stated, "Nothing which is not already in the brain can be put there by ESB."

Because of the possibilities of ESB, Delgado sees the need to(2)

Reprinted from Edward A. Sullivan, "Medical, Biological, and Chemical Methods of Shaping the Mind," *Phi Delta Kappan*, April 1972, pp. 483–486; by permission of the publisher.

develop an educational system that is based on the knowledge of our biological realities, an education that would attempt to: First, establish good "automatisms" in the child and, second, as he matures, permit his thinking capability to evolve without being subjected to unknown forces and impulses which may overpower his rational intelligence.

Other research is being done in the area of biofeedback, the process which occurs when the activities of an organism are modified continuously by the interaction between its signals or output and the environment. Every human task depends upon biofeedback. As you read this sentence or turn the page, sensory data, fed back to your brain, indicate the next step to be taken (in this case, the reading of the next word) in a largely unconscious process.

Until a few years ago physiologists believed that we were regulated by two distinct nervous systems, one giving us voluntary control of muscles and the other, the autonomic nervous system, controlling such "involuntary" acts as heart rate and blood pressure. New advances in the study of biofeedback have shown that these "involuntary" acts can be regulated by an individual(3). This is possible through the use of electronic instruments (e.g., the electromyograph) which inform the individual of changes in heart rate, blood pressure, or muscle contractions by amplifying the signals given off as these changes occur. The individual, then, can listen to the changes taking place within his system. By being instantly aware of these changes as they occur, it is possible for the individual to recognize cues which indicate that a change is taking place and, as a result, develop control over the autonomic nervous system. It has been shown that it is possible, using biofeedback, for a person to conquer the symptoms of hypertension by means of mental processes without the use of drugs. The treatment consists primarily of education in blood pressure control. Even patients with serious cardiac problems can learn to control their heart rate and blood pressure. Psychologists have also been able to relieve people of a number of fears through biofeedback. Ailments such as headaches and insomnia have also been overcome through this process(4).

Can life be changed for the better if we are able to teach children in their first years of school how to develop autonomic control? It might lessen the tensions that eventually evolve into disease. If so, teaching autonomic control can become just as important as teaching children to read.

Biofeedback has also been used as an educational tool to free slow readers of their main difficulty, the silent mouthing of words. Slow readers are placed individually in a laboratory with an electrode over their Adam's apple and are given a book to read for an hour. Whenever the reader mouths a word silently his larynx tenses and a noise is switched on. Because the noise is so unpleasant, slow readers, both children and adults, learn to abandon silent mouthing of words in 45 minutes(5).

Another area of research is the study of the biology of human violence. Dr. Vernon Mark, a neurosurgeon at Boston City Hospital, and Dr. Frank Ervin, a research psychiatrist at Massachusetts General Hospital, have been working to refute the theory that an individual misbehaves because something is wrong in his environment. The theory postulates that if the environment can be changed, then the behavior can be changed. Drs. Mark and Ervin feel that, while environment and upbringing are important factors, the arrangement and functioning of the brain cells are a coequal factor in producing behavior. Their experience has convinced them that a large percentage of repeatedly violent people suffer from certain types of epilepsy or other brain defects that make them behave the way they do. Dr. Ervin hopes that at some time in the near future it will be possible to teach victims of brain damage, through biofeedback, to use the proper nerve circuits to prevent seizures which lead to violence(6).

Dr. Ervin is also developing a thirty-minute screening test for violence-prone individuals. Screening devices of a slightly different nature have been developed already. Examples are the Glueck Scale developed by Sheldon and Eleanor Glueck to determine the probability of young children becoming juvenile delinquents and the profile which has been developed for airline clerks and security men to spot prospective airplane hijackers. It is Ervin's hope that the test he develops will be administered to all who are brought before the courts accused of violent crime, those involved in repeated assaults against others, and habitual traffic offenders. However, when a similar proposal to screen all children between the ages of 6 and 8 for potential antisocial behavior was made to the White House in 1970 there was a great deal of opposition to it.

At present the violent are punished by being sent to prisons or to custodial care institutions, where they are generally neglected(7). It is Dr. Ervin's belief that many of these people may have treatable brain disorders with definite physiological causes. If this is so, then it should be possible to develop a method to diagnose, to treat, and even to prevent the problem of violent behavior.

Doctors who treat people with brain disorders have noted that many people who commit violent crimes are repeat offenders. It has also been noted that many of the conditions which go with poverty and deprivation can lead to brain damage. Such damage may occur in childbirth if good medical care is lacking. Malnutrition, often present in poverty areas either prior to or after birth, can also result in brain damage. At the Johns Hopkins University Hospital doctors have noted that brain injuries to children are more common in the slums than in the rest of the community. A probable factor is the greater incidence of fights and accidents among slum children.

The conditions of poverty seem to contribute more than pressure and frustration to produce violence. If it is true that the conditions of poverty— lead poisoning, malnutrition, poor pre- and postnatal medical care, beat-

642

ings, fights, high accident rates, etc., all of which can cause brain damage—do lead to violent behavior, then there is no real point to attempting rehabilitation of the violent unless such rehabilitation cures the brain damage.

Preventive rehabilitation is also necessary. This would involve as one phase the removal of the conditions which cause brain damage. One such condition is lead poisoning. Lead poisoning is caused for the most part by the ingestion of lead-based paint peeling from walls and furniture. In many cities children suffering from lead poisoning are hospitalized and treated and then sent home for further exposure to the lead source. In New York City nearly $2.5 million has been allocated to deal with the problem of lead poisoning. Most of the funds have been applied to the medical detection and follow-up of lead poisoning cases. Medical teams go from door to door taking blood samples. Where cases are detected care is given and funds are made available for house repairs to get rid of the lead paint. The latter step is crucial, for prevention depends on eliminating the lead paint.

As noted, another cause of brain damage is malnutrition. Studies have shown that among the poor a disproportionate number of children are mentally retarded. The poor also have a higher infant mortality rate, a higher incidence of infectious and chronic diseases, and a great number of premature and low birthweight infants. The common denominator of all these ills seems to be malnutrition. Studies in nutrition have shown that the earlier in life that the malnutrition occurs the more severe is its effect and the less likely is recovery(8).

Studies have also shown that the performance of children on psychological tests is related to nutritional factors. Preschool and school children in Mexico showed positive correlation between performance on the Terman-Merrill, Gesell, and Goodenough draw-a-man tests and body weight and height(9).

There is good evidence of the relation between an expectant mother's nutrition and intelligence of her offspring. When the mother-to-be receives a proper diet as well as vitamin supplements, the IQ of her children as measured at the ages of 3 and 4 surpasses that of children whose mothers do not receive an adequate diet or vitamin supplements(10).

In a study conducted by Harmeling and Jones(11) it was found that school dropouts had an average birth weight lower than that of slow learners. The slow learners, in turn, had an average birth weight lower than that of "normal" learners. The reason for the finding appears to be that infants who are malnourished in utero weigh the least at time of birth. Malnutrition before birth, as noted previously, can lead to brain damage. It can also lead to premature birth.

Current research(12) suggests that some of the effects of malnutrition may be offset by programs of environmental stimulation or increased by environmental impoverishment such as exists among many people living in the inner city.

Programs to prevent malnutrition are difficult for school officials to devise and implement, for a variety of political and economic reasons. However, schools should find it relatively easy to educate teen-age girls about the importance of a proper diet, especially if and when they become pregnant.

Greater availability and use of surplus foods would of course help to alleviate the problems of malnutrition among the poor. Yet we still find ourselves as a nation destroying or storing surplus foodstocks when people are going hungry.

The above summary suggests that what is needed to effect necessary change is not so much more doctors or hospitals but more preventive programs—programs in which people help themselves. The Community Medicine Department of Mount Sinai Hospital in New York City realizes that housing, nutrition, accident prevention, sanitation, clean water, clean food, and clean streets and homes have produced more advancement in health than all the doctors and hospitals combined. It has therefore developed a corps of people to clean up, repair, and maintain deteriorated housing in slum areas(13). An important part of the program is teaching people to take care of themselves.

The health index of a community is positively correlated with its poverty level—the more poverty, the more medical problems. The health index of a community is more than its mortality rate. It also includes the incidence of crime, violence, delinquency, drug addiction, alcoholism, and the like(14). Until more preventive programs are developed, there seems to be very little chance of effecting change.

A whole new field of research is opening up in the area of chemical influence on brain processes and learning. Kenneth Clark, in his presidential address to the American Psychological Association in Washington last September, stated that recent studies of electrical and chemical control of the brain

> suggest that we might be on the threshold of that type of scientific, biochemical intervention which could stabilize and make dominant the moral and ethical propensities of man and subordinate, if not eliminate, his negative and primitive behavioral tendencies.

Clark has proposed the development of "psychotechnology," the study of ways in which new drugs may be used to subdue hostility and aggression and allow more humane and intelligent behavior to emerge.

The first priority in psychotechnology, according to Clark, would be the development of a medication that national leaders would take to diminish their tendencies to respond to an international crisis by initiating a nuclear war.

Clark's second priority would be the use of similar drugs on a wider scale for those in elective office and the military. There would be a standard

644

dosage for all individuals. Clark has also suggested the creation of an association of behavioral and neuropsychological scientists to prevent the undesirable use of drugs already developed and yet to be developed.

As would be expected, there has been a great deal of opposition to Clark's proposal, the main theme being that the type of control possible through drugs and psychotechnological techniques can never be the solution to the problems that beset humanity. Shades of *1984* and *Brave New World!*

Linus Pauling(*15*) has stated that normal mental functioning depends on the presence of molecules of many substances—the B vitamins, vitamin C, uric acid, and other substances normally present in the brain. According to Pauling, the average person gets enough of these substances in his daily diet or produces enough of them through his own body chemistry, while the mentally ill person either does not produce enough of them or uses them up too quickly. Mental patients may thus be suffering from a type of deficiency disease, according to Pauling. The cure, obviously, is proper chemical balance.

Bernard Agranoff(*16*) has demonstrated that there is a connection between the consolidation of memory and the manufacture of protein in the brain. His studies have led him to "view learning as a form of biological development." According to Agranoff(*17*),

> One may think of the brain of an animal as being completely "wired" by heredity; all pathways are present, but not all are "soldered." It may be that in short-term memory, pathways are selected rapidly but impermanently. In that case protein synthesis would not be required. . . . If the consolidation of memory calls for more permanent connections among pathways, it seems reasonable that protein synthesis would be involved.

It has also been theorized that the learning process depends upon a permanent alteration of RNA (ribonucleic acid) inside the nerve cell. Experiments have shown that learning produces an increase of RNA in brain cells(*18*). Dr. Ewen Cameron, director of the Veteran Administration's Psychiatry and Aging Research Laboratories at Albany, New York, has fed yeast RNA to patients with poor memories. He and his patients were certain that the RNA did help their remembering processes.

James McConnell has demonstrated the chemical transference of learning in the experiments he performed with planaria and rats. Rats were trained to push levers in a cage and then run to another location for a reward. When the brains were removed from these rats and ground up and injected into other rats, this learning was transferred to the untrained rats.

From experiments such as those mentioned above the following conclusions can be drawn in regard to the chemical basis of learning: (1) Memory is a chemical process and drugs can limit or improve memory. (2) Chemicals can either speed up the learning process or prevent the learning process from taking place. (3) Learning of a basic nature can be transferred from one animal to another by using chemical means only.

If it is true that knowledge is obtained by changing the RNA molecule inside the cell, it should be possible to identify the particular chemical changes that produce particular behavioral changes in human beings. Once this occurs it should be possible to synthesize the chemicals needed to produce the change and inject them directly or give them in pill form. This could be the so-called "smart pill" for which many generations of students have longed.

Dr. Sidney Cohen of the UCLA Medical School has indicated that, in functional terms, human intelligence involves three different skills. These are: (1) the ability to pay attention or concentrate; (2) the ability to form a permanent memory trace—in the form of changed RNA molecules or in the form of protein manufactured under the direction of RNA; and (3) the ability to develop a retrieval system by which the memory is scanned and focused.

Cohen believes that all three processes can be improved chemically, leading to the improvement of thinking abilities. The "smart pill" envisioned by Dr. Cohen may be several pills influencing the various processes involved in learning. It is also likely that such pills would work best with improved psychological methods of training the mind, according to Cohen.

Dr. Georges Ungar(19) of the Baylor University College of Medicine has isolated, identified, and possibly synthesized the first component of what may be a system of molecular coding by which information is processed in the brain. Ungar has begun experimenting to duplicate for man chemicals which tell mice what to do when they are injected into their brains. He hopes by doing this to improve the brain functions of the mentally retarded and senile.

An area of concern currently being examined is the use of amphetamines to control hyperkinesis in school children. Amphetamines—the so-called pep pills—have been used for many years to treat the hyperkinetic child(20). Such children cannot sit still, have a very short attention span and are generally behavior problems in school. Amphetamines, which are stimulants, seem to act like sedatives for these children, allowing them to control their behavior. The amphetamine actually does not act as a sedative; it acts in an unknown way to enable the hyperkinetic to focus his attention and control his muscles. The amphetamines result in learning improvement for from one-half to two-thirds of the pupil hyperkinetics taking them(21).

Dr. Maurice Laufer believes that hyperkinesis is a physically based problem that has something to do with chemical transmissions in the brain but is not necessarily the result of brain damage. The brain is just not functioning as it should(22).

There has been some fear that children taking the amphetamines would become addicted to them. But recent evidence indicates that amphetamine addiction, if there is any, is primarily psychological rather than physical. Children taking amphetamines under medical supervision perceive the drugs as medicine which will eventually be given up. It would seem that the dangers of addiction are minimal for the hyperkinetic child receiving skillful medical treatment.

The fear has been expressed by many critics of the use of amphetamines that they are being used to control and suppress behavioral problems which result not from hyperkinesis but from a poor home life or from boredom with school. This is a valid fear. Nevertheless, it should not prevent the use of amphetamines. Rather, it should lead to greater care in seeing to it that these drugs are prescribed only for those students who are hyperkinetic.

There is still another area of research with overtones of *1984* and *Brave New World*. Embryos are now being fertilized in vitro and grown to the multicelled stage(*23*). One hope of biochemists involved in this research is that, since a number of genetic defects originate in the improper splitting of the chromosomes at early stages, observation of cell division will lead to discovery of the cause of the improper splitting.

Joshua Lederberg, a Nobel Prize winning geneticist at Stanford University, has predicted that within ten to fifteen years a human being will be produced by "cloning"—a process in which a cell from a single human being could be made to give an exact infant duplicate of the adult who donates the cell(*24*). Cloning would allow for human mass production; science would be able to order up carbon copies of individuals now alive.

The ramifications of such a development, if Lederberg is right, are truly incalculable. The whole society might be transformed if genetic deficiencies could be eliminated by in vitro reproduction or by cloning.

Much research has been done in medical, biological, and chemical methods of shaping the mind. More is coming. Educators are just beginning to notice this research. It is the area of development which seems to offer greatest hope for the future of education. It is also an area of great danger, for all powerful discoveries are dangerous if misused. We are indeed on the verge of a brave new world.

References

1. Maggie Scarf, "Brain Researcher Jose Delgado Asks—What Kind of Humans Would We Like to Construct?," *The New York Times Magazine*, November 15, 1970, pp. 46–47ff.
2. Ibid., p. 170.
3. Gay Luce and Erik Peper, "Mind over Body, Mind over Mind," *The New York Times Magazine*, September 12, 1971, pp. 34–35ff.
4. Ibid., p. 134; also Harold M. Schmeck, Jr., "Control by Brain Studied as Way to Cure Body Ills," *The New York Times*, January 10, 1971, p. 1ff.

5. Luce and Peper, op. cit., p. 132.

6. Richard A. Knox, "Violence: As Likely from Faulty Brain as Faulty Upbringing," *The Boston Sunday Globe,* November 29, 1970, p. 4-A.

7. The film *Titicut Follies,* a documentary, shows the shocking neglect and abuse of those who are confined to such institutions.

8. Aaron M. Altschul, "Food: Proteins for Humans," *Chemical and Engineering News,* November 24, 1969, p. 70.

9. Rita Bakan, "Malnutrition and Learning," *Phi Delta Kappan,* June, 1970, p. 528.

10. Ibid., p. 529.

11. James D. Harmeling and Marshall B. Jones, "Birth Weights of High School Dropouts," *American Journal of Orthopsychiatry,* January, 1968, pp. 63–66.

12. Mark R. Rosenzweig, Edward L. Bennett, and Marian Cleeves Diamond, "Brain Change in Response to Experience," *Scientific American,* February, 1972, p. 29.

13. Earl Ubell, "Are We Spending Money for the Wrong Care?," *The New York Times,* February 28, 1971.

14. "Biomedical Enginneering Pace Slows Up," *Chemical and Engineering News,* October, 1970, p. 30.

15. Linus Pauling, *Vitamin C and the Common Cold.* San Francisco: W. H. Freeman and Company, 1970, pp. 20–22.

16. Bernard Agranoff, "Memory and Protein Synthesis," *Scientific American,* June 1967, p. 115.

17. Ibid., p. 120.

18. Ibid., p. 121.

19. "Small Peptide Induces Fear of Darkness in Rats," *Chemical and Engineering News,* January 11, 1971, p. 27.

20. An excellent description of the hyperactive child can be found in Mark A. Stewart's article, "Hyperactive Children," *Scientific American,* April, 1970, pp. 94–98.

21. Earl Ubell, " 'Pep Pills' to Quiet the Over-Peppy Child," *The New York Times,* March 14, 1971, p. E7.

22. Randall Richard, "Drugs for Children—Miracle or Nightmare?" *Providence Sunday Journal,* February 6, 1972, p. B-13.

23. R. G. Edwards and Ruth E. Fowler, "Human Embryos in the Laboratory," *Scientific American,* December, 1970, p. 45.

24. Ellen L. Sullivan, "Test-Tube Baby Cloud Gathers," *Boston Sunday Globe,* January, 1971, p. A9.

Operational Concepts

1. Educators would do well to keep abreast of the ongoing medical and biochemical research that has practical implications for learning.

2. Present precepts of learning and teaching could well be altered by the results of current chemical and biological research into the learning process.

3. Research suggests that certain types of biochemical intervention, such as the administration of amphetamines to hyperkinetic pupils, can modify classroom behavior and facilitate learning.

4. Genetic research has led scientists to a new understanding of human intelligence and its components.

5. It may be possible to teach students to control the tensions that inhibit learning by helping them to develop and use autonomic control techniques.

Implications

A great deal of attention has recently been given in the popular psychological magazines to the use of psychotherapeutic drugs. Not infrequently sensational hokum has been pondered along with legitimate scientific findings for the sake of literary sensationalism. This would hardly seem necessary, since the legitimate evidence itself is truly mind-boggling.

The research into biochemical educational intervention is fascinating and the prospects unquestionably exciting. Nevertheless, it seems clear that it will be a long time before researchers can develop techniques useful to educators. Moreover, even if such technology were available now, it is unlikely that they would be used in the present social and educational milieu. Nevertheless, it is to be hoped that curriculum designers, educational administrators, and theorists will follow the research developments with interest and an open mind.

Rose Mukerji

TV's Impact on Children: A Checkerboard Scene

Television holdouts are now a rare and endangered species. "We don't even have a TV set" was briefly the badge of the independent-minded spirit withstanding the ubiquitous boob tube or idiot box. More Americans have succumbed to its lure than to any other electrical appliance. Televison is now a pervasive and, thereby, a substantial element in our environment.

In our most judicious moments, we acknowledge that our worst fears have not materialized. The haunting possibility that television would pre-empt the teacher's role, and thus the teacher's job, has been laid to rest. The great expectation that television would so revolutionize education in its broadest sense that persistent problems of organized education would be solved has also not come to pass.

Although its potential educational power has not yet been realized, television has had an unmistakable impact on the lives of children. In trying to assess the nature and extent of this impact, researchers no longer have the luxury of studying "before and after TV." Children in the middle years (now in elementary school) have been weaned on television hearing, if not watching. In a brief period of twenty years, children in the early childhood years are now the second TV generation.

This discussion will attempt to sort out the significance of television, and to some extent film, as a medium for influencing learning, both cognitive and affective, and as an agent in the socializing process of children from age 3 to 12. To some extent, distinctions will be made between the two groups of children: early childhood (children 3 to 7) and middle childhood (8 to 12).

In considering TV's impact on children in the early and middle years, it is necessary to take into account all television: commercial, public, and educational or instructional; children's programs and adult programs which they watch; and the inescapable commercials of American television.

Reprinted from Rose Mukerji, "TV's Impact on Children: A Checkerboard Scene," *Phi Delta Kappan,* January 1976, pp. 316–321; by permission of the publisher.

There is a growing body of research on various aspects of television. Some studies concentrate on the relative teaching effectiveness of such television techniques as graphics and three-dimensional images. Other studies examine the effect of violence. Still others probe the influence of programs purporting to foster sound values and attitudes.

As a subject that people talk about a great deal, television has generated considerable empirical data about its influence on children. Educators, particularly, derive hypotheses about TV's impact from their strong professional base of learning and child development theory. It is, therefore, reassuring to find that, in summary, television in the lives of children is a complex scene. It is to be expected that contradictory judgments are being made about its influence.

COGNITIVE LEARNING

Early research efforts were designed to measure rather limited informational items, as scores from television and nontelevision instruction were compared. In summary, the findings indicate that television learning of this nature is equal to, or slightly superior to, nontelevision instruction(1).

More recently, considerable data have been gathered in systematic research in early childhood television learning related to the nationally and internationally broadcast "Sesame Street." Educational Testing Service research shows a positive relationship between amount and frequency of viewing and gains made on items tested: recognition, matching, and labeling of letters and numerals; identification of body parts; and classification by size, form, and function(2).

It is interesting to note that other independent research findings challenge the interpretation of results presented by ETS. Herbert Sprigle set out to test two hypotheses suggested by the Research Department of the Children's Television Workshop(3). Stated as goals, these were: (1) "Sesame Street" can prepare poverty-level children for first grade, and (2) it can substantially narrow the achievement gap between the poor and the middle-class child. Sprigle suggests that the "Sesame Street" curriculum did not reach these goals. He adds:

> The findings of the two-year study of "Sesame Street" graduates, the findings of the adult/child communication patterns of the program, the examination and evaluation of the philosophy, adult behavior, and attitudes toward learning and children fail to identify any redeeming features of "Sesame Street" as an educational program. The evidence suggests that the label "education" is misleading and deceptive.

One finds little if any controversy about the efficacy of television in enhancing learning for elementary or middle-age children. But there is considerable ferment about the role of television in concept development and cognitive learning by *young* children.

Studies and theory emphasize the centrality of the sensory style of learning among young children. As Milton Schwebel notes(4), the seminal work of Piaget makes clear that many diverse and related concrete experiences are required for young children to develop concepts about their world. He states further:

> It is absolutely necessary that learners have at their disposal concrete material experiences (and not merely pictures) and that they form their own hypotheses and verify them (or not verify them) themselves through their own active manipulation. The observed activities of others, including those of the teachers, are not formative of new organizations in the child.

It would be simplistic to place the entire burden of the learning process on direct experience. Certainly an important part is played by imitation of others, by stimulating suggestions gained from TV viewing, and by efforts to sort out ideas verbally in a social context. But development of concepts and understanding of relationships by the young child rely primarily on his active structuring in a complex, real environment.

Since much of a child's learning takes place through the medium of play, and since play is a young child's primary vehicle for forming the symbolic meaning of what he is experiencing, there is reason to be concerned about the long hours which some youngsters spend in front of the TV set. After all, the time spent watching television is taken from the time when a young child would otherwise play. According to Eleanore E. Maccoby, as long ago as the early days of TV in 1951, approximately one and a half hours a day shifted from active play to passive viewing(5). It gives one pause to think of the great increase in TV watching among young children today.

Although to this point the discussion has centered on cognitive learning, it should be noted that the separation of cognitive from affective learning is made only as a convenience for emphasis. Actually, all learning is basically entwined and has components of intellectuality and emotionality. With this understanding, we move on to consider the impact of television on affective learning.

AFFECTIVE LEARNING

Three dimensions of affective learning of particular import here are: (1) feelings and emotions, (2) modeling, and (3) fantasy–reality.

Feelings and Emotions

In the early days of television for children, little attention was given to consciously incorporating the subject matter of emotions and feelings, either directly or by implication. Not that this arena was considered un-important. On the contrary, it was generally agreed that, in the early years, children are trying to manage a crucial aspect of growth in which they move from powerfully egocentric behavior to that in which they begin to understand and to manage their feelings. The demands on them to cope with their feelings in ways acceptable to other people are great.

In response to the question, "Why not feelings and values in instructional television?" I have expressed the view that television *should* deal with a variety of emotions honestly(6). It should present important feelings such as fear and anxiety as well as those of delight and love. Television, as a channel for dramatic form, is uniquely suited to engaging children in the drama of life, just as outstanding children's books have succeeded in doing.

It is interesting to note that, about ten years ago, the 1966 Award for Excellence in Children's Programming was awarded by National Educational Television for a program in the "Roundabout" series titled "Living or Dead?" The citation spoke of the courage shown in dealing with such a delicate, emotional subject in straightforward, yet sensitive, terms for young viewers age 3 to 5. In an evaluation of this series, "Living or Dead?" (a very controversial program among adults) was mentioned most frequently by children as one they liked, referring to it by their own title, "The Dead Bird." Teachers and parents reported their surprise when many children incorporated the emotional content of the program into their play over an extended period of time.

A long-running early childhood series, "Mister Rogers' Neighborhood," has as its hallmark the position that children are best served when programming evokes the inner drama of children's feelings. Much of the success of this program rests on children's acceptance of a caring adult who demonstrates that feelings are mentionable as well as manageable.

Programs for elementary children have generally related directly to conventional subject matter while their designers explored more effective ways of presenting these subjects. One outstanding television series, "Inside/Out," is geared to health education but provides a "feelings" approach to the subject. It deals with day-to-day problems and emotions of children from *their* point of view. There are programs on common topics such as the bully, the joker, growing in responsibility and freedom, and competition between brothers and sisters. Included are topics that generally have been hush-hush in school, such as a death in the family, divorce, child abuse, and a crush on the teacher.

The viewers are involved emotionally as well as intellectually in the problems and situations encountered on television. Suggested follow-up discussions and activities make a direct tie between children's viewing and their own ideas, choices, values, and behavior. In the middle years, when the gang or peer group is a powerful molding force, group viewing has a particular advantage because it encourages the interplay of ideas and

654

positions so characteristic of upper-elementary youngsters. In dealing with feelings and emotions, one is naturally led to consider, also, how models of behavior are an integral part of affective learning.

Modeling

The significance of television for both younger and older children rests, in part, on its ability to provide models for their identification and imitation. However, they still need *live* people to help them develop as social beings and to serve as models for identification.

With middle and older children, we need to look at the models which blanket the television scene. What images do they identify with—the daredevil image of Evel Knievel? The flamboyant dress of the latest rock star? The impossible power of the Six-Million-Dollar Man? The "Kung Fu" hero? The action man on adult drama? One has to answer in the affirmative, and the answer is far from comforting.

In this connection, an ingenious study was carried out by Stanley J. Baron and Timothy P. Meyer. They posed a morally ambiguous problem and asked children to give their own solution. They also asked the children how their favorite television characters would solve it. There was extensive agreement between the two solutions, indicating strong identification with the television model. These findings concur with Urie Bronfenbrenner's theory that children are turning more and more to peers and television characters as behavior models for identification purposes(7).

On a more positive note, Maccoby states that the media provide a child with experience free from real-life controls, so that, in attempting to find solutions to a problem, he can try out various modes of action without risking injury or punishment(8).

Fantasy and Reality

At the same time that television provides models for identification and imitation, it also provides grist for a child's fantasy life. Fantasy is not the same for younger and older children. In the young child, it is intertwined with his developing mode of thinking. He is not able, consistently, to distinguish between fantasy and reality (often a disturbing condition to adults, who are fearful that a youngster is a chronic liar). In this uncertainty, he is only following a normal path of moving from a magical conception of the world to one which is more rational.

In its efforts to engage children's imagination, television has frequently added to a child's confusion by portraying live adults who talk to inanimate objects and expect them to reply. "Mister Rogers' Neighborhood" has, in recent productions, sought to make a clearer distinction between fantasy and reality. Children are invited to "pretend" as the scene shifts from the reality set to the "neighborhood of make-believe." The fact that young children often confuse fantasy and reality is no reason for adults to add further to their confusion through television programming.

When older children create fantasies in which they themselves are active, they do it quite consciously and without confusion. Television can stimulate fantasies which, in turn, may lead to creative and imaginative expression by youngsters. Special effects made possible by television technology offer new and unique visual stimuli which may expand viewers' perceptions. These children can also express their own fantasies through explorational use of the newer media. Television, along with other recreational forms such as drama, fiction, and film, provides a respite from reality. Certainly no one would gainsay the need for fantasy and its attendant aesthetic experience in one's life, provided, of course, that it *is* an aesthetic experience.

On the other hand, there is some indication that fantasies are related to an individual's unfulfilled needs and frustrations. Do fantasies merely reflect frustration, or do they assist in working out solutions to frustrations? There is danger when children retreat from real-life encounters into excessive television fantasy in order to avoid facing problems of reality.

Maccoby raises another possible danger, suggesting that externally controlled fantasy on television builds up motivation and satisfies it with relatively little delay(9). One thing that children must learn during the socialization process is to suffer delay in their satisfaction—to keep a motive at work over long periods of time. Maccoby is concerned that mass media experience may run counter to this training and build up habits of premature closure.

In summary, although there can be value in the fantasy nature of identification with television characters for younger and older children alike, they both need to balance their television fantasy encounters against real experiences with live people.

In this brief discussion of television and children's learning in the interrelated cognitive and affective domains, it is clear that the potential and real impact on young and middle children is a checkerboard of positive and negative influences. The same can be said of television as a socializing factor in children's lives.

SOCIALIZING EFFECT

Children's ideas about the social world and how people relate to each other are influenced by television. Their developing sense of social values also receives some input from television images. Since social behavior is affected by one's emerging ideas and values, it is only natural that, to some extent, television will have a socializing effect on children. Research supports this observation. Children who watch programs depicting interpersonal violence display increased aggressiveness, but television can also encourage socially valued behavior. This discussion will consider some of the research and current points of view concerning television violence and children, as well as prosocial television and children.

Violence

The question of the impact of television violence on children has been one of the most widely studied and discussed aspects of television. In the wake of the assassinations of Robert F. Kennedy and Martin Luther King and during the spread of campus riots, President Lyndon Johnson, in 1968, appointed a National Commission on the Causes and Prevention of Violence, headed by Milton Eisenhower. The commission report pointed out that television is not the sole culprit. However, it did conclude that violence on TV encourages violent forms of behavior and fosters moral and social values about violence in daily life which are unacceptable in a civilized society. In one memorable line, it said, "If TV is compared to a meal, programming containing violence clearly is the main course"(10).

In 1969, Senator John O. Pastore, chairman of the Senate Communications Subcommittee, set in motion the surgeon general's investigation—an exhaustive three-year study costing $1 million—dealing with the impact of televised violence on children. Robert M. Liebert, a psychologist at the State University of New York and a principal investigator in the study, found(11):

> The more violence and aggression a youngster sees on TV, regardless of his age, sex, or social background, the more aggressive he is likely to be in his own attitudes and behavior. The effects are not limited to youngsters who are in some way abnormal, but rather were found in large numbers of perfectly normal American children.

This conclusion arises from analysis of more than fifty studies covering the behavior of 10,000 children between the ages of 3 and 19.

Subsequent studies confirm the findings of the 1972 surgeon general's report. Leifer and Roberts, studying four groups of preschoolers with different treatments, found that young children apparently had difficulty extracting the themes of good or bad *consequences* of aggression and of good or bad *reasons* for aggression from the aggression and counteraggression in each program. Thus the *amount* of aggression in the program became the significant factor influencing their subsequent behavior(12).

Despite the surgeon general's report that there are now sufficient data to justify action, not everyone accepted the conclusion. Edith Efron, a contributing editor of *TV Guide*, speaks out strongly in opposition(13):

> The sex and violence pack is out again, baying with full throat, blaming crime on network plays. It is a tiresome fact that crime antedates network TV [and she goes back to Cain and Abel to prove it]. There is only one reason

657

today to pay the slightest attention to this claque, and that is: It is now brandishing "scientific" studies at us which allegedly "prove" that the sight of TV violence can indeed cause real-life violence.

Referring to the measured tones of the research report which deal in tendencies and qualifications rather than in absolutes and unequivocal proof, she adds:

> Now sensible people, facing this kind of intellectual nonsense, will simply put on their hats, go home, and settle down to a jolly evening with "Kojak," "Mannix," "Cannon," and company, who, if they have any virtue in common, [have] the capacity for lucid deduction.

Not unexpectedly, the specter of government censorship began to loom on the horizon. The cry of "civil liberties and censorship" was raised. Frederic Wertham, a psychiatrist known for his long-time concern with children and violence, says(14):

> The battle for civil liberties should not be fought on the backs of children. The argument that protecting children from harmful media exposure is an infringement of civil liberties has no historical foundation. . . . It has never happened in the history of the world that regulations to protect children—be they with regard to child labor, food, drink, arms, sex, publications, entertainment, or plastic toys—have played any role whatsoever in the abridgment of political or civil liberties for adults.

Violence on television continues to be a subject of concern to the television industry. The NBC network president states: "Our Broadcast Standards require that 'violence will be shown only to the extent appropriate to the legitimate development of theme, plot, or characterization. It should not be shown in a context which favors it as a desirable method for solving human problems, for its own sake, for shock effect, or to excess' "(15).

In 1975, network broadcasters, as members of the National Association of Broadcasters, ratified an agreement to introduce the "family hour' between 7 and 9 p.m. starting in September. According to Robert D. Wood, president of CBS/TV, it is "an attempt to program a specific part of our schedule so that the whole family can enjoy television together without being disturbed or embarrassed"(16).

This move has been received with some skepticism. It is perceived by most experts as a subtle carte blanche for "business as usual" or, as one writer put it, "gore as before." Despite the passage of years after the surgeon general's report, the 1974 annual report on television violence by George Gerbner and Larry Gross of the Annenberg School of Communications at the University of Pennsylvania states that levels of TV violence have remained unacceptably high(17). No wonder that skeptics question the impact of the cosmetic Bandaid of a two-hour family slot when radical surgery is required.

Television violence and children should continue to command our concern. However, we must also turn our attention to the potential for prosocial influence through television.

Prosocial

The early childhood years are ones for reaching out beyond the home and family into more complex and diversified relations with many unpredictable people. Underlying a child's ability to grow as a social person is his capacity for feeling, for empathy, for caring, and for identifying with others. Young children begin this difficult journey of social development; middle children continue it; adults pursue it the rest of their lives.

Can the viewing of prosocial television by children influence them toward prosocial attitudes and behavior? Empirical data in this area are being corroborated by several research studies. For example, regular "Sesame Street" programs showing children and adults sharing and helping each other were used to compare prosocial behavior of children who watched the program with those who did not. It was found that the viewers were more likely to cooperate and share than children who did not view these segments(*18*).

In another study with nursery children, Lynette Friedrich found that(*19*)

> systematic viewing of "Mister Rogers' Neighborhood" effected significant changes in their free play behavior in two areas of personality development: (1) self-regulatory behavior—children increased in task persistence and showed greater ability to carry out responsibility without adult intervention; and (2) prosocial interpersonal behavior—children showed increased cooperative play, increased ability to express feelings, and increased sympathy and help for others. The changes in prosocial interpersonal behavior were significant for children from lower-social-class homes. The increase in self-regulatory behavior was found in the entire sample.

Fostering prosocial attitudes and behavior in children who inescapably live in a multicultural country and world is an urgent responsibility for television. In a recent study commissioned by the Corporation for Public Broadcasting under the auspices of the Advisory Council of National Organizations, one of two underlying recommendations was as follows:

> The Corporation for Public Broadcasting should recognize and support the principle of cultural pluralism which is rooted in our common concerns as humans as well as the differences which enhance the strength and diversity of the American people.

It is gratifying to note that progress has been made in educational programs for children in the past ten years in support of the principle and value of cultural pluralism. An early entry on the national scene was "Roundabout," which had as its central, sustaining character the realistic young black, Jim Jeffers. The "Ripples" series for younger children and the "Inside/Out" series for middle children sustained multicultural values throughout. "Big Blue Marble" is a recent series for older children which is made up of segments showing interesting children's activities in various countries. Both "Sesame Street" and "The Electric Company" feature interracial and intercultural casts.

Underlying the multicultural content and multiethnic casts of all of these programs is the assumption that these qualities will help develop positive attitudes toward various races and cultures among viewers. This assumption has received some support from recent research. In national studies, children who watched "Sesame Street" for two years had more positive attitudes toward school and members of various races than did children who watched less(20).

Two nationally distributed current series have brought a bilingual, multicultural approach to children's television. They are "Villa Alegre," produced in California, and "Carrascolendas," from Texas. In both cases, the languages used are English and Spanish. "Carrascolendas" states as its principal objective(21):

> To cultivate in each child an awareness of the contributions of his own and other cultures to America, and to provide each child with a rich reper-toire of living skills that can enhance his potential for optimally effective living in a multicultural America.

While there is progress in educational and public programming for children, commitment to prosocial themes and multicultural valuing cannot be said to characterize television in general. Commercial television has been severely criticized for its distorted picture of real life. Yet this is what children watch. With what effect?

Leifer says(22):

> TV, whether or not it accurately reflects our social system, does contrib-ute to forming this social system. At the very least, it helps to socialize a new generation of children into an already existing pattern. To the extent that TV does not reflect reality, it socializes children into a fictitious social system.

Stereotyping

It is to be expected that any medium which must telegraph characters, a story line, and a resolution in a short half-hour or hour will rely on stereotypes and caricatures for quick identification. However, when we examine television stereotypes, we see how prejudicial they can be. For example(23):

660

White Americans make up the overwhelming majority of TV characters. Indians and Africans are barely represented. The typical role of Italians and blacks is an insult to all of us, not only to these groups. And what about the roles of men and women? The TV screen is a sexist screen where the man is not only more evident, but also superior. . . . Working women are more often victims of aggression than married women.

And who are the models of success on TV? The clever, highly unorthodox lawyer . . . the brutal police officer . . . the "private eye" operating outside the law. Ordinary workers are frequently depicted as coarse and stupid, there for laughs.

We object to these distortions; we deplore this stereotyping. At least we say we do. Yet there is a disturbing question that remains to haunt us: Why are these television shows so popular? Why do they continue and multiply season after season? Do we, in our silent hearts, cherish these stereotypes and the excitement of forbidden violence? Are we, by our actions, adding to the negative impact on the checkerboard scene of children and television?

CHILDREN AS PRODUCERS

So far, we have been focusing on children as consumers of television fare, pointing up the tremendous influence, both positive and negative, it has on them. However, there is another facet which deserves attention: children as producers of material using the media of television and film.

Children have traditionally used art media to express who they are and to know more deeply who they are. Too often, in restrictive school settings, they have failed(24).

Many children are, unfortunately, turned off by their stifling experiences or unfortunate failures with traditional art media. With other media, they have a second chance. Technology has opened channels for children to capture their unique expressions in newer media. Less encumbered by stereotypes, these media can rekindle a child's eagerness to express himself and thereby continue forming himself with a conscious sense of affirmation.

Children seem intuitively at home with the unique character of television and film—its all-at-once sound and movement without barriers of time and distance. Perhaps they "know" these dimensions because they are so similar to their own play, which readily defies and controls the limits of time and space.

Having grown up with television, it is not surprising that children all over the country respond enthusiastically by contributing skits, riddles, films, and other "ZOOM-ies" to the unusual children's series, "ZOOM," which incorporates them into the programs. The on-camera children also play a significant role in putting together this nationally distributed public television show—no small accomplishment for middle and older children.

Within a school setting, the Children's Video Theatre has developed a project for child-created television in the inner city(25). Programs were produced by fifth- and sixth-graders and were shown monthly on local Community Antenna Television (CATV). The project reaffirmed that engaging poor achievers in video production can improve academic performance, especially in the language arts.

The demands of television production touch all curriculum areas. Unlike other forms of expression, television and film are group enterprises, requiring social skills and understandings as well as intellectual and aesthetic ones. To conceive, execute, and evaluate anything as complex as television or film making requires children to tap and develop all of their resources. Planning, researching, recording, script writing, making storyboards, learning techniques for handling the technology, scouting and "seeing" locations, interviewing, communicating, selecting, editing, designing, constructing, titling, recording sound and music, coordinating efforts under pressure, adapting, revising, persisting, and sharing the successes and disappointments—all of these come into play in a single television or film production.

Although impressed by its potential, those who have worked with children and media are, nevertheless, aware that it is no easy road leading from failure to success. But, as one creative teacher and her film associate, carrying on a project with sixteen children age 5 to 9 (nine of whom were considered failures in school), reported(26):

> As we had suspected, the camera turned out to be an excellent tool. It served not as an end in itself, but rather as a means to help "open up" the children and give them a nonverbal, nonthreatening means to begin to perceive themselves as more worthy and to see themselves in relation to their world; a means to look again, observe, question, differentiate, clarify, and, in the broadest sense, become more effective learners.

These few examples underscore the power of direct involvement in the creative arts, in this case television and film, as an essential means by which children can more fully develop their human potential. Through such involvement, they become not just pawns to be pushed onto positive or negative squares on the checkerboard—they become important players.

CONCLUSION

The dynamics of the media, and television in particular, are still in a healthy state of flux and development. We are nowhere near approaching a final score where television and children are concerned. That television has a tremendous influence on children is clear. Whether that impact is more positive than negative depends, to some extent, on the determination with which concerned adults help to tilt the balance in favor of children.

References

1. Godwin C. Chu and Wilbur Schramm, *Learning from Television: What the Research Says* (Washington, D.C.: National Association of Educational Broadcasters, 1967).
2. Gerald S. Lesser, *Children and Television: Lessons from "Sesame Street"* (New York: Random House, 1974).
3. Herbert A. Sprigle, "Who Wants To Live on Sesame Street?" *Young Children,* December, 1972.
4. Milton Schwebel and Jane Raph, eds., *Introduction to Piaget in the Classroom* (New York: Basic Books, 1973).
5. Eleanore E. Maccoby, "Television: Its Impact on School Children," *Public Opinion Quarterly,* Fall, 1951.
6. Stanley J. Baron and Timothy P. Meyer, "Imitation and Identification," *AV Communication Review,* Summer, 1974.
7. Urie Bronfenbrenner, *Two Worlds of Childhood* (New York: Russell Sage, 1970).
8. Maccoby, op. cit.
9. Eleanore E. Maccoby, "Why Do Children Watch Television?" *Public Opinion Quarterly,* Fall, 1954.
10. Neil Hickey, "Does TV Violence Affect Our Society? YES," *TV Guide,* June 14–20, 1975.
11. Robert M. Liebert, John M. Neale, and Emily S. Davidson, *The Early Window: Effects of Television on Children and Youth* (New York: Pergamon Press, 1973).
12. Aimee Dorr Leifer and Donald F. Roberts, "Children's Responses to Television Violence," in J. P. Murray, E. A. Rubenstein, and G. A. Comstock, eds., *Television and Social Behavior,* vol. 2 (Washington, D.C.: Government Printing Office, 1972).
13. Edith Efron, "Does TV Violence Affect Our Society? NO," *TV Guide,* June 14–20, 1975.
14. Frederic Wertham, in Hickey, op. cit.
15. "Violence!" *TV Guide,* June 14–20, 1975.
16. Ibid.
17. Hickey, op. cit.
18. D. Lynn McDonald and F. Leon Paulson, *Evaluation of "Sesame Street" Social Goals: The Interpersonal Strategies of Cooperation, Conflict Resolution, and Different Perspectives,* ERIC Document ED 052824, April, 1971

19. Lynette K. Friedrich, "The Use of Television in Early Childhood Education," proceedings of the International Council of Educational Media, Munich, 1974.

20. Gerry A. Bogatz and Samuel Ball, *The Second Year of "Sesame Street": A Continuing Evaluation* (Princeton, N.J.: Educational Testing Service, 1971).

21. "Carrascolendas" Television Project, KLRN-TV, Austin, Texas, 1975.

22. Aimee Dorr Leifer, Neal J. Gordon, and Sherryl Browne Graves, "Children's Television: More than Mere Entertainment," *Harvard Educational Review,* May, 1974.

23. Liebert, Neale, and Davidson, op. cit.

24. Rose Mukerji, "Creating and Becoming," in *Children Are Centers for Understanding Media* (Washington, D.C.: Association for Childhood Education International, 1973).

25. John LeBaron and Louise Kanus, "Child-Created Television in the Inner City," *Elementary School Journal,* April, 1975.

26. Roberta Harris, "A Child's-Eye View," in *Children Are Centers for Understanding Media* (Washington, D.C.: Association for Childhood Education International, 1973).

Operational Concepts

1. Children's ideas about the social world and human interaction are strongly influenced by their television experience.

2. Although television viewing may stimulate imaginal thought, perceptions derived solely from television can be deleterious when not balanced with adequate real experience.

3. In view of the amount of television to which children typically are exposed and the resulting impact upon their attitudes and beliefs, it is of great importance that television programs be designed to foster prosocial behavior.

4. Since childrens' values are influenced by experiences in and out of school, the curriculum must take external events into account.

Implications

Although the extent is not yet completely understood, it seems certain that the overall influence of television on children is substantial. As long as this remains the case, the school must take steps to counteract potentially harmful consequences. First, the effort to protect children from excessive exposure to crime, violence, and other possibly harmful viewing must be sustained. In addition, parents, in whose hands control ultimately rests, must be cautioned against a lackadaisical attitude regarding what they permit their children to view. Third, at least some provision should be made in the formal curriculum to counterbalance the undesirable television influences to which children are regularly exposed. Insofar as prosocial behavior is already a major objective of schooling, some such counterbalancing activity occurs as a matter of course. Nonetheless, sensitive teachers will want to take advantage of opportune moments in the course of their regular instruction to go beyond the existing provisions and reaffirm the tenets of ethical behavior.

James J. Gallagher

Problem-Solving Strategies for the Gifted

TEACHING FOR DISCOVERY

The work of Piaget, well-known child psychologist, has had an increasing influence on American psychologists and, through them, on educational psychology. His major point of interest to us is his concept of stages of intellectual development. He believes that children's thought processes and operations go through distinct changes at various age levels. These levels are shown in Table 1.

Let us suppose that we have four children ages 3, 7, 10, and 15, all of whom are of average intellectual ability. What would Piaget's stages mean in terms of their reaction to various situations—for example, watching a tea kettle whistle?

TABLE 1 Stages of Intellectual Development

APPROPRIATE AGE LEVEL	THOUGHT PROCESS
1½ to 4 years	Development of symbolic and preconceptual thought.
4 to 7 or 8 years	Intuitive thought leading to the threshold of the "operation."
7 or 8 to 11 or 12 years	Concrete operations are organized. These are groupings of thought concerning objects that can be manipulated or known through the senses.
11 or 12 years through adolescence	Formal thought is perfected and "its groupings characterize the completion of reflective intelligence."

SOURCE: From J. Piaget. Piaget's theory. In P. Mussen (ed.), *Carmichael's Manual of Child Psychology*. Chicago: Rand McNally, 1970, pp. 703–732.

Reprinted from James J. Gallagher, *Teaching the Gifted Child*, © 1975; by permission of Allyn and Bacon, Inc., Boston.

The 3-year-old might say, "It is singing a song to me," thus revealing the egocentric and preconceptual thinking of his age. The 7-year-old might say, "When the kettle is on the fire and it has been there for a while, then the kettle begins to whistle." One can see in this statement the beginnings of logical association, but further inquiry would probably reveal that the essentials of the situation still escape the child at this age.

The 10-year-old might say, "The stove heats the water, which makes steam which pushes against the opening and makes the kettle whistle." This certainly makes more logical sense, but it still lacks depth and larger organization. The 15-year-old might say, "Heat causes expansion of the molecules and thus an increase in pressure." This is generalizing the situation beyond the immediate and the observable, and is the mark of the adult intelligence.

Naturally, the kind of response a child gives depends not only upon his age but also on his intellectual ability and his previous experiences with the situation.

It has been a common observation of American educators and psychologists, as well as of Piaget, that children below the chronological age of 10 or 11 cannot produce the formal structure of thought required for the *traditional* exposition of complex mathematical or physical concepts. This has led to the erroneous conclusion that, since formal thought cannot be elicited at a young age, the ideas themselves should not be presented to children before the age of 12, or thereabouts.

Advocates of new curricular programs have pointed out that, although young children cannot *produce* the formal language necessary for exposition, they can effectively *operate* on the ideas. The results of this line of reasoning are sometimes quite amazing. They lead to teaching primary-aged children the elements of set theory, geometric theorems, and complex physical concepts, such as the attraction of bodies and time–space continua.

This is possible because the children are not being asked to present the material in logical structure but, rather, they are enabled to operate on the information through problem solving. Important generalizations can be introduced in social studies and language arts in the same fashion. It remains a possibility that different types of instruction might improve the young gifted child's capacity even for formal logic.

Another goal of those who propose the use of the discovery method is to train gifted children to adopt a set or attitude about the search for knowledge itself. The proponents complain that the average textbook is not organized according to the way in which the scientist or scholar actually performed the experiments or thought through the problems. Textbooks are usually arranged in logical order, proceeding systematically from one point to the next, whereas the actual thinking processes of the scientist or scholar himself are often chaotic, intuitive, and occasionally incoherent. By presenting material in a carefully organized structure, it is possible for the student to gain understanding of that structure without being equipped with the set or attitude necessary to the discovery of further knowledge.

Learning or Mimicry?

Too much emphasis cannot be placed upon the importance of the set or attitude that the teacher establishes in students by the manner in which he approaches a topic. Two major teaching strategies can be identified by observing in most classrooms. A teacher can take the general attitude that "Truth in all its ramifications is yet to be discovered." The alternative strategy is presented by the teacher with the set or attitude that "Truth will be revealed to you in due time." Such strategies, presented day after day over a considerable period of time, can steer the students in predictable directions. If the teacher holds to the second strategy—that truth will be unfolded step by step—the natural student strategy would be to find out what it is that the teacher has in mind. Thus, the student's main job would be to get inside the structure that the teacher has in mind, rather than to attempt to build a structure of his own.

However, student strategy is quite different if the first strategy is adopted. If the truth is still considered relatively elusive, then it is up to the student, as much as to the teacher, to discover as much about this phenomenon as possible. In the process of doing so, the student is forced to develop a structure or organization of the subject himself, rather than merely to attempt to mimic the teacher's structure.

Discovery in Science

Teachers and educators of gifted children must come face to face with the central fact that one of their goals is to stimulate an attitude or approach toward the world, as much as to provide an infusion of knowledge of specific content. If teaching methods and the educational program are effective, one would expect the gifted child to come forth from that program not only with large bodies of information but with an enthusiasm for "questing," for searching out new knowledge. Somehow in this experience, a child should gain a love for the "hunt," a desire to search for knowledge with the same kind of enthusiasm that prior generations of youngsters had for the hunt for wild animals.

How can this attitude or motivation be engendered by the teacher? There are strong suspicions that certain types of teacher behavior in the elementary schools are not very conducive toward the building of such an attitude. It has been found that, in typical classrooms, teachers will ask from eight to ten times as many questions as will the children. Theoretically, it should be the children who are searching, questioning, and inquiring into new ideas. Should it be the teacher's role to be continually testing the extent of knowledge of the children?

The essence of *guided discovery*, then, can be stated in the following points:

1. The teacher has in mind a general principle that has to be learned by the student. This is an essential and limiting requirement in itself. It means that the teacher has already conceptualized, in his own mind, the topic to be discussed.
2. The teacher then constructs examples, each one of which would illustrate some elements of the concept.
3. These problems are then presented to the students with the number of examples varying according to the needs of the particular group. In some instances, one or two examples might be sufficient, whereas, in others, it might demand maximum ingenuity and patience to illustrate the concept.
4. Students are encouraged to demonstrate their understanding through the application of ideas or problem solving, rather than through verbalization. The case against verbalization is based on two factors: (a) too early verbalization of the principle would tend to short-circuit the other students' discoveries, and (b) too early verbalization tends to be poorly stated, and organized in such a form that attention must then be paid to the preciseness of the verbalization itself, often resulting in loss of the concept and its meaning.

All this presupposes a teacher flexible enough to veer from the point he had in mind to others to which the students' inquiry might lead. It matters little in what order the anchor points of a conceptual structure of mathematics or social studies are discovered, so long as they are all present at the end.

The prime limiting factors in the successful use of this technique are the intellectual flexibility of the teacher and the teacher's own conceptualization of a content area. Fortunately, both these factors are trainable to a large extent. It seems entirely likely that increased knowledge of an area in itself can lead to increased flexibility in the teacher, just as lack of knowledge can lead to rigidity.

Evaluation of the Discovery Method

Kagan presents four major arguments in favor of the discovery method as a desirable teaching technique(*1*):

1. Studies of both animals and young children indicate that the more active involvement required of the organism the greater the likelihood of learning. . . . A major advantage of the discovery strategy is that it creates arousal and as a result maximal attention.
2. Because the discovery approach requires extra intellectual effort, the value

of the task is increased. . . . It is reasonable to assume that activities become valuable to the degree to which effort is expended in their mastery.

3. The inferential or discovery approach is likely to increase the child's expectancy that he is able to solve different problems autonomously. . . .

4. The discovery approach gives the child more latitude and freedom and removes him from the submissive posture ordinarily maintained between teacher and child.

These arguments are based on solid educational and psychological principles. Nevertheless, it would be more reassuring if there were direct experimental evidence as to the value of the technique.

The discovery method, despite its inherent attractiveness, is not without its cost. Perhaps the largest cost of all is that of *time* and increased teacher preparation. Guided discovery means careful teacher preparation in choosing the examples to be used to attain the concepts. In addition, there is the time required for the student to follow the path to the expected discovery. Thus, a principle that could be quickly stated, along with several cogent examples by the instructor in a formal presentation, must be evoked from the students through the discovery method, which might take four or five times as long. Eventually, the decision has to be made as to whether the gain obtained is worth the cost involved.

In the author's opinion, the discovery method generates obvious enthusiasm and excitement in preadolescent children that is not obtained through more formal presentation. The discovery that is useful, however, is not random discovery but the discovery within an organized and structured framework that the teacher already has in mind. This does not mean that the children will not come up with some surprising associations that even the teacher had not considered, but it is important that the teacher of gifted children—those who most likely will be dealing in the world of thought in their adult life—be able to use this pedagogical technique effectively whenever it seems appropriate.

Reference

1. J. Kagan, "Impulsive and Reflective Children: The Significance of Conceptual Tempo," in J. Krumboltz (ed.), *Learning and the Educational Process,* Chicago: Rand McNally, 1965, pp. 133–161.

Operational Concepts

1. Although children below the age of 10 generally are not able to deal with the formal structure of complex concepts, they can make constructive use of the ideas inherent in these concepts.

2. A major advantage of the problem-solving activities and of learning through discovery is that the learner acquires a taste for inquiry and a predilection for "searching out" answers.

3. The curriculum must not only expose children to a body of essential information, it must also provide repeated opportunities for the raising of questions, the exploring of new ideas, and the seeking of solutions to problems.

4. In using inductive teaching and fostering student problem-solving capacities, the teacher should look for evidence of effective reasoning rather than for any one particular response from the student.

5. Problem-solving activity tends not only to deepen the student's conceptual understanding of an idea, but also to nurture a capacity for independent, self-directed learning.

Implications

The advantages of discovery learning—over the excessive emphasis upon factual accumulation characteristic of most traditional curricula—have been widely discussed in the professional literature for more than a decade. Yet when present practice is scrutinized, one is led to conclude that the discovery has been talked about to a far greater extent than it has been applied. For this reason, Gallagher's statement, although familiar to many readers, has been included in the *Handbook*.

Efforts to improve the curriculum and to take advantage of new research evidence have been hampered, on the one hand, by the traditional resistance to change, and, on the other, by the inclination of advocates to distort a useful idea into a full-blown fetish.

In the curriculum, as in life itself, balance is crucial. A program of instruction based upon effective learning alone would fail to serve all our purposes, just as a program that belabored memorization, drill, and rote learning to the exclusion of problem-solving activity would deprive the learner of essential intellectual development. What is to be avoided, consequently, is the trap of "either–or".

The student cannot effectively attack a problem without an understanding of the facts involved. Similarly, if the facts learned are not put to use in subsequent problem-solving efforts, their potential value is wasted. To sum up, then, the healthy curriculum provides times and places for inductive as well as deductive learning experiences.

James Bosco

Behavior Modification Drugs and the Schools: The Case of Ritalin

Over the last ten years, various drugs have been increasingly used to modify the behavior of hyperactive children. Of these, methylphenidate hydrochloride (Ritalin) is perhaps the most common. The trend raises new and complex problems for school administrators and teachers. As more is understood about brain chemistry and the neurophysiology of learning, new drug interventions will be possible. The educational, social, and ethical problems will intensify.

The purpose of this article is to present educationally relevant information about Ritalin and to suggest the implications for school system policy and procedures.

ORIGIN, NATURE, AND USE

Methylphenidate hydrochloride was patented in 1950 by the CIBA Pharamaceutical Company under the name Ritalin. Ritalin is classified as a stimulant and is related to the amphetamines. In addition to its use with hyperkinesis, Ritalin in tablet form is indicated for the treatment of drug-induced lethargy, mild depression, and apathetic or withdrawn senile behavior, according to the *Physician's Desk Reference*. As the list of uses indicates, although classified as a stimulant, Ritalin produces a different effect on children than on adults. The action of the drug on brain chemistry is not fully understood, but it has been known since 1937 that stimulants can produce a "subduing effect" on children(*1*). Ritalin falls under Schedule II of the Controlled Substances Act, the most restrictive schedule for marketed drugs, which limits the quantity and the number of refills which can be prescribed, to provide close monitoring of use.

One of the problems attending the use of Ritalin is the diagnosis of hyperkinesis. There is a considerable volume of literature on the etiology of

Reprinted from James Bosco, "Behavior Modification Drugs and the Schools: The Case of Ritalin," *Phi Delta Kappan,* March 1975; by permission of the publisher.

hyperkinesis and problems in diagnosing it, yet much remains unknown. In general, the major symptoms of the hyperkinetic syndrome are "an increase of purposeless physical activity and a significantly impaired span of focused attention which may generate other conditions such as disturbed mood and behavior within the home, at play with peers, and in the schoolroom," according to a Department of Health, Education, and Welfare pamphlet published in 1971.

The hyperactive syndrome, while found in adults, is of considerably more concern when exhibited by school-aged children. Mark Stewart says:

> Many adults exhibit the same cluster of symptoms [associated with hyperkinesis in children]. In adult life, however, certain of the basic characteristics—high energy, aggressiveness, lack of inhibition—may be helpful in one's work, whereas in childhood, when one is required to sit still at a desk and concentrate on studies for long periods, the restlessness associated with the syndrome may be a great handicap and give rise to severe problems(2).

Other experts(3) contend that the problems which lead to the use of a Ritalin regime often (if not generally) occur within the school setting. The close relationship between the school environment and the use of Ritalin is demonstrated by the procedure some physicians follow of discontinuing medication during the summer vacation.

EFFECT ON SCHOLASTIC, SOCIAL VARIABLES

Since children are frequently treated with Ritalin because of behavior disorders observed in the school setting, one of the significant issues is drug effect on scholastic and behavioral variables. Empirical information concerning such variables has been furnished by a number of researches. Studies have been reported using subjects of average and above-average IQ as well as below-normal intelligence. A variety of behavior, aptitude, and perceptual-motor tests has been used, with some tests used in more than one investigation.

These studies reveal different patterns of significant effects of the drug. While there is reason to believe that the use of Ritalin for hyperkinetic children may have an effect on social variables (e.g., teachers' ratings), the studies do not provide a clear understanding of ways in which the drug affects scholastic variables under different conditions. Variability with regard to differences in diagnosis, age, sex, IQ, or severity of illness confounds the analyses. Multivariate analyses which would be most useful in the design of studies of the effects of Ritalin have not generally been employed.

The attitude of physicians toward the drug is influenced strongly by their clinical experience with it. It is not uncommon for the physician to receive reports from parents of a dramatic abatement in the scholastic or behavioral problems of the child. These responses may provide compelling evidence about the drug for the physician, yet such subjective and unsystematic information cannot supply the needed rigorous analysis of drug effect which is furnished by properly designed research.

THE SOCIAL CONTEXT

Attitudes and beliefs of other individuals significant to the child (e.g., parents, teachers, peers) may be salient factors in treatment programs using Ritalin. Its use is a social as well as a medical phenomenon. Therefore, it is reasonable to expect that interactions with significant people in the child's environment may complicate or facilitate treatment. A 1971 HEW conference report on the use of stimulant drugs in the treatment of behaviorally disturbed young school children expressed concern about the child being stigmatized as "stupid," an "emotional cripple," or a "drug-taker"(4). This report also presented broad guidelines for the manner in which physicians, school personnel, and parents should cooperate in treatment programs.

Teachers and administrators may differ sharply in their attitudes toward stimulants. A national poll of superintendents (N = 700; response, 40 percent of sample) indicated little approval (6 percent) for the use of behavior modification drugs in 1971. Forty-eight percent indicated disapproval, and the remaining 46 percent were uncertain(5). If the findings of this study were valid and attitudes have not changed, administrators are not generally favorable toward the use of such drugs. (Given the low return and lack of information about the survey design, the validity is questionable.)

In a recent study by Stanley Robin and James Bosco, a 20 percent sample of regular (nonspecial education) elementary-level teachers in a large Midwestern city school system was studied. These data revealed that teachers were generally favorable to the use of the drug. There was little strong opposition, such as was demonstrated in 1971 by administrators. Further, almost all of these teachers (97 percent) claimed to know what Ritalin was, and two-thirds had one or more children in their class on a Ritalin regime. They had little accurate information about the drug, however, and there was no consensus concerning their function in treatment programs involving Ritalin. A third of them approved a passive role, another third believed in an active and cooperative role, and the other third gave miscellaneous and uncertain responses. This study suggests that allegations of widespread "pushing" of the drug by teachers are unfounded. More problematic is the lack of consensus concerning ethical teacher practice relative to the use of stimulant drugs and the lack of communication and cooperation among physicians, teachers, and parents of children using stimulants.

James Bosco

IMPLICATIONS FOR EDUCATION

The use of Ritalin has several implications for education which require increased consideration within the educational community. I shall offer and discuss four major propositions.

1. *The use of Ritalin or other stimulants with hyperkinetic children is an issue with explosive potential within many school systems.*

Schools and teachers are usually central in the controversy on stimulant drug usage. Legally, the responsibility for prescribing a drug falls upon the physician, but the controversy created by drug usage for hyperkinesis has generally been focused on teachers. A 1973 article in *Time* titled "Classroom Pushers" is indicative. It began as follows(6):

> About five years ago, teachers heard the welcome news that small doses of amphetamines and other psychoactive drugs could turn hyperactive children into willing learners. As a result, an estimated 300,000 children are now taking these drugs—and many should not be.

Even though the 300,000 children mentioned in *Time* received a drug through the use of a physician's prescription, the article links drug treatment to teachers. The fact that physicians are susceptible to inappropriate pressure from teachers elevates the importance of proper conduct on the part of teachers and other school personnel. Fairly or unfairly, when physicians accede to pressure from school people regarding drug treatment, the wrath of the community and the media falls more heavily on the teacher and the schools than on the physician or the medical profession.

The time for school administrators and boards of education to remedy error is before battle lines are drawn. While this makes sense both educationally and politically, there is a tendency to let "sleeping dogs lie," to avoid initiating activities which focus community attention on a problem.

Barrett Scoville, acting director of the Food and Drug Administration's Division of Neuropharmacological Drug Products, said recently, "Psychotropic drugs with abuse potential which are given to children present as complicated a mixture of loaded issues as exists in the field of drug evaluation"(7). There is little wonder that incidents related to stimulant drug use erupt in school systems. The ingredients for an explosion exist within many U.S. schools. We can expect additional eruptions if nothing is done.

2. *The role of school personnel is extremely important in screening and referring hyperkinetic children, yet clearer definition of the role is required.*

Hyperkinesis is not a figment of the imagination of perverse physicians or incompetent teachers; it does exist. The diagnosis of hyperkinesis, however, remains a difficult problem. The way in which a teacher sets norms

677

for behavior affects the amount of hyperactivity she sees. Another complicating factor is that the pattern of behavior we call hyperactive may be produced by factors other than minimal brain dysfunction: boredom, poor teaching, etc.

The problem of diagnosis was demonstrated in a study reported by Thomas Kenny et al. in 1971(8). They reported that an appreciable number (58 percent) of children referred for treatment as hyperactive may not be. Further, even with comprehensive diagnostic procedures there will be some disagreement among diagnosticians. (In the Kenny study, 29 percent of the children referred for hyperactivity were diagnosed by some but not all of the three diagnosticians who examined them. In 58 percent of the cases, the child was judged to be not hyperactive by any of the staff members who examined him.)

Given the complexities of diagnosis, medical authorities such as Gordon Millichap and Leon Eisenberg(9) have stressed the need for systematic diagnostic procedures involving physical, neurological, and psychological tests. Only through careful diagnostic procedures is it possible to identify situations where drugs are appropriate. Clearly, the physician is the person best trained to make such a determination.

Since hyperkinesis is not easy to diagnose, we were disconcerted to learn that 96 percent of the teachers in one of our studies(10) felt they could identify the syndrome in their classrooms. Teachers seem overly confident about their abilities to identify hyperkinetic children. More preservice and inservice instruction for teachers on the distinction between pathological and normal behavior is needed.

We found that approximately 70 to 80 percent of teachers inform parents, the principal, and the school specialist when they recognize a hyperactive child. The way teachers present the information to parents is quite important. An appreciable number recommend contact with a physician and mention the possibility or desirability of Ritalin usage. Even cautious and qualified statements by a teacher, if they include a drug name, are undesirable and dangerous. Yet we should not be surprised to encounter inappropriate behavior on the part of teachers if the standards for behavior are not clarified and disseminated. At the same time, it is important that teachers not be made so cautious that they neglect to call parents' attention to behaviors in the classroom which may require a visit to a physician.

3. *Teachers and school authorities need to have a clearer understanding about their responsibilities with regard to children on a stimulant drug regime.*

Confusion about the role of teachers and the relationships among parents, physicians, and teachers in Ritalin treatment has created a complex but understandable problem, partly because the problem is unprecedented. Never before has such extensive use been made of a drug to treat a condition which often is primarily evident and primarily dysfunctional within the classroom. The problems are complex because the boundaries of the medical and educational professions are considerably more blurred in this situation than they are when school children are being treated for other medical problems such as heart disease, diabetes, or leukemia. Moreover, values in the society concerning psychoactive drugs (as well as the proper use of medication in general) impinge upon the problem.

Some states have enacted legislation to govern what teachers can and cannot do with regard to drugs administered during school hours. Information about legal standards for teacher conduct should be disseminated to teachers, parents, and physicians. Beyond the legal requirements, the ethical responsibilities of teachers in drug treatment programs require additional clarification, since drug treatment of hyperkinesis entails both medical and educational expertise.

Along the same lines, channels of communication among teachers, parents, and physicians need to be developed. Since treatment is frequently sought because of a problem which is manifested within the school, and because the drug which is used metabolizes in such a way that its action is mainly observable during school hours, teachers have a unique and important role in monitoring the effect of treatment. Differences in customs and norms of the educational profession and the medical profession hinder communication. The logistics and substance of cross-professional communication need to be developed. Factors such as the status differential between teachers and physicians, the differences in training and perspective, and the way each professional works affect communication. Edward L. Birch's recommendation for the establishment of a school district task force with representation from the medical and educational professions as well as from parents deserves consideration(*11*). Such a task force could furnish guidelines for teachers on the proper procedures to be followed upon recognizing a child they believe to be hyperkinetic. Also, procedures for communication about drug effects on the child's work in the classroom could be devised.

Since children may be stigmatized if put on a drug regime, attention should be directed to the problem in teacher training and inservice programs. (This suggestion is not meant to disparage concern about the increase of drug usage within our society. A teacher or administrator may be concerned with this problem without forming an attitude toward particular children on Ritalin.)

4. *Education should contribute to the elimination of hyperactivity.*

Although educators are not usually qualified to explore the medical aspects of hyperkinesis, they are qualified to investigate the organizational and curricular characteristics of the educational system which may promote hyperactivity. There has been considerable speculation about the extent to which teacher practices and the structure of schools promote hyperkinesis. The social climate of some classrooms and the practices of some teachers

679

may contribute to the development of symptoms like those which result from minimal brain damage. If such a relationship does exist, modification of classroom management is an obvious must.

CONCLUSIONS

In conclusion, I would like to emphasize several specific recommendations.

1. Some states have enacted legislation regulating the behavior of teachers and other educational personnel in drug treatment programs. These laws may concern the storage and administration of drugs within public schools. School system administrators should communicate and interpret these laws to teachers.

2. Teachers should avoid such statements as, "I think Billy's work and behavior would benefit if he took Ritalin." Teachers are not qualified to make such judgments; in order for a physician to make a proper diagnosis, a careful and thorough examination is necessary.

3. The decision to recommend medical consultation should not be made until there is reasonable assurance that the child's problem does not stem from inadequacies in the teacher or other aspects of the school environment. Drug therapy is not appropriate when the cause of the problem is boredom or inappropriate standards set by teachers.

4. Physicians who issue prescriptions for stimulant drugs on the basis of a brief interview with a parent and a cursory examination should be avoided when there is suspicion of hyperkinesis. Certainly no school official should channel parents to physicians who simply ratify the teacher's diagnosis and prescription. Many communities have physicians who specialize in the treatment of learning and behavior problems of children. Such persons are most likely to provide proper treatment.

5. Educators and physicians should collaborate in the development of monitoring systems for children being treated with drugs because of learning and behavior disorders. There are many differences between physicians and teachers in language and perspective. Thus there is little reason to expect that interprofessional communication will be easy. In some communities instruments for providing information from the teacher have been standardized. The effective treatment of learning disorders with drugs requires an unprecedented level of coordination between physicians and teachers. School officials can begin the process of communication leading toward coordination by requesting an opportunity to meet with physicians in staff meetings held within the local hospital or in meetings of specialists (e.g., pediatricians).

6. School system administrators should be aware of the numbers of children who are being advised by the school to seek medical treatment for learning-related problems. Schools or classrooms with unusually high re-

ferral rates should be investigated to determine if school personnel are overly reliant on the use of drugs to solve classroom problems.

References

1. Charles Bradley, "The Behavior of Children Receiving Benzedrine," *American Journal of Psychology*, November, 1937, pp. 577–88.
2. Mark Stewart, "Hyperactive Children," *Scientific American*, April, 1970, pp. 94–98.
3. Maurice Laufer and Eric Denhoff, "Hyperkinetic Behavior Syndrome in Children," *Journal of Pediatrics*, April, 1957, pp. 463–74; James Worrell and William Bell, "Management of Hyperactive Behavior in Children," *Northwest Medicine*, January, 1971, pp. 43–46; and Gordon Millichap, "Drugs in Management of Hyperkinetic and Perceptually Handicapped Children," *JAMA*, November, 1968, pp. 1527–30.
4. Office of Child Development and the Office of the Assistant Secretary for Health and Scientific Affairs, "Report on the Conference on the Use of Stimulant Drugs in the Treatment of Behaviorally Disturbed Young School Children," Department of Health, Education, and Welfare, Washington, D.C., 1971.
5. "Debate on 'Drugging' for Classroom Control," *Nation's Schools*, July, 1971, p. 39.
6. "Classroom Pushers," *Time*, February 26, 1973, p. 65.
7. Barrett Scoville, "Governmental Perspective in the Evaluation and Regulation of Stimulant Drugs for Hyperkinetic Children," unpublished paper presented at the AERA meeting, Chicago, Ill., April, 1974.
8. Thomas Kenny et al., "Characteristics of Children Referred Because of Hyperactivity," *Journal of Pediatrics*, October, 1971, pp. 618–23.
9. Millichap, op. cit.; Leon Eisenberg, "Principles of Drug Therapy in Child Psychiatry with Special Reference to Stimulant Drugs," *American Journal of Orthopsychiatry*, April, 1971, pp. 317–79.
10. Stanley Robin and James Bosco, "Ritalin for School Children: The Teacher's Perspective," *Journal for School Health*, December, 1971, pp. 624–28.
11. Edward L. Birch, "Ritalin as Problem and Solution: Perspective of a School Administrator," paper presented at the AERA meeting, New Orleans, La., March, 1973.

Operational Concepts

1. In recent years, it has become increasingly common to use various psychotherapeutic drugs for the purpose of modifying the undesirable classroom behavior of hyperactive children.

2. Many teachers feel they can intuitively distinguish between a normal and a pathologically hyperactive child, but diagnosis of true hyperkinesis is difficult, requiring extensive neurological, physical, and psychological testing.

3. Since school personnel play a significant role in screening and referring hyperactive children, it is of great importance that teachers and administrators become knowledgeable about the hyperkinetic syndrome, its characteristics, and its responses to the various psychotherapeutic drugs that may be prescribed in its treatment.

4. Where hyperactivity is suspected, a careful examination of the classroom climate is desirable, if only to ascertain that the behavior is not attributable to some external factor.

Implications

Although hyperactivity is not a curricular concern per se, the preceding commentary has been included largely because of the current high interest regarding the use of psychotherapeutic drugs in the schools for diagnosed hyperkinetic pupils. Hyperkinesis obviously creates behavioral problems for both the pupil and the teacher; for some, drug therapy has provided a solution to these problems. There is, of course, a clear distinction between the medically prescribed treatment of a specific physiological disorder and indiscriminate use of drugs for any child posing a behavioral problem.

Virtually every teacher must, at one time or another, cope with student restlessness and inattentiveness; indeed, boredom is the time-honored indication that the pacing or content of the instruction is inappropriate. Hence, in the case of marginally hyperactive children, the line separating those who should be treated by a physician and those who simply need different learning activities is easily blurred. The identification of better criteria with which to distinguish between the two cases would seem to be a fitting target for further research.

Teacher Development

Lilian G. Katz

Developmental Stages of Preschool Teachers

Preschool teachers can generally be counted on to talk about developmental needs and stages when they discuss children(1). It may also be meaningful to think of teachers themselves as having developmental sequences in their professional growth(2).

There may be at least four developmental stages for teachers. Individual teachers may vary greatly in the length of time spent in each of the four stages outlined here and schematized in Figure 1.

STAGE 1: SURVIVAL

During Stage 1, which may last throughout the first full year of teaching, the teacher's main concern is whether she can survive. This preoccupation with survival may be expressed in questions the teacher asks: "Can I get through the day in one piece? Without losing a child? Can I make it until the end of the week? Until the next vacation? Can I really do this kind of work day after day? Will I be accepted by my colleagues?" Such questions are well expressed in Ryan's enlightening collection of accounts of first-year teaching experiences(3).

The first full impact of responsibilities for a group of immature but vigorous young children (to say nothing of encounters with their parents) inevitably provokes teachers' anxieties. The discrepancy between anticipated successes and classroom realities intensifies feelings of inadequacy and unpreparedness.

During this period the teacher needs support, understanding, encouragement, reassurance, comfort, and guidance. She needs instruction in specific skills and insight into the complex causes of behavior—all of which must be provided on the classroom site. On-site instructors may be senior staff members, advisors, consultants, or program assistants who know the

Reprinted from Lilian G. Katz, "Developmental Stages of Preschool Teachers," *The Elementary School Journal*, Vol. 73, No. 1, 1972, pp. 50–54.

beginning teacher and her teaching situation well. Training must be constantly and readily available. The trainer should have enough time and flexibility to be on call as needed. Schedules of periodic visits that have been arranged in advance cannot be counted on to coincide with crises. Cook and Mack(4) describe the British pattern of on-site training given to teachers by their headmasters (principals). Armington also tells how advisors can meet the needs of these teachers(5).

STAGE 2: CONSOLIDATION

By the end of the first year the teacher has usually decided that she can survive. She is now ready to consolidate the gains made during the first stage and to differentiate tasks and skills to be mastered next. During Stage 2, teachers usually begin to focus on individual children who pose problems and on troublesome situations. The teacher may look for answers to such questions as: "How can I help a shy child? How can I help a child who does not seem to be learning?"

During Stage 1, the beginning teacher acquires a base line of information about what young children are like and what to expect of them. By Stage 2, the teacher is beginning to identify individual children whose behavior departs from the pattern of most of the children she knows.

During this stage, on-site help continues to be valuable. A trainer can help the teacher by exploring a problem with her. Take the case of a young

FIGURE 1 Stages of Development and Training Needs of Preschool Teachers

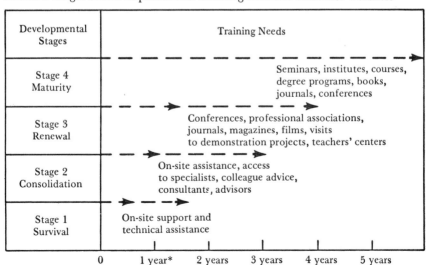

*Time periods approximate.

685

teacher from a day-care center who was eager to get help and asked: "How should I deal with a clinging child?" An on-site trainer can observe the teacher and the child at the center and arrive at suggestions and tentative solutions fairly quickly. However, without firsthand knowledge of the child and the context, an extended give-and-take conversation between the teacher and trainer may be the best way for the trainer to help the teacher interpret her experience and move toward a solution of the problem. The trainer might ask the teacher, "What have you done so far? Give examples of some experiences with this child during this week. When you did such and such, how did the child respond?" Other suggestions for helping children are offered by Katz(6).

At this stage, the teacher may find that she needs information about specific children or about children who pose problems. It will be helpful if she has a wide range of resources. Psychologists, social workers, health workers, and other specialists can strengthen the teacher's skills and knowledge at this time. Exchanges of information and ideas with more experienced colleagues may help teachers master the developmental tasks of this period. Opportunities to share feelings with other teachers at the same stage of development may reduce some of the inadequacy and the frustration the beginning teacher feels.

STAGE 3: RENEWAL

Often, during the third or fourth year of teaching, the teacher begins to tire of doing the same things. She asks questions about new developments in the field: "Who is doing what? Where? What are some of the new materials, techniques, approaches, and ideas?" Perhaps what the teacher has been doing for each annual crop of children has been adequate for them, but she herself finds the seasonal Valentine cards, Easter bunnies, and pumpkin cutouts no longer interesting. If it is true that a teacher's own interest in the projects and the activities she provides for children contributes to their educational value, then her need for renewal and refreshment should be taken seriously.

During this stage, teachers find it rewarding to meet colleagues from various programs on both formal and informal occasions. Teachers at this developmental stage are particularly receptive to experiences in regional and national conferences and workshops. Teachers at Stage 3 profit from membership in professional associations and participation in their meetings. Teachers are now widening the scope of their reading, scanning magazines and journals, and viewing films. During this period they may be ready to take a close look at their own classroom teaching through video-tape recording. This is also a time when teachers welcome opportunities to visit other classes, programs, and demonstration projects.

Perhaps it is at this stage that the teachers' center has the greatest potential value(7, 8). Teachers' centers are places where teachers can meet to help one another learn or relearn skills, techniques, and methods. At these centers, teachers can exchange ideas and organize special workshops. From time to time specialists in curriculum, or child growth, or any other area of concern are invited to the center to meet with teachers.

STAGE 4: MATURITY

Some teachers may reach maturity, Stage 4, within three years; others need five years or more. The teacher at this stage has come to terms with herself as a teacher. She now has enough perspective to ask deeper and more abstract questions, such as: "What are my historical and philosophical roots? What is the nature of growth and learning? How are educational decisions made? Can schools change societies? Is teaching a profession?" Perhaps she has asked these questions before. But with the experience she now has, the questions represent a more meaningful search for insight, perspective, and realism.

Throughout maturity, teachers need an opportunity to participate in conferences and seminars, and perhaps to work toward a degree. Mature teachers welcome the chance to read widely and to interact with educators working on many problem areas on many levels. Training sessions and conference events that teachers at Stage 2 enjoy may be tiresome to the teacher at Stage 4. Similarly, introspective and searching seminars that teachers at Stage 4 enjoy may lead to restlessness and irritability among the beginners at Stage 1.

It is useful to think of the growth of preschool teachers (and perhaps other teachers, also) as occurring in stages, linked generally to experience gained over time.

The training needs of teachers change as they gain experience, as they move from one stage to another. The issues dealt with in the traditional social foundations courses do not seem to address themselves to the early survival problems that are critical to the inexperienced teacher. However, for the maturing teacher, those same issues may help deepen her understanding of the total complex environment in which she is trying to be effective.

The location of training should change as the teacher develops. At the beginning of the new teacher's career, training resources must be taken to her so that training can be responsive to the particular (and possibly unique) developmental tasks and working situation she faces in her classroom. As the teacher moves on past the survival stage, training can move to the college campus.

The timing of training should be shifted so that more training is available to the teacher on the job than before it. Teachers say that their preservice education has only a minor influence on what they do day to day in their classrooms. The complaint suggests that strategies acquired before employment may seldom be used under the pressures of the job.

It is often said that experience is the best teacher. To make sure that the beginning teacher has informed and interpreted experience should be one of the major roles of the teacher trainer.

Notes

1. Lilian G. Katz and Mary K. Weir. *Help for Preschool Teachers: A Proposal.* Urbana, Ill.: ERIC Clearinghouse on Early Childhood Education, 1969.

2. This paper was produced pursuant to a contract with the Office of Education, U.S. Department of Health, Education and Welfare. Contractors undertaking such projects under government sponsorship are encouraged to express freely their professional judgment. Points of view or opinions stated do not, therefore, necessarily represent official government position or policy.

3. Kevin Ryan (editor). *Don't Smile Until Christmas: Accounts of the First Year of Teaching.* Chicago, Ill.: University of Chicago Press, 1970.

4. Ann Cook and Herbert Mack. *The Head-teacher's Role.* New York: Citation Press, 1971.

5. David Armington. "A Plan for Continuing Growth." Newton, Massachusetts: Educational Development Center (mimeographed, no date).

6. Lilian G. Katz. "Condition with Caution," *Young Children.* In Press.

7. Arlene Silberman. "A Santa's Workshop for Teachers," *American Education, 7* (December, 1971), 3–8.

8. Stephen K. Baily. "Teachers' Centers: A British First," *Phi Delta Kappan, 53* (November, 1971), 146–49.

Operational Concepts

1 Artistry in teaching develops slowly over time.

2 As teachers develop a pedagogical style, they progress through sequential stages: a stage in which survival is the dominant objective; a stage in which attitudes, skills, and knowledge are consolidated; a stage in which acquired techniques are refined; and, finally, a stage in which authentic maturity is reached.

3. Because of these sequential stages, professional in-service educational opportunities should be offered that fit the particular developmental stage of a given teacher.

4. Craftsmanship in teaching is a highly individualized matter, requiring balance between natural style and learned technique.

5. Inherent ability is of great importance, but teachers, as a general rule, are "made" rather than "born." Consequently a fundamental obligation of school administration is to nurture continuous professional improvement among teaching staffs.

Implications

Each teacher's progression through the several stages of professional development tends to be highly idiosyncratic. Much has recently been written about the best approach to the preparation of teachers and a good deal of controversy generated over, for example, the merits of liberal versus competency-based training.

An effective administrator must seek to determine the particular stage of development of each teacher and—in cooperation with the teacher—plan desirable growth experience. Otherwise, much of the in-service activity will be irrelevant. The present failure to individualize professional improvement probably constitutes the most serious weakness of many staff development programs.

Gene Stanford
Albert C. Roark

Beyond the Classroom

"Escape . . . The real classroom is outside!" urges a poster produced by the Environmental Studies Program. Its advice is sound, and in recent years more and more students and teachers are heeding it. In some cases, students (and teachers) are taking the advice literally and dropping out of a classroom-bound system they feel can offer them little of value, perhaps agreeing with Mark Twain, who said, "I never let school interfere with my education." In other cases, students and teachers are working together to fashion new educational experiences that take them into the world outside the confines of the classroom.

WHY LEAVE THE CLASSROOM?

Until recent decades, when it became fashionable for young people to spend most of the first third of their lives in school, young people did most of their learning of how to live and what the world is like through direct experience in their communities. At a very early age children were expected to contribute significantly to the work of keeping the family going. They learned the skills they needed for adult success by working alongside their parents or other adults. School was reserved for learning only those things that a person couldn't learn outside.

However, schools have more and more begun to include in their curricula subject matter that could more easily and effectively be learned otherwise. Instead of learning about our political system by attending rallies, committee meetings and party caucuses, a student takes a "course" in something known as "civics," in which he reads about the political system and discusses it in class (and tries to pass a test on it). The result is that students all too often make a distinction between what they learn in the classroom and the "real" world outside. A student who can recite fifty grammar rules and correctly fill in dozens of workbook pages con-

Reprinted from Gene Stanford and Albert C. Roark, *Human Interaction in Education,* © 1974; by permission of Allyn and Bacon, Inc., Boston.

tinues to pair singular subjects and plural verbs when talking to his friends at the local hangout. Or, an A student in science leaves garden tools outside overnight, not realizing that they will rust from the dew.

One reason, then, for providing students with experiences outside the classroom is to give them a chance to transfer what they have learned in the safe confines of the classroom to the world of reality. The classroom can be seen as a sort of sheltered environment, in which new behaviors can be learned and practiced without the penalties that failure might bring in the world outside. The classroom "microsociety" can give students a safe introduction to new knowledge or new behavior and a chance to try it out. But he then needs an opportunity to transfer the skills to the situation in which he ultimately needs to utilize them—the world of everyday life.

Activities outside the classroom also have the advantage of providing a wider diversity of experiences than are possible within the school. Some learning experiences are simply not possible in the classroom—physical or financial limitations make them impossible. The classroom-bound student who wants to experience what the inside of a canning factory is like has but one choice—to read about it. However, the vicarious experience of reading will be so much less effective in helping the student learn that he may feel he might as well have not wasted his time. We—and a host of other educators from John Dewey to Edgar Dale—feel that the more direct the learning experience, the more permanent the learning will be. Even in the mid-nineteenth century, Thoreau was suggesting that students(*1*)

should not play life, or study it merely, while the community supports them at this expensive game, but earnestly live it from beginning to end. How could youths better learn to live than by at once trying the experiment of living? Methinks this would exercise their minds as much as mathematics. If I wished a boy to know something about the arts and sciences, for instance, I would not pursue the common course, which is merely to send him into the neighborhood of some professor, where anything is professed and practised but the art of life; to survey the world through a telescope or a microscope, and never with his natural eye; to study chemistry, and not learn how his bread is made, or mechanics, and not learn how it is earned; to discover new satellites to Neptune, and not detect the motes in his eyes, or to what vagabond he is a satellite himself; or to be devoured by the monsters that swarm all around him, while contemplating the monsters in a drop of vinegar. Which would have advanced the most at the end of a month—the boy who had made his own jackknife from the ore which he had dug and smelted, reading as much as would be necessary for this—or the boy who had attended the lectures of metallurgy at the Institute in the meanwhile, and had received a Rodgers penknife from his father? Which would be most likely to cut his fingers? . . . To my astonishment I was informed on leaving college that I had studied navigation!—why, if I had taken one turn down the harbor I should have known more about it.

FIGURE 1 Cone of Experience

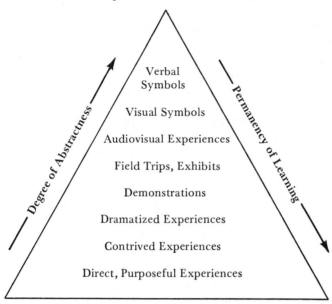

Dale(2) has suggested the Cone of Experience (Figure 1) as a graphic means of comparing the relative effectiveness of several types of learning activities.

It is interesting to note that the approaches to learning that are utilized most frequently by most of us—verbal symbols (discussion, lecture) and visual symbols (reading)—are those that Dale claims lead to the least permanency of learning. On the other hand, direct experiences are the most effective. If we accept Dale's position, we will attempt to give students direct experiences with the subject matter as often as possible. For some educational goals we can provide these direct experiences in the classroom. But in a great number of cases, we must look beyond the classroom if we hope to provide direct experience.

ACTIVITIES OUTSIDE THE CLASSROOM

When choosing activities to help achieve educational objectives, the teacher's first question should be, "Can I give students direct experience with the subject matter?" If the direct experience can be provided within the confines of the classroom or school, fine. But if direct experience is possible only outside the school, the teacher should look for ways to make it available to students. Some possible approaches are suggested below. Only if a direct experience—inside or outside the classroom—is impossible (learning about the geological features of the moon through direct experience is an example) should the teacher resort to a more abstract experience—simulations, audiovisual presentations or reading.

Interactive Field Trips

The field trip has traditionally been a passive experience, accomplishing little of value except giving students and their teacher a chance to escape from the routine of daily life in the school. Usually students are cautioned not to talk or otherwise cause disturbance—as they shuffle along on a guided tour of the local city hall, a museum or a newspaper plant. The experience has rarely been any more involving than viewing a movie on the same topic—and often less effective because of the difficulty of seeing over the heads of other students on the tour. Yet, the field trip is potentially an effective learning experience—if students are allowed to become involved through interaction with the environment they are visiting. We are choosing to call this type of experience an *interactive field trip*.

Assume, for example, that your students are studying the rise of mass production in American industry. By fortunate circumstance, just two blocks down the street is a General Motors plant that assembles Chevrolet trucks. An excellent opportunity for your students to see mass production in action, you muse. If you call the plant's public relations department and ask for a tour of the plant for your students, you are likely to end up with a field trip of the traditional sort. Students will see some interesting things, but will have no personal involvement in the experience. On the other hand, you might ask the public relations department if it would be possible for your students to talk with some of the workers on the line— perhaps during a coffee break. The workers are likely to be delighted that someone is interested in their work and considers it valuable enough to bring a class of sixth-graders to look at and talk about. In addition, students will have a chance for human interaction to add personal significance to their tour of the plant. They can ask the workers whether they enjoy their work, how it feels to do the same repetitive job over and over, and so forth. Such an experience can have a profound effect on students' attitudes toward various occupational groups, as well as helping them in their own vocational exploration and understanding of mass production.

The key to planning an interactive field trip is to look for ways for students to interact with the human beings involved. Usually this consists of a chance to ask questions, but it can also extend to allowing students to participate in the process—sitting in the driver's seat, pressing the button at the right time, sliding down the fire pole or whatever. Actual participation may be difficult to accomplish with a big group. For this reason it mighe be useful to allow students to go on their own individual interactive field trips. A middle school we have worked with allows ninth-graders to spend two hours each Monday visiting some place that they would like to learn about. One student, for example, spends his time at the courthouse, where he is allowed to visit various offices, to do simple clerical tasks and to ask as many questions as he wants.

The Environmental Studies Project of the American Geological Insti-

694

FIGURE 2

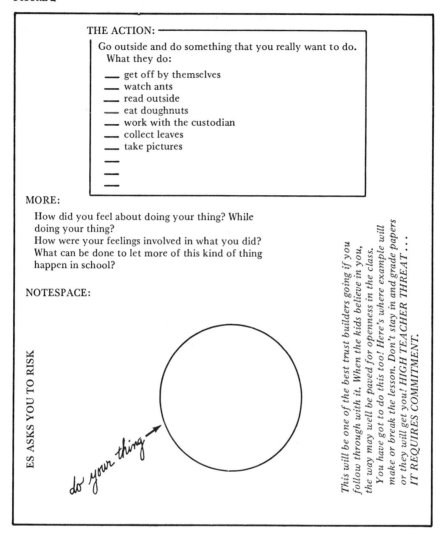

THE ACTION: ——————

Go outside and do something that you really want to do.
What they do:

___ get off by themselves
___ watch ants
___ read outside
___ eat doughnuts
___ work with the custodian
___ collect leaves
___ take pictures
___
___
___

MORE:

How did you feel about doing your thing? While
doing your thing?
How were your feelings involved in what you did?
What can be done to let more of this kind of thing
happen in school?

NOTESPACE:

ES ASKS YOU TO RISK

do your thing →

This will be one of the best trust builders going if you
follow through with it. When the kids believe in you,
the way may well be paved for openness in the class.
You have got to do this too! Here's where example will
make or break the lesson. Don't stay in and grade papers
or they will get you! HIGH TEACHER THREAT ...
IT REQUIRES COMMITMENT.

tute has been creating ideas for active-involvement experiences outside
the classroom suitable for students at any grade level. Their Environmental Studies Packets (see the list of Additional Resources at the end of
this chapter) comprise a set of cards; on each card is a suggested activity,
along with follow-up possibilities and helpful hints to the teacher. Two
such cards are reproduced in Figures 2 and 3.

Exchange Programs

In a pluralistic society such as ours, students need frequent contact
with people of different backgrounds. Many schools are providing this experience by establishing exchange programs between schools. A class in

a suburban school might spend a week at an inner-city school, living with families of the inner-city students, who themselves are visiting the suburbs at the same time. A school in a small conservative town might arrange an exchange with a school in a cosmopolitan northern city.

Cross-Age Teaching

In numerous schools across America students leave behind not only their classroom but their role as students—as they devote themselves to the teaching of younger students. Fifth-graders are helping second-graders with arithmetic; high school students are conducting art lessons for third-

FIGURE 3

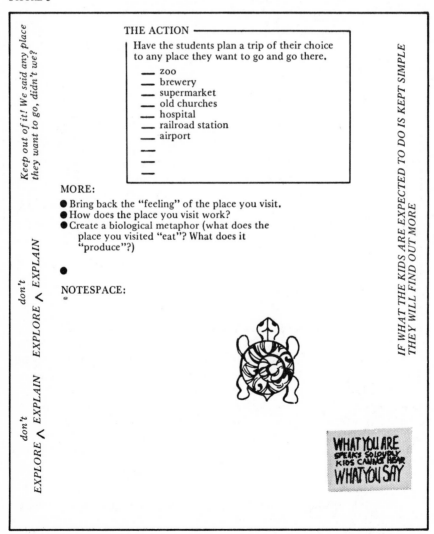

graders; college students are tutoring sixth-graders with reading difficulties. The combinations are almost limitless, but all involve a student becoming "teacher" for a while. The benefits are far more significant than merely relieving some teacher of part of his work load. The older student who is serving as "teacher" learns not only subject matter but also interpersonal skills. He starts to understand more about the process of learning and thus gains skills he can use in his own learning.

In some schools, cross-age teaching is an informal process—with a student utilizing some of his unscheduled time to help younger students. In other schools, the process has become highly structured—with the "teachers" receiving a thorough orientation and obtaining school credit for their work. Gartner, Kohler, and Riessman provide a current summary of the various approaches to cross-age teaching that are being utilized(3).

Shadowing

How can you give students direct experience and insight into what it's like to be a surgeon, a college professor, a bricklayer, a telephone operator, a union organizer or a beauty shop operator? It may not be feasible to let a student be a "surgeon-for-a-day." Yet, even though he may not be able to "walk in the other man's moccasins," he can walk in his footprints. That is what shadowing is all about.

The student literally "shadows"—that is, follows around—the person whose role he is interested in learning more about. The experience can last for one day, a week or a month. Here are some general guidelines for a shadowing program in which college students shadowed a professor of their choice. They can easily be modified to suit shadows of any grade level.

1. The student and faculty member agree on a week (five days) for shadowing.
2. The student and faculty member agree on what situations will be private (e.g., shadow is asked to leave office because of confidential conversation).
3. The shadow attends meetings, conferences, classes; and listens to conversations, interviews, advising sessions and other daily activities of the faculty member. The shadow may travel with the faculty member on a consulting or speaking trip.
4. The faculty member shares his mail, decisions, problems and general thoughts with his shadow.
5. The faculty member attempts to inform the shadow of his areas of interest and expertise; he gives the shadow bibliographies and recommends books in his area. The shadow may read as many as three books during the week if he is interested.
6. It is recommended that the shadow spend at least four hours per day (twenty hours total) with the faculty member other than in classes, and

that the shadow attend all of the faculty member's classes during the week.

7. The student will write a paper, synthesizing his experiences on completion of the week and have it approved by the faculty member.

Sensitizing Modules

The concept of "sensitizing modules" was introduced by Simon and elaborated on by Kirschenbaum. These are brief experiences that put the student into interaction with the environment in some way. For example, Simon(4) suggests the following modules (particularly suitable for middle-class suburban students):

> Sit in the waiting room of the maternity ward of (a large hospital). Strike up a conversation with other people in the waiting room. Try to distinguish which patients are charity cases and which are not. Spend 30 minutes in the emergency ward. Keep out of the way, but note carefully what happens.
>
> Go to magistrate's court and keep a list of the kinds of cases brought before the magistrate. Who are his customers? How are they handled? What lesson about our economy can you learn here?
>
> Wear old clothes and sit in the waiting room of the State Employment Office. Listen, observe, talk to the people sitting next to you. Read the annoucements on the bulletin board, etc. Try to overhear an interview if possible.

Kirschenbaum suggests a large number of module ideas, including the following(5):

> Try to call City Hall with a complaint that your landlord did not give you heat, or has not repaired a roof leak, or that the toilet is not working. Better yet, find a neighbor with a real complaint and offer to help him get it fixed (p. 37).
>
> In teaching elementary children the period of world exploration and the discovery of America, one teacher had her children go out and actually "discover" new parts of the city. One instruction was to "find a new faster route to the ball field." She stayed a half block behind them, but they had to do the discovering themselves. And the gap between Columbus and their own risk-taking world in the city was narrowed (p. 38).
>
> One high school class studying the Second World War took a trip to a Veteran's Hospital where the students interviewed many of the patients (p. 38).

The "sensitizing module" can be almost any experience that puts the students—individually or in teams—in direct interaction with their environment. Insofar as possible, it should include the opportunity for the

698

student to *do* something rather than passively looking, and should include the opportunity for interaction with other human beings.

On-the-Job Training

Some of the most exciting educational programs that we have visited have been designed to give the "non-college-bound" high school student practical vocational skills. Classroom-confined academic subjects are reduced to a minimum, and the student spends the greatest part of his day at a local business firm or industry, receiving on-the-job work experience. It is not hard to begin feeling as though it is the college-bound student who is suffering educationally—as well as psychologically. While students in the "lower tracks" are allowed to have direct experiences with the real world, the average and honors students are often forced to learn about the world second-hand. It is not surprising, then, that many of the students identified as potential dropouts are those with high ability and achievement scores. They are wise enough to realize that most of the "dropout" programs will give them a much more meaningful educational experience than what most classrooms filled with highly motivated students can offer.

It is unfortunate that practical work experiences are not provided for the "upper-track" student as well as the potential dropout. In our experience, a school which encourages—or even allows—the "good" students to learn a marketable skill and receive on-the-job experience is almost nonexistent. (One of the first exceptions will be described later in this chapter.) We feel that virtually every student should graduate from high school with a skill with which he can support himself and with at least one semester's experience in the world of work.

References

1. Henry David Thoreau, *Walden: Essay on Civil Disobedience* (New York: Airmont Publishing Co., 1865).
2. Edgar Dale, *Audiovisual Methods in Teaching* (New York: Dryden, 1969).
3. Alan Gartner, Mary Kohler, and Frank Riessman, *Children Teach Children* (New York: Harper, 1971).
4. Sidney, Simon, "Sensitizing Modules: A Cure for 'Senioritis,' " *Scholastic Teacher,* Sept. 21, 1970, pp. 29, 42.
5. Howard Kirschenbaum, "Sensitivity Modules," *Media and Methods,* Feb. 1970, pp. 36–38.

Operational Concepts

1. If learning is to be maximally effective, students must have opportunities to apply what is learned within the classroom to the world outside.

2. Many of the potentially most useful learning experiences are situated in the community proper.

3. Conventional curricula are based largely upon visual and verbal symbols, which are among the least permanent forms of learning.

4. As a general rule, the more direct the learning experience, the greater its permanence.

5. Direct learning experiences should be used wherever circumstances permit; correspondingly, indirect learning experiences should be used only when more direct learning is not feasible.

Implications

Interest in community-based learning has gained strength in the recent past. In a celebrated argument, James Coleman has gone so far as to contend that the present school is obsolete, and that in the future the young should acquire a considerable portion of their learning by participating in the life of the community.

Whether the convictions of Coleman and similar-minded critics are viewed as rational or irrational, the evidence seems to suggest that greater involvement in the mainstream of organized social life is highly desirable.

The chief impediment to a curriculum that includes direct community-based experience lies in the formidable logistical problems. It is infinitely easier to educate citizens in a specially designated facility, using books and other symbolic material, than to engage them productively in ongoing events in the community environment. Yet, that which is formidable is not necessarily impossible; as technology advances, it may be feasible to overcome many of the organizational impediments. In the interim, we are well advised to relate the lessons of the classroom as closely as possible to the real world, and to balance symbolic learning with direct experience wherever possible.

Classroom Management

William I. Gardner

Management of Some Recurring Problem Behavior Patterns

TEMPER-TANTRUM BEHAVIORS

All young children engage on occasion in temper-tantrum behavior whenever they do not have their own way, do not receive expected positive consequences, when placed in conflict situations, or when something interferes with their ongoing, goal-directed behavior. The temper tantrums include a combination of anger and aggressive behaviors such as crying, screaming, thrashing about, attacking others verbally or physically and self-directed aggression. Children with developmental difficulties are even more likely to engage in such frustration behaviors as their disabilities frequently increase the difficulty of task accomplishment. As a result, they are faced with more barriers to goal attainment and generally exhibit low tolerance to frustration.

How the Behavior Develops

Parents, teachers, and others are more prone to "feel sorry" for the young child with learning and behavior problems whenever he is experiencing difficulty and to provide him with extra attention or assistance during a temper outburst. It is not unusual under these circumstances for the adult to reduce the requirements or to give in to the child. In this manner the child learns that a successful way to stop the adult from requiring him to do something is to engage in temper tantrum behavior. Stated more technically, the child's temper-tantrum behavior has been strengthened under these conditions through a combination of negative and positive reinforcement. The behavior not only removes an aversive condition (negative reinforcement) but also may result in increased attention in the form of soothing comments and sympathy (positive reinforcement).

As it will be illustrated, such behavior patterns under certain learning conditions can become quite frequent and, under the slightest provocation, rather intense. It is also true that the temper outburst can become discriminative, occurring only in the presence of certain people or only under highly specific conditions.

John, a four-year-old physically handicapped boy, has been given candy on numerous occasions recently as his mother was under emotional stress and used the candy as a means of keeping John happy and quiet. John learned to come to mother and ask for candy at an increasingly frequent rate. These requests had been reinforced since they produced the candy which the child promptly ate.

Mother, becoming concerned when John began to be fussy about his food at mealtimes and when he began to leave too much food on his plate at dinnertime, decided to cut out the candy between meals and to provide it only immediately after meals.

When John asked her for candy between meals, she refused him, explaining her new plan. Although logical, it did nevertheless represent a removal of a reinforcing event which previously had been provided following John's request for it. This change in mother's procedure, an extinction one, produced a frustration reaction. He began fretting and, failing to obtain the candy, sat down on the floor and began crying. Mother, feeling sympathy for him and feeling guilty that she had upset him, gave in after a few minutes of his sobbing and provided him with the candy, with the declaration, "This is the only piece that you will get until dinner."

This episode is repeated many times over the next few weeks. Mother is able to stick to her resolution on occasion to cut the candy out between meals. At other times, she gives in immediately saying, "Oh, okay. Just one piece, though." On still other occasions she makes unsuccessful attempts to withstand the temper outburst. The longer she waits, the louder the crying and the more vigorous the thrashing about becomes. The child kicks the floor and pounds on mother with his hands. Mother becomes afraid that he will hurt himself and gives him the candy to quiet him down. In this manner John is reinforced for increasingly vigorous temper-tantrum behaviors. The less intense temper-tantrum behavior which appeared initially following withholding of the candy had failed to produce the reinforcer. More intense forms were shaped gradually in the child as these more vigorous temper tantrums, and only these, resulted in the mother giving in and providing the candy.

Behavior Management Program

When setting up a program to alter temper-tantrum behavior, the parent or teacher should follow these guidelines:

1. Define precisely the behaviors which make up the temper tantrum. Define the time, place and social setting in which these behaviors occur. What produces or precipitates the temper tantrums?

2. Obtain some measure of the strength of the behavior. How many temper tantrums occur per morning, day, or during other designated time periods? How long does the outburst last once it begins? How intense is it? It is necessary to obtain some objective measure of the strength of the temper tantrums prior to initiation of a behavior management program in order to determine if the program is being effective.

3. Describe what occurs in the child's environment as the tantrum behavior occurs. What happens whenever the child engages in such behaviors? These consequences most likely are serving to maintain the tantrums and thus must be evaluated carefully.

4. If the program involves a change in reinforcement schedule or in the contingency, inform the child that the reinforcing event or activity will no longer be provided except at designated times or following designated behavior. Do this prior to the occasion in which the reinforcer is usually available to the child, that is, prior to frustration, so that the child knows what to expect under the new arrangements.

5. If the temper tantrums are more likely to occur at certain periods of time or in certain situations, attempt to get the child involved in behaviors which will reduce the possibility of frustration and the resulting temper tantrum.

6. If the child does not understand language, demonstrate to him (in those instances where this is possible) what he must do to obtain the desired consequence or some appropriate substitute.

7. Do not provide reinforcement following the initiation of temper-tantrum behavior. Let the temper tantrum run its course. After a few occurrences the length and intensity of the tantrum will typically decline. The child may be placed in a room by himself. If the teacher remains in the room to insure that the child does not harm himself or damage property, care must be exercised to keep attention at a minimum. Even looking at the child or responding to him in any manner may only intensify and prolong the tantrum.

8. Provide both the withdrawn reinforcer or one of comparable value and positive social attention (approval, praise, playful interaction, affection) at other times during the day when the child is involved in appropriate behavior.

9. Reinforce the child richly in those instances in which he demonstrates appropriate behavior in the face of frustrating conditions. As he begins to decrease the frequency of temper-tantrum behavior, provide him with frequent praise and approval for being a "big boy" or "big girl."

10. Be prepared for long and loud temper tantrums on the first few occasions of this behavior being placed on extinction. Remember that giving in, even occasionally, will greatly prolong the episodes.

11. If the child is left alone during temper tantrums, be sure that there is minimal possibility that the child's behavior will require that you provide him with attention. If the child inflicts minor injury which you attend to, the possibility exists that such behavior will be strengthened.

12. Inform the child of the consequences of the tantrum (e.g., "John, you can cry if you wish. I shall leave you until you finish.") Be consistent in fulfilling stipulations (e.g., "You cannot come out of your room until you have stopped your crying"; "You may join the class again after you choose to stop your tantrum").

13. Do not let the child's temper tantrum arouse your sympathy or guilt. He will survive. If you provide him with sufficient acceptance and affection at other times in a natural manner, any emotional trauma that he may experience or any feelings of being rejected or mistreated will be short-lived. In fact, by being consistent in your treatment of temper-tantrum behavior you will assist the child to develop a concept of responsibility for his own behavior. As his temper tantrums begin to occur less frequently, his concept of himself as a person who has self-control will be enhanced.

14. It is also crucial that the social environment recognizes the manner in which chronic temper-tantrum behaviors can be strengthened and avoids the trap in the future.

As noted initially, all children engage in temper-tantrum behaviors on occasion as things do not go right for them. These tantrums become exececessively intense and chronic, however, only under conditions where they are too frequently reinforced by the social environment and other competing behaviors are not provided sufficient reinforcement.

NEGATIVISTIC BEHAVIOR

Some children are actively negativistic to many requests made by parents and teachers. *Stubborn, oppositional, noncompliant,* and *passive-aggressive* are other terms used to describe a behavior pattern which is accentuated by "No," "I don't want to," or "I'm not going to do that." Usually these verbal negatives are accompanied by whining and other similar obnoxious behaviors which accompany the failure to comply with or to fulfill the requests made by others—peers, older siblings or adults.

Some children are more passive in their noncompliance. They do not verbally refuse to comply or engage in whining or other disruptive emotional behavior—they just do not perform. They drag through the requested behavior for an inordinate period of time, or may postpone action until the request is finally presented in a harsh and threatening manner.

The child with various types of developmental difficulties frequently comes to control the household and to attempt to control the school environment. Parents and teacher may spoil the child by permitting him to set the pace. If the child objects to adult requests, these requests too frequently are removed and the child is permitted to do as he pleases. On those occasions when adults do attempt to obtain compliance, the child responds with increased negativism, much to the surprise of the adults because "we require very little of him. I don't know why he objects so much to our few requests."

It is not unusual to observe that parents, teachers, and others do not respond or relate to the negativistic child too frequently. Most of the interaction occurs when the adult is presenting requests or is attempting to enforce compliance. This becomes such an unpleasant experience that both adult and child tend to ignore each other due to the limited positive reinforcement associated with interaction. It is also true that many noncompliant children do not seem to pay attention. Whenever a request is made, the child sits as if he did not hear the request. He has found it more comfortable to turn the social environment off as it frequently is unpleasant to him.

How the Behavior Develops

It should be recognized initially that no child will comply with adult requests on every occasion. However, it is evident that the social environment, regardless of intentions to the contrary, can teach a child to be excessively noncompliant by gradually shaping this behavior pattern over a period of time.

The child's negativistic or noncompliant behavior has been strengthened as it has resulted in the termination of the adult request, has postponed compliance, or has resulted in excessive attention from parent or teacher as she attempts to nag him, reason with him, or argue with him.

The following situation illustrates such noncompliant behavior. Mother calls from the kitchen, "It's time to take your nap. Put your toys away." Johnnie quickly replies, "I don't want to," and begins to fuss. Mother, not feeling well and not up to a battle with Johnnie, makes no reply and lets him continue his play activity. After thirty minutes or so she makes another attempt and suggests in a calm voice as she walks into the playroom, "Johnnie, don't you think it is time for your nap now?" Johnnie screams, "No, no, I won't," and begins to cry as he scoots across the room. Mother becomes upset, storms out of the room and yells, "Just do what you want to then." Mother's actions are teaching Johnnie that he should refuse and put up a fuss when requests are made of him because these behaviors will result in the termination of the unpleasant requests.

Another child may be taught to resist passively or to ignore requests if such behaviors avoid or postpone termination of pleasant activity or initiation of requested unpleasant activity. The child at school may be playing in the sand box and be requested to join the group for music period. The child ignores the request and makes no move, or if he acts as if he did not hear what the teacher requested, he can prolong his pleasant activity.

On other occasions, the teacher will nag the child. The request will be repeated, "Sue, get your mat and prepare for naptime." "Sue, I told you to get ready for your nap." Finally, in aggravation, the teacher yells in a harsh manner, "Get your mat this second or I'll send you out of the room." The child may prepare for naptime after this demand; however, the teacher's approach may also have two other effects. It may teach the child that compliance with teacher requests is unnecessary unless the teacher becomes angry. Additionally, the teacher is reinforced for yelling at the child since the behavior did provide a solution to the problem. As a result the teacher is more likely to yell under similar conditions of the child's noncompliance.

When a teacher repeats a request a number of times prior to requiring the child to initiate, persist at, or complete an activity, two learning processes are possibly in operation which strengthen negativistic or noncompliance behavior. First, refusal results in continued attention from adults as they repeat the requests or otherwise reason with, argue with, or scold the child. Second, if the requested activity is unpleasant (complete a difficult visual-motor task, pick up your toys, stop playing and prepare for work), refusal serves to postpone the initiation of the unpleasant activity. This has an immediate effect of strengthening the refusal behavior.

As noted earlier (and as is true in many problem situations) the major behavior which results in social attention for the child is that of being negativistic. As the child becomes more negativistic, he is left alone more and more at other times because "he is such a brat," or "he's such an unpleasant child."

Some children have also been taught that after refusal, parents will occasionally bribe them into compliance. Under these conditions the children are reinforced for refusal as a result of the subsequent bribe. As the reward is not provided on every occasion, the behavior becomes even more difficult to eliminate due to the intermittent nature of the reinforcement.

Behavior Management Program

The adult attempting to alter the behavior of a noncompliant child should consider these suggestions:

1. Define precisely the behaviors which are viewed as negativistic. When do they occur, where, and under what conditions? What are the major types of requests which produce negativistic behavior? Is the child negativistic most of the time or mostly under certain time or situa-

tion conditions? Identify occurrences of compliance and attempt to identify those factors which distinguish compliance from negativistic behavior.

2. What is the strength of the negativistic behaviors? In obtaining a record of the number of times negativistic behaviors occur during designated periods of time, also note the types of requests and the manner in which they are presented to the child. A child may have developed highly discriminating negativistic behaviors; that is, he may be negativistic with mother or the teacher aide but not with father or the teacher.

3. What happens after negativistic behavior? Attention should be given to the cueing as well as the possible reinforcing events. Does the social environment repeat a request a number of times prior to becoming firm and requiring the behavior? If so, the initial requests are redundant and have no appropriate behavior control function. What are the consequences of the negativistic behavior?

4. Make no request of a child that he is not fully expected to fulfill. Do not change requests after the child balks. Insure that the child follows requests even if it becomes necessary to actively assist him; if the child refuses, take it in a matter-of-fact manner. Perhaps the teacher may take him by his hand and gently guide him through the activity to demonstrate to him that he should comply with the request the first time it is made. This may be a novel experience for the child since, as suggested earlier, the child has been trained to respond only after persistent requests from adults.

Stay *calm* in this activity. It is highly likely that the child will put up a fuss. If the teacher becomes too emotional, the child's emotionality will be intensified. If the child complains or cries, he should be ignored. Sufficient physical guidance or verbal prompts should insure that the initial request is fulfilled.

If, under this new approach, the child becomes too disruptive (highly emotional and physical), it may be necessary to postpone his compliance until a later time. However, he should not be permitted to continue the activity which the request interrupted.

5. Be prepared to reinforce compliance with natural social consequences ("Thank you for putting your mat up"; "You are a big help").

6. If a child is being requested to terminate or disrupt some activity which he enjoys, *provide a lead time.* "John, after you finish the next picture, put your toys away." "Sue, we'll go wash our hands after the sand stops falling," as the teacher places a five-minute sand timer on the finger-painting table. Again, do not become upset if a child shows displeasure. This is a natural reaction; do not reinforce it with an excessive reaction. Act as if it did not occur and provide a model of more positive emotional reaction. Assist the child by providing initial

support, "Come on, I'll get you started." Take a child's hand or put an arm around him.

7. Be pleasant. Sudden, curt, demanding, or harsh requests will most likely provoke increased negativism.

8. Be positive and definitive. Instead of "John, how would you like to take the trash out, please," or "Would you get the paper for me," state, "John, take the trash out," or "Hand me the papers on my desk. I would appreciate it."

9. If the child is engaging in an undesired behavior such as talking too loudly, provoking a younger peer or the like, suggest some alternative activity which he also enjoys. "Jack, get the puzzle out and play a game with me. That yelling hurts my ears."

   If the behavior is one that the child understands is taboo, suggest a natural negative consequence of continuing the behavior. "John, if that does not stop immediately, you will be sent to the quiet room." Also, suggest some alternative acceptable behavior. Again, *be prepared to fulfill the stated consequence.* If the child continues, send him to the quiet room. Without a follow-through, the child will merely learn that the threat is an empty one and he will not be influenced by it; he will learn to ignore it.

10. It becomes important, as implied earlier, that the child is in fact able to comply with the request made. Demanding in an unrealistic manner that the child behave in a given manner only intensifies his difficulties.

11. Be prepared to reinforce cooperative compliance behavior in many situations. Identify those instances in which the child is most likely to comply and reinforce the child richly for his cooperative behavior. Label his compliance in a positive manner. "Thank you for doing that. You are a big help." Provide him with a concept that fulfilling adult requests is a pleasant activity. "I appreciate your helping me." "Thank you for picking up your toys. That's a big help."

12. Again, reinforce the child consistently for compliance. Do not assume that the child should comply merely out of gratitude, love, appreciation, respect, or the like. Don't be afraid to express pleasure. Only under such conditions can a child learn to express his happiness.

13. It may prove helpful in cases of high rates of noncompliance to use a time-out procedure in combination with one of reinforcing compliance and other desired behaviors. Wahler has found in his work with children with oppositional behavior patterns that differential social reinforcement of cooperation behavior may not result in reduction in noncompliance. This perhaps is a result of the relatively ineffectual nature of adult social attention. The child has found little in his interaction with teachers and parents that has been pleasant. Wahler and Patterson and his associates have reported successful re-

duction of inappropriate behaviors in highly oppositional children with a skillful use of a time-out procedure combined with the differential reinforcement of cooperative behaviors.

A reduction in the oppositional behavior following use of a time-out procedure provides the adults and child with oportunities to relate to each other in a more positive manner. The parents and teachers will attend to and enjoy the child more as he is no longer so obnoxious. The child will like his teachers and parents more because they no longer are yelling at him or are angry at him.

14. It may be valuable to initiate a token system in which the child would be reinforced immediately for compliance behavior. This may be needed with children who do not appear to care much for adult attention. If a token system is used, start it in a setting in which the child is likely to comply. Gradually extend the token system into problem behavior areas as the child is assured that compliance will result in reinforcing events. Extend it into more difficult areas as the token system becomes more influential.

DEPENDENCY

Children with developmental difficulties are quite prone to develop behavior patterns of dependency. Some dependent children are unable to do much without the presence or assistance of adults, require an excessive amount of adult attention and support, and are apt to become fearful or excessively docile or inactive when adults are not prodding or assisting them. As the child grows older, he clings to mother or teacher, prefers to stay with an adult instead of being with other children, and may even insist on sitting next to teacher or even sleeping with parents. Under these conditions, adults are constantly available for assistance of one kind or another and generally to "do for the child" whenever a problem arises.

How the Behavior Develops

Children with developmental difficulties are likely to learn patterns of dependency as a result of (1) the difficulty which such children have doing things they see others doing or which the social environment requires of them and (2) the tendency which adults and older siblings have to provide too much assistance to the child when he is confronted with difficulty. Stated differently, children are taught by others to be excessively dependent. Children with physical, cognitive, and sensory handicaps of one kind or degree often do require the assistance of others. However, if the adult continues to do for the child, or encourages the child to seek his assistance, even with those things that the child could do or learn to

710

do himself, the child becomes excessively dependent. Whenever the adult does for the child that which he could do himself, the child is being reinforced for not doing, for being passive and dependent.

Many parents of handicapped children overprotect their children. They do not expose them to the range of experiences required for adequate development. Whenever the parent is not present, the child is helpless. Being helpless earns the solicitous attention of mother, teacher, and others. This is quite satisfying to some adults since they feel important and needed when asked for help by a dependent child.

The following example illustrates the development of dependency behavior. Jane, a retarded child with physical handicaps, experiences difficulty in dressing, self-feeding, and in walking. Mother did everything for her, providing her with excessive attention and assistance. Whenever Jane faced a problem, she would call for mother. She seldom let mother out of her sight. However, when a new baby, Sue, was born, mother was no longer available for the constant solicitous attention. The child's dependency behavior no longer produced mother's immediate attention. Jane was placed under a change in schedule of reinforcement, a process which produces emotional or frustration behavior if imposed too suddenly. As a consequence Jane engaged in long crying episodes and exhibited extreme jealousy and aggressive outbursts toward her young sister. The mother's close attention on occasion following the crying episodes only served to strengthen this behavioral reaction.

Dependency, once developed, can be maintained at high strength merely by infrequent reinforcement. Consider the following interaction between child and adult. "Help me." "No, do it yourself." The child whines, stalls, pleads, grumbles. On occasion the adult feels sorry for the child, is in a hurry, gets aggravated at the child's demands, and does provide the requested assistance. Such assistance serves to strengthen the whining, stalling, pleading and grumbling, and thus prolongs these behavior patterns.

Some children have a difficult time leaving mother. Whenever mother is out of sight, leaves home, or leaves the child at school, the child cries excessively. This type of pattern is highly likely when mother is the child's sole or major source of positive reinforcement. Such children have a history of obtaining little reinforcement without mother being present. Mother has hovered over the child, attended to her, encouraged the child's dependent behavior. As a result other persons or situations become relatively unimportant. In some cases, it also may be true that the child has experienced several unpleasant experiences (has been punished or frightened) when away from mother.

Under these conditions, the child becomes highly upset when mother is not present as her absence represents a withdrawal of reinforcement. As noted earlier, a child is quite likely to display disruptive emotional behavior whenever a familiar reinforcing event (in this case, mother) is no longer available. The child may sob, scream for mother to return, and display other fearful behavior. If the crying results in mother's return, the behavior can become a predominant one whenever mother attempts to leave or is absent. Parents frequently go to extremes to meet the child's requirement of no separation as they "feel so badly when I leave him crying like that." It is not unusual under such conditions for children to learn to cry intensely or for prolonged periods of time since these actions have resulted in the reappearance of the parents. Some parents attempt to leave their crying child but return after varying periods of time during which the child is crying. The child thus learns to persist at his crying and mother will return.

Montenegro provides a description of a six-year-old boy who would begin to "cry and shout desperately" when mother left him in kindergarten. They boy, Romeo, had seldom been away from his mother. He had never been left with a baby-sitter. He always got his way with mother. If she did not comply with his wishes, he would engage in tantrum behavior until he got his way. The mother bathed the boy, helped him dress, and sometimes gave him his food. He had no sources of social reinforcement independent of parents.

Behavior Management Program

The following program provides suggestions for dealing with the dependent child:

1. Define the child's dependency in specific observable behavioral terms. Identify both what the child does in various specific situations as well as what he should be doing. Distinguish between those things that the child can do but does not do with sufficient independence and those behaviors that should occur but which the child has never exhibited.

2. Obtain objective measures of the dependency behavior. For example, what percentage of the time does the child remain undressed after being requested to dress without assistance? How many times does the child cry when left alone? How long does he cry after he is left alone?

3. What happens when the child requests "Help me," or "Show me how," or "I can't do that," or some similar indication of dependency? Does the social environment do for the child too frequently? Some social learning experiences have encouraged and strengthened the dependency. Develop some hunches about what has created and reinforced these behaviors.

4. As has been emphasized in previous chapters, a child with learning and behavior problems can learn to be independent in many behavioral areas if the learning experiences permit this. It is essential that the parents and teacher be aware of what the child is able to do or could learn to do and to provide a systematic series of experiences designed to

712

strengthen these behaviors. Why should a child dress or feed himself if the adult world does this for him? Why should he assume responsibility for cleaning up his mess if the adult does it for him?

It often happens, as suggested earlier, that the adult has been too busy, too impatient or too overprotective to permit the child to develop independence in those areas that are within his realm of possibility. In some cases the adults may have expected the child to engage in behaviors which were beyond his level of development at the time or which required considerable vigilance on his part. The child, failing these tasks, may have engaged in dependency behavior which the adults reinforced. New tasks may come to be viewed as aversive. The child may avoid them by displaying dependency behavior.

It may be difficult for a child to do certain things. It may require considerable effort for a child to finish a task. But the child can learn "I can do" only if permitted to do and is reinforced for his efforts. Thus, the initial step in decreasing the dependency of a child is to adopt the position that the child can in fact be more independent and self-sufficient if *realistic* expectations are set and *appropriate* learning experiences provided.

5. Refrain from reinforcing the child for dependency behavior. However, do not suddenly withdraw all assistance: this could be too upsetting to the child. Identify a limited number of behaviors initially and reinforce him for increased independence in these areas.

6. As the child acquires new behaviors of independence (dresses himself, picks up his toys, remains in the room while mother runs an errand, plays with a small group of peers while teacher is engaged with another group), have the child engage in these activities frequently in order to give the child experience in obtaining positive consequences associated with doing for himself. Label the child's independence as being "big boy," "strong," "able," and with other competency terms. Have other persons in the family and school environments recognize the independence and attend to these. As new skills develop, adopt a policy of ignoring dependency behavior and reinforcing competing independent behavior. If a child cries excessively when he has a minor accident, does not have his way, or the like, such behavior should be ignored. Whenever the child is not crying, he should be attended to for being a "big boy" or "big girl." It is not being suggested that a child should not be provided comfort on occasions when he is frightened or is really hurt. Be certain that there is a distinction between these occasions, however, and those in which the child uses this means of getting attention for dependent behavior. Again, do not suddenly withdraw directions or support. Gradually move from a position of directing his dependency behavior toward one of providing less and less assistance as the child becomes able to do for himself.

7. In handling separation crying, either when left in bed at night or at various places and times during the day, the following procedures should be initiated:

   (a) Insure that the child will not have frightening or otherwise unpleasant experiences when left by the adult.

   (b) Increase the range of social reinforcers provided the child. Have other people, especially peers, interact with the child and provide pleasant activities and events.

   (c) As the child begins to respond to other reinforcing events, separate adults more and more.

   The specific procedures used will depend upon the strength of the crying and related behaviors and upon the presence and number of other dependency and fearful behavior patterns. If separation crying is one of numerous dependency reactions, a program emphasizing gradual separation should be followed as new independent behaviors are acquired. If the behavior is an isolated pattern, separation at specific times in familiar and comforting settings may be initiated early in the program.

8. It may be necessary initially to reinforce the child for trying. Following this, reinforce progressively more complex approximations of the desired independent behavior. Consistency becomes important. It is important to recognize that many children may be able to accomplish certain tasks (has the skills of dressing, self-feeding, playing without adult present) but will not do these things independently of the adult. The task is to reinforce independence in these areas. In other cases, the child may be unable to accomplish certain tasks as he has not acquired the necessary basic skills. In both instances, specific behavior objectives denoting increasing independence must be identified and provided frequent and consistent reinforcement.

9. Provide the child with experiences in making simple decisions. Give him two foods and permit him to select one. Offer two puzzles and have him select one. Let him select one of two shirts or her select one of two dresses provided. Be prepared to accept and reinforce the child's choices. In this manner the child's independence is being enhanced.

EXCESSIVE AGGRESSIVE BEHAVIOR

Some children are described as aggressive, hostile, and having associated patterns of negativism and general noncompliance. These behavior patterns not only interfere with the child's learning of more appropriate ways of behavior but also disrupt others in the social environment. Children are often unpredictable, embarrass parents, create turmoil because they tease and fight siblings and peers, will not comply with parental or teacher re-

714

quests, and engage in temper tantrums when aggravated. These behavior patterns may occur in isolation or in various combinations. Unfortunately for child, family, and those in the school setting, some children are characterized by all.

When this combination occurs, parents and teachers frequently are puzzled, discouraged and overwhelmed. They frequently feel that something is wrong with the child which causes him to behave in this manner. It is not unusual for parents and others who attempt to manage the child to be drawn into a battle with the child. Similar patterns of shouting, striking out, and temper-tantrum-like behavior result.

The major difference between the behavior of the aggressive child and other children is that the behavior rate or intensity of the aggressive child is greater and he engages more frequently in such behaviors in inappropriate situations. Most children are noncompliant at times, display temper tantrums, and attack others either verbally or physically in the normal course of development. When these events become too frequent or when an aggressive episode becomes highly intense and prolonged, the home and school environments usually become concerned and begin to look for factors which may account for these behavior patterns.

How the Behavior Develops

Teasing, yelling, and attacking others (hitting, shoving, verbally abusing) are behaviors acquired by children because they produce consequences which are either positively or negatively reinforcing. In most instances, yelling "Stop that or I'll poke you" increases in strength as the threat removes an unpleasant source of teasing from siblings or peers. Hitting, kicking, and biting become major reactions to situations which interfere with the child's plans or activities as these behaviors remove the interruption. The child may learn to be aggressive as these behaviors terminate a range of unpleasant situations (teasing and reprimanding from others).

The child pushes another child and gets a toy. He is reinforced for pushing. A child yells when his big brother attempts to recover his book which Frank is reading. Frank's yell brings a demand from father, "Let Frank keep the book." In this way the child is trained to yell whenever his brother interferes with him.

It has been observed that the crying which hitting another child may produce serves as a powerful reinforcer to the child who does the hitting. It frequently does become a secondary positive reinforcer to the aggressive child as crying so frequently becomes associated with getting his way. If a child "gets away with" hitting, pushing, demanding, grabbing —the aggressive child causes another child to cry and he gets the toy, book, tricycle, privilege, following such behaviors—these ways of behaving will become more frequent and may become the more dominant form of peer control.

715

It is understandable that parents and teachers are sometimes puzzled by the persistence of aggressive behavior in some children. "Why, I'm always scolding or spanking Jim for hitting his younger brothers, but he keeps doing it in spite of the punishment. He's good for a while but I can't spank him all the time."

In a recent study of an overly aggressive child, it was observed that Jim attacked his younger siblings four or five times in a morning. Almost invariably the younger boys would begin crying. Most frequently, Jim would win the argument before mother would appear and would get the toy, TV choice, food or reinforcing event from the other boys. Mother fluctuated considerably in her handling of the problem. Frequently she would ignore the fracas. At other times, she would yell at Jim and threaten to punish him if he did not stop being naughty. Even less frequently, usually after the fighting became intense, she would lose her patience, scold Jim and send him to his room. But for every punishment, Jim was reinforced many times by the crying of his younger brothers and by the positive events which his hitting produced. The inconsistent manner in which mother was handling the problem merely compounded the problem. She was becoming a grouch, was losing her temper, and was yelling in a manner similar to that which she was attempting to eliminate in Jim.

Aggressive behavior also may be strengthened by the social attention which it creates. Parents and teachers come running when a child attacks another child. Also, whenever the child is aggressive toward adults he is sure to obtain considerable attention. The fact that the adult attention may be a reprimand is not a factor in many cases. As emphasized earlier, it is not unusual for such attention to have a strengthening effect on the behavior that produces it. Also it is probably true that both positive and negative reinforcement underlie the development of high-rate aggressive behavior, with negative reinforcement being the major process involved.

An additional factor involved in development of aggressive behavior is imitation. Children are more likely to engage in aggressive behavior if parents, siblings, peers, or teachers display aggressive behavior. It is not invariably true that aggressive children have aggressive parents or teachers. It is true, however, that aggressive children frequently have parents or teachers who have behaved quite inconsistently in their handling of the child's aggressive behavior. On occasion, adults will punish such behaviors, sometimes rather harshly. But on too many other occasions such behaviors are ignored, overlooked, tolerated, or permitted to occur and be reinforced.

Behavior Management Program

Control of aggressive behavior might be achieved by following this management program:

1. As behaviors which may be viewed as aggressive vary considerably, the initial step in a behavior management program is to define the

behaviors and describe the time, place, and social settings in which these events occur. The program is designed to deal with the behaviors—hitting, pushing, yelling, smart talk—and not with aggression. It is necessary to specify the behaviors which are creating difficulty.

2. The second step is to obtain some measure of the frequency with which the behavior occurs. Children will not suddenly stop being aggressive. However, if aggressive outbursts are well-defined and measured prior to and during the behavior management program, the adults can readily determine if the rate of aggressive behavior is being reduced. The objective is to lower the rate of aggressive behaviors to a tolerable level.

3. Third, prior to initiating a program, observation should be made of precisely what the behavior produces. Does the child get his way? Does he get attention which he otherwise would not obtain? Do the adults in the environment become upset with the child and engage in disruptive emotional behavior? Any of these and similar events may be maintaining the behavior.

4. How frequently does the child receive positive social reinforcement for behaving appropriately? It is likely that the excessively aggressive child gets little positive social attention. Adults and peers have learned to turn him off because he is so obnoxious so often. They avoid interaction with him when he is behaving satisfactorily in fear of creating a situation in which he will behave aggressively. He is likely to be attended to only when he behaves aggressively, and then only inconsistently.

5. The child should not get his way following aggressive behavior; he does not get a toy which was snatched from another child, or does not get his choice of records after screaming at another child. That kind of behavior must not result in positive consequences. When this extinction procedure is initiated, be prepared for emotional outbursts from the child. Recall that whenever certain behavior no longer produces reinforcing consequences, a frustration reaction is highly likely for a period of time. These periods will decrease in frequency and intensity, however, as the child experiences no positive consequences following aggressive behavior.

6. In initiating a behavior management program, inform the child of the new rules which will be in effect. Ignore complaints. Do not argue with the child or attempt to defend the rules. Whenever possible, involve the child in a discussion of his aggressive behaviors and in the desirable consequences associated with more socially appropriate behavior. Encourage him to set new behavioral goals and to select positive consequences to be obtained by nonaggressive behaviors.

7. It frequently becomes valuable to impose some negative consequences following inappropriate aggressive behavior. This is especially needed at times in which it is impossible to remove all positive consequences

717

for aggressive behavior and in those instances of high strength and frequently practiced behaviors. Under the condition of consistency, such contingent and predictable consequences also provide the child with a realistic relationship between inappropriate social behavior and unpleasant consequences. A five- to ten-minute time-out procedure has been used successfully with many aggressive children.

8. As emphasized earlier, it is essential that the punishment procedure be accompanied by a plan for reinforcing the child frequently for appropriate behavior. Be sure to identify specific behaviors to reinforce which may serve to take the place of the aggressive behavior. These may include such activities as playing with children, sitting quietly, complying with requests, cooperating with peers, watching without disruption, taking his turn, sharing his materials. Upon initiation of the punishment procedures, it is critical that additional effort be made to recognize and positively reinforce appropriate behaviors. Otherwise the relationship with adults will be one predominantly associated with punishment. As the reinforcement value of social praise or approval provided by parents and teachers is relatively weak, it would be desirable to utilize reinforcers of a concrete nature such as trinkets, toys, or candy. A token system might be initiated to make available a wider range of reinforcing events. In addition, after some success has been realized and the child's aggressive behavior shows a noticeable decrease, the token system would permit the easy use of a response-cost procedure.

   Frequent pairing of social praise and approval with the presentation of the token and other tangible reinforcers is essential as a means of increasing the reinforcement value of these social events.

9. Make a point of reinforcing desired behaviors in other children while the child with excessive aggressive behaviors is observing. This demonstration of appropriate behaviors which produce valuable positive consequences may well increase the likelihood of these behaviors on the part of the observer.

10. Be as consistent as possible in managing the new contingencies. Whenever deviations of the rules occur, regardless of the time and place of infraction, provide the negative consequence. Children learn to be aggressive in highly selective situations—public places such as church, grocery store, bus; when visitors are present—because this behavior has resulted in immediate reinforcing consequences. These immediate consequences become highly influential in strengthening aggressive behavior and serve to offset the suppressing effects of punishment which is inconsistently provided but at a much delayed time. At the same time, be sure to immediately and frequently reinforce desired reactions.

11. It is best to initiate the behavior management program at home and at school. There is no basis for expecting behavior which changes in one

setting to change spontaneously in another. It may occur to some degree but unless both environments change the manner in which aggressive behavior is handled, there is no basis for expecting a generalized change.

12. Demonstrate to the child and have him rehearse those socially acceptable behaviors which will produce reinforcing consequences comparable to those produced by the aggressive behavior. Some children have had little practice in engaging in nonaggressive behaviors in some conditions. Tell him, show him, have him observe other children engaging in the desired behaviors, physically guide or prompt him through desired behaviors, have him role-play or otherwise rehearse the behaviors —and be sure to provide positive reinforcement for these.

13. Remain calm as the behavior management program is implemented. If the teacher becomes angry, loud, explosive, loses his temper, or otherwise loses his control, he is merely providing an aggressive model. Firmness and consistency produce much better results.

Operational Concepts

1. Although different children may exhibit the same behavioral patterns, the etiology of the behaviors, as well as the current stimulus, may be quite different for each.

2. The same behavior, developed into a habit pattern, can be prompted by different stimuli at different points in time.

3. The identification of problem behavior depends not only on the perceptions of the observer, but also on his values and expectations.

4. Variation in teacher attitudes with regard to what constitutes desirable or undesirable behavior is often confusing and misleading to the pupil.

Implications

Because of the enormous importance that teachers, administrators, and parents assign to coping with problem behavior in children, a comparatively large piece of Gardner's work has been included in the *Handbook*. The virtues of his analysis are obvious: the major categories of problem behavior are identified; the forces contributing to their development are discussed; the basic elements of related theory are incorporated; and—perhaps of most practical benefit—specific teacher strategies are suggested for each of the problem-behavior categories.

Although Gardner has organized his ideas with serious problem behavior children in mind, precisely the same coping strategies are appropriate with less serious behavioral problems.

The author himself takes pains to remind the reader that his recommendations, although based upon solid clinical evidence, are more suggestive than prescriptive. Errors frequently occur in the diagnosis of a behavioral problem; individual children frequently do not fit the standard pattern; and the classroom organization or personal idiosyncrasies of a given teacher may inhibit the effectiveness of a particular tactic. For these and a number of other reasons, the recommendations are not to be regarded either as foolproof or as the most desirable course of action in all cases.

William I. Gardner

Influencing Behavior Patterns

The home and school environments of the child contain a wide range of events which influence *how* a child will behave as well as *when* and *where* these behaviors are likely to occur. A brief look at a preschool classroom might reveal the following activities:

> The teacher, Mrs. Schmidt, points to a puzzle and suggests, "Put the dog together, Phil." Susan jumps out of her chair and yells at Jim who is in the play area across the room. The teacher aide, Miss Debany, seated with three children in another section of the room, smiles at Jill and exclaims, "Oh, you can really color well." Mrs. Schmidt exclaims, "Scott, stop that and sit down!" Jill smiles at Tom when he gives her a toy.

Within this brief time span, a number of things are occurring which illustrate the dynamic aspects of the social learning process. The environment contains many events which may assume various roles in this process.

Some of these events facilitate learning; others may actively interfere with effective learning. Some events come to influence the time and place of specific patterns of behavior. Other events serve to strengthen and to insure that specific behaviors will be maintained. Still other events serve to discourage a child from engaging in certain behavior. Some events influence unsettling emotional reactions while others serve to soothe and satisfy the child. There are certain rules which, when followed by the parent and teacher, will influence child behavior in a specific manner. The effective adult, whether parent or teacher, whether in the home or in a more formal school setting, uses these rules to insure that the child will learn those behaviors which he should acquire.

CLASSES OF ENVIRONMENTAL EVENTS

Events Influencing Emotional Behavior

Many events in the environment influence the child's *emotional* behavior. A child who behaves in a fearful manner around strangers repre-

Reprinted from William I. Gardner, *Children with Learning and Behavior Problems,* © 1974; by permission of Allyn and Bacon, Inc., Boston.

sents an example of the influence of such events. The fear response occurs whenever strangers are present. The fearfulness developed out of the child's previous experiences and can be understood in terms of certain learning principles. The same principles accounting for the development of this fearful behavior can be used to influence more positive emotional characteristics of the child. For example, these principles can be used in structuring learning experiences to insure that a child learns to like an activity or to enjoy a person.

Positive Reinforcing Events

Other events in the environment influence the development of a wide range of self-help, motor socialization, language, and similar behavior patterns. Such events influence behavior when they occur after the child does something. These consequences which follow behavior and strengthen it are called *reinforcers* or *reinforcing events* (see Table 1).

The child will learn to behave in that manner which results in these reinforcing and similar pleasant consequences. Jill's smile, which followed Tom's sharing of his toy, increases the likelihood of such behavior on his part in the future. The smile may serve to reinforce or strengthen this behavior.

It is valuable to recognize that the type of reinforcing events which are most effective in promoting learning vary greatly from child to child and under certain circumstances, from one time to another for any specific child. A consequence such as adult approval or praise may be highly reinforcing to Melissa but be of little interest to her playmate, Toni. A teacher's smile at a given time in a child's development may be highly reinforcing for one child but not so for another child. Adult attention may be highly enjoyable to a child on most occasions, but at times for the same child such attention may have a neutral or even an aggravating effect.

Discriminative Events

A third class of environmental events fulfills a *discriminatory* role. These antecedent events come before behavior occurs and serve to signal

TABLE 1

BEHAVIOR	PLEASANT (REINFORCING) CONSEQUENCES
Tom gives Jill the toy car.	Jill smiles at Tom.
John looks at the teacher when she calls his name.	The teacher smiles and suggests, "You may put your work up."
Sue says the word "Ball" when shown a picture of a ball.	The language therapist enthusiastically exclaims, "That's right!"
Sara puts her toys away.	Mother hugs her and exclaims, "What a big helper you are!"

the time and place at which certain behaviors are likely to result in certain consequences (see Table 2). The same behavior occurring at other times or in other places may not result in positive consequences and thus would be less likely to reoccur under those circumstances. The child who does behave appropriately by engaging in the desired behavior at the right time and place is said to be behaving in a discriminating manner. He learns not only how to behave, but also when or under what conditions to engage in various behaviors.

A teacher's request, "John, finish your work," has acquired influence over the behavior involved in work completion as this behavior pattern has been reinforced (resulted in desirable consequences) on numerous occasions in the past. Behaviors other than those involved in work completion, under these conditions, have not resulted in similar positive consequences and are less likely to interfere with work completion.

Aversive Events

Another class of events has painful or unpleasant characteristics. These events may have quite different effects on the behavior of a child depending upon whether the behavior is followed by (1) the *occurrence* of these unpleasant consequences or (2) the *removal* of these unpleasant consequences.

Punishing Events

Behavior which results in the occurrence of unpleasant consequences is less likely to be repeated under similar conditions in the future. Behavior which results in the loss or reduced availability of pleasant consequences is also less likely to reoccur. The arrangement whereby such unpleasant consequences follow certain behaviors is called *punishment* (see Table 3).

John's behavior of pulling the toy away from Joe was followed immediately by the painful consequence of being hit in the stomach. Sue's whining behavior resulted in her loss of the privilege of watching TV. In both instances of punishment, the behavior which produced the unpleasant consequences would be less likely to reoccur under similar conditions in the future.

TABLE 2

ANTECEDENT (CUE)	BEHAVIOR
Jill sees the candy.	Jill reaches for the candy.
The teacher says, "Mindy, look at me."	Mindy looks at the teacher.
The teacher says, "John finish your work."	John returns to his desk and begins working.
Mother announces, "Dinner is ready."	Sue stops her coloring and runs to the table.

TABLE 3

BEHAVIOR	UNPLEASANT (PUNISHING) CONSEQUENCES
John pulled the toy away from Joe.	Joe hit John in the stomach.
Sue began to whine when asked to get ready for bed.	Sue lost her privilege of watching the late movie on TV.
Jill moved from the table when asked by the teacher to remain seated.	The teacher aide promptly placed Jill in a chair in the corner facing the wall. She could not interact with the class for ten minutes.
Steve refused to put the toys on the shelf.	Mrs. Jones required Steve to sit at his desk during recess period.

Negative Reinforcing Events

Other behaviors may be followed by the removal of unpleasant conditions which are present at the time the behavior occurs. As a result, these behaviors are more likely to reoccur under similar circumstances in the future. The procedure by which behavior is influenced through removal of unpleasant conditions is called *negative reinforcement.*

In each case in Table 4, those behaviors which terminated the unpleasant conditions were strengthened. Sara's calling her mother, Don's whining, Jill's crying, and teacher's frowning and threatening all are more likely to occur under the same or similar circumstances in the future since each removed an unpleasant condition; Cathy stopped teasing Sara, Nan gave the book to Don and left the room, Mother stayed with Jill, and Jack stopped talking.

Neutral Events

Numerous events in the life of the child may have no systematic effect on his behavior. Many of these *neutral* events can acquire, however, any of the behavior influence characteristics noted above. A neutral event

TABLE 4

UNPLEASANT CONDITION	BEHAVIOR AND CONSEQUENCE
Cathy is teasing Sara.	Sara calls her mother. Cathy stops teasing.
Nan attempts to take the book from Don.	Don begins to whine. Nan turns the book loose and leaves the room.
Mother announces that she is leaving Jill with a sitter.	Jill begins to sob and clings to Mother. Mother stays at home.
Jack is talking too loudly during independent work period.	Teacher frowns at Jack, shakes her finger at him and threatens to punish him. Jack stops talking.

may become aversive, reinforcing, may come to produce either positive or negative emotional behavior, or may serve as cues for other behaviors. The actual characteristics acquired will depend upon the manner in which these neutral events are associated with other events which presently influence behavior in a specific manner.

A teacher may request, "Sue, look at me." The child may continue playing with her toys and give no indication that the verbal request had any influence on what she was doing. In this instance, the request was a neutral stimulus event since it had no specific influence on the child's behavior.

If the teacher wishes to change the influence which the verbal request has on the child, she may follow a procedure of *behavior shaping*. This may involve the following steps: (1) the child is physically guided, or prompted, through the response pattern of looking at the teacher following the verbal cue "Sue, look," and (2) after looking at the teacher the child is provided an immediate consequence such as a pat on the back, a piece of food, or some other event which is reinforcing to the child. After a few repetitions of this sequence, the neutral event of "Sue, look at me," may come to function as a specific discriminative cue. The child learns to look up whenever teacher makes a request. This learning takes place as the behavior of looking at the teacher immediately following these specific cues results in positive consequences.

As another example, a teacher's praise initially may have little consistent reinforcing effect on Tim's behavior. However, after frequent association of teacher's praise with other events, which are in fact reinforcing to Tim (such as a pat on the back or food), the teacher's approval may become reinforcing. In this manner, a neutral event may become highly effective in strengthening and maintaining other behavior patterns of the child. The procedures of behavior shaping and the method of increasing the reinforcement qualities of neutral events will be described in more detail in later chapters.

Social Models

The social models in the child's life are another important class of events which influence the behavioral patterns of the child. He may develop desirable and undesirable behaviors alike through *imitating* the observed behavior of those around him. If the peers, siblings, or adults in the child's life are loud, anxious, short-tempered, and aggressive, the child is quite likely, through imitation, to adopt some of these behavior patterns. If the social models are relaxed and pleasant, the child is more likely to acquire these behavioral patterns. In view of the possible influence of behavioral models, adults must behave in the presence of their children as they wish the children to behave. If most effective behavior development is to occur, children must be exposed to the appropriate behaviors of other children and adults.

Behavioral Contingencies

It is useful to think of the relationship which exists between behavior and its environmental consequences as representing a *behavioral contingency*. A statement of a behavioral contingency includes a specification of the behavior which will produce a specific consequence. The behavioral contingency may refer to relationships which involve either positive or negative consequences. The behavior management program is designed so that the teacher may control many of these behavioral contingencies. She may arrange for positive consequences to follow desired behavior or she may decide to remove positive consequences following inappropriate behavior. She may arrange for aversive events to follow or be presented contingent upon inappropriate responses or she may arrange for the removal of aversive consequences following desired behavior. To the extent that she has control over present contingencies or can influence future contingencies, the teacher will be able to influence the development and reliable occurrence of desired behaviors.

INCONSISTENCY CREATES PROBLEMS

Inconsistency by parents and teachers in requiring certain behaviors from the child creates conditions for development of inappropriate ways of behaving. A child may learn to voice excessive and unwarranted objection to teacher and parental requests by the inconsistent manner in which the objections are handled by these adults. A teacher who fluctuates between following through at times on what she requires the child to do and in giving in to the child's objection (e.g., stalling, negativistic comments, whining, crying) at other times is merely teaching the child to object inappropriately to those teacher requests which he does not like. These experiences teach the child to become uncooperative, to whine, or to engage in temper tantrums or attention-getting behavior. These inappropriate behavior patterns occasionally pay off; they remove the unpleasant requests made by the teacher. The child learns not to pay too much attention to what adults say or else he learns that responsibilities or agreements do not have to be honored. Rules and limits are not taken seriously since they apply only part of the time—and then only inconsistently.

Children with learning and behavior problems should be provided with well-delineated restrictions and freedoms. A child who knows what to expect—what various behaviors will result in what specific consequences—is a child who will be free to use his resources for positive learning experiences. He will not spend excessive time "objecting," "testing the limits," or attempting to find out if mother or teacher is really serious this time when she makes a request.

It is probably true that a child who does experience learning and behavior difficulties requires, even more than the nonhandicapped child, a consistent and supportive learning environment if he is to avoid learning an excessive number of undesirable behavior patterns. In view of this situation, both parent and teacher should be highly selective in the behavioral expectations which are set for each child at any given time. They should have a sound basis for their expectations of each child so that there is reasonable assurance that the child can engage in the behaviors expected under the specific conditions provided. With this assurance the adults will be justified in their expectations on most occasions and will provide the child with a consistent, predictable, and successful learning experience. After favorable experiences in a structured and consistent environment, the child will become assured that requests will not be made that will be impossible or too difficult for him to fulfill. The child will become a more cooperative, self-assured, and successful learner.

CLASSES OF PROBLEMATIC BEHAVIOR

The major goals of an early education experience are (1) to influence the development and consistent occurrence of an increasingly complex set of new behavior patterns and (2) to eliminate or reduce in strength behavioral reactions which create problems for the child and others in this social environment. A child is viewed as having problems whenever he does not learn or behave as he is expected to by the home or school environments. If the child does not behave as expected, teachers, parents, and others comprising the child's social environment will react in a manner which reflects their disappointment or concern. These expectations by parents and teachers may be based on a variety of chronological, mental, physical, legal, ethical, or other considerations. A four-year-old child is expected to do certain things in relation to specific situations. He is expected to feed himself, to dress with minimal assistance, to play with other children, to have language skills permitting verbal interaction. A child with a mental age of three is expected to be able to discriminate a doll from a ball upon verbal request and to color a picture with reasonable accuracy.

Behavioral Deficits

Regardless of the basis for these, parents and teachers do expect a child to behave in a specified manner both in structured learning or performance situations and in unstructured settings. The child is given a spoon and encouraged to feed himself. He does not do so. Another child is given a box of blocks of various shapes and colors and asked to sort the red circles and blue squares in a separate pile. He fails to complete this task even though he does seem to distinguish red from blue. A third child does not pay attention to the teacher during language class. He wanders around the room instead. Josh sits and stares in a blank fashion at a cartoon movie while his peers respond with laughter and animated pleasure. All of these children exhibit *behavioral deficits* when viewed from the point of view of what the social environment expects or wishes the child to be able to do. Each child in these examples does not behave in the manner expected of him by the situation. A discrepancy exists between what the child does and what the situation requires. He either lacks the necessary skills, or, if they are present, the skills occur in an inconsistent and unacceptable manner.

Basis for Behavioral Deficits

Depending on the behavior deficits which he presents, a child may be described as exhibiting a general learning deficit, perceptual–motor deficits, language deficits, deficits in self-care behaviors, or a combination of these and other problems. Within any of these behavior areas, the deficits may represent one or a combination of the following:

1. *The desired behavior may be completely absent.* The child may never have engaged in the behavior. The child may never have been able to distinguish a red ball from a blue ball or to write his name. He may be unable to engage in certain behaviors at a given time because he never has had an opportunity to learn the desired behaviors. He may not be able to dress himself because mother has always done it for him. He may be unable to engage in simple perceptual–motor tasks or in social interaction as a result of high-rate stereotyped behavior such as body rocking. He may be unable to use scissors, to distinguish red from green, or to speak in complete sentences because he has never been exposed to an environment which provided for the development of these behaviors.

In other instances the learning experiences which were provided may have been inadequate to teach that child the behavior patterns which were desired but absent. Mother may have attempted to teach the child to distinguish red from blue or to see the difference between a circle and a square, but failed to accomplish her goal as a result of the way in which she presented the task. The educational goal in these instances where the desired behavior is absent is to provide a more satisfactory teaching program to insure the development of the absent behavior.

2. *The desired behavior may be in the child's repertoire but may not occur on a consistent basis.* The child may be able to engage in the behavior but does not. He has done so on some occasions in the past. The child may not want to dress himself or be interested in playing with other

729

children even though he has dressed himself previously and has played with other children on past occasions. The goal is to increase the consistency of the behavior by associating its occurrence with reinforcing consequences.

3. *The desired behavior occurs only under restricted conditions.* The child will talk when mother is present but will not talk to anyone else when mother is absent. The child can read simple stories, but will not do so when other children are present. The goal in such instances is to insure that the behavior will also occur in a number of other appropriate conditions.

4. *The desired behavior may be in the child's repertoire but occurs only under conditions of frequent reinforcement.* Under less favorable conditions the behavior becomes erratic or does not occur at all. Hal will complete his table work when the teacher sits next to him and praises him frequently. He seldom completes a task when the teacher is not present. The goal is to insure that the behavior will be maintained under conditions of less frequent reinforcement.

It is true that behavioral deficits may reflect neurological or other physical conditions which restrict or greatly impede the learning or performance of the desired behavior. Care must be exercised in assuming, however, that behavioral deficits are in fact totally a result of physical limitations. The child with obvious neurological, sensory, or physical impairment may well be able to acquire new behavior patterns and to engage in them under normal conditions if provided carefully designed learning experiences. The goals of an early education program for children with deficit behavior patterns are obviously (1) to provide appropriate learning experiences which will result in the child's acquisition of desired behavior patterns which he presently does not have, and (2) to insure that these are maintained and do occur with consistency under appropriate conditions.

Excessive Behavior Patterns

Other behavior patterns create problems due to their *excessive* nature. Children who are demanding, who cry too easily or too frequently, who talk too much or are too loud, who are too fearful, or who are too aggressive toward their peers demonstrate excessive behavior patterns. In other instances behavior is excessive if it occurs in too many inappropriate situations. The child shows poor discrimination. Such excessive behavior patterns may not only disrupt other children and adults but also may interfere with the child's ability to learn new behaviors or to engage in other more appropriate behaviors. As an example: a child who is disruptive during music period may well have appropriate skills of attending; during Sesame Street, he may attend for long periods of time. The teacher knows from this observation that he can sit still and participate in group activities under certain conditions. But under the conditions of the music period, the disruptive behavior is stronger than the desired behavior of attending.

At the same time, such excessive behavior patterns frequently interfere with the development of more appropriate ones. During the time the child is talking loudly he cannot be listening to what the teacher is saying and thus misses his language lesson. He cannot learn the new concepts which the teacher is presenting.

It may well be that a child "knows better" than to engage in excessive behavior patterns. The child may be able to verbalize what he should do in a situation, and even be successful in engaging in such behaviors on occasion. But on other occasions inappropriate behavior occurs. The child displaying such inconsistent behavior patterns should not be viewed as naughty or intentionally disruptive. His behavior is the result of social-learning experiences and is acquired in the same manner that more appropriate behavior is acquired. The disruptive behavior pattern at times is under stronger environmental influence than is the appropriate behavior. This may reflect a difference in the previous reinforcement experiences under varying combinations of cues which become associated with the contrasting behavior patterns.

In viewing the excessive behavior patterns of young children, it also is important to recognize that most behavior is not excessive in any absolute sense. Although some behaviors are excessive regardless of where or when they occur, many behaviors may be excessive if they occur in one setting, while not being inappropriate for other situations. Additionally, some excessively occurring behavior may be quite adaptive and even characteristic of many children, but for a given child it becomes inappropriate due to its extreme rate of occurrence. Asking for teacher assistance may be encouraged for all children in a class when unusual difficulty is encountered, but seeking teacher assistance may be viewed as maladaptive when a child engages in this tactic on numerous occasions throughout the school day.

It may be true that specific behavior becomes excessive because a child has numerous behavior deficits in relation to the requirements of specific situations. The child may not have the required behavior in his repertoire; therefore, he engages excessively in what he can do. A child may engage in temper tantrum behavior because he does not have the skills demanded in a situation. Similarly, he may withdraw into stereotyped hand waving, become aggressive, begin to cry, or become hyperactive because the competing appropriate behaviors are not in his repertoire.

Some excessive behavior patterns may occur in a wide range of situations. "He always talks too loudly." "He is too aggressive in all his peer interactions." Other excessive patterns may be specific to situations or to types of situations. "He only becomes hyperactive and distractible when required to interact verbally with adults. At other times he is calm and is able to stick to his work."

Excessively occurring behaviors frequently are puzzling to the teacher due to the apparent self-defeating character of such behaviors. It is difficult to understand what is accomplished. In some instances excessive behavior patterns appear to persist in the absence of any discernible positive consequences. These patterns become even more puzzling when they persist in the face of obvious punishment. "I reprimand him every time it occurs, but it doesn't seem to do any good. He still persists in taking things away from his peers," or "I can't understand why he continues to refuse to cooperate with his peers. They reject him and won't play with him for a while." There is a tendency for many teachers to view such behaviors as resulting from some internal psychic pathology or as reflecting some "deep-down disturbance."

Again, it may be that the child simply has no suitable alternative behaviors available. While the reinforcing consequences associated with the excessive behavior may be minimal, these consequences are sufficient to maintain the excessive behavior patterns simply because the child has no alternative behaviors available for producing more desirable consequences. He must repeat perseveringly the behaviors that are available even though these do not produce the desired positive consequences.

In summary, the "inappropriateness" or the "excessiveness" of a behavior is not an inherent or all-or-none characteristic of the child's behavior. Each gains meaning only in relation to the requirements or expectations of specific situations.

The goals of an educational program designed to deal with excessive patterns are:

1. Teaching the child new discriminations so that behaviors will occur under appropriate conditions and only under appropriate conditions.
2. Reducing the frequency or intensity of excessive behaviors to a level that is acceptable by teaching the child a range of appropriate behaviors which can be used as alternatives to the excessively occurring behaviors.
3. Eliminating selective behaviors so that these will seldom or never reoccur.

732

Operational Concepts

1. Events in the home and school environments strongly influence how a child will behave in the classroom.

2. The learning stimuli responsible for the development of undesirable behaviors are precisely the same as those which can be used to encourage desirable behavior.

3. The motivating and reinforcing events that promote desirable learning vary considerably from child to child. Moreover, they may also vary from time to time for the same child.

4. For constructive behavioral development to occur, children must be exposed to the desired behavior in other children and adults.

5. All behavior is rooted in some cause; what we regard as bad or disruptive conduct is a result of social-learning experiences and is acquired in much the same way as approved behavior.

Implications

   As all teachers know, the odds of being assigned a classroom of children who all behave properly all the time are extremely remote. As a result, a significant aspect of teaching involves the reshaping of inappropriate behavior and the encouragement of desirable actions. The canons of behavioral psychology dictate that good behavior can be fostered through specific conditioning. Whether or not one chooses to embrace the totality of Skinnerian theory, the wisdom of practical experience suggests that constructive action on the part of the teacher is infinitely more effective than action which is merely punitive.

   The system of influencing behavior patterns that Gardner proposes is based upon identifying the behavioral problem, inferring its probable cause, and invoking specific management procedures. Gardner's system is similar, of course, to the techniques which gifted teachers have informally or intuitively always employed. If allowances are made for reasonable trial and error in selecting preferred teacher response to behavioral problems, it is likely that the tactics described will be highly efficient. From the standpoint of the teacher, consequently, the critical thing to remember is that both good and bad behavior are spawned by particular events, experiences, and conditions.

Don E. Hamachek

Strategies for Achieving Positive
Classroom Management

FIVE FACTORS THAT INFLUENCE
CLASSROOM BEHAVIOR

A healthy approach to discipline is one that is more comprehensive than merely maintaining order in the classroom. It is more comprehensive because it includes considerations that also involve personal, social, and environmental factors that influence a student's behavior. The five factors that we'll consider briefly in the pages to follow include: (1) situational and environmental factors, (2) teacher-related factors, (3) academic and curriculum factors, (4) students' personality and growth factors, and (5) group factors.

Situational and Environmental Factors

Social-class conflicts, irresponsible parents, and bad family conditions are among those obvious influences that trigger emotional problems that may be reflected in classroom misbehavior. These are conditions that are external to the immediate school situation and that, unfortunately, the school cannot directly change. There are, however, at least three conditions that are more intrinsic to the school itself and that, as research shows, can have a powerful influence on school behavior.

Size of the school system is an important consideration. Size of the school system is one of those important intrinsic conditions. For example, research indicates that the typical teacher in a large school system copes with almost twice as many severe behavior problems as a teacher in a small or medium size school system. The frustrations of crowded living conditions, racial conflicts, heterogeneity of class membership, and limited dollar resources for upgrading the instructional program are all factors that have been identified by sociologists as affecting the behavior of students in large city schools.

Class size and composition can affect behavior. Class size and composition is another situational condition influencing classroom behavior.

Reprinted from Don E. Hamachek, *Behavior Dynamics in Teaching, Learning, and Growth,* © 1975; by permission of Allyn and Bacon, Inc., Boston.

Research data clearly shows that as the size of the class increases, discipline problems multiply. Group interaction research indicates that as a group grows larger it becomes less able to satisfy the demands of all its members for recognition, affection, and social interaction. This in turn makes it necessary for the teacher to impose more rigid controls, while at the same time reducing the opportunities for responding positively to any one student.

Administration and school organization are strong forces. Administration and school organization is a third situational factor affecting the behavior of students. For example, if the school administration and parents stress the importance of routine, order, and quiet, and rate teachers in terms of how well these objectives are achieved, then many teachers, for the sake of their own survival, may feel forced to bypass psychologically healthier methods of student management and use more punitive and coercive techniques to maintain control. The net effect of this approach is twofold: (1) it drains a teacher's emotional energy, and (2) students start behaving in counter-aggressive and impulsive ways.

Teacher-Related Factors

Classroom misbehavior is sometimes the consequence of a teacher's personality characteristics and manner of relating to students. Some teachers, for example, are so rigidly locked in to doing things a certain way that they unwittingly establish a climate for misbehavior by establishing rules that violate the conditions of growth. They may insist upon total subservience to authority, long periods of enforced concentration, and other patterns of behavior inconsistent with the natural exuberance and energy level of growing children. When restrictive requirements exceed the limits of a youngster's tolerance, they may trigger reactions that are more a rebellion against unreasonable constraints rather than an expression of personal problems unrelated to school.

Lack of experience and a generation gap may cause problems. A teacher's capacity to tolerate or accept or handle misbehavior is influenced by a number of personal factors, which may be interesting for you to know about. For instance, it has been found that teachers who are in good physical health seem to be better able to cope with misbehavior than those who are in poor health. In addition, it has been noted that teachers under twenty-five and over sixty years of age seem to have the most difficulty with discipline problems. Lack of experience is very often associated with the disciplinary problems of younger teachers, while with older teachers it seems to have more to do with greater rigidity and loss of touch with the values and behavior standards of the younger generation. Although it doesn't have to be this way, it does seem to be true that once a teacher reaches his fifties or so he may have to make a special effort not to allow his memories of the "way things used to be" to cloud his perceptions of how young people change from generation to generation.

Too much emphasis on control and punishment is detrimental. Research also shows that some teachers' insistence on control and order in their classes occurs at the sacrifice of qualities of personal warmth. In one investigation, for example, observers sat in on the classes of 118 teachers and wrote down the first remark these teachers made at the start of each minute of a twenty-five minute period. Altogether there were four observation periods, and a total of 100 statements was collected for each teacher. These statements were then rated by other researchers in terms of whether they indicated a concern with achievement, control, management, or affiliation. The ratings were in turn related to other measures of teacher-behavior, including the general impression teachers made on observers. The results of this study are shown in Table 1.

TABLE 1 Classroom Behaviors That Tend To Be Related to Certain Teacher Types

TYPE OF TEACHER			
A	**B**	**C**	**D**
Cold and Controlling (as contrasted with warm and permissive)	Vigorous and Dynamic (as contrasted with dull and quiet)	Insecure and Anxious (as contrasted with confident)	Much Academic Activity (as contrasted with little academic emphasis)
TYPE OF CLASSROOM BEHAVIOR ASSOCIATED WITH EACH TEACHER			
Activities very orderly	Stimulating	Uncertain	Systematic
Much direct control	Excitable	Disorganized	Much direct control
Delegates little authority to students	Gives support	Much evidence of emotional frustration	Emphasized learning
Low affiliation motivation	Vigorous	Dull	Functions often as a source of knowledge
Frequently punishes	Functions often as a source of knowledge	Excitable	High achievement motivation
Aloof	Very verbal	Frequently punishes	
Harsh		Negativistic	
Inflexible			
Hostile			
Dull			
Much evidence of emotional frustration			
Negativistic			
Neuroticism			

SOURCE: N. E. Wallen et al., "Relationships Between Teacher Needs and Teacher Behavior in the Classroom." *Journal of Educational Psychology*, 54 (1963):23–32. (Copyright 1963 by the American Psychological Association. Reprinted by permission.)

Note that the teachers who were perceived as cold and controlling tended to behave toward students in ways that were perceived as punitive and rigid. Their classes were dull and monotonous, and there appeared to be little concern for students' academic achievement. This does not mean that a concern about control is a negative quality, but it does raise the issue about how control is used. Notice that Teacher A maintains order more or less for its own sake, or because he finds disorder personally upsetting. Teacher B, on the other hand, uses control procedures to support a systematic program of classroom learning. The insecure and anxious teacher exercises rather little direct control and punishes often (probably out of frustration), whereas the vigorous and dynamic teacher controls less by threat and punishment and more by the intrinsic holding power of an interesting class and stimulating presentations.

However we look at it, teacher-related factors play a significant part in the sort of discipline problems that occur in a classroom. Wise teachers realize this and make a point of being as aware of themselves as possible in order to minimize the possibility of being the instigator of unnecessary problems. As one teacher expressed it, "It's difficult to cure a problem if you've caused it in the first place."

Academic and Curriculum Factors

Many discipline problems may be traced to an academic curriculum that imposes learning tasks that are unchallenging, unstimulating, and unrelated to students' needs. When coupled with an educational organization that literally forces youngsters to achieve at a certain level before they are either physically or psychologically prepared to do so, the result is an open invitation for the development of discipline problems.

Compulsory education laws that keep youngsters in the classroom many years after they have reached the limit of either their academic educability or interest have created some unhappy problems for teachers. Without judging the merits of compulsory attendance laws, it is evident that we need to acknowledge the futility of trying to cram additional academic learning of the traditional kind into youngsters, who are either unwilling or unable to learn, and instead teach them skills that will contribute to their usefulness as citizens in everyday life.

These observations are not meant to imply that all teachers should be indicted for bad teaching or that all schools are insensitive to the needs of the youths. The fact is that many children and adolescents pursue school-related activities with eagerness and enthusiasm, and many teachers are challenging and stimulating individuals. Yet we cannot deny that significant numbers of children experience feelings of repeated frustration and failure (remember, over one million youngsters drop out of school each year), which generalize into negative attitudes toward the school and are acted out in classroom misbehavior.

Students' Personality and Growth Factors

Even when the curriculum offerings are suitable and varied, the teachers skillful artists, and the administrative organization satisfactory, there will be classroom disciplinary problems because of certain personality and growth characteristics of students. We know, for example, that a youngster's physical condition may be responsible for his misbehavior in school. Lack of sleep, a poor diet, parent conflicts, or an incipient illness may make a child nervous, irritable, unable to concentrate, or difficult to manage in a classroom.

Problem behavior and normal growth consequences are sometimes confused. We would do well to keep in mind that there are some aspects of perfectly normal behavior that can lead to problems of control and management if they are not properly understood. Take, for example, the following account of behavior commonly observed among preadolescent youngsters(*1*):

> With the onset of puberty there is an increasing tendency to withdraw from the parents, to exaggerate friendship with peers, and to idealize adults other than parents. Affective restraint and personal habits that had been acquired and maintained for the parents' sake begin to deteriorate. Unaccountable giggling, laughing, and crying fits, and unexpected coarseness in behavior contrast sharply with the composure of latency.

Sometimes teachers overact to youngsters who behave this way, forgetting that the behavior may be motivated more by the natural consequences of growth than by angry feelings toward either the teacher or school. What we have to do is learn how to temper control with flexibility, and we have to remember that not all misbehavior is abnormal but merely symptomatic of a particular growth period. There are many times when youngsters have difficult growing experiences that may be reflected as an inability to sit still, lack of attention, irritability, or other reactions that can be annoying. The solution to problems created by growth is not to be found through an attack upon behavior but, rather, through a better understanding of the psychological growth pains that a youngster is experiencing.

Fritz Redl, a clinical psychologist with over forty years experience with problem children, has made the point that teachers and youth workers create unnecessary problems for themselves because they fail to understand that much of the so-called "defiant" behavior of children and adolescents is both appropriate and normal. There is what Redl calls "developmental defiance," which, rather than being in any sense abnormal, is a youngster's healthy inclination to defend his own integrity against the wrong demands made by others. In Redl's words(*2*):

> We want Johnny to be respectful to his teacher but we don't want him to run after the first designing bum that offers him candy just because the

man is an adult and looks like a mixture of Abe Lincoln and Santa Claus. On the contrary, we want our children to retain the capacity for *intelligent rebellion*—courage to stick to what they believe in even against strong-armed pressure and the fear of becoming unpopular with the mob.

Actually, a lot of behavior usually termed *defiance* is exactly the opposite. The fifteen year old who participates in smashing the school's windows because he is afraid of being called a sissy is not a *defiant* youngster. He's a coward, an overconformist, a frightened adolescent with no convictions of his own. The fact that he is a sucker for the wrong sort of acclaim does not change the fact that submission rather than defiance is the problem at hand.

Not all "defiant" behavior means the same thing. From a clinical point of view, then, we have to look deeper than surface behavior to know what the problems really are in any specific "defiant act." Where behavior falls into the category of "developmental defiance," we are presented with an educational challenge, and we must be cautious not to be lulled into too hastily diagnosing it "delinquent" or "abnormal."

Then there is what can be termed *reactive defiance*. If you pour a foul-tasting substance down someone's throat, his organism will likely rebel by choking sensations to ward off the unpleasant intrusion. Vomiting under such conditions is not symptomatic of illness but, rather, a healthy defense against hurt from the outside.

A lot of youthful "defiant" behavior falls into the same category. That is, rather than being the outgrowth of a corrupt personality, it is more a defense used by a healthy person against the kind of treatment that shouldn't happen to a snake but that often does happen to school age youths. For example, in a classroom of normal students bored out of their heads by inane teaching methods, the intelligent ones will be the first to become "hard to handle." Their misbehavior is a defense against the devitalizing impact of excessive boredom. If a child with deep-rooted fear of adult violence (perhaps he sees so much of it at home) gets hit by a teacher, the resulting outburst will not be the consequence of a "warped personality" but his frantic defense against the possibility of being overwhelmed by a frightening adult. This sort of "reactive defiance" calls for a consideration of not only what is wrong with the youngster, but also of what is wrong with what we're doing to him.

To be sure, there are many occasions when a student misbehaves that he is, in fact, disturbed or sick or delinquent and what he needs are strict, firm controls or an immediate referral to the school system's mental health personnel. To know the difference between normal reactiveness and abnormal coping, we must first of all be empathic, sensitive observers of child-adolescent behavior, thoroughly grounded in the basic dynamics of each growth stage. We must also recognize that a classroom group can influence behavior, an idea to which we now turn.

Don E. Hamachek

Group Factors

There is little doubt that individual behavior is influenced by the complex, shifting tides of interpersonal relations within the classroom group. Inasmuch as group forces may make a student a bully or a scapegoat, a leader or an isolate, the effects of group climate and the psychological forces operating within a group are matters that have specific implications for the management of child behavior.

Dynamics of group contagion. A group develops distinctive attitudes and patterns of behavior that make its members act as a collective unit. This force is so strong that individuals tend to bow to majority opinion, even when the majority is wrong. This is an important insight into group life because it means that a teacher must be skillful in handling a group's behavior if he hopes to control the behavior of particular individuals within it. The idea behind this insight is that group contagion, or the spread of behavior through a group, can radically alter the behavior of individual group members. We have all seen how the behavior of normally restrained individuals can change dramatically at, say, a football game or pep rally or even an out-of-town convention. Redl has referred to this phenomenon as a form of group psychological intoxication. It is the sort of group contagion that can cause a group of students to lose their sense of proportion, move them to enthusiasm or hostility, spread unrest or irritation through a group, or weld them solidly together for a joint purpose.

References

1. J. S. Kestenborg, "Phases of Adolescence, Part II. Prepuberty Diffusion and Reintegration," *Journal of Child Psychiatry* 6(Oct. 1967):577–614.
2. F. Redl, "Our Troubles with Defiant Youth," *Children*, 2(Jan.–Feb. 1955):5–9.

Operational Concepts

1. The classroom behavior of students is affected by size, composition, and classroom organization.

2. Excessive emphasis upon control and ill-advised approaches to punishment in themselves frequently are detrimental influences.

3. Discipline problems also arise out of (1) learning material that lacks challenge, stimulation, and relevance, and (2) learning assignments that, for one reason or another, foster student failure.

4. The problem behavior of an individual student frequently stems from a psychologically prompted need to be defiant.

5. The classroom behavior of children is influenced by the prevailing group dynamics inasmuch as individual children often adjust their actions in accordance with peer pressures and group expectations.

Implications

It is interesting to note that year after year, in poll after poll, parents identify "discipline" as their predominant concern with the schools. Teachers, too, particularly in the beginning stages of their career, are likely to find classroom control the primary source of anxiety and frustration.

Children are not always disposed to behave in an ideal manner, and all teachers must occasionally deal with "problem children," but the rules of effective classroom management are not particularly complex. When steps can be taken to achieve a defensible class size and a reasonably harmonious composition of personalities; when the teacher invokes sensible standards of student behavior; when the learning content is made appealing and each student is given some hope of success; and when the teacher responds to particular behavior problems diagnostically, seeking to understand the underlying causes and choosing remedies accordingly, the odds of achieving a successfully managed classroom are very high.

All in all, it would be difficult to find better practical advice than that set forth by the author.

Self-Concept

Don E. Hamachek

The Effect of Early School Failures on Self-Image

Three Reasons Why Elementary School
Success Is Important

Early school success is crucial for three basic reasons: (1) subsequent success is not only easier to build onto early success, but it also seems more possible to the student; (2) early success gives him not only a sense of competence and accomplishment, but also establishes a precedent with which he can strive to be consistent; (3) early school success makes any later school failures more bearable because they are more likely to occur within a consolidated self-system buttressed by achievement and fortified by personal accomplishment.

As noble or as worthy as early school success may be, it unfortunately is not available to all children. Two widely used practices, letter grading and nonpromotion, doom thousands of children to failure at a very time in their lives when they are apt to be most lastingly influenced by it. Both of these practices are notorious for their negative effects on a young child's self-concept development, motivation, and subsequent achievement. Let's examine more closely why . . . .

Effects of Elementary School Letter Grades
on Self-concept Development

Letter grades enter into many aspects of the mental health and self-concept development of elementary pupils. For bright children with high achievement needs, letter grades are no problem. They usually receive high marks and enjoy the challenge of competing for them. For many other children, however, letter grades are continual reminders to them that they are not doing as well as the others and that they are slow learners. As one second grader expressed it after receiving four D's and one F on his report card, "I must really be dumb." In ways like this, a child's *perform-*

Reprinted from Don E. Hamachek, *Behavior Dynamics in Teaching, Learning, and Growth,* © 1975; by permission of Allyn and Bacon, Inc., Boston.

ance gets translated into *feeling* and over a long enough period of time the perception of "dumbness" is converted into a *conception* of "dumbness," which is far more difficult to change.

Alexander has correctly noted that low marks function more as a threat of failure than as motivation for improvement. More often than not they are actually punishment for previous failure, poor past environment or emotional problems. As a young elementary school child continues to experience failure, he begins to perceive himself as a poor achiever. Once a negative self-perception sets in, he will, in all likelihood, continue to perform at a low level no matter what his ability.

Not all students are ready for the same learning at the same time. In spite of a certain amount of lip service to the documented evidence that supports the concept of wide individual differences in growth among elementary age youngsters, some schools doggedly persist in behaving as if all children were ready for the same curriculum at the same time. Nothing could be further from the truth. As one small example of the wide disparities in academic readiness among elementary children, a typical fifth-grade class may reflect a range of reading skills all the way from those who are still at the second-grade level to those who are reading at the high school level. In fact, reading test data indicated that we might expect to find as many as 42 percent of a fifth grade reading below grade level. This does not necessarily mean that students in this 42 percent group are less smart than their fellows; it may only mean that developmentally they still have some growing to do and have not yet completed the business of putting it all together in order to cognitively handle the symbol manipulation necessary for reading at grade level.

All in all, the letter-grade system in elementary schools, particularly if it is based on norm-referenced measurement, is an almost certain method of guaranteeing that up to 40 percent of all elementary age children will be exposed to failure, and thus encouraged to incorporate a failure attitude as a part of their self-image during the most impressionable years of their development.

Effects of Elementary School Nonpromotion Practices

A popular education assumption underlying the practice of nonpromotion is that the retained student is re-covering material, is better able to overcome his deficits in subject-matter savvy than he would be were he passed on and exposed to new material. Research has consistently shown that such an assumption is built more on myth than fact. Some of the evidence:

1. The average repeater learns no more in two years than does the average nonrepeater of the same mental age in one year.
2. Nonpromotion does not reduce the range of abilities within a particular

grade level; that is, grades with a high proportion of repeaters are as apt to have as wide a range of ability differences as grades with a low proportion of repeaters.

3. Failed students during two years following failure do not progress significantly greater than promoted matchees during the single year spent in the next grade.

4. A policy of "achieve or fail" seems to have a more negative effect on students who are being retained than those who are not. Although there is a trend toward increased achievement in the school with an "achieve or fail" policy, the increase is limited largely to those who are in no real danger of being retained anyway.

5. Achievement does not decrease when students cease to be threatened by the possibility of nonpromotion; e.g.,
   a. No difference in reading ability was found over a ten-year period when a school changed to a 100 percent promotion policy.
   b. Children who were told at the beginning of a school year that all would be promoted did as well on comprehensive achievement tests as those who were reminded throughout the year that they would not be promoted if they didn't do good work.

6. Retention of students because of their inability to achieve academically can have undesirable effects on their personal-social adjustment.

7. Teachers and peers tend to develop unfavorable attitudes toward nonpromoted students, which encourages nonpromoted students to develop increasingly more negative attitudes toward school and even an eager anticipation towards dropping out.

8. Of those who repeat beyond the first grade, about 35 percent show some improvement, about 53 percent show little or no improvement, and about 12 percent do poorer work.

9. Lack of motivation and subsequent poor school achievement is positively related to a student's experience with nonpromotion; e.g.,
   a. Of those students dropping out between grades eight and nine, all had experienced nonpromotion at least once and over four-fifths had experienced nonpromotion twice.
   b. Out of 2,000 children who began first grade at the same time in the same school system, 643 dropped out before completing high school. All but five of these dropouts, 638, or 99 percent, had been retained in the first grade. As a combined total, these 643 students failed a total of more than 1,800 grades during their first six years of school. This averages out for each dropout failing every other year for six years.
   c. Over 74 percent of the dropouts in one school system repeated at least one grade as compared to only 18 percent among students who graduated from high school.
   d. More than 1,200 students in grades 6 and 7 from fourteen representative schools in a North Carolina study were investigated to differenti-

ate between repeaters and nonrepeaters. Results showed that those who had been retained were reading a 6.8 grade level; those repeating one grade scored a 5.2 level, and those who had repeated two or more grades dropped to a 4.5 grade level. On mathematics achievement, non-repeaters averaged in the 27th percentile; those repeating one grade in the 10th percentile; and those repeating two or more grades dropped to the 5th percentile. All in all, the data do not indicate that retention helps a student "catch up" academically—the usual justification for having students repeat. Failing was also found to have a strong influence on a student's feeling of self-worth. For example, on all the subscales of the *Tennessee Self-Concept Scale,* students who repeated grades scored lower than those who had not. Students repeating two or more grades scored far below the mean on each subscale.

New Perceptions May Lead to New and Improved Behavior

A pioneer in the area of relating self-consistency to school performance was Prescott Lecky, who was one of the first to point out *that low academic achievement may be related to a student's conception of himself as being unable to learn academic material.* He observed, for example, that some children made the same number of errors in spelling per page no matter how difficult or easy the material. These children spelled as though they were responding to a built-in upper limit beyond which they could not go. It occurred to Lecky that they were responding more in terms of how they *thought* they could spell than in terms of their *actual* spelling abilities. He arranged to have a group of these children spend some time with the counselor who helped them explore their feelings about their spelling abilities. As a consequence of these discussions and despite the fact that these children had no additional work in spelling whatever, there was a notable improvement in their spelling! There was less improvement for some children than for others, but the general trend was in the direction of better spelling. One can only speculate about the dynamics at work here, but it does not seem unreasonable to suggest that as the childrens' spelling *confidence* increased, so, too, did their spelling *skills.* In other words, as they acquired new perceptions of their spelling abilities, they also acquired new consistencies, which is to say that as a child moves from believing he is a poor speller to believing he is at least a better speller than he thought he was, his performance changes in the direction of being consistent with his new perception.

Behavior Reinforced Early Tends to Remain Stable Over Time

The purpose for understanding something about the nature and expressions of self-consistency is not merely an academic one. Psychological research and developmental evidence suggests that basic personality styles begin early in life, which means that whether we are teachers or other professional people or parents we can be alert to signs indicating the possible direction of a child's growth. Too often we wait for a child to "grow out of" his shyness, or aggressiveness, or lack of motivation, or speech problem, or whatever without realizing that we are confusing the symptom of a possible personality defect for what is frequently called "just a stage he's going through." Behavior that is established early and reinforced while the child is young is likely to remain stable over time and serve as the seedbed in which one's basic ideas about himself are nurtured. The fact that a child's personality structure is established early and tends to remain stable over time would suggest that, if we are to have a positive effect on a child's self-image development, then we must do this while he is going through his formative years. Sensitive parents and psychologically tuned elementary level teachers working in conjunction with extended guidance and counseling programs in elementary schools would surely be a constructive step in the right direction.

SELF-CONCEPT AND RELATIONSHIP TO ACADEMIC ACHIEVEMENT

The self is a complicated subjective system that a student brings with him to school. A student perceives, interprets, accepts, resists, or rejects what he encounters at school in the light of the way he sees himself as a person generally and as a student specifically. Indeed, there is a mounting body of evidence to suggest that a student's performance in an academic setting is influenced in both subtle and obvious ways by his concept of self. For example, Roth, investigating the role of self-concept in achievement, observed: ". . . in terms of their conception of self, individuals have a definite investment to perform as they do. With all things being equal, those who do not achieve, *choose* not to do so, while those who do achieve, *choose* to do so"(1).

A Low Self-Image May Lead to Underachievement

If a child starts with a negative self-image about his ability to do school work, we might expect to find explicit signs of low or poor academic achievement during the early elementary years. For instance, Shaw and McCuen reasoned that if it is true that academic underachievement is related to basic personality structure, then such behavior is, indeed, likely to occur during the early school years. To check this out they took a group of eleventh- and twelfth-grade students who had been in the same school system since the first grade and who scored in the upper quarter of an intelligence test administered in the eighth grade and divided them into achiever and underachiever groups, which were separated for males and females; thirty-six male achievers, thirty-six male underachievers, forty-five femals achievers, and seventeen female underachievers. The mean grade point averages were computed for each group at each grade level. They found that there were significant differences between male achievers' and underachievers' grade point averages at the first grade. The grade point difference between the two groups increased at each grade level from grade three up to grade ten, where there was a slight decrease. There were no significant differences between female achievers and underachievers before grade nine, although nonsignificant differences were apparent in grade six. These differences between the two groups of girls continued to increase through grade eleven. So, as you can see, underachievement for boys can begin as early as the first grade, is definitely present by third grade, and becomes increasingly more serious into the high school years. For girls the problem may exist as early as grade six and is definitely present and of increasing importance from grades nine to eleven.

A Positive Self-Concept Is Necessary But Not Enough

In the second phase of a longitudinal investigation of the relationship between self-concept of ability and school achievement that began with the study cited above, Brookover and his associates found that self-concept of ability was a significant factor in achievement at all levels, seventh through tenth grade.

In the third and final phase of this longitudinal project, which studied the same students from the time they were seventh graders through grade twelve, the following observation regarding the relation of the self-concept of ability to achievement was made(2):

> The correlation between self-concept of ability and grade point average ranges from .48 to .63 over the six years. It falls below .50 only among boys in the 12th grade. . . . In addition, the higher correlation between perceived evaluations and self-concepts tends to support the theory that perceived evaluations are a necessary and sufficient condition for [the growth of a positive or high] self-concept of ability, but [a positive] self-concept of ability is only a necessary, but *not* a sufficient condition for achievement. The latter is further supported by the analysis of the achievement of students with high and low self-concept of ability. This revealed that although a significant proportion of students with high self-concepts of ability achieved at a relatively lower level, practically none of the students with lower (less positive) self-concepts of ability achieved at a high level.

The research reported by Brookover and his associates is important for several reasons. One, it points out the important impact that "significant" people can have on the self-concept of a growing child. Since the self begins early in life and is nurtured in a framework of social interaction, a substantial dimension of any person's feelings about himself is derived from his incorporation of the attributes he perceives other people assigning to him. It is through an individual's long immersion in an interpersonal stream of reflected appraisals from people important to him that he gradually develops a view of himself that he strives to maintain. And number two, the Brookover research serves to remind us that it takes more than a positive self-concept in order for there to be high academic achievement.

References

1. R. M. Roth, "Role of Self-Concept in Achievement," *Journal of Experimental Education,* 27(1959):265–281.
2. W. B. Brookover, E. L. Erickson, and L. M. Joiner, "Self-Concept of Ability and School Achievement, III," Final Report of *Cooperative Research Project 2831,* U.S. Office of Education (E. Lansing, Mich.: Human Learning Research Institute, Michigan State University, 1967), pp. 142–143.

Operational Concepts

1. The successful adaptation to life situations depends more upon how one feels about one's personal qualities than upon the nature of the qualities themselves.

2. An individual's self-concept, that is, the totality of attitudes toward the self, begins in early childhood and develops gradually.

3. Feelings regarding success and failure are influenced by personal aspirations and by what is taken to be important.

4. The capacity to tolerate failure and avoid permanent damage to one's sense of self-esteem is enhanced when there has been a personal history of general success.

Implications

Hamachek argues persuasively for more humane schooling. Since most dropouts leave school because of repeated failure, although they usually have the intellectual ability to complete the designated course of study, the need for corrective action is obvious.

If the child is to have a successful school career, learning achievement at the elementary level is crucial. Logic suggests, therefore, that teachers and administrators work zealously to avoid academic and socialization failure during the early grades.

It seems probable, also, that poor grades and nonpromotion contribute heavily to a negative self-concept. The needed change, obviously, does not lie in rewarding poor achievement with a good grade; rather, it lies in greater efforts on the part of school personnel to assure authentic learning success. In short, if we recognize that all children do not learn in the same way, that some learn more slowly than others, and if we take steps to actually accommodate these differences, the problem of school failures and dropouts should diminish markedly.

Donald S. Arbuckle

Existential Humanistic Counseling

CHARACTERISTICS OF EXISTENTIAL COUNSELING

I would think that there are several crucial characteristics which distinguish existential counseling from other theories or methodologies:

1. The basic issue in the discussion of any "kind" of counseling, including existential counseling, has to do with the nature of humanity and the relationship of humans to the culture they have produced. The behavioral and deterministic view sees humans as conditioned sets of behaviors, and their life and living can thus be predicted and controlled, for good or evil. On the other hand, the world of the existential counselor is subjective rather than objective, and humans are streams of consciousness and experiencing, and thus cannot be predicted and measured and controlled.

When Osipow and Walsh describe what they call "facilitative-effective" counseling, I would see this as being very much akin to existential counseling. They say that this viewpoint "has the higher human objective of facilitating normal development and individual creativity. . . . Its counseling activities encourage the client to look inward and develop, through verbalized introspection, insights into his behavior that can be used to foster growth." In contrast to this, the "interventionistic-cognitive" counselor focuses "on the development of methods to identify causes of client ineffectiveness, peer performances or discomfort, and toward the elimination of undesired behaviors and the introduction of new and more effective behaviors by means of learning principles"(1).

The existential counselor would also feel that when Maslow refers to humanistic qualities such as boldness, courage, freedom, spontaneity, perspicuity, integration, and self-acceptance(2), he is talking about qualities that can be developed, by each one of us, from within.

Rogers raises a very pertinent point when he comments(3):

The issues of personal freedom and personal commitment have become very sharp indeed in a world in which man feels unsupported by a supernatural religion, and experiences keenly the division between his awareness and those elements of his dynamic functioning of which he is unaware.

Hitt described the behavioral model in this way(*4*):

Man can be described meaningfully in terms of his behavior; he is predictable; he is an information transmitter; he lives in an objective world; he is rational; he has traits in common with other men; he may be described in absolute terms; his characteristics can be studied independently of one another; he is a reality; and he is knowable in scientific terms.

As contrasted with the existential model(*5*):

Man can be described meaningfully in terms of his consciousness; he is unpredictable; he is an information generator; he lives in a subjective world; he is irrational; he is unique alongside millions of other unique personalities; he can be described in relative terms; he must be studied in a holistic manner; he is a potentiality; and he is more than we can ever know about him.

Another way of looking at it might be to say that existential counseling views a human as being basically an inner rather than an outer person. Our inner self is our real self, and to a greater or lesser extent our outer behavior reflects the kinds and the degree of our conditioning. The greater the gap between the two, the more artificial our life becomes. Ideally, the *me* that I reflect to *you* should be the phenomenal me with which *I* live. In a very literal sense, the level of the actualization of my self will be minimal if there is a great discrepancy between the me that I present to me, and the me that I present to you. The extent to which you, of course, can be open to receive the me that I am communicating to you is affected by the degree and the kinds of conditioning to which you have been subjected.

Behavioral counseling, too, would appear to consistently separate the culture from the people who have created it, as if somehow the culture, impinging upon, modifying, and controlling human beings, was separate and apart from those human beings. Skinner, in talking about the improvement of culture by people, comments that "the ultimate improvement comes from the environment that makes them wise and compassionate"(*6*), but at the same time he says, "The man that man has made is the product of the culture that man has devised"(*7*). It would seem to me that Skinner is simply saying that the environment, the culture, is people, past and present. Thus when someone agrees, rationally, that he is racially prejudiced, what he is saying is that people, past and present, have taught him to be that way. It would seem that a logical counselor reaction to this would be, "Well, how about you, now? Is this you, is this the way you want to be, and if it isn't what will you do about it?"

Skinner is partially correct when he says that "the individual remains merely a stage in a process that began long before he came into existence and will long outlast him"(8). But the past, nevertheless, is still people, and my life, *for me,* is not "merely" a stage, since it is the only life that I now experience. Thus I must accept responsibility for the degree to which the dogmas of the past shackle me, limit my freedom, and make me blind to the reality of the existence of my self and my fellow humans. All of us can try to come closer to understanding and being open to experiencing who we are, but this continuing struggle is a basic part of our existence. Indeed, it *is* our existence. It is hard to peel off the layers, not only of our own span of living, but also those which have been squeezed into us and onto us over the centuries.

2. It is fairly obvious that another crucial difference between existential counseling and the more behaviorally oriented therapies has to do with this question of objectivity and subjectivity. It is likely, too, that this is one of the reasons for the difficulty in communication, since the existential counselor tends to view the behaviorist in a subjective way, while the behavioral counselor is equally puzzled, and sometimes irked, as he views the existentialist through what he perceives as his objective eyes. It may possibly be like the problems that would arise if a poet and an engineer tried to develop a love affair. They might respect each other, but they would have a very difficult time getting together, both literally and figuratively!

Barclay is discussing phenomenology, but he is talking about the world of the existential counselor when he says "the world of subjective phenomena and facts, as contrasted with the world of scientific and objective reality"(9). Dreyfus is talking in the same vein when he says, "The counselor must expose himself, and, therefore, cannot maintain the scientific objective attitude of the physical scientist. He cannot view the client as an object to be manipulated, exploited and explored"(10). So too, are Schell and Daubner when they say(11):

> The realistic counselor should help his client perceive his problem situation as it "really" is and as it appears to others. The phenomenalist counselor cannot do this; instead, he can only try to enter the client's subjectivity and to help him deepen and enrich his unique perception of the problem situation.

Kemp discusses this inner subjective world of the self, the *Eigenwelt,* as presupposing self-awareness, self-relatedness, and self-transcendence, possessed only by human beings. He describes this as the potential for grasping what something, such as a snow-topped mountain, a ballet, or a personal relationship, means to us. "In our false attempt to be more scientific, more truthful," he says, "we lose the sense of reality in our experiences"(12).

The existential counselor helps the individual to develop a sharper awareness, a keenness, a sensitivity to what is going on around him and in him. In a way, the senses of such a person become more highly developed—a mountain is more than rock and snow, drenching rain is not just water, a flower is more than a yellow object. Even more important is the sensitivity to all of the ways in which a fellow human tries to communicate with us—sometimes desperately trying to tell us something that so often we do not hear. This is touching the reality of our experience.

A thread here too, is *believing,* and certainly believing is subjective. It is often the object of the scorn, and the amusement, of the scientist who sees himself, and the world, in what he actually *believes* is an objective manner. While he might say that he knows, his moment-by-moment life and living is overwhelmingly affected by what he *believes* he knows. A startling and tragic example of this mistaken impression of the infallibility of supposed knowledge is to be found in a book on Robert S. McNamara and his Vietnam adventure by Trewhitt(*13*). McNamara, a brilliant man, had the best that was available in the technology of the day, and he applied it. His predictions were scientifically sound, his analysis logical and correct. He knew, without doubt, what would happen in Vietnam when certain procedures and pressures were applied. But what he knew would happen didn't happen, and I would think that this was because he was too much of an objective man. He discounted the irrationality of human beings, and his own ability to be aware of, let alone control, the multiplicity of variables that are to be found in each human being. The Vietnamese, possibly, were like the British of 1940. They were the only ones who didn't know that they were beaten and that their cause was hopeless! Both *believed* otherwise.

3. The subjectivity of existential counseling is related to another aspect, namely, the stress on the experiencing of me, now, rather than the talking about me yesterday or tomorrow. Many individuals, sadly, live their lives without ever becoming open to this human experience. If I am a highly defensive person who cannot risk looking at me, I will probably talk about others yesterday or tomorrow; with more certainty I may talk about others today; if I am still more certain I may talk about me yesterday or tomorrow; and if I am beginning to feel capable of taking a risk, if I feel I may be worth something, I may even go beyond talking about me now, but actually experience me, now. This would mesh into the ideas of Kell and Mueller, who say that(*14*)

> we think it is rare that significant changes in human behavior occur without an effective experience. Change in behavior in regard to other humans, the interpersonal dimension, as we understand it, almost invariably calls for an effective, and often, conflicted experience.

This movement toward the experiencing of self now is not, of course, limited to the period of counseling. Indeed, if the only time this ever took place was during the counseling period, the prognosis would be somewhat dismal. Clients may talk, with much feeling, about changes they have experienced as occurring in them. I can remember a young woman who had been seeing me for a year, coming in, flushed and excited and pleased, sort of bursting out, "You know, I've been having the craziest feelings this week—I'm actually coming together—and I'm scared—because I'm going to let go of what I used to need and had to hang on to, but I don't need it now—but it's real scary letting it go" and her whole person expressed her excitement and her joy and her fear.

Or a man, who had been seeing me for a year and a half, who came in tightlipped and hostile, and almost immediately accused me of betraying him, and thus making it clear that he was originally right in feeling that he could never trust anyone, even me. I did not try to convince him he was wrong, but tried rather to help him to accept the responsibility for either trusting me or not trusting me. He left, still tight-lipped, and I wondered if I would see him again. A letter I received a few days later told me what happened. Halfway home he became so overcome with feeling that he pulled off to the side of the road and wrote me a letter. The letter indicated that his reaction to me was his last attempt to somehow get back to the way that he was, to use me as the rationale. My putting the responsibility on his shoulders helped him to see what he was doing, and now the past was really gone, and he could move ahead.

Or a session where the client was a woman who had never been able to feel anything but revulsion, even though her head did not agree with her body, toward men, because of several dreadful childhood experiences with men, especially with her father. At the end of the session, as we both stood up, we moved spontaneously toward each other and held each other tightly. It was tender and it was loving, and it was real. She had experienced something she had never been able to allow herself to experience before.

4. The experiencing of the client cannot take place without the involvement of the counselor as a person, as a fellow human being, and thus the person of the counselor is of crucial importance in existential counseling. Such counselors could hardly be acceptant of behavior modification as described by Madsen and Madsen: ". . . behavior modification means changing behavior by rewarding the kind you want to encourage and ignoring or disapproving the kind you want to discourage. Used with understanding, it is an effective caring way to control behavior in school"(15). Such a "counselor" would sound very much like one of the controllers of the future as perceived by Skinner, who says that "we must delegate the control of the population as a whole to specialists—to police, priests, teachers, therapists, and so on, with their specialized reinforcers and their codified contingencies"(16).

A lesson of history, of course, is that too often, shortly after we have "delegated" control of a part of our lives to others, we awaken to discover that we have lost control. Man can be individually free if he is willing to accept the responsibility that comes with freedom. If he does not, it is clear that the world of controllers described by Skinner will indeed become our fate. If we, for example, continue to spew forth children, as unfortunate accidents of the sex act, into an overpopulated and uncaring world; if we continue to blindly pollute and destroy the environment that is part of our life; if we eat up our limited natural resources as if they would continue forever; if we accept the horrors of war as one of those things that cannot be avoided—then indeed, we will soon be in the hands of the controllers. We will continue to exist, but we will not live. But we do have the choice. We can live the life of individual freedom if we are capable of accepting it. Skinner feels that homo sapiens is not capable of accepting this responsibility. I do. It's as simple as that.

Krumboltz and Thoresen are, of course, correct when they say that behavioral counselors are human beings like any other counselors, and they are equally concerned about the welfare of the client(17). Nonetheless, the behavioral counselor does tend to stress method and techniques over the person, and he feels free to use any techniques which will achieve the desired behavioral goals. As Krumboltz and Thoresen say, "If one technique does not work, he tries something else"(18). There is not here the personal exposure and involvement of the counselor with the client such as that implied by Jourard when, in talking about clients, he says that(19)

> they have become so estranged from their real selves that they are incapable of making these known to their associates in life. I don't see how we can reacquaint our patients with their real selves by striving to subject them to subtle manipulation.

In some ways, I would think of the behavioral counselor or the behavioral engineer as being somewhat like a surgeon. He can have a tremendous impact on us—indeed, he can be the determiner of whether we live or die—but he need have no personal contact with us, since he is concerned only with our behavior, just as the surgeon is concerned only with the physical body. Human intimacy is difficult and complicated enough with anyone, but certainly one who controls us is hardly one with whom we can comfortably and honestly become intimate. We do not sleep easily with those who hold our destiny in their hands.

The existential counselor, on the other hand, is intimately involved in a personal human experience with another person. It is essential that such a counselor have a clear understanding of the meaning of this human involvement, since intimacy is usually initiated for self-satisfaction, rather than for the satisfaction of the other. If I am to become intimately involved with a client it behooves me, for the sake of the client as well as for my own sake, to have a clear understanding of just why I am doing what I am doing.

Intimacy also implies that the counselor is experienced in life and living, and not just a personally removed scholar of life and living. There are confrontations in existential counseling—verbal, physical, personal. In a very literal sense, there will be a transference of feelings from the client to the counselor and from the counselor to the client. These feelings are part of the humanness of the counselor and the client, and they are faced and shared. They are not analyzed to determine their real meaning by the personally aloof expert, as in the more traditional psychoanalysis, nor are they considered to be a form of resistance to be worked out under the direction of the therapist.

The human involvement of the existential counselor as a person also means that he must share some of the responsibility for what happens. It would seem inevitable that the existential counselor, possibly more than any other kind of counselor, would serve as a model of a human being for the client. This, needless to say, is a very grave responsibility, but it should be faced and accepted as a reality of existential counseling.

References

1. Samuel H. Osipow and Bruce W. Walsh, *Strategies in Counseling for Behavior Change* (New York: Appleton-Century-Crofts, 1970), p. 19.

2. A. H. Maslow, *Toward a Psychology of Being* (New York: Van Nostrand Reinhold, 1962) p. 136.

3. Carl R. Rogers, *Freedom To Learn* (Columbus, Ohio: Charles E. Merrill, 1969), p. 260.

4. William D. Hitt, "Two Models of Man," *American Psychologist*, 24:651–658 (July, 1969).

5. Ibid.

6. B. F. Skinner, "Beyond Freedom and Dignity," *Psychology Today*, 5:37–80 (August, 1971).

7. Ibid.

8. Ibid.

9. James R. Barclay, *Foundations of Counseling Strategies* (New York: Wiley, 1971), p. 15.

10. Edward Dreyfus, "The Counselor and Existentialism," *Personnel and Guidance Journal*, 43:115–120 (October, 1969).

11. Edith Schell and Edward Daubner, "Epistemology and School Counseling," *Personnel and Guidance Journal*, 47:506–513 (February, 1969).

12. C. Gratton Kemp, "Existential Counseling," *Counseling Psychologist*, 2:2–30 (Fall, 1971).

13. Henry L. Trewhitt, *McNamara: His Ordeal in the Pentagon* (New York: Harper & Row, 1971).

14. Bill L. Kell and William J. Mueller, *Impact and Change: A Study of Counseling Relationships* (New York: Appleton-Century-Crofts, 1966), p. 66.

15. Clifford K. Madsen and Charles H. Madsen, Jr., "What Is Behavior Modification?" *Instructor*, 8:44–48 (October, 1971).

16. B. F. Skinner, op. cit.

17. John D. Krumboltz and Carl E. Thoresen, *Behavioral Counseling* (New York: Holt, Rinehart and Winston, 1969), p. 3.

18. Ibid.

19. Sidney Jourard, *The Transparent Self* (New York: Van Nostrand Reinhold, 1964). p. 74.

Operational Concepts

1. Existential counseling emphasizes the adaptive quality of human beings, the importance of experience, and humanistic values.

2. Existential counseling is predominantly subjective, allowing the counselor to stress sensitivity to the external environment.

3. Existential counseling is concerned more with the present and future than with the past.

4. Existential counselors engage in authentic relationships with their counselees, avoiding manipulation and direction.

5. In the counseling relationship between student and adult, the counselor's attitudes and values are fully as important as counseling technique.

Implications

With the legitimation of children's rights and the growing acknowledgment of adolescent interest in self, existential counseling has come into its own. The student, in short, is a person subject to the full range of human insecurity and must, therefore, be seen as a person rather than as an innominate creature to be regimented.

The counseling and guidance of children from minority groups, in particular, both by counselors and classroom teachers, is closely related to recent interest in the incorporation of ethnic studies in the curriculum. In a sense, the objectives of ethnic studies and counseling are similar: students should (1) deepen their understanding of their cultural background, (2) view their heritage with pride, (3) recognize the problems that sometimes accompany membership in a minority group, and (4) develop and sustain a healthy self-image.

There are clear curricular implications for nonminority children as well. Recent research, for example, suggests that efforts at court-enforced integration have been a spectacular failure. But despite the failure, it is probable that both whites and blacks have developed more tolerance for each other's preferences and a greater willingness to live and let live. It follows, then, that the school must seek to nurture in succeeding generations attitudes of mind that permit different groups to coexist in harmonious fashion.

What is of greatest importance, however, in the counseling of all students is a willingness to accept their existing concerns as the primary point of departure, and an effort to facilitate their capacity for self-directed emotional growth.

Anthony F. Gregorc
Richard A. Dempsey

The Developmental Staffing Model: Differentiated Staffing for Human Motivation

Of the many innovative ideas sweeping the nation today, none is more promising or more controversial than differentiated staffing. Educators, boards of education, and laymen alike are coming to grips with the complex questions surrounding differentiated staffing. What is it? How can it best be implemented? Who will be involved in the planning? What will be its impact on people? These are some of the questions that will be subject to debate during the next decade. Not since the one-room red schoolhouse gave way to graded education has an educational innovation had such a potentially dramatic impact on the staffing organization patterns of schools.

MENTAL HEALTH

Robert Boyd[1] defined the elements necessary for mental health in an organization. They are given in Table 1.

ORGANIZATIONAL DESIGN

The search for an organization that could fulfill these beliefs and expectations led to the following design, which is envisioned as a molecule with lines of communication established between and among all component parts. The design attempts to convey the various roles that interrelate in the educational process within a school. This design illustrates the spirit of an organization, that is, individual specialists have a responsibility to work together to help the student and one another to succeed.

The conceptual drawing in Figure 1 portrays an instructional module within which teachers interrelate with students. An instructional module

Reprinted from Anthony F. Gregorc and Richard A. Dempsey, "The Developmental Staffing Model: Differentiated Staffing for Human Motivation," in Arthur D. Roberts (ed.), *Educational Innovation*, © 1975; by permission of Allyn and Bacon, Inc., Boston.

TABLE 1

THE ORGANIZATION MUST:	THE PERSONAL RIGHTS OF INDIVIDUALS ARE:
A. Define and publish the structure and procedures of the organization	A. To be heard
	B. To be evaluated clearly and specifically
B. Specify job responsibilities	C. To receive specific instructions
C. Identify a structured reward system	D. To have one's talents and concerns appreciated
D. Give instructions clearly and concisely	E. To be trained to meet the expectations of the organization
E. Provide knowledge regarding the political and economic forces affecting the people's existence	F. To function independently insofar as it does not adversely affect the clientele (students) or the organization
	G. To receive enough money to maintain personal dignity
	H. To be permitted to interact with coprofessionals
	I. To be treated with human dignity

could consist of an English department or an interdisciplinary teaching team. The leadership, human services, and physical environment components provide the teachers, students, parents, and one another with skills and knowledge noted. The people in the modules and components interact at will. It would be well to note that each subdivision of a component represents the needed areas of expertise. It is conceivable that a single person could provide the necessary skills in one or more subdivisions.

The *instructional module* (Figure 2) is under the direction of an executive teacher who has line authority and is accountable for the growth and development of the students and teachers involved in his or her module. Assisting the executive teacher are master teachers who are research or teacher trainer specialists, staff teachers who perform traditional classroom duties, and associate teachers who, while performing traditional duties, are receiving basic professional training. Teacher aides are also available to assist the module as the need arises. The instructional module houses responsibility for activities aimed at students, at the learning activities, and at staff members. An English instructional module, for example, is responsible for the quality of English instruction in a given school. Individual members of the module are differentiated in such a manner that diagnosis, prescription, evaluation, research, curriculum development, etc., are handled within the respective unit.

The module is designed to provide a home base where "satisfiers" can be achieved. It further provides opportunities for developing a feeling of belonging and for gaining opportunities to learn the norms of excellence.

FIGURE 1 Developmental Staffing Model

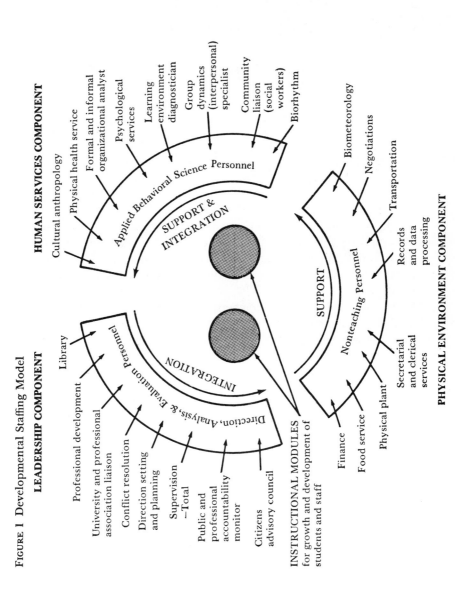

LEADERSHIP COMPONENT

HUMAN SERVICES COMPONENT

Cultural anthropology

Physical health service

Formal and informal organizational analyst

Psychological services

Learning environment diagnostician

Group dynamics (interpersonal) specialist

Community liaison (social workers)

Biorhythm

Applied Behavioral Science Personnel

SUPPORT & INTEGRATION

Library

Professional development

University and professional association liaison

Conflict resolution

Direction setting and planning

Supervision —Total

Public and professional accountability monitor

Citizens advisory council

Direction, Analysis, & Evaluation Personnel

INTEGRATION

INSTRUCTIONAL MODULES for growth and development of students and staff

SUPPORT

Biometeorology

Negotiations

Transportation

Records and data processing

Nonteaching Personnel

Secretarial and clerical services

Physical plant

Food service

Finance

PHYSICAL ENVIRONMENT COMPONENT

765

FIGURE 2 Instructional Module—Activities Analysis

The *Physical Environment Component* is responsible for the support of the entire system. It consists of business affairs agents, bus drivers, custodians, cooks, physical plant maintenance personnel, secretarial helpers, and audiovisual personnel. Also included in this component would be a negotiator who is concerned with working conditions including salaries. This view is consistent with Herzberg's hypothesis.

The *Human Services Component* is responsible for emotional support and integration of people as they work together. Within this component are behavioral scientists who apply theory and research derived through the various behavioral sciences to help students, parents, and teachers achieve their purposes.

Among the behavioral scientists are individuals skilled in analyzing the social and psychological state of both the clients of the school and those individuals influencing the learning environments experienced by the system's clients. Others are skilled in the analysis of the cultural environments of the school and community. Specialists in the development and execution of social–psychological systems intervention models are also available to serve as counselors and consultants to the student, teachers, administrators, parents, and others influential in the life of the child. The foci of this component are on the social learning base. This means, of course, that members of this team can and will have varying theoretical orientations, e.g., Skinner, Maslow, Piaget, Rogers, etc. The techniques used are appropriate for the resolution of both intra and interpersonal concerns and are aimed toward execution units: (1) the individual, (2) a group or collective, or (3) the entire school organization as a social system.

Also included in the unit are those other personnel charged with concern for the physical health and well-being of the student. The student approaches school as a personal totality. Recognition of this factor requires adequate response and concern for those health concerns that affect his ability to learn.

The human services component supervisor reports directly to the school administration. He is charged with the promotion of the learning climate of the school to the end that the educational opportunities of the child may be maximized. His concern is directed toward providing conditions under which those physical and emotional attributes that influence maladaptive behavior will not occur. The institutional mental and physical health of the students is thus translated into the goal of maximizing student learning opportunities.

The *leadership component* is charged with integrating the entire system internally and also with keeping the system in harmony with the community. It is the central "thermostat" for the system. It functions by maintaining communication with the community and within the system. This component is also responsible for maintaining a "reality check" for the system, i.e., keeping the components apprised of what is new, how each is being viewed, and how each is performing. Elements of this component include the administration, teacher recruitment and training, the library, and a community advisory board that would include members of the board of education. (Note the aggressive nature of the librarian. This person can be a sparkplug to new ideas.)

This component provides training in the development of accountability models and the reporting of results. Further training is provided in conflict resolution and specific needs as identified by teachers. At this juncture, it may be helpful to the reader if we now focus our attention on some of the important aspects of differentiated staffing as well as on the advantages and shortcomings of the model.

As with any innovative concept, certain conditions or facets must be in existence in order for differentiated staffing to become operationally effective. These components include:

1. The planning and development of the differentiated staffing model must involve teachers, from the inception of the idea to its implementation.
2. As the model evolves the learning needs of youth should determine the staffing pattern.
3. Improved instruction rather than budgetary economics should be the goal.
4. Board of education and community support must be obtained.
5. Goals and objectives must be established.
6. Job descriptions must be developed.
7. Evaluative criteria must be developed and modified as the planning continues.
8. Adequate time must be allowed for total staff planning.

9. Administrators and teachers must be willing to share jointly in decision making.

10. It is understood that increased salaries will be paid for increased responsibility and training, and not be confused with merit pay.

As with any innovative idea, there are both advantages and disadvantages to differentiated staffing. The authors have listed some of the more obvious of each in order not only to put differentiated staffing in its proper perspective, but also, to highlight the fact that it has definite merits as well as pitfalls that should be anticipated.

ADVANTAGES OF DIFFERENTIATED STAFFING

1. Differentiated staffing provides for varied instructional responsibilities for teachers, thus utilizing their professional talents and range of experiences.

2. Teachers become key components in the decision making process.

3. When teachers become involved in making decisions that affect them, they also become more committed to teaching.

4. Differentiated staffing provides for compensation based on talent and responsibility, a condition that is more acceptable to laymen and boards of education.

5. It provides for more curricular flexibility than is permissible in a more traditional setting.

6. It permits beginning teachers to be assimilated more gradually into the school routine, thus reducing the possibility of failure.

7. Paraprofessionals relieve teachers of many of the more mundane but necessary tasks that must be performed in every classroom.

8. Students will have contact with many adults, and they can draw on the skills and talents of these adults.

9. Differentiated staffing reduces the gap between administrators and teachers.

10. It belies the idea that all teachers are alike.

11. Teachers are given the opportunity to determine how far they want to go on the career ladder, how much salary they wish to strive for, and how many months they wish to work each year.

12. Differentiated staffing generates a sense of purpose and an atmosphere of teamwork.

13. Lower echelon teachers are more secure because they can be relieved of many of the tasks that they do less well than others.

14 Differentiated staffing provides competent teachers with the status and salary they would not ordinarily receive unless they left the classroom for the administrative ranks.

768

15. It brings about a truly individualized teaching–learning program by identifying specific teaching–learning objectives.
16. It identifies criteria for preservice and in-service training programs for educational personnel.
17. Differentiated staffing leads to better manageability of educational variables.
18. It opens the educational system to new ideas from outside the educational paradigm.
19. It attracts and holds more talented teaching personnel.
20. It operationalizes the results of educational research and facilitates innovation.

DISADVANTAGES OF DIFFERENTIATED STAFFING

1. Differentiated staffing can be used as a pretext to initiate merit pay for teachers.
2. It can become a haven for teachers with limited ambition and those who wish to hide their incompetence under the cloak of team effort.
3. It can become a way in which administrators reward their favorites.
4. Parents may want to go only to the teacher at the top of the hierarchy for advice and consultation about their childrens' problems.
5. A strong differentiated staffed school can make some administrators very insecure especially when many of the educational decision-making prerogatives are transferred to teachers.
6. Some-teachers may want the status and additional compensation connected with the plan but may be unwilling to fulfill the job requirements.
7. Professional preparation in the form of amassed credits and degrees will be less important than demonstrated competency.
8. Seniority is much less important to the concept of differentiated staffing than it is in traditional settings.
9. Those lower on the career ladder may be more effective teachers than those above them, which may create strained staff relations.
10. The twelve-month schedule may discourage some of the more competent teachers from seeking the higher echelon positions.
11. It may be argued that there is more concern about staff organization than about the learning needs of youth.
12. Many teachers may resent following directions given them by colleagues who for years have been their peers.
13. Good teachers do not necessarily make good leaders.
14. Teachers at the lower levels of the career ladder will receive no increase in status or compensation.

15. It may be argued that differentiated staffing tends to foster fragmentation rather than teamwork.
16. Administrators and teachers must be retrained to function in a differentiated staffed model.
17. Teachers who do not know how to use the talents of paraprofessionals effectively may waste considerable time and money.
18. Paraprofessionals may threaten teachers especially if the paraprofessional is a member of a minority and communicates with the minority children more effectively than the teacher.
19. New job descriptions and methods of evaluation must be framed in conjunction with teachers.
20. The planning costs related to differentiated staffing may prohibit schools from adopting this system.

SUMMARY

Differentiated staffing, in spite of its disadvantages and possible pitfalls, suggests new solutions to the problems related to the improvement of learning and teaching. It proposes an entirely new way of organizing for education, a change from the lock-step model that has served educators for seemingly endless generations.

Differentiated staffing is a challenge to the career teacher to shed the cloak of quasi-professionalism for a full professional status with all of its responsibilities and privileges. It is a challenge to the educational administrator to harness the desire of teachers for a greater voice in "the system" in order to deploy their maximum talents. It is a challenge to boards of education to let their professional staffs initiate substantially new programs with increased quality. And it is a challenge to teacher organizations to provide the necessary impetus needed to help the professional break away from the image of Ichabod Crane so that they can take a new, more professional stance in the family of professions.

The authors feel that the advantages of differentiated staffing far outweigh the disadvantages and that the proposed model is light years ahead of the model that has served public education in past decades. But if education is ever going to catch up to societal needs, and rise from the level of a white-collar skilled trade to that of a true profession, a major breakthrough must soon be implemented. In order to do this, teachers are going to have to be provided a real career opportunity in the classroom.

Reference

1. Robert E. Boyd. "Mental Health Characteristics of Organizations," mimeographed, University of Illinois, 1972.

Operational Concepts

1. The goals and needs of individuals and organizations can be made compatible.

2. Since schools are organizations that function through the use of human resources, and since human resources also have human needs, the school organization must endeavor to satisfy these needs.

3. With skillful management, the bureaucratic structure of the school organization can be reduced, thus contributing to higher job satisfaction and professional productivity among personnel.

4. The art of teaching can be sub-divided into various specializations. Since individual practitioners vary in their natural aptness the assignment of teachers to the specialization in which they are particularly adept offers obvious benefits.

5. Differentiated staffing presents both advantages and disadvantages, but ordinarily the former outweigh the latter.

Implications

Like many other innovations discussed in the *Handbook*, the concept of differentiated staffing is neither new nor adequately tried. Administrators—and, for that matter, teachers themselves—have long recognized that individuals are more adept at some pedagogical tasks and less adept at others. The logic of accommodating special strengths, consequently, is difficult to refute.

The principal deterrents to the use of differentiated staffing assignments, as the early experiments demonstrated, lay in increased programming complexity, in the need for substantially greater physical movement on the part of the teacher or the students, and in the unfortunate fact that some aspects of teaching are more attractive than others. Nonetheless, the advantages seem to outweigh the disadvantages, and differentiated staffing must be regarded as a useful device whose prime has yet to come.

Samuel G. Sava

Instructional Methods: Individually Guided Education

To an audience wearied by a decade's overuse of the word "innovation," it may come as a pleasant surprise if I describe individually guided education (IGE) as a highly innovative program without a single new idea in it. Every component of the program has been borrowed from somewhere else. In a field sodden with "breakthrough concepts," "fresh insights," "revolutionary modes of conceptualizing," etc., IGE stands out as the thieves' market of education: everything we have to sell, somebody else used to carry around in his pocket. The Institute for Development of Educational Activities (/I/D/E/A/) may be remembered fifty years hence as the Fagin of pedagogy—dispatching Oliver Twists into the stacks of educational research to pilfer pedagogical theorists of their intellectual wallets.

This characterization of IGE does an injustice to the original research and the painstaking developmental work performed by /I/D/E/A/ staff members, but it has an element of truth in it. I resort to obvious exaggeration not only to solicit the reader's interest, but to make a valid point: it is not the concepts embodied in IGE that make it an innovative program, *but the way in which those concepts are put together.* Having watched /I/D/E/A/'s staff assemble various jigsaw bits of research into a harmonious picture, I would argue that figuring out how to put a useful idea to work is at least as difficult as having that idea in the first place—perhaps more so.

Simply defined, IGE is a process for allowing teachers to alter instructional method to accommodate the individual needs, capacities, and interests of each student. IGE is not a curriculum, but a *process.* We believe—to reduce this distinction to an easily comprehensible form—that IGE can be used equally well to teach the old math or the new math. We maintain that, regardless of instructional aim or content, IGE enables teachers to teach and children to learn more effectively.

Enough, however, of what IGE is *not.* What, apart from the very general description offered above, *is* it?

Individually guided education joins two separable strands of educational inquiry: (1) how can teachers manipulate the components of instruction to accommodate the distinctive needs of individual students, and (2) how does any school improvement program succeed? I will comment separately on the importance of each question and describe our efforts to answer them.

INDIVIDUALIZING EDUCATION

Individualizing education is another pair of "buzzwords" from the sixties. At the risk of appearing more transparent than anybody with a doctorate should, and at the risk of boring readers who already have a firm, well-supported understanding of this concept, I will try to explain what these well-worn words mean.

No teacher can attain the venerable age of 24 without realizing that his/her pupils vary remarkably in such characteristics as intellectual and emotional readiness to understake certain forms of learning, personal interest in the instructional content offered, and personal skill at fulfilling the learning tasks required. Nor can any parent: although the offspring of a husband and wife share the same genetic endowment and similar environment upbringing, their children differ; one "likes" history, and another "likes" math and, usually, their separate likes or preferences will be reflected in the success that they attain in these subjects.

So much is obvious. Yet our schools—often for reasons of administrative convenience and organizational sanity—treat all children of the same age as if they had the same learning preferences and capabilities. Every child who has attained the age of 6 by a certain date is assigned to the first grade, and is expected to "master" or, at least, "pass" a stipulated body of knowledge judged appropriate for American children at that age. In practice, only a few children *master* the body of learning proposed for their absorption, and they receive A's; the majority digest it in varying degrees, which educators classify with letter grades ranging from B to F, or—in a well-intended but nonetheless soul-chilling set of euphemisms for the parent reading the report card—in such categories as "making steady progress," "needs improvement," or "parent–teacher conference recommended."

The fact is that children *do* differ, and there is little point and considerable injustice in subjecting them all to the "same treatment" and expecting them all to turn in roughly the same learning performance. What IGE does, in essence, is to enable teachers to devise *optimal learning conditions to match the distinctive learning traits of each child*.

This goal is not unique to IGE; many other programs during the past decade have aimed at it. The crucial factor is determining how a school's resources can be deployed in changing patterns to accommodate individual difference. /I/D/E/A/ began by identifying the ways in which youngsters differ from each other in their "learning personalities."

First, they differ in their genetic endowment and family cultural traits, by which we mean the intellectual ability and propensity toward learning that each child brings with him when he first walks through the schoolroom door. The school can do nothing about genetic endowment and very little about family cultural traits passed on to children. What it *can* do, however, is seek to make the most of this raw material.

Other categories of individual difference include the following:

1. *Learning style:* the preference of children for one medium of instruction or instructional procedure over another. For example, some learn readily from the printed word; others respond better to a film or teacher's lecture. Some children grasp a principle well after it has been stated and explained to them; others are uncomfortable with abstract explanations and need tangible objects, ranging from simple items for counting to reasonably sophisticated laboratory demonstrations, before they can understand. Still others learn best through a form of debate, in which alternative principles to explain a phenomenon or alternative answers to a question can be argued about and rejected one by one.

2. *Learning mode:* children also differ in their response to the *instructional setting.* In the typical (less typical today than ten years ago, but still dominant) classroom situation, one teacher directs the learning activities of a fixed, unvarying number of children, approximately twenty-five. For different purposes, however, children can be grouped in other modes: (a) *independent,* with the student working alone, seeking teacher help when needed; (b) *one-to-one study,* essentially tutoring, from a teacher, teacher aide, or another student; (c) *small group,* three to fourteen students working on a common objective, with or without a teacher present; and (d) *large group,* several classes (14 to 200 students) for informational and motivational purposes in which student–teacher interaction is relatively unimportant or will be handled later, in smaller groups.

There is nothing startling here. The importance of such alternative groupings is the flexibility that they offer a school staff in responding to individual difference. For example, seventy-five children spanning two or more age-groups, and working on the same type of subject matter, might be grouped in this fashion:

5	students, each with a project, working alone on independent study.
10	students, working with one teacher on a special assignment.
50	students, assembled for a lecture, film, or other large-group presentation by one teacher, and
<u>10</u>	students, working with a teacher skilled at diagnosis of learning problems.
75	students, 3 teachers

This particular grouping is solely for purposes of illustration. The actual pattern will shift from one instructional purpose to another.

Finally, it should be emphasized that these alternative groupings are not intended to merely supplement the usual twenty-five-to-one classroom, but to supplant it.

One last aspect of individual difference should be noted: teachers are individuals, too, and, as such, differ in their teaching "styles" as well as in their teaching abilities. Some are adept at large-group presentations; others sympathize with the learning difficulties of below-average students and derive personal as well as professional satisfaction from helping such youngsters; other teachers are impatient with "slow learners." Although every teacher should, of course, try to turn in his or her best performance under all conditions, each is human; IGE tries to deploy these differences for instructional advantage, rather than assuming that all teachers are alike.

THE LEARNING COMMUNITY: PUTTING THE PIECES TOGETHER

The individual differences cited above have long been recognized, and various educators have devised methods for dealing with them. Among the concepts advanced that would meet the problems posed by individual difference are, for example, the following:

1. *Nongraded instruction,* which permits a youngster to be placed in each subject according to his attainment and learning ability, rather than by the single index of age.
2. *Team teaching,* which permits teachers to pool their abilities, contribute varying perspectives to assess and diagnose the progress of the same students, and share teaching responsibilities to take advantage of the strengths, and minimize the weaknesses, of each teacher.
3. *Continuous progress,* which permits a youngster to advance as rapidly as he can—or as slowly as he must—in *each* subject, rather than being locked into an unvarying instructional pace prescribed by the school calendar.

These and many other solid ideas were available to educators in 1965, when /I/D/E/A/ was established. The problem, in the institute's view, was that each was tried in isolation; rarely were they integrated into a coherent, instructional whole designed to make use of several methods, *simultaneously,* for tailoring instruction to the individual learner's needs.

Beginning in 1967, /I/D/E/A/ launched a developmental effort entitled "Enhancing Differences." Broadly, this program had two purposes:

1. To investigate and, if the results were favorable, to adapt a new mode of school organization.

2. To develop comprehensive methods for training teachers in the techniques necessary to evaluate student differences and vary instruction to make it appropriate for each learner.

The school organization model, in essence, shifted traditional student–teacher assignment patterns to permit team teaching, nongraded assignment and instruction of students, continuous progress, and cooperative planning by school principals and staff for maximum utilization of school resources. The difference between this organization and that of the traditional, "egg-crate" school in which students were assigned by age, is probably best illustrated (see Figure 1 and Table 1).

FIGURE 1

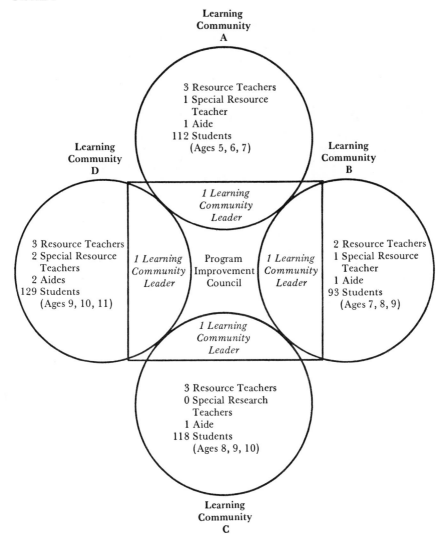

TABLE 1 Organization of a Hypothetical Graded Elementary School with 20 Teachers and 600 Pupils

| KINDERGARTEN | | PRINCIPAL | | | | | |
	FIRST	SECOND	THIRD	FOURTH	FIFTH	SIXTH
	1 teacher 30 pupils of age 6	1 teacher 30 pupils of age 7	1 teacher 30 pupils of age 8	1 teacher 30 pupils of age 9	1 teacher 30 pupils of age 10	1 teacher 30 pupils of age 11
1 teacher 30 pupils of age 5	1 teacher 30 pupils of age 6	1 teacher 30 pupils of age 7	1 teacher 30 pupils of age 8	1 teacher 30 pupils of age 9	1 teacher 30 pupils of age 10	1 teacher 30 pupils of age 11
1 teacher 30 pupils of age 5	1 teacher 30 pupils of age 6	1 teacher 30 pupils of age 7	1 teacher 30 pupils of age 8	1 teacher 30 pupils of age 9	1 teacher 30 pupils of age 10	1 teacher 30 pupils of age 11

The IGE organization model was an immensely useful framework for achieving the goals of individualized education. Like any framework, however, its effective operation depended on humans well trained in its intelligent use. To design such training was the second aim of "Enhancing Differences."

The fundamental problem underlying this teacher-training component of "Enhancing Differences" was well expressed by its director, John Bahner of /I/D/E/A/:

> A few gifted teachers have always known how to accommodate individual difference. We must find out how the average teacher can be trained to do deliberately, consciously, and in a step-by-step fashion what the gifted teacher does by instinct.

With the cooperation of school districts in Florida, Michigan, New York, and Ohio, "Enhancing Differences" went forward for about three years until /I/D/E/A/, with the assistance of a number of educational institutions, believed it had a program suitable for widespread adoption. Development of that program was a learning experience for /I/D/E/A/ staff, as well as for principals and teachers in the cooperating schools—and, on occasion, immensely frustrating for both. Some salient points of their findings and of the resultant program deserve special mention:

Clinical Approach to Teacher Training

Through "Enhancing Differences," /I/D/E/A/ staff became convinced that typical methods of training teachers in improved techniques—mostly through course work—were insufficient. IGE workshops stress a learn-by-doing approach that involves work with students concurrent with assistance from another teacher who has mastered the process.

Continuous Appraisal of Students

If proper attention to individual difference is to be maintained, and if continuous progress of students is to be realized, appraisal of student achievement and student response to varied instructional strategies must be carried on throughout the year—not just once at the beginning of fall semester and again at half-year. Each IGE teacher learns a continuous cycle of appraisal with four components:

1. *Initial assessment* of student ability, using various means.
2. *Development* of an individualized learning program, based on ability, interests, learning needs, and learning styles.
3. *Evaluation* of the youngster's response to this individualized program.

4. *Revision* of the program as necessary to improve the original prescription: retaining its successful components, and substituting new ones for components that have not worked.

Underlying all these ideas is the notion of what /I/D/E/A/ termed "manipulative factors." Neither principal nor teachers in any school can control a number of factors in the overall instructional situation: the school's budget, its size, its location, and the number of staff and students assigned there, for example, are determined by a central administration staff and the school board. However, a number of school factors *can* be "manipulated" by the principal and teachers: *where* instruction is to take place, *when,* with *what number* and *mix* of students, and so forth.

In addition, as a condition of their participation in the IGE program, IGE schools receive an unusual degree of autonomy from their school boards in allocating resources. Although the school's general budget is fixed by the school board, for example, principal and staff can shift resources from one budget category to another to suit their instructional strategy. Such manipulative factors may be minor when viewed individually, but in the aggregate, we believe, they can have a substantial impact on instructional quality.

WHY SOME EFFORTS TO IMPROVE SCHOOLING HAVEN'T WORKED, BUT CAN

At about the same time that /I/D/E/A/'s developmental staff went to work on "Enhancing Differences," the institute's research staff went to work on the second of the "two separable strands of inquiry" mentioned above: how does any school improvement program succeed? This is a simplified formulation of the complex investigation pursued by John I. Goodlad (director of research for /I/D/E/A/, and dean of the Graduate School of Education at the University of California at Los Angeles) and his colleagues. An integral part of the same question, for example, is "What makes school improvement programs fail?" Between those extremes is a whole spectrum of factors that incline a program toward or away from success.

However one states the basic question, the crucial concern underlying our research was a recognition that many excellent ideas for improving education, after being introduced in the schools and tried for a year or two, were later abandoned. "Enhancing Differences," we hoped, would offer schools a comprehensive, workable program for individualizing education. Unless we understood the dynamics of educational change, however, it seemed likely that "Enhancing Differences" would go the melancholy way of many other worthwhile programs.

As a laboratory for its investigation, the research staff obtained the cooperation of eighteen schools in eighteen different school districts in

Southern California. Ideally, the institute hoped, the principals and staff of all eighteen would have volunteered beforehand to commit themselves to educational change. In reality, /I/D/E/A/'s researchers learned later, a few of the eighteen had been arbitrarily chosen by their district superintendents as "volunteers." Owing to roughly equal amounts of good will, hard work, and good luck, however, the "volunteers" did participate in the five-year Study of Educational Change and School Improvement (SECSI) with the spontaneity necessary for valid research into change processes.

A few words may be in order about SECSI's[1] research design. *First,* /I/D/E/A/ purposely chose schools from different school districts to avoid undue influence from any single school superintendent and school board; clearly, there was no point in studying schools committed to "change" if they were all receiving direction from the same source.

Second, the school board and superintendent in each district were briefed on SECSI's purpose and research design, and agreed to give its participating school a high degree of autonomy; while remaining a member of its own school district for financial and legal purposes, each SECSI school was largely free to make its own operating and instructional decisions.

Third, the schools chosen were carefully selected to present a typical cross section of American schools. These were not "lighthouse" schools—centers of innovation and excellence in the past. They ran the gamut from suburban affluent to urban poor (white, chicano, black) and included some rural schools.

Fourth, although this was not recognized for a while by the researchers, the union of a respected California institution of higher education with a national foundation in a single research project proved beneficial in enlisting and retaining school participants for the project. The participation and reputation of UCLA suggested that the research was in the hands of "neighbors" who knew Southern California schools, understood their problems, and were seriously interested in a sympathetic study of obstacles to improvement; the participation of a foundation with educational interests implied that this research would lead to something more than just another report.

Fifth, the study sample (eighteen schools) was mainly determined by two factors: (1) the size of the /I/D/E/A/ research staff available for regular visits to the schools, and (2) the number needed to represent a reasonable microcosm of American education.

At the outset, /I/D/E/A/'s research staff did not promote any specific program for school improvement. It asked the staff in each school to examine their own problems, to select the general directions for change that they considered appropriate to their teaching–learning situation, and to set about achieving the goals that they had chosen for themselves.

1 The inevitable question about this acronym will rise in most readers' minds, and the answer is yes, the project was referred to by staff and participants as "Sexy."

As SECSI progressed, each school staff began to encounter problems in attaining the objectives it had proposed for itself—and it began turning to /I/D/E/A/ staffers for answers. After all, weren't they "the experts," the "consultants" imported to make innovation run smoothly?

The answer was "no." /I/D/E/A/ was there not only to find out what made change work in a cross section of schools, but to find out what *prevented* it from working. Furthermore, although a temporary infusion of "consultants" from UCLA, /I/D/E/A/, or elsewhere might be able to provide some answers, this type of support would ultimately have to be withdrawn when the research ended. It was gradually impressed on each school staff that they would have to learn to solve their *own* problems.

As time went on, however, two things happened: (1) each school staff found through trial, error, and hard work that it had a greater capacity for solving its own problems than it had previously thought, largely because, in the past, it had relied on outside consultants or school-district specialists for advice and had not tested its own problem-solving capabilities; and (2) each school recognized that it was not alone in its predicament; there were seventeen other schools and each of them was running into problems, too. Perhaps, the eighteen school staffs began to reflect, somebody at one of the other schools has solved a problem we're groping with, or we've solved one that still puzzles them, and we can share expertise. Perhaps, in sum, regular, workaday classroom teachers and administrators can learn to serve as *consultants to each other.*

By this gradual process, the League of Cooperating Schools, which had existed on paper from the beginning of SECSI, took shape as an operating reality with regular meetings, joint seminars, informal phone calls—and even its own newspaper, featuring classified ads that offered (or asked for) help with instructional and organizational problems.

The entire history of SECSI makes an intriguing detective story in the processes of educational change—so much so, in fact, that McGraw-Hill Book Company decided to publish history, procedures, and findings in a seven-volume series. Although no article can adequately summarize a five-year project, the following conclusions stand out as particularly important, and as particularly suited to integration with the "Enhancing Differences" program:

1. *The focal point for school improvement must be the individual school.* Orders from the top—from the superintendent level—to "innovate" are too easily frustrated by the individual culture of each school, the distinctive mix of personnel, resources, personalities (not only of principal and teachers, but also of students), and needs that give each school a "teaching–learning profile" that is as distinctive as a fingerprint. Only a school whose principal and staff *want* to improve will do so. At the other end of the scale, the lone teacher who wants to change will sooner or later be discouraged if a majority of his or her colleagues hold a contrary viewpoint. Only a school staff *united* in its *commitment to improvement* and its *agreement*

on the *direction of change* has the critical mass of resources to make a new approach succeed.

2. *Thus, the principal is a key agent of change.* Since the individual school, not the school district or the individual classroom, is the focal point for improvement, only the school's chief administrative officer can bring all its human and material resources to bear on innovation. This finding places a new burden on the school principal, but it also opens up new possibilities for professional leadership in a much-disparaged educational post. Viewed from a more interesting, professionally challenging perspective of genuine leadership, the principal is the guy or gal who, by helping teachers define what they need, what they want to do, and how they intend to get there, supplies the tangible and intangible resources needed to make innovation tick. He or she is partly the teachers' leader, partly their servant—and he or she values both jobs.

3. *However, the individual school will find it difficult to make improvement efforts succeed in isolation from other schools.* For good reasons and bad, schools and their staffs see themselves as competing with other schools in the same district for approval. Schools committed to improvement, SECSI found, pose a threat to other schools in the same district that hew to outdated methods of instruction: if the improvement-minded school succeeds, it is likely to gain attention, obtain a larger share of school board resources, and its personnel are more likely to obtain promotion or salary increases. To combat these possibilities, noninnovative schools and their staffs adopt defense mechanisms designed to minimize the successes of the innovative school and magnify its failures. One principal involved in the SECSI study reported, for example, that his school was referred to as "The Funny Farm" by other principals in the district. Slight as such criticism may sound, the subtle as well as obvious forms it takes can harm the morale of a school staff and jeopardize their success.

4. *Therefore, the improvement-minded school should ally itself with other schools similarly committed to educational change.* In part, such alliances help solve the morale problem of schools that feel themselves isolated from other schools within the same district. More significantly, however, these alliances—"leagues" in IGE parlance—permit the sharing of problems and expertise that converts classroom teachers into occasional consultants to other schools within their field of specialization.

5. *But "change" itself can become frozen; schools need a process for constantly appraising and revising their solutions to constantly shifting educational problems.* Virtually every practice to be found in the schools today was at one time an "innovation." It is crucial to educational progress that school staffs learn when a once-new idea has outlived its day and must be replaced. Through its observations of and work with the eighteen LCS schools, /I/D/E/A/ researchers developed and refined a problem-solving process called DDAE—for dialogue (analysis by the teachers of commonly encountered problems, research on methods to solve them, and discussion

783

of alternative possibilities), *dec*ision making (reaching consensus on one or more of the possible solutions), *a*ction (implementing the solution or solutions selected), and *e*valuation (determining whether the solution worked, to what degree, and how its effectiveness can be increased through modification).

SECSI, in sum, produced a *strategy for change.* Both its purposes and its findings were well characterized by John Goodlad:

> There is no great trick in improving a few schools, given adequate resources. But such efforts tell us little or nothing about how to proceed next time with minimum resources and maximum impact. Further, such efforts are rarely self-renewing. . . . Perhaps we will have self-renewing school systems (as well as self-renewing schools) when schools, having learned how to help themselves, will then help one another.

By the time developmental work on "Enhancing Differences" was completed, /I/D/E/A/ had the two interrelated components of its school improvement program: first, a coherent program for tailoring instruction to individual needs, and, second, a change strategy to make that program work. It joined the two into a single change program: IGE.

A set of *thirty-five IGE "outcomes"* is intended to help a school staff measure its progress toward incorporating genuinely individualized learning into daily school practices. The specific number thirty-five may sound excessively mechanistic, an attempt to introduce pseudoscientific precision into an area that—like all human endeavors—is exceptionally difficult to quantify. The outcomes express necessary conditions for individualizing education according to IGE procedures; in and of themselves, however, they do not guarantee the result. They are probably best regarded as a kind of thermometer for a school; taking its temperature at many spots does not guarantee overall health, but it can detect specific maladies that require attention.

IMPLEMENTATION

Guided by the strategies evolving from the "study on change," /I/D/E/A/ proceeded to develop an implementation strategy.

The key element of the strategy was, and is, the participation of "intermediate agencies"—colleges, universities, local school districts, state boards of education, and even one federal agency (the Bureau of Indian Affairs)—that would act as recruiters for schools, provide IGE training, and establish "leagues" of IGE schools for mutual support. These intermediate agencies, in sum, performed much the same functions for their schools that the UCLA–/I/D/E/A/ staff performed for the original League of Cooperating Schools in the latter stages of SECSI.

784

The implementation scheme for IGE, in outline, works like this:

1. An intermediate agency, having reviewed and approved IGE goals and processes, is appointed by /I/D/E/A/ for a given geographical area, ranging from a city, county, archdiocese (parochial schools), state, or— in the case of the Bureau of Indian Affairs—a larger but specialized jurisdiction.

2. The intermediate agency recruits schools for the IGE program under special conditions: (a) the school principal and staff must review IGE goals and processes and be willing to commit themselves to the program; (b) the local school board must agree to give the individual school's principal and staff relative autonomy within broad legal and financial boundaries.

3. A number of schools (normally five to fifteen) within a convenient, "commutable" distance from each other are organized into a single IGE league.

4. To each league is assigned an IGE "facilitator," a staff member of the intermediate agency who undergoes rigorous training in facilitator workshops sponsored by /I/D/E/A/. This facilitator, in turn, establishes training programs for the principals and staff in his or her league, maintains communication among the schools in that league, and promotes their common progress toward achievement of IGE goals and processes.

5. Finally, through periodic meetings and workshops, facilitators and institute staff review problems, monitor progress, and update IGE concepts. From beginning to end of the implementation chain, all parties, including the institute, assume that IGE is not a static "package," but a constantly developing program that requires constant review and renewal.

PRESENT STATUS

It is important to emphasize, as a preface to the statistics that follow, that IGE is a financially *self-sustaining program*. The only expense borne by /I/D/E/A/ are those for salaries and expenses of its immediate staff. All other expenses, including training for facilitators, travel and other expenses incident to operation of the leagues, and purchase of necessary IGE materials, are borne by the IGE schools and intermediate agencies. IGE schools receive no financial subsidy from /I/D/E/A/.

In 1970, there were 2 intermediate agencies and 125 schools participating in the project. By September, 1973, there were 84 intermediate agencies and more than 1,000 elementary schools participating. As of this writing (March, 1975), 148 intermediate agencies serving 1,200 elementary and secondary schools in 35 states are taking part in IGE in the United

States; another 41 American-sponsored schools in 29 foreign countries have also elected to adopt IGE. Finally, the institute is engaged in discussions with education officials of 7 foreign nations who have expressed interest in translating IGE programs into their languages for adoption in native schools.

Quantitatively speaking, at least, IGE has therefore been a success. There is, no doubt, a certain "bandwagon" effect that operates in any new approach, a collective hopping aboard various well-promoted programs by school officials out of fear of being left behind. By the early 1970s, however—the period during which IGE got started and began registering its rapid expansion—educators had become much more skeptical of innovation's glittering appeal. Moreover, far from being a bonanza for the wheelers and dealers of grantsmanship, IGE offered nothing but hard work and the possibility of providing children a better way to learn and teachers a better way to teach. The fact that so many schools have adopted IGE speaks well not only for IGE, but for the willingness of American educators to invest considerable amounts of energy into a process that, upon examination, holds out the promise of improving their teaching effectiveness.

But numbers tell only part of the story. How has IGE stacked up qualitatively?

EVALUATION

At mention of the word *"evaluation,"* or upon being asked, "How do you know that your program is better than anyone else's?" educators tend to shuffle their feet restlessly, look off at a distant corner of the room, and suddenly remember a dentist's appointment, which requires their immediate departure. The reason for this reaction, known to psychologists and even ornithologists as *avoidance behavior* (birds as well as people take to flight when suddenly made uncomfortable), is not that educators have no answers, or that the answers are unfavorable, but that evaluation of educational achievement is an astonishingly tricky business, one that requires a considerable background in understanding a program's goals and nature.

Inasmuch as this book is intended for educators, I will presume some of this background and at least a modicum of sympathy for the problems of evaluation. Rather than cop out entirely on the difficulty of evaluation, however, let me point out just three problems in evaluating IGE, which will suggest the intricacy of qualitatively appraising the program:

1. *IGE schools are in different phases of implementing IGE.* Some schools will obviously be more advanced in implementation than others, even though all have some right to consider themselves "IGE schools."

2. *IGE school staffs differ in their understanding of, and ability in, implementing IGE.* If all school staffs were uniform in intelligence, energy, and application, every school that adopted IGE in 1970 should be in roughly the same state of program adoption as every other school that adopted IGE in 1970. Until we discover a method for stamping principals, staffs, and IGE facilitators out of a common dough with cookie cutters, however, humans will persist in individual difference, and IGE schools will continue to differ in their *quality* of program implementation.

3. *IGE is a process, not a curriculum.* At present (as mentioned above), IGE recommends no specific content. In consequence, not all IGE schools apply IGE processes to the same areas of learning.

/I/D/E/A/'s own staff has constantly monitored IGE implementation since the program's inception. More importantly for readers who want external evaluation as some guarantee of objectivity, bearing in mind the constraints mentioned above, let us look at some results of evaluation by organizations outside the institute. Three institutions (all under contract to /I/D/E/A/) were asked to look at IGE from different perspectives. Belden Associates, a marketing-research firm, was asked to conduct a national survey of parents, students, teachers, and administrators on their assessment of IGE. A team from the University of Nebraska was asked to design a method for analyzing costs associated with IGE and to evaluate pupil and teacher attitudes in IGE schools. Finally, the University of Missouri's Center for Educational Improvement was asked to do a case study of IGE implementation in a single school. The results given below single out some highlights of probable general interest, but are by no means exhaustive.

Both administrators and teachers in high-IGE schools (i.e., those

TABLE 2

OVERALL RATINGS OF IGE	ADMINISTRATORS	TEACHERS	PARENTS
Excellent	68%	42%	34%
Good	28	53	42
Fair	1	3	8
Poor	—	1	4
Don't know, or no answer	3	1	12

TABLE 3

		YEARS IN IGE SCHOOL	
STUDENT ATTITUDES	TOTAL	ONE YEAR	TWO YEARS OR MORE
Learned more this year than last	75%	75%	77%
Learned same amount	20	21	19
Learned less	5	4	4

which had made the most progress toward achieving, in both quality and quantity, the IGE "outcomes") expressed more favorable attitudes toward the program than those in low-IGE schools. Parents in both had roughly the same attitudes.

IGE EFFECTS ON CHILDREN

Among teachers:

1. Believe academic performance had improved: 60 percent.
   Performance is poorer: 4 percent.
2. Thought students were enjoying school more: 77 percent.
   Students were enjoying school less: 19 percent.
3. Believed behavior had improved: 31 percent.
   Believed behavior was worse: 16 percent.
4. Thought IGE worked equally well for fast and slow learners: 74 percent.
   Thought it was better for fast: 16 percent; better for slow: 10 percent.
5. Thought IGE worked equally well for culturally advantaged and culturally different children: 75 percent.
   Thought it better for advantaged: 8 percent; better for different: 7 percent.

Among parents:

1. Felt their children had learned more under IGE: 43 percent.
   Learned less: 5 percent.
2. Believed their child had enjoyed school more under IGE: 40 percent.
   He or she had enjoyed it less: 6 percent.
3. Were "very satisfied" with their youngster's progress under IGE: 59 percent.
   Were dissatisfied: 4 percent.
4. Believed that IGE teaching methods were superior to those used before: 61 percent.
   Thought better before IGE: 10 percent.

Among children:

1. Thought school subjects were more interesting: 58 percent.
   Liked them less: 5 percent.
2. Liked their teachers better: 35 percent.
   Liked them less: 9 percent.
3. Enjoyed school more this year: 55 percent.
   Enjoyed school less: 11 percent.

COSTS OF IGE, ACCORDING TO PRINCIPALS

1. No additional budget provided: 64 percent.
2. No more than 5 percent additional provided: 17 percent.
3. No more than 10 percent additional provided: 7 percent.
4. No more than 15 percent additional provided: 2 percent.
5. At least 15 percent higher than non-IGE schools provided: 7 percent.

NEGATIVE REACTIONS TO IGE

The primary reason for dislike of IGE reported by both administrators (27 percent) and teachers (36 percent) was the amount of time required for implementation. Administrators (12 percent) and teachers (15 percent) claimed that they are understaffed for IGE, and 16 percent of the teachers reported difficulty "in meeting the needs of children." No other negative factors were reported by more than 9 percent of either group.

SUMMARY

Individually guided education blends research into individual differences as reflected in learning with intensive teacher training in methods to accommodate individual differences, plus a strategy for change designed to make educational innovation and improvement a self-renewing process. Statistics on the rate of adoption indicate rapid and widespread acceptance, particularly since IGE has not been promoted on a scale approaching that of some better-known innovations. In addition, parent, teacher, administrator, and student attitudes toward IGE are overwhelmingly favorable. Reported costs do not seem to stem directly from IGE-related expenditures, but from a decision by school boards as to the size of the investment that they wish—or feel necessary—to make. IGE is being conducted with apparently equal success in modern, architecturally flexible schools and in traditional "egg-crate" schools.

The theoretical base underlying IGE has been researched, both by /I/D/E/A/ and by other organizations. Its practical processes—for individualizing of education by teachers, for inculcating school staffs with techniques for constantly analyzing and renewing their change efforts, and for supporting change through such mechanisms as mutually reinforcing schools organized into leagues—were developed through intensive research and development with typical schools. Although these processes require a higher level of effort on the part of principals and teachers, this greater effort has not proved a hindrance to adoption of IGE.

In less parsimonious, more enthusiastic terms, /I/D/E/A/ believes that the program represents a responsible means for individualizing learning for children and youth, and for making continuous improvement a way of life within our schools.

SPECIAL NOTE

As indicated in the introduction to this paper, concepts in the /I/D/E/A/ Change Program for Individually Guided Education have come from the work of many institutions. The institute has drawn from the efforts of other programs, such as the Ford Foundation-sponsored Harvard Teaching Teams' Projects from 1959–1964. Another source has been the Wisconsin Research and Development Center for Cognitive Learning.

An early outcome of the Wisconsin Research and Development Center's "Project Models" (maximizing opportunities for development and experimentation and learning in the schools) was the creation of thirteen nongraded instructional and research units as replacements for age-graded classrooms and schools of Madison, Jamesville, Milwaukee, and Racine, Wisconsin, beginning in 1966. This effort marked the beginning of the multiunit elementary school, which was subsequently tested in a variety of situations.

Through an agreement in 1969, results of the center's experience with the multiunit organizations were combined with /I/D/E/A/'s research and development efforts to prepare in-service materials relating to IGE. /I/D/E/A/ and the center define their respective programs differently, however, and use different implementation strategies and materials. Both institutions use the term "individually guided education."

Some of the intermediate agencies and schools participating in the /I/D/E/A/ change program also participate in the Wisconsin Research and Development Center's Program.

Operational Concepts

1. The focal point for educational improvement is in the individual school.

2. The principal is a key agent of change.

3. The implementation of a new educational procedure, particularly one involving different instructional methodology, is both difficult and complex; a sustained period of time is therefore essential for a successful transition.

4. Educational change is more easily accomplished when groups of schools initiate program modifications in concert.

5. It is doubtful whether any prescription for change can be permanently viable; instead, schools must continuously seek new solutions to the problems that arise.

Implications

Viewed in the large, the IGE experiment is significant on several counts. First, as a comparatively long-term and large effort at school improvement, it provides a number of insights into the sociology of school organizations and the process of institutional change. The instructional systems used by schools, for example, are not easy to alter. Although schools are relatively unique in that they are staffed by administrators and teachers of varying educational and philosophical persuasions, schools must remain within the range of ideological expectations that prevail in a given community. Put another way, the evidence seems to suggest that as long as schools adhere to a typical instructional structure, modification and improvement can occur without much resistance. But when the attempted changes go beyond the customary structure, many of the factors commonly associated with "institutional deviance" are brought into play.

The IGE experiment is also significant in that it espoused a specific goal (greater individualization) and a specific process (internal reorganization) for the achievement of its goals rather than substantive shifts in the content of instruction. Thus, its basic intent was to do better what was already being done. As a consequence, it achieved greater success than probably would have occurred if more fundamental realignments in the instructional organization had been sought.

Two other points are worthy of mention: the history of IGE reinforces the long-respected belief that even low-risk change requires careful nurture and support, and it demonstrates that the "bandwagon effect," wherein the principle of safety in numbers is evoked, can be used to considerable advantage in educational reform.

Although the author is commendably cautious in the claims made for IGE's achievements, one suspects that the process through which greater individualization was achieved also served to diminish the fear of change itself and, as a result, prompted a number of other small-scale improvements not described. The effort was also beneficial, then, in the sense that successful change is likely to beget a continued interest in improvement.

792

Donald W. Protheroe

The Instructional Uses of Junk in the Classroom

Item: The new teacher, at her wit's end to know how to motivate a nonreading, nonwriting fifth grade boy, brought an old lawn mower engine to school, along with a few simple tools borrowed from her boy friend. The nonreader–writer was interested and wanted to take the engine apart. The teacher confided to the youngster, however, that she didn't know how to take the motor apart and she doubted that the other youngsters in the class knew how either. Would he use paper and pencil and list the steps he was to follow in taking the engine apart?

The result was that the boy disassembled the engine and then drew up a list, complete with a diagram that showed how he had taken it apart. Later he made this list even more sophisticated by naming bolt and wrench sizes, types of screwdrivers he had used, etc. Since the engine was now apart, the nonreader–writer was then asked to make a second list showing how to reassemble the engine. The proud boy's lists and diagrams, although rudimentary to be sure, were hung on the classroom wall above the engine.

Item: It has been shown that when encouraged to manipulate a series of threaded pipes (about eighteen inches long, complete with T's, nipples, elbows, and unions), young children tend to thread the pipes together in a random fashion. Even though they give little thought to the original intent of the pipes, the youngsters apply the skills of matching and sorting, use fine motor control in threading the pipes into fittings, and become familiar with the names of the various pieces.

So? Kids playing with junk? What does this have to do with schooling? Sounds like it might be fun, but it's certainly not part of the mainstream of "modern" education.

Critics and theoreticians, however, disagree. Charles Silberman, for one, suggests that junk or scrap materials such as bottle caps, leather scrap, spools, spindles, etc., may be used with more traditional art materials to teach aesthetics. The various subjects that are part of aesthetics are not

Reprinted from Donald W. Protheroe, "The Instructional Uses of Junk in the Classroom," in Arthur D. Roberts (ed.), *Educational Innovation,* © 1975; by permission of Allyn and Bacon, Inc., Boston.

"frills to be indulged in if there is time left over from the 'real' business of education."

Lev Vygotsky, in *Thought and Language*(*1*), has articulated a rationale that suggests a vital use of junk in language development. Words in the education of children first play the role of *means* through which concepts can be formed. Later they become the *symbols* for concepts. For example, in the case of the plumber's union, the child will call it by name, if he first hears someone else call it by name. However, he may not realize, when he first uses the word, that union means the joining of two separate elements. But having had the experience of joining pipes in union, he can more easily understand the abstraction of the word "union" as it applies or refers to the union of states, labor organizations (unions), etc.

The intent is not to "teach" union with the pipes, but to have the child experience the act. For, as Vygotsky explains it, "The language of the environment, with its stable, permanent meanings, points the direction the child's generalizations will take." The teacher needs to be aware of and use many different experiences from various fields in order to broaden the language experiences of each youngster.

This process of broadening, however, needs to be put into workable terms. Roger Brown, in *Words and Things*(*2*), speaks of what he calls the "Original Word Game." Two people are required to play the game: "one who knows the language, and one who is learning."

Brown indicates the game is made up of at least four steps:

1. "The tutor names things in accordance with the semantic customs of his community." With the pipes, for example, the young child tends to say, "Give me that crooked thing" (the elbow). To which the tutor may reply, "Yes, that would be a good place to put the elbow."

2. Having heard the "crooked thing" named as "elbow," the child may use the term "elbow" and is ready for the second step. "The player forms hypotheses about the categorical nature of the things named." The child may determine that the elbow in the pipe is similar in some way to his own elbow. (Some children have been observed holding their elbows horizontally to their shoulders and swinging their forearms to illustrate this categorization.)

3. The player "tests his hypothesis by trying to name new things correctly." For example, the child may generalize that the plumber's "Tee" is also an elbow because it, too, can change the direction of the pipe. The tutor (another child, the teacher, etc.) "corrects" him by using the term "Tee" to name the new object. The learner may then learn a new, related, category; not only is the Tee like the elbow, it is different in some way. Perhaps it is more like the letter "T" he finds in his study of sound–letter relationships.

4. "The tutor compares the player's utterances with his own anticipations of such utterances and, in this way, checks the accuracy of fit between his own categories and those of the player." If, for example, the

child uses the word "joiner" for the elbow or Tee, the tutor recognizes that the child knows something about the function of the two objects. But the tutor continues to improve the accuracy of fit in terms of his own linguistic background and preference for specificity, and may indicate to the child that the more precise "elbow" or "Tee" is preferable. Hopefully, these "corrections" in the classroom will be made as naturally as they are in most life situations. (Consider your language learning when you tell your automobile mechanic that the "big round thing on top of the engine" rattles. He inspects the engine and informs you that the air cleaner is loose. When you describe the incident to your friends you use the precise term "air cleaner" instead of the inexact "big round thing.")

Brown reminds us that the tutor is not one person, but a variety of people. In fact, this is life as it goes on around the learner. The learner encounters new experiences and new languages in face-to-face confrontations with new people and through sources such as television, radio, billboards, newspapers, books, and the like. Each of these contacts calls for the learner to improve his linguistic reference categories (words) for nonlinguistic referents (things).

The use of junk capitalizes on children's enthusiastic interest in the technological environment. As a result, it expands language learning and the possibilities of concept formation. Children *are* interested in go-carts, minibikes, bicycles, washing machines, etc. And these interests can be used to serve the goals of the school.

In this chapter we want to give you some ideas of how to use junk. It's easy enough to come by; every child in class can help you collect it, and it rarely costs anything. The following categories and examples are by no means exhaustive. They are simply "starters" to help you in your own development of the uses of junk.

MECHANICAL JUNK

"Mechanical junk" consists of cast-off appliances, vehicles, motors, engines, tools—any mechanical equipment or machinery in parts or whole. It is not necessary for the equipment to be in good working order.

Mathematics

Mathematical concepts are fundamental to anything mechanical. Let's look at some uses of mechanical junk in math:

1. An old telephone. Dial a name. What does it add up to? Find simple sums.
2. A bicycle tire. Read the tire. What math is involved? (1.75×26 indicates that the tire is $1\frac{3}{4}$ inches wide and 26 inches in diameter.)

3. How could you measure the school yard with the tire? (Discover the relationship of circumference to distance traveled by cutting a tire in two.)
4. A roller from a scrapped wringer-washer. With the roller, measure the height of a door. (Area may be calculated, too.)
5. Nuts and bolts. Nuts and the heads of bolts are (in the United States) generally identified in fractions. Children can soon learn to distinguish, for example, between nuts measuring 9/16ths and 5/8ths, *and* select the appropriate wrench to fit.
6. Gears. Ratio may be explored by using the front and rear sprockets of bicycles. (The rear sprocket from a five- or ten-speed bicycle is especially good.) An automobile differential or transmission is a more sophisticated version of the same principle.

Matching, Sorting, Classifying, Categorizing

1. Nuts, bolts, screws. Sort all of the carriage bolts, stove bolts, round head bolts, flat head, wood screws, sheet metal screws, hex head and square head nuts, etc.
2. Engines, parts. Put the head on an engine properly. Insert the crankshaft and camshaft.
3. Electrical appliances. Observe how toasters, waffle irons, clothes irons, and small electric room heaters are similar (heating elements).
4. Wheels and axles. Discover relationships between doorknobs, cranks on wringer-washers, hand drills, screwdrivers, etc.
5. Two clothes irons: one aluminum, one cast iron. Hypothesize which is heavier. Test your hypothesis.
6. Devices for carrying liquids. Group pipes (copper and galvanized), hoses (various sizes and diameters), roof gutters.

Language Development

1. An old telephone. "Dial" words.
2. Parts of engines. Name parts, and speculate on names and functions of parts (connecting rod, valve, wrist pin, cam lobe, camshaft, head, etc.).
3. Concrete objects and abstractions. Derive concepts such as automobile universal joint and universality, or plumber's union and union of states, labor union, etc.
4. Toaster, waffle iron. Take them apart, and list the stops in disassembly and reassembly.
5. Two clothes irons. Write descriptions of each, noting the similarities and differences.

Science

1. A lawn mower engine. Learn scientific principles of construction and operation.
2. Lawn mower engine, or outboard motor. Learn scientific principles of construction, or operation of two-cycle and four-cycle engines.
3. Engines. Contrast operation and construction of diesel engine, two-cycle, and four-cycle engines.
4. Automobile parts.
   a. Fuel pump. Learn principles of operation.
   b. Carburetor. Discover the Venturi tube principle.
   c. Clutch. Learn principles of friction and pressure.
   d. Battery, generator. Discover transformations of energy.
   e. Transmission. Trace changes in direction of force.

NATURAL JUNK

The category natural junk is made up of nests, hives, tree stumps, leaves, limbs, roots, snakeskins, etc.

Art

1. Sculpture. Driftwood, small stumps, unusually shaped limbs, etc.
2. Wall plaques. Old boards varnished and used as mountings for
   a. Textures. Bark scraps, stones, shells, seeds.
   b. Pictures. Scenes made by arranging pine cones, berries, acorns, other seeds, grasses, shellfish, etc.
3. Christmas decorations.
4. Scenes, dioramas. Twigs, branches, roots, leaves, etc., to represent real-life landscapes.
5. Shells. Paint scenes on shells (use India ink or fine felt-tip markers).
6. Sketching. Use burnt pieces of wood. Sketch on bark, paper, old boards, etc.

Science

1. Nests. Disassemble nests, then try to reassemble them.
2. Hives. Examine insect homes, and speculate on population.
3. Nests. Collect various types. Speculate on sizes of birds. Chart areas for nest locations, etc.

Mathematics

1. Seeds. Use them as counters.
2. Plants. Make strip graphs to record growth.
3. Seeds. Record distances from location of seed to tree or plant.

CLOTHING JUNK

The clothing junk category is made up of any cast-off clothing. Of special interest is antique clothing or replicas. Uniforms, especially hats and shoes easily identifiable as belonging to a particular organization, occupation, or profession, are especially valuable.

Classifying, Categorizing, Matching

1. Uniforms. Ask children to group uniforms: nurse, soldier, sailor, etc.
2. Shoes. Ask children to arrange shoes for different sports: golf, football, baseball, basketball, fishing, etc.
3. Hats. Arrange hats by function: for protection, for identification, etc.
4. Pairs: rights, lefts, etc. Arrange appropriate activities.
5. Textures. Ask children to identify fur, wool, silk, rubber, etc., by touch.
6. Men's and women's shirts: how can you tell them apart?

Social Studies

1. Period clothing. Dress as a teenager in the 1950s.
2. Other countries. Dress as Mexican, Japanese, etc.
3. Study occupations. Dress as a doctor, soldier, carpenter, etc. Why is a special type of clothing worn?
4. Special occasions. Dress to attend a formal party, a wedding, etc.
5. Inclement weather. Dress for rain, snow, hot weather, cold weather, etc.

Role Playing

1. You and a classmate dress in costumes of countries at war. Arbitrate your differences.
2. Create a country with a certain climate, customs, etc. How would you dress?
3. You are going on an overnight camping trip. What clothing will you take along?
4. You have just won a trip to Anchorage, Alaska. What clothing will you take with you?

Science

1. Warm clothing. Why is darker colored clothing warmer than light colored? Why are several layers warmer than one heavy garment?
2. Rain gear. What makes a garment water-repellent, or waterproof?

STORE JUNK

For generations children have learned math skills and concepts from grocery stores set up in elementary school classrooms. Too often, however, the store has been thought of as appropriate for primary age youngsters only. Studies in comparison shopping, unit pricing, cost of living, origin of produce, etc., are only a few of the activities that older children might explore in the fourth through eighth grade store.

Make your store using some of the suggestions indicated in the furnishings section of this chapter. Visit supermarkets to obtain items such as large signs, stands, etc., from displays. Don't forget bag, boxes, and shopping carts. Make money from construction paper and bottle caps. The use of discount coupons, "green stamps," government food stamps, checks, etc., should also be part of your merchandising program. Here are some suggestions:

Mathematics

1. Sets. Ask children to select a set of all dairy products, canned goods, produce department items, etc.
2. Comparisons. One brand of tomato paste is ten cents per can; another brand is nine cans for eighty-nine cents. Which is the better buy?
3. Discounts. Coupons received in the mail or cut from advertisements range from five cents to fifteen cents off. How can you save in doing your family's shopping? (How does the grocer get reimbursed for accepting the discount coupons?)
4. Sizes. How big is a number ten can? How does Jumbo differ from Giant or Family size? Which one should you buy for greatest economy?
5. Estimating. With only fifteen dollars to spend, how can you avoid embarrassment when paying for your grocery cart's contents?

Science

1. Classifications. Shop for foods representative of a balanced diet for a family of four.
2. Preservatives. Study materials used to retard spoilage in food.

3. Calories. Which foods have the highest calorie values? The lowest?

4. Refrigeration. Which foods would spoil if the electricity were out for a long period of time?

5. Origins. Which products in the store can be traced in full or part to the cow? To the chicken? To the pig?

6. Diet foods. How do diet foods differ from foods made from nondiet recipes?

Social Studies

1. Origins. Which products are manufactured or packaged in your city or state? Which products are produced in other countries? Which countries? Why? Trace the steps in the manufacture of a can of corn. How many people and what materials combined to provide the finished product?

2. Map study. Use a product to initiate map study. Use city maps for local products, world maps for foreign products, etc.

Language Arts

1. Role playing

   a. You are a clerk in this store. While you are pricing cans your friend comes in and you discover him shoplifting. What should you do?

   b. While shopping you meet a friend. You begin to chat and the conversation shifts to the high cost of food. Act out the scene.

   c. You are the store owner and have just hired a new clerk. This morning you explain his duties and show him where things are.

   d. You are a customer and suspect that the cashier has made an error in adding up your bill. What do you do?

   e. You take your groceries home and discover that your eggs have been broken by careless bagging. What might you do?

2. Creative writing

   a. Naming. You and a friend have just become owners of this store. What will you name it? Why?

   b. Description. Describe your life as a carton of milk.

   c. Advertising. Each week this store features a special product. Select a product and develop an effective advertisement.

   d. People. Write a character sketch of one of your favorite customers.

3. Reading. Children are often familiar with name brands from hearing and seeing them on television. Use product packages to develop certain reading skills.

CONCLUSION

Erik Erikson terms the psychological stage of development that includes ages five through twelve the Age of Industry. During this period the child has to be active: tinkering, manipulating, taking apart, putting together, building, tearing down, and building up. If this is so, the classroom teacher should strive to accommodate these characteristics by deliberately designing and redesigning a rich learning environment that gives children much to explore and react to.

The teacher can capitalize on this stage of development by determining, through observation, what the children are interested in and, with the help of "junk" materials, constructing a classroom environment that will expand the child's language and concept development.

References

1. Lev Vygotsky. *Thought and Language.* Cambridge, Mass.: M.I.T. Press, 1962.
2. Roger Brown. *Words and Things.* New York: Free Press, 1966.

Operational Concepts

1. Children in the years between the ages of 5 and 12 often have a fondness for the manipulation of concrete objects, for arranging, tinkering, fixing, and so on.

2. To the extent that circumstances permit, teachers should satisfy these desires by providing an opportunity for manual activity in their instructional plans.

3. The imaginative teacher can make substantial use of commonly available, inexpensive objects (junk) in enhancing the learning environment.

4. The "handling" of material objects—particularly when an intellectual purpose is involved—offers a means of perpetuating concept development in language, social studies, mathematics, and science.

Implications

There are several advantages to the use of "junk" in the classroom. First, the provision for "hands-on" experience (allowing children to experiment with objects) can materially enrich the physical stimulation of the classroom. Second, time spent in such activity tends to increase the practical relevance of schooling; a familiarity with the workings of an electric toaster, for example, may diminish the fear of mechanical objects as well as teach something about electricity. Third, the opportunity to deal with concrete objects permits the child to learn through nonverbal activity and reduces the extensive emphasis upon abstract symbols. For these reasons alone there is much to commend in the writer's point of view.

Values Education

Kenneth H. Hoover

Developing Values

Based upon his own unique experiences, each individual develops guides to human behavior. These are called values. Values are continually being modified as experience accumulates. The teen-age years are characteristically a time of questing or searching for reliable guides to behavior. Values which were once accepted without question come into full critical analysis.

Every teacher is a purveyor of a value system. Even the most traditional teacher emphasizes certain facts over others by any number of gestures, incidental comments, and inflections in assigning a high or low value to certain ideas. The issue is whether students will develop values accidentally or whether they will be provided a learning atmosphere which lends direction and support to their efforts.

FUNDAMENTAL PROPERTIES

Values exist at different levels of commitment. From a mere positive feeling about something one may develop a compelling urge to persuade others to his way of thinking. It becomes apparent then that values may be expressed in different ways. A number of value indicators may provide clues for value clarification and development.

What Role Do Attitudes and Interests Play in the Acquisition of Values?

Attitudes are predispositions to behave in a prescribed manner. An individual may say he is for or against something as a result of impulse or

Reprinted from Kenneth H. Hoover, *The Professional Teacher's Handbook: A Guide for Improving Instruction in Today's Secondary Schools,* © 1976; by permission of Allyn and Bacon, Inc., Boston.

804

observation of others. He may have given little thought or analysis to the attitude, however. An attitude may become a guide to behavior (value) in any number of ways. Ideally it should be carefully examined and reexamined in the presence of valid data. All too often, however, an attitude becomes fixed on the basis of erroneous assumptions and little or no data. Unfortunately, those values which are acquired illogically may be as difficult to dislodge as those which are the product of critical examination.

All individuals have passing interests which may be discussed or even pursued temporarily. In a sense, this is the manner in which one becomes informed about many things. Eventually, if the needed reinforcement is not provided, one interest will be replaced with another. The interest of teen-agers may vary considerably from one month to the next. Interests do provide clues or indicators of values, however.

How Do Beliefs and Convictions Enter into Value Formation?

High school students freely express their beliefs and convictions. Generally such expressions represent an invitation for discussion and analysis. Essentially, this represents a youngster's way of saying, "I would like to explore further in this area." Perhaps he senses the need for developing a stable value in the area. Thus a verbal expression of a belief may be no more than a mere indication of an emerging value. It provides an avenue through which a value may be developed as a result of careful examination.

How Are Feelings Associated with Values?

Feelings or emotional reactions are closely associated with values. Values which are highly prized tend to create within the individual a certain amount of anxiety. Thus he may feel compelled to persuade others to his way of thinking. Feelings, however, do not necessarily reflect values. They are often of a temporary nature and are easily dissipated through reflection. Feelings represent a basic component of values, however. Accordingly, one can approach value teaching through either the affective or the cognitive dimension. There is considerable evidence suggesting that until feelings are examined little progress in value restructuring can be expected.

How Persistent Are One's Values?

Values are the basic component of an individual's personality. As such they tend to change rather slowly over a period of time. Nevertheless, a teacher must bear in mind that values are products of experience. Since experience is continuous, values too are modifiable. If a value makes an individual unhappy, perhaps creating worries and problems, with appropriate guidance it may be altered. It has been observed that values per se are not so damaging as the tenacity with which they are held.

What Are the Basic Ingredients of Values?

When an individual is asked to make a decision (a choice between alternatives) he is asked to think. When he is asked how he feels about that choice an appeal is made to his emotions. The process of valuing includes both domains.

In discussing the affective domain Krathwohl concedes that the attainment of a cognitive goal may result in attainment of an affective goal as well(1). He points out, however, that this process does not necessarily occur when he says that "the development of cognitive behaviors may actually destroy certain desired affective behaviors. . . . For example, it is quite possible that many literature courses at the high school and the college levels instill knowledge . . . while at the same time producing an aversion to . . . literary works."

PROCEDURES FOR DEVELOPING VALUES

Some people contend that teachers must indoctrinate students with the basic values of our democracy. Others are convinced that values cannot be taught at all—that they are somehow "caught" in the home, the church, and the school as individuals interact with others and with life in general. As a result, the schools have all too often steered clear of any systematized procedure for teaching values. This seems strangely at odds with the obvious needs of today's youth, who must cope with unprecedented value contradictions and complexities.

The teaching of values, like other instructional methods, involves a process of reflective thought. Since values are intimately associated with emotional responses (e.g., attitudes, interests, feelings, beliefs, etc.), unusual precautions are necessary. As Raths and his associates point out(2), "we may raise questions but we cannot 'lay down the law' about what a child's values should be."

How Are Value Problems Identified?

Value problems arise constantly, both incidentally as learners interact one with another and in connection with the content of every course of study. In either case one must look for value indicators in areas involving aspirations, purposes, attitudes, interests, beliefs, and so forth.

Value indicators of the incidental variety are usually statements such as the following:

1. Import duties should be enacted to protect our farmers.
2. The American Indian must be taken off the reservations.
3. When I'm old enough I want to join the Navy.
4. I like to read poetry.

As the foregoing suggest, many such statements reveal what one stands for, what he supports, what he prefers to do, what his ambitions may be.

An appropriate problem for discussion, "What steps should be taken to minimize the air pollution in our industrial centers?" is clearly one involving values. In mathematics, the problem, "What procedures should be followed in switching from the English to the metric system?" is also one of values. The reader will note that the problem itself assumes a given value position. Thus a prior question might well concern itself with whether or not such action or policy changes are needed.

How Are Value Problems Analyzed?

The initial phase of resolving problems usually takes one into a consideration of existing data or facts. Not only must the facts be recognized but they must be *evaluated* as well. Simon and Harmin contend that content material can and should be treated at three different levels: facts, concepts, and values(3). To illustrate: What steps should be taken to make the U.S. Constitution functional in our own lives?

Fact questions:

1. What essentially is the subject of the constitution?
2. Who were the signers? What special interests did they represent?
3. How did it differ from the Articles of Confederation?
4. Why are the first ten amendments called the Bill of Rights?

Concepts level:

1. The constitution set the pattern for democratic forms of government.
2. The constitution provides for a system of checks and balances.
3. The Bill of Rights attempted to correct social injustices.
4. The constitution is an evolving concept, as reflected in amendments and Supreme Court decisions.

Values questions:

1. What rights and guarantees do you have in your family? In school?
2. Is your student government able to function democratically?

3. Should a student editorial board have the final say about what is printed in the school paper or the yearbook?
4. How can you initiate needed changes within the democratic framework?

It should be noted that value questions usually are of the "you" variety. They are designed to make content functional in the lives of the learner.

How Are Alternatives Evolved?

Following an analysis and evaluation of the existing state of affairs, possible alternatives are introduced and evaluated. Some alternatives are usually suggested or implied in text materials; others may be apparent from the data analysis. It is important, however, for the learner to advance beyond the obvious. He should be encouraged to apply his own creative imagination to the problem. Some creative and provocative solutions or alternatives relative to the foregoing problem might be: (1) rewriting the constitution, (2) passing certain constitutional amendments, (3) suspending the constitution for specific purposes.

Again, the values level of analysis would be employed to personalize the discussion. For example, "If you were rewriting the constitution what changes would you make?" "Should the president (or your school principal) ever be 'above the law'?" In each case the consequences must be carefully weighed.

How Are Choices Affirmed?

A choice in the realm of values is held in high esteem if it is to become a true value. Unless one prizes, cherishes, or is happy with his choice, he is not willing to affirm his stand publicly. After a choice is finally reached, the learner must perceive ways of making his value functional in his own life. The teacher's role is to guide the student in discovering possible and practical applications. For example, "What immediate and specific steps in altering your student government rules may be taken?"

What Activity Is Appropriate?

The logical conclusion to a values discussion is some form of action. Values, by definition, are guides to human behavior. Sometimes such action is ill advised simply because the learner does not fully understand the legitimate avenues of action open to him. A student strike, for example, initiated by the acts of a few can deny education to a majority. Less drastic forms of behavior may involve some reading on the subject, forming friendships or organizations designed to nourish the values(s), collecting and spending money for the cause, conducting a letter-writing campaign, floating petitions, and the like. The teacher will want to guide students in reorganizing and evaluating possibilities for action relative to values.

References

1. David R. Krathwohl et al., *Taxonomy of Educational Objectives: Affective Domain* (New York: David McKay Co., Inc., 1964), p. 20.
2. Louis E. Raths, Merrill Harmin, and Sidney B. Simon, *Values and Teaching* (Columbus Ohio: Charles E. Merrill Publishing Co., 1966), p. 37.
3. Sidney B. Simon and Merrill Harmin, "Subject Matter with a Focus on Values," *Educational Leadership,* 26 (October 1968): 34–9. Used with permission of the publisher.

Operational Concepts

1. It is likely that values education will receive increasingly heavy emphasis in the future.

2. Citzenship education should include the analysis of moral and ethical issues.

3. Students resent the hypocrisy that is conveyed when school practices violate the values that are taught in formal lessons.

4. Preaching is of limited utility in the development of enduring values.

Implications

Reflecting the cyclical nature of curriculum development, interest in values education, relatively high several decades ago, has waned considerably in recent years. An abrupt shift is occurring, however, and extensive developmental activity is likely in the immediate future.

At the moment, however, affairs are somewhat muddled. Expert opinion ranges from those who are convinced that values cannot be taught at all, to those who favor a variety of conflicting beliefs regarding the optimum methodology.

In this first of three excerpts from Hoover's work, extensive attention is given to the technique of values clarification. Although the technique has many useful features and is popular among committed users, a number of theorists seriously question its merits.

There are, in addition, strong disagreements between curriculum designers who contend that the schools should emphasize conventional values, and others who are convinced that students must have the right to formulate their own moral conceptions.

Within this confusion, nonetheless, several implications are seemingly incontrovertible: values should be approached cognitively; the curriculum must in one way or another cause the student to identify, analyze, and reformulate basic values and beliefs; the powerful influence of the learner's early experience must be acknowledged; the impact of out-of-school experiences must be recognized; and, as best they can, the schools must endeavor to satisfy community expectations.

James A. Peterson
Dick Park

Values in Career Education: Some Pitfalls

The concept of career education has recently emerged as a possible solution to some of our national ills. We propose to examine this concept in the light of current cultural developments, noting some possible pitfalls and focusing upon some of the significant determinants of the potential influence of career education.

Any analysis must heed several considerations. First, we live in a transitional culture: As a society, we are moving away from one predominant value system toward another. In such times much ambiguity, confusion, and conflict can be expected, with a tendency toward subverting the new by incorporating it within the old.

Second, we are faced with depletion of natural resources while population continues to grow; hence we must acknowledge that "old" solutions based on ever greater industrial production and growth no longer work.

Third, we are reexamining our humanistic values; the trend is toward valuing persons over things.

A basic question is whether education will continue simply to transmit the culture of the larger technological supersystem or, on the other hand, collaborate with other systems in the modification of culture, focusing upon the need for a shift from currently self-defeating industrial values to humanistic values.

Since the industrial revolution in the early eighteenth century, the production sector of our society has increased its influence and control, particularly in the United States, where most of our policy decisions are now made to increase production. Many social systems once independent of industry—religion, government, labor, and education, for example—have now become subsystems of the production suprasystem.

In complex societies such as ours, conflict and tension develop at the interface of coexisting systems where people, decisions, or activities overlap. This stress can either strengthen both systems or increase the strength of one while weakening and subordinating the other. In the latter case, one becomes a subsystem, a mere component of the more powerful system

Reprinted from James A. Peterson and Dick Park, "Values in Career Education: Some Pitfalls," *Phi Delta Kappan*, May 1975, pp. 621–623; by permission of the publisher.

and, at the extreme, loses its identity, with an accompanying deterioration of its goals and values. However, such a confrontation between two systems can take another direction. Dialogue may bring about a clarification and formation of revised values and goals.

THE EDUCATIONAL AND INDUSTRIAL SYSTEMS

Industrialization demanded acquisition of the basic literacy and computational skills required in the factory or the marketplace. Education met the challenge by making its services compulsory and placing the three Rs at the center of the curriculum. With the evolution of needs from unskilled to highly skilled technicians, expectations grew for a more comprehensive vocational curriculum. As a result, the educational system is in danger of surrendering even more of its individuality.

Career education, the most expansive human resources development program the government has ever proposed, could, depending upon the value systems which it espouses, be the near final step in subordinating the education system to the production system. It is possible that historians of the future will look upon our time as another Dark Age, this time blanketed by industry rather than the church.

There are, however, alternatives. It is almost inevitable that, as systems grow, their boundaries begin to overlap and they merge into super-systems. This is not *necessarily* bad. The growing interchange between education and the other sectors of society is potentially beneficial. The question is, Can education enter into collaborative efforts—yet preserve humanistic values and goals?

Historically, education has varied in form and content. In a hunting society, formal schools did not exist. Learning amounted to socialization. Children learned to be adults, productive workers. After agriculture was invented, man's caloric output began to exceed his needs, freeing some people from work. Had it been an egalitarian system, it would have freed everyone equally. Instead, schools (from Greek, *scholē*, leisure) arose to teach an elite class how to spend its leisure time. What was taught was not merely instrumental or functional, supporting the status quo.

New tools and ideas, often generated by those freed from toil, ushered in the industrial age. These new and continually changing technologies required skills that could not be transmitted informally. Schooling became compulsory—to serve industrialization. While industrialism increased leisure, it also increased specialization and alienation or lack of value and fulfillment in most men's work. A gap grew between man's work and his leisure. Social obligation often denied personal fulfillment.

Education tried to span this gap, to meld a "liberal" curriculum that allowed men to grow and evolve with an "applied" curriculum to fulfill industry's needs. The schools were saddled with conflicting expectations: Teach the student to work, but keep him out of the job market for twenty years; liberate his mind, but make him a productive citizen, willing to work at meaningless, absurd jobs(1).

Schooling imposes an artificial zone between childhood and adulthood. Adolescents are told not to act like children, but they are not permitted to function as adults. They are told to be responsible but are not given real responsibilities.

Career education may help eliminate, or reduce, this discontinuity in our educational efforts. However, while it is desirable to create a smoother transition from child to adult, we cannot merely revert to the socialization processes of primitive societies where the child learns the roles and skills of the adults. In our rapidly changing world, adult role models, especially instrumental ones, become increasingly obsolete.

INDUSTRIAL VALUES IN THE CLASSROOM

Our industrial value system rests upon competition as a motivating factor; each individual measures his "success" by how much better he is than others. Within this system there must always be losers—and a resulting alienation from self. Thus each "winner" has a subtle investment in keeping the system as it is. This same value system dominates our classrooms.

Education is a value-laden activity, and educators must be aware of what they are promoting. Unexamined values are easily and often unknowingly smuggled into the classroom; schools have taught many lessons advantageous to industrialism besides the three Rs. Students have been coerced to compete with one another in striving for "success." To succeed, one must conform and do what is acceptable to the authorities; one must act "responsible." Failure in this system is dangerous and helping others is often seen as cheating; children learn quickly that it is every man for himself. To get lower grades is to have less worth as a person, which results in frustration, lowered self-esteem, and other-directedness(2). Success in others becomes defeat for self; suspicion and distrust lead to hostility and alienation. Many students simply give up, overcome by eroded self-confidence and feelings of inferiority.

As Alvin Toffler recognized, the whole school system seems to be an ingenious machine to produce the kind of adults industry desires through regimentation, rigid seating patterns, grouping, grading, and bells to announce changes of time(3).

POST-INDUSTRIAL EDUCATION

The struggle between the values of work and leisure, vocational and liberal education, and childhood and adulthood is difficult to resolve in

814

industrial society. Yet these values can and must merge in the fourth stage which we are entering—postindustrial man.

Buckminster Fuller and John McHale both address themselves to the new possibilities our technology has opened(4), while Dennis Meadows et al. warn of catastrophe due to population and industrial growth(5). Though these two philosophies are in opposition in many respects—in their perception of abundance or scarcity of resources, for example—they have three things in common: They start with a global and systematic view; they see a necessity for radical value change; and they see production work decreasing and becoming of less value.

The challenge is no longer to have enough workers to produce enough goods. The problem is one of planning, design, distribution, and redefinition of human usefulness and work. As little as 4 to 10 percent of our present work force may eventually be able to supply all of our material needs. McHale says, "Work, as previously defined, is no longer the central life interest. It has lost its relation to the compulsive work ethic, to the principle of nationality and efficiency, and the notion of time as money— that is, as a scarce commodity and socially significant unit"(6).

Much of the discontent in the work force comes not from lack of preparation to do meaningful work, as some career educationists hypothesize, but from the realization that the work is meaningless. Both Paul Goodman and Martin Bronfenbrenner have recognized the dehumanizing effects of the codification, featherbedding, and planned obsolescence which have replaced meaningful labor(7). Educators must not prepare individuals for work that is meaningless or that may not exist in the future.

We are not saying, however, that education must return to its old goal of preparation for leisure. The goal of education is no longer for students to learn how to spend their leisure or how to work, but rather to learn how to live a richer, more satisfying life. Postindustrialism necessitates a redefinition of careers, an incorporation of more humanistic values. Work— as time clocked, sacrifice made, or industrial output—is no longer a good in and of itself. And education must not be segregated from the business of living; it must be "pervasively viewed as an *ongoing* aspect of living itself"(8).

Educators must realize that the least skilled workers, who are also least prepared to adapt to a new definition of careers, will be hit first by increased automation and cybernation. The primary values of a whole culture do not change overnight. As Bronfenbrenner noted(9):

> We dare not foresee our work–leisure evaluation either changing rapidly enough to extract us from our present troubles, or being enforced stringently enough to drive people off relief into whatever substandard jobs and wages they would perforce accept. . . .

In the interim we must "batter down the multitudinous economic walls, from apprenticeship rules to occupational licensing and professional standards, which keep so many pleasant and rewarding jobs closed to so many 'other Americans' "(*10*). We need to recognize and value learning through experience as well as learning in a structured academic setting.

In a postindustrial era, the amount and type of work will change, as will the way in which work is defined and valued. The current focus upon the collection and distribution of energy and natural resources as well as the manufacturing and marketing of goods will give way to the delivery of information, services, and experiences(*11*). Educators must be sensitive to the potential for careers emerging in these areas. While technology will be fundamental in this emerging period, industry need no longer be the center of our activities or values.

THE CHALLENGE

The design and implementation of a comprehensive career education program will require an awareness of the changing needs of individuals and of society. We are presented with a challenge: the opportunity to reassess our values and alter the type and meaning of our careers. Career education can hasten the progress of several desirable trends: (1) the softening of the distinction between work and leisure; (2) a switch in society's needs from the production of goods to the delivery of services; (3) a decrease in the status of specialization and professionalism, allowing a broader base for work opportunities; and (4) a deemphasis upon the "marketability" of a career while emphasizing its potential for social self-realization. (For example, how many career educators encourage field trips to study volunteer programs?)

Educators must confront the coexisting systems; analyze the implicit and explicit values, goals, and behaviors of those systems; clarify their own values; explore with others the most desirable and feasible futures for our world, country, and schools; assess present and future needs; state valuable goals; and decide where and how much they can collaborate with these other systems without compromising their values and goals.

Career education provides an opportunity to begin this process. Education should and must be more responsive to its environment and all other societal systems in it. While increasingly fulfilling the needs of other systems, such as family, community, religion, recreation, and industry, it must also maintain its own unique purposes. Education must pursue an influential, not a passive, role in relation to our society, yet retain its individuality and autonomy, not in the interest of self-preservation, but for the health of the entire system.

The many proponents of career education have correctly evaluated schools as inadequate, largely irrelevant, and poorly motivated. They see higher and "liberal" education as an elitist expectation being foisted upon many who have differing skills and needs. They want to incorporate purposiveness, relevancy, continuity, and individual planning and decision making into the educational system. They admit that education and career choice cannot be valueless, and recommend decentralized goal setting and implementation of career programs. They encourage "hands-on" learning models and elimination of the walls between the school, home, community, and economic systems.

Despite all of these points of agreement, career education could have many outcomes—some of which are antithetical—depending on the values which prompt and direct its implementation. This ordering and selection of values will be the ultimate test for career educationists and the career education movement.

How much emphasis will be given to corporate, production, and concentration values, and how much to human, consumer, and distribution values? How much importance will be given to means and how much to ends? How much will we focus upon competition, striving, property rights, and social conformity on the one hand, and cooperation, gratification, personal rights, and personal expression on the other? How much do we want simply to create better employees rather than change careers to improve people's lives?

Retaining our society's historical emphasis on industrial values would obviously be the easiest course. A shift in focus toward more humanistic values will require insight, courage, commitment, and strong leadership.

References

1. Paul Goodman, *Growing Up Absurd* (New York: Random House, 1960), p. 14.
2. Jules Henry, *Culture Against Man* (New York: Random House, 1963), Chap. 8.
3. Alvin Toffler, *Future Shock* (New York: Random House, 1970), p. 400.
4. Buckminster Fuller, *Utopia or Oblivion* (New York: Bantam Books, 1969); and John McHale, *The Future of the Future* (New York: Ballantine Books, 1971).
5. Dennis L. Meadows et al., *The Limits to Growth* (New York: Universe Books, 1972).
6. McHale, op. cit., p. 317.
7. Paul Goodman, op. cit., pp. 19–21 and Martin Bronfenbrenner, "Economic Consequences of Technological Change," *Values and the Future* (New York: Macmillan, 1971), p. 463.
8. McHale, op. cit., p. 319.
9. Bronfenbrenner, op. cit., p. 464.
10. Ibid.
11. Toffler, op. cit., Chap. 10.

Operational Concepts

1. Without proper precaution, career education could contribute to the subordination of the educational system to the production system.

2. Career education programs must ensure that students acquire the vocational skills that are likely to be needed in the future.

3. Students should be helped to view work as a means of "social self-realization" as well as a source of income.

4. The industrial ethos of the past may no longer be suitable, and career education programs must therefore reflect emerging new relationships between work and leisure.

Implications

A good many social critics have argued that the existing curriculum serves to perpetuate an orthodoxy of beliefs which allow the power elements of the society to control the citizenry. Reflecting upon the arguments of Paul Goodman, Buckminster Fuller, Martin Bronfenbrenner, and others, the authors fear that career education could become the handmaiden of the corporate structure. Whether or not these fears are justified, their recommendations for career education would seem to make abundantly good sense. They propose, in the main, that work be viewed as a vehicle for self-fulfillment, that those now in schools who will constitute the future work force be exposed to humanistic values, and that programs in career education be geared toward a contemporary rather than an obsolete job market. These arguments, seemingly, are difficult to fault. Further, they tend to espouse the proposition that, since schooling is intended to equip the young to meet adult responsibilities, the total curriculum, not just career education, must be involved in shaping students' attitudes and beliefs regarding the place of work in a rewarding life-style.

Open Education

Ian Westbury

"Open" Education and the Technology of Teaching

Two insistently maintained sets of principles run through the literature advocating "open" education; one set draws upon a conception of the relationship of the child to his learning environment; the second makes certain stipulations about the role of teacher vis-à-vis the child. The two sets run something like this:

STUDENTS AND THEIR LEARNING

1. Children's innate curiosity leads to exploratory behavior that is self-perpetuating.
2. The child will display natural exploratory behavior if he is not threatened.
3. Play must not be distinguished from work as a predominant mode of learning among children.
4. When children are interested in exploring the same problem or the same materials, they will often choose to collaborate in some way. Similarly, when a child learns something which is important to him he will wish to share it with others.
5. Concept formation proceeds very slowly, children learn and develop intellectually not only at their own rate, but in their own style, and intellectual development takes place through a sequence of concrete experiences followed by abstraction; verbal abstractions should follow direct experiences with objects and ideas, not precede them or substitute for them.
6. Errors are necessarily part of the learning process; they are to be expected and even desired for they contain information essential for further learning.

Reprinted from Ian Westbury, " 'Open' Education and the Technology of Teaching," *Journal of Curriculum Studies*, Vol. 5, No. 2.

TEACHERS AND THEIR TEACHING

1. Teaching must proceed from the interests and capabilities of pupils.

2. The teacher must take an active role in the classroom and seek to understand and direct the pupil's interests in order to attach these to subject matters that might not ordinarily interest him.

3. Learning must be sustained; the teacher must bring out in children the interests that underlie sustained involvement in learning.

4. The teacher cannot, in the nature of things, find an ideal match between the "interests" and "abilities" of pupils, and a program for such a match cannot exist. The teacher's task is to search for meaningfulness in the activities, whatever they may be. More important, though, the teacher must create a situation in which the child is willing to project himself into an activity so as to bring his own innate resources and innate sense of orderliness into play.

5. The teacher can only do these things if he provides an environment in which (a) children can move from activity to activity as they wish and need to, (b) the activities *available* for children are rich in educative potentiality, and (c) there is a balance of activities available in the classroom—raw materials, structured materials, reading materials, materials for dramatic play—which truly communicate to the pupils who live in *specific* classrooms(1).

The creation of an environment that will support student-initiated learning is the most important task of the "open teacher." The selection of materials that become, in their turn, the bases for student activities is the most important planning task of the teacher. In the classroom the teacher must guide students through the activities he has made available with vigor and authority.

Three problems lurk in this conception of the open teacher's tasks. As Ronald Barth has pointed out, by selecting the activities available to students the teacher controls the scope of the curriculum in the classroom. The kinds of activities the teacher chooses determine in their turn the quality and intensity of the learnings available to students. The kinds of decisions the teacher makes about when and how students should move from one activity to another determine the breadth and depth of the curriculum that students experience(2). In these problems we have the issues of *coverage, mastery,* and *management,* even if the environment of the room and the teacher's attitudes allay the issue of *affect.* What coping strategies (to use the term suggested earlier) does the current literature on open education offer to escape the dilemmas that these issues present to teachers in conventional classrooms(3)?

> The topic of provisioning . . . is central to an educational philosophy that stresses the importance of choice for children. . . .

Sand not only lends itself to all kinds of numerous measurement operations (sifting, pouring, weighing), but provides a rich variety of tactile, aesthetic, and conceptual materials as well. Wet sand feels and acts differently than dry sand. Dry sand is good for making pictures and designs; wet sand affords the added possibility of three-dimensional construction. . . . Whole towns and road systems can be constructed, and those in turn may become the subject of mapping exercises as children learn to represent their three-dimensional sand town on a two-dimensional plane. . . . In short, the potential for developing quantitative operations and concepts; artistic ability; notions of city planning; rudimentary principles of architecture, engineering, drafting, and mapping; and symbolic representation skills—are all inherent in sand and water.

We can adopt two stances as we read material of this kind. We can ask whether or not we believe that prescriptions for method couched in terms such as these are meaningful given our view of the problems presented by the realities of the classroom, or we can accept the claims of proponents of open education that open classrooms work and then proceed to ask how they might or can work. Let me address both of these problems.

If the view of problems of managing the conventional classroom that I outlined above stands, prescriptions for teaching methods of the kind that I have been citing clearly fail to address the complex realities of the classroom. We are not given any set of concrete strategies that tell us how the involvement of many students in tasks is sustained, how involvement is actually transformed into mastery of a conventional (or even unconventional) kind, or how the teacher manages the series of simultaneous learning settings that are implicit of open classrooms. We are not told how the need for very active planning on the part of teachers can be reduced so that open teaching can become a method suitable for teachers of only average interest in teaching. We are not given any insight into the concrete optimizing strategies by which the tradeoffs between management, mastery, and coverage are secured, or interest is made compatible with coverage, or how mastery is built into materials.

Likewise, we are given no real understanding of the concrete theoretical principles that should underlie the provisioning of the open classroom. Coverage and mastery are addressed in terms of productive and "unproductive" materials, but this distinction seems to cut directly across conceptions of interest and involvement. As Ronald Barth writes(4):

We find open educators inconsistent and even somewhat confused on the question of criteria for selection of materials. On the one hand there is some confidence that any activity on which the child is fully engaged and interested is productive and will result in learning, and on the other hand there is an inclination to make distinctions between productive and "unproductive" materials.

Two different sets of classroom goals are implied in this ambiguity, but no clear coping strategy for trading between these goals is hinted at so that we could have a feel for what we should be doing were *we* trying to run an open classroom. The examples we are given of method are singularly unhelpful in this search for clarity: it is undeniable, for example, that a sand tray has potential for developing quantitative operations and concepts, artistic ability, etc., but how does the teacher go about extracting real learnings of this kind from a sand tray, and how does she do this when she has other groups doing similar open-ended tasks? Without an understanding of how these things are done, without a sense of the classroom strategies that an open teacher should employ in situations of this kind, we have no way of generating a picture of what such a teacher might do in other similar situations.

These objections to the hortatory literature can be met, however, by the claim that, while, admittedly, concrete teaching strategies are not set forth clearly, a picture of the character of the open classroom is adequately sketched in this writing. This claim is true, to some extent at least, but when we seek to penetrate the kind of characterizations that we are offered by such writing the same kind of inadequate specification emerges(5).

Thus we can see that the open classroom, with its centers of activity (reading corner, math corner, sand tray, and the like) and its emphasis upon physical movement of students among many different kinds of activity as the interests of individual students change, permits a manipulation of both time and space by the teacher. Students can move between activities and spend as much time as is appropriate with a single class of activities. The insistent emphasis within the literature of open education on the need for intrinsic involvement by students in relatively freely chosen activities may meet the problem of involvement that conventional self-paced instruction faces. The emphasis on warmth and honesty in encounters between students and teachers and the emphasis on teacher–student enquiry offers the possibility—so often missed amid the managerial problems of the conventional classroom—of liberating a task-focused emotionality in the classroom that can, in its turn, engender both intrinsic and productive work, i.e., learning(6).

This kind of analysis of the nature of the open classroom gets us, as I have suggested, some way in our search for understanding of how such a classroom should work. But only some of the way! We can still ask what vague notions like intrinsic involvement or aspirations like warmth or honesty of encounter mean in the world of the classroom and its routines. And what of the demands of mastery and coverage? As Ronald Barth has pointed out, activities can be intrinsically rewarding and motivating without being educative(7):

> There are many activities in which children engage, such as learning to
> play the piano, which are tedious, laborious, and even painful. Others, such

as playing ball, are fun, unrestrained, and carefree for most children. Both may be characterized by active involvement with materials, but they have considerable differences, as any child knows. One appears, from the adult point of view, to be "work" and the other "play."

Open educators meet this problem by eschewing any attempt to claim that piano playing (i.e., work) was more educative than playing ball (i.e., play); rather they would attempt to distinguish between activities using such terms as "educationally productive" and "educationally unproductive" and then seek to show how productive such activities as ball playing can be. However, if we assume that "educational productivity" can be defined as a goal for any activity, the pedagogical issue remains of showing how productivity can be secured from activities, i.e., of showing how coverage and mastery can be effected given some specified activity. We can grant that almost any activity (and particularly those chosen *by* children) can be turned to some educative purpose, but we need to ask how the teacher goes about turning activities to educative purposes and how the teacher goes about building *educative* purpose into otherwise educationally neutral activities. As I have already suggested, we can concede that quantitative operations and concepts, artistic ability, notions of city planning, or principles of architecture and the like are pregnant in any sand tray, but how should a teacher go about extracting these purposes from the sand tray, and particularly how should he go about doing this when he has other groups in his classroom doing similar tasks?

The literature of open education seems to give two different answers to these questions: one of these answers is of little theoretical interest and, on the face of it, would seem to imply the presence of a rock on which open education might founder; the other answer is of great theoretical and practical significance.

The simple solution to this problem of input, and that implied by the sand tray example, is to station a teacher or a teacher substitute near all productive or potentially productive activities with the implication that he should intervene to turn an activity to productive ends. A learning activity thus becomes externally paced, although the experience itself, from the viewpoint of the students, might well have intrinsic qualities. The problem with this solution lies in its trivial character: it is merely an extension of the existing classroom practices to smaller activity centers. Given the real problem of management in a decentralized classroom environment, this solution demands either that classrooms be manned more intensively than they are at present or that teachers must expend greater than normal energy on teaching. The implications of either of these possibilities for the institutional viability and cost of open education have not been widely discussed.

These rocks can be avoided, to some extent at least, by recognizing that there are problems in any attempt to run an open classroom and by then facing the theoretical issue of what the problem of the open classroom is. Thus, although activity units can be decentralized in the interests of organizational and pedagogical flexibility, the classroom goals of coverage and mastery of subject matters of one kind or another nevertheless remain; the open classroom has to teach its students, and if, for any reason, the teacher cannot do this, then something else has to. This something else must, of course, be materials of some kind.

We can gain some glimpses of what this claim might mean and how this problem might be met—although not in the hortatory literature of open education. Let me attempt to demonstrate this possibility by means of a simple illustration from the nursery school.

David Olson has reported the development of an educational toy that is an effective means of teaching the concept of diagonality to preschoolers but, at the same time, makes no demands on the teacher. His toys were placed in a nursery school with the request that teachers were not to provide any instruction on how to make the patterns but merely to keep the toys, properly assembled, on the shelf; they were to let the children play with them as they would with any other toy in the school. After seven months, control and experimental children were tested on their mastery of the concept of the diagonal; 64.1 percent of the experimental group received maximum scores on the test for diagonality as compared to 39.6 percent of the control group; even the unsuccessful children in the experimental group went about their attempts to solve the task problems with strategies that were superior to those used by the control children(8).

Olson's toy seems to offer a way of avoiding the pitfalls that are pregnant in the open classroom notion. Little teacher energy was expended on injecting specific instruction on the diagonal into the classroom setting; the toy itself was responsible for specific instruction and the toy itself exerted its own motivational press on students. The toy was, in other words, self-instructional and thus imposed no special demands on the teacher.

I have emphasized this one in some way trivial example of materials-induced instruction because I believe that the open classroom can only be made to work if devices of this kind become the primary instruments of routine explicit instruction in these classrooms, thus leaving the teacher free to address the demands of classroom management and nonroutine instruction. I am arguing, in other words, that the open classroom can only be regarded as a real and plausible alternative form of schooling if the teacher can be relieved, to a substantial extent, from traditional responsibility for mastery and task attention. As a corollary to this belief, I would argue that the effective development and dissemination of the open classroom notion demand that significant attention be given the issues entailed in the development of devices of this kind; the conventional American literature advocating open education gives little attention to these issues and, by this omission, gives a false impression of the issues and problems in open teaching.

In fact one can argue that the open classroom movement in Britain has been, in practice, grounded in the development of a technology similar to that implied by Olson's toy. Materials such as Dienes's *Multibase Arithmetic Blocks* or *Cuisinaire Rods* are packages of toylike stimuli developed for teaching elementary mathematics. The literature that surrounds these packages provides the bases for teacher understanding of what they should do with these toys and, indirectly at least, provides the basic discourses that the teacher is to use in his classroom as he operationalizes an "open" method. This literature is, if my inference is correct, the *real* literature of open education, and the issues that this literature raises are the real issues in open education. As Zoltan Dienes writes in his discussions of open mathematics teaching(9):

> Let it be immediately understood that decentralization does not mean chaos: nor does it mean any abrogation of the teacher's responsibility as regards the conduct of the class. The way this responsibility is discharged will, however, be different in a decentralized classroom from the way it is discharged in a centrally controlled one. The children must feel with certainty that the teacher is in charge of things, but at the same time *he has arranged that information can reach children without his intervention. The children must also feel that they can check their own or each other's work in an independent manner, and they will consult the teacher if some problem arises which they are unable to solve by themselves.*

Unfortunately, there are too few written discussions and too few written prescriptions for method in areas outside mathematics for one to feel at all confident that the pedagogic problems of the open classroom will readily and rapidly be solved *in practice*. And the solutions to the theoretical problems with open education that I raised earlier will have to wait until we see the character of the practical solutions.

THE TECHNOLOGY OF TEACHING AND THE GOALS OF SCHOOLING

A conception of knowledge as a content which can be stored in books that can be opened for and by students controls, of course, the goals of the conventional school. The methods employed in the conventional classroom are designed to perform this task; in the classroom the book is, in one sense, an aid to the teacher, but, in another sense, it is the sole object of the teacher's attention—other methods, discussion, most audiovisual aids, and the like, are devices that the teacher can use to ease the approach to the book. The real work of conventional schooling is focused on the book or on proxies drawn from books(10). It is this conception of tasks of education that legitimizes the methods of the conventional classroom—those methods that I discussed earlier. They are designed to open, more or less systematically, the boxes of knowledge symbolized by subjects to students. The existing classroom draws upon a technology of books and teacher talk to effect these goals.

The open classroom movement, of course, is an assault on the validity of this conception of knowledge and of methods that have their legitimacy in an image of schooling as information giving and box opening. Thus, at the heart of Dienes's prescriptions for mathematics is a conception of all mathematical thinking as experiential and intuitive, not formal(11).

> Take the multiplication concept. Take the two blocks illustrated below, one in each hand, and ask a six-year old child: "The long one is how many times as big as the small one?"

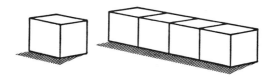

> A great many times the answer will be 3 not 4. This is because the child cannot yet appreciate the relationship 1:4 between the two objects (analytical thinking), but starts with the small object and mentally builds 3 more of them to make the long one (constructive thinking). Such a child needs a lot more practice in making the long piece with the little pieces. It is only through such practice that he can be led to analytical thinking; constructive exercises have to precede the analytical insight. It may be that some children will never reach the analytical stage: the great challenge to the teacher is that of devising ways and means of making the whole of mathematics available to such children.

Similar activities are required, Dienes argues, for *all* mathematical concepts and for all levels of mathematical thinking: for each new instructional goal a child must experience the concept that we wish him to learn before abstraction and generalization can become possible. And at each successive stage of generalization and abstraction, appropriate experience is required before the child can move to yet-higher-level abstraction. Teaching methods must conform to this understanding of the nature of mathematics; the student must be allowed to learn mathematical structures through an inductive examination and manipulation of physical and game-like embodiments of the concepts we are seeking to teaching them. In his words(12):

> In the natural concept formation process, which goes on uninterruptedly all the time, artificially structured games are rarely played, and, if they are, the structure itself is supposed to provide the amusement, as in a game of chess. Nevertheless, experiences have their own structures and so some experiences will tend to lead towards a concept more quickly than others. The

> "play" quality of these early experiences is probably a powerful stimulus towards the attainment of concepts, and a careful selection of these play experiences could accelerate such growth considerably. . . . Unfortunately, these natural situations and games do not take us all the way. . . . As higher and higher order concepts are aimed at, the number of life situations that could usefully lead up to them diminishes. Eventually, we are faced with having to teach concepts for which they have absolutely no background in experience at all. . . . Clearly, if we still wish to teach the child to form concepts as a result of experience, then we must provide him with artificial experiences to lead up to these more complex concepts and processes.

Dienes's materials are an attempt to engineer ways in which play- and game-like materials can be used in classrooms as the basis for mathematical experience. They represent a technological form which can be used to support a classroom environment that is appropriate to attainment of the "proper" goals of school mathematics.

This conclusion brings us back to the claims of open education, but in a somewhat different context. For Dienes, play-like school experience is a tool that he uses in the classroom to achieve a congruence between the demands of mathematics and the psychological capabilities of children to learn this demanded form of mathematics. These goals of means and ends require him to search for an appropriate organizational structure for the classroom; to effect play the classroom must be a different place than the conventional room: he needs to group children by interest, level of cognitive maturity, level of learning, and the like, and place them close enough to *experience* for them to truly manipulate the materials he puts before them. He can do all these things if he moves students through activities over *both* time *and* space, but only if pedagogical control is transferred to materials that are both self-instructing and, as far as possible, self-managing.

This discussion of Dienes's pedagogy can be generalized in some important ways. His invocation of an intuitionist metamathematics represents an awareness of the place of the person as an active agent in both mathematical knowing and learning. This turning of the person into the act of knowing represents one of the crucial understandings of twentieth-century philosophy. For us there is no content that is not inextricably entangled in the act of questioning. As Marjorie Grene writes, we understand that knowing is a form of doing, and "it is the full, concrete, historical person who is the essential agent of knowledge"(*13*). We believe that our discourses are discourses about a world, but this world is a world that is created by the questions we ask, not a world that is given. For us there is no content that is not inextricably entangled in the act of questioning. As a consequence of this awareness, a manifestation of what Father Ong has called our recognition of "the interior aspects of the person"(*14*), most of our current reconstructions of knowledge, most of the ways in which we conceptualize what knowledge is, give a higher priority to the question and the act of asking questions than they give to the bodies of answers that we have to past questions. This is the import of, say, Collingwood in history, Polanyi in epistemology, Kuhn in science, Piaget in psychology, and Dewey. For us the *encyclopedia*, the ordered body of accumulated knowledge, is not the symbol of knowledge; instead we attempt to symbolize our conceptions of the knowledge most worth having by talking of masteries of the methods by which new questions can be asked of subject matters or by which discoveries of new subject matters can be achieved. Moreover, our awareness of the many forms of knowledge has led us to ask why *this* man is asking *this* kind of question; and our psychological awareness has led us to ask why I (and we and they) habitually ask this kind of question. These questions have shifted easily and naturally into the further, specifically psychological question of "How do I (or we or they) learn to ask questions of this kind?" This whole chain of questions and the considerations about teaching that it implies is, of course, totally disquieting to anyone who thinks about schooling. This prescription for instruction that the chain implies—"Teach students to think"—is old hat, but, as we know all too well, the schools do not do these things. Schools are as obsessed with the *encyclopedia* of content as they ever were.

One source of the failure of the schools to take the point of prescriptions that students must be taught to think is to be found in the classroom itself, in its structures, and ultimately in the technology that needs and makes possible given structures. The technologies of the conventional classroom—the recitation, the lecture, the textbook—were designed to teach the eighteenth- and nineteenth-century *encyclopedia* of established facts and established doctrines. In their time these technologies *were* responsive to the goals that the schools were designed to enact. However, these technologies are not responsive to the goals that are implicit in our present conceptions of what the schools should do; we cannot execute the program of teaching implicit in Dewey, Kuhn, or Piaget within the structures and given the materials and methods of these old forms.

It is this conclusion that brings us back to open education. The ideology of open education articulates goals that the conventional school cannot address. The structures of the open classroom, derived from the methods of the preschool or kindergarten (where students cannot conform to the institutional demands of the classroom), are designed to meet needs that the structures of the conventional classroom cannot fulfill. But prescriptions for structure alone do not tell us how the *work* of the classroom, the tasks associated with mastery, coverage, management, and affect, can be performed. Dienes has shown us some ways in which aspects of this work might get done, but his technologies are only a beginning.

If we want to execute a new program in the schools, we must develop an array of new ways and new means that are real alternatives to the tried and true method of the conventional classroom. We must see what new purposes imply for the classroom and focus our attention on this latter problem. Infant methods as developed by Montessori and the English

Froebel movement offer us one, clearly viable set of models that we can ransack for our new needs. We can equally readily explore how we can turn the principles that lie behind these procedures and artifacts to more complex purposes. But this source of ideas is too limited in scope to cope in any sustained way with the real problem of implementing a new conception of the goals of schooling. We need to turn as well to technologies such as advertising and the computer, and to television, and to such understanding as we have of play, of the nature of learning, of the potentialities of group interaction. Most important of all, we must address the question of what new purposes mean when we face the problem of initiating millions of children into the forms of discourse and behavior that "education" connotes.

I wish to acknowledge the assistance of Jon Abrahamson and Ilene Harris in developing many of the ideas outlined in this paper. For valuable criticism of earlier drafts of the paper, I would like to thank my colleagues Robert Dreeben and Benjamin Wright.

References

1. See Ronald S. Barth, "Open Education—Assumptions About Learning," *Educational Philosophy and Theory*, 1 (1969), passim; Anne M. Bussis and Edward A. Chittenden, *Analysis of an Approach to Open Education*, Educational Testing Service, Report No. PR–70–13, August, 1970, passim; and Charles Rathbone, "Examining the Open Education Classroom," *School Review*, 80 (1972), pp. 521–49.

2. Barth, op. cit., pp. 32–34.

3. Bussis and Chittenden, op. cit., pp. 37, 39–40.

4. Barth, op. cit., pp. 33–34.

5. Rathbone, op. cit., does offer a characterization of the open classroom that meets this stricture.

6. For a discussion of the potentialities inherent in the class as a group, see Herbert A. Thelen, "Work Emotionality Theory of the Group as an Organism," in *Psychology: A Study of a Science*, Vol. 2, Sigmund Koch (ed.) (New York: McGraw-Hill, 1959).

7. Barth, op. cit., p. 32.

8. David R. Olson, *Cognitive Development: The Child's Acquisition of Diagonality* (New York: Academic Press, 1970), Ch. 9.

9. Zolton P. Dienes, *Mathematics in the Primary School* (London: Macmillan and Co., 1966), pp. 208, 209. (Italics added.)

10. For this argument, see Walter J. Ong, S.J., *Ramus, Method and the Decay of Dialogue* (Cambridge, Mass.: Harvard University Press, 1958), Ch. 13.

11. Zoltan P. Dienes, "The Growth of Mathematical Concepts in Children Through Experience," *Educational Research*, 2 (1959), p. 12.

12. Ibid., p. 16.

13. Marjorie Grene, *The Knower and the Known* (New York: Basic Books, 1966), p. 158.

14. Walter J. Ong, S.J., "Introduction: Knowledge in Time," in *Knowledge and the Future of Man,* Walter J. Ong, S.J. (ed.) (New York: Holt, Rinehart and Winston, 1968).

Operational Concepts

1. The objectives of open education differ from those of the traditional curriculum.

2. Since effective instructional methodologies must be congruent with educational purpose, the techniques of open and conventional education cannot serve the same ends.

3. Used by a sensitive and expert teacher, lecture and recitation can be adapted to a variety of classrooms and learning contexts; they afford the teacher considerable flexibility in catering to student differences.

4. The primary test of an efficient classroom method lies in its capacity to achieve a reasonable compromise between multiple and sometimes competing classroom objectives.

5. Students engaged in self-directed learning activities normally create more management problems for the teacher than students involved in teacher-directed activity.

6. In devising a curriculum appropriate to our time, we must make use of teaching procedures drawn not from open and conventional practices alone, but from other sources as well.

Implications

Because of its extraordinary scope, Westbury's essay could have been placed in any of the *Handbook's* sections. The arguments are thought provoking and sobering. He suggests that in our unbridled search for novel solutions to our problems, we may have imprudently discarded valuable old servants. Noting that public education will always be constrained by organizational and financial limitations, as well as by a range of alternative purposes, Westbury is of the opinion that lecture and recitation, because of their efficiency and effectiveness, are among the most valuable tools at the teacher's disposal. Most classroom observers probably would agree with his conviction that aimless classroom discussion has little virtue, and with his contention that, in the hands of a skillful teacher, lecture and recitation can be used to considerable advantage since they facilitate the teaching of traditional subject matter, lessen management problems, and permit the teacher to adjust the pedagogy to the particular nuances of the learning situation. One suspects, incidentally, that by "lecture" Westbury means that organized presentation of carefully selected ideas of importance, and that within the term "recitation" he includes dialogues among teachers and students.

The resulting implications are clear: teacher trainers, supervisors, and principals should be cautious about indicting teachers who rely heavily upon lecture and recitation. Correspondingly, in-service training activities that sharpen the teacher's ability to employ lecture and recitation may have considerable merit. Whether teachers talk too much (as often has been charged) may remain a point of dispute; nonetheless, one can scarcely contest the argument that when they do talk teachers should talk as effectively as possible. Of greatest moment, however, we are warned that we must choose our dominant educational missions with care, maintain an eclectic spirit, and fashion usable teaching methodologies out of a wide array of potential resources.

Concept Teaching

Kenneth H. Hoover

Gaining the Concepts

The mental images that we carry around in our heads are known as concepts. *A concept is a mental picture of an object, event, or relationship derived from experience.* Concepts help us classify or analyze; they help us associate or combine as well. These "mental images" gain meaning from subsequent experiences. As meaning becomes firmly established, we develop *feelings* about an idea or concept.

In the educative process concepts are thought to form the basic *structure* of content areas. An understanding of the structural dimensions of a field of knowledge provides the learner with a frame of reference for thinking and for evaluating future experiences.

The structural properties of each teaching unit normally consist of from six to eight major concepts. These are the basic ideas which provide the focal point of instructional activities. Unit goals are derived from such concepts.

Concepts are derived from content. They are usually formulated as brief, concise statements. In essence, they are the basic ideas which hold a unit together. Thus the first step in unit planning is identification of the basic unit concepts (ideas) to be sought. To illustrate from a unit in a class in general business (Sales Promotion and Advertising):

1. Customer satisfaction is the most important product.

2. Customer needs are the prompters for purchasing decisions.

3. Advertising can be an effective means of preselling products.

4. Advertisements use customer motives that can be restated in the personal selling approach.

5. The customer market is in a state of constant change, and therefore continuous study is required to stay abreast of current developments.

6. Differences in the structure and style of a product can be stated as sales appeals.

Reprinted from Kenneth H. Hoover, *The Professional Teacher's Handbook: A Guide for Improving Instruction in Today's Secondary Schools,* © 1976; by permission of Allyn and Bacon, Inc., Boston.

FUNDAMENTAL PROPERTIES

Concepts exist at many different levels ranging from highly abstract symbols to complex generalizations. They are also of different types. The specific level and type to be sought is dependent upon the nature of the content area to be studied.

How Do Concepts Differ with Respect to Level?

The recent expansion of knowledge has focused attention on the importance of analysis, generalization, and application of knowledge. Rather than emphasizing specific content materials as ends in themselves, teachers have attempted to guide students in the processes of reduction of content learnings to basic ideas which, in turn, can be expanded or generalized to a wide variety of problems and situations. Three distinct concept levels are necessary for such an instructional approach.

Unit Themes

At the most abstract level are unit themes (concepts). They are usually incorporated in the unit titles in such a manner as to provide direction for unit planning. Each instructional unit is based upon one such theme. For many years teachers struggled with subject-matter units, activity units, process units, and the like with relatively little satisfaction. Unit themes seem to provide the necessary cohesion and direction long sought by those who would make learning most realistic. Instead of a unit on Julius Caesar, for example, a worthwhile literature unit theme might be *ambition.* As Chase and Howard point out, such a unit would begin with a study of contemporary issues of vital concern to youngsters(1). Stress would be placed upon development of concepts of ambition and the characteristics which compose it. Julius Caesar would provide a basic content reference; indeed the unit would appropriately culminate with an intensive study of Julius Caesar. Instead of a unit on reproduction, a unit theme in science may be developed around the basic theme of interdependency of all body systems. Thus content emphasis is shifted from subject matter as an end in itself to its appropriate place as a means to attainment of more basic learnings.

Unit Concepts

Each unit theme, in turn, is broken into six to eight unit concepts. Based upon content, they provide the basic threads of a unit. The practice of writing out each unit concept, *in advance of the instructional experience,* provides much needed direction for unit planning. Furthermore, such a practice provides a useful safeguard against neglect or omission of important aspects of the unit. To illustrate from a unit in a class in general business (Sales Promotion and Advertising):

1. Customer satisfaction is the most important product.
2. Customer needs are the prompters for purchasing decisions.
3. Advertising can be an effective means of preselling products.
4. Advertisements use customer motives that can be restated in the personal selling approach.
5. The customer market is in a state of constant change, and therefore continuous study is required to stay abreast of current developments.
6. Differences in the structure and style of a product can be stated as sales appeals.

Such unit concepts are often referred to as the structural properties of a unit and provide the basis for derivation of unit goals.

Lesson Generalizations

Each lesson is based upon a unit concept, previously identified by the teacher. A lesson culminates in the derivation of a number of important generalizations (concepts). Lesson generalizations should be derived *by students* as an outgrowth of a given experience. Collectively they will embody the unit concept. To illustrate from a lesson on health:

> *Concept:* Use of drugs may permanently damage an individual's health and well-being.

Lesson Generalizations:

1. LSD users may incur permanent brain damage.
2. While under the influence of LSD, a person loses his ability to distinguish between reality and fantasy.
3. Use of LSD may render an individual emotionally dependent upon the drug.

What Are Some Basic Concept Types?

Concepts vary from axioms and propositions in mathematics to hypotheses and conclusions in science. Although the specific nature of concepts is dependent upon the nature of the unit under investigation, Pella has identified three basic types(2).

Classificational

This is the most common type germane to classroom instruction. Its function is basically that of defining, describing, or clarifying essential

836

properties of phenomena, processes, or events. It is often based upon the classification of facts into organized schemes or patterns. To illustrate in the field of science: An insect is an animal with six legs and three body cavities. It should be noted that the student is most appropriately provided a series of learning experiences which will inductively lead him to such a principle. For example, he might be asked to inspect a number of specimens, noting characteristics. He may conclude that there is a group of organisms which share this characteristic. We *classify* this group as insects.

Correlational

This type of concept is derived from *relating* specific events or observations; it consists of prediction. According to Pella, it consists of the formulation of general principles(3). To illustrate in the field of science: When voltage is constant, the electrical current varies with the resistance. It will be noted that the concept consists of an *"if . . . then"* dimension. Involved is a *relationship* between two variables.

Theoretical

A theoretical concept facilitates the explanation of data or events into organized systems. It involves the process of advancing from the known to the unknown. Examples: Unemployment leads to social unrest; indiscriminate bombing tends to stiffen enemy resistance; an atom is composed of electrons, protons, neutrons, and other particles. A theoretical concept goes beyond the facts, but must be consistent with the known facts.

The list of concepts which follows has been derived from many different instructional units in various content fields. The reader is urged to classify each according to concept type. It should be noted that some concept types are more typically found within a given field than are other types. In the social science area, for example, theoretical concepts usually predominate.

1. Ill-advised public expression may adversely affect statesmanship.
2. As population increases pollution problems are increased.
3. The world's population is increasing at a geometric rate.
4. The conditions of the times influence the nature of literary contributions.
5. Definitions, assumptions, and previously established principles become the basis for developing proof.
6. Equations resemble a scale; both sides must be equally balanced.
7. Absence of law leads to anarchy.
8. States and local boundaries unnaturally divide regions which share common governmental problems.

9. One's wardrobe reflects his life style.
10. The frequency with which household equipment is used is related to convenience of storage and its arrangement in the work center.

CONCEPT ATTAINMENT

Development of methods and techniques of guiding students in the formation of concepts is one purpose of this book. It seems necessary at this point to lay a foundation for the various teaching methods to be introduced in subsequent chapters. As indicated earlier, there seem to be certain cognitive processes which are normally employed when an individual thinks. In this section each step of the analytical thought process is described. Although the steps will not always be followed in the order presented, nor all steps necessarily employed on each occasion, the classroom teacher should be aware of the sequence as a basis for preparation of classroom experiences.

How Is the Problem Stated and Clarified?

A problem arises when an individual encounters difficulty in his regular activities. He recognizes that the concepts at hand somehow do not fit the observed events. This may produce a vague feeling of dissatisfaction with things as they are—from unhappiness with a definite snarl in the progress of events, or from mere curiosity. In any event, this is when the problem should be stated in as precise a manner as possible.

Frequently the teacher formulates a realistic problem from the unit concept which he has previously identified. As cited earlier, a concept in the area of general business was: Customer satisfaction is the most important product (of sales promotion and advertising). From this basic idea the teacher may formulate the problem: How might a customer feel when he is pressured into buying a product? He then decides upon an instructional method or technique which seems most appropriate for guiding students in solving the problem.

It should be noted that the teacher is involved in at least two separate creative acts: (1) the identification of important ideas (concepts) that are to be the "residue" of teaching and (2) the designing of appropriate learning situations in which the concepts may be derived. One logically follows the other. If the concept is poorly formulated, it will become evident when one attempts to plan specific learning experiences. To illustrate with [a] concept [from] the area of home economics, "Each family functions differently." In order to provide an appropriate learning experience, one must focus upon a particular area of family relationships. An appropriate problem might be: What policy should govern the financial aspect of family living? Again, various methods and techniques provide possible avenues for grappling with such an issue. The concept might have been more appropriately stated as follows: The management of family finances is dependent upon the personalities of the family members. Thus the teacher works constantly back and forth from concept to method as he engages in preinstructional activities.

In many instances students will be encouraged to develop their own problems for study and analysis. Problems may arise from ongoing class activities, or they may be planned with the help of the teacher. Any preplanned experience is subject to modification as the need arises.

How Are Facts Sorted and Analyzed?

The terms of a problem must be clarified, cause and effect relationships must be examined, and the importance of the issue must be established. This involves identifying and evaluating all the important facts and relationships which bear upon the problem. Students are prone to confuse personal opinion with facts and to confuse their opinion about facts with the facts. They also tend to jump to conclusions on the basis of limited evidence. Students, as well as most adults, tend to seek facts which will support a given point of view. Data on all sides of a question must be perused in the interest of intellectual honesty.

One of the most crucial aspects of the instructional process is the task of guiding students in their selection and analysis of facts. A common misuse of textbooks has contributed to an attitude of the text as the final answer. This also contributes to reliance upon the teacher as a final source of authority. It must be remembered that concept seeking is a searching, an inquiring process. Therefore the teacher must encourage students to seek widely for facts or data; he must guide students deliberately to uncover facts which will contribute to widely differing points of view. In discussion of the facts, students need to listen, need to actively pursue contrasting hypotheses and trace their ideas to their conclusions ("if . . . then"). As indicated in later chapters, buzz groups contribute to such an analysis. Students must be assisted in keeping to the problem and supporting their contentions with evidence. Whenever possible the student should compare conclusions based on personal experience with those drawn from the evidence.

How Are Hypotheses Developed?

Once the problem has been stated and clarified, the individual has already moved into the "next step" in the analytical thought process. At this point he develops some hypotheses—bold guesses or hunches with respect to his problem. For the untrained individual there may be a tendency to accept the first guess (hypothesis) as correct. Thus further thinking is blocked. The trained individual delays reaction and deliberately "casts about" for several possible solutions. *It is important to remember that hypotheses are necessary as a guide in the acquisition of facts.* Hypotheses, of course, are based upon the facts in the original situation from which the problem grew.

Hypotheses cannot be guaranteed or controlled; they just appear. There are techniques, however, for minimizing ordinary inhibitions built up from past experience. One of these, brainstorming, for example, is discussed in another chapter.

What Is the Role of Inference in Analytical Thought?

From an analysis of facts the individual formulates tentative conclusions. His ideas may be in the form of possible explanations to account for a chain of events, or they may represent several possible courses of action. An *inference* is a leap from the known to the unknown. This *movement* from present facts to possible (but not present) facts represents the heart of the thinking process. Each individual is continually making inferences as he grapples with large and small difficulties of his daily existence. Since the process is so commonplace there is a tendency to jump to unwarranted conclusions. It is the function of the instructional process to guide students in making *tested* inferences.

Both deductive and inductive reasoning processes normally are used in problem-solving experiences. Involved in the process of making inferences are assumptions. An assumption is anything taken for granted—anything assumed to be self-evident. A teacher may offer considerable assistance by requesting students to state their implicit assumptions, thus making them aware of them.

How Are Conclusions Tested?

Although the processes of reflection ultimately result in a decision, the complexity of many instructional problems may render an immediate decision impossible. In any event, however, the learner is encouraged to evolve pertinent generalizations (concepts) from the experience. These will not be identical to the major concept which gave rise to the problem. Rather, they will be supporting concepts which collectively encompass the major concept.

Lesson generalizations are derived by students. They are made most meaningful when written out and illustrated. Provision also must be made for their application to new situations, with emphasis on exploration of relationships, comparisons, and prediction of consequences.

What Is the Role of Intuitive Thinking in Concept Formation?

Any treatment of the processes of concept formation would not be complete without some attention to those thought processes which do not seem

840

to follow the scheme outlined on the preceding pages. It has long been reecognized that many of the really great contributions to human knowledge have come in sudden flashes of insight. Frequently after an individual has labored over a problem for hours, days, or even weeks the idea suddenly meshes. This very often occurs after the problem has been put aside. It was Archimedes who supposedly jumped from the bathtub shouting "Eureka" at his sudden discovery. Jerome Bruner describes the process as *intuitive thinking*.

Whether intuitive thinking follows a definite pattern or not is not known. Most writers, however, suggest that too much emphasis on the formal structure of analytical thinking processes is detrimental to intuitive thought. Routinized activities of any sort seem to be detrimental to the process. Bruner, however, stresses the complementary nature of the two when he says:

> Through intuitive thinking the individual may often arrive at solutions to problems which he would not achieve at all, or at best more slowly, through analytic thinking. Once achieved by intuitive methods, they should if possible be checked by analytic methods, while at the same time being respected as worthy hypotheses for such checking. Indeed, the intuitive thinker may even invent or discover problems that the analyst would not. But it may be the analyst who gives these problems the proper formalism(4).

Accounts of thought-in-progress by individuals who have made singular intuitive leaps are beginning to accumulate. From this evidence a few characteristics of the process are beginning to emerge.

1. The idea comes as a sudden flash—a "Eureka."
2. It usually comes after a problem has been put aside, often when least expected. Thus an incubation period is necessary.
3. The Eureka does not seem to follow any logical sequence of steps.
4. It seems to be built upon a broad understanding of the field of knowledge involved.
5. Individuals using this process seem to be characterized by bold guessing. They seem to have the ability to cut through the conventional, the mundane, the expected.
6. They seem to be willing to abandon false hypotheses no matter how well they are liked.

How Do Teaching Methods Relate to Analytical and Intuitive Thought Processes?

The preceding analysis of how we think has not been presented to suggest a formal outline to follow during the instructional process. A general, flexible scheme is not only possible but necessary. It means that teachers should conduct their classes so that students learn to take the steps as the normal way of going about learning, without self-consciousness. In an atmosphere that is reflective in quality, thinking may be expected to break out at any moment. As Burton, Kimball, and Wing so ably express the point, "The mind, contrary to widespread belief, has natural tendencies to generalize, to draw inferences, to be critical, to accept and reject conclusions on evidence"(5). The student learns to think through thinking. He needs guidance in perfecting this ability to select and clarify problems, to hypothesize, to secure and analyze facts, to make inferences from data, and to reach valid conclusions. The task of the school is to provide ample opportunity to exercise the process of thinking, to the end that the natural tendencies to reflect and to draw inferences will be transformed into attitudes and habits of systematic inquiry.

A final word of caution is in order, however. To ask teachers to emphasize thinking is not to suggest that they keep students so occupied at all times. As indicated throughout this book, there is a valid place for drill, for lecture, and even recitation at times. The point is made, however, that whatever is done in the classroom should occur in a pervasive atmosphere of reflective behavior.

In the development of the various instructional approaches in this book, the reflective or problem-solving process has been used as a guiding theory of teaching. To suggest that such a theory is complete, however, would amount to gross oversimplification. Always they are viewed as avenues which follow the normal processes of inquiry. The patterns are flexible and offer ample leeway for each instructor to bring his own personal creativity and Eurekas into the picture. Still, their validity rests upon this unifying structure of how we think. Classroom instruction for too long has been a haphazard venture into techniques which seem to work. Some systematized, unifying structure is needed. This is seen as the natural cognitive process of thought. It accommodates intuitive thought processes as well.

References

1. John B. Chase, Jr., and James Lee Howard, "Changing Concepts of Unit Teaching," *The High School Journal*, 47, no. 4 (February 1964): 180–7.
2. Milton O. Pella, "Concept Learning in Science," *The Science Teacher,* 33 (December 1966): 31–4.
3. Ibid.
4. Jerome S. Bruner, *The Process of Education* (Cambridge, Mass.: Harvard University Press, 1961), p. 58.
5. William H. Burton, Ronald B. Kimball, and Richard L. Wing, *Education for Reflective Thinking* (New York: Appleton-Century-Crofts, Inc., 1960), p. 292.

Operational Concepts

1. The essence of learning is embodied in the concepts that stem from organized study.

2. As human knowledge expands and the resulting need to establish curricular priorities becomes more acute, determining the significant concepts associated with a body of information is increasingly important.

3. Systematically reinforced concepts allow the student to integrate acquired knowledge with maximum efficiency.

Implications

A majority of the textbooks published during the last decade, particularly those of the most recent vintage, tend to stress the importance of teaching critical concepts. More must be done, however, to integrate students' knowledge and understanding across disciplinary lines. For example, there are geographic, economic, political, sociological, and psychological concepts that bear upon humankind's penchant for war. It is therefore essential that teachers compensate for artificial fragmentation by interrelating the material whenever possible.

Correspondingly, where the activities of the classroom do not rely upon the textbook as the basic learning device, as is the case, for example, in true open classrooms and in various alternative curricula, the need to organize the student's learning into an interlocking network of cognitive insight is even more pressing. For these reasons, it is to be hoped that, as long as schools make use of tests and examinations, the emphasis in these evaluations will be upon conceptual understanding rather than factual recall.

Francis P. Hunkins

Formulating Effective Questions

How can we use knowledge about the types of questions to improve our teaching? How can we get our students involved in asking effective questions?

BECOME KNOWLEDGEABLE

The first step in formulating effective questions is to become knowledgeable about the types of questions. Because we tend to overlook the obvious, one reason that our questions may not be as effective as they might is because we may have assumed a knowledge about questions that we really did not possess.

ANALYZE

The next step is to analyze the educational situation within which we find ourselves. Part of this analysis centers on the student. What is the student's background, his readiness for particular types of learning? What are his interests, both present and potential? Knowledge of the student is central to planning what types of questions to use with particular students. Some means of acquiring this knowledge are by observing the student in class, analyzing his anecdotal records, and by his test scores. The reader must know many other ways by which to obtain information on students.

Another dimension of analysis studies the situation within which one is to conduct a lesson. What are the particular times or teaching arrangements within which the lesson will be taught? What facilities does one have at his disposal? The situation may involve team teaching that could allow a certain type of question planning. Or the situation may refer to individualized study or pupil team learning or large group instruction or

Reprinted from Francis P. Hunkins, *Questioning Strategies and Techniques,* © 1973; by permission of Allyn and Bacon, Inc., Boston.

working with programmed materials or field trips. Will the situation allow for certain types of questions to be used effectively? If we wish to use questions of analysis we will have to provide adequate time for dealing with such questions. If the situation only allows for a three-minute response to a question, then we, as a rule of thumb, might as well not plan to use analysis questions. Such questions demand more time for student response.

The educational environment affects our educational activities. While our actions and questions are not completely influenced by our surroundings, we must consider the facilities within which we are to work. Educational materials also exist as part of the educational arena. If we wish to ask questions stressing synthesis, specifically formulating a generalization, the educational situation must enable students to discuss, or to consult resource materials, or view filmstrips or meet with the teacher, or view maps and charts. The educational environment cannot be a sterile room with one map, a basic text, and chairs arranged in a row for total class discussion. This sort of environment is not likely to stimulate students to effectively engage in synthesis. Questions can challenge and direct students' activities, but the environment can facilitate or retard the success with which a student meets the challenge of questions.

CONSIDER GOALS AND OBJECTIVES

This step closely relates to the previous one. It may even be done at the same time. After we have come to know our students and their needs and interests and have defined our teaching situation and the facilities, we need to ask ourselves what are the basic goals of our school, or of education in general. We can then see if the information gained in the previous step relates well to the overall aims of the school. If one school's aim is to foster independent thinkers, which would be an aim of the discovery curriculum, we need to ascertain if the students indicate a readiness for such a goal. If not, we need to structure lesson activities, materials, and questions that would develop readiness. Once this is done we can plan strategies to extend pupils' competence as independent thinkers.

Consideration of goals, which are long-range phenomena, is crucial for overall direction to our teaching, our questioning. The discovery curriculum cannot effectively function without such goals. Some of these goals have been implied previously: independent learner, process-oriented learner, active learner, a humanistic learner, an appreciative man. It is evident these goals overlap. Goals should not only suggest definite end products, they should also allow for the unexpected, the different. Those of us concerned with discovery curriculum need to realize that we should be more concerned with beginnings rather than endings. In the discovery curriculum we want our questions to spur students to active search; we wish our questions to encourage students to begin to understand their world. We need to know direction, but we don't wish to become narrow in looking at the school's goals. A discovery curriculum should foster diversity, not undue conformity among the students.

Once goals have been defined in somewhat flexible terms, we can then consider objectives. Again we need to think of objectives as guides which will need continual alteration to meet the unique needs of persons in the discovery curriculum. Objectives need to be identified and put in behavioral terms to assist us in our evaluation. However, objectives also need to consider the vague, the unplanned, the creative reaction. Objectives to cover these dimensions of discovery curriculum are rather difficult. We do not wish to limit students' learning in attempts to have them all behave in predictable ways. We need balance between objectives behaviorally stated and objectives which can be more open ended.

In considering goals and objectives we need to plan questions that will facilitate student attainment of the said goals or objectives or point the students in the designated directions. For students to analyze data independently they will need questions at the analysis level. We will need to schedule time for the student to dig, to analyze. Often we give lip service to having students analyze and then provide them with questions that only demand comprehension.

Questions are not asked solely to check if students remember what we presented the previous day. Questions should be handles that students apply to gain better grips upon information, upon understanding reality. The objectives we plan should reflect this "handle" use of questions. Objectives should guide the planning and selection of questions.

CONSIDER QUESTION TYPES

What type or types of questions can I formulate to achieve the objectives, the aims of both the school and the student? Here we use Bloom's Taxonomy as a guide or some other guide and check question examples. How do the questions I have tentatively planned compare with the examples presented? Are they worded so that students will be capable of responding to them? Are we considering the types of questions needed to fit the objectives and overall lessons planned? If our objective is to have students comprehend certain written materials, then we need to be sure that comprehension questions are placed crucially in the lesson's planned sequence. If our objective is student formulation of generalizations (synthesis), then our questions need to be at this level. We need to continually check tentative questions against some type of guide, at least initially, when dealing with questions.

Not only must we consider question types, we must consider the effects, potential effects, that certain types of questions will have on students. The effects can relate to both the cognitive and affective domain. Will the question as you have worded it really cause the particular student to analyze a particular situation? Or will such a question, if asked at this time, produce frustration with his performing the task? Knowing the effects that certain questions will elicit can allow us to plan with some precision the total learning situation. It will allow us to anticipate various reaction avenues.

CRITERIA

In considering question types, we also need to think about criteria for selecting content and experiences. The content should relate to the achievement of objectives; it needs to be supportive of higher order abstractions; it needs a high interest potential; it should be relevant to the student's needs; it requires necessary support materials; it needs to be feasible in terms of cost, time required to learn, and ease of implementation.

When working with formulating questions, we need to keep such criteria in mind. The questions we plan are vital elements of the content. They must assist in the achievement of objectives; they need to facilitate the development of higher order abstractions, concepts, and generalizations. The questions, if they are to effectively stimulate pupils to various levels of cognition, will require adequate materials for effective student reaction to questions. Questions require time. When we plan questions, we need to ask if the questions we are asking are feasible in terms of the time scheduled. If we have twenty minutes, we are not likely to be able to engage pupils in reacting to high-level questions. However, it is possible to ask high-level questions on one day and not expect a response until the end of the week. We need to get away from the practice of expecting an answer to all our questions three minutes or less after we ask them.

Criteria for effective questions not only relate to the criteria for selecting content and activities. We should also use criteria specifically relating to forming the questions. Perhaps the first criterion for an effective question relates to its wording. Does the question's wording make clear what it expects, both cognitively and affectively, from the student? Can the student understand what the question means? Remember that a question's wording can be misleading from a cognitive standpoint. All questions beginning with "How" and "Why" are not high-level questions. Therefore the wording of the question should be done in relation to the pupil's prior experience and the current class situation. Does the wording of a question allow the student to respond with optimal productivity? Does the wording of the question provide the student with adequate directions for the task? Does the question's wording provide unnecessary clues for the student? Does the question's wording allow the student to see the relationship of this particular question with ones previously asked? Of course, if the question is one of numerous objective types, such as multiple choice, matching, completion, the rules for such construction should be followed.

Rather than go into detail as to how to write these various "mechanical" types, I would recommend one review a tests and measurement text. I would like to stress, however, that knowing how to write a multiple choice question with discriminating options does not mean that one can write a high-level question. Multiple choice questions can be at the knowledge level, or they can be at the synthesis or evaluation levels.

A question such as "react to the situation" may not be very effective in that the student has inadequate information as to how to proceed or exactly what the task is. A tighter phrasing is, Comparing the two situations, what are the major commonalities? Or, Considering the information, what are some conclusions you can formulate? These questions are still some- what general, but the student does realize that he has to end with some conclusions.

How much information to provide the student in the wording of the question depends upon the particular learning situation and what cognitive level you wish to emphasize. Usually, the more clues in the wording as to what the student is to do the lower is the cognitive level. Perhaps when dealing with the writing of questions, a prime criterion is that of clearness. Does the wording facilitate effective student functioning? If the question is to stimulate analysis and the student misinterprets and just regurgitates information, then the question needs revision or it needs to be planned for another lesson sequence.

Operational Concepts

1. Questions are a useful device for enhancing learning.

2. Through appropriate questions, teachers can assist students to extend their reasoning from facts to concepts to generalizations.

3. Because different types of questions serve different functions, teachers must select questioning strategies in accordance with their purpose.

4. The determination of appropriate questioning strategies is a sophisticated teaching skill which is best developed through systematic training and practice.

5. Requiring students to formulate significant questions about a problem is in itself an effective teaching maneuver.

Implications

Although theories on the use of effective questioning techniques have been widely discussed in the professional literature, observations of contemporary classes yield sparse evidence that the theories have been widely applied. All teachers ask questions of their students, but the wrong questions are sometimes asked, and often for the wrong reasons. To question intelligently, the teacher must have a thorough knowledge of the subject and (if only intuitively) the thought processes through which students normally reason. Even more importantly, the teacher must have a specific instructional purpose in mind.

The ability to make skillful use of questions is a crucial element in effective teaching. Once mastered, the ability is readily transferred from subject to subject and topic to topic. As a consequence, staff development activities aimed at the cumulative cultivation of effective questioning techniques are virtually indispensable. For when classroom time is spent in pursuit of answers to wrong or trivial questions, precious learning opportunity is wasted.

Kenneth H. Hoover

Processes of Inquiry

FUNDAMENTAL PROPERTIES

Like most other instructional approaches, the processes of inquiry approach is representative of systematized problem solving. Unlike some other approaches, however, this technique is based upon current student needs and interests rather than upon organized bodies of subject matter as a starting point. Indeed, the processes of reflective thought are applied by the entire group. The topics which follow represent essential conditions necessary for effective application of the method.

Why Is a Democratic Framework Important?

Inquiry experiences are conceived within a framework which may be new to both student and teacher. Teacher-imposed activities and assignments are replaced by problems and projects often suggested by students themselves. A competitive class climate is replaced with a climate of cooperative group interaction as students pursue different aspects of a complex problem. All legitimate areas of choice must be identified (by either or both student and teacher) and then resolved by the class group. The teacher's role is relegated to that of a participating guide. His task is that of guiding students in their objective consideration of issues; sometimes acting as a resource person; sometimes discouraging or even rejecting suggested actions which would carry students beyond the particular problem under investigation; sometimes offering suggestions and advice of his own. The basic objective is that of supplying guidance, assistance, and support at every step of the way *without* unnecessarily imposing his wishes or authority upon the group.

Reprinted from Kenneth H. Hoover, *The Professional Teacher's Handbook: A Guide for Improving Instruction in Today's Secondary Schools,* © 1976; by permission of Allyn and Bacon, Inc., Boston.

Why Are Immediate Applications Important?

In selecting an appropriate topic for inquiry, attention must be directed to the immediate concerns of adolescents. Some areas of school work are more directly related to the group than are others. There are areas within almost all subject fields, however, in which immediate parallels can be found. If such parallels can be made apparent to students, *prior to a thorough investigation of the topic,* such an experience may be effective.

Why Is Flexibility Important?

Adolescents feel real concerns in many areas of their daily existence. If the inquiry (inductive) experience successfully touches their lives, the quantity and quality of questions will be almost overwhelming. Textbook units will no longer seem adequate, as questions tend to cut across topical areas. Some questions may seem more directly related to courses other than the one under consideration. The answers to other questions will be difficult to find. A few questions may be embarrassing or even appear to go beyond the realm of prudence acceptable to school authorities.

Both teacher and students must be flexible in such matters. The teacher must be willing to revise his thinking with respect to units and courses, recognizing that conventional lines are often extremely arbitrary. Questions which seem inappropriate for class consideration frequently can be reworded to incorporate the basic idea in a more acceptable form. Biology students who are studying reproduction, for example, may want to know the "safe" days during the menstrual cycle when conception cannot occur. A more appropriate question might be, "What are the factors which may influence the ovulation period?" Thus by inference the student understands the basic idea or concept involved. Sometimes a teacher will find it necessary to exclude questions which more appropriately may be treated in a different context or which are remotely related to the area or subject. An explanation of such matters is desirable.

What Resource Materials Are Needed?

The diversity of questions will usually render textbooks inadequate. One must search through journals, encyclopedias, yearbooks, and the like. Frequently, personal interviews with individuals knowledgeable in the area are appropriate; sometimes school trips and individual experimentation are needed. The teacher, anticipating such needs, must make preliminary arrangements for study groups in a variety of settings. Key books must be placed on study reserve; potential resource people must be contacted. If resources are limited, it may be desirable to restrict the experience to one class group at a time. Since students will be working somewhat independently of the teacher, expected rules of conduct must be clearly established.

What Are the Time Requirements of the Method?

The processes of planning, researching, and reporting take time. Developing questions, establishing study groups, and researching a given area usually necessitates a time span of at least one and a half weeks. Reporting, review, and evaluational activities will likely involve another one and a half weeks. On the other hand, most teachers have found that three and a half or four weeks' duration is about the maximum time that interest in a given problem area can be maintained. (When used for the purpose of developing a "set" for inquiry, the experience may merely involve a few minutes of a single class period.)

INQUIRY PROCEDURES

The processes of inquiry generally follow a logical sequence of problem solving. The basic objective is to guide the learner in his exploration at every step along the way. Above all, the learner must anticipate each phase of the experience well in advance of the activity and plan accordingly. The procedure which follows is suggestive only.

How Is the Problem Identified?

With inquiry processes, as here conceived, the teacher identifies the problem *area*. He then attempts to develop interest in the area. This may be accomplished in a variety of ways, including such techniques as a short lecture, discussion, film, resource speaker, or oral report. For purposes of illustration, a specific example from high school biology is employed. Let us assume that the unit is entitled "The Human Body" and the particular topic *which the teacher has selected* is the circulatory system.

> Teacher: Our next topic for exploration is the circulatory system. Let us read —————— books for an overview or broad picture of the problem. Then we will let Bill give us a ten-minute report on "The Heart and You."

The reading is designed to acquaint the students with the general area, while Bill's report will open up definite avenues of interest. He is directed to touch upon such aspects as heart diseases, disorders, and malfunctions. Such an activity is designed to provoke student thought in the area.

How Are the Issues Clarified?

Once the proper foundation has been established, students are urged to formulate questions which they would like answered. Emphasis is placed upon realistic, practical problems, rather than upon questions which they think the teacher wants them to ask.

Teacher: From our general inspection of the circulatory system what sub-headings or divisions seem appropriate? For example, Bill suggested many diseases which may affect the circulatory system. What are some other areas which might be worthy of exploration?

The class then suggests five or six groupings. Some of them might be:

1. Organs of the circulatory system
2. Diseases
3. Disorders or malfunctions
4. Conditions which affect the heart
5. First aid in relation to the heart

Teacher: Now, as an assignment, you will be provided an opportunity to list specific questions which you would like to have answered as we study the circulatory system. Your questions will determine what we will study, so make sure they represent what you really want to know. You might want to work with others on this assignment. It is not necessary that you submit questions, nor is there any specific number requested. If there are no questions, just write me a note to this effect. To assist us in organizing our thoughts, we will refer to the general areas listed. Some may develop questions in each area, while others may be interested primarily in only one area.

The next day questions are grouped and refined. To save time, it may be desirable to appoint a committee for this purpose. When the list of questions has been compiled, the teacher should make copies available to each person.

How Are the Learning Activities Planned and Developed?

Students at this point are assigned to subgroups, usually on the basis of choice. Subgroups of five are preferred. Each subgroup is expected to select a leader and a recorder and to develop a study plan. Each subgroup considers informational sources, along with methods of investigation, reporting and evaluation. Students should give some consideration to all phases of the project so that they can more fully grasp the total task ahead. The teacher moves from group to group, to guide and direct as necessary. For example, students may need guidance in rephrasing and expanding some of the questions. "Why do we want to know about the diseases which affect the circulatory system? How can we use the information in our daily lives?" The teacher may find it necessary to assist some groups to develop an appropriate division of labor. Does each person know his specific responsibility? Are the tasks appropriate for the individuals involved?

At the outset the teacher will want to suggest the amount of time available for the project. Time allotments for each group report must be established early. By providing for some flexibility in this respect, students are encouraged to use their own imagination relative to unique and creative ways of reporting to the class. They will then need assistance in carrying out such plans.

How Are the Data Collected?

The instructor, well in advance of need, should have placed key library references on reserve, made arrangements for some of the class in the library schedule each day, and looked into the possibilities of field trips and other resources.

While investigating a variety of problems, the groups will have different resource needs. These require careful supervision, a great deal of trust in students, and a cooperative attitude on the part of other teachers and administrators. The wise teacher will set the stage carefully. The first five minutes of every work period might well be devoted to brief progress reports and plans for the day's activities. Copies of the reports should list problems needing attention. The teacher quickly determines which problems need immediate attention. A short class discussion on how to find information may be in order, especially for groups inexperienced in the procedure.

If a project is to have a two-week duration, four class periods may be devoted to collection of data. A major portion of another period likely will be needed for specific preparation of the reporting procedures to be employed.

What Reporting Procedures Are Employed?

Although a group may have accomplished a great deal in planning and research activities, the value to the class group depends on how well findings are shared with others. Somewhere in the process the entire class might profitably set up standards for this phase of the project. Each group can be asked to consider the problem before planning its specific method of reporting. A master list is then distributed to the chairman of each group. One class listed eight points essential to an appropriate presentation:

1. Material presented should relate to the goals established.
2. Presentations should involve all members of the group in some way.
3. Presentations will be brief, preferably not exceeding fifteen minutes.
4. Presentations should not be read.
5. Other class members should be allotted time for questions. If a key question cannot be answered, some member of the group should be designated to find the answer.
6. As a general rule, technical material should be omitted from presentations. When it is necessary, however, it should be reproduced for the class.
7. Sources of information should be available.
8. Contradictory evidence should be presented as impartially as possible.

Following each presentation the teacher may lead the class in a general review for the purpose of expanding, clarifying, or correcting important points. It is seldom possible to have more than two group presentations in one class period of fifty-five to sixty minutes. Sometimes keen interest may be indicated, suggesting the desirability of extending discussion to a full class period.

How Are Generalizations Derived?

As a culminating activity the teacher will want to conduct a review of the entire project. This will involve recalling the major concepts and procedures employed and expanding to related areas. The activity, usually extending over a period of some two class periods, serves the important function of organizing and clarifying basic ideas which have been developed gradually over a period of several class periods.

How Is the Experience Evaluated?

Early in the cooperative experience, students are asked to give some consideration to evaluational techniques. As indicated previously, they assist in establishing standards of reporting. They may want to participate in some sort of group evaluation. Perhaps a group mark, derived by students, may be combined with an individual mark administered by the teacher. Whatever procedure is employed should be developed jointly by teacher and students.

Operational Concepts

1. Although inquiry learning is widely known as a theoretical construct, teachers tend to make only limited use of its potential.

2. A judicious balance between inductive and deductive learning is far more advantageous to the student than reliance upon either one or the other.

3. A critical aspect of teaching judgment lies in the linking of proper teaching methods with particular objectives and subject matter.

Implications

Three segments of Hoover's writing have been incorporated in the present section, for two reasons: first, each effectively synthesizes the major principles related to the topic; and second, each of the three methods are underutilized in current practice.

Inquiry learning, sometimes referred to as heuristic teaching or the discovery method, is a powerful instructional tool precisely because it requires the learner to organize his understanding of a phenomena into a workable and cohesive pattern. It is, moreover, a learning procedure that students can use in many aspects of their lives, long after their formal education has been concluded. The discovery of meaning through thoughtful analysis is, in short, both an effective way to learn and a valuable skill to acquire. To advocate that the curriculum should enable the child to learn how to learn is to advocate substantial practice in inquiry learning.

Discovery Method

Anita Simon

Teaching Without Telling: A Structural Change in the Classroom

At the present time, one estimate of the half-life of scientific knowledge is between ten and twenty years. Thus, even if a student could immediately master all the new scientific knowledge produced by the scholars of the world, within ten to twenty years half of that knowledge would be obsolete. This suggests the need for a fundamental change in the traditional model of the classroom in which the teacher is the producer and distributor of knowledge and the student is the consumer. The race to find more and more efficient ways to help the student become a more and more efficient consumer has already been lost.

Innovations from research on small-group processes suggest a model for the classroom in which the pupil becomes the producer and distributor of knowledge and the teacher functions as one of a number of resources. However, practical procedures to help the classroom teacher shift the focus of pupil activities from consuming to producing and distributing are in short supply. Therefore, even if a teacher believes, in theory, that teaching is different from telling, it is difficult for him to find concrete tools in the literature to help him shift his role.

Although educational theory clearly implies that there is a difference between teaching and telling, a simple experiment will demonstrate that this difference is more theoretical than real. Take a walk down the hallway of a nearby school building, and note what each teacher is doing as you pass her door. Research, and common sense, predict that in most cases the teacher will be telling something to the class.

Professional methods courses often try to provide practical techniques to help teachers teach without telling. Those devices, however, are usually nonverbal aids that encourage an active teacher to feed information to relatively passive pupils. Such devices as audiovisual aids, charts, graphs, and demonstrations do not affect the underlying structures of the classroom in which a teacher, or teacher substitute, "gives" and pupils "absorb."

The model of the classroom in which the teacher is the active agent most of the time is founded on the assumption that, when students first confront new content, they feel uninvolved and unmotivated; the teacher therefore must motivate students by *doing* something to cause them to become interested in the content before they will want to learn. Under this model, the teacher must be active because she has the responsibility for motivating students by saying or doing something *to* them to get them ready to learn.

Herein is described in detail one specific method for helping the teacher share the responsibility for dispensing knowledge with her class. This involves changing the structure of the classroom, and an example is offered as a model for one sort of change in the role of the teacher.

Research on small groups indicates that when people have a share in the decision-making process, involvement, commitment, and group productivity are greater than when the decisions are made for them(*1*). These findings have obvious implications for the classroom. Changing the structure of the classroom is one method for increasing class involvement, thereby potentially increasing student achievement.

Classroom structure refers to the patterns of influence in the classroom, as revealed, for example, by the physical seating arrangements of the students, by who talks to whom, by who supports, rejects, or ignores whom, by who can say and do what kinds of things, etc. Thus, a classroom in which the students can legitimately speak only with the explicit permission of the teacher has a different structure than one in which the students can freely talk to each other or to the teacher without first waiting for the teacher to acknowledge a raised hand. And a classroom in which all the suggestions come from the teacher has a different structure than one in which students help plan their own work.

One kind of structural change is a change in the physical seating arrangement. Even this simple shift can affect pupil behavior and attitudes, as teachers who have attempted to solve "discipline problems" by moving pupils from seat to seat in an academic version of Chinese Checkers well know.

Learning to change the structure of a classroom group is not a common part of the teacher education curriculum and, therefore, not a familiar concept to most teachers. Teachers, like anyone else, are not likely to want to plunge into the unfamiliar, particularly with as many as thirty not-so-willing pupils viewing new procedures with suspicion. Therefore, creating a structural change, i.e., working with small groups, is relatively uncommon, particularly at the high school and college levels. This is the case even when the technique offers major advantages for the teaching–learning process.

Teachers who are uncomfortable with the idea of working with small groups generally agree that pupils do talk more in groups, but believe that the talk is irrelevant to the topic assigned. Another serious problem lies in the difficulty of integrating the ideas emanating from each small group so as to provide a common learning experience for the entire class.

Planning for structural change offers a partial solution to these problems. But the planning demands a different procedure than that teachers normally use to construct lesson plans for a particular piece of content or a particular skill.

AN EXAMPLE OF STRUCTURAL CHANGE: PLANNING A COMMUNICATION LESSON

Teacher planning begins with the teacher selecting the major concepts or themes he would like his students to learn from each segment of the unit. It specifically does *not* allow the teacher to determine the facts the students must learn in order to master these concepts. An additional part of the teacher planning is scheduling the flow of activities to help the student use his own personal interests to achieve the goals for the lesson.

For example, suppose that the unit topic to be studied is the development of national communication media in the United States. The teacher's first decision is to select underlying main themes on which he wishes to focus. In this case, let us suppose that the teacher wishes to focus on the social and cultural conditions present during a period of radical innovation and the conditions that allow for national acceptance of these new inventions. The planning would look something like a flow chart ranging over the number of weeks necessary to complete the unit, and would end with detailed specifications of both process, audience, and content.

Example of Planning

Session 1: Total Class

1. Announcement of the topic.
2. Selection of small groups around those topics.

Class and teacher together list all the communication media they can think of. The teacher will ask the students to group together those media that they think are similar, with criteria for judging similarity, and to select a representative media from each group to study in detail. For example, the class may select the radio, movies, and computers as examples of three main groups of media.

Session 2: Total Class

The class and the teacher decide on a uniform series of questions to be answered by all groups; for example,

1. Were there great men or specific inventions involved in the process of development?

2. What was happening in the country to cause these inventions to come at this specific time?

3. What was happening to cause these inventions to be accepted at this specific time? (Had similar inventions been ignored before?)

4. What were the cultural resistances to the development? That is, what fears did people express concerning the effects on the community or the country if the media became popular?

5. What did happen to the culture (community, state, nation) as a result of the development of this media? What do you think would have happened had the media not been developed?

Session 3

Assign topics and people to six small groups, which for the average-sized classroom of thirty to thirty-five pupils would be five to six in a group (Figure 1).

Session 3a, b, . . . , n: Small-Group Work

Each group has the task of planning for and carrying out its assignment, which is twofold:

1. Answer the questions developed by the class about their specific media.
2. Prepare to teach the classmates about their media.

FIGURE 1

Two groups studying computers	
Two groups studying movies	
Two groups studying radio	

Teaching Without Telling: A Structural Change in the Classroom

Session 4

It is at this point that the usual planning for group work ends, leaving the teacher with the job of integrating the product of six groups in a manner that holds the interest of the class. This job is at least as difficult for the teacher as the one he would have faced had he planned for teaching the three units himself from the beginning. At this point, planning to capitalize on the structural rearrangement of the classroom becomes useful. Unlike the usual product of group work, which is to learn specific content and to be able to demonstrate that the content is learned by passing a test, the product of this group work is to be used as raw materials for the next class task. This changes the student focus from consumer of material to producer and distributor. An example of structural change that gives each pupil a teaching responsibility follows:

Once the computer, radio, and movie groups have completed their tasks, the teacher restructures the students into groups of three people each, one each from a group representing each media. The new group structure is illustrated in Figure 2.

The task selected for the second set of groups must serve two functions: (1) It is important that the task be continuously meaningful not just to the student who is reporting at the time, but to every student in each group. (2) The task must encourage the students to generalize from the data

FIGURE 2

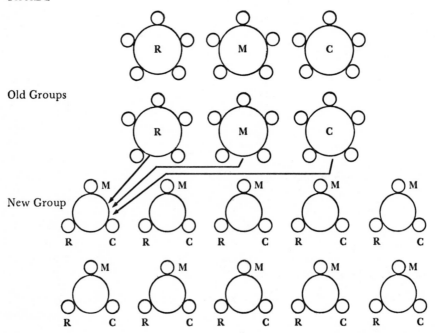

Old Groups

New Group

collected instead of merely sharing facts with each other. In other words, the task for the new groups should require the students to collaboratively process the data from the three group members. An example of such a task is to have each new group form a list of similarities and differences in their answers to the original questions. This will require that each student learn the "fact level" information of the others in his group, but places primary emphasis on the process of abstracting common elements and noting similarities and differences in the three reports. Another task might be that of constructing hypotheses about the history of the development of a fourth communication medium for later group testing.

This use of a pupil group to process the data acquired by a different group of pupils provides an opportunity for teachers to help students learn to use facts, to evaluate data to draw conclusions, and to suggest hypotheses for further testing, rather than remaining on the fact level for the entire unit.

Session 5

The teacher at this point has a number of options open to him.

1. He can conduct a full class discussion in which the groups report their findings. In classes in which the author has watched this process, much excitement and speculation were generated as group after group reported similar generalizations.
2. He can have each group display its results on large sheets of paper, and have a representative panel discuss similarities and differences.
3. He can form new groups of students or select a panel to prepare a plan for pulling together the findings of the small groups.

Session 6

A final stage, if desired, would be group evaluation in which the class is given the opportunity to develop criteria for "good" test questions and valid grading procedures. In addition, the pupils can, as a class or in small groups, evaluate the unit's strengths and weaknesses and/or make suggestions for improving the class process of working together.

The key difference between a plan for using groups and teaching via structural change is that the teacher uses the class, either as a total group or in small groups, to process and evaluate the products of other groups of pupils. The potential of the process is severalfold:

1. The dismal research findings that the majority of pupil thinking in the classroom is at fact level may be changed through students processing their own data.

2. Students learn because the learning will be of further use to themselves and to their classmates instead of being of use to pass a test or complete an assignment.

3. Students learn to develop standards for evaluating their own and others' work, because they are given the opportunity of comparing their work with others and to form criteria for evaluation.

4. Students' pleasure in working with friends is channeled into work instead of into informal, nonacademic activities.

5. The teacher is freed from being the giver of content to become a diagnostician of individual and group needs and a resource for content and group process problems. He therefore has time to conduct total class or small-group lessons on issues such as effective roles for good group work, library facilities, criteria for evaluating data collection, test question construction, and other learnings usually ignored in the process of teaching the content.

6. Since there is less risk in asking for clarification of a point from a peer in the relative security of a small group than from the teacher in front of the entire class, students may feel freer to actively explore content in a small group.

7. One way of thinking about discipline problems is as a conflict of wants between student and teacher, with the student wanting to do something the teacher (or school culture) does not want him to do, and vice versa. Since this method allows the pupil more responsibility in determining his own classroom activities, with increased commitment to the legitimate goals of the classroom, there will presumably be less push to satisfy his needs by becoming a "discipline problem," in the sense of wanting to do that which the teacher or school culture does not want him to do.

A common educational cliche is that the teacher is the person in the classroom who learns the most about any unit. If there is truth to this saying, it may be due to the teacher's felt responsibility for learning enough to teach the unit. In this case, the responsibility for teaching is a motivating force working on the teacher. Structural change lets the teacher capitalize on this sort of motivating force by allowing students an active role in the classroom process. By using pupils to help produce the content of the classroom, the teacher may find that the pupils in the class learn almost as much about the units as the teacher does.

Reference

1. Kurt Levin. "Group Decision and Social Change," in T. Newcomb and E. Hartley (eds.), *Readings in Social Psychology*. (New York: Holt, Rinehart and Winston, 1947).

866

Operational Concepts

1. Observers generally agree that many teachers lecture excessively.

2. Wherever possible, students should learn through active rather than passive means.

3. Incentive, commitment, and relevance are all increased when the learning activity has a purpose, and when students share in the acquisition and communication of the information.

4. Instruction often can be arranged so that students "process" their own data.

5. Learning aimed at the fulfillment of the student's own purposes is more satisfying and lasting than learning aimed primarily at compliance with a teacher's demands.

Implications

The instructional procedures described by the author are a useful illustration of the ways in which a number of discrete learning tactics can be woven into a different and infinitely more productive teaching methodology. It is significant, for example, that although the primary learning objectives in the method described by the author are teacher-determined, the students have considerable autonomy regarding the particular actions through which the learning is to be accomplished. The method, moreover, makes use of individual, small-group, and large-group instruction, and permits the learners to evaluate the usefulness and applicability of information that they themselves have acquired. As a consequence, the teacher's pedagogical activity is aimed at facilitating student self-direction rather than dispensing knowledge.

More than anything else, the teaching model demonstrates how the imaginative practitioner can invent instructional methods that not only achieve the desired cognitive ends but also help to make the classroom more stimulating and exciting.

Kieran Egan

Discovery Learning Through Structural Communication and Simulation

Expecting a student to learn by discovery in an entirely open-ended situation is expecting him, among other things, to replicate independently the work of many of the creative geniuses of the past. It is an ambitious teacher who would feel confident that leaving the student thus "to discover" represents a fruitful learning situation. Normally, of course, the teacher tries to limit and structure the environment in such a way that the student is encouraged to perceive relationships which we know exist and which it is desirable for that student to learn. This limited discovery, when it works out well, can be a powerful stimulus to learning and the desire to discover more. But it is not easy to "limit and structure the environment in such a way. . . ." Indeed, only by using such vague general statements has it been possible to state what sounds like a great idea. Lacking materials or techniques, we are left merely with the frustration of yet another beautiful ideal.

I want to describe a revolutionary new technique which brings this ideal into the realm of the practical. To focus the description, I will write about the teaching of history, but teachers of other subjects will be able to make an easy translation as they read. The technique is called "structural communication" and has been developed in England over the past four

FIGURE 1

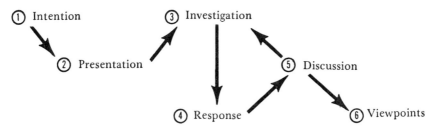

Reprinted from Kieran Egan, "Discovery Learning Through Structural Communication and Simulation," *Phi Delta Kappan*, April 1972, pp. 512-513; by permission of the publisher.

years. Development work is being done on other aspects besides the one I will consider here. It has two connected, unique features which offer the potential to realize the ideal of discovery learning in a form that can be made widely available.

Most teachers would agree that one aim of teaching history is to engage the student in thinking historically, not merely in memorizing the products of historians' scholarship. Ideally the student should be able to simulate, on an appropriate scale, the kind of thinking the historian does. Thus the student should be engaged in organizing knowledge in the light of a particular viewpoint; in constructing coherent pictures from random data, statements, concepts, generalizations; in employing evidence to resolve a problem; etc. It is this kind of intellectual activity that structural communication engages the student in.

Simulation units are a development from structural communication study units, and their overall structure is similar. Figure 1 names the various sections of a simulation unit and charts the normal pathway a student follows when working through the unit.

Each unit can be entirely self-contained; thus structural communication is a programmed method of teaching but, as we shall see, it is unlike any other programmed instruction technique. It is based on ideas drawn from Gestalt psychology rather than S–R theory, and it seeks to engage the higher synthesizing intellectual abilities.

In the diagram, the sections "intention" and "viewpoints" are more or less self-descriptive. The intention locates the simulation unit in its curriculum context. The viewpoints at the end allows the authors of the unit to state explicitly their particular viewpoint, or biases, in the subject matter dealt with. The presentation contains the subject matter with which the student is to interact. This may take many forms—a field-trip experience, a novel or play, or the more usual specially prepared text. The unique features of the technique are to be found in the interaction of the remaining three sections—investigation, response matrix, and discussion.

The kind of intellectual activity the student will engage in depends heavily on the kind of challenge posed to him and the means allowed for him to respond. If he is presented with a set of prepared answers of which he has to choose one, it takes great ingenuity on behalf of the programmer to ensure that the student's intellectual activity is not trivial. The object is to stimulate synthetic thought, not teach simple facts. In the example, note the Investigation and response matrix. You will see how the inventors of structural communication have tried to develop a challenge and response medium that encourages the higher level intellectual activities.

The simulations are set up as problems which the student is challenged to solve. Sometimes it has been found best to construct the problems as case studies containing a problem situation. In a typical Investigation section, about four situations may be simulated. The means of resolving the problems are provided in the matrix of items called the response matrix. Such a matrix may be seen as a random "semantic field" if considered from no specific viewpoint. Once viewed "through" the problems, however, it may be seen as capable of logical ordering. The student resolves each problem by composing a response from the matrix, using as many of the items as he feels are required to construct a coherent answer. A specific item may be found useful in constructing responses to two or three or even four of the problems, and, if the authors have done a good job of "structuring," such an item will play a different role in each. For each problem, the matrix items will fall into different patterns and relationships. Thus the problems serve as organizing principles which the student then has to apply to the random matrix. As he composes a coherent response from the matrix, so the structures inherent in the material emerge.

Before considering the kind of simulation situations that may be set up, let us look at the next stage of the simulation unit—the discussion. Having made his response, the student will have marked—on a piece of scrap paper, on a prepared form, or in a punchcard—the numbers corresponding to the items which he thinks best combine to resolve the problem posed. Inferences will be drawn from certain inclusions, omissions, patterns, etc., in the response. To put it simply, if a student omits a couple of important factors, it may be inferred that he is misunderstanding that part of the problem which those factors illuminate. A look at the discussion guide will give you some idea of the kind of things the authors may test for in a response.

By setting simple tests (of this form: "If you included in [or, omitted from] your response items 3, 7, or 18 . . ."), the authors can allow for, and catch, most of the more common kinds of error, as well as much more subtle misunderstandings which may show up in specific incoherent patterns or failures to perceive certain relationships. Having constructed tests for these, the author may then guide the student to specially prepared comments aimed directly at the error or misunderstanding. Alternatively, the author might want to test not for misunderstandings but for biases with regard to the subject matter, and the comments may be aimed at presenting alternative cases. Or again, they may simply be discussions at greater depth based on the student's response. The possibilities are very numerous; research is still proceeding on ways to take advantage of the new power offered by this technique.

Let us now get back to the simulations as set up in the problems. The example problems indicate two kinds of simulation. Problem 1 asks the student to put himself in the place of a historian explaining two specific occurrences. Problem 2 asks the student to put himself in the place of historical characters and show what factors he would consider significant in the events of the time to explain the situation outlined.

Other units which are still undergoing field trials employ the simulation to engage the student in arguing different viewpoints from the same matrix. Thus he will be asked to take the part of both a conservative and

871

liberal in separate problems and use the response matrix to support either case. This teaches, among other things, how the shift in viewpoint affects the relationships of item to item, as well as the changed significance of various factors. (Not a bad intellectual exercise in times of increasing rigidity of opinions.)

More complex units have been developed which use the problems to develop a story (in *The Anglo-Saxons,* a murder that leads to an inter-village feud). The student uses his data about life in Anglo-Saxon times to develop a strategy of actions which he would take at the point where the story stops to allow his intervention. The discussion section then takes account of his response, his particular combination of "actions," and leads the story on from there. Any number of interventions of this kind can be allowed for, and research is continuing into the development of more complex stories which teach and engage the student in this way.

At the Center for Structural Communication, Kingston-upon-Thames, England, mechanical devices are being developed to automate this technique. Most prominent is the "systemater," a complex minicomputer which records and processes responses, displaying texts and comments on a screen and highlighting the student's developing response by a pattern of lights.

Much smaller information processors are available which can read punched cards. Working with these, the student uses a simple hand-punch to make his response. This response is then processed by the machine, directing the student to the appropriate comment or activity. The punched card also serves as a record of the student's response, of course, and may be used for assessment of his ability to organize the items from the response matrix into coherent wholes.

Much research is being done on investigating further uses of structural communication, and work is beginning in a few centers in America. Already it seems evident that this new technique offers a considerable contribution to education. It seems likely that further research should refine and increase the power of the method.

Operational Concepts

1. When the objective is to provide an intellectual understanding of specific concepts, unstructured inquiry has severe limitations.

2. Perceptual learning is the primary device through which teachers assist learners to coordinate large volumes of factual information; the ability to organize knowledge for subsequent use is, therefore, a major aim in conceptual learning.

3. Simple computer applications can be used to help teachers diagnose particular errors in students' conceptual reasoning.

4. Teaching methods that enable students to develop skills in organizing information, in synthesizing this information for a particular purpose, and in using the synthesized information in problem-solving activity have great instructional value.

Implications

Since the mid-fifties, curriculum workers have been intensely interested in methods that could be used to enhance conceptual understanding. During the sixties, a variety of textbooks were based upon an organized sequence of key constructs. As a consequence, much of the teaching that now goes on, particularly in the social sciences and literature, is of a conceptual nature.

The device of structural communication through simulation is commendable on several grounds. The use of a "random matrix" of prepared answers that can be used in working out solutions to problems offers great flexibility. Moreover, when time and student ability permit, there is no reason why students cannot be asked to create their own matrix of answers. The method can be used with equal success in chemistry, geography, political science, and a number of other subjects. In the teaching of values, for example, the procedure's capacity to teach simultaneously substantive information, heuristic thought, and problem-solving skills would offer great advantage. It is precisely these activities, one suspects, that must underscore a rational attempt to teach students a moral basis for behavior.

It should also be noted, finally, that the imaginative teacher will find it easy to construct variations of the method simply by altering the major elements: (1) the simulation of a problem; (2) a body of relevant information; and (3) a means of analyzing and comparing students' responses.

David J. Irvine

Specifications for an Educational System of the Future

Restructuring the American educational enterprise to meet the demands of the future involves not only improving what exists but also creating new organizations and methods. Simply adjusting the educational system to meet new conditions is not sufficient. Concerted efforts must be made to plan for the future. But what kind of future? What kind of education?

Rather than try to predict what the educational system of the future will *be,* one may take as an appropriate starting point the specification of what the system *should be able to do.* In this way alternative solutions are more likely to be considered without focusing prematurely on any given solution and thus becoming locked into it.

The remainder of this article is made up of a set of suggested specifications of what the educational system of the future should be able to accomplish. Following each specification is a brief rationale upon which it is based.

1. *The educational system of the future must be able to deal with large numbers of students.* The requirement needs no justification. The rapid increase in world and national population is testimony enough. Advances in medical science are likely to make us underestimate, even today, the extent to which population growth will become a factor in educational planning of the future. Developing technical skills required in a modern society will require large proportions of the growing population to stay in school for longer periods of time, thus multiplying the effects of population growth.

2. *The system must accommodate itself to new and different population patterns.* The traditional boundaries between cities, suburbs, small towns, and rural areas are rapidly being erased or rendered inappropriate to the realities of population concentrations. The residents of a suburb may have more at stake in the government of the city in which they work than of the town in which they live. Systems of government which integrate the

Reprinted from David J. Irvine, "Specifications for an Educational System of the Future," *Phi Delta Kappan,* February 1972, pp. 382–384; by permission of the publisher.

interests of several municipalities may be required in the future. Educational systems will need to reflect this same trend.

Even state boundaries are becoming anachronisms. Washington, D.C., now covers portions of Maryland and Virginia as well as the District of Columbia in everything but name and legal designation. Newark and New York City share airports and problems even though they lie in different states. What kind of governmental arrangement will be suitable for the megalopolis which will extend between Richmond and Boston by the year 2000? What kind of educational system will serve it?

In addition to these changes, population will most likely be concentrated in certain areas of the country. The population density of New York City will, in the future, be found in perhaps a dozen areas of the United States. Will, then, the ills of education now apparent in New York City be visited upon these other areas? Or can we, by planning and ingenuity, anticipate the problems and solve them before they become all but insoluble?

3. *The system must be capable of utilizing new technological developments for educational purposes.* In order to cope with the greatly increased numbers of students, educational systems will need to find ways of bringing educational services to greater numbers of students without a proportional increase in manpower and money. Teaching machines and computer-assisted instruction are two examples of technology available today to multiply the effect of human teachers. Greater use of these developments, as well as the creation of other innovations, will help stimulate greater learning among more students.

In addition to the pressures of large numbers of students, the rapidly rising cost of education demands attention. Education is one of the most highly labor-intensive industries. In the manufacturing industries, higher wages have been justified largely by the greater productivity of workers. This increased productivity has been to a great extent due to the application of technology to manufacturing. There has been no parallel increase in productivity in the service industries such as education. Yet, in order to remain competitive, wages in these industries have risen in proportion to those in the manufacturing industries. If education is to increase productivity and thereby blunt the "taxpayers' revolt," it must seek ways to extend the impact of the individual teacher to greater numbers of students.

4. *The system must capitalize on the many other educational forces which exist in society.* Another strategy for increasing the productivity of educational organizations is to break down the artificial barriers between the institutions which we commonly identify as "educational" (for example, schools, libraries, museums, and colleges) and the many other repositories of information, skills, and processes within the community. Programs which use the total community, including the business community, rather than restrict themselves to the usual "educational" institutions,

876

may provide many advantages, not the least of which is greater learning for the money.

5. *The system must be able to bring learners in contact with a wide variety of realistic learning experiences.* In spite of the many educational media now available, the bulk of learning is stimulated through the use of books, lectures, and rather simply conceived student–teacher interactions. The present calls for less reliance on such a narrow range of instructional approaches; the future will demand it. As we begin to apply more effectively what we know about human learning, we will utilize multisensory media which provide analogs to the real situations for which learners are being prepared.

6. *The system must accommodate itself to changes in the natural resources available to man.* Many natural resources which we have until recently taken for granted are being changed. The most notable of these are air and water. Sources of energy and raw materials may change in their availability, costs, and efficiency. As a result, man will need to learn new ways of utilizing his resources as well as new ways of adapting himself to the conditions which confront him. The educational system will be subject to these influences while it is developing adaptable learners.

7. *The system must be capable of coping with increased amounts of information.* The explosion of knowledge in almost every field of human endeavor requires that we develop ways of processing information so that it does not become unmanageable. Information systems are vulnerable to information overload. We can foresee the day when educational systems become so swamped with knowledge that students are exposed to confusing, perhaps almost random, bits of the total sum of knowledge. In addition, the very means of collecting, processing, storing, and disseminating information are likely to become clogged.

Organization of knowledge is becoming as important as facts. We cannot rely on each learner to supply his own organization. He must be taught how to organize his knowledge without being provided an inflexible organization which destroys creative thinking.

8. *The system must be concerned with economy of learning.* The increased amounts of information available and the accelerating change in the world will also require that a great deal of learning be squeezed into limited time. The student should not have to tolerate slow ways of teaching when faster and equally effective ways exist. Greater resourcefulness in integrating human and technological instructional capabilities will utilize human beings in those jobs they do best—synthesizing complex fields of information and feelings, for example—while freeing them from tasks at which they are relatively inefficient, such as storing and retrieving information.

9. *The system must emphasize the development of learning skills.* The two preceding specifications have brought into focus the problems of in-

creasing amounts of information. This characteristic of our time, plus the accelerating pace of change, will militate against the schools' being able to transmit all necessary learning.

Change is taking place at an accelerating pace, and the nature of change is changing. New knowledge does not merely pile onto old knowledge; it changes the old knowledge. Man's work changes not only because a machine now does his work faster and better, but also because machines are doing jobs which were not feasible using raw manpower. It is becoming less and less likely that the learning one goes through at one stage of his life will be completely adequate for a later stage. For this reason the individual must have the necessary learning skills available when he encounters learning situations throughout his lifetime.

10. *The system should progressively involve the learner in making decisions about his educational program so that ultimately the learner controls his own learning.* As learning becomes a lifelong process, the learner must have, in addition to learning skills, the ability to plan and decide on his own learning needs. An educational system which provides for decisions to be made *for* the learner without involving him in the decision-making process is likely to produce docile, indecisive individuals. The system of the future must help the individual learn to make decisions; the most obvious starting point is in his educational program.

11. *The system must develop broadly educated specialists.* The high level of technology which our society will attain in the next few decades will require technical training of many citizens. Decisions in business, education, and government will require both technical knowledge and a grasp of the "big picture." The size of the population of the world, the complexity of the world, the speed of communication, and the intricate organizational patterns of our institutions will require a broad education. The technician must be a "universal man," and leaders must know much technical detail of the operations they command.

12. *The system must emphasize human relations.* In a very real sense, modern communication and transportation are rapidly making us neighbors to people in all parts of the world. Communication satellites have illustrated dramatically the possibilities of instantaneous transmission of pictures and sound. The "Town Meeting of the World" is a reality.

Technical advances in transportation have brought us in more rapid contact with other people. In addition, more individuals now have the economic resources to travel within their own countries and to other countries.

The increasing mobility of the population brings people of diverse backgrounds together, and it brings more people into already congested areas. Crime in urban areas is probably less a function of a "breakdown in law and order" than it is a function of more people being in contact with more people, geometrically increasing the possibility of conflict.

878

13. *The system must provide the means by which individuals can determine overriding purposes in their lives.* Many of the traditional influences which gave meaning to our lives have lessened in their impact. Today we see the influence of the family lessened by distance if not by a changing definition of the concept of marriage. The church is experiencing growing (or more accurately, shrinking) pains. An individual's work may also come to direct his life less, if shorter working hours and distance of work from home are guides.

To remedy these losses in guidance, the individual will have to depend more heavily on his own inner resources. His purpose in life will be more nearly a product of his own efforts than it is of family, church, or other traditional influences.

14. *The system must help individuals break down the dichotomy between work and play.* In order to accomplish his life purposes, the educated person of the future will have to look at work and play as part of a total plan: Work will be challenging; play will be work in the sense that it is meaningful rather than merely time consuming.

Shortened work hours and increased leisure time must be part of the individual's life plan. Escaping from work merely to have more time to fill with entertainment is neither constructive nor satisfying.

15. *The system must help each individual, regardless of characteristics and previous condition, to release the potential he possesses.* Society, that faceless monolith which is really *us*, forces patterns of behavior which are inimical to individual development. Discrimination, whether it is based on race or on tradition, is still discrimination. The woman who causes raised eyebrows by entering a male-dominated occupation is as surely the victim of discrimination as is the black trying to enter a white-dominated occupation; but society is also a victim, since it may be deprived of the benefit of the woman's and the black's best talents.

The system can help overcome discrimination by preparing individuals to realize their potential; but it must also help by preparing society to accept the best of each individual.

Man has been interested in the future ever since he has been able to conceive of a time dimension. To dream of the future is to extend history beyond the present.

However, modern man has moved beyond merely dreaming about the future. He predicts the future with a degree of accuracy. He plans for the future. And by planning, and acting upon his plans, he assists in fulfilling his predictions.

Shaping the future—or as Bennis has aptly phrased it, "inventing relevant futures"(*1*)—may be the most important role for leaders of the educational enterprise during the balance of this century. Imaginative planning and vigorous action are imperative to maintain a viable educational system. The educational system of the future will be shaped by men in purposive fashion, or it will, by default, be shaped by accident, tradition, and the senseless forces of the environment.

Reference

1. Warren G. Bennis, "A Funny Thing Happened on the Way to the Future," *American Psychologist,* July, 1970, pp. 595–608.

Operational Concepts

1. New technological apparatus will be utilized in the schools of the future.

2. Because of a growing number of constraints, the efficiency of the educational system must be increased.

3. In the time ahead, alternatives to the traditional school will become more essential, a greater range of curricular options will be required, and provisions for self-directed learning will need to be expanded.

4. In view of the probable social conflicts, stresses, and tensions that lie ahead, schooling must strive to increase the ability of people to communicate effectively with one another.

Implications

Much thought has been given to the types of schools the society is likely to need in the coming decades. As the essay demonstrates, however, preparing for the future is in large measure a matter of dealing with the emerging problems of the present. Projections regarding future needs are necessarily conjectural. Indeed, it is the fact that societies can and do take steps to reverse undesirable trends that causes so many future predictions to eventually prove inaccurate. To predict is to anticipate; to anticipate is to be forewarned; and to be forewarned is to take preventative measures. If only for this reason, the article's fifteen recommendations have considerable interest. For both the school administrator and the curriculum designer, they offer a sensible estimation of things to come and an outline of those steps which are most likely to constitute rational preparation.

Carol B. Barnett

Sexism in the Curriculum: A Study in Discrimination

Sexism, discrimination by members of one sex against the other, is based on the assumption that one of the sexes is superior to the other. In our society, as in most, this assumption has led to the exploitation of the female population by the male. Sexism has existed for so many years—as far back, at least, as our written history—that it is viewed by most as not discrimination at all, but as a natural phenomenon of "man's" condition. The notion that men and women are inherently different, biologically, psychologically, emotionally, and intellectually, is subscribed to by both men and women, despite the fact that in every age and in every culture there has been evidence to the contrary.

Because of its long and, until recently, rarely challenged tautology, sexist ideology has permeated all our institutions—political, social, economic, legal, and educational. Efforts to initiate change resulted, for a long time, in little, if any, modifications. Lawmakers had truly developed a body of "man-made" laws, created *by* men, *for* men. Many who did see the injustices of the law preferred not to give up or share their powers with others (women); and many others, more steeped in nonconscious sexism, did not even see the inequities of the system. When women did fight and win certain rights (suffrage in 1920), they were stopped from exercising their newly earned power in any consequential way by a greater force: public opinion about what is and is not "appropriate" female behavior. These pressures, plus the hard 5th Avenue sell about the good life of the American wife in her kitchen with its double sink, kept woman "in her place."

Therefore, legislation is not enough. It can prohibit practices but not the beliefs, attitudes, and values that affect and infect human behavior. To create an egalitarian society, we must raise the nation's consciousness by an investigation into what sexism is, how it manifests itself throughout society, how it detrimentally affects both men and women, and what can be done about it.

Sexism in Education

Although sexist thinking exists throughout all our institutions, its presence in our schools is the most pernicious and abhorrent: pernicious because it is here that children first encounter sex discrimination in an organized fashion, thereby giving legitimacy to the concept of male-ness and female-ness; it is more abhorrent because it is *exactly* here, in the schools, that we should be widening students' perceptions and options, not limiting them.

"Our educational system is sexist." "Our schools' curriculae are discriminatory." Such statements as these are responded to with varying degrees of ennui, scepticism, or hostility. The sceptics say, "Where is this sexism which you say exists in our schools? If you can't show it to us, then it isn't here." The bored have seen it, worked to implement the Educational Amendments Act and Title IX, but are fully aware that despite a trickling of lawsuits challenging sexism in education, nothing much has happened. Thinking, even among liberals, is still quite traditional. The hostile either do not understand what all the fuss is about, and are, therefore, threatened and angry, or understand only too well and, because of vested interests, prefer not to see any changes made at all. In such a climate it is difficult to find sympathetic listeners or readers who can objectively evaluate the degree of discrimination in our curriculum, recognize its long-range detrimental implications upon individual potential and societal productivity, and actively work to remedy the situation.

"Our curriculum is sexist." So, what *is* curriculum? Is it only the content established by the school and school board policies? Or does it include what is learned informally through continuous contact with students, teachers, and administrators, and through experiences with the school's rituals and rules? Obviously, the curriculum is *all* of these; it's what the school teaches, formally or informally, explicitly or implicitly, by omission as well as by commission. It is the sum total of everything the school teaches.

DISCRIMINATION IN THE FORMAL CURRICULUM, AN EXCLUSIONARY PROCESS

One-Sex Schools

It seems impossible to believe that in 1976 students might be refused access to particular schools because of their race, or that minority students would be denied entrance to desirable vocational educational programs because of the demand for such programs by nonminority students. But if the word "sex" is substituted for "race," we see that such practices are common today and that they are not only performed openly but are righteously defended. Women throughout the country *have* been and continue to be excluded from elite high schools and vocational–technical schools purely on the basis of sex. Let us consider some examples:

884

Before 1969, the New York City Board of Education did not admit girls to Brooklyn Technical High School or to Stuyvesant High School of Science and Mathematics, two of New York City's most prestigious high schools. The board was sued in a state court but avoided a judicial decision by admitting the plaintiff, Alice de Rivera. In 1971, 446 girls in a student body of 2,322 were enrolled at Stuyvesant and 180 girls in a student body of over 5,000 were admitted to Brooklyn Technical High School(1).

A report on New York City schools in 1971 disclosed that there were more high schools for boys than for girls in the city, and that course offerings for girls in both coed and all-girl schools were far more restricted than those for boys(2).

Of the seventeen vocational–technical schools in New York City in 1971, eleven were open to males only and offered training for jobs that were generally better salaried and had strong union support(3). The segregated schools in New York City prevent girls from taking courses in seventeen different vocational fields that are offered to boys. Girls are still not admitted to the Food and Maritime Trades School, the only school in New York City where one can study to be a chef(4).

One-sex high schools are not limited to New York City; they exist throughout the country. A comparison of Boston's two trade high schools, one for girls and the other for boys, reveals that boys can choose courses from a wide selection, whereas those offered to girls are few and developed along strictly traditional lines. Furthermore, the average expected wage for trades taught at the girls' school is 47 percent less than that for trades taught at Boston Trade High School for Boys(5).

Baltimore, Philadelphia, Detroit, and New Orleans all have sex-segregated public schools. Not until recently did Boston's schools become coeducational, the result of a new state law prohibiting sex discrimination in elementary and secondary schools.

Differential Admission Standards

Differential admission standards is another form of curricular exclusion. Although somewhat less conspicuous than one-sex schools, the objective is the same: to keep girls out. In 1974, Lowell High School in San Francisco was taken to court because female applicants were being judged for admission on different criteria than were male applicants. The assistant superintendent of the school district publicly justified the discriminatory practices as "necessary in order to keep the girls from overrunning the special school"(6). The courts decreed that the use of higher admission standards for females violated the Equal Protection Clause of the Fourteenth Amendment(7). In similar cases (i.e., Bray v. Lee)(8), the courts have found in favor of the plaintiffs, stating that the schools had denied female applicants, solely on the basis of sex, their constitutional rights to an education equal to that which a qualified man might receive.

One-Sex Classrooms

Although it is more than twenty years since the Supreme Court decreed that "separate is not equal," there are still many who fail to see the relevancy of this statement in relationship to the sexes. Educators who would never suggest segregating students into separate classes for blacks and whites, propose, implement, and support sex-segregated classes. Their "research" is proudly submitted to "reputable" journals where they are published, void of any editorial comments. Consider the following:

The Coeburn School in Brookhaven, Pennsylvania, in 1970(9) established sex kindergarten classes: two for boys, two for girls, and two mixed. The decision to do so was based on the assumption that boys and girls have inherently different interests: "girls are becoming feminized . . . they enjoy dressing up in clothes, having tea parties, and playing with dolls." Not only were these educators concerned with "biologically determined" differing interests, but with the fact that girls, upon entering school, are socially, physically, verbally, and emotionally months ahead of boys. "Competing with girls . . . may be injurious to the boy's young self-concept." Boys, therefore, were given muscle-building activities in order to develop physical coordination; "male" tasks to perform, such as building and repairing; "male" materials to work with, like clay, rock, and wood; they listened to "male" stories, about railroads, spacemen, cowboys, and animals. Boys made maps, puppets, Indian replicas, played in team games, and developed a cooperative spirit. They had work benches, riding trucks, wagons, animals, and balls. Dolls, playhouses, and kitchen equipment were moved out of their classroom. The researchers did not mention what kind of equipment the girls were using in their segregated classes. They did say, however, that the all-girl groups were more verbal than the boys (who wouldn't be when working in a vacuum?); more critical in their behavior (but their criticism should have been directed toward the educators rather than each other); and displayed greater mimicry of their teachers. Unlike the boys, they desired more frequent changes of activity (bored, no doubt), and did not request frequent repetition of familiar stories as the boys did (how many times can one listen to "Goody-Goody Two Shoes"?).

The researchers found great differences in the boys. They were more enthusiastic, cooperative, and excited about school. The girls, on the other hand, were more critical of each other and demonstrated more competitiveness within the group. The researchers felt that both boys and girls had, so far, benefited from the separation into programs "tailor-made" for each sex!

Obviously, the needs of the children as individuals were completely ignored in the experiment. Boys and girls were both thrust into culturally determined stereotypic roles, based upon misconceptions about "appropriate" sex role behavior. Unfortunately, one-sex classes at the elementary level are not limited to this one experiment. Others have been developed at Wakefield Elementary School, Fairfax County, Virginia(*10*), and in Greeley, Colorado(*11*).

Classroom exclusion on the basis of sex is much more common, though, at the secondary school level. At San Francisco's Vocational High School, for example, courses offered to female students include commercial art, drafting, dry cleaning, electronics, food preparation, power sewing, and restaurant services. Available to male students are such courses as aircraft mechanics, construction crafts, and automotive mechanics. A female student seeking to enroll in a traditionally male class may be admitted if she is persistent, but she will be openly discouraged(*12*).

In Sanchez *v.* Baron et al.(*13*), the plaintiff challenged the New York City School Board's policy that prevented women from taking shop courses. In Della *v.* Gaffney(*14*) women were excluded from auto mechanics. The principal of the school in question said(*15*),

> Whether we agree with this or not, auto mechanics is still predominantly a male occupation. If we open the regular school program to girls, then for each girl in the class, a boy doesn't have a chance to enter.

More than half the women in public vocational programs are being trained in home economics and one third of them are studying office skills, while vocational courses leading to higher paying jobs in industry are often closed to them(*16*).

Separate But Not Equal

Nowhere has discrimination in the public school curriculum been more pervasive than in the sports arena. In 1970, the Minneapolis schools appropriated $197,000 for boys' athletics and $9,000 for girls'(*17*). In Ann Arbor, Michigan, two high schools spent $68,025 on boys' interscholastic activities in 1972 and $6,296 for girls'(*18*). A school in Palo Alto, California, budgeted $550 for girls' athletics compared to $45,000 for boys'(*19*). San Francisco schools budgeted 6 percent of the money allocated for men's sports to the women's. In addition, the women's program included only two team activities, volleyball and gymnastics; the men's athletic program consisted of sixteen to seventeen teams per school(*20*).

The amount of money spent on boys' and girls' sports is only one index of discrimination. Availability of equipment is another. Swimming pools, basketball and tennis courts, and recreation areas are generally less available to girls(*21*). Another indicator of inequality in physical education is the amount of pay or released time given to coaches of boys' and girls' teams. Female coaches, if paid at all, are given a small percentage of what their male counterparts receive. Women officiators are rare(*22*). Female students have routinely been denied the opportunity to enter interscholastic athletic competitions, often the road to lucrative scholarships and opportunities.

Sexism in the Curriculum: A Study in Discrimination

Exclusionary curricular practices, all the way from one-sex classes to one-sex schools, have had permanent negative effects upon the lives of both boys and girls. Channeling women into less interesting and economically less rewarding positions deprives them of those personal freedoms that we guarantee to all "men" in our constitution. Survival skills are necessary not only for economic reasons, but for psychological and emotional reasons as well. Those who do not become instrumentally (vocationally) independent feel powerless to control their own lives, a condition that often creates psychological anxiety and depression. Equality in job training is not an issue of minor concern for women. According to Sylvia Porter(23),

> Seven of the total 35 million women in the working force are single women workers, most of them working to support themselves or others. Another 6,300,000 are widowed, divorced, or separated from their husbands, and these millions—particularly the women who also are rearing children—also are working for what the Labor Department calls "compelling economic reasons." Then, there are the 3,700,000 married women workers with husbands who had incomes below $5,000 at latest reporting date, and an additional 3,000,000 with husbands who had incomes between $5,000 and $7,000. These women, says the Labor Department, are "almost certainly working because of economic need." On top of these millions are 1 million wives with husbands not in the labor force and more than 500,000 wives with unemployed husbands—women working or seeking work because many are their family's sole support.

Although the debilitating effects of exclusionary curricular practices on men is, obviously, not as great as it is on women, men are, however, affected, too. It is no longer a luxury to have a wife whose skills bring a fair price in the marketplace and can therefore share in the family's responsibilities. In an age of steadily rising costs, the husband whose wife is not working is often forced to take a second job in order to make "ends meet." Additional time away from the family takes its toll on all members. A wife who is professionally productive brings other benefits to a family. Because she is making contributions outside the home (not to lessen the important contributions that women make *in* the home or that men could make in the home), she is cooperatively interacting with other people, receiving not only economic rewards but the emotional "stroking" that we all need. More often than not, the man whose wife is at home all day finds himself completely responsible for her intellectual, emotional, and psychological needs. Such a burden can lead to resentment—not to mention an ulcer or two.

Sexist policies in physical education courses, with its coexistent emphasis on boys' athletics, have not necessarily been to the boys' advantage. Thomas Turtko, professor of psychology at San Jose State and codirector of the Institute for Study of Athletic Motivation at Santa Clara, California, says(24),

888

> I continually meet athletes who are burned out. They are disillusioned
> about sports. They feel sports absorbed them and they had no time for any-
> thing else.

Turtko would like to see the demise of organized sports for children. He
believes that too many parents see themselves as "Vince Lombardis" and
put undue pressures on their children(25):

> The major thing is that we have to become aware, as parents, that some
> of us are physically abusing our children through sports. More tragically,
> we're psychologically abusing them.

Many young men, by going along with a system that stresses "jock
power" in the schools, may be doing themselves irreparable damage in two
ways: (1) they limit their energies to the sports field, neglecting development
of cognitive skills, and (2) they grow up believing that the road to success
and ego gratification is the "macho" way, leading them to development of
unhealthy and unbalanced personalities.

For girls, discrimination in physical education classes has not only
limited their professional options and kept them from the money with
which to further their careers, but often deters them from establishing
lifelong patterns of physical exercise.

Boys and girls should be free to take advantage of educational resources—currently delineated along sex-role lines—entirely in accord with
individual differences in interest and aptitudes.

SEXISM IN THE INFORMAL OR HIDDEN CURRICULUM

Informal curricular discrimination is more insidious than formal discrimination because it is covert and, therefore, more difficult to detect, isolate, and exorcise. It exists, for the most part, outside of formal school
policies and perpetrates itself upon the nonconscious ideological beliefs of
teachers, administrators, parents, and students. It is manifested in *de facto*
segregation in classes, from kindergarten through the twelfth grade;
through teacher–student interaction, based upon beliefs about inherent
differences between boys and girls; through curricular materials; and by
the administrative hierarchy.

Segregation by Sex Within the Classroom

Segregation by sex begins innocently and innocuously enough in
nursery and kindergarten rooms where the *children* may not be segregated
but where the toys that they play with *are* separated. "Masculine" toys may
be in a "Blue Room" or a "Noisy Corner," whereas those toys associated

with girls may be placed in a "Pink Room" or a "Quiet Corner." Predictably, most boys will be found in the noisy room, ramming trucks into one another, building forts with blocks, and killing off Indians with plastic pistols. The girls will be in the pink zone, dressing up, playing with dolls or a new microwave oven. For the normally curious boy who wanders too closely to the girls' area, there are hoot calls and cries of "sissy." The boy quickly returns to his voluntary male ghetto. Even in "progressive" schools that pride themselves on "freedom of choice," there is, even as early as nursery school, no real choice at all. Children have already learned to avoid materials and toys that are stereotypic of the opposite sex(26). Freedom of choice does little more than perpetuate the *status quo*.

There is segregation on the playgrounds, where boys avoid contact with girls and where girls avoid contact sports. Teachers segregate students by sex and pit them against each other in competitive games and on attendance slips, where it makes as much sense to divide lists into black and white students as it does to divide them by sex. They are segregated in music, where boys play band instruments predominantly and girls play strings and light brass; in art, where boys draw trucks and girls butterflies; in the classroom where boys run the mechanical equipment and lift chairs while girls pass out paper and water the plants.

This constant division of people arbitrarily by sex creates a polarity that is detrimental to the cognitive and affective development of all children. More and more, boys and girls see themselves in diametrically opposed roles, rarely working together in a cooperative effort. Such dichotomous positioning not only deters them from working with each other in a school situation, but affects their ability to interrelate in a larger society—whether at work or in the home.

Student–Teacher Interaction

Sexist ideology is manifested every day in the classroom as teachers interact with their students. All teachers have well-developed sex-role expectations (and these expectations are the same whether the teacher is a man or a woman)(27, 28). Boys are expected to be dominant, independent, and assertive; girls, submissive, dependent, unassertive, orderly, and conforming. Although different kinds of behavior are expected from boy and girl students, teachers demand from all students *that* behavior which is characteristic of the stereotypic female pattern. Typically, male sex-role traits are rejected(29, 30). Why? Because the "school as an institution socializes teachers to place a high premium on pupil control"(31). Most teachers feel, unfortunately, that learning cannot take place unless the class is passive and conformist. This syndrome is especially true for new teachers who are uncertain and nervous as they face their first classes. An authoritarian position is, therefore, the least threatening and most comfortable, especially because the teacher is generally a product of such an autonomous system her/himself. Once this teaching style has been established, it is difficult, if not impossible, for the teacher to change.

We see, then, that teachers, on the one hand, *expect* boys and girls to behave differently; yet, they insist that both boys and girls conform to the schools' feminine values. This dichotomy produces different kinds of interactions between teachers with boy and girl students. Consider the following:

1. Boys have a greater number of teacher–student contacts of all types(*32, 33*).
2. Boys have significantly more (80 percent) disapproval contacts with teachers than girls do(*34–37*).
3. Boys get significantly more praise from teachers than girls do(*38, 39*).
4. Teachers give more attention, especially in direct instruction, to boys(*40*).
5. Teachers call on boys more frequently than on girls(*41*).
6. Boys are involved in more teacher-initiated contacts, particularly of the behavioral kind(*42*).
7. Boys have more positive contacts with teachers(*43*).
8. Boys who are behavioral problems interact significantly more with teachers than boys who are *not* behavioral problems, and significantly more than *all* girls(*44*).
9. Of the prohibitory remarks passed to the students, 40 percent was for inattention. Another 40 percent of total disapproval of girls was for lack of knowledge or skill as opposed to 26 percent for the boys(*45*).
10. Boys were disapproved of for violating rules 17 percent of the time as compared to 9 percent for the girls(*46*).
11. Teachers reward creative behavior in boys three times as often as they do with girls(*47*).
12. Teachers make more supportive remarks to girls(*48*).
13. Teachers are supportive of low social power girls (those unable to get others to follow them) but not of low social power boys(*49*).
14. Teachers like aggressive boys as much as they do dependent boys(*50*).
15. Teachers dislike aggressive girls most of all(*51*).
16. Teachers are able to identify satisfied girls rather than satisfied boys. Teachers are more able to identify dissatisfied boys rather than dissatisfied girls(*52*).
17. Teachers express concern for low achieving girls while rejecting low achieving boys(*53*).
18. When teachers disapprove of boys, they register that disapproval in a harsh voice; with girls, they use a normal or moderate tone(*54–56*).

A deficit picture begins to emerge for both sexes. Girls are "rewarded" for conformity by receiving significantly less teacher-contact hours. Furthermore, by conforming to school rules and expected behavior patterns, a disproportionate number of critical remarks having to do with knowledge and/or skills are wagered against them. This seemingly overweighted attack on their intellectual competence may help to explain the fact that, when boys and girls of equal ability and achievement levels are asked to evaluate themselves, girls are significantly lower in self-concept, feelings of general adequacy, and in popularity, whereas boys have an exaggerated opinion of themselves and their capabilities(57). As boys and girls progress through school, both their opinions of boys become higher; their opinions of girls, lower(58). High school girls, although they make better grades than high school boys, are more likely to believe that they do not have the ability to do college work(59).

These feelings of inferiority, combined with the kind of "success" girls have achieved by conforming, may account for the fact that female students are reluctant to "make waves" by initiating teacher contact or questioning or challenging their teachers. Consequently, they fall further and further into classroom passivity. But "playing it safe" takes its toll in the long run. Upon entering school, girls are, intellectually, way ahead of boys(60). They maintain their advantage through the early grades, but by the time they reach high school their performance on ability tests begins to decline. Girls—as they become dependent upon other people for their feelings of "self"—become less creative, analytic, and independent in their thinking. "Dependency interferes with certain aspects of intellectual functioning"(61).

Because the masculine "virtues" are diametrically opposed to the school's preferred student characteristics, it challenges and punishes the boy's sex-typed behaviors. Bentzen studied referral patterns in the elementary schools for over a year and found that, out of 919 referrals, 628 were boys—two boys for every girl. The highest number of referrals was in the first grade where boys were referred three times as often as girls and eleven times as often for social and emotional reasons(62). For those boys who do not conform, there is a double penalty: (1) so much energy is spent in rebelling that they fail to accommodate themselves to a learning situation; and (2) they are given even lower grades than their measured achievement scores would justify(63–65). A feeling of futility may begin to develop. They may either decide to attack the system even harder or just give up—intellectually. The cycle may not be broken until they drop out of school.

For those who do conform, there are long-lasting positive results, since the masculine characteristics are related to intellectual development and self-actualization. But for all those who do, many do not.

Another deficit on the boy's side develops as boys discover that the other students and the teachers admire aggressive boys, and that conformity, as exemplified by the girls, is dull, albeit safe. The female sex-role characteristics, such as nurturing, touching, feeling, and loving, are consequently rejected, leading frequently to the development of unstable personality types. Eighteen-year-old boys who scored low on masculinity also scored lower on the California Adjustment Inventory than did boys who scored high on the masculinity scale. Twenty years later, however, these same boys—then men—presented a different picture. The high masculine boys scored lower on the adjustment inventory, and the reverse was true for the low masculinity boys(66). Kagan found that highly sex typed individuals invested a lot of psychological energy into maintaining their sex-typed image. In contrast, "the more androgynous person could shift roles when the situation demanded without any threat to the ego"(67). Furthermore, high masculinity positively correlates with anxiety and proneness toward guilt; low masculinity correlates with warmth, emotional stability, sensitivity, bohemianism, and sophistication(68). It would appear that, except during adolescence when the male subculture values masculinity, sex-typed interests do not increase the male's psychological adjustment; in fact, they may retard it.

The effects on women who attain toward the stereotypic feminine sex role are just as pernicious. Maccoby(69) found that women with high feminine sources were anxious and poorly adjusted. Those whose whole self-concept was dependent upon the responses of others in their lives lived in a state of anxiety—sometimes close to oppression.

Sustained and systematic efforts to reedify the sex role and student-role expectations of the average teacher could inundate the system with needed change, whereas revamping the content of curricular materials might not. An "aware" teacher could *use* sexist teaching materials to point out misrepresentations and inequities in the content, whereas a teacher who is functionally sexist—no matter what materials he/she uses—will continue to interact with boy and girl students differently, thereby voiding any improvement in the curricular materials.

CURRICULAR MATERIALS

Not only do teacher–student interactions affect students' perceptions of themselves, but so do the texts that they use. Surveys of public school and library books reveal the following:

1. Of 134 school readers, published by fourteen major publishing companies, consisting of 2,760 stories in all, stories of boys to girls were 5:2; adult male stories to female were 3:1; male biographies to female were 6:1; male folk or fantasy to female, 4:1(70).

2. For men, 147 role possibilities were presented, compared to 25 (all traditional) roles for women. Only three working mothers were shown(71).

3. Men were found significantly more out of doors and in business; women were found significantly more in the home or the school(72).

4. Professors, doctors, and presidents of companies were all male(73).
5. The American Library Association's choice of Caldecott winners (picture books) for the past five years showed 11:1 pictures of men over women. Not one adult woman had a job or profession(74).
6. Of the Newberry Awards for children's books, stories about boys outnumbered stories about girls 3:1(75).
7. Social studies texts for grades 1–3 showed men in 100 different jobs and women in 30 (all traditional). All leaders were men(76).
8. An analysis of eight currently popular texts on the U.S. government used in the senior high schools listed 1,103 men as compared to 33 women in the index; 533 men were quoted as compared to 5 women; 53–71 percent of the human figure illustrations depicted men as compared to 3–9 percent for the women. Cartoons denigrated women(77).
9. In a study of social studies texts, *no* women were portrayed outside the home except as a teacher or nurse(78).
10. In history and government courses, little or no space is given to the importance or influence of women. Their presence is by and large ignored(79).

It is obvious that schools not only socialize children in a general way, but they also exert a powerful and limiting influence on the development of career choices. Instead of encouraging girls to broaden their horizons, they specify attitudes, modes of acting, and traditional outlets for achievement, all limiting their choices and future potential. Furthermore, not only is the view of women presented through curricular materials stereotypic, but it is unrealistic. The survey of 134 elementary school readers (2,760 stories) by the Central New Jersey NOW organization in 1970 showed only *three* working mothers; yet 38 percent of our total work force of women have children under 18.

For boys, career choices are implied as well, although along far broader lines. The male nurse, the airline steward, the male interior decorator are implicitly forbidden. Only the most secure of egos would challenge public opinion. Boys, having rejected the female role, also smother the mother instinct and channel their drives almost entirely along instrumental lines. To view oneself entirely or disproportionately in professional terms leads to an existence as precarious for men as dependency on "others" does for women.

Consider the business-driven man who is retired at age 65 and finds himself within 24 hours moved from identity to anonymity—according to his socially determined criteria of "worth."

Noneducation of the male along expressive lines and noneducation of the female along instrumental lines leaves both of them ill equipped to deal with the many emotional and economic demands society and families make of them. Androgynous persons who have inculcated both male and female sex-typed characteristics into well-rounded beings will have the most flexibility and success in adjusting to an ever-changing, ever-expanding world. It is the school's task to encourage flexibility by increasing options, not to limit them. To do so, the schools must provide children with equal access to what has been traditionally sex typed cultural and educational experiences, and this can only occur through intervention into both the formal and hidden curriculums.

Teaching materials, texts, films, workbooks, posters, tapes, etc., have all presented a stereotypic view of men and women in our society, delineating to young, impressionable children "appropriate" behavior and career choices, and thereby preventing them from developing interests and professions that are in line with natural interests and abilities. The construct of sex role should be reduced to its biological essence; but because boys and girls are treated differently from the time they are brought home from the hospital in their respective blue and pink blankets, we may never know what *is* truly biologically different rather than culturally determined. But from an educational perspective, sex-linked genetic differences are, for the most part, irrelevant.

Sexism has been and continues to be part and parcel of the curriculum. Those steps that need to be taken to counteract its discriminatory practices are as broad and diverse as the problem itself. The federal agencies must enforce Title IX provisions and initiate further steps to mandate nondiscriminatory practices. The state departments of education, in addition to also enforcing the letter and spirit of Title IX, should encourage school boards to adopt instructional materials that offer a balanced view of minorities and women, encourage the promotion of women into top administrative posts, and ensure that all instructional materials coming from state educational agencies are free of sex biases. Local school boards should analyze personnel policies, seek a greater number of female superintendents, and initiate in-service workshops that familiarize teachers with existing sexism. Of greatest importance, however, individual teachers must conduct their classes in ways that eliminate sex bias and sexist thinking, and encourage both boys and girls to view one another as "people" rather than members of the opposite sex.

References

1. NYC Chapter of NOW, "1971 Report on Sex Bias in the Public Schools."
2. Ibid.
3. Ibid.
4. Citizen's Advisory Council on the Status of Women, "Needs for Studies of Sex Discrimination in Public Schools."
5. Bryan, Gail, "Discrimination on the Basis of Sex in Occupational Education in the Boston Public Schools,"paper, Boston Commission to Improve the Status of Women, 1972.

6. Kauer, Ralph, Assistant Superintendent, San Francisco Unified School District, as quoted in *Associated Press Dispatch,* September 22, 1971.

7. Berkelman *v.* San Francisco Unified School District, 1974.

8. Bray *v.* Lee, Mass., 1972.

9. Strickler, R. W., and Phillips, Cynthia, "Boys Are Different," *The Instructor,* December, 1970, 50–54.

10. Lyles, Thomas, "Grouping by Sex," *National Elementary Principal,* 46:2, November, 1966, 38–41.

11. "No Girls (or Lady Teachers) Please," *Nation's Schools,* April, 1969, 68–69.

12. Martinez Susanne, "Sexism in Public Education: Litigation Issues," *Inequality in Education,* 18, October, 1974.

13. Sanchez et al. *v.* Baron et al., New York, U.S. District Court, 1971.

14. Martinez, Susanne, op. cit.

15. Ibid.

16. Citizen's Advisory Council on the Status of Women, op. cit.

17. Emma Willard Task Force on Education, "Sexism in Education," December, 1971.

18. Campbell, Rita, *Campus Report,* April 18, 1973.

19. Ibid.

20. Ibid.

21. NYC *v.* Junior High School 217, 1971.

22. Campbell, Rita, op. cit.

23. Porter, Sylvia, *News Gazette,* Champaign, Ill., February 21, 1975.

24. Turtko, Thomas, *News Gazette,* Champaign, Ill., February 1, 1976.

25. Ibid.

26. Elton, Charles, and Rose, H., "Traditional Sex Attitudes and Discrepant Ability Measures in College Women," *Journal of Counseling Psychology,* 14:6, November, 1967.

27. Levy, J., "The School's Role in the Sex-Role Stereotyping of Girls: A Feminist Review of the Literature," *Feminist Studies,* 1:1, Summer, 1972, 5–23.

28. Letivin, T. E., and Chanarme, J. D., "Responses of Female Primary School Teachers to Sex-typed Behaviors in Male and Female Children," *Child Development,* 43, 1972, 1309–1316.

29. Feshback, N., "Student Teacher Preferences for Elementary School Pupils Varying in Personality Characteristics," *Journal of Educational Psychology,* April, 1969, 126–32.

30. Good, T., and Grouws, D., "Reaction of Male and Female Teacher Trainees to Descriptions of Elementary School Pupils," Technical Report No. 62, Center for Research in Social Behavior, University of Missouri of Columbia, 1972.

31. Lee, P. C., "Male and Female Teachers in Elementary Schools: An Ecological Analysis," *Teacher's College Record,* 75, 1973, 79–98.

32. Brophy, J. E., and Good, T. L., "Teachers Communication of Differential Expectations for Children's Classroom Performance: Some Behavior Data," *Journal of Educational Psychology,* 61, 1970, 365–374.

33. Spaulding, R. L., "Achievement, Creativity, and Self-concept Correlates of Teacher–Pupil Transactions in Elementary Schools," Cooperative Research Project No. 1252, U.S. Department of Health, Education, and Welfare, Office of Education, 1963.

34. Lee, P. C., and Wolinsky, A. L., "Male Teachers of Young Children: A Preliminary Empirical Study," *Young Children,* 28, 1973.

35. Hess, Robert, Shipman, V., Brophy, J., and Bear, R., "The Cognitive Environments of Urban Preschool Children: Follow-up Phase," Report to the Children's Bureau, Social Security Administration, Department of Health, Education, and Welfare, 1969.

36. Good, T., Sikes, N., and Brophy, J., "Effects of Teacher Sex and Student Sex on Classroom Interaction," *Journal of Educational Psychology,* 1973.

37. Brophy, J., and Good, T., *Individual Differences: Toward an Understanding of Classroom Life.* New York: Holt, Rinehart and Winston, 1974.

38. Meyer, William, and Lindstrom, D., "The Distributions of Teacher Approval and Disapproval of Headstart Children," Report to the Office of Educational Opportunity, 1969.

39. Felsenthal, H., "Sex Differences in Teacher–Pupil Interaction on First Grade Reading Instruction," paper, American Education Association, 1970.

40. Spaulding, R. I., op. cit.

41. Brophy, J., and Good, T., op. cit.

42. Ibid.

43. Good, T., Sikes, N., and Brophy, J., op cit.

44. Spaulding, R. L., op. cit.

45. Ibid.

46. Ibid.

47. Torrance, E. P., *Guiding Creative Talent.* Englewood Cliffs, N.J.: Prentice-Hall, 1963.

48. Letivin, T. E., and Chanarme, J. D., op. cit.

49. Ibid.

50. Ibid.

51. Ibid.

52. Ibid.

53. Good, T. L., and Brophy, E., "Behavioral Expression of Teachers' Attitudes," *Journal of Educational Psychology,* 63, 1972.

54. Jackson, P. W., and Lahaderne, H. M., "Inequalities of Teacher–Pupil Contacts," *Psychology in the Schools,* 4, 1967, 204–208.

55. Waetjen, W., "Is Learning Sexless?" *Educational Digest,* September, 1962.

56. Spaulding, R. L., op. cit.

57. Sears, Pauline S., "The Effect of Classroom Conditions on the Strength of Achievement Motive and Work Output of Elementary School Children," Cooperative Research Project No. OE–873, U.S. Department of Health, Education, and Welfare, Office of Education, 1963.

58. McKee, J., and Sherriffs, A., "The Differential Education of Males and Females," *Journal of Personality,* 35:3, September, 1957, 356–371.

59. Cross, Patricia, "College Women: A Research Description," *Journal of National Association of Women Deans and Counselors,* 32:1, Autumn, 1968, 12–21.

60. Oetzel, R. M., "Classified Summary of Research in Sex Differences," in Maccoby, Eleanor (ed.), *The Development of Sex Differences.* Sanford, Calif.: Stanford University Press, 1966.

61. Maccoby, Eleanor, "Sex Differences in Intellectual Functioning," in Maccoby, Eleanor (ed.), *The Development of Sex Differences.* Stanford, Calif.: Stanford University Press, 1966.

62. Bentzen, F., "Sex Ratios in Learning and Behavior Disorders," *National Elementary Principal,* 46:2, 1966. 80–35.

63. Ibid.

64. Davidson, D., and Lang, G., "Children's Perceptions of Their Teacher's Feelings Toward Them Related to Self-perception, School Achievement, and Behavior," *Journal of Experimental Education,* 29, 1960, 107–118.

65. Doyle, W., Hancock, G., and Kifer, E., "Teacher's Perceptions: Do They Make a Difference?" paper, American Education Research Association, 1971.

66. Mussen, P., and Rutherford, E., "Parent–Child Relations and Parental Personality in Relation to Young Children's Sex Role Preference," *Child Development,* 34, 1963, 589–607.

67. Kagan, J., "The Emergence of Sex Differences," *University of Chicago School Review,* 80:2, February, 1972.

68. Ibid.

69. Maccoby, Eleanor, op. cit.

70. New Jersey Task Force, NOW, Princeton, N.J., 1970.

71. Ibid.

72. Saario, T. N., Jacklin, C. N., and Little, C. K., "Sex Roles Stereotyping in the Public Schools," *Harvard Educational Review,* 43:3, August, 1973.

73. Ibid.

74. Nilsen, Alleen Pace, "Women in Children's Literature," *College English,* May, 1971.

75. "A Feminist Look at Children's Books," *School Library Journal,* 17:5, 1971, 18–24.

76. Frisof, Jamie, "Textbooks and Channeling," *Women, A Journal of Liberation,* Fall, 1969.

77. MacLeod, Jennifer, and Silverman, Sandra, *You Won't Do.* Pittsburgh, Pa.: Know, Inc., 1973.

78. DeKrow, K., "Look Jane, Look, See Dick Run and Jump! Admire Him!" In Anderson, S. (ed.), *Sex Differences and Discrimination in Education.* Worthington, Ohio: Charles A. Jones, 1972.

79. Trecker, Janice Law, "Women in U.S. History High School Textbooks," *Social Education,* March, 1971.

Operational Concepts

1. A sizable number of schools are sex-segregated.

2. In athletics and other nonacademic areas, curriculum provisions for boys and girls are often separate and unequal.

3. Traditional misconceptions as to differences between males and females are reflected in some curricular materials.

4. Despite improvement in the recent past, some teaching still conveys sexist values.

Implications

Custom and habit are not easily altered. Although considerable effort has been expended to eradicate curricular sexual bias, strong vestiges remain. Laws have been passed, lobbying coalitions have been formed, and most administrators have sought to eliminate inequities. Yet, because of attitudes and beliefs deeply engrained in both male and female educators, the traditional myths regarding sex roles in society tend to filter, directly or indirectly, into the curriculum.

Because there is little question as to the undesirability of sexism, and because most teachers are intellectually opposed to its existence, time alone, in all probability, will improve the situation. This is not to say that deliberate attempts to identify and remove prejudicial bias should not continue. The odds are good, in fact, that the overt manifestations of the problem will be removed in the not too distant future. But the more covert aspects, buried in the mind sets of people, will undoubtedly disappear somewhat more slowly. What is of greatest importance, obviously, is that the schools convey to boys and girls alike a sense of equality.

Judith R. Vicary

Toward an Adaptive Developmental Education

> *We do not feel our knowledge. Nothing could better illustrate the flaw at the heart of our civilization. . . . Knowledge without feeling is not knowledge and can lead only to public irresponsibility and indifference, and conceivably to ruin.*
>
> (MacLeish, 1970, p. 11)

These strong words regarding the outcome of an incomplete learning process, one without feeling, were deliberately chosen as a beginning to this discussion of an adaptive developmental education. They were selected not as a dire warning, nor as a criticism of an educational system, but as an indicator of a need that is of immediate and primary concern to today's educators and the community they serve. In this time of economic constraints, accompanied by a chorus for outcome measures and accountability, it is appropriate, necessary, even urgent that the goals of our educational processes be reexamined, and perhaps redefined or reemphasized. The place of affective learning or development, if any, must be clearly, honestly, and openly described in relation to the total goals of education, for debate, refinement, and eventual acceptance or rejection by a community and its educational leadership.

Recent authors have dealt with such statements of educational objectives. Weinstein and Fantini (1975) state that "Education in a free society should have a broad human focus, which is best served by educational objectives resting on a personal and interpersonal base and dealing with students' concerns" (p. 102). The Elementary School Teaching Project proceeded based on the "assumption that the broad objectives of American education must include the preparation of students to engage in constructive personal and social behavior" (Weinstein and Fantini, 1975, p. 103). Arthur Combs (1975) summarizes these goals in *Educational Accountability: Beyond Behavioral Objectives*.

> Modern education must produce far more than persons with cognitive skills. It must produce *humane* individuals, persons who can be relied upon to pull their own weight in our society, who can be counted upon to behave

responsibly and cooperatively. We need good citizens, free of prejudice, concerned about their fellow citizens, loving, caring fathers and mothers, persons of goodwill whose values and purposes are positive, feeling persons with wants and desires likely to motivate them toward positive interactions. These are the things that make us human. Without them we are automatons, fair game for whatever crowd-swaying, stimulus-manipulating demagogue comes down the pike. The humane qualities are absolutely essential to our way of life—far more important, even, than the learning of reading, for example. We can live with a bad reader; a bigot is a danger to everyone (p. 91).

If society is indeed dependent on formal education to assist its members in becoming better individuals, for their own sake as well as for the benefit of their fellowmen, then it appears that our educational process has not yet reached successful fulfillment of that goal. The ultimate outcome measures, it would seem, are the resultant behaviors of the individuals who pass through the educational system, as they are required to do by law. Therefore, if schools are truly to influence behavior, it is necessary "to redefine both the school's role and function" (Rubin, 1973, p. 28).

HISTORICAL PERSPECTIVE

Historically, one primary result sought from the educational system has been the perpetuation of the social system. The technological and knowledge explosions of the past three decades alone have meant that replication of learning and experience is no longer sufficient for either the individual or for his larger world. John Gardner identified the need for an "ever-renewing society," representing its ability to modify and change to meet the new, both in problems and in opportunities.

The question that Carl Rogers (1968) raised of whether man can survive this change, as we see it spiraling daily, has been and is being dealt with repeatedly, from *Future Shock* to doomsday predictions (Whitehead, 1969):

> Our sociological theories, our political philosophy, our practical maxims of business, our political economy, and our doctrines of education are derived from an unbroken tradition of great thinkers and of practical examples from the age of Plato . . . to the end of the last century. The whole of this tradition is warped by the vicious assumption that each generation will substantially live amid the conditions governing the lives of its fathers and will transmit those conditions to mould with equal force the lives of its children. We are living in the first period of human history for which this assumption is false (p. 11).

The psychological implications of man's changing role, responsibility, and coping mechanisms do threaten both the educational content and the process as they have been known. Present and future affluence, leisure, and differing vocational roles are examples of these developments and are becoming appropriate considerations for educators. Another change, seen in the new role definitions through the feminist movement, also requires recognition in both course content and direction. It is not sufficient to open shop classes for girls! Additionally, the alienation and ennui of youth raised with (or by) television, both in and out of the classroom, represented by the psychological withdrawal through drugs, alcohol, dropouts, crime, or violence, have panicked parents and created pressures on the school system to *do* something.

The prime responsibility presently for societal problem solving does appear to be delegated to, or accepted by, the public school systems. A review of historical content and emphasis in American schools indicates that an early concern, in addition to academic subjects, even in colonial America was on development of character and values, criteria considered essential to the continuation of societal standards. (Lessons of that era, often with a strong religious–moral orientation, can be seen in colonial primers that exhort the reader to high principles and worthy behaviors— all of which they must be able to spell!) Actually, the view of what knowledge was needed for life's activities (work) limited the content available for many. For that reason, girls did not regularly learn the subjects that boys did, and only pioneers, like Mary Lyon, often considered radicals by their contemporaries, advocated the full development of the female mind. Social classification and stratification were implicit in the content available during the 1700s and 1800s, and may have been considered appropriate when there were limited positions available for the occupational, social, and power elites.

The mental discipline or facility psychology as a theory of learning transfer (of the late 1870s) had a profound effect on curriculum theory, with the form of a discipline, rather than the content, of primary importance. In the 1890s different societal needs were felt and all youth were to be considered in educational concerns; less academic curricula and more emphasis on manual arts and domestic science, for example, resulted. Thorndike's work on transfer, resulting in the identical elements theory of the 1920s, affected education through the selection of subjects for inclusion in the curriculum. Subjects had to be justified on the basis of the *specific* skills, knowledge, and understanding that they provided, a revolutionary concept. Trade courses with simulated learning situations were one outcome. The behavioral research in the 1930s suggested another frame of reference for curricula, based on the transfer of principles in learning. A "core" curriculum emerged in the 1930s that protested the identical elements theory. Humanistic concerns were evident in innovations of that period.

One message from John Dewey had been heard, and a progressive trend appeared with a conscious effort to respond to each person's psychological growth and development. The learner's emotional nature was

903

considered along with his mind. Dewey (1973) in *Democracy and Education* wrote,

> Knowledge is humanistic in quality not because it is *about* human products in the past, but because of what it *does* in liberating human intelligence and human sympathy. Any subject matter which accomplishes this result is humane, and any subject matter which does not accomplish it is not even educational (p. 223).

However, the pendulum swung back toward superior cognitive development following the advent of Sputnik in 1957. The resultant stimuli produced defensive responses to the public fault-finding in education, and schools embarrassedly removed any nonpractical subject areas. The National Defense Education Act passed by the U.S. Congress in 1958 was designed to meet changing societal needs, ones for scientific and technological superiority. Through it, superior students received financial aid; funds bought teaching materials for states; graduate fellowships were provided; research aided curricula development; vocational education, counseling, and testing programs also benefited, as did teacher training in "critical areas." Now, the pendulum has again swung, from the lopsided emphasis on cognition to meet America's needs of that period toward an emphasis on the "whole individual," meaning both factual knowledge acquisition and affective–mental health development.

PHILOSOPHY AND RATIONALE

As part of the present search for what to teach and how, there is currently a new interest in affective (sometimes labeled humanistic) education designed to meet societal needs and to reduce pressures put on schools by the developmental crises of today's students. Recently, affective development has only been attended to in terms of its contribution to the cognitive domain; thus, a large amount of work in the affective domain was either ignored or overlooked. However, it is important to examine some of these largely ignored developmental affective concepts and incorporate them with the cognitive elements into a learning model not as a secondary consideration, but as a matter of primary focus or equal attention.

Two educators who have not overlooked the importance of the affective domain, Gilchrist and Roberts (1974), note, "We cannot teach someone to think without concurrently having him develop feeling about his thinking. Feeling, intuiting, sensing and thinking interact inevitably" (p. 45).

Piaget's (1932) position is similar: "Affectivity or its privations can certainly be the cause of acceleration or delay in cognitive development.... Actually the affective and cognitive mechanisms always remain indissociable although distinct ..." (p. 12).

Krathwohl et al. (1964) also see the impact of affect on cognitive development. "If the student is not able to achieve certain of the objectives (affective) which would be properly categorized here at the same time that he achieves cognitive objectives, his ability to accomplish the cognitive behaviors will be imperfect, academic, and ultimately, in life, of much less value than they would otherwise be" (p. 31). We clearly cannot ignore either the cognitive or affective levels of children's development.

Weinstein and Fantini (1970) also state a premise for an affectively based education model. "Significant contact with pupils is most effectively established and maintained when the content and method of instruction have an affective basis" (p. 10).

They go on later to note that "Unless knowledge is related to an affective state in the learner, the likelihood that it will influence behavior is limited" (p. 28).

Arthur Combs (1975) concurs, saying that "Information will affect a person's behavior only in the degree to which he has discovered its personal meaning for him" (p. 125). Alpren (1974) adds that "Another way of summing up the curriculum input desired by those with affective concern is that they believe it imperative to help youngsters today see themselves, other people, and institutions as schools have never before attempted to do" (p. 221). A common element to these writings does stand out: "The belief that 'affect' is not so much a domain as a dimension of human experience, and more generally that affective and cognitive learnings are so inextricably tied together that the educational neglect of either will adversely modify or limit the development of the other" (Ecker, 1975, p. 361).

CRITICISMS OF AFFECTIVE EDUCATION

The implications for education of these positions endorsing planned-for affective development have, or are, being recognized by a range of educators and programs. However, many have based incomplete, undeveloped, and hasty efforts (often formulated because of a local crisis or community pressure) on such statements. Education's new directions appear often, therefore, as a sudden, unfounded fad, with a bandwagon, snake-oil remedy type of proselytizing resulting. The lack of well-defined curriculum goals and materials reveals the need for more "investigative description and dialogue," and articulation of thinking, as well as planned processes. Otherwise, the real strengths and contributions of affective learning–development may become lost, along with its weaknesses or insufficiencies, because of the confusion, misconcepts, and incompleteness of many of its approaches and proponents.

Douglas Heath (1972) aptly summarized the advent and defects of this phenomenon:

The affective education movement is a response to deep currents of student dissatisfaction with and alleviation from the education they are receiving. "Affective education" is more a rallying slogan with several different measures than a well-defined program for action. It is a diffuse, poorly formulated gutsy reaction to the excessive and exclusive academicism that has dominated our educational values since Sputnik. Affective education is in danger of becoming an ephemeral fad. As a movement, it risks encouraging the same types of excesses that our faddish enslavement to academic excellence committed. If we do not understand the causes for its dramatic flowering in the past several years, we may snuff out the spirit of affective education through judicious excess (p. 353).

Resistance and even backlash frequently follow this misinformation and confusion; in fact, legislation is pending in several states that would make it illegal for schools to teach about values, feelings, needs, etc., and injunctions have already halted the introduction or continuation of a variety of affectively oriented curricula. A bill (McCurk, 1974) introduced in the Maryland Senate in both 1974 and 1975, and to date unreported out of the Finance Committee, states:

(2) The primary responsibility of the school is to develop the intellectual capabilities of the child. The school has neither the responsibility nor the right to intervene in all areas of personal development and exceeds its authority as a servant of the people paid by public taxes if it attempts to do so. . . .

(5) No employee of a school and no person brought into a school by the administration may seek to subvert parental authority by acting as a change agent of attitudes, values, and religious or political beliefs of the students. . . .

(C) Pupils may only be tested for intelligence quotient, proficiency in basic skills and academic subject matter. Any testing pertaining to pupil attitudes, parent attitudes, or personal information pertaining to the pupil and his family, or as concerns their habits or values, including personality inventories, value appraisals, psychological inventories or diagnostic tests shall be given only after receiving written parental permission to give such tests. Any such tests shall be made available to the parents or guardian upon request if their child is to be tested.

(E) (1) No psychological or psychiatric methods shall be practiced in the public schools. This prohibition includes role playing, sensitivity training or any other method dealing with or probing psyche of the pupil. "Sensitivity training" is defined as group meetings, large or small, to discuss publicly a pupil's intimate and personal matters, opinions, values or beliefs; or to act out emotions and feelings toward one another in the group, using techniques such as self-confession or mutual criticism (pp. 2–3, Senate Bill No. 196).

At least two other states, Michigan and California, have had similar legislation proposed.

The State Department of Education in Pennsylvania has been testing fifth-, eighth-, and eleventh-grade students in relation to its ten goals of quality education. About 80 percent of the questions involve attitudes, in areas such as self-knowledge, understanding of others, and positive attitudes toward learning. The EQA director, J. Robert Coldiron (1975), stated that "You can't get away from the fact that attitude has an influence on learning" (p. 12). Nonetheless, the American Civil Liberties Union and some concerned parents and educators disagree with the attitude testing, calling it an invasion of privacy and damaging to children who are sensitive about revealing their innermost thoughts. They have succeeded in removing any identities from the tests, but many people are still striving to stop the assessment program. Fred Heddinger (1975), executive director of the Pennsylvania School Boards Association, stated, "As soon as you begin large scale testing programs that deal with things beyond reading, writing and basic skills you get into the arena of where do you draw the line, how far do you go and who really knows enough to formulate the proper questions?" (p. 12).

A recent issue of *Learning* (Divoky, 1975) also dealt with the role of affective subjects and materials.

> Loving teacher, classroom preacher,
> How do your children grow?
> With psychic probes; affective goads—
> I cultivate kids row by row (p. 22).

Divoky (1975) summarizes the concerns for the proliferation of mental health–affective–humanistic programs, saying "The field is amorphous, the goals and objectives unmeasurable, the rhetoric often incomprehensible" (p. 22), and yet mental health is becoming an assumption and a staple of the school curriculum. Some of these approaches she calls "a Disneyized view of emotional life with boppy slogans and easy answers" (p. 23). These concerns *are* legitimate, as Heath (1972) has implied, and even some of the strongest proponents of affective development would agree with Divoky's assessments and questions.

Whether schools should be taking on the emotional and moral development of youngsters is an overwhelming question, yet one that has barely been considered in the rush to buy programs. Should schools—given their limited and spotty success in meeting the more measurable and modest goals of teaching reading and computation skills—really undertake the enormously more difficult and complicated responsibilities that affective education implies? Should teachers—who pretend to no higher level of ethics or sensitivity than any other citizen—try to become humanists/psychologists/social workers/exemplars of values? The not atypical teacher who wrote "I love you" at the top of all her *good* student papers after attending an affective workshop comes to mind. This is not to say that individual teachers with particular strengths—a special rapport with youngsters or an ability to deal with controversial social issues, say—shouldn't use these talents in their classrooms, just as they would call on a talent for music or carpentry. But what is being suggested by many is that all teachers have the job of publicly probing and examining the emotional health and values of each one of their students, and then, armed with little more than hunches and blind faith, deal in some vague, prescriptive way with what they find.

Even if the school could provide professionally competent personnel and material in these areas, does the state—through its institution of compulsory education—have a right to intervene further into the lives of its children, well beyond its traditional mandate? It is one thing to have public services available in the community for voluntary use; it is quite another to make them a part of the school program all children attend by law. It is one thing to create a happy, relaxed learning environment; it is quite another to demand from each child a level of mental well-being that "makes it" in the eyes of the beholder. . . .

Once the school takes on a mental health function, there are no limits to what it needs to know and record and share with other agencies. The new federal Family Educational Rights and Privacy Act, designed to protect against such infringements, isn't capable of dealing with situations where the social worker works with children in the school setting and makes her records about them for a different agency, or where the school staff includes a counselor funded by a Law Enforcement Assistance Administration project who makes one set of student records at the school and another at his office at the police station. The information flows as through a sieve, unstoppable (pp. 25, 27).

The questions raised here do need better answers, for the development of a sound philosophical and societal goal for education, from a strong research base and with programs and materials carefully designed to meet these goals. Educators must recognize the range of concerns evident in both conservative and liberal viewpoints, from the Council for Basic Education to the American Civil Liberties Union. The "backlash movement," with walls reappearing in open schools (Reston, Virginia; New Ipswick, New Hampshire), to "law and order" classrooms, with single-file, adult-supervised hall passages, and dress codes (Prince George County, Maryland) represent valid viewpoints, alternative needs, and possibly an impetus to educators to "develop . . . thoroughly, systematically, and continuously, an integrated conceptual framework, a theory" (Stewart, 1975, p. 686).

To understand the range of dimensions currently seen as affective education, representative models, both of affective content and climate, can be examined. These are illustrative examples and are not meant to be all inclusive.

AFFECTIVE MODELS: CONTENT OR CLIMATE

In one area of content, the integration of affective dimensions with regular academic curricula, George Isaac Brown's *Human Teaching for Human Learning* (1971) includes Figure 1. He explains that complete learning recognizes personal relevancy by being

> personally meaningful, when we have feelings about it, whatever "it" may be. There has been concern in the educational establishment for motivating learners, but this is usually only fancy wrapping on the package. If the contents of the package are not something the learner can feel about, real learning will not take place. We must attend not only to that which motivates but to that which sustains as well (p. 10).

The paradigm of Figure 1 integrates the personalization of both abstract and factual data with the cognitive subject content; such a confluent education approach includes:

1. External structure, which integrates subject matter and personal awareness.
2. An intellectual component.
3. Abstract knowledge or information (Brown, 1975).

FIGURE 1 What I Discover About Myself Is What Makes History

COGNITIVE		AFFECTIVE	
(Subject content)		(Emotional content)	
STRAIGHT COGNITIVE	**ABSTRACT COGNITIVE**	**ABSTRACT AFFECTIVE**	**STRAIGHT AFFECTIVE**
Columbus visited the New World in 1492	Beginning of the "Modern Age"	What makes man seek the unknown?	What have I discovered about myself?

History is man's endeavors.　　　　　What is in all men is in me.

EDUCATION HUMAN

Similarly, Raths et al. (1966) use the phrase "values level teaching" to describe the third or affective level of traditional subject content. Their model's base is the facts level (see Figure 2), a strictly cognitive approach. The second part of the pyramid is designated concepts, with values level at the peak. An example of a lesson in these three levels is outlined below.

Facts Level

- What was the religious problem that the Pilgrims faced?
- Why did they go to Holland?
- Why did the Pilgrims decide to leave Holland?
- What was Plymouth Rock?
- What did the Indians do to help the Pilgrims?
- How did they celebrate the first Thanksgiving?

Concepts Level

- What is religious prejudice?
- How did cultural assimilation affect the Pilgrims?
- Why was emigration such an important decision for them?
- What rituals were important to the Pilgrims?
- How were these incorporated into their changed style of life in the New World?

Values Level (Simon, 1971)

- Have you ever seen prejudice?
- What did you do?
- Have you ever been the victim of prejudice?

Figure 2

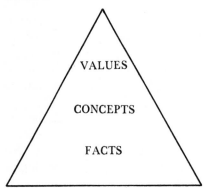

910

- What is your cultural background?
- How much do you know about your cultural heritage?
- What do you care enough about in your life, your rights, that if removed, would cause you to leave our country?
- Who would you say good-bye to; who is important to you?
- Which is harder—to give help or receive help?
- Name ten traditions that are meaningful to you.

It is important to recognize that such values level teaching also does not negate the factual level. Knowledge and skills are also desired directions and outcomes, and academic development need not be sacrificed for affective growth. Both are goals and can be viewed as mutually compatible. Facts are examined in terms of concepts, and these are ultimately internalized through the values level. The current popularity, particularly with teachers, of Raths et al. (1966) and their values clarification concept illustrates a void that previously existed and is being partially filled by this approach. Many good teachers have been doing this kind of teaching, even on a "gut" level, for generations. The values clarification process applied to education crystallized terms and directions; as a result, methods have been developed to implement and adapt these concepts. *Clarifying Values Through Subject Matter* (Harmin et al., 1973) is a good example of a practical handbook for the teacher. Subjects thus integrated range from mathematics to industrial arts, social studies to biology.

The previously described subject content areas were concerned with the enrichment of regular curricula subjects. The other major content level is materials themselves with an affective or mental health content. The *Dimensions of Personality* (Limbacher, 1970) *Series* (DOP), with K–12 levels, is one such example. DUSO, *Developing Understanding of Self and Others* (Dinkmeyer, 1970), and *The Magic Circle* (Human Development Institute, 1970) are similar educational applications of affective content as seen in mental health principles. Basic to the material is the theme of self-concepts; the way a child sees himself is considered "the most important single factor affecting behavior" by Combs et al. (1971, p. 39). Dinkmeyer, probably best known for his *Developing Understanding of Self and Others* (1970) kit, stated that ". . . only as the child understands himself, his needs, his purposes, and his goals is he free to become involved and committed to the educational process" (1971, p. 67). Other writers who also agree on the value of a positive self-concept to positive behavior and learning include Hamachek (1965), Morse (1964), and Coopersmith (1959). Although both psychologists and philosophers at the beginning of this century (William James, Alfred Adler, George Mead) examined the role of feelings of personal worth in relation to happiness and effectiveness, systematic research in these areas has been of recent origin. However, it was more or less accepted that self-confidence and an optimistic assessment of one's abilities were significant factors in success and interpersonal relations. In 1961, Wylie's *Self-Concept: A Critical Survey of the Pertinent Research Literature* surveyed several of these interdirected constructs, especially self-concept up to that time, looking at the theme through Fromm and Freud, and McClelland and Maslow, among others.

Hansen and Maynard (1973) later examined the more current research on a range of youth self-concept behaviors, such as counseling, school, anxiety, drugs, and vocational development. They reported that a number of studies, like that of Hogan and Green (1971), for example, found a direct correlation between school achievement and self-concept. Although other current studies also have similar findings, a question is frequently raised concerning which comes first: is a positive self-concept the product of or the producer of successful achievement? One important study dealing with this issue was reported by Thomas et al. (1969). Parents were shown how to help their children develop a more positive self-concept; substantial improvement in self-concepts did result during and immediately following the program. However, the increase in achievement of these students occurred six to twelve months after the parent intervention, lending weight to the "positive self-concept produces higher achievement" direction. Carleton (1963) found that significant self-concept improvements, with indicated permanency, correlated with greater reading progress in a group of second, third, fourth, fifth, and sixth graders.

In addition, the total way a child behaves can also reflect his sense of self-esteem. Favorable responses to challenge or troubled conditions and success achievement are likely to result from positive self-concepts (Coopersmith, 1967). McCandless (1961) found that anxiety, adjustment problems, reduced popularity, and defensiveness were evident with poor self-concepts. Therefore, it seems beneficial to the child both as a learner and as a person that he be helped to develop a more positive self-concept.

Glasser, Bills, and Dinkmeyer are among a body of educators, researchers, and psychologists who suggest that, although a child's self-concept is begun in the preschool years, much of it is formed during elementary and middle school years, and the total school experience is crucial to this development. Materials like DUSO kits and DOP are popular affective content teaching tools for this purpose, and research has been done which confirms that these programs have been successful in significantly improving the self-concepts of children (Koval and Hales, 1972; Eldridge et al., 1973; Swisher and Piniuk, 1973).

In the realm of learning environments, the models of classroom climate–environment range from interior design arrangement, as seen in the student seating of Figure 3, to communication evaluations, as in the Climate Index (Withall, 1967).

The Climate Index includes seven categories of evaluation of teacher responses as follows:

912

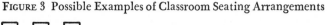
FIGURE 3 Possible Examples of Classroom Seating Arrangements

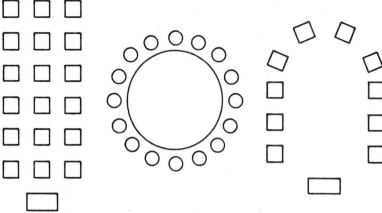

1. Approving and commending.
2. Accepting and clarifying.
3. Problem structuring.
4. Neutral.
5. Controlling.
6. Reproving and deprecating.
7. Teacher self-supportive.

This phenomenon of a classroom atmosphere is evident and even obvious to students. Their statements that "Miss Smith's room always seems happy" or "It's so dismal having math with Mr. Jones" are accurate commentaries usually backed by adult observations. The attitude, atmosphere, and effect are all summarized in the *climate* of the learning environment. Its importance operationally was summarized as follows (Withall, 1969):

> influencing the sense of common purpose of a group of individuals, the meaningfulness of the group or individual problem is attacked, and the degree of self-involvement or participation by the individual. Climate probably affects the degree of freedom, spontaneity and range of roles available to each individual within the limits set by the problem and the group . . . (p. 403).

The classroom has been found to be one of the most important places for a child's attitude and behavior development (Henry, 1947). Research in group dynamics (Getzels et al., 1968) and leadership styles (Lewin et al., 1939) was the foundation for studies of teachers' attitudes and behavior in determining classroom climate and student interactions. Recent research has emphasized the correlation between the learning environment and the success of both cognitive and affective learning. Kahn and Weiss report that

Walberg's series of studies found that affective aspects in the classroom can predict the educational action therein (Kahn and Weiss, 1972).

The above examples of both cognitive–affective and affective content, as well as of classroom climate, are frequently considered on an either/or basis as meanings for affective education. When both content and process have been joined, it has often been on only a one-by-one basis, as evidenced by the DUSO kit (Figure 4).

Brown (1971) and Simon's (1971) models cited earlier enlarged the possibilities to include one by two components (Figure 5).

The restrictions of considering these content models without the integration of climate dimensions are responsible for both misunderstanding of the fullest possible range of adaptive developmental education and for the reluctance or inability of teachers to revise or redirect their teaching with such affective techniques and materials. Four frequent positions taken even by the most interested or affectively oriented teachers are as follows: "I'd like to work on affective development with my students but

1. . . . my principal/superintendent/school board/team leader doesn't believe in/allow these open classrooms.
   or
2. . . . I'm just not that warm fuzzy/emotional/outgoing kind of person.
   or
3. . . . we don't have any of those materials available in our school/class/building/district.
   or
4. . . . the cognitive learning/subject matter/facts are too important to ignore by concentrating on the affective."

However, the affective component of learning should *not* necessitate

1. Unstructured/undisciplined classrooms.
   or

FIGURE 4

	CONTENT
CLIMATE	Affective
Facilitative	DUSO

FIGURE 5

	CONTENT	
CLIMATE	Affective	Cognitive-affective integration
Facilitative	DUSO	Values level teaching

914

2. Rogerian (Carl or Mr.) personalities.
   or
3. A supply depot/closet/library full of puppets/games/toys.
   or
4. The abolition of mental processes/knowledge/skills.

ADAPTIVE DEVELOPMENTAL MODEL

Therefore, in order to explain and illustrate a continuum-based definition of affectively integrated education, with a full range of methods, materials, subjects, and environments, the following eight-cell model of adaptive developmental education is presented. Continuing the earlier cell paradigm, these eight cells (Table 1) include both content and climate components. The content of the subject matter may be described as either cognitive or affective. However, there is a further delineation, the *orientation* or *integration,* according to the approach chosen by the educator, in presenting the materials. Either content area can be approached from a strictly facts level, the cognitive orientation, or from a personal relevance, a feeling level or affective integration.

The classroom climate dimension, as shown on the y axis, indicates either a teacher-managed environment, *directive,* or a student-involved one,

TABLE 1 Rating of Process and Content

		SUBJECT CONTENT			
		COGNITIVE		AFFECTIVE	
		COGNITIVE ORIENTATION	AFFECTIVE INTEGRATION	COGNITIVE ORIENTATION	AFFECTIVE INTEGRATION
Climate	Directive	(No affective component) $0-0_0$ a	$0-0_1$ c	$0-1_0$ e	$0-1_1$ g
	Facilitative	$1-0_0$ b	$1-0_1$ d	$1-1_0$ f	$1-1_1$ h

Key:
Left number, climate.
Right number, content.
Subscript, orientation.
1, with facilitative and/or affective component present.
0, with facilitative and/or affective component absent.

915

facilitative. Recognizing that each of these represents a range of possible situations, some of the determining factors should be noted. The desk arrangement is an obvious component; another less obvious but often even more visible one in its total manifestation is the administrative preferences for particular learning situations. Group projects, with students simultaneously involved in a variety of activities, incorporate facilitative possibilities, as do movable- and moved-seating arrangements and participatory investigation and learning. The directive atmosphere often includes undertaking tasks assigned by the teacher to the entire class, to be worked independently, each at his own desk. The above examples are to be considered only illustrative and not totally descriptive; a facilitative climate can exist through a teacher's methods, for example, despite bolted-in-place desks and bell-initiated class marches in the library. In Table 1, the presence of an affective component in any cell is indicated by a 1, its absence by 0, with the left number referencing the climate axis, the right the content component. The content subscript measures the orientation–integration aspect.

In Table 2 the *process analysis* summarizes the origin, direction, and procedure in the learning process. The *affective integration* shows how the content is internalized for the student by the inclusion of his or her feelings, attitudes, and values. Tables 3, 4, 5 and 6 detail examples on the ele-

TABLE 2 Process Analysis

		CONTENT			
		COGNITIVE		AFFECTIVE	
		COGNITIVE ORIENTATION	AFFECTIVE INTEGRATION	COGNITIVE ORIENTATION	AFFECTIVE INTEGRATION
Climate	Directive	*Teacher directs content and tasks*			
		Student examines subject through teacher lecture and class recitation — a	Student examines subject through structured internalized personal strategies and written reports — c	Student examines subject through teacher lecture and class recitation — e	Student examines subject through structured internalized personal strategies and written reports — g
	Facilitative	*Teacher facilitates participation and self-expression*			
		Student participates in group discussion–interaction through expression of facts, concepts, and ideas — b	Student participates through expression of feelings, attitudes, and values — d	Student participates in group discussion–interaction through expression of facts, concepts, and ideas — f	Student participates through expression of feelings, attitudes, and values — h

TABLE 3 Content Analysis, Elementary Level: Topic, Nutrition

		CONTENT			
		COGNITIVE		AFFECTIVE	
		COGNITIVE ORIENTATION	AFFECTIVE INTEGRATION	COGNITIVE ORIENTATION	AFFECTIVE INTEGRATION
Climate	Directive	Teacher leads: presentation on the basic food groups and examples of each. **a**	Student writes: keep a record of *all* the food you eat, by food group, for three days. Is this meeting your body's nutritional needs? **c**	Teacher leads: half the world population is undernourished and malnutrition kills millions of people each year. **e**	Student writes: how I think the U.N. or other agencies should try to solve the world food crisis and allocate the supplies. **g**
	Facilitative	Class discussion: discuss how our bodies digest food and use the different kinds of nutrients. **b**	Group discussion: discuss how and what you feel and the way you act when very hungry; very full; craving a food; learning to like a food. How do babies react? Adults? **d**	Role play: children trick or treating for UNICEF and explaining the program to people. **f**	Group discussion: pretend you are a mother or father who can't get enough food for your child. Now pretend you are your own mother telling you to eat your dinner. Discuss how each of these parents feels. **h**

mentary and junior–senior high levels of how health education and social studies topics could be taught using each of the eight process–content cells. Both the intrapersonal and interpersonal are more evident in the cells where an affective component is present. However, the need for a cognitive base is evident as a requirement for participation in the affective cells. Role playing would be impossible, for example, without an information stage from which to act

Seven of the eight cells have some degree of affective consideration, indicating the wider range of possibilities actually available to a teacher than the earlier models suggested. It is of importance to note that cells a through h are not listed in a rank ordering nor is a "best way" intended. Rather, the fullest possible range of education can be recognized and de-

TABLE 4 Content Analysis, Junior–Senior Level: Topic, Drugs

		CONTENT			
		COGNITIVE		AFFECTIVE	
		COGNITIVE ORIENTATION	AFFECTIVE INTEGRATION	COGNITIVE ORIENTATION	AFFECTIVE INTEGRATION
Climate	Directive	Teacher leads: definition and classification of drugs. a	Student lists: list 10 major benefits to man-kind of drug discoveries in the past 100 years. c	Teacher leads: all people throughout history have had and used drugs for various purposes. e	Student writes: why young peo-ple and adults use drugs today and what other ways they can meet those needs. g
	Facilitative	Class discussion: What are the historical and current uses and purposes of drugs? b	Group discussion: what you would have thought of the values of and claims for heroin when it was introduced. Methadone? d	Role play: students discuss-ing before a party the pros and cons of trying the drugs they know will be available there. f	Group discussion: how I make decisions now and in the future concern-ing my own use of any drugs. h

scribed. An individual teacher can choose, within the limitations of administration and materials, a cell or cells in which he or she is most comfortable and able, and in which his or her learners respond best. Indeed, within one day, teaching period, or topic several cells may be chosen to accomplish specific learning goals. Content, desire, naturalness, willingness, frequency, sincerity, and acceptance are among the factors to be considered in a teacher's choice of and ease with any one of the cells.

The implications of this model are of particular importance in terms of the number of choices available, both to individual teachers and to the administration, principals, and curriculum personnel. An affectively oriented teacher need not put away those techniques in a more directive school; three content-option possibilities are available (see cells c, e, and g). The teacher who needs, or whose students seem to need, a restrictive climate may minimally use an affective integration with cognitive materials (cell c), personalizing the learning to each student. And, obviously, within a facilitative environment, cognitive emphasis is likewise available.

918

TABLE 5 Content Analysis, Elementary Level: Topic, Space Explorations of the Americans and Russians

		CONTENT			
		COGNITIVE		AFFECTIVE	
		COGNITIVE ORIENTATION	AFFECTIVE INTEGRATION	COGNITIVE ORIENTATION	AFFECTIVE INTEGRATION
Climate	Directive	Teacher leads: the space voyages of the Americans and Russians, Sputnik, etc. a	Student lists: what are five benefits for people that have come from space travel? c	Teacher leads: people all have curiosity and various ways of exploring. e	Student writes: why I would (or would not) like to travel in space someday. g
	Facilitative	Class discussion: why are people interested in going into space? What other explorations have people tried in the past? b	Small group discussion: decide what feelings and thoughts you would have had as a Russian astronaut when the first American landed on the moon. d	Class role play: an astronaut's explanation to his children of why he wants to be an astronaut and what he hopes to accomplish by going into space. f	Small group discussion: what am I curious about? what would I like to explore or learn more about? why? h

In summary, it would seem, ideally then, that experiencing a range of cells would create for a student maximal opportunities to learn on both the cognitive and affective levels with a range of integration of the two. And for the teacher it would result in a range of techniques to meet classroom–student needs and school district requirements, as well as personal needs and competencies. Any subject area can be approached through this design; when the content, climate, and process are thus integrated with the subject area, an adaptive learning experience may occur. In this, provision is made additionally for both the affective and cognitive levels to be integrated, and an *adaptive developmental education* is being offered. Such a total approach should help meet the needs of today's learners and tomorrow's world, what Silberman (1970) concludes is of major importance to the future.

What tomorrow needs is not masses of intellectuals, but masses of educated men—men educated to feel and to act as well as to think.

TABLE 6 Content Analysis, Junior-Senior Level: Topic, Columbus's Explorations to the New World

| | | CONTENT | | |
| | | COGNITIVE | | AFFECTIVE | |
		COGNITIVE ORIENTATION	AFFECTIVE INTEGRATION	COGNITIVE ORIENTATION	AFFECTIVE INTEGRATION
Climate	Directive	Teacher leads: Columbus's voyages, dates, etc. a	Student lists: justify 20 results you think important from Columbus's explorations. c	Teacher leads: all men have a psychological basis for their need to explore and develop. e	Student writes: what I most want to explore. g
	Facilitative	Class discussion: what made men in that era seek the unknown? are there any parallels today? b	Small group discussion: come to a consensus on what would you have felt and thought as a member of Columbus's crew? as a native meeting Columbus in the New World? d	Class role play: Columbus's explanation to his doubting friends of his desires to explore, and what he hopes to accomplish. f	Small group discussion: what unknowns do I seek? what do I want in life? what are the benefits in this seeking? what are the advantages? h

References

ALPREN, MORTON. Curriculum Significance of the Affective Domain. *Theory into Practice,* Vol. 13, November 1, 1974.

BROWN, G. I. *Human Teaching for Human Learning: An Introduction to Confluent Education.* New York: Viking Press, 1971.

———. *The Live Classroom.* New York: Viking Press, 1975.

COLDIRON, J., *in* Margasak, L. Attitude Testing in Schools Faces Challenges. *Central Daily Times,* August 15, 1975, p. 12.

COMBS, A., *in* READ, D., and SIMON, S. (eds.). *Humanistic Education Sourcebook.* Englewood Cliffs, N.J.: Prentice-Hall, 1975.

———, AVILA, D., and PURKEY, W. *Helping Relationships: Basic Concepts and the Helping Professions.* Boston: Allyn and Bacon, 1971.

COOPERSMITH, S. A Method for Determining Types of Self-esteem. *Journal of Abnormal Social Psychology,* 59 (1959), 87–94.

———. *The Antecedents of Self-Esteem.* San Francisco: Freeman, 1967.

DEWEY, J., *in* RUBIN, L. *Facts and Feelings in the Classroom.* New York: Viking Press, 1973.

DINKMEYER, D. *Developing Understanding of Self and Others* (DUSO). Circle Pines, Minn.: American Guidance Source, 1970.

———. Top Priority: Understanding Self and Others. *Elementary School Journal,* 72 (1971), 62–71.

DIVOKY, DIANE. Affective Education. *Learning,* October, 1975, 20–28.

ECKER, D., *in* READ, D., and SIMON, S. (eds.). *Humanistic Education Sourcebook.* Englewood Cliffs, N.J.: Prentice-Hall, 1975.

ELDRIDGE, M. S., BARCIKOWSKI, R. S., and WITMER, I. M. Effects of DUSO on the Self-concepts of Second Grade Students. *Elementary School Guidance and Counseling,* 7 (1973), 257–260.

GETZELS, J. W., LIPHAM, J. M., and CAMPBELL, R. F. *Educational Administration as a Social Process: Theory, Research, and Practice.* New York: Harper & Row, 1968.

GILCHRIST, R. S., and ROBERTS, B. R. *Curriculum Development a Humanized Systems Approach.* Belmont, Calif.: Fearon Publishers, 1974.

HAMACHEK, D. (ed.). *The Self in Growth, Teaching and Learning: Selected Readings.* Englewood Cliffs, N.J.: Prentice-Hall, 1965.

HANSEN, J., and MAYNARD, P. *Youth: Self-concept and Behavior.* Columbus, Ohio: Charles E. Merrill, 1973.

HARMIN, M., KIRSCHENBAUM, H., and SIMON, S. *Clarifying Values Through Subject Matter.* Minneapolis, Minn.: Winston Press, 1973.

HEATH, D. H. Affective Education: Aesthetics and Discipline. *School Review,* 18 (1972), 353–372.

HEDDINGER, F., *in* MARGASAK, L. Attitude Testing in Schools Faces Challenges. *Centre Daily Times,* August 15, 1975, 12.

HENRY, N. B. (ed.). Science Education in the American Schools. *The Forty Sixth Yearbook of the National Society for the Study of Education,* Part 1. Chicago: The Society, 1947.

HOGAN, E., and GREEN, R. L. Can Teachers Modify Children's Self-concepts? *Teachers College Record,* 72 (1971), 423–26.

Human Development Institute. *Magic Wide: An Overview of the Human Development Program.* La Mesa, Calif.: The Institute, 1970.

JONES, R. M. *Fantasy and Feelings in Education.* New York: Harper & Row, 1968.

KAHN, S. B., and WEISS, J. The Teaching of Affective Responses, *in* TRAVERS, R. M. (ed.). *Second Handbook of Research on Teaching.* Chicago: Rand McNally, 1972.

KOVAL, C. D., and HALES, L. W. The Effects of the DUSO Guidance Program in the Self-concepts of Primary School Children. *Child Study Journal,* 2 (1972), 57–67.

KRATHWOHL, D. R., BLOOM, B. S., and MASIA, B. *Taxonomy of Educational Objectives Handbook II: Affective Domain.* New York: David McKay Co., 1964.

LEWIN, K., LIPPETT, R., and WHITE, R. Patterns of Aggressive Behavior in Experimentally Created Social Climates. *Journal of Social Psychology,* 10 (1939), 271–299.

LIMBACHER, W. *Dimensions of Personality Series*. Dayton, Ohio: Pflaum Standard, 1970.

MacLEISH, A., *in* RESTON, J. The Forgotten Factor. *The New York Times,* November 29, 1970, E, p. 11.

McCANDLESS, E. B. *Children and Adolescence*. New York: Holt, Rinehart and Winston, 1961.

McCURK, S. Bill Number 196, Senate of Annapolis, Maryland, January 9, 1974, 1–3.

MORSE, W. Self-concept in the School Setting. *Childhood Education,* 41 (1964), 195–198.

PIAGET, JEAN. *The Moral Judgment of the Child*. Great Britain: Routledge Press, 1932.

RATHS, L., HARMIN, M., and SIMON, S. *Values and Teaching*. Columbus, Ohio: Charles E. Merrill, 1966.

READ, D., and SIMON, S. (eds.). *Humanistic Education Sourcebook*. Englewood Cliffs, N.J.: Prentice-Hall, 1975.

ROGERS, C. *Interpersonal Relationships in the Year 2000*. Lecture given at the Esalen Institute, January 10, 1968.

RUBIN, L. *Facts and Feelings in the Classroom*. New York: Viking Press, 1973.

SILBERMAN, C. *Crisis in the Classroom*. New York: Random House, 1970.

SIMON, S. *Values Level Teaching*. Speech given during Values Clarification workshop in Rochester, N. Y., 1971.

———, HOWE, L., and KIRSCHENBAUM, H. *Values Clarification*. New York: Hart Publishing Company, 1972.

STEWART, J. Clarifying Values Clarification: A Critique. *Phi Delta Kappan,* June 1975, 684–688.

SWISHER, J., and PINIUK, A. *An Evaluation of Keystone Central School District's Drug Education Program*. Pennsylvania Governor's Justice Commission, Region IV, 1973.

THOMAS, S., BROOKOVER, W., LAPERE, J., HAMACHEK, D., and ERICKSON, E. An Experiment to Modify Self-concept and School Performance. *Sociological Focus on Education,* 3 (1969), 55–67.

TRAVERS, R. M. (ed.). *Second Handbook of Research on Teaching*. Chicago: Rand McNally, 1973.

WEINSTEIN, G., and FANTINI, M., *in* READ, D., and SIMON, S. (eds.). *Humanistic Education Sourcebook*. Englewood Cliffs, N. J.: Prentice-Hall, 1970.

WHITEHEAD, A., *in* POSTMAN, N., and WEINGARTNER, C. *Teaching as a Subversive Activity*. New York: Dell Publishing Co., 1969.

WITHALL, J. Creating a Climate for Learning, *in* Ishler, R. E., and Inglis, J. O. (eds.). *On Student Teaching*. Toledo, Ohio: University of Toledo, 1967.

———. Evaluation of Classroom Climate. *Childhood Education,* 45 (1969), 403–408.

WYLIE, R. *Self-concept: A Critical Survey of the Pertinent Research Literature*. Lincoln, Neb.: University of Nebraska Press, 1961.

Operational Concepts

1. Affective learning and development should be integrated within the overall instructional program.

2. Cognitive and affective growth are essential objectives in a well-balanced curriculum.

3. Affect strongly influences both cognitive learning and emotional development.

4. The goals of affective education require (1) well-defined objectives, (2) appropriate instructional materials, and (3) specialized evaluative procedures.

Implications

The approach to adaptive education described by Vicary demonstrates the inherent relationship between affect and cognition. There are, in short, affective dimensions of cognitive learning as well as cognitive aspects of affective development.

Classroom observers have long been sensitive to the particular "feel" of a learning situation. Expert teachers, whether out of knowledge, experience, or intuition, are adept at cultivating classroom ambience. Less expert teachers, conversely, are often impaired by negative feelings among students or "atmosphere," to use the writer's term, that reduces both the spirit and quality of a lesson.

Although some teachers and some learners are more comfortable in a restrictive climate that has a relatively rigid organization, the writer suggests that, even in a highly structured environment, learning can be personalized. It is this personalization, characterized by instruction that is maximally apt and relevant for each child, that constitutes the ultimate objective of individualized instruction.

The typical teacher, in this connection, faces two overriding difficulties: first, how individual learner needs can accurately and conveniently be determined; and, second, once determined, how they can be accommodated with reasonable efficiency. These two skills might well serve as a central component in all preservice and in-service professional training since they are at the heart of expertness in teaching. Both skills, moreover, are learnable, in that they are based upon particular clusters of techniques.

John A. Dow
Maurie Hillson

An Individualized Curriculum Program for Continuous Personalized Instruction

Any given group of children represents different rates of learning, styles, and modalities. However, until very recently, surveys of the status of programs of individualized instruction have shown that the practice of tailoring instruction to individual student needs and learning characteristics is not very widespread.

The 1964 Yearbook Committee of the Association for Supervision and Curriculum Development introduced its book, *Individualizing Instruction*, with the belief that "achieving individualization which effects release of human potential has long been an important function of classroom teachers"(1). Indeed, they are correct. Individualization is one of the educational tenets of our democracy. That is, the strength of our democracy depends on the development of each individual's potential in order to bring about his independence as a citizen.

Individually prescribed instruction (IPI) is a concrete, observable, and describable approach to achieving what has been a desirable education concept for many years. It is based on stated behavioral objectives correlated with diagnostic instruments, curriculum materials, and teaching techniques. The purpose of this paper is to critically analyze the present individually prescribed instruction program that has been developed and is being implemented by Research for Better Schools, Inc. (RBS) of Philadelphia and to assess various aspects of the implementation and evaluation strategies. In order to do this with some measure of competence and success, one needs to set the program materials and their manner of use, along with the impact they have achieved, into a somewhat larger educational context. Moreover, there needs to be a definition of the implementation in relation to what the individualization of instruction means in the first place.

LESSER AND LARGER LEARNINGS

One must be alert to two sets of distinctions concerning individualized instruction. First, individualized instruction can mean that the teachers involve themselves on a personal one-to-one basis with each pupil. This essentially is a tutorial program. It can and usually does insist on the tailoring of instruction to the specific and particular needs and abilities of the pupil. Individualized instruction can also mean the establishment of an individual curricular pattern within the school, using a grouping procedure that embraces "look-alike" learners. Regardless of the process, the key to understanding these ideas lies in the word *instruction*. The *instruction* in individualized instruction may refer to either *act* or *content*.

Secondly, individualized instruction can refer to the levels of learning being addressed in the educational process, the *lesser* learnings and the *larger* learnings(2). Lesser learnings are usually described as those based on skill mastery. They are incorporated in programs where the pupil moves through a process of growth based on achieved and measurable competency at each level of his current work. The first generation of IPI materials and programs produced at the Learning Research Development Center at the University of Pittsburgh was closely tied to the principles of programmed instruction for the achievement of this level of mastery.

Larger learnings relate to and may be endemic to the whole arena of activities concerned with the development of human beings. These learnings are based on the concept that individualization is really seeking the achievement of learning to learn. This second level of individualization, which deals with the larger learnings and seeks satisfaction in the fundamental area of basic human needs, encompasses most of the vital areas of life itself: feelings, beliefs, emotions, creativity, self-concept, sound mental health, and the whole range of problems and questions that lead to the satisfaction of human needs. With these distinctions in mind one has a framework or design for analyzing or evaluating certain extant approaches to the individualization of instruction.

The fundamental criticism of IPI since its inception in 1963 and continuing to this day, in spite of sweeping programmatic changes, is that the process it embraces of sequencing materials, detailing specific educational objectives, organizing methods of approach to the attainment of these objectives, diagnosing the pupil prior to his addressing the area of concern, and constant evaluation and guidance of the pupil's work as he progresses through the prescribed curriculum flies in the face of those humanistic values and constructs that underpin the search for the establishment of the larger learnings. The criticism that abounds in the literature over the ten years of IPI's existence, along with the companion criticism of the correlative concept of instruction based on behavioral goals and outcomes, seems to boldly state that to seek attainment of stated behavioral objectives based on diagnostic approaches related to and correlated with curriculum materials and teaching techniques is to achieve only narrow outcomes. These outcomes, so goes the argument, are at odds with the broader or global humanistic goals—ill-defined and imprecise as they may be—of knowing who you are, loving, creating, enduring, or just simply being. From congeries of collected materials, insights, based on visits, discussions, and intense involvement in action-oriented educational innovation, any reasonable assessment of the above stated position vis-à-vis outcomes must mark the argument arrant nonsense. Because one seeks to have a pupil achieve competence in a substantive area of the curriculum, it does not necessarily follow or indicate that the other areas of living and learning are not addressed.

The very opposite may be the case. It is becoming quite obvious that, as our knowledge about self-concept grows, our insight about school achievement and its relationship to a healthy self-concept also grows. The humanistic surge places great emphasis on the student's personal and subjective evaluation of himself. This in turn has been found to be a dominant influence on his success in school. Although the "self-theory" hypothesis needs to be continually and carefully researched, nothing to this date contravenes the overwhelming body of contemporary research that insists that there is a high and significant relationship between academic achievement and self-esteem.

It is obvious that both lesser and larger learnings can be the outcomes of IPI. Because mastery of skills is pursued, development of humanistic growth is not necessarily contradistinctive. Evidence from inner-city schools as well as from the more affluent suburban schools attests that it is well nigh impossible to achieve larger outcomes if lesser outcomes are not first established.

To achieve both the lesser and larger outcomes of education, it also becomes obvious that there needs to be a fundamental modification of the school and the process of schooling(3). As it stands now, many schools primarily place emphasis on cognitive subject matter acquisition. There is no doubt that this thrust is necessary. Knowledge and use of subject matter are essential in the development of others areas of life. However, it is also apparent that there is a changing nature to subject matter as it has been known. Conventionally trained teachers freqently do not achieve depth in the subjects that they are asked, or forced, to teach. It is important, therefore, that, if the education of the child is to change, there must be a change in the "stuff" of the curriculum, the "manner" by which the teacher teaches, and the ways in which the child can learn. In addition to the change in subject matter, there is a distinct and growing emphasis on change in the concept of "school" itself. The school is becoming an open rather than a closed institution. The school is moving from a unified and uniform institution to a diversified one. The school is becoming an immediate, highly related institution rather than a remote one. The school is becoming a more experiential institution than a symbolistic one. The school is now more interested in the whole set of life concerns rather than simply the cognitive academic area. And, finally, the school as an institution is moving toward becoming more reality oriented in all its activities so that there exists a fundamental relationship between life and learning.

OPEN EDUCATION AND INDIVIDUALLY PRESCRIBED INSTRUCTION

If one accepts these fundamental movements in education and sees them as being highly related to the larger learning that we have discussed above, one should also look at various aspects and components within these movements. Materials and strategies produced by RBS under their IPI program perpetuate and support these fundamental innovative thrusts.

To move toward open education institutions, certain kinds of assumptions about openness and the activities that take place must be made.

It must be assumed that an open learning situation will have a rich environment. It will be saturated with a collection of items, manipulative as well as intellectual, that will allow the children to choose and engage in activities that will be of high interest to them.

If the school is to be open, children will be able to explore in an unthreatened atmosphere. They will be able to make important choices affecting their own learning. In an open situation children are able to develop, as they move through any of the programmatic activities, their own styles of learning according to their own rate. The growth of a youngster will advance to higher levels as these levels are established by his competency in actual performance. His performance, of course, can be evaluated in many ways: by his actual performance on materials that are embedded in the curriculum; through various kinds of tests in evaluative situations in which he presents or uses the material that he has learned; or by assessing his behavior by careful and direct observation. The work that he performs successfully will be a fundamental point of evaluation of the work that he knows.

By evaluating the IPI programs, and by studying their implementation in the school, it becomes readily apparent that the activities inherent in those programs are of such a nature that students can direct their own learning. In reading, for example, at both the primary and intermediate levels, looseleaf notebooks contain lesson plans for each selection in the program. The objectives, materials, suggested assignments, and evaluation questions are all set down as guidelines. They are deliberately open ended so that the teacher can judge when he or she should adhere to or depart from a particular assignment. The teacher then, along with the youngster, is involved in an instructional program that permits high individualization of elementary reading. The material has been developed in sequence. The reading skills are organized into units and levels of work, and the materials are closely correlated with diagnostic instruments. The self-paced progress of the child through a program geared to his personal interest and abilities is a critical factor in the whole area of opening education. It is a positive step toward helping the child achieve a commitment to learning that is of interest to him.

Studying the IPI programs in action leads to the conclusion that there is a fundamental growth and an independent pursual of learning on the part of the child. When watching children work, both in reading and mathematics, one sees intense activity. There seems to be a high level of appropriateness in the material that each youngster addresses. The teacher serves as a consultant and moves about the classroom helping when called on by the child. One becomes immediately aware of the fact that the questions students ask of the teacher are generally relevant or related to simple rather than complex problems. This leads to the tentative assessment, if not the obvious fact, that the prescriptions based on the diagnosis are fairly accurate and that children do work at the most appropriate and pertinent level of their diagnosed ability of the moment. Rarely does one see youngsters involved in a question and answer situation with the teacher on problems where children display a fundamental lack of understanding. There is no problem, in a program such as IPI, based on the observations we have made, of engaging the children in academic work.

A source of criticism over the years had been that the IPI primary reading program was built around programmed texts. However, this criticism can be easily countered. There are new and quite varied materials available now so that children can move away from that previously constrained feature of the program. For example, all the program material is heavily supplemented by special study booklets and audio tapes. In the IPI intermediate reading program one sees specially prepared materials as well as library and commercial resources being brought heavily into play. In fact, when one moves into the intermediate program, selected readings become the most desirable vehicle in developing the child's independence. The paperback books that are available are keyed to a specially developed continuum of skills. Selections vary from very simple picture stories to lengthy novels. The materials are categorized and, within the category, broken into levels of accomplishment. The child is able to choose what he reads. He also can choose within a framework which is appropriate to his reading level so that he can master materials and problems, rather than become frustrated by them. This is an individualized open-ended reading experience.

When we observed this program in action we were very impressed by the fact that youngsters could move from their particular classroom locations to a skills center. The movement from one area to another was rapid and achieved with simplicity. Walls that had not been removed in one building we observed, even though we would have to classify the education as "open," did not interfere with the movements of the children. They came and went as they pleased and *needed to,* without the attendant problem of conventional discipline. They went to the skills center, which was in a different part of the building. They would go to various areas within the rooms where the prescriptions and materials were stored. They were able to help themselves to various materials made available for their use to pursue their individual programs of activity. Teachers did not issue orders for silence or quiet. There was no need for it. The level of noise in a given classroom and in the other areas did not bother anyone because everybody was heavily involved with his own learning activity. The noise was simply the "busy" noise of something akin to a business office when people are on the move doing the kinds of things called for in their work.

One of the more current and basic themes of education is vertical or family grouping. This is what we know as multiage grouping through the elimination of grade assignments. If this is desirable, and we think that it is, the materials offered by RBS in their various IPI programs support this prospect extremely well. The IPI programs are based on a learning continuum that is independent of grade assignment. This offers many opportunities for interage grouping. However, regardless of the grouping arrangement employed, each student knows exactly where he is on the learning continuum and what he must do to master a particular objective or achieve a desired outcome. The IPI programs include placement tests, pretests, curriculum-embedded tests, and posttests. These essential diagnostic tools are used to place the student at the appropriate level of his work and to isolate areas of particular learning difficulty. This, along with student–teacher conferences, enables the student to share his understandings of and reactions to what he has read or accomplished in a one-on-one relationship with the teacher. Additional conferences with peers give students an opportunity to share their experiences with other members of the class. This one-to-one relationship between teacher and student is evident in all IPI activities, whether in mathematics or reading.

Teachers rarely lecture to an IPI class. Rather, they devote their time to instructing small groups and individuals, evaluating learners' needs, writing student prescriptions based on diagnosis, and developing opportunities in which the individual youngster will be able to show his growth in learning. Diagnosis and evaluation are continuous, specific, and highly individualized. They involve the use of well-prepared materials and diagnostic tests and are carried on in both group and individual bases. Careful record keeping shows individual progress. The odious use of comparative markings is no longer used. Individualization emphasizes the process of continuous progress on the part of an individual, not on the part of a group as a whole.

If one were to subscribe to a curriculum and the instructional theories that are attendant to "opening" the school so that individual growth is enhanced, then some of the following concepts have to be adapted.

In the area of *general curriculum* the school must have a clearly written statement of curriculum philosophy and curriculum objectives. It must be able to produce documents that indicate the essential prerequisites of adapting the curriculum, its study, and the activity involved in its implementation. If we keep that in mind and look at IPI, we see in its curriculum materials the rationale from which the skills are developed. We see how the components were derived. We see how the placement test is given to determine the appropriate instructional level and how specific weaknesses are recognized. And we see how the student will be able to use the instructional material to pursue his individual learning task. In the *selection, organization, and treatment of individualized learning tasks,* the above considerations are extremely important. The organization of materials can and does vary in many instances. However, the availability of several instructional sources from which to select material to help the student attain specific learning objectives is essential to the IPI program. By using a program that is *arranged longitudinally,* based on the *identification of essential learning elements,* and that has both continuity and sequence, the student can move forward in accomplishing his learning objectives. Although the materials accompanying skill areas in the IPI programs vary in length, they all contain review, teaching, practice, summary, and test pages. They are supplemented by teacher tutoring, peer-to-peer tutoring, small and large group instruction, cassette tapes, film strips, and other manipulative materials. In this manner, differentiated treatment of the curriculum areas can be employed, and in the broad content areas such as reading, key concepts can be identified, thus encouraging systematic mastery. Throughout the learning sequence, the student is involved in achieving process goals. Nothing in the IPI materials is contrary to the development of the larger learnings involving the skills of inquiry, evaluation, interpretation, and the application of ideas. Nothing in the IPI materials is contrary to the most important of all larger learnings, that of "learning how to learn." The IPI materials in mathematics and in reading embrace the concept of *balance and integration of curriculum elements.* This is accomplished through the identification and organization of centers of ideas. Their proper use and implementation is described in well-conceived curriculum guides and materials. For example, in the primary reading program we have the organizing features of prereading, decoding, and transition. The use of self-instructional readers and accompanying tape books allows for early reading instruction without the use of separate skill sheets or additional instructional materials. Reading readiness is an organizing element within the prereading activity. The specifics of reading are taught during the reading readiness period. Also, the child is prepared for work in his first book, tne prereader. The child moves then to decoding, where he learns to translate printed symbols into meaningful speech sounds. Throughout this activity the teacher monitors the student's progress toward the objective, both subjectively and objectively. During the transition stage, continued instruction in decoding and comprehension takes place, as well as the reinforcement of silent reading. By analyzing the student's prescription, each day the teacher can diagnose and evaluate the student's performance. The prescription becomes a daily lesson plan for both student and teacher. Intermediate reading, which stresses the maintenance, reinforcement, and improvement of skills in these defined areas, employs separate skill sheets and supplementary materials to aid the student in mastering important reading skills.

In the IPI mathematics continuum, materials are arranged in learning areas: numeration, place value, addition and subtraction, multiplication, division, fractions, money, time, systems of measurement, geometry, and applications. These have been subdivided into levels of difficulty. The student, after taking a battery of placement tests that measure his competency in each of the learning areas, begins his work in the unit that is most appropriate for his particular learning level. Sixty-one pretests in the continuum reveal the youngster's particular needs. On the basis of the pretests, the teacher writes a prescription specifying the skill to be mastered and the materials that the student should use. When the student has completed his assigned prescription, he takes a posttest to show his competence. Without the aid of these diagnostic instruments, a student would receive instruction for an objective that he has already mastered or for an objective for which he is lacking prerequisites. The student does not work in every skill in every unit, only in those which he needs. Intraindividual differences in areas of learning evident in the progress of most children are taken into account when this kind of diagnosis is applied. The continuity and progression of each child's learning and the internalization of that learning allows him to find order and meaning for himself. The logical order of learning from simple to complex, concrete to abstract becomes clear. Here again we see the integration and proper balance of learning. Through the application and repetition of skills and concepts to ensure adequate understanding and mastery, the desired learning is achieved and the opportunity for individualized growth enhanced.

In the development of IPI, great care was taken to build into the program materials that would generate self-motivation on the part of the student. Program activities are deliberately in keeping with the interests and learning styles and patterns of the student. The child's initial experiences are particularly crucial to continued motivation. Motivation is sustained by the continuity and frequent reinforcement of learning growth and experiences. More importantly, because of the child's proper and pertinent placement in IPI, success becomes a matter of fact. Put another way, the learner internalizes his learning through his success, and this leads to yet more learning. The challenge and "pressure" in IPI come from the child himself, not from an authoritarian external source. IPI's strong emphasis on various relationships, child-to-teacher, teacher-to-child, child-to-child, and the like, continuously supports the learner's active involvement and effort.

Integral to the IPI program are the careful continuous diagnosis and evaluation of learning problems and progress. It is through these elements that true individualization comes into play. Individualization is found in the priming and pacing of learning, in the instructional materials and

932

resources available to the learner, and in the approaches and instructional techniques.

With all of the above serving as a basis for discussion about whether or not the IPI programs can indeed serve to enhance larger learnings as well as the lesser learnings, now one needs to step back momentarily and look at the programs in relation to the ways that they have been successful or not successful in achieving this.

In the earliest application, IPI was based upon the fundamental concepts of programmed instruction. Somewhere along the line, however, the problem of program materials and the whole area of programmed approaches to learning became confused. It was difficult to understand the differences between programmed instruction, as such, and the use of programmed materials per se. Many schools in the initial rush toward programmed instruction adopted programmed texts and materials. Few, if any, adopted the necessary changes in classroom operation and school organization that would support a programmed approach to learning. Also, only a few schools that made use of programmed materials adopted, or indeed even recognized, the need for careful diagnosis, individual student pacing, evaluation of individual achievement, and individualized plans of study vital to the use of programmed instruction. Many school systems simply adopted programs and allowed pupils to go through them without paying any attention to a whole host of other inputs necessary to the real success of programmed instruction. The result of all this, rather than achieving an individualized, well-thought-out learning procedure that would be related to the growth of the child, was chaos. Many people equate individualized instruction with the concept of letting each pupil work as fast as he can or wishes. They stop at that point. Very little analysis and individual prescription are involved. The concern is only for rate.

The maladaptive use of IPI or its materials can obviously doom a program. The prospects of IPI have always been clear: that is, to create environments of individualized instruction that would provide for the fundamental and tremendous differences that we all know are extant in student achievement, aptitude, interest, and a host of other characteristics. IPI is an attempt to provide for these differences within a school system that is generally committed to the goal of mass education. Just reflect on Gasparini's statement(4):

> The key to successful innovation is training and sustaining personnel. For too many years the assumption has been that a teacher graduate has been trained to teach—so teach. New programs have been brought in with little or no teacher input, dumped by administration on the teachers, and operated on the assumption that something magical will happen and the program will commence to function well. When it does not and all too many times this is the case, the innovation is blamed when actually the implementation is at fault.

An Individualized Curriculum Program

In describing the "Project for Individually Prescribed Instruction (Oak Leaf Project)," Lindvall and Bolvin observed that(5)

> the task involved in setting up a program for individualizing instruction is one of formidable proportions in terms of the teaching materials and evaluation instruments that must be developed, the details of instructional procedures that must be spelled out, and the reorientation of personnel involved.

It becomes very obvious that merely to take materials and not to develop, at the same time, new physical arrangements, and new teachers' roles in diagnosing, planning, preparing, working with pupils individually, and supervising adults will lead to chaos. When students become more actively involved in the learning process by assuming responsibility for their own development, a whole program of a different nature emerges. The teacher who cannot fit into this new role comfortably and who does all his or her work from a frontal classroom position is likely to savor little success from what might otherwise have been a well-thought-out approach to dealing with individual needs.

However, in schools where the extant practices are based upon an awareness of and a commitment to the concepts of individualization, the arrangement works very well. The planning sessions that sustain a teacher after he has been trained can provide a means for ventilating problems and finding solutions. They aid in the fundamental growth process of moving toward openness. The orientation that teachers give children, plus the more thorough consideration given to class organization and operation, helps achieve high levels of success in many of the areas having to do with the larger learnings in education. Additionally, the programs as they are successfully implemented become internal catalysts for other changes both in attitude and performance by teachers. Individualized approaches to learning bring together the two concepts of mastery and humanistic feelings.

However, much of this would be without any value if there were no evidence of academic growth. RBS is now gathering data on the effects of the IPI programs on academic growth. One example of effective use of IPI in an urban environment is described in a recent RBS publication(6):

> St. Gregory's School is in the heart of Philadelphia's inner city. Its students come from a low income population. . . . Since the implementation of IPI in 1970, student achievement scores have steadily climbed upward. In 1972, results from tests administered to 130 students in grades three through seven showed that over half the students had advanced one or more grade levels in reading and over a third had advanced one or more grade levels in mathematics in one year. Seventh grade scores placed students at or very near grade level.

Two inner-city schools in Wilmington, Delaware, reported similar success. The Harland School reported, after completing its second year with the reading program, that, based on an expectancy of six months gain for six months of instruction(7):

> The observed differences either exceed the expected difference or are not significantly different from the expected difference. That is, all grades did as well as expected on the achievement tests and grades three and four exceed expectancies on all sub-tests of the Comprehensive Set of Basic Skills.

There are other studies of academic achievement of youngsters in IPI programs that could be cited. However, to be fair, one must also indicate that the findings from numerous studies using various standardized instruments have been mixed. A major contribution being made by RBS is the attempt to bring together as much of the research as possible through the Nationwide Network of School Districts and related activities. The conclusions drawn from the data on academic progress indicate that IPI pupils are progressing through the continuum and that, generally, IPI pupils achieve at about the same level or slightly above comparison with school pupils on standardized tests(8). It should be noted, however, that standardized tests are not really appropriate for the evaluation of an individualized program such as IPI(9).

The ever-revolving IPI material and rearrangements of classroom operation brought about by the interplay of materials, teachers, and children represent a dynamic concept. It can be said that to rely on standard instruments of measure that are static in nature and to impose them on a dynamic multifaceted system is to end up with a collection of materials hardly valuable for stating the real worth of a given program(10). What all this seems to indicate is that the field of education cries for more precise measures for the new and the innovative, rather than making new and innovative systems fit the already achieved conventional mode.

The other areas of pupil growth, such as self-concept and behavior, likewise rely upon measures that are not wholly valuable. These do, however, reveal significantly higher scores on all measures of creative tendency, self-concept, and attitude toward the school for IPI pupils. Therefore, one can state that IPI does have a positive effect on pupil self-concept. The majority of studies that were conducted in the demonstration schools by independent evaluators found that the students do display positive attitudes toward math and reading, like school better, demonstrate more dependent positive actions, and have an enhanced self-concept. These findings are reported by Maguire(11). He indicates that parental opinions were generally favorable to the program, that the teachers' attitudes were favorable, and that childrens' attitudes were favorable. Students had a more positive additude toward arithmetic than those in the control group. Teachers were more positively disposed toward innovation and individualization than their colleagues in the control group. The classroom allowed for more extended student interaction with teachers than did classrooms in the control schools. Parents were more favorably impressed with the program and more than half would even favor an increase in taxes to support the program. Also, parents freely gave of their time to help with the many clerical chores that the program demands.

And what are the expansive prospects of a program such as IPI? Individualization may very well be the prerequesite educational theme needed to assure learning in a democracy. If this is so, it remains for us to think about and create learning activities that are fresh, alive, exciting, and powerful for the individual learner.

Individualization should not be thought of as a fad. It should not be thought of as limited programmed instruction, singly oriented and singly purposed in its implementation. Rather, it should be thought of as the development of a systems approach to learning that will result in the pupil becoming able to conduct his own learning. This requires the acceptance and careful use of items that can help in doing this—programmed instruction and materials, computerized aids in instruction, collaboration in learning and teaching, reorganization of the classroom to make it more flexible, and yet undiscovered methodologies and schemes for enhancing the whole teaching–learning situation. Additionally, it requires total staff involvement in the planning and presentation of materials so that they more nearly fit the needs of the teachers and the pupils of the community. It requires a clear commitment to setting up clearly defined learning and instructional objectives. It requires a clearer understanding of the total learning process. It requires a careful rethinking and a complete understanding of the various skills and subskills that go into a curriculum area. It requires a long-range view of the continuously evolving growth of the pupil. And it requires a clear understanding of the integrative nature of curriculum and learning. Finally, but most importantly, the expansive prospects of individualized instruction shall only be realized if constant feedback is used for improving the program. Systematic evaluation of relevant data for continued improvement is a must. The success and future modification of IPI, based upon this feedback, may be the keystone upon which the whole effort will be judged.

References

1. *Individualizing Instruction*, 1964 Yearbook, Association for Supervision and Curriculum Development, p. 7.
2. These two definitions related to individualizing instruction are fully discussed by Alexander Frazier in "Individualized Instruction," *California Journal for Instructional Improvement*, 2 (March 1968), 31–44.
3. For an excellent updated discussion of this, see the whole issue of *Phi Delta Kappan* "Special Issue: Alternative Schools," 54 (March 1973).

4. John N. Gasparini, "History of IPI in Allenwood," unpublished, June 23, 1972.

5. C. M. Lindvall and J. O. Bolvin, "The Project for Individually Prescribed Instruction" (The Oakleaf Project), Learning Research and Development Center, University of Pittsburgh, 1966, p. 5.

6. "The Schools and Individualized Instruction: Six Perspectives." Philadelphia: Research for Better Schools, 1973, p. 11.

7. "I.P.I. Reading Program—Harland School," Wilmington, Delaware.

8. G. W. Fairgrieve, "Evaluation of the IPI Math Program at McMorrow School," St. Louis, Mo.; Larry Johnson and D. R. Ostrum, "Second Year Evaluation," IPI Mathematics Project, Hall School, Minneapolis, Minn., 1971.

9. David M. Shoemaker, "Evaluating the Effectiveness of Competing Instructional Programs," *Educational Researcher,* 1 (May 1972), 5–8, 12.

10. T. J. Rookey and Alice Valdes, "A Study of Individually Prescribed Instruction and the Affective Domain." Philadelphia: Research for Better Schools, Inc., October 1972.

11. T. O. Maguire, "Evaluation of the IPI Project," *Alberta Journal of Educational Research,* 17 (December 1971) 255–273.

Operational Concepts

1. Emphasis upon specific educational objectives need not inhibit the acquisition of larger conceptual understandings.

2. True conceptual understanding is prohibitive if the learner lacks a prerequisite body of factual information.

3. If authentic educational reform is to occur, the substance of the curriculum, methods of instruction, and the basis of evaluation must all be altered.

4. In addition to improving cognitive achievement, the individualization of instruction may also contribute to a healthier self-concept among learners.

Implications

As in the case of many other educational issues, the arguments for and against individualization are difficult to evaluate. Some children, for example, learn effectively without individualization; others do not. Furthermore, teachers vary considerably in the extent to which they are able to manage the intricacies of adjusting to differences among learners. Little is to be gained, consequently, from abstract debates on comparative advantages and disadvantages.

It would be a great deal more profitable to focus attention upon those children who clearly need individualized help. Over the past years, a great deal of work has gone into the development of alternative instructional methods and materials. These are of great utility with some children and largely unnecessary with others. Experts have estimated that roughly 20 percent of students require individualized attention; the remaining 80 percent are able to learn effectively through standardized procedures. It would be most sensible, therefore, to individualize whenever and wherever it is clearly advantageous.

Index

Index

Index

Index

Index

953